REVOLUTIONARY VIRGINIA
THE ROAD TO INDEPENDENCE

Volume III

The Breaking Storm
and the Third Convention, 1775

A Documentary Record

John Murray (1732–1809), fourth Earl of Dunmore, twenty-fifth and last royal governor of Virginia, 1771–1776. When in 1765 Sir Joshua Reynolds thus depicted his subject, it may not have been with prescience that he stroked in the background; but whether so or not, His Lordship's future was to be one of storm. Oil copy by Charles X. Harris, 1929. (Courtesy of the Virginia Historical Society)

REVOLUTIONARY VIRGINIA
THE ROAD TO INDEPENDENCE

Volume III

The Breaking Storm
and the Third Convention, 1775

A Documentary Record

Compiled and Edited by ROBERT L. SCRIBNER
With the Assistance of BRENT TARTER

Published for
Virginia Independence Bicentennial Commission
University Press of Virginia

THE UNIVERSITY PRESS OF VIRGINIA
Copyright © 1977 by the Rector and Visitors
of the University of Virginia

First published 1977

ISBN: 0-8139-0685-7
Library of Congress Catalog Card Number: 72-96023

Printed in the United States of America

Contents

Preface

THE 316 documentary entries within the present volume (10 of which are "imported" to round out items that otherwise would be incomplete) are derived from 35 basic sources. Of these sources, 23 are manuscripts, 7 published works, and 5 newspapers. It is believed that the greatest value in the present volume will be found in the manuscripts of the third Virginia Convention—the extant portions of John Tazewell's journal and minutes, and a number of loose papers—for they combine to present a more nearly complete and accurate account of the proceedings of that assemblage than ever heretofore has appeared in print.

Those proceedings are the logical and necessary counter to British policy as correctly interpreted and clumsily pursued by a royal governor. They are also in a very real sense the summation of the sentiments held and publicly expressed by the local committees of correspondence. As was true in Volume Two of the present work, in Volume Three it is the newspapers that provide the great majority of extant transactions of the committees. But whereas in the predecessor volume the number of committees for which records were found was forty-two, in the present volume the number is expanded to forty-eight. This expansion of itself may not be without significance, because with war already being waged, it is not likely to be a committeeman with a noticeably tender neck who will thrust it into the noose of publicity.

Four other changes between the contents of the two volumes will be noticed. First, with the reports of the Essex County committee on 26 April 1775 of the public sale of goods, the committees quit the business of holding auctions. The flow of goods after application of the imports article of the Continental Association has been dammed. Thereafter commerce and trade, under the restrictions of the Association and the watchful eyes of the committees, is left to the merchants.

Second, the mayors and the Common Halls of Williamsburg and of Norfolk, effectually assuming the functions of committees, yet with the sanction of legal authority, constitute themselves a new patriotic force and enter the lists, the first to joust with a governor, the second with a British naval captain.

Third, the independent companies of gentlemen volunteers, given the breath of life by the second convention and designed to replace the moribund militia units, are constituting themselves still another force. Only a sampling of the records of these companies is presented; but that sampling will suffice to demonstrate that the third convention is to be called upon to alter the nature of that force and to reduce it to obedience and accountability, lest a monster worse than the British Royal Army conceivably evolve.

And fourth, there is in this volume much more of a western orientation than in the first two. That is not to say that all eyes are not upon Philadelphia for the meeting of the second Continental Congress, or elsewhere along the Atlantic seaboard for the occurrence of important events. It is to say that all eyes are not upon Philadelphia or the seaboard exclusively. In part the western thrust arises from the sessions of the last House of Burgesses, from 1 to 24 June 1775, and the desire of the members to do delayed justice to the unpaid veterans, the widowed and orphaned dependents, and the creditors of Dunmore's War; and this unsatisfied concern becomes an inheritance of the third convention. The thrust also arises from the fact that whether in House or convention (or, indeed, in Congress), the westerners are resolved to be heard, and the easterners are almost as anxious as they that the frontiers be pacified, that patriotic firepower may be concentrated in the East.

Too, with a firming of patriot attitudes, there will be found in the records an amount of harshness hitherto not really characteristic of Virginia. It is true that in the colony men failing to adhere to the terms of the Continental Association or to conceal loyalist views will continue to be ostracized, with nothing worse (and even occasional forgiveness) to follow. But John Sherlock of Accomack County recants with such "calm reflection" as is induced by staring down the lengths of leveled gun barrels. William Clarke vows to silence his tongue, to quit Dunmore County within twenty-four hours, and not to return within a year. The "Cloathes" torn from his back, John Schaw escapes from a mob and seeks refuge up a chimney in the house of a Norfolk alderman. And tarred and feathered, Anthony Warwick rides out of Smithfield under a pelting of antiquated eggs.

In presenting this volume, the compiler-editors would be remiss were they not to acknowledge an indebtedness for assistance rendered by the staff of the Virginia State Library. The nature of the work considered, this debt is particularly owed to members of the Archives Division. Those members have responded with unfailing efficiency, and with a courtesy that the compiler-editors aspire eventually (it is a matter of finding the time) to requite.

A last word is in order. As though the problems of the cataloguing phase of library science were not already sufficient, the purist will accord to the deceased William J. Van Schreeven credit as being co-compiler of this and later volumes. Although the present compiler-editors flatter themselves that they would have found, as they will continue to find, all or nearly all extant sources desirable to comprise the documentary portions of this and successor volumes, they have discovered and anticipate to discover that Mr. Van

Schreeven's extensive notes are invaluable guides to the nature and where-abouts of documents already or yet to be examined.

R. L. S.

Virginia State Library
October 1975

Apparatus

IN THE present volume angle brackets ⟨ ⟩ are employed to enclose proper names and titles or their missing parts and occasionally to enclose dates, punctuation marks, and words or portions of words that were abbreviated in a confusing fashion. This bracketing treats of elements none of which originally appeared in either a given manuscript or printed source.

Unless otherwise specifically noted, regular brackets [ ] are employed to supply words, syllables, letters, or punctuation marks that are torn, faded, cut from, or smeared in a source. The elements thus bracketed were either obviously or conjecturally in the source when penned or printed. In instances of editorial conjecture an interrogation point is enclosed within the bracket.

Chronology

1775

March 28	Lord Dunmore issues proclamation forbidding election of Virginia delegates to second Continental Congress.
March 30	King George III assents to New England Fisheries Bill restricting trade of northern colonies.
April 1	Daniel Boone and advance party of Transylvania Company establish Boonesborough on Kentucky River in Fincastle County, Virginia.
April 13	King George III assents to bill to restrict trade of New Jersey, Pennsylvania, Maryland, Virginia, and South Carolina—a companion piece to act of March 30.
April 19	British military expedition through Lexington to seize munitions at Concord is driven back to Boston by Massachusetts militia in daylong skirmishing.
April 21	Lord Dunmore's removal of gunpowder from Williamsburg public magazine precipitates angry exchange with city Common Hall.
April 22	Election of delegates to Continental Congress by New York Provincial Convention secures triumph of radicals.
April 28	News of events at Lexington and Concord arrives in Fairfax County, Virginia.
April 29	Six hundred armed men massed at Fredericksburg in readiness to march on Williamsburg disperse at request of Peyton Randolph.
April 30	News of events at Lexington and Concord reaches Williamsburg.
May 2	Addressing armed volunteers in Hanover County, Patrick Henry is elected captain to conduct march on capital.
May 3	Lord Dunmore issues proclamation denouncing "commotions" caused by removal of gunpowder.
May 4	Patrick Henry procures £330 from Receiver General Richard Corbin in compensation for gunpowder and disbands volunteers.
May 4	Captain George Montagu of His Majesty's Ship *Fowey* threatens bombardment of Yorktown if inhabitants hinder movement of sailors and marines to Williamsburg.
May 6	Lord Dunmore issues proclamation charging Patrick Henry with "outrageous and rebellious Practices."

May 9	Spotsylvania County committee calls for meeting of third Virginia Convention.
May 10	Second Continental Congress assembles in Philadelphia and elects Peyton Randolph president.
May 10	Colonels Ethan Allen and Benedict Arnold capture Fort Ticonderoga on Lake Champlain in New York.
May 12	Lord Dunmore issues proclamation for General Assembly to convene on 1 June to consider Lord North's proposals for reconciliation.
May 12	Call is issued for speedy election of delegates to third Virginia Convention.
May 12	Colonels Allen and Arnold seize Crown Point on Lake Champlain.
May 15	Continental Congress unanimously resolves united colonies be put in a state of defense.
May 17	Arnold takes St. John's, Ontario.
May 23	Settlers at Boonesborough meet in convention and adopt plan of government.
May 24	Peyton Randolph retires from presidency of Continental Congress to return to Virginia and is succeeded by John Hancock of Massachusetts.
May 25	Generals Sir William Howe, Sir Henry Clinton, and John Burgoyne arrive in Boston to reinforce General Thomas Gage.
May 25	Williamsburg independent company of volunteers pledges services anywhere on continent in defense of American liberty.
May 29	Continental Congress adopts address to inhabitants of Canada inviting their joining "fellow-sufferers" in the common cause.
May 31	Peyton Randolph is effusively received on arrival in Williamsburg.
June 1	In response to summons of 12 May, General Assembly convenes in Capitol, and Peyton Randolph is reelected speaker of House of Burgesses.
June 3–4	Breaking into Williamsburg powder magazine, three of a number of youths are wounded by discharge of a spring gun, leading to exchange between governor and burgesses.
June 5	House of Burgesses unanimously approves work of second Virginia Convention.
June 8	At 2:00 A.M. Lord Dunmore and family slip out of Williamsburg to take up residence on board H.M.S. *Fowey* off Yorktown.
June 9	Continental Congress advises Massachusetts Provincial Congress to establish a government independent of royal authority.
June 10	Virginia General Assembly adopts Thomas Jefferson's resolutions rejecting Lord North's proposals for reconciliation.
June 12	General Gage proclaims Massachusetts under martial law.
June 14	Continental Congress votes embodiment of six companies of "expert riflemen," of which two companies are allotted to Virginia.
June 15	Continental Congress unanimously elects George Washington commander in chief of Continental Army.
June 17	British win Pyrrhic victory at Bunker Hill near Boston.
June 21	Governor's Council joins House of Burgesses in rebuking Lord Dunmore for abandoning seat of government and rendering transaction of public business impracticable.

June 22	Continental Congress votes emission of $2,000,000 in bills of credit to finance Continental Army.
June 23	Inhabitants of Williamsburg request neighboring counties to send volunteers to help protect city.
June 24	House of Burgesses having appointed commissioners to treat with Indians in Ohio Valley, General Assembly adjourns, never again to meet with a quorum.
June 26	Peyton Randolph issues call for third Virginia Convention to meet at Richmond on 17 July 1775.
June 29	Lady Dunmore and children sail for Great Britain.
June 29– July 6	On behalf of Lord Dunmore, Major John Connolly conducts treaty at Fort Pitt with spokesmen for Six Nations and Delaware tribes of Indians.
June 30	Continental Congress adopts articles of war for Continental Army.
July 3	General Washington assumes command of army at Cambridge, Massachusetts.
July 5	Continental Congress adopts "Olive Branch Petition" to King George III.
July 6	Continental Congress adopts "Declaration of the Causes and Necessities of Taking up Arms."
July 8	Continental Congress adopts address to "Inhabitants of Great Britain."
July 8	Georgia Provincial Congress votes to send delegates to Continental Congress, bringing to thirteen the number of united colonies.
July 9– August 10	On behalf of Commissioners appointed by Burgesses on 24 June, Captain James Wood conducts meetings with various Indian leaders in Northwest, inviting them to treaty scheduled for Fort Pitt on 10 September 1775.
July 15	Captain Daniel Morgan leads company of Frederick County riflemen across Potomac River at Harper's Ferry en route to Washington's camp at Cambridge.
July 16	Lord Dunmore takes up residence on board man-of-war off Norfolk.
July 17	Third Virginia Convention meets at Anglican Town Church in Richmond and elects Peyton Randolph president.
July 20	Resolution of Continental Congress leads to observation of day of humiliation, fasting, and prayer throughout colonies.
July 24	Earl of Dartmouth, secretary of state for the colonies, instructs northern Indian agent Colonel Guy Johnson to cause his charges to take up hatchet against patriots.
July 26– July 29	Independent companies of volunteers at Williamsburg send out parties to seize king's revenues.
July 28	Continental Congress adopts address "to the people of Ireland."
July 31	Continental Congress rejects Lord North's proposals for reconciliation.
August 1	Continental Congress adjourns until 5 September 1775.
August 5	Virginia Convention elects Patrick Henry colonel of first Virginia regiment and commander in chief of colony's armed forces.
August 11	Virginia Convention elects Peyton Randolph, Richard Henry Lee, Thomas Jefferson, Benjamin Harrison, Thomas Nelson, Jr.,

	Richard Bland, and George Wythe deputies to Continental Congress.
August 12	Captain John Macartney of H.M. Sloop *Otter* threatens to bombard Norfolk in response to mob violence.
August 15	Virginia Convention elects Francis Lightfoot Lee deputy to Continental Congress, vice Richard Bland, declined to serve.
August 16	Virginia Convention authorizes "dissenting Clergymen to celebrate divine worship and to preach to the Soldiers" of their persuasion mustered under convention authority.
August 17	Ill health forces Peyton Randolph to retire from presidency of Virginia Convention; he is succeeded by Robert Carter Nicholas.
August 17	Convention elects Committee of Safety composed of Edmund Pendleton, George Mason, John Page, Richard Bland, Thomas Ludwell Lee, Paul Carrington, Dudley Digges, William Cabell, Jr., Carter Braxton, James Mercer, and John Tabb.
August 21	Convention enacts ordinance for defense and protection of colony.
August 23	King George III proclaims thirteen colonies to be in state of rebellion and treason.
August 24	The membership already elected, the convention enacts ordinance creating the Committee of Safety.
August 25	Convention provides for levying of taxes and emission of bills of credit.
August 26	Third Virginia Convention adopts address to public and adjourns.
August 26	Committee of Safety holds first meeting in Richmond.

Part One   The Next Gale from the North, and
a Curtain Descended

Tuesday, 28 March–Saturday, 24 June 1775

Tuesday, 28 March–Saturday, 24 June 1775

An Introductory Note

ON 28 March 1775 His Excellency John Murray, fourth Earl of Dunmore, Viscount Fincastle, Lord Murray of Blair, &ca., governor of Virginia and vice admiral of the same, issued a proclamation.[1] Commanded by his king, he forbade the election of Virginia deputies to attend the second Continental Congress. That assemblage was scheduled to convene in Philadelphia on 10 May to consider what next to do should by that date there be no redress of what His Lordship was pleased to call "certain pretended Grievances." But, as the governor wrote to Lord Dartmouth, secretary of state for the colonies, the proclamation had "no other effect than exciting the further insults of the Enemies of Government here, in their free Animadversions upon Administration, and giving them occasion to urge, to the People, a Stronger Necessity of Continuing their unwarrantable Practices."[2]

His Excellency may have been reporting accurately. If so, the "Enemies" chose in the main to animadvert orally. At least very little comment on the proclamation reached print. It was rather as though the fatuity of the document was beneath serious notice. Owing to the tardiness with which the king's command had been received, the attempted interdiction followed by three days the election by the second Virginia Convention of Peyton Randolph, George Washington, Patrick Henry, Richard Henry Lee, Edmund Pendleton, Benjamin Harrison, and Richard Bland as a delegation to Congress.[3] And as though to emphasize the paralysis of the regal pleasure in Virginia when unconstitutionally invoked, John Dixon and William Hunter in their *Virginia Gazette* of 1 April 1775 silently subjoined the prohibitory proclamation to the convention proceedings of 27 March. On that final day of session Thomas Jefferson was elected Randolph's alternate, and there was adopted a resolution that "the said Deputies, or any four of them, be a sufficient number to represent this colony in General Congress."[4]

Legally governor of all Virginia and her appendages, treated with every outward form of respect due his nominally exalted station, and even praised by the extralegal second convention for "his truly noble, wise and spirited Conduct on the late Expedition against the Indian Enemy,"[5] Dunmore was nevertheless frustrated by the knowledge that when glancing from a window of his Williamsburg Palace, the field of his vision exceeded that of his real power. That was a knowledge especially goading to one so near the throne that he boasted of his companionship in more youthful years when both he and the present king had been under the tutelage of John Stuart, third Earl of Bute.[6] Because of that relationship

His Lordship's own were married to his sovereign's constitutional concepts. But it was a union that left the governor unable to grasp or interpret the constitutional concepts of the colonials to his sovereign. Yet worse than this, in a contest with the Virginia patriot leaders, His Excellency had too few weapons in his personal arsenal. He was at best a carpet knight, an embodied set of manners acquired at the court of St. James's or in the drawing rooms of London, with no understanding of what beyond the externals of etiquette there remained of a gentleman. In consequence, his "honor" was a thing to be served, when served at all, by its own convenience—for deceit could always be made a "duty" to the king—and in this wise his plighted word could not be trusted past the breath that uttered, or the pen that inscribed, it.

Much of history is a record of grand achievements by great knaves. Their achievements are brought about sometimes by vigor, sometimes by biding time. But whether they achieve by aggression or wile, such knaves are intelligent. Psychologically incapable of passiveness, His Lordship could exert vigor. His intellect, however, was such that assuming he ever tried to, he could not accurately assess the narrowness of its circumscription. These are the harsh judgments of those who did not admire him, it is true, but those who knew him best admired him least.

Thus did this former lieutenant of His Majesty's Third Regiment of Foot Guards combine activity and impotence in an effort to render his master's "Enemies" less potent than himself and by that new relativity to find ground on which to resurrect the king's authority. To him it seemed that simple.

The resolution of the late convention "of raising a body of armed Men in all the counties," he informed Lord Dartmouth in a letter dated 1 May 1775, "made me think it prudent to remove some Gunpowder which was in a Magazine in this place, where it lay exposed to any attempt that might be made to seize it, and I had reason to believe the people"—for which read "Enemies"—"intended to take that step." [7]

This decision arrived at, the governor procured the keys to the Magazine (or munitions depot) from the keeper and gave them to Lieutenant Henry Colins, commanding His Majesty's armed schooner *Magdalen*, which lay some four miles down the James River at Burwell's Ferry. The governor's orders were that the lieutenant secretively remove the gunpowder, load it aboard the schooner, and transport it to H.M.S. *Fowey*, a man-of-war stationed off Norfolk. The Magazine, which is one of the restored buildings in the old colonial capital, had been erected some sixty years before for the storage of a quantity of powder that "our late sovereign Lady Queen Anne, of her grace and bounty, was pleased to bestow" for the defense of the colony and which needed protection from the acquisitive and the elements, lest it be "imbezzled" or "spoilt." If not in the best repair, in April 1775 the octagonal building was still structurally sound, was enclosed by a high wall, and could be entered only by opening a heavy gate—notwithstanding which, ere Dunmore's business with the Magazine should be done, many would pass through the opening. [8]

Between three and four A.M. on Friday, 21 April, Lieutenant Colins and a detachment of fifteen marines crept through the dark capital streets with "his Excellency the Governour's" horse-drawn "waggon." Unchallenged, they succeeded in loading fifteen half barrels of gunpowder when someone deserving a better footnote in history espied them and spread the alarm. There being no further need or opportunity for furtiveness, Colins and his men presumably leapt aboard the wagon and went clattering posthaste out of town; at least they were not intercepted.

Now drums were beating, shouting citizens assembling, and the local independent company of gentlemen volunteers falling into ranks. As the word spread, tempers rose, and a mob prepared "to repair to the palace, to demand from the Governour a restoration of what they so justly supposed was deposited in this magazine for the country's defence." At the same time, "continual threats" were reaching Dunmore that the mob was clamoring for his life and that of "every person" assisting him should he refuse "to deliver the Powder immediately into their custody."[9]

But cooler heads prevailed. Peyton Randolph was in town, and if Robert Carter Nicholas was not, he soon would be. Although no such scene has been documented, it little strains the imagination to envision Mr. Speaker thrusting his ample person into the midst of the lantern- and torchlit turmoil, calling for quiet and for sober discussion. Neither he nor Nicholas would desire the incident to become such as would undermine the efforts of the forthcoming Continental Congress to reach an accommodation with Great Britain, or if accommodation could not be reached, to denigrate the fair name of the Old Dominion. It was thus eventually agreed that a remonstrance should be made to the governor, "in a decent and respectful manner," and that the municipal governing body, the Common Hall, should be forthwith assembled. Mayor John Dixon and his conferees thereafter prepared an address requesting that the powder be returned.[10] The written document they took to the Palace ("leaving their armed force"—the independent company—"at a little distance," Dunmore dourly noted), and Randolph handed the paper to His Excellency. The governor was inwardly surprised, the contents being "milder in terms" than he had anticipated. But "still," he fulminated to Lord Dartmouth, "from the manner in which it was presented," the entire action could "be deemed, if not a treasonable proceeding at least nothing less than one of the highest insults, that could be offered to the authority of his majt'ys Governt."[11]

In a paragraph of their address the city fathers advanced as a reason for the need of the powder the prevalence of rumors that can be interpreted in two different ways: either a slave insurrection was being fomented or "diabolical" notions of murdering individual masters had been implanted in the minds of the enthralled blacks. His Lordship snatched at his own interpretation and replied that he had himself heard of "an insurrection in a neighbouring county" (he later specified Surry) and for that very reason had caused the powder to be removed for its "perfect security." But if it should be needed in Williamsburg, it would be returned "in half an hour"—a delivery which, though offered on his "word and honour," was by this time impossible to effect.[12]

Though disappointed that the governor's response was not "more explicit and favourable," Randolph, Nicholas (who was now definitely present), and the other gentlemen of the Common Hall reassured the burghers and, "unexpectedly" to Dunmore, wrought their dispersal. With emotions cooling, quiet returned to the town; and even Lieutenant Colins came back to walk the streets unmolested, for he, after all, had acted as an officer in obedience to orders, not as the instigator of the incident.[13]

That weekend the three Williamsburg gazettes printed the formal exchange between Common Hall and governor. But a crucial omission was any statement to the effect that His Lordship's reply had mollified the citizenry. Thus were the hinterlands still to be heard from, and for the chief magistrate the portents were not good. Parties of "armed Men were continually coming into town from the adjacent Counties the following days," he complained, "and offering" unspecified "fresh insults." [14]

The matter was becoming less simple than the former lieutenant of H.M. Third Regiment of Foot Guards had foreseen. He had contrived a situation where whispers fed upon themselves and grew into open talk. He was, it was said, converting the Palace into a fortress and arming not only his household but even the Indian hostages brought back from his western campaign. Some declared that he was capable of summoning the royal naval craft upstream to bombard the capital. Others contended that the man would go so far as to arm the slaves! For this talk His Excellency could in large part thank himself, because in lieu of ability to act he substituted indiscreet oral outbursts.

To Dr. William Pasteur, who was at the Palace on Sunday morning, 23 April, he said that "tho' he did not think himself in Danger," yet if "injury or insult" should be visited on him, Lieutenant Colins, or his confidential secretary, Captain Edward Foy,[15] then "by the living God," he would "declare Freedom to the Slaves, and reduce the City of Williamsburg to Ashes." He had no doubt, he continued, that he would "have a Majority of white People and all the Slaves on the side of Government, that he had once fought for the Virginians, and that, by God, he would let them see that he could fight against them" and within a short time "depopulate the whole Country." How he would arrange to fight against the Virginians with a "Majority" of them on his side, and at the same time persuade them to depopulate themselves he neglected to divulge.[16]

In Fredericksburg the "very disagreeable intelligence" of the removal of the gunpowder arrived on Monday morning, 24 April, while the independent company, commanded by Captain Hugh Mercer, was gathered for drill. The company voted unanimously to summon its counterparts from surrounding counties, to solicit the advice of Colonel George Washington, and "to hold themselves in readiness" to move on Williamsburg "as light horse" on Saturday, 29 April. On Wednesday, 26 April, Mann Page, Jr., ex-burgess, burgess-elect, past conventioner, and conventioner-to-be, set out with two companions for the capital in order to ascertain whether it would be necessary or desirable for the assembling volunteers to ride. On that same day Colonel Washington "Went up" to Alexandria "to meet the Indt. Company." This typically economical diary entry is all that survives of that meeting, but the colonel probably counseled caution until more exact information could be obtained.[17]

Twenty-four hours after leaving Fredericksburg, Mann Page, Jr., and his colleagues arrived in Williamsburg, encountered a rider on a like errand from Hanover County, and went immediately to see Peyton Randolph. Page reported that "upwards of 2000 men" would be at the Spotsylvania County town by Friday night, 28 April, ready to march. Mr. Speaker said no. Matters were entirely under control; the capital was quiet; though the offer of assistance was appreciated, it was unnecessary; and the governor continued to give private assurances that if the powder should be needed, it would be made available. In such circumstances, "violent measures" might "produce effects" of "which God only" could forsee the consequences. Randolph signed a letter to that effect for Page, and the courier and his fellow riders turned their mounts northward—"vowing vengeance of their enraged Confederates against me," Dunmore misinformed Dartmouth, "and I am consequently in hourly expectation of their appearance." The trio was back in Fredericksburg late on Friday, surely nigh exhausted, for they had covered well over 200 miles in a little in excess of forty-eight hours.[18]

Before Randolph's letter reached Fredericksburg, another horseman, coming from the North, rode into town with the first reports of the shot soon to be heard round the world. Notwithstanding the electrifying nature of these tidings, moderate opinion prevailed. Not only was the information fragmentary but from no practical viewpoint could Massachusetts be benefited by the descent of armed Virginia horsemen on their own capital. Although Colonel Washington did not go to Fredericksburg, he seems to have communicated advice very much in harmony with Randolph's. On Saturday the twenty-ninth, then, 102 officers, committee members, and other worthies voted that the 600 (not 2,000) men assembled should not march. Instead, there was composed a fiery resolution denouncing the governor's action, a vow to resist ministerial tyranny "at the utmost hazard of our lives and fortunes," and a promise to remain in constant readiness to reassemble.[19]

If momentarily relieved, His Lordship was not therefore happily circumstanced. His comings and goings about Williamsburg were peaceful enough, and he frequently walked unattended the quarter of a mile from the Palace to the house of that stanchest supporter of royal prerogative, the colonial attorney general, John Randolph. But beyond listening to learned oral disquisitions on how misled the "people" were, it is doubtful that the governor learned much of their "designs," for Mr. Attorney General was later to testify that he was not given to "mixing much" with the populace. Too, John Pinkney had somehow got hold of an "Extract" of one of His Lordship's confidential letters to Lord Dartmouth, and printed it in his *Virginia Gazette* of 28 April 1775.[20] The publication was certain to raise a storm of protest and crimination, and there would be no way to reply, except by proclamation, which would be but to repeat a stormy cycle. Then to add to the restlessness and humiliation of the chief executive, of the Virginia delegates deputized to attend the second Continental Congress all but Patrick Henry set out for Philadelphia. Peyton Randolph left Williamsburg on 29 April, Washington (having packed his handsome militia uniform as though expecting the worst), Mount Vernon as late as 4 May. And because of rumors of the planned seizures of their persons set afoot by the proclamation of 28 March 1775, the delegates all went escorted by armed independent companies, roundly huzzahed en route by the misled people.[21]

And Henry? He on 2 May 1775 was at Newcastle, which, no longer extant, was then a considerable Hanover County port town lying on the Pamunkey River some nineteen miles northeast of Richmond. Thither he had summoned the committee and the gentlemen volunteers of his county. This was the same day that Dunmore, citing "COMMOTIONS and insurrections" resulting from his "constitutional right" to dispose of the gunpowder as he deemed best, was seeking the advice of his Council as to what next to do.[22] It was the same day that Robert Carter Nicholas was forwarding to the North Carolina Committee the information that call it what you would, Great Britain and the Colony of Massachusetts Bay were at war.[23]

Despite its being but three days since the council at Fredericksburg had disbanded, with the result of its deliberations yet to reach public print, Henry undoubtedly knew what the outcome had been. Express riders were kicking up clouds of dust throughout the colony and transporting facts, allegations, and fictions with extraordinary speed. He apparently consulted with no one likely not to be of his own mind—the conservatives would attempt to put off forever the inevitability of tomorrow, until tomorrow should overwhelm them. So with the volunteers convened, Henry proceeded to deliver himself of one of his explosive speeches. His admiring biographer William Wirt did not presume to duplicate the speech but recaptured its essence from the fading memories of the orator's auditors. In his "harangue"—that is Wirt's word—Henry bristled with moral indignation at Dunmore's "plunder of the magazine in Williamsburg." He demonstrated that the theft was but part of a "corrupt and tyrannical" ministerial scheme to spare no force in imposing "wretched debasement" on the colonies. And with vivid imagery he guided the gathered warriors across a divided Red Sea toward the promised land of "American liberty," every foot of their forward march shielded by "a pillar of cloud by day" and guided at "night by a pillar of fire."

Swept off their emotional footing, the captain of the company resigned, and the volunteers acclaimed the speaker their Moses. If he had not already done so, Henry then wrote, or more likely had the committee of correspondence write, to the independent companies of nearby counties proposing that they share in acquiring the "never-fading laurels" he had promised his own followers.[24]

Yet Henry's plans are not exactly clear. In his speech he had spoken of "a rapid and vigorous movement, to compel the restoration of the powder," with the alternative of "a reprisal on the King's revenues in the hands of the receiver-general, which would fairly balance the account." [25] But did rapidity and vigor mean compulsion by threatening or even seizing the governor? If His Excellency should be threatened, threatened with what—something worse than seizure? Or if the alternative should prove impracticable and the governor not injured or killed but seized, what then should be done with him? And if he should offer stout resistance, would the cause best be served by turning Williamsburg into a battlefield? None of these questions was to be answered, because it would in fact be reprisal that was brought to pass.

Commencing the march, Henry set about concurrently testing the worth of his option. He detached Ensign Parke Goodall with sixteen men to swing eastward to Laneville in King and Queen County. That was the sumptuous seat of Receiver General Richard Corbin. Goodall's orders were either to procure £330 sterling, the estimated value of the powder, or failing that, to take Corbin prisoner and, "with all possible respect and tenderness," to bring him to Doncastle's Ordinary (or tavern) in New Kent County, some sixteen miles from the capital. There the main body would be encamped.[26]

On Tuesday, 3 May, Henry and his command reached and bivouacked at Doncastle's. Subsequently the "army" was described as totaling "150 men and upwards, all well accoutred," of "very martial appearance," and "all men of property." The historian John Daly Burk, who wrote while many of the Revolutionary actors were still living, declared that Henry's "force was estimated at 500 men." Whatever its number, however, it most assuredly could not have approached the "five thousand men at least" reported by Wirt as "believed" either to be encamped or "crossing the country to crowd around" Henry's "standard." [27]

Neither did His Lordship know the number of Henry's cohort, but the very existence of the force was a menace rubbing on nerves already raw. This third day of May 1775 was for the governor a busy but not an especially good one. With the advice of his Council, he issued a proclamation, probably all the while suspecting its futility, in which he attempted to justify his removal of the powder, affirmed his anxiety "to restore peace and harmony to this distracted country," and called on "all his majesty's liege subjects" to "exert themselves in removing all discontents, and suppressing the spirit of faction, which prevail among the people."[28]

There was something inconsistent in bidding "all" of His Majesty's subjects to remove discontents and suppress faction among the "people" who were their discontented and factious selves. With the colony admittedly "distracted" and the capital swept by rumors and speculations, it was almost equally inconsistent (if the report be true) of His Lordship to say to Mayor Dixon: "I will be damned, if I were in your place, if I would not march out the town volunteers, and tell Henry's men, 'As the other companies' "—those lately represented at the council in Fredericksburg—" 'have been prevailed upon to stop, and as we are satisfied about the affair of the powder, you must not and shall not enter our town, which is now in peace and quietness.' " But instead of fighting the governor's battle for him, the mayor convoked the Common Hall, which advised him to send messengers to Captain Henry in an effort to dissuade him from invasion.[29]

Ensign Goodall the while was cantering with his detachment to the ordinary, which he reached about sunset. On the previous night he had halted at Laneville "some hours after bedtime" and had thrown a guard around the receiver general's mansion. Near daybreak Mrs. Corbin appeared and assured him that Colonel Corbin was in Williamsburg. No, her husband did not keep public moneys at his residence but at his office in the capital. If, however, the ensign wished to assure himself, the house was "open to search." A gentleman, the ensign needed no further assurance.[30]

Others were arriving in camp. "Messenger after messenger" was hurried to Doncastle's importuning Henry not to resume his march. Dunmore had sent his lady and their children to the safety of the *Fowey*, which had "come round" on 23 April "to York, from Hampton road"; he had mounted cannon before the Palace; and he swore to fire on the town "the very moment one hostile Virginian should enter it." And it was being buzzed about that at the signal of his fire, the *Fowey* would "perpetrate the same atrocity" on Yorktown. That his noble opponent might not learn the strength of his command, Henry ordered the messengers detained. But there came into camp one man whom he could not detain. That was Carter Braxton, who had ridden down from Edmundsbury, Edmund Pendleton's estate in Caroline County. At Bowling Green he had witnessed Pendleton, Benjamin Harrison, and Peyton Randolph, pausing on their way to Congress, dissuade the independent company from moving against the capital. He hoped in consequence that Henry could be halted "upon the strength of this precedent." But Henry was given to making his own precedents: either the powder must be returned or its loss compensated with money. An understanding was reached. Braxton would go to Williamsburg and exert his influence on Richard Corbin. His prospects should be fair, for the receiver general was his father-in-law. In the meantime, Henry would remain in place pending Braxton's return.[31]

Braxton found his father-in-law's official finances involved and the older man reluctant to accede to his proposition. But with the aid of Thomas Nelson, Sr., president of the governor's Council and secretary of the colony, accession was finally won and a bill of exchange procured. Or, according to His Excellency, "a certain Patrick Henry," notoriously "a man of desperate circumstances," and his accomplices "found means, by threatening the person, family and property of his Maj'ty's Receiver General, Mr. Corbin, to extort the sum of 330 pounds from him." Although by this statement Dunmore was quenching his wonted thirst for exaggeration, Braxton might in part have agreed with him, as the latter's actions in the third Virginia Convention were to disclose.[32]

Whatever the cause—perhaps because of faulty loyalist intelligence—the governor had persuaded himself that with or without concessions on his part, Henry intended to attack the Palace at dawn on the fourth of May. Hence, before he knew or could know of the Braxton-Nelson-Corbin negotiations, he "wrote privately" to Captain George Montagu, commanding the *Fowey*, requesting that he send a detachment to his assistance. Dunmore was further informed that Henry had sent a letter to "the People of the County of York" bidding them to "prevent, at all events, any succour being sent" to the governor from the *Fowey*, and to cut off his line of withdrawal should he seek to "retreat to the Man of War." In this case His Lordship's intelligence may have been more accurate. But notwithstanding such vigilance as a letter may have roused, a total of forty-three sailors and marines, led by a captain and a lieutenant, disembarked without detection near midnight the third and marched to Porto Bello, the governor's plantation on Queen's Creek in York County, about six miles from the capital. It was there that their presence seems to have been discovered.[33]

Captain Montagu, meanwhile, was worried. It was later to be reported that he had no firearms for his men and sent them on their mission equipped only with cutlasses, swords, and bayonets. "It is imagined," wrote John Pinkney, with mock seriousness, "they were to be supplied from the spoils of the vanquished." It was much more probable that Dunmore had promised to provide them with muskets, of which he had an ample stock in the Palace—provided only that the detachment could reach him. In seeking to assure himself that it would, Montagu sent a letter to Thomas Nelson, Sr. But at the time of receipt of the letter at his house, that addressee was either in Williamsburg or on his way to Doncastle's Ordinary, whither he rode with Braxton. "THE town of York being somewhat alarmed," apparently by the very fact that the captain had addressed the president-secretary, the York County committee procured a copy of the letter and learned that should the sailors and marines be "molested and attacked," the *Fowey* would fire on the town.[34]

The practicality of this means of communication is elusive. The captain neither made certain that Nelson would receive the letter nor that he would receive it at a given time. Although it was desirable that the movement of the sailor-marine force should be expeditious, the movement could not be kept secret once the contents of the letter were known. Yet fending off molestation and attack could not be guaranteed until the contents were known widely. But the letter did serve a purpose—to the patriots, enabled once more to reveal the cloven hoofs of His Majesty's servants.

Hearing that the detachment had resumed its march, Captain James Innes, commanding the Williamsburg independent company, assembled his men. But Captain Foy was making the rounds, going from house to house, stating that the force would not enter the municipality but would come in through the gardens at the rear of the Palace, and pledging that as soon as His Lordship's personal safety was assured, sailors and marines would depart. The "people wavered." So did Captain Innes. And the detachment slipped into the Palace, but not, according to one of Pinkney's "correspondents," who was present in fact or imagination, until several marines, grown flabby from confinement aboard the *Fowey*, "tumbled into a ditch, which it was necessary to cross."[35]

The departure of the tars and sea-soldiers was delayed until Monday, 15 May, a considerable time after it was certain that Patrick Henry had withdrawn and his troops were dispersed. Feeling for the moment secure, Dunmore on the sixth affixed his signature to another proclamation. His target was the selfsame Henry and his "deluded Followers." They had, His Excellency averred, "lately" placed themselves "in a Posture of War," excited "great Terrour" in "all his Majesty's faithful Subjects," committed "Acts of Violence," extorted £330 from His Majesty's receiver general, and reduced the colony to a situation where there was "no longer the least Security for the life or Property of any Man." The governor therefore strictly charged all Virginians to have nothing to do with "the said *Patrick Henry*" or his abettors but to oppose "their Designs by every Means." [36]

Reading the proclamation in Philadelphia, Edmund Pendleton accurately judged it "Waste Paper, a mere Subject of Ridicule." With Henry's progress to Philadelphia a triumphal march, approval of his recent action, along with concommitant flayings of almost every activity of the governor by those grown inexplicably comfortable in their "Terrour," was soon reaching the gazettes; and over those patriots to whom Henry's conduct was highly questionable there descended a cloud of silence. To Dunmore the result must have been infuriating. He hated many Virginians. But of them all he probably most hated Henry, whom he described as "one who has been very active in encouraging disobedience and exciting a spirit of Revolt among the People for many years past." Yet had His Lordship taken employment as Henry's publicity agent, he could not have raised his client to an eminence more lofty, and he may even have assured his enemy's election by the third Virginia Convention as commander in chief of the colony's two-regiment "army." [37]

The scene in Virginia was now that of a drama the script of which was being written by the actors themselves as they played their respective roles. Each actor was a free agent, except as he was molded by his constitutional ideology and his personal limitations. But consistency is, after all, a requisite of characterization.

On Friday, 12 May, to the unfeigned "great joy of the inhabitants," the highly esteemed Countess of Dunmore, "with the rest of the Governour's family," returned from the *Fowey* to the Palace. She and the children were doubtless glad to leave cramped quarters, but the exchange was not for the palatial spaciousness they once had known. Edgy in the still-garrisoned abode, the head of the household was "expecting every moment to be attacked" and was supposing that he and his family might be seized and held as hostages, though as to hostages for what he was not quite clear.[38]

It was also on 12 May that His Excellency issued another proclamation. This one roused no controversy. It at long last convoked burgesses elected nearly eleven months past to meet in General Assembly in Williamsburg "on the first *Thursday* in the next Month," or 1 June 1775. The governor said only that the purpose of the convocation was "for the Dispatch of public Business." [39] It was true that there was much long-neglected public business clamoring for dispatch. But few were the Virginians who did not understand that the most important "Business" would be consideration and acceptance or rejection of Lord Frederick North's "Proposition for Conciliating the Differences with America," designated also by other phrases but most popularly as "the Olive Branch."

Around 4:00 P.M. on 20 February the prime minister had risen in the House of Commons and after an introductory speech moved "that when the Governour, Council, and Assembly, or General Court, of any of his Majesty's provinces or colonies in America, shall propose to make provision, according to the conditions, circumstances, and situation of such colony, for contributing their proportion to the *common defence* (such proportion to be ratified under the authority of the General Court or General Assembly of such province or colony, and *disposable by Parliament*) and shall engage to make provision also for the *support of civil government, and the administration of justice* in such province or colony, it will be *proper*, if such proposal *shall be approved by his Majesty, and the two Houses of Parliament*, and for so long as such provision shall be made accordingly, to *forbear*, in respect of *such* province or colony, to levy any duty, tax, or assessment, except only such duties as it may be expedient to impose for the regulation of commerce; the neat ⟨net⟩ produce of the duties last mentioned to be carried to the account of such province, or colony, respectively." [40]

Whatever was the motive of the noble lord in introducing a conciliatory resolution so unlikely to conciliate only he knew. He probably aimed to divide the opposition and to unify the greatest number of Britons behind a policy of applied force by demonstrating that conciliation on any terms then acceptable to the majority of Britons was impossible to achieve. The king viewed even this resolution lukewarmly as evidencing weakness. So contrary was the resolution to the general policy of the ministry that North's own supporters were confused. Likewise was the loyal opposition bewildered. Some contended that the resolution yielded too much. Others argued that it yielded nothing at all. But following a week of strident debate and the exercise of masterly political skill that caused factional lines to vanish, His Lordship rammed the measure through the Commons by the amazing majority of 261 to 85.[41]

Lord Dunmore did not state precisely when he received an official copy of the Olive Branch resolution, but he did state that the gist of "so fair an opening for reconciliation" was public knowledge in the colony for a considerable length of time before receipt. Then late in April the contents of North's proposal were printed in the Williamsburg gazettes.[42] What would the colonial reaction be? It was probably more coincidence than occult forewarning, but between 2:00 and 3:00 P.M. on 22 May three successive storms lashed the lower Tidewater with hailstones, most of them "as big as pigeons eggs, some much larger," and broke windows, "particularly at the palace, which lost upwards of 400 panes." [43] Three days later the Richmond County committee found that the North scheme of conciliation offered "no kind of redress," and on 27 May the committee of Frederick recommended to the county burgesses-elect that they "oppose such proposal to the utmost of their abilities." [44]

His Excellency was gloomy. "The Newspapers," he wrote Dartmouth, "have already begun to prejudice the people" against "Lord North's Plan." He had "little or no good expectations" from the forthcoming meeting of the General Assembly. Influential burgesses were as one with the ringleaders in other colonies, defiant of the constitution and parliamentary law, given to applauding each other's felonies, and having thrown off "every inclination to an accommodation," driving relentlessly toward their true object, "Independence" of the mother country. As for the mass of the "People of this Country," they were paying almost reverential regard "to the Laws established by the General Congress" and were beyond "the influence of reason." [45]

Nevertheless, the play must go on. It went on with a touch of high drama. The pending opening of the Assembly had necessitated Peyton Randolph's quitting the presidency of Congress, and he set out for Virginia "this Morning early" on 24

May. Six days later he reached Ruffin's Ferry, some thirty miles from the capital. There he was met by Carter Braxton and a cavalry detachment of the Williamsburg volunteers, determined to protect him from possible seizure by royal agents. Two miles from the town the group was joined by the infantry company, and around sunset the procession made its way in the governor's sight and hearing to Randolph's house midst tolling bells, illuminations, and acclamations. Then the volunteers, "with many other respectable Gentlemen, assembled at the Raleigh, spent an hour or two in harmony and cheerfulness, and drank several patriotic toasts." [46]

The next day the volunteers presented Randolph with a formal address, pledging their lives to defend him against the "malevolent daemons" they supposed were plotting his capture and legalized murder. This message was not lost on His Excellency. Cooped up in his Palace, he had heard that there were "daemons" in Congress too, and they had directed the "people" to make "reprisals," in consequence of which "if any lives of Americans are lost, or their persons seized, in the course of these unhappy divisions, the same is to be retaliated upon the officers of Governt wherever they are to be found." Obviously, Mr. Speaker's security and good health were not the least of His Excellency's concerns. [47]

When the General Assembly convened on 1 June, all was conducted with wonted courtesy and decorum. All of the traditional forms were maintained. The House of Burgesses unanimously reelected Peyton Randolph speaker and sent a messenger to the council chamber to announce the fact to the governor. His Lordship sent his own messenger to bid the members of the House attend him. Once they were in his presence, they stood with outward signs of respect. But there was a difference in the attire of many who heretofore had come elegantly vested. It having been bruited that the noble trickster seated at the head of the table intended by a sudden return of the sailors and marines to capture and imprison the burgesses, "a Number" had come to Williamsburg armed to the teeth and now were "in the habits of the Men Intituled American Troops, wearing a Shirt of Coarse Linnen or Canvass over their Cloaths and a Tomahak by their Sides." [48] The noble trickster of course pretended not to notice and said: "Gentlemen of the Council, Mr. Speaker, and Gentlemen of the House of Burgesses, I have called you together to give you an Opportunity of taking the alarming State of the Colony into your Consideration, and providing Remedies against the Evils which are increasing therein." So much he had been induced to do, he added, because actions of king and Parliament "no longer admit of a Doubt that your well-founded Grievances, properly represented, will meet with that Attention and Regard which are so justly due to them."

He then took up the subject of Lord North's Olive Branch, which he labeled "a benevolent Tender," and stated that "It must now be manifest, to all dispassionate People, that the Parliament, the high and supreme Legislature of the Empire," had only the "Enjoyment of equal Rights, Privileges, and Advantages," of all His Majesty's subjects in view, and he did not believe that the "Principle" that all of the parts should contribute to the whole had ever "been denied by the People of his Majesty's Dominion of Virginia."

Delivering himself of the sophism that any money forced from the colony would be a "Gift" to be considered "in the completest Manner, free," he concluded this phase of his address by expressing the hope that the Assembly would "imitate the Example of Justice, Equity, and Moderation" that had "actuated the House of Commons in their Resolution," to the end that it might be held "by his

Majesty not only a Testimony of your Reverence for Parliament, but also as a Mark of your Duty and Attachment to your Sovereign."

On one other subject he touched. That was to recommend that the House "fall upon Means of paying the Officers and private Men" who had served in the Indian war that bore his name.[49]

Returned to its own chamber, the House ordered that a fair copy of "the said Speech do lie upon the Table," presumably alongside the members' collective "Reverence for Parliament." [50]

So long had it been since a General Assembly had met that there was a veritable mountain of work for the House to consider even before it could begin deliberation on Lord North's "benevolent Tender." There were lapsed laws to be revived and reinvigorated. Standing and special committees had to be appointed and shoals of petitions and memorials taken up and investigated: for the redress of grievances against allegedly arrogant vestries acting illegally; for the redistribution of estates of deceased subjects; for the rectification of disputed county boundaries; for the authorization of more ferries; for the restraint of hogs roaming the streets of Staunton. And in implementation of such necessities, the House labored on until Saturday, 3 June, when it "adjourned till Monday Morning next ten of the Clock." [51]

His Lordship's penchant for action was now again to find expression. During the night of that Saturday a number of young men (among whom it was said was Mayor Dixon's son) "intending to furnish themselves with"—that is, to steal —"arms," entered the Magazine. One of the youngsters chanced to touch a string. A gun loaded "eight fingers deep with swan shot" suddenly discharged. One youth was wounded only slightly. But a second was "terribly hurt in the shoulder." And a third lost one finger and was maimed in another, which rendered him unable thereafter to ply his undesignated trade.[52]

Immediately Williamsburg was in an uproar of indignation. Assuming that everyone could pretty well guess the identity of the fiend who had arranged for this mayhem, John Pinkney wrote, "We are informed that a certain noble lord is engaged in writing a treatise on the art of war, for the instruction of the *general officers* employed in the reduction of America." With an engineer so skillful at their disposal, Thomas Gage and his colleagues in Boston could, without the sacrifice of a single British regular, wipe out any American army by encircling it with concealed spring guns. Pinkney did, however, think some timid townspeople overwrought in their belief that the noble lord had planted a "subterranean train" of powder from the Palace to the Magazine and could at whim blow up the town.[53]

Alexander Purdie was less certain of identity, but he was no less, and perhaps more subtly, inflammatory in stating that had any of the young men been killed, "the perpetrator, or the perpetrators, of this diabolical invention, might have been justly branded with the opprobrious title of MURDERERS." John Dixon and William Hunter vouched the information that investigation showed a second spring gun to have been emplaced and "double charged," and that the hellish death machines were "said to have been contrived by L——d D——e." [54]

The implication that Dunmore was the inventor of the spring gun, an old device, was nonsense. But, as he never failed to remind others, he was the official custodian of the Magazine, and his failure to post notice that the life of anyone entering it would be endangered rendered him culpable. For, as the

House would subsequently admonish, "an unfortunate Culprit might have been hurried into Eternity without a Moment's Time for reflection." [55]

When the burgesses met again, on Monday, 5 June, the subject of conversations may easily be supplied by supposition rooted in logic. Later that day Speaker Randolph would on order appoint a committee "to inspect the public Magazine in this City, and inquire into the Stores belonging to the same and make report thereof to the House." But on being called to order, the House first had other business. The most significant was presentation and unanimous approval of a reply to the address delivered by the governor on the opening day of session. In measured terms this response cast the whole of the blame for "the alarming Situation of our Country and the Evils brought upon us" on the obstinately unconstitutional policies of the British ministry. It obliquely accused His Lordship of having "strangely" misrepresented the colony to the authorities in England. It charged governor and ministry with having impeded the course of justice and having distressed the course of trade. It stated that certain Virginia inabilities were not locked in mystery, because "Money, my Lord, is not a plant of the native Growth of this Country." And it promised to consider Lord North's Olive Branch "with that Calmness and Impartiality" that its "great Importance" merited.[56]

Although as the burgess for the College of William and Mary, Attorney General John Randolph was present during some days of session, the unanimity with which the reply was adopted renders it inconceivable that he was in attendance during much of the session of this Monday. He would have approved neither of the philosophy of the reply nor of the phraseology in which it was couched. He would not on this same day have participated in the unanimous action of the House in "intirely and cordially" approving the proceedings and resolutions of the first Continental Congress. Nor in the unanimous and warm commendation of the conduct of the Virginia delegation to that Congress. Nor in the unanimous approval of the proceedings of the second Virginia Convention, which he had refused to attend, and which in some measure was the bestowal of legal applause by the House upon itself when performing in an extralegal capacity.[57]

On 6 June there was a tart exchange between His Excellency and the House respecting gubernatorial behavior and that of the committee appointed to inspect and report on the condition of the Magazine. Having been put at a considerable disadvantage in this correspondence, on the seventh he shifted stance and assured the burgesses that his only thought had been to infringe no "Rule, or omit any Ceremony due to your House." On that same day the capital was again thrown into tumult, this time by a report that the sailors and marines were returning and that Captain Colins, having slipped the cable of the *Magdalen*, was sailing up "the River with a number of boats in which there was said to be a hundred armed men at least." There followed a parade of agitated townsmen along the well-trod paths leading to the Magazine, and soon the remaining serviceable muskets were being passed from hand to hand. The committee of inspection appointed on the fifth described the latest acquirers as "some Persons, unknown," but by passing around the word that no questions would be asked (though, complained Dunmore, "so heinous an offence" deserved severe punishment), managed to retrieve a few of the pieces. The committee also had Captain Innes post a guard at the Magazine, an action that His Lordship challenged as being a usurpation of executive authority, though with some justification he thought it a bit late, "as there remained nothing" in the depot that "required being guarded." [58]

Flying rumors and seething citizens were by now causing nervousness among members of His Lordship's Council. Isolated from the mainstream of events as several of them had been made to feel, unfortunate in their attempt to pacificate,[59] and fully aware that with the establishment of a new order, their days of power would be ended, they yet clung to their posts and worked as best they could. Meeting hastily, they recorded in their journal their having heard that the "Marines and Sailors belonging to his Majesty's Ship the Fowey, were expected to be at the Palace this day, by the Governor's orders." Reports were rife that Williamsburgers and the men of adjoining countries were "greatly alarmed" and "determined to attack the said Marines and Sailors if they should come." It was therefore "ordered" that Richard Corbin and Robert Carter, a former councilor residing in the town, "wait on his Excellency" and desire him in the name of the Council, by countermanding his order, to prevent "the great Calamity which would otherwise ensue."

When approached, His Excellency "appeared to be astonished." He had given no such "order." He knew of no intention to send sailors and marines to the Palace. And if sending them was anybody's "design," he would certainly prevent it.[60]

The governor in his letter of 15 May to Lord Dartmouth had already considered the possibility of having "to retire towards the Town of York," where he might throw up "a little entrenchment" or "at worst" establish his headquarters aboard the *Fowey*. In his opinion the time for "retirement" now had been reached. True it would be that the burgesses were to tell him, "A proper Guard, at the publick Expense, would have been at your Service, had you judged it necessary." He may himself have thought of that possibility and rejected it, for in a moment initiated protection might evolve into protective custody.[61]

As the detested representative of a corrupt and tyrannical authority, Lord Dunmore would soon rouse his detractors to vie in merriment with tales of his discomfitures and embarrassments. Some would even brand him a physical coward. It is highly doubtful that he was. He was of that privileged class of Britons who while seeking aggrandizement and producing too few statesmen, yet boldly shed their blood on battled fields and seas that if not they individually, then their class should remain firmly secured. What seems most probable in his own case is that although capable of initiating an aggressive campaign in the open, he was not of a mold to endure a war of nerves, and his imagination feasted and grew large on phantoms. Had he been a childless widower or a bachelor without commitments of guardianship or support, he might at this time have acted differently. Even then, however, he would have been in the situation, as he professed to believe, of being "fallen upon," with the result that the colony would be plunged "into the most horried calamities" and "the breach with the mother Country" thereby rendered "irreparable." [62]

When, then, in the evening of 7 June 1775 he walked to John Randolph's house, his going thither may of itself have been an act of courage. He knew that arms were in the hands of "some Persons, unknown" and could not be certain that at any moment he might not be gunned down by a shadowy figure fading into the darkness. Suppose that vengeance-minded kinsmen or friends of the two young men seriously wounded by the discharge of the spring gun were to seek to even the score. The burgesses might think this highly improbable, but a person so unexcitable as Edmund Pendleton believed that because of the spring-gun incident, His Lordship "might well fear what he must have been conscious he deserved, Assassination." [63]

What Dunmore and John Randolph discussed in the evening of that seventh day of June is unrecorded. On a previous occasion the attorney general had advised the governor that in his opinion "his Person was in no danger," and Randolph, who was an authority on the penalties incurred by unpopularity, had not yet changed his mind. But apparently the subject did not arise during the present conversation, and unaccompanied and unaccosted, the governor returned to the Palace. [64]

On 8 June the House resumed business with the expectation that in order to present an address respecting certain matters raised in his speech of the opening day of session, His Lordship would receive the burgesses in the council chamber at 1:00 P.M. It was with astonishment therefore that after having transacted a good deal of business, the House received from him, as transmitted through the Council, a message announcing that he and his family were aboard the *Fowey*. Mr. Attorney General was inclined to impute the nocturnal flight to Lady Dunmore's "Timidity of her Sex" (he did not say as perhaps played upon by her husband) in fearing injury might "be done to her or her Family." He could not conceive what else had motivated the governor's withdrawal unless His Lordship had credited "Reports" of which he had himself heard nothing. [65]

But whatever he may or may not have heard, Dunmore asserted that he was "fully persuaded" that he, his lady, and their children were in constant danger of "falling sacrifices to the blind and unmeasurable fury which has so unaccountably seized upon the minds and understandings of great numbers of People." He trusted that the Assembly would appreciate this reason for his change of residence; and he would remain accessible in the discharge of his office and contribute everything in his power "if opportunity be given me to restore that harmony, the interruption of which is likely to cost so dear, to the repose, as well as to the comfort of every individual." [66]

The House immediately resolved itself into Committee of the Whole. Plainly the members believed that assigning Lady Dunmore and the children to roles as potential victims of either mob or individual violence was not only poor casting but an aspersion on the honor of the colony. The members did not believe that the governor himself was in jeopardy, and in a return address they offered "cheerfully" to accede to "any measure that may be proposed proper to the security of yourself and family." They added that it was "impracticable" to carry on the business of legislation "with that dispatch the advanced season of the year"—an allusion to the need of gathering in their harvests—required, what with the *Fowey* moored twelve miles down the York from the Capitol. For these reasons and because it would be the "most likely means of quieting the minds of the People," they urged the return of himself and his loved ones. With these sentiments His Lordship's own Council concurred and appointed two unidentified members to join Archibald Cary, James Wood, Mr. Attorney General, and Carter Braxton to wait on him with the address. [67]

It is not improbable that the cause for his flight was exactly what the Scottish earl-governor stated it to be. He may also have had larger objects in view. Flight was the abandonment of an ancient post and might seem a cowardly recourse. But it presented to him the opportunity for what was most appealing, action—a strategic withdrawal—for he may have conceived that from his new post he could with increased flexibility maneuver his king's "Enemies" into false positions, despite which possible purpose, among those "Enemies" were some of the most politically astute minds in the colony.

The House the while labored on, making every effort to bring bills, of which there now were many, to completion. Then on 10 June it received Dunmore's reply to the address of the eighth. He defended his departure, citing "commotions among the People, and their menaces and threats (an enumeration of which I forbear, out of tenderness)." Loose talk was not deed, but he had heard talk enough to justify his "suspicion" that such words might well end in "Crime." The remainder of the reply was an ultimatum: He must be reinstated in the "full powers" of his office, the courts entirely reopened, the independent companies disarmed and dissolved, the arms restored to the Magazine, and the "ferment" ended. "I shall have no objection," he said, "to your adjourning to the Town of York, where I shall meet you, and remain with you till your business is finished." But, he added ominously, unless the House should "seize this opportunity" to adopt Lord North's conciliatory proposition, all else must fail.[68]

Subscribing to the Olive Branch was precisely what the burgesses did not intend to do. Peyton Randolph had on 2 June appointed a committee of twelve "to draw up an Address, to be presented to the Governor upon the said Resolution" of the House of Commons. Robert Carter Nicholas was the chairman. But Randolph, returned from Congress, wished Virginia to produce a reply that would "harmonize with what he knew to be the sentiments and wishes of the body he recently left." He feared that Nicholas would produce one of those mealy-mouthed hemmings and hawings fraught with the obsequious phraseology so much the mark of conservatives educated in an earlier tradition and not yet convinced that the hour was eleven forty-five. So Randolph "pressed" Jefferson to "undertake the answer."

This Jefferson did. Because the terms of North's proposition were known, having already appeared in the three Williamsburg gazettes,[69] Jefferson may by tacit agreement have begun work even before appointment of the committee, and thus to the startlement of others on that body, have presented his manuscript before there was time to catch a conservative breath. On 10 June Archibald Cary, ninth-named of the committee, reported the draft to the House, which immediately went into "a Committee of the whole House." With the aid of Mr. Speaker, Cary and Jefferson carried the address "through the house with long and doubtful scruples from Mr. Nicholas and James Mercer," the second-named vice-chairman of the drafting committee. Nicholas and Mercer threw "a dash of cold water" on the document, "here & there, enfeebling it somewhat," but without weakening its essential power. Approval guaranteed, Jefferson departed on the eleventh for Philadelphia to attend the Congress. On 12 June the House of Burgesses adopted the resolution. Jefferson in his recollections years later indicated that the address was accepted "with unanimity or a vote approaching it." But it was not with unanimity, for the house journal does not so record it.[70]

Even if somewhat enfeebled, the nine-paragraph address to the governor was so clearly phrased that none could misunderstand it, and if respectful to His Lordship, it was blunt. In adopting it, the House disclosed not only that it resented new grievances superimposed on those grown encrusted but that the great majority of burgesses no longer in principle descried any distinction between "internal" taxation and the regulation of "external" trade and thought themselves

as Britons equally entitled to "a free Trade with all the World." That majority
had also come around to Jefferson's view that Parliament had no constitutional
authority "to intermeddle" in any phase of colonial life: "for us, not for them, has
government been instituted here," and "we conceive that we alone are the judges
of the condition, circumstances and situation of our people, as Parliament are of
theirs." Lord North's leafless Olive Branch was, therefore, rejected in whole, but
"Because the proposition now made involves the interest of all the other Colonies," Virginia could do no other than await the decision of the Continental
Congress, to which she was "bound in honor as well as interest to share one
general fate with our Sister Colonies, and should hold ourselves base deserters of
that union to which we have acceded, were we to agree to any measure distinct
and apart from them." [71]

Jefferson on 21 June presented his credentials to Congress. On 22 July he was
appointed vice-chairman of a committee that, consisting also of Benjamin Franklin, John Adams, and Richard Henry Lee, was directed "to take into consideration, and report on the resolution of the House of Commons, Feby. 1775,
commonly called lord North's motion." The Virginia document had been printed
in the *Pennsylvania Gazette* on 28 June and was being roundly applauded. Its
author was therefore requested to draft another for the committee, and for that
reason presentation of the report on 31 July revealed a "similarity of feature in
the two instruments." [72]

While this sequel was being played out to the northward, Richard Bland returned from Congress, "charged with some important business from that august
body to be laid before the Assembly of this colony." The business, which he
divulged on 14 June, was important indeed, relating as it did to securing the
western frontiers. Bland presented to the House a petition to Congress from
"several Persons in that part of the County of *Augusta* which is on the West side
of the *Allegany* Mountain." The petitioners were extremely uneasy. Lord Dunmore had promised the Northwest Indians to meet them in the spring of 1775 at
Fort Pitt, to restore to them the hostages of the tribes defeated in the late war,
and with all the tribes to conclude a final peace. But though the petitioners were
kept in the dark, "unable to discover the design of Government," they suspected
that "the Commandant in that Quarter" [73] was under instructions to assemble the
Indians "so soon as he could" and while winning them to the royal cause, "to
enfranchise the Slaves, on the condition they would rebel against their Masters."
The West Augustans had appealed to Congress because both the colonies of
Virginia and Pennsylvania were involved, and it was believed that the Assembly
of neither could "provide adequate remedies early enough." But for a number of
reasons, this was a touchy subject, and Congress referred the matter to the delegates of the two colonies and, adopting their recommendation, transmitted the
document or a copy of it to the House of Burgesses, to which it was now submitted "with all convenient expedition." [74]

The parts of a picture seemed all coming together, however much might be
fact, however much surmise, however much fantasy: a governor in seclusion
giving ear to evil counselors of suspected identity plotting no patriot knew
exactly what; intrigue in the West and the possibility of new Indian incursions;
schemes to rouse the slaves to a murderous uprising; and a public magazine deliberately denuded of serviceable munitions. Then on 15 June the governor replied to the Jefferson composition of the twelfth. He was brief: "Gentlemen of

the House of Burgesses, It is with real concern I can discover nothing in your address that I think manifests the smallest inclination to, or will be productive of, a reconciliation with the Mother Country." [75]

Did these few words signify the end? Not quite. For the burgesses must needs keep the faith with their constituents and hold the stage until denouement, and that still required the writing of much script. On the next day, 16 June, James Mercer, chairman of the committee of inspection, presented and successfully moved the adoption of an address in which the governor was informed that "the Public Magazine is now repaired, and in fit Condition for the Reception of Arms and Ammunition." He was requested, therefore, to order the gunpowder "lately removed from thence" to be returned in keeping with his written "promise." But more, in consideration of the possibility of a renewal of Indian warfare and of an insurrection of slaves "encouraged, merely from a Notoriety of a total Deficiency of our public Stores of Arms and Ammunition," to draw on the ample funds provided for that purpose, and "immediately" to purchase and stock the Magazine with 2,000 stand of arms, five tons of powder, and twenty tons of lead, "with a sufficient Quantity of other Military Stores." [76]

Next there was the task of responding to His Excellency's reply received on the tenth, in which he had defended his flight and laid down his ultimatum. Robert Carter Nicholas presented the lengthy response on 15 June, when the House adopted it unanimously. Unanimity can mean only that if present, John Randolph discreetly withdrew. By adopting, the burgesses declared that they had received His Lordship's reply "with equal Concern and Amazement." Their honors impugned, they were "driven" into the "disagreeable necessity of inquiring, minutely, into the Causes of the late Disturbances in this Country." They would not rub salt into His Excellency's exposed sensibilities, but they could not but contrast his administration with that of his immediate predecessor, "the truly noble" Norborne Berkeley, Baron de Botetourt, who examining every subject "to the bottom," discountenanced "Tale-Bearers and malicious informers" and gloried in observing Virginia in "Tranquility and Happiness." [77]

Dunmore and his family had been received in the colony with every manifestation of respect and joy. If now His Lordship discovered any "Alteration of Sentiments or behaviour" in those over whose destinies he presided, it might be to his advantage "to search out the reason of it." The House then proceeded to spare him the trouble: He mistakenly believed that respect was obtainable by force: he lacked dignity; he was not exemplary in his conduct; he was uncandid; and he "too easily" credited the whispers of "designing Persons, who, to the great injury of this Community, possess much too large a share of your Confidence," [78] with the result that to judge by his letters of 29 May and 24 December 1774, his pronouncements to the Colonial Office were masses of misrepresentation.

The burgesses went on to review the course of constitutional and political developments since 1773, contesting every foot of the way the governor's allegations and presenting the patriot case for the first two Virginia conventions, the Continental Congress, the associations, the county committees, the independent companies, actions following the removal of the gunpowder, tumults that had rocked the capital in particular and the colony in general, and their own rejection of the North Olive Branch.

"The important Business of the Assembly, my Lord," they concluded, "has been not a little interrupted by your Excellency's Removal from the proper Seat of your Government." The reassembling of the legislature in Yorktown would be "extremely improper," both because accommodations would be inadequate and, more importantly, because Williamsburg alone was "established by Law" as the site for holding a General Assembly. For these reasons, it would be best were the governor to return with his family to the Palace.[79] But with such an address in hand, such a governor would have returned only at the head of a brigade.

Late in the session of 20 June His Excellency's reply to James Mercer's report of five days before was received. The reply was a flat refusal to return the gunpowder to the Magazine; a reiteration that Williamsburg as "an improper place for the residence of the Governor"; an accusation that the House was trying to bring "legal and Constitutional Government at this unhappy Conjuncture, into discredit among the People"; and a statement that "Army Powder and other Military Stores" would be placed in the Magazine only when the "legal executive Power of Government" should be "restored."[80] If reported accurately, it may have been at this time that "Old Dick Bland" exploded and proposed that somehow His Lordship's person be seized, talking "very fluently in the house about hanging him." This at least was the report that, sifting down to Norfolk, would within another four days be repeated by James Parker, who though never inclined to let an effervescent story lose a bubble, seems generally to have been well informed. Parker heard also that Thomas Whiting "made some foolish Speeches to the Same purpose."[81] But Parker did not advise his correspondent as to how the burgesses could bring "Government" into a discredit exceeding that it already experienced among the "People," or how the governor's "executive Power" was to be restored without a governor.

On 21 June the Council joined the House in trying to persuade Dunmore to return to Williamsburg for the signing of bills in the "accustomed Mode" and again mentioned the "advanced Season of the Year," which required "our Presence in our several Counties." The joint appeal drew an unwontedly quick reply, received the next day, but the governor remained adamant; he would not return. And as for bills, not having "been made acquainted with the whole proceedings of the Assembly"—although before the rising of the legislature a governor of Virginia seldom was—he knew of "none of importance."[82]

There was one that he would consider important by his own testimony. In his address to the Council and the House on the opening day of session, he had said: "I must recommend to you to fall upon Means of paying the Officers and private Men employed in repelling the late Invasions and Incursions of the Indians, and I make no doubt you will think their Services on that Occasion deserving of your Attention."[83]

He needed "make no doubt," and the Assembly had fallen upon "Means," in a bill passed by the House on 15 June and concurred in without amendment by the Council six days later; and John Randolph was chosen to bear that bill and others to the *Fowey*. The attorney general returned to the House on 23 June. The governor had objections. The militia-payments bill would impose duties on imported slaves, a fact that would almost certainly incur the royal disallowance; and there was no suspending clause, although the bill provided for an emission of paper money. Thus "the Miscarriage of a Bill I had very much at heart cannot be attributed to me." Should the Assembly feel unable to remove these objectionable features, he would nevertheless "transmit the Bill to his Majesty and desire leave to it, though in regard to the Duty upon Slaves I should not, I think, obtain it." He saw nothing wrong in the other bills so far submitted to his examination and was ready to give his assent to them whenever the Assembly desired, with the implication that any signing would have to take place aboard the man-of-war or under her guns. If any other bills were ready, he would welcome their delivery "in like manner that the whole may be passed together." And then, having fastened upon the nuisance value of his earlier suggestion, he requested that the clerk be ordered to lay before him a copy of the journal of the House "before the time be fixed for passing the Bills." [84]

Speaker Randolph immediately appointed a committee of six, with Robert Carter Nicholas as chairman, to prepare what would prove to be the final address of a Virginia House of Burgesses to a royal governor. Although the journal shows the document to have been presented on the heels of the appointment, this would have been an impossibility, and since no other business was to be transacted that day, it is probable that the House recessed until a designated hour.

The address that Nicholas introduced was adopted without recorded amendment. It expressed "Concern" that His Lordship should be under any "Difficulty" in assenting to the militia-payments bill. Investigation had shown that to do the justice the governor had so much at heart, the "extreme Scarcity of Cash in the Country" left the only means of supply that of "a speedy Emission of Paper Money," and the inclusion of a suspending clause "would defeat the very purpose, for which the Bill was intended as it would withhold that Relief, so immediately necessary to the comfort and support of many of our poor Inhabitants, who are in the utmost Distress for want of it." In discharge of the relief, it had been conceived that a 10-percent duty on imported slaves would be least "burthensome." It was not recalled that such a duty had ever been objected to by His Majesty, while it had been understood that one not exceeding that percentage was "perfectly agreeable to his royal Will and Pleasure."

Once again the imperative need to harvest was mentioned. His Lordship was therefore "entreated" to meet the Assembly at the Capitol on the morrow. It was hoped that he did not still entertain "any groundless fears" that he would be in the "least Danger." Yet if he did (Bland's and Whiting's tempers having apparently been brought under control), the House would pledge its honor "and every thing sacred" that his person would be secure. If, however, he saw fit to deny even this "just Request," it was hoped that he would be pleased to commission President Thomas Nelson, Sr., to assent to such bills and resolves as Dunmore should himself approve.

Since from time immemorial it had been "customary" for governors to "signify their Pleasure as to adjournments," the burgesses wished not "to take Things out of their old Channel." For that reason, it was trusted that His Excellency would express "approbation" should they adjourn themselves to "some Day in October next," a time most convenient for them to reconvene and when "the sickly Season of the Year will probably be over."

The members of the House did not wish to conceal from the governor "one Tittle" of their journal. But penning "a full and immediate Transcript" would be impossible. They might have added that he knew a great deal of the contents already, as many entries consisted of a voluminous correspondence in which he had been writer or addressee. Instead, they observed that his request was "unusual," but they would forward such of their proceedings as had appeared in newsprint (which he probably had already read).

The final address was ordered delivered to the governor by John Randolph and Andrew Lewis. A better couple could not have been appointed. The former, though His Excellency's friend, stood as one with the other burgesses in believing him in no physical danger and could counsel him on constitutional and legal points at issue. The latter, the hero of the Battle of Point Pleasant, could most authoritatively present the case for the "poor Inhabitants" reduced to distress by Dunmore's War.[85]

It is doubtful that a governor possessing steadier nerves and wisdom of at least second magnitude would have betaken himself to the seclusion of the *Fowey*. At the present juncture it would seem that a governor possessing wisdom of at least third magnitude would have thrown aside the hitherto presumed advantages of isolation. Such a governor would by this date have divined that in no way was he outmaneuvering the burgesses. If not wholly seeing, he would have sensed that continued isolation could end only in severing the last delicate link by which the colony remained in civil attachment to the Crown. He might have left his family behind, but he would himself have returned to the "proper Seat" of government and there confronted and attempted to resolve; and if though with courtesy and tact failing to resolve, he would have retrieved the earlier, fair reputation men had wished to assign him, and he would have been honored even by those who opposed him. To His Lordship, however, the entreaty of the House was but an attempt to inveigle him to place himself "again in their Power." [86] But "Power" to do what? The future would not record that the availability of the Earl of Dunmore in His Majesty's service brought great cunning to the royal councils or glorified the British arms by the glint of a single bayonet.

Returned, Randolph the next day—it was Saturday, 24 June 1775—rose in his place and read the governor's written "Answer." If Mr. Attorney General had attempted to convince, and Colonel Lewis to persuade, they had failed. For the reasons previously advanced, His Lordship refused to assent to the militia-payments bill, and now disowning his promise to transmit the proposed legislation to the king, though without approval, he commented that "the blame of its not passing now into Law" could not be made to "lie upon" him. As for the plighted honor and everything held sacred by the House, in a damning indictment of himself, he brushed them aside with the statement that the "well grounded cause" he had for believing himself unsafe in Williamsburg "increased daily." He would, in consequence, be ready to receive the burgesses on the Monday following at his "present residence" for the purpose of signing such bills as met his approval. The desire of the House "not to take things out of their old Channel" he treated with a parenthetical sneer that rasps down the years of over two centuries: "(as if you had such Power)." But, rather contradictorily, if the House wished to adjourn, let it begone; he would determine the date of reconvocation when he pleased.[87]

He was never to have the opportunity to proclaim a reconvocation of the General Assembly. The House resolved itself into a "Committee of the whole House," Richard Bland presiding, "to take into Consideration the state of the Colony." The unanimity with which the resultant five resolutions were adopted strongly suggests that after the first reading, John Randolph was granted leave: the first two resolutions he could not have endorsed. In the first the House resolved that Dunmore's requiring the members to attend him on board a man-of-war was "a high Breach of the Rights and Privileges" of its body. In the second it resolved that the "unreasonable delays" he had caused in enacting legislation, and the "evasive Answers" he had returned to "sincere and decent Addresses" indicated that he meditated an armed attack and that the people should prepare their defense. In the third it resolved that the king should be supported in all his rights and prerogatives "as founded on the established Laws and Principles of the Constitution." In the fourth it resolved that the bands of "Amity" with fellow subjects in Great Britain should be preserved and strengthened. And in a fifth it resolved that it was with "deepest concern" that it had been deprived of the chance to make "the most ample Provision" for the suffering poor of Dunmore's War.[88]

But there were measures that could be taken. With or without the governor's approval, every effort must be made to secure the western frontiers. The Council joined the House in voting the appointment of commissioners "to ratify the Treaty of Peace with the Ohio Indians, and for defraying the expense thereof." [89] And Speaker Randolph appointed ten commissioners to "examine, state, and settle the Accounts of the pay of the Militia, and of all Provisions, Arms, Ammunition, and other necessaries, furnished the said Militia of the Counties" and to "report the same to the General Assembly." [90]

Lord Dunmore heard of other transactions unrecorded in the journal and petulantly informed Lord Dartmouth that "the Treasurer has taken upon him, without any Warrant from me, and without the Authority of any Law, to pay out of the Publick Money Committed to his Care the Burgesses, and the Speaker their Wages, and such other claims as the House of Burgesses thought proper, amounting to a large Sum of Money." [91]

"*And then the House adjourned until* Thursday, *the twelfth day of* October *next, at ten of the Clock in the Morning.*" [92]

This was finis. The House had played its role well, with sincerity, character, and dignity, and in making its final bow needed apologize for no lack in its performance. There would be other dramas to come, some even with scenes in which, however sanguinary, His Lordship would provide a species of comic relief. But as for royal government in Virginia, save where its authority could be pinned down by bayonets, after 161 years the drama in which it had held center stage was ended, and the curtain descended forever.

1. See 28 Mar. 1775 below.

2. British Public Record Office, Colonial Office, Group 5, Class 1353, folio 110; hereafter cited as P.R.O., C.O. 5/1353, fol. 110.

3. William J. Van Schreevan and Robert L. Scribner, comps., *Revolutionary Virginia: The Road to Independence*, ed. Robert L. Scribner (Charlottesville, 1973–; hereafter *Rev. Va.*), II, 276–77.

4. Ibid., II, 385.

5. Ibid., II, 376.

6. John Page, "Memoir," *Virginia Historical Register* . . . , ed. William Maxwell, III (July 1850) 148–49.

7. *Rev. Va.*, II, 374–75; H[enry] R. McIlwaine and John Pendleton Kennedy, eds., *Journals of the House of Burgesses of Virginia* (13 unnumbered vols., published in reverse sequential order, Richmond, 1915–1905; hereafter *JHB*), *1773–1776*, p. xviii.

8. William Waller Hening., ed., *The Statutes at Large; Being a Compilation of All the Laws of Virginia, from the First Session of the Year 1619* (13 vols., Richmond, etc., 1809–23; facsimile reprint, Charlottesville, 1969; hereafter *Statutes at Large*), IV, 55–57; *JHB, 1773–1776*, pp. 223–24; Ivor Noël Hume, *1775: Another Part of the Field* (New York, 1966), p. 138.

9. P.R.O. C.O. 5/1353, fol. 137; *Virginia Gazette* (Purdie), 21 Apr. 1775, supplement; *JHB, 1773–1776*, p. xviii.

10. See 21 Apr. 1775, The Capital, 1st entry.

11. *Va. Gazette* (Purdie), 21 Apr. 1775; P.R.O., C.O. 5/1353, fol. 137; *JHB, 1773–1776*, p. 231.

12. See 21 Apr. 1775, The Capital, 2d entry; 27 Apr. 1775 below.

13. See 27 Apr. 1775 below; P.R.O., C.O. 5/1353, fol. 138; *JHB, 1773–1776*, pp. 231–32.

14. *JHB, 1773–1776*, p. xviii.

15. EDWARD FOY, probably somewhere in his 40s, was a battle-tested veteran of the Seven Years' War in Germany. To Landon Carter's taste disturbingly taciturn, Foy was the "confidential inmate, counselor, and private secretary" and "speech-writer" of His Lordship, and some thought that when the unusually tall captain pulled strings, his short and noble employer danced. It might have been better for the employer had he indeed been the employee's puppet. At least Foy thought so, for then some of the "disgrace attending" the employer's "proceedings" would not have occurred. Foy would continue to "revere" Dunmore's countess and the children, but if contempt for the earl-governor was not at this time already built, it would soon be under steady construction (Noël Hume, *1775*, pp. 22, 24–25, 205, 265–67; *Va. Gazette* [Pinkney], 6 Oct. 1775; Jack P. Greene, ed., *The Diary of Colonel Landon Carter of Sabine Hall, 1752–1778* [2 vols., Charlottesville, 1965], II, 837; Edmund Randolph, *History of Virginia*, ed. Arthur H. Shaffer [Charlottesville, 1970], p. 196; Marvin L. Brown, Jr., and Marta Huth, trans. and eds., *Baroness von Riedesel and the American Revolution: Journal and Correspondence of a Tour of Duty, 1776–1783* [Chapel Hill, N.C., 1965], p. 11 n. 52).

16. *JHB, 1773–1776*, p. 231.

17. Hugh Mercer et al. to William Grayson, 24 Apr. 1775 (copy), and to George Washington, 25 Apr. 1775, Grayson et al. to Washington, 26 Apr. 1775, all in George Washington Papers, Library of Congress, microfilm in Virginia State Library; *Va. Gazette* (Purdie) 28 Apr. 1775, supplement; John C. Fitzpatrick, ed., *The Diaries of George Washington, 1747–1799* (4 vols., Boston and New York, 1925), II, 193.

18. *Va. Gazette* (Purdie), 28 Apr. 1775, supplement; ibid. (Dixon and Hunter), 29 Apr. 1775; 27 Apr. 1775 below; Douglas Southall Freeman et al., *George Washington: A Biography* (7 vols., New York, 1948–57), III, 414; *JHB, 1773–1776*, p. xviii.

19. Freeman, *George Washington*, III, 414–15 and n. 88; James T. Flexner, *George Washington: The Forge of Experience* (Boston, 1965), pp. 229–30; Washington to Charles Lewis et al., 3 May 1775, transcript in autograph diary and Revolutionary memoranda of Dr. George Gilmer, Virginia Historical Society; *Va. Gazette* (Pinkney), 11 May 1775; 29 Apr. 1775, Spotsylvania Council.

20. See 28 Apr. 1775, Royal Chief Magistracy.

21. *Virginia Gazette, or the Norfolk Intelligencer,* 4 May 1775; Dunmore to Dartmouth, 1 May 1775 (copy), P.R.O., C.O. 5/1353, fols. 139–40; Dunmore to Samuel Graves, P.R.O., Admiralty (hereafter Adm.) 1/485, pp. 174–75; Dunmore to Thomas Gage, 1 May 1775, in William Bell Clark and William James Morgan, eds., *Naval Documents of the American Revolution* (Washington D.C., 1964–), I, 258–59; *Va. Gazette* (Purdie), 28 Apr. 1775, supplement, 12 May 1775, supplement; Flexner, *George Washington: The Forge of Experience*, p. 331.

22. See 2 May 1775, Royal Chief Magistracy.

23. See 2 May 1775, Va. Committee.

24. William Wirt, *Sketches of the Life and Character of Patrick Henry* (9th ed., rev., Philadelphia, 1845), pp. 156–58; 3 May 1775, New Kent Co. Committee and n. 22; 9 May 1775, Hanover Co. Committee and n. 5, Orange Co. Committee and n. 6.

25. Wirt, *Patrick Henry* (9th ed.), p. 158.

26. Ibid., p. 158; John Daly Burk, *The History of Virginia, from Its First Settlement to the Present Day* (3 vols., Petersburg, 1804–5), Skeleton Jones and Louis Hue Girardin, continuators (Vol. IV, Petersburg, 1816), III, 415 n.; 9 May 1775, Hanover Co. Committee and n. 1.

27. *Va. Gazette* (Pinkney), 4 May 1775; ibid. (Purdie), 5 May 1775; Burk, *Hist. of Va.*, III, 412; Wirt, *Patrick Henry* (9th ed.), p. 159.

28. See 3 May 1775, Royal Chief Magistracy.

29. Burk, *Hist. of Va.* III, 414–15, 415 n.

30. Jones and Girardin, *Hist. of Va.*, IV, 13; Wirt, *Patrick Henry* (9th ed.), p. 158; 9 May 1775, Hanover Co. Committee and n. 1.

31. Wirt, *Patrick Henry* (9th ed.), p. 159; Burk, Jones, and Girardin, *Hist. of Va.*, III, 415 IV, 13 n.; *Va. Gazette* (Purdie), 28 Apr. 1775, supplement.

32. Jones and Girardin, *Hist. of Va.*, IV 13 n.; *Va. Gazette* (Pinkney), 25 May 1775; *JHB, 1773–1776*, p. xxii; 10 Aug. 1775, Third Va. Convention, Procs. and n. 8; 25 Aug. 1775 and n. 7.

33. Burk, *Hist. of Va.*, III, 416–17; *JHB, 1773–1776*, p. xxii.

34. *Va. Gazette* (Pinkney), 4 May 1775; *JHB, 1773–1776*, p. 270; 4 May 1775, York Co. Committee.

35. Burk, *Hist. of Va.*, III 417; *Va. Gazette* (Pinkney), 4 May 1775.

36. *Va. Gazette* (Purdie), 19 May 1775; 6 May 1775 below.

37. David John Mays, ed., *The Letters and Papers of Edmund Pendleton, 1734–1803* (2 vols., Charlottesville, 1967), I, 103; 6 May 1775, n. 4, final para.; *JHB, 1773–1776*, p. xii; 5 Aug. 1775 and nn. 6, 7.

38. *JHB, 1773–1776*, pp. xxi, xxii.

39. *Va. Gazette* (Dixon and Hunter), 13 May 1775.

40. Ibid. (Purdie) 28 Apr. 1775, supplement.

41. Alan Valentine, *Lord North* (2 vols., Norman, Okla., 1967), I 357–61.

42. *JHB, 1773–1776*, p. xxiii; *Va. Gazette* (Pinkney), 28 Apr. 1775, supplement; ibid. (Purdie), 28 Apr. 1775, supplement; ibid. (Dixon and Hunter), 29 Apr. 1775.

43. *Va. Gazette* (Purdie), 26 May 1775, supplement.

44. See 25 May 1775, Richmond Co. Committee; 27 May 1775 below.

45. *JHB, 1773–1776*, pp. xxii, xxiii.

46. Worthington Chauncey Ford et al. eds., *Journals of the Continental Congress, 1774–1789* (34 vols., Washington, D.C., 1904–37; hereafter JCC), II, 58; *Va. Gazette* (Dixon and Hunter), 3 June 1775.

47. See 31 May 1775, Williamsburg, 1st entry; *JHB, 1773–1776*, p. xxii.

48. Burk, *Hist. of Va.*, III, 421; P.R.O., C.O. 5/1353, fol. 161.

49. *JHB, 1773–1776*, pp. 174–75.

50 Ibid., p. 176.

51. Ibid., p. 186.

52. *Va. Gazette* (Purdie) 9 June 1775, supplement; James Parker to Charles Steuart, 12 June 1775, Charles Steuart Papers, National Library of Scotland, microfilm in Virginia State Library.

53. *Va. Gazette* (Pinkney), 8 June 1775.

54. Ibid. (Purdie), 9 June 1775, supplement; ibid. (Dixon and Hunter), 10 June 1775.

55. *JHB 1773–1776*, p. 260.

56. Ibid., pp. 187–88.

57. Ibid., pp. 190, 191.

58. Ibid., pp. 193, 193–95, 201, 214, 224, 271; *Va. Gazette* (Pinkney), 8 June 1775.

59. For the futile address of the Council to the people and the condemnation of the address by 3 county committees, see 15 May 1775, Royal Magistracy and nn. 1, 2.

60. H[enry] R. McIlwaine et al., eds., *Executive Journals of the Council of Colonial Virginia* (6 vols., Richmond, 1925–66; hereafter *Exec. Journs. Coun. Col. Va.*), VI, 58; *JHB, 1773–1776*, pp. xix, 198; Louis Morton, *Robert Carter of Nomini Hall: A Virginia Tobacco Planter of the Eighteenth Century* (Williamsburg, 1941), pp. 44, 205.

61. *JHB, 1773–1776*, p. 261.

62. Ibid., p. 206.

63. Mays, *Letters and Papers of Pendleton*, I, 113.

64. *JHB, 1773–1776*, pp. 232, 259.

65. Ibid., p. 232.

66. Ibid., p. 206.

67. Ibid., pp. 208, 280.

68. Ibid., pp. 214–15.

69. See pp. 11–12 and nn. 39–41 above.

70. *JHB, 1773–1776*, pp. 176–77, 211–14, 219–21; Paul Leicester Ford, comp. and ed., *The Works of Thomas Jefferson* (Federal ed., 12 vols., New York, 1904–5) I, 16–17.

71. *JHB, 1773–1776*, pp. 219–21.

72. *Rev. Va.*, II, 385; *JCC*, II, 202, 224–34; P. L. Ford, *Works of Jefferson*, I, 19–20.

73. The "Commandant in that Quarter" was Dr. John Connolly, for whom see pp. 151–52 n. 6 below.

74. *Va. Gazette* (Purdie), 16 June 1775; 16 May 1775, Augusta Co. West, 2d entry.

75. *JHB, 1773–1776*, p. 245.

76. Ibid., p. 250.

77. "But," admitted Edmund Randolph in retrospect, by June 1775 "probably no British viceregent, not Botetourt himself, had he been on earth, could have gained ten revolters from their country's cause" (Randolph, *Hist. of Va.*, ed. Shaffer, p. 197).

78. In addition to the supposedly invidious Capt. Edward Foy, 32-year-old Rev. Thomas Gwatkin was thought to have the governor's ear and to be the sort of divine in whom Rasputin, casting about, would later espy his proper prototype. For rather more publicity than Gwatkin needed, see 8 June 1775, Royal Chief Magistracy and n. 6, Williamsburg and nn. 10–12.

There was apparently more that the House might have stated but because of its respect for the Countess of Dunmore could not. When visiting in Williamsburg in July 1774, Lt. Col. Augustine Prevost heard reports that His Lordship was "a consumate rake" who paid little attention to "his Lady" but according to "the scandalous chronicle," found greater pleasure in the embraces of a paramour. As for dignity, when campaigning with Dunmore in the West 2 months later, Prevost was asked by a surprised Delaware chief who was the "old litle man yonder" romping around "like a boy." The British officer found Dunmore a "jolly, hearty companion" but adjudged him as a governor or a field commander "the most unfit, the most trifling and the most uncalculated person living"; and he predicted that "the anals of Virginia will show the truth of one, & the event of his conduct in the later capacity will suficiently evince that of the other" (Nicholas B. Wainwright, ed., "Turmoil at Pittsburgh: Dairy of Augustine Prevost, 1774," *Pennsylvania Magazine of History and Biography*, LXXXV [Apr. 1961], 123, 142, 143).

79. *JHB, 1773–1776*, pp. 253–62.

80. Ibid., pp. 270–71.

81. Parker to Charles Steuart, 24 June 1775, Steuart Papers, National Library of Scotland.

82. *JHB, 1773–1776*, pp. 274, 276.

83. Ibid., p. 175.

84. Ibid., p. 278.

85. Ibid., pp. 279–80.

86. P.R.O., C.O. 5/1353, fol. 168.

87. *JHB, 1773–1776*, p. 280.

88. Ibid., pp. 281–82.

89. See 19 May 1775, Third Va. Convention and n. 3; 9 July, n. on provenance; 11 Aug., Third Va. Convention and n. 6.

90. *JHB, 1773–1776*, pp. 282–83.

91. P.R.O., C.O. 5/1353, fol. 171.

92. *JHB, 1773–1776*, p. 283.

Tuesday, 28 March 1775

Royal Chief Magistracy

By his Excellency the Right Honourable JOHN *Earl of* DUNMORE, *his Majesty's Lieutenant and Governor General of the Colony and Dominion of Virginia, and Vice Admiral of the same.*

A PROCLAMATION.

Virginia, to wit,
WHEREAS certain persons, styling themselves Delegates of several of his Majesty's Colonies in America, have presumed, without having his Majesty's Authority or Consent, to assemble together at Philadelphia in the Months of September and October last, having thought fit, among other unwarrantable Proceedings, to resolve that it will be necessary that another Congress should be held at the same Place on the 10th of May next, unless Redress of certain pretended Grievances be obtained before that time, and to recommend that all the Colonies in North America should chuse Deputies to attend such Congress, *I am commanded by the King*, and I do accordingly issue this my Proclamation, to require all Magistrates and other Officers to use their utmost Endeavours to prevent any such Appointments of Deputies, and to exhort all Persons whatever within this Government to desist from such an unjustifiable Proceeding, so highly displeasing to his Majesty.[1]

Given under my hand, and the Seal of the Colony, this 28th Day of March, in the 15th Year of his Majesty's Reign.

Dunmore.

GOD SAVE THE KING.[2]

Virginia Gazette (Pinkney), 30 March 1775

1. "And thereupon the said Lords Spiritual and Temporal and Commons, pursuant to their respective letters and elections, being now assembled in a full and free representation of this nation, taking into their most serious consideration the best means for attaining the ends aforesaid, do in the first place (as their ancestors in like case have usually done) for the vindicating and asserting their ancient rights and liberties declare . . . That it is the right of the subjects to petition the king, and all commitments and prosecutions for such petitioning are illegal" (The Bill of Rights, 1689, in Andrew Browning, ed., *English Historical Documents*, gen. ed. David C. Douglas [London, 1955—], VIII, 123.

2. "Had the above proclamation made its appearance but a day sooner," scoffed Alexander Purdie in his *Va. Gazette* of 31 Mar. 1775, "it very probably would have

been honoured with some strictures from the Delegates of the people, who were convened in Provincial Congress at Richmond, and broke up the 27th late in the afternoon."

Monday, 3 April 1775

Gloucester County Committee

Reading and Unanimous Approval of Resolves

AT a meeting of the committee of Gloucester county, at the courthouse of
the said county, on Monday the 3d of April 1775, WARNER LEWIS, Esq; was
unanimously elected chairman.

The resolves of the Convention, held at the town of Richmond the 20th of
March 1775, were read, and unanimously approved of.

Resolved, that the thanks of this committee be presented to THOMAS
WHITING, and LEWIS BURWELL, Esquires, our worthy Delegates, for their
faithful discharge of the important trust reposed in them.

It being late before a sufficient number of members assembled, to proceed
upon business, the committee adjourned to Tuesday the 25th instant.

Virginia Gazette (Purdie), 28 April 1775

Prince William County Committee

Public Apology by Mr. Travers Nash

At a meeting of the committee for the county of Prince William, held at the
house of Thomas Young, in the town of Dumfries,[1] on Monday th[e] 3d of
April, 1775.

FOUSHEE TEBBS, esquire, in the chair.

MR. Travers Nash having been called before the committee for a breach of
the third article of the continental association, and having expressed great sorrow and contrition for his conduct, and, signed the association, together with
an apology to be published in the gazette, it is the opinion of the committee
that he be reprimanded by the chairman, and discharged without further
censure.

"I do acknowledge, that once since the beginning of last March I made use of tea, contrary to the continental association, for which I am sincerely sorry, and ask pardon of the public.[2]

Travers Nash."

A true copy.   Evan Williams, clerk.

Virginia Gazette (Pinkney), 1 June 1775

1. In the source of the name is printed "Drumfries."

2. The 3d article of the Continental Association adopted by the first Continental Congress on 20 Oct. 1774 read:

"As a non-consumption agreement, strictly adhered to, will be an effectual security for the observation of the non-importation, we, as above, solemnly agree and associate, that, from this day, we will not purchase or use any tea imported on account of the East-India company, or any on which a duty hath been or shall be paid; and from and after the first day of March next, we will not purchase or use any East-India tea whatever; nor will we, nor shall any person for or under us, purchase or use any of those goods, wares, or merchandise, we have agreed not to import, which we shall know, or have cause to suspect, were imported after the first day of December, except such as come under the rules and directions of the tenth article hereafter mentioned" (*JCC*, I, 77).

Wednesday, 5 April 1775

King and Queen County Committee

Public Sale at Todd's Warehouse

PURSUANT to an order of the committee for *King and Queen county*, and agreeable to the tenth article of the continental congress, will be sold, at public sale, for ready money, at ⟨William⟩ *Todd's* warehouse, on *Wednesday* the fifth day of April next, several PACKAGES of *European* GOODS, imported in the ships *Alexander* and *Venus*, from Liverpool.[1]

By order of the committee,
John Tunstall, Clerk.

Virginia Gazette (Pinkney), 30 March 1775

1. The 10th article of the Continental Association read:

"In case any merchant, trader, or other person, shall import any goods or merchandise, after the first day of December, and before the first day of February next, the same ought forthwith, at the election of the owner, to be either re-shipped or delivered up to the committee of the county or town, wherein they shall be imported, to be stored at the risque of the importer, until the non-importation agreements shall cease, or to be sold under the direction of the committee aforesaid; and in the last-mentioned case, the owner or owners of such goods shall be reimbursed out of the sales, the first cost and charges, the profit, if any, to be applied towards relieving and employing such poor inhabitants of the town of Boston, as are immediate sufferers by the Boston port-bill; and a particular account of all goods so retained, stored, or sold, to be inserted in the public papers; and if any goods or merchandises shall be imported after the said first day of February, the same ought forthwith to be sent back, without breaking any of the packages thereof" (*Rev. Va.*, II, 191). No report of the present sale has been found.

Thursday, 6 April 1775

Essex County Committee

Announcement of Public Sale of Goods

AND at a committee, held for the county of Essex, by special summons from the chairman, on the 6th of April, 1775: Mr. John Rowzee informed the committee that he had imported in the Venus, captain Peirt, master, from Liverpool, who arrived since the 1st of December last, and before the 1st of February, two parcels of goods, amounting, as per invoice produced, to £.9 4 6 sterling, including the charges, and desired that the same might be sold agreeable to the tenth article of the continental association,[1] it is therefore ordered that John Lee, Muscoe Garnett, Robert Reynolds, Henry Garnett, and John Henshaw, or any three, do sell the said goods to the highest bidder, giving notice of the time and place of sale, and that they reimburse the said John Rowzee, out of the sales, the first costs and charges, and if any profit shall arise, that they retain such profit in their hands for relieving such poor of Boston as are sufferers by the Boston port bill, subject to the direction of this committee.[2]

Virginia Gazette (Pinkney), 1 June 1775

Sussex County Committee

Thanks for Pains and Trouble

At a committee held for the county of Sussex, at the courthouse, on Thursday the 6th of April, 1775,

PRESENT

THOMAS PEETE, chairman.

And 27 other members of the said committee.

THE proceedings of the Provincial Congress, lately held in the town of Richmond, and county of Henrico, were laid before the committee by the late delegates for this county;[3] and the same being read, and maturely considered, the committee came to the following resolution:

Resolved, that the thanks of this committee, in behalf of themselves and their constituents, the good people of this county, are justly due, and are most unfeignedly given, to the Congress in general, and to our late worthy delegates in particular, for the great pains and trouble they have been at, and wisdom shewn in their consultations and resolves, and to assure them that this committee will adhere strictly to the spirit of the resolves of the said Congress.

Signed by order.

Thomas Peete, chairman.

John Massenburg, clerk.

Virginia Gazette (Purdie), 5 May 1775

1. For the 10th article of the Continental Association, see 5 Apr. 1775, n. 1.

2. The result of the sale is under the date heading of 26 Apr. 1775.

3. The "late delegates" for Sussex County at the second Virginia Convention were Henry Gee and David Mason (*Rev. Va.*, II, 337).

Friday, 7 April 1775

Virginia Select Committee of Correspondence

A Quest to Distinguish Friends

At a Meeting of the Select Committee of Correspondence in the City of Williamsburg on Friday the 7th of April. 1775.

Ordered that Letters be prepared to the Delegates for the Province of New-York, and to Isaac Low Esq: agreable to the Resolution of the late Convention.[1]

A Letter was accordingly prepared to the Delegat[es] which being read was approved, as follows.

Gentlemen,   Williamsburg Virga. April 7th. 1775.
    The late Convention of the Representatives of this Colony judging it essential to the Common Interest of America, that every proper Means should be used to preserve our Union of Sentiments amongst the Colonies, and, in Case of Defection, that they should be able to distinguish their Friends, came to a Resolution of which we have by this Conveyance transmitted a Copy to the Committee of Correspondence of New York[.] That we may omit no Means of obtaining the most authentic Information, we take [the liberty?] of inclosing you a Copy of the same Resolution, and shall hold ourselves much obliged, if you will be pleased to exert your particular Endeavours to enab[le] us to make a satisfactory Report to our next Convention or Assembly.
                            We are, very respectfully, yr. mo. obt. Sts.

To Isaac Low, James Duane,
    John Jay, Phil⟨ip⟩: Livingston,
    John Alsop, Will⟨iam⟩: Floyd,   Peyton Randolph
    Henry Wisner, John Herring   Ro. C. Nicholas
    & S⟨imon⟩. Boerum Esqs.   Dudley Digges

    And also a Letter to the Committee of Correspondence for New York, as follows.[2]

Gent.   Wmsburg. Virga. April 7th. 1775
    The inclosed Resolutions of our late Convention will fully explain the Reason for our troubling you with this Letter. We have only further to express ou[r] earnest Wishes that you would be pleased, by the earliest opportunity, to furnish us with the most authentic Information, that we may be able to make a satisfactory Report to our next Convention or assemb[ly.] [3]
    We have the honor to be Gent. your respectful humble Servants.
To the Committee of   Peyton Randolph
Correspondence for New York   Ro. C. Nicholas
                                                 Dudley Digges

                    Virginia Committee of Correspondence MS minutes, the whole, including signatures, in hand of John Tazewell, clerk (Archives Division, Virginia State Library) [4]

Chesterfield County Committee

Promotions and Censures

                                        CHESTERFIELD, *April* 7, 1775.
    AT a meeting of the committee for Chesterfield county,[5] the proceedings of the Convention were read, and unanimously approved of.

Resolved, that we will, as soon as possible, promote and further the establishment of manufactories for the making of linen, cotton, and woollen cloth; and that we will give encouragment to such persons as shall excel in the preparation of materials necessary for carrying on such manufactories; and also that subscriptions be opened in this county, by the several members of this committee, for raising a fund to support such manufactories as may be determined on in consequence of the foregoing resolution.[6]

Mr. John Brown, of Norfolk, having, by his behaviour, incurred the censure of the people of this colony,

Resolved, that we will not hereafter transact any business, or have any connexion, with the said John Brown.

Capt. Sampson, of the ship Elizabeth, from Bristol, having, by his conduct, incurred the general contempt and resentment of the good of the people of this colony,

Resolved, that we will not hereafter have any intercourse with the said Sampson, nor contribute to, or, as far as in us lies, permit the loading of any ship which he may now or hereafter be concerned with; and it is recommended to the inhabitants of this county to adopt these resolutions.[7]

Ordered, that these, and the resolutions relative to the manufactories, be printed.

A true copy from the minutes.
Jerman Baker, clerk.

Virginia Gazette (Purdie), 5 May 1775

1. The "Resolution of the late Convention," apparently introduced by Thomas Jefferson, was adopted on the same day, 24 Mar. 1775. It instructed the Committee of Correspondence to address its colonial counterpart in New York, or by seeking "otherwise," to procure "authentic information" as to why the New York Assembly on 23 Feb. had voted, 17 to 9, not to send delegates to the second Continental Congress. Why, as is implied, separate letters should be sent to the former New York delegates (among whom the cautious Low had been one) and to Low as an individual is not clear, but the explanation may lie in the fact that at this time he was also chairman of the Committee of Sixty, which was guiding antiministerial policies and activities in New York City (*Rev. Va.*, II, 370–71; Joseph Bucklin Bishop, *A Chronicle of One Hundred & Fifty Years: The Chamber of Commerce of the State of New York, 1768–1918* [New York, 1918], pp. 26, 28–29, 150; Thomas Jones, *History of New York during the Revolutionary War* . . . [2 vols., New York, 1879], I, 34, 35, 38, 42–43, 46; Thomas Jefferson Wertenbaker, *Father Knickerbocker Rebels: New York City during the Revolutionary War* [New York, 1948], pp. 36–37, 38–40, 56).

2. As the creature of the suspect General Assembly, the New York Committee of Correspondence, which had been appointed on 20 Jan. 1774, was by that very appointment and its own subsequent actions itself not above suspicion. It would not be psychologically amiss, however, to let the members of the committee know that in Virginia suspicion was much alive (*Rev. Va.*, II, 129–30 n. 5, 137, 138 n. 1).

3. A reply to neither letter has been found, unless that of 5 May 1775 from Henry Remsen, deputy chairman of the New York Committee of One Hundred, be considered a response to the letter seemingly sent separately to Isaac Low.

4. For the provenance of the manuscript minutes, see *Rev. Va.*, II, 17. The scant minutes appearing within the present volume have previously been printed by William P. Palmer et al., eds., *Calendar of Virginia State Papers and Other Manuscripts* . . . (11 vols., Richmond, 1875–92; hereafter *Cal. Va. State Papers*), VIII, 13–14; and *JHB, 1773–1776*, unnumbered p. 288.

5. The Chesterfield County committee had been elected on 25 Nov. 1774, when "a great Number" of freeholders were reported to have assembled at the courthouse (*Rev. Va.*, II, 176); but their number was not great enough to keep disgruntled petitioners on 20 Aug. 1775 from protesting to the third Virginia Convention that the committee was not truly representative.

6. On its final day of session, 27 Mar. 1775, the second Virginia Convention had "Resolved unanimously that the setting up & promoting woollen[,] cotton[,] & linen manufactures ought to be encouraged in as many different Branches as possible; especially coating, Flannel, Blankets[,] Rugs or Cover lids, Hosiery, & coarse Cloths, both broad and narrow" (ibid., II, 382).

7. The acts of ostracism were extensions of condemnation laid down by the Norfolk Borough committee on John Brown on 2 Mar., and on Capt. John Sampson on 21 Mar. 1775, for violating the Continental Association (ibid., II, 307–8, 354–55).

Saturday, 8 April 1775

Caroline County Committee

Condemnation and Summonses

At a Called Comittee the 8th. of April 1775

Present 19 of the Committee

Robert Johnston having notice to appear before the Committee, appeared And after hearing the Complaint against him & the Witnesses they are of Opinion he has violated the Association in vending his goods at a higher price than customary for a year preceding the Association. Ord. the Case be published & that he be allowed to trade on the same terms that other Merchants do in the County that do break the Association [1]

On Information of Alex⟨ande⟩r. Parker⟨,⟩ Ord. Rodham Kennon have notice to appear at the next meeting of the Committee

Ordered John Long & Joseph Cooper have notice to appear as Witnesses against Rodham Kennon.

The Committee appoint Thursday next It being Court day to choose Delegates to represent this County for a Year [2]

> Committee MS minutes in hand of Samuel Haws, Jr., clerk (original in Henry E. Huntington Library and Art Gallery of San Marino, Calif., by permission of which institution reproduced from photocopy kindly supplied Virginia Independence Bicentennial Commission) [3]

Norfolk Borough Committee

A Desire to Pay Particular Attention

Committee Chamber, April 8, 1775.

The Committee, being informed that some persons within this borough had raised the price of their goods, do hereby desire all merchants, shopkeepers and retailers of goods within their jurisdiction, to pay particular attention to the following article of the Association, to wit,

"That such as are venders of goods or merchandise will not take advantage of the scarcity of goods that may be occasioned by this Association, but will sell the same at the rates they have been respectively accustomed to do for twelve months last past; and if any venders of goods or merchandise shall sell any such goods on higher terms, or shall in any manner, or by any device whatever, violate or depart from this agreement, no person ought, nor will any of us deal with any such person, or his or her factor or agent, at any time thereafter, for any commodity whatever." [4]

Of any breach of this ninth article the Committee are bound to take notice, and publish the delinquent to the world; they therefore give this public caution that none may plead ignorance.

By order of the Committee.
William Davies, Secretary.

> *Virginia Gazette, or the Norfolk Intelligencer,* 20 April 1775

Southampton County Committee

Thanks, Collections, and Elections

At a committee held at the courthouse for the County of Sohampton on Saturday the eighth day of April 1775 agreeable to the 11t. article of the Continental Congress [5]

Present   Edwin Gray⟨,⟩ Ch⟨airman⟩.   Joshua Nicholson
                           Thomas W⟨illia⟩mson   Thomas Edmunds
                           Rich⟨ar⟩d Kello   Benjamin Ruffin jr.
                           James Ridley   Thomas Blunt
                           George Gurley
                           Benjamin Ruffin⟨, Sr.⟩
                           Peter Butts
                           Benjamin Clements⟨, Sr.⟩

The proceedings of the Committee being read and Considered resolved that this Commee. do intirely approve of the proceedings of the late convention held at the town of Richmond on the 20th. March & that they will with the greatest energy recommend [the sev]eral measures then agreed to by such Convention to the people [of this?] County

Resolved that the several members of this Committee in their respective districts endeavour (by subscriptions) to collect the sum of ten Pounds for promoting the making of salt & the sum of fifteen Pounds for the use of the delegates in the General congress to be held in may next⟨, and⟩ that such money as may be collected be immediately paid by the several collectors into the hands of Edwin Gray & Henry Taylor to be by them transmitted to R⟨obert⟩ C⟨arter⟩ Nicholas Esqr. for the Purposes aforesaid [6]

Resolved that monday the 17th. of this instant be appointed for the election of delegates at the Courthouse of this County to represent this county in provincial congress[.] [7] Ordered that a copy of this resolution be transmitted to the Clergymen in the Different parishes of this County & that the Clerk of this Commee. advertise the same at the Courthouse door at the next Court. Ordered that Mr B Clements jr. Mr Benj Ruffin jr. & Mr. Joshua Nicholson or any two of them be appointed to Conduct the election of the sd. delegates

Resolved that the thanks of this Committee be given to Edwin Gray & Henry Taylor our worthy and patriotic delegates & assure them that we are perfectly satisfied with their conduct in the execution of their important trust & that they have demeaned themselves intirely to the satisfaction of this committee

Resolved that this commee. be adjourned to thursday the 13th. day of April this instant

                                                                    EDWIN GRAY

> Committee MS journal in hand of Samuel Kello, clerk, with Gray's autograph signature (original in office of county clerk of Southampton County, photocopy in Virginia State Library) [8]

1. The "same terms" was a euphemism for a penalty set forth in the 9th article of the Continental Association as more explicitly stated this same day by the Norfolk Borough committee.

2. "Thursday next" was the 13th, under which date heading Rodham Kennon will be found paying attendance on the committee.

3. For the provenance of the Caroline County manuscript minute book, see *Rev. Va.*, II, 167. The portions of the minute book appearing within the present volume have previously been edited by H[enry] R. McIlwaine and printed in the *Bulletin of the Virginia State Library*, XVII (Nov. 1929), 130–31.

4. The quotation closely follows article 9 of the Continental Association as adopted by the first Congress on 20 Oct. 1774 (*Rev. Va.*, II, 212 n. 1).

5. The 11th article of the Continental Association read:

"That a committee be chosen in every county, city, and town, by those who are qualified to vote for representatives in the legislature, whose business it shall be attentively to observe the conduct of all persons touching this association; and when it shall be made to appear, to the satisfaction of a majority of any such committee, that any person within the limits of their appointment has violated this association, that such majority do forthwith cause the truth of the case to be published in the gazette; to the end, that all such foes to the rights of British-America may be publicly known, and universally contemned as the enemies of American liberty; and thenceforth we respectively will break off all dealings with him or her" (ibid., II, 169 n. 5).

6. On 27 Mar. 1775 the second Virginia Convention resolved "that the delegates from the several counties in this colony, as also from the city of Williamsburg and the borough of Norfolk do without delay, apply to their respective counties and corporations for fifteen pounds current money and transmit the same as soon as collected to Robert Carter Nicholas, Esq; for the use of the deputies sent from this colony to the General Congress" (ibid., II, 385). The "General Congress" referred to was the second, which would convene in Philadelphia on 10 May 1775. Henry Taylor and Edwin Gray would deliver Southampton County's £15 to Nicholas on 12 June 1775 (MS Cash Book, 1770–76, Treasurer's MS Item no. 16, Archives Division, Va. State Library, unpaged).

7. Although the Southampton County committee conducted the election of delegates, no result of the poll was entered by Samuel Kello in the committee manuscript journal; but on "monday the 17th." Edwin Gray was reelected. Probably, as a "worthy and patriotic" representative, Henry Taylor was also, but he would not attend the third convention.

8. For the provenance of the Southampton County committee manuscript journal, see *Rev. Va.*, II, 319. The portions of the journal appearing in the present volume have previously been edited by H[enry] R. McIlwaine and printed in the *Bulletin of the Va. State Library*, XVII (Nov. 1929), 142–43.

Tuesday, 11 April 1775

Albemarle County Committee

Resolutions respecting Independent Military Companies [1]

Resolved that the companies when raised should not be led to duty without the voice of the committee

Resolved that every person that inlists shall be obliged to go after the determination of the Committee, unless he gives sufficient proof by two witnesses of his Inability.[2]

Autograph diary and Revolutionary memoranda of
Dr. George Gilmer (Virginia Historical Society)

1. The assignment of this date is arbitrary. It precedes by a week the date, also arbitrary, of the "Termes" laid down for enlisting in the Albemarle "Independent Companies," and Lt. George Gilmer's address to the "First Independent Company."

2. On 24 Dec. 1774 Lord Dunmore wrote to Lord Dartmouth, secretary of state for the American colonies, that "Every county, besides, is now arming a company of men, whom they call an independent company, for the avowed purpose of protecting their committees, and to be employed against government, if occasion require." After an excerpt of this letter appeared in Pinkney's *Va. Gazette* of 28 Apr. 1775, the Norfolk Borough committee on 4 May challenged the governor "to name the county where the committee had proceeded so far as to swear the men of their independent company to execute all orders which they should give them." His Excellency would have been hard put to document his case. In the main he was wrong, but just as he was shooting in the dark, so was the borough committee, as the above unpublicized resolution demonstrates. And another instance of the governor's partial correctness may be cited: On 25 Aug. 1775 Richard Adams would report to the third Virginia Convention that the evidence was that in Chesterfield County the officers of the county independent company "were chosen by the committee of the said county, and directed to raise the men, in consequence of which they were accordingly enlisted" (p. 489 below).

Thursday, 13 April 1775

Third Virginia Convention

Call in York County for Election of Delegates for One-Year Terms

THE freeholders of York county are desired to meet at the courthouse on Tuesday the 25th instant (*April*) to elect delegates to represent them the ensuing year.[1]

Virginia Gazette (Pinkney), 13 April 1775

Caroline County Committee

Of Gaming and Ammunition

At a meeting of the Committee the 13th. of April 1775 [2]
Present 15. of the Committee

Rodham Kennon appeared before the Committee having had notice and from the testimony of Alexander Parker & Danial Barksdale It appears to this Committee He has violated the Association in Gaming at his house[.] Ordered the Case be published in both the Virginia Gazettes [3]

All the Gentlemen of the Committee are appointed to form themselves in districts & collect two shillings for every Tithe in this County as recommended by the late Convention to purchase Amunition for the use of the said County [4]

> Committee MS minutes in hand of Samuel Haws, Jr., clerk (Henry E. Huntington Library and Art Gallery of San Marino, Calif.)

Southampton County Committee

Chearful Payment and Future Strict Compliance

At a Comme. held at the Courthouse for the County of Sohampton on thursday the 13th. April 1775 agreeable to the 11th. article of the Continental Congress [5]
Present

	Edwin Gray⟨,⟩ Ch⟨airman⟩	Thomas Blunt
	Thomas Williamson	Thomas Edmunds
	Richard Kello	Joshua Nicholson
	James Ridley	John Thomas Blow
	Henry Taylor	
	Benjamin Ruffin⟨, Sr.⟩	
	Benjamin Clements⟨, Sr.⟩	
	Benjamin Ruffin⟨, Jr.⟩	

This Commee taking under their Consideration the necessi[ty] of providing the militia with powder and lead & despai[ring] of Collting a sum sufficient for that Purpose from the peo[ple] *of this County* in a short space of time Resolve therefore that each member of this Commee. now will most chearfully pay the sum of ten Pounds to Edwin Gray & Henry Taylor or either of them on or before the 1st day of may next for the Purpose aforesaid [6]

Resolved that *Edwi*n Gray & Henry Taylor do inform the absent members of this Commee. of the proceding resolution & request them to contribute the aforesd. sum of ten Pounds

Resolved that Edwin Gray & H Taylor or either of them do so soon as they shall have received the money so subscribed or any other sums that may be voluntarily advanced for this purpose make application to the Committee appointed by the late Convention to procure ammunition for as much Powder and lead as the money they may have received will amount to in the Proportion of one Pound of Powder to four Pounds of lead [7]

Silas Kirby James Ingraham Josiah Kirby & Jno. Simmons voluntarily appeared before this Commee. & acknowledged that they had been guilty of violating the 8th. article of the association by gaming at the said Kirby's & that they had been guilty of an error in so doing & were convinced of its evil tendency & were willing to refund all the money by them there won & having assured this commee. of their future strict compliance *with their strict compliance* with the several articles of the association of the continental congress [8] Resolved therefore that the Persons aforesd. have been guilty of violating the association But this commee. in consideration of their orderly behaviour before & since this breach of the association & candid behaviour before this Commee. hope the public will join with them in not consider[in]g them as enemies to American liberty

Resolved that the powder & lead when procured shall be stored in such convenient place or places as shall be agreed on by this Committee & be liable to any further direction of same

[Resolved] that the clerk of this *Commee.* transmit a copy of the [proceed]ings of this day to M⟨ess⟩rs. ⟨John⟩ Dixon & ⟨William⟩ Hunter [request]ing them to publish the same [9]

Edwin Gray Ch.

> Committee MS journal in hand of Samuel Kello, clerk, with Gray's autograph signature (Office of county clerk of Southampton County)

1. The summons to elect delegates for the "ensuing year" was issued in response to the final action of the second Virginia Convention, on 27 Mar. 1775, when that body "recommended to the people of this colony to choose delegates to represent them in Convention for one year, as soon as they conveniently can" (*Rev. Va.*, II, 386).

2. The meeting was held in compliance with the "appointment" of 8 Apr. 1775.

3. Although "Ordered" by the previous meeting of the committee to appear as the prime "Witnesses against Rodham Kennon," John Long and Joseph Cooper seem to have relinquished that honor. The violation was of the 8th artcle of the Continental Association, which read:

"We will, in our several stations, encourage frugality, economy, and industry, and promote agriculture, arts and the manufactures of this country, especially of wool; and will discountenance and discourage every species of extravagance and dissipation, especially horse-racing, and all kinds of gaming, cock-fighting, exhibitions of shews, plays, and other expensive diversions and entertainments; and on the death of any relation or friend, none of us, or any of our families, will go into any further morning-dress, than a black crape or ribbon on the arm or hat, for gentlemen, and a black ribbon and necklace for ladies, and will discountenance the giving of gloves and scarves at funerals" (ibid., II, 224).

Any issue of "both the Virginia Gazettes" in which Kennon's indiscretion may have been given notice is missing.

4. On 25 Mar. 1775 the second Viriginia Convention adopted the "Opinion" of a committee "That in order to make a further & more ample Provision of Ammunition it be recommended to the Committees of the several Counties that they collect from their Constituents in such Manner as shall be most agreable to them so much money as will be sufficient to purchase half a pound of Gunpowder, one pound of Lead, necessary Flints and Cartridge paper, for every Titheable person in their County; that they immediately take effectual Measures for the procuring such Gunpowder, lead, Flints and Cartridge paper, & dispose thereof when procured in such Place or Places of Safety as they may think best. And it is earnestly recommended to each Individual to pay such proportion of the Money necessary for these purposes as by the respective Committees shall be judged requisite" (ibid., II, 375).

It is to be noted that although the Caroline County committee on 8 Apr. had set this Thursday, "It being Court day," for the election of convention delegates to "represent this County for a Year," no further mention of the fact occurs in the minutes. In all probability, however, the election was an event of this day; but whether on this day or later, Edmund Pendleton and James Taylor were reelected, and on 11 May, William Woodford would be elected an alternate for Pendleton, who on 25 Mar. had been chosen by the Virginia Convention to serve as a deputy to the second Continental Congress (ibid., II, 376).

5. For the 11th article of the Continental Association, see 8 Apr. 1775, n. 5.

6. Although acting under the same recommendation as was the Caroline County committee (n. 4 above), the Southampton County committee applied its own interpretation as to how the recommendation should be implemented.

7. On 25 Mar. 1775 the second Virginia Convention had adopted the proposal of a committee that for county committees not "apprized" of the "most certain and speedy method of procuring" munitions there be appointed "one General Committee" through which requests and purchase money could be channeled for procurement. The members of the committee were Robert Carter Nicholas, Thomas Nelson, Jr., and Thomas Whiting (*Rev. Va.*, II, 375–76). Nicholas will be found taking action pursuant to that resolution under the date heading of 16 June 1775.

8. For "the 8th. article of the association," see n. 3 above.

9. A "copy of the proceedings of this day" was printed in their gazette by Messrs. Dixon and Hunter on 6 May 1775.

Monday, 17 April 1775

Isle of Wight County Committee

A Case of Serious Consideration

At a meeting of the Committee for the County of Isle Wight at the Court House of the said County on

Monday the seventeenth day of April in the year of our Lord Christ one thousand seven hundred and seventy five,

Present John Scarsbrook Wills Chairman, Josiah Parker, Brewer Godwin, Richard Hardy, John Day, Arthur Smith, The Reverend Henry John Burges⟨s⟩, Thomas Peirce, John Mallory, Tristram Norsworthy Junr, Goodrich Willson ⟨Wilson⟩, and William Davis⟨,⟩ Gent⟨lemen⟩.

Convention re-solves approved of by Com. & to be put in Exc.

The Committee taking into their Serious Considera-tion the resolves of the late Provincial Convention held at Richmond in the County of Henrico do most heartly approve of them and resolve to do all in their power to put them in execution by every persuasive means.

Captains of Militia to collect money to pur-chase Gun Powder & to acct. with Comm.

Resolved that it be recommended to the several Cap-tains of the Militia in this County to make application to their respective Companys for one shilling and eight pence current money or any sum that they may gen-erously contribute towards purchasing Amunition for the use of this County and that they also personally apply to such persons who are not on the muster Roll in their several Districts for the purpose aforesaid and that the said Captains account for the money so received with this Committee and render an account of the several persons who shall contribute for the purpose aforesaid.[1]

Ten other Gent. to be added to the Comm. &c.– – – –

Resolved that on account of the small number of Members in our Committee It is recommended that ten other Gentlemen be nominated and added to this Com-mittee to assist them and that they be elected by ballot on thursday the fourth day of May next.

Delegates to be Elected &c.

Resolved that the freeholders of this County have notice given them by Proclamation or otherwise and they are desired to attend at the Court-house in the Town of Smithfield on Thursday the fourth day of May next in Order to elect delegates to represent them (when called upon) in Colony Convention for one year.[2]

Sub Committee to wait on Merchs. to pur-chase Powder

Resolved that Richard Hardy, Thomas Peirce, and Arthur Smith Gent. be appointed a Sub. Committee and do wait on the Merchants in the Town of Smithfield and purchase all The Gun Powder they may have to spare for which this Committee are ready to pay two shillings and six pence per pound immediately.

Sub Committee's report after waiting on the Merchants in

The Sub Committee appointed to wait on the Mer-chants in the Town of Smithfield returned & made the following report, to wit, "That they had made applica-tion to an assistant Storekeeper of Mr. George Purdie in

Order to pur-
chase Powder———
Sub Committee
to wait on Geo:
Purdie to pur-
chase Powder &c.

John Sym agreed
to deliver up his
Powder &c.————

the said Town who informed them that there were in the Store a small quantity of Gun Powder but as he had no Order from his employer he would not sell it.—Resolved therefore that Thomas Peirce, Arthur Smith and Josiah Parker Gentlemen do wait on the said George Purdie so soon as he shall return to Town and purchase the same and make report thereof to the next Committee,[3] And the said Sub Committee also made report that John Sym a Merchant in the said Town declared to them that he had about three pounds of Gun Powder and that he was willing to spare part of the same on any emergency reserving a sufficiency for the use and protection of his own family.[4]

The Minutes of these proceedings were signed

"John Scarsbrook Wills Chairman"

Committee MS minutes, the whole, including Wills's signature in hand of Francis Young, clerk (Office of county clerk of Isle of Wight County)[5]

Middlesex County Committee

Alleged Refusing and Reviling

AT a meeting of the committee for the county of Middlesex on Monday the 17th of April, 1775, a complaint being lodged against one Thomas Haddin, an inhabitant of the said county, for refusing to sign the continental association, and reviling the same; whereupon the committee ordered him to be summoned to appear before them the 22d of May.[6]

Virginia Gazette (Pinkney), 15 June 1775

Richmond County Committee

John Fowler to John Pinkney: An Open Letter

Mr. Pinkney,

Lowry's Point, Rappahannock,
April 17, 1775

As I have, for a time past, been on a voyage some distance from home, that piece in Mr. Purdie's paper, of the 17th of last February, handed to him from a chairman of a respectable committee, has but lately fallen into my hands.[7]

Forbearing to reply would be acknowledging faults that I have not committed, and the expence of an answer, I fear, will purchase displeasure. However, as it will appear that I did all in my power to prevent those disagreeable disputes, I do, with the more confidence, ask leave to lay before your readers what are no more than matters of real fact:

The occasion of the chairman's piece happened in consequence of my endeavouring to oblige some of our former customers on Rappahannock river, who had petitioned that their grain might be received in payment of their debts. It was necessary that some person, acquainted with those accounts, should attend, and for his employment a parcel of goods, duly imported (of which the chairman was satisfied) were put on board a vessel at Alexandria, and she dispatched round for the purpose above. I never understood that any of the goods were complained of, on Rappahannock, but a set of real buck handle knives and forks, which were sold for 8s. Some very large sieve bottoms sold at 1s. 6d. and bar iron. The bar iron was put on board to be used in Gloucester, on our own accounts; my apprentice on board had directions to retail what of it might be left at 4d. per lb.

A person came on board to purchase the fourth part of a ton, and was informed that if he paid for it in commodities he must give after the rate of £.30 per ton. I retail iron at home for 4d. per lb. but have never traded in that article till within the last nine months. I have proved to many that the sieve bottoms cost 10s. sterling per dozen. As to the knives, if they were of our first quality, of the above sort . . .[8] and that the price received was set on them by Mr. Philip Vass, while he acted as our assistant, which are more than two years past.

Under these circumstances, a constable, and six or eight men, some of them armed, were dispatched in quest of the vessel, which they boarded whilst under sail, with little or no wind; they proceeded to haul down the sails, let run the anchor, and then ordered that all on board should attend them to the courthouse; the constable adding that he had orders to bring off every white man, if there were twenty. The master on board begged time only to shift his clothes, but was denied it.[9] The vessel, with very considerable property, was left to the mercy of what weather might have happened, not a sail handed, nor soul on board.

On trial, no invoices were asked for, none were produced. Mr. James Samford, a man of strict probity, sent word to the committee that he had bought of the same sieve bottoms, and at the very same price before our goods had been removed from this river. His message was openly delivered before the committee by the gentleman that had been on board to purchase iron, who, at the same time, personally declared, that he saw nothing on board, save the iron, but what was as low as they could be had elsewhere. The knives were had before the committee, and allowed to be reasonable.

How then were those matters proved? Or give me leave to ask, how it was possible they could be proved, since it is notorious that I have been removed from Rappahannock more than fifteen months? But the chairman said that such and such goods cost this or that price, and is he to be mistaken?

By mere chance I happened at Richmond courthouse, in my way down the country, on the day of this trial, and but a short time after, the committee had risen, and did, in the presence of most of the members, assure them that it was in my power to acquit myself of their charge, and that about this time I most certainly would do so, by producing my invoice, which I have now brought for the perusal of such as wish to be better satisfied.

The chairman informs your readers that on account of the non-age of my apprentice, the committee did agree not to act with rigour against him. If their determination was too pacific, it was by no means a fault in that gentleman, as it is well known what he proposed for their resolve was, that if the vessel was not gone out of the river in twenty-four hours (winds permitting) any person should be at liberty to set fire to and burn her up.

Have not hasty resolves been productive of fatal consequences? The great indulgence, at last agreed on, was in consequence of the petition of my apprentice being approved of by a majority of the committee, less inclined to rigourous proceedings than the chairman was. Has the rigid proceeding the chairman alludes to been recommended by the wisest assembly that ever were convened on our part of this globe? [10] From whence, then, is the authority? [11]

John Fowler

Virginia Gazette (Pinkney), 18 May 1775

1. If the resolution was intended to be a compliance with the recommendation of the second Virginia Convention respecting the collection of money for the purchase of munitions (13 Apr. 1775, n. 4), the method hit upon by the Isle of Wight County committee was even less guided by the letter of the recommendation than had been that of the Southampton County committee on 13 Apr. 1775.

2. Although the committee set in motion the events leading to the reelection on 4 May of John Scarsbrook Wills and Josiah Parker as convention delegates, Francis Young made no entry of the results in the manuscript minute book. He would, however, on 15 May 1775 report the election of 10 new members to the committee itself.

3. The mood of the committee is noticeable from the fact that the subcommittee was not instructed to pay the slightest heed to any "Order" George Purdie had given his "assistant Storekeeper"; but no report by the subcommittee appears in the manuscript minute book. On 27 July 1775 Purdie would find himself more directly involved when summoned to answer charges of transgressing the Continental Association "by selling Needles at a double price."

4. Whether John Sym delivered up any gunpowder is problematical. By 15 May 1775 he would have "removed his Merchandize" from Smithfield to Norfolk.

5. For the provenance of the Isle of Wight County committee manuscript minute book, see *Rev. Va.*, II, 235. The portions of the minute book appearing within the present volume have previously been edited by H[enry] R. McIlwaine and printed in the *Fifteenth Annual Report of the Library Board of the Virginia State Library, 1917–1918* (Richmond, 1919; hereafter *15th Annual Library Report*), pp. 44–48.

6. Refusing to answer the summons on 22 May 1775, Thomas Haddin would subsequently acquire a temporary notoriety.

7. In Alexander Purdie's *Va. Gazette* of 17 Feb. unfavorable notice had been cast upon John and George Fowler, Alexandria merchant-shippers, by determination of

13 Jan. 1775. On that date young John Blatt, Jr., a Fowler apprentice, was hailed before the Gloucester County committee, to which he confessed that in discharging instructions, he was guilty of violating "the resolves of the general congress, in advancing upon the price" of goods. Despite his "promise not to do the like again," on 6 Feb. 1775 he was summoned to appear before the Richmond County committee. When he did so the next day, he was found guilty of continuing to sell goods "at an extravagant price." Again he was excused on the basis of his youth and was bade begone from the Rappahannock as fast as his craft could sail (*Rev. Va.*, II, 234–35, 279, 280–81). The chairman of the "respectable committee" of Richmond County was Landon Carter of Sabine Hall.

8. At this point several words are indecipherable.

9. The "master on board" the sloop *Liberty* was Charles Marshall.

10. The first Continental Congress.

11. It would have been completely out of character for Colonel Carter not to reply. He will be found doing so under the date heading of 26 May 1775.

Tuesday, 18 April 1775

Albemarle County Committee

Agreement of Gentlemen Volunteers [1]

Terms of Inlisting

We the subscribers volunteers in the Independent Companies for the county of Albemarle, do most Solemnly bind ourselves by the sacred ties of virtue, Honor & love to our Country, to be at all times ready to execute the command of the committee, in defence of the rights of America (unless incapacitated) agreeable to the underwritten resolves.

1st We resolve should we fall or fly back on being called into service to be held unworthy the rights of freemen & as inimical to the cause of America

2 That each man Elected to the office of Captain Lieutenant or Ensign & refusing to accept the same oblige himself to pay 25 £ for the first, 15 £ for the second, 10 £ for the latter to be disposed of by the Committee for the use of the company.

3 We oblige ourselves to obey the commands of the officers by ourselves elected from the Inlisted Volunteers, to Muster four times in the year or oftener If necessary. To provide Gun shotpouch, powder horn to appear on Duty in a hunting shirt.

List of Officers and Soldiers listed under the above agreement:

⊙ [2]   Charles Lewis Captain

⊙   George Gilmer ⎫
⊙   John Marks   ⎬ Lieutts:

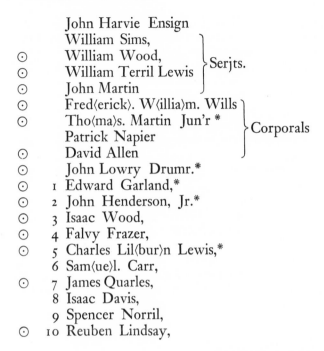

John Harvie Ensign
William Sims,
⊙   William Wood,   ⎫
⊙   William Terril Lewis ⎬ Serjts.
⊙   John Martin   ⎭
⊙   Fred⟨erick⟩. W⟨illia⟩m. Wills ⎫
⊙   Tho⟨ma⟩s. Martin Jun'r * ⎬ Corporals
     Patrick Napier   ⎪
⊙   David Allen   ⎭
⊙   John Lowry Drumr.*
⊙ 1 Edward Garland,*
⊙ 2 John Henderson, Jr.*
⊙ 3 Isaac Wood,
⊙ 4 Falvy Frazer,
⊙ 5 Charles Lil⟨bur⟩n Lewis,*
   6 Sam⟨ue⟩l. Carr,
⊙ 7 James Quarles,
   8 Isaac Davis,
   9 Spencer Norril,
⊙ 10 Reuben Lindsay,

Autograph diary and Revolutionary memoranda of
Dr. George Gilmer (Virginia Historical Society)

Lieutenant George Gilmer to the Albemarle County First Independent Company of Gentlemen Volunteers A Reconstructed Address

Editorial note. The following address is reconstructed from four pages in the source cited. Each page is badly torn at its outer margin, and the original written contents are thus incomplete. In this exceptional instance, the present editors have bracketed in missing phrases, words, or characters on a basis of what is obvious or what they conceive the absent elements to have been. The author's extant spelling is left untouched. The editors have also substituted their own punctuation, for although a fair copyist, Lieutenant Gilmer in his own inditements presumed that when in doubt, one was free to insert a comma; and he was very frequently doubtful.

Also with many emendations, the address has previously been edited by Robert A. Brock and printed in *Collections of the Virginia Historical Society,* new ser. (12 vols. in 11, Richmond, 1833–92), VI, 77–80. Editor Brock indicated torn portions in the recto of the leaves by employing asterisks, but with a grasp of physics transcending that of the present editors, he contrived to reproduce whole clusters of words from the verso of the selfsame tears.

In 1778 George Mason stated that the "first independent Company formed in Virginia, and indeed on the Continent" was constituted from a plan of organization that he drew up for Fairfax County; and it is possible that as did Gilmer around this date, Mason addressed the Fairfax unit at some time between 17 and

26 April 1775 (Robert A. Rutland, ed., *The Papers of George Mason, 1725–1792* [3 vols., Chapel Hill, N.C., 1970], I, 214, 215–16, 229–32, 434). Colonel Mason was not, however, destined to be a fighting soldier.

Nor, despite the dedication of his "Arms, life, & fortune" to the defense of his "Country," was Lieutenant Gilmer. The son of a recently deceased Williamsburg physician of the same name, Dr. GEORGE GILMER had lived in Albemarle County for less than a decade. As a boy he had spent seven years in England, and after studying at the College of William and Mary, he returned for a five-year sojourn in the isles, this time in Edinburgh, where he studied medicine at the university. In December 1766 he announced that he would pursue "the practice of medicine and the art of midwifery" in Williamsburg. There he married and was physician to Governor Norborne Berkeley, Baron de Botetourt, as later he was to the Jeffersons of Monticello and the Madisons of Montpelier. Despite his dispensing commas as though from a salt spoon, Gilmer was well versed in the classics and in languages and owned a large library of classical authors and Latin medical books. At this time he was thirty-two years old (*William and Mary College Quarterly* [hereafter *Wm. and Mary Qtly.*,], 1st ser., XV (Apr. 1907), 226; Richard Beale Davis, *Francis Walker Gilmer* [Richmond, 1939], pp. 4–10; Wyndham Bolling Blanton, *Medicine in Virginia in the Eighteenth Century* [Richmond, 1931], pp. 75, 79, 86; *Va. Gazette* [Purdie and Dixon], 4 Dec. 1766).

Gentlemen Soldiers,

On your disposition this day much may [depend] respecting our own fate. This alternative [is now] before us, either to become the voluntary & abject slaves of a wicked administration, or to live free as the air we breath. The choice is easily made, but remember the maintaining this happiness must depend on a peculiar magnanimity and resolv[e] which must be firm, unanimous, and permanent. We must not only emulate the Roman name but surpass it, if possible, when in its greatest lustre. We must now exert to the utmost Valour, prudence, & love for our Country—that valour void of rancour & revenge; observe that prudence which may be necessary, devested of every selfinterested motive; with that love for our Country that to die in its defence shall be our highest ambition & most exalted virtue.

Let us this day unite hearts, hands, & [spirits] to oppose any power that shall attem[pt to subvert] our lives, liberties, or properties. Inst[ead of permitting] any divisions amongst us, let us no[w divest ourselves] of every illiberal & party prejudice, [and let us] act as one in working our own salva[tion. Let] us behold integrity as an inestimab[le jewel] & rejoice in poverty with freedom rathe[r than to] submit to the power of corruption, whi[ch we can] neither purchase [n]or restrain o[urselves by vir]tuous act. [God for]bid there shall be one amongst us of [suc]h confined views or sordid principles as to overlook or dispise danger at a distance or be regardless of evils that do not Threaten an immediate or contingent fall on himself. If there should unfortunately be such a wretch in hearing, if he is not devested of every feeling, he can not wai[t] till calamity infests his own dwelling for provocation to take up arms in defence of his liberty could he place himself in the situation of a once opulent Bostonian whose property is wrested from

him by the hands of Tyranny & oppression. Let him behold his house filled
with Soldiers against his consent, whose brutal [be]haviour, unpunished insults, & boundless [insol]ence distroy his peace. Can he behold [his wife] &
children abused with all [the insol]ence of Gage's[3] myrmidons [and be an
u]ndisturbed Spectator? If such [a mo]nster should be found, let's fix [a
stigm]a on him that may distinguish [him] from the brave & worthy, avoid
[his s]ociety, let him exist by himself [with] his own reflection (if he can be
capa[ble of] any) to torture him.

Let me observe to you, Gentlemen, [that] our warmest thanks are due to
the [Continental] Congress in General, our Delegates both in Congress &
Convention in particular for their spirited behaviour & the noble plan they
have laid for our conduct, which may, if rigidly observed & persisted in, remove all our difficulties without the horrors of Carnage & bloodshed (but
should this be unavoidable heaven forbid that any terrors should afright us or
make us value life too high to run any risks of loseing it) knowing no power
on earth can Antidate our doom. Let us therefore promote, as much as in us
lies, the rigid observance of the Association & by every method in our power
discountinance non associators. We shall in this manner effectually demonstrate our veneration for the system and our highest esteem for its founders.

We stand immediately obliged to the Gents: that composed the Richmond
Convention for their noble and judicio[us plan of] preservation, a plan
w[hi]ch, if exe[cuted] with the Spirit it deserves, [will] prove a terror to all
our e[nemies] & oblige them to declare s[ure our s]uccess, which heaven
avert, that we [at l]ast deserved it.

There can not be an individual capable of murmur at the plan proposed.
Let us immediately shew our Alacrity & willingness to Contribute our pro-
portions for our own & the benefit of the community. The Convention recommended to the committees to adopt what mode appeared most proper for
the purpose. Your Committee, in compliance with that recommendation, think
it proper to require one Shilling & Sixpence per poll for making a proper
defence should we be invaded or otherwise attacked.[4] It will clearly appear
to every reasonable person that all who are to reap the advantages should bear
their share of the burden & not shift it from their shoulders to the few generous Spirits that are to be found amongst us. The 10th of may is the latest
time fixed for this Collection, but why pos[t]pone it one moment? Those
who [have] wherewithall Pay in immediately. [Thos]e who have not, bor-
row, for we m[ay be taken] by surprise & Unprovided[, which] would be a
horrid reflection on a [spiri]ted & resolute people.

We are also, Gentn., directed by the Convention to practice the Exercise
apointed by his Majesty [in] 1764.[5] There may be [some] who think the
military anticks & ceremonies altogether useless, others who may disapprove
of some particular parts of these evolutions; but, Gentlemen, as it is an impracticable matter to please or satisfy the whim & inclination of everyone, it
is most righteous that we Should endeavour to make ourselves masters of this
exercise & thereby comply with the recommendation of the Convention,
which will be better than to gratify any of our private dispositions. It must be

evident to every one that being frequently under arms will enure us to the fatigue, obeying the word of command will learn a Soldier his duty, & by meeting frequently we shall acquire an acquaintance with each other, & I hope, a friendship, & by an uniform exercise, we shall become more active & less subject to Confusion or [of] injuring one another. Our pa[tience] will probably prevent some [other] evils that are but too much to [fear.]

My Good Soldiers, let me beg [you] to look on this matter with a serious eye & to make yourselves masters of every art of war with the quickest dispatch.

Gentln., you behold me before you with my Tomahawk girt about me, & tho I am but too sensible of my awkwardness, yet your esteem shall animate me to its proper use. & give me liberty now, Soldiers, to plight my honour to you that my abilities shall not only be exerted to make myself Master of the necessary parade of war but of the really usefull branches of that Intricate Science.[6] & I do now dedicate my Arms, life, & fortune to the protection of my Country & the service of the first Company of Independents for the County of Albemar[le,] with this firm resolve—never to bury the Tomahawk untill liberty shall be fixed on an immoveable basis thro the whole Continent.

Ibid.

1. The date for this item and the one that follows it is arbitrary. It follows by a week the suppositional date on which the Albemarle County committee assumed command of the companies to be raised within the limits of its purview, and precedes by 11 days the date on which, it being impossible to assemble the committee, the company voted whether to march to Williamsburg.

2. A note by Gilmer states that "Those marked with the chemical character for gold ⊙, marched from Charlottesville, or joined us on the way to W'msb'gh, in order to demand satisfaction of Dunmore for the powder, and his threatening to fix his standard and call over the negroes." Next to the names of those who "had powder" Gilmer drew symbols for the asteroid Pallas, for which asterisks are here substituted. The list of "Officers and Soldiers" is identically extended by R[obert] A. Brock in *Collections of the Virginia Historical Society*, new ser., VI, 82–84, and by Edgar Woods in *Albemarle County in Virginia* . . . (Charlottesville, 1901), p. 364, but these extensions were made by drawing from other data and do not appear in the manuscript under the present date heading.

3. Lt. Gen. Thomas Gage.

4. For the recommendation of the second Virginia Convention, see 13 Apr. 1775, n. 4.

5. On 25 Mar. 1775 the convention had recommended that infantry companies be formed, particularly in the piedmont and western counties, and that company personnel "endeavour as soon as possible to become acquainted with the military Exercise for Infantry appointed to be used by his Majesty in the Year 1764." The reference was to *The Manual of Exercises, as Ordered by His Majesty* (London, 1764); see *Rev. Va.*, II, 242, 244 n. 3, 375.

6. Gilmer here placed an asterisk to indicate a 2d footnote, in which he wrote, "Chevalier Folard says war is a trade fo[r a serv]ant, & a science for men of Gen[ius.]" Jean Charles de Folard (1669–1752), soldier and theorist, had contended

that victory on the battlefield would most surely result from a combination of fire-power and replacement of the extended line of battle by large, massed formations of troops; but it was to be the gradual increase of firepower that would render massed formations impractical.

Wednesday, 19 April 1775

Third Virginia Convention

Election of Delegate in Williamsburg

LAST Wednesday the inhabitants of this city met at the courthouse, to choose a Delegate, agreeable to the recommendation of the late Convention, for one year.[1] when the Hon. PEYTON RANDOLPH, Esq; was unanimously elected. At the same time, a very liberal subscription was made for our suffering fellow subjects at Boston, in cash; which will be remitted to them together with our first donation,[2] by the hands of the Hon. the Speaker, who sets off, next Saturday se'ennight,[3] for Philadelphia, to preside at the General Congress.[4]

Virginia Gazette (Purdie), 21 April 1775

1. For the election of delegates "for one year," see 13 Apr. 1775, n. 1.
2. On 24 Mar. 1775 the second Virginia Convention had "Resolved unanimously, that the Committees of the several Counties and Corporations in this Colony do exert themselves in procuring and continuing Contributions for supplying the Necessities, and alleviating the Distresses of our brave & worthy Fellow-Subjects of Boston now suffering in the common Cause of American Freedom, in such manner and so long as their Occasions may require" (*Rev. Va.*, II, 371). It would appear that by "Commit-tees" the convention meant those of correspondence. In at least 8 instances such county committees are known to have acted also as committees of donations for the relief of the suffering poor of Boston. Ordinarily, however, the donations were collected by separate ad hoc committees, again with the qualification that the membership of both committees of correspondence and donations was hardly distinguishable (ibid., II, 261 n. 8, 321 n. 10). In the present instance the collection seems to have been taken spontaneously (though probably following an appeal by the successful candidate) when the "inhabitants" were assembled to elect a delegate. There is no record of a "first donation" by the inhabitants of Williamsburg.
3. A contraction of "sevennight," or one week.
4. The confidence that Randolph would be chosen to "preside" at the second Con-tinental Congress was well placed.

Thursday, 20 April 1775

Third Virginia Convention

Election of Delegates in Spotsylvania County

SPOTSYLVANIA, April 2. This day the freeholders of this county met at the courthouse, to choose Delegates, agreeable to the recommendation of the late Convention, for one year, when GEORGE STUBBLEFIELD and MANN PAGE, jun. Esquires, were unanimously elected.[1]

Virginia Gazette (Dixon and Hunter), 20 May 1775

1. For the recommendation of the second Virginia Convention that delegates be elected "for one year," see 13 Apr. 1775, n. 1.

Friday, 21 April 1775

The Capital

Municipal Common Hall to Governor Dunmore
An Humble Address

My Lord,

We, his majesty's dutiful and loyal subjects, the mayor, recorder, aldermen, and common council of the city of Williamsburg, in common-hall assembled, humbly beg leave to represent to your excellency that the inhabitants of this city were this morning exceedingly alarmed by a report that a large quantity of gunpowder was in the preceding night, while they were sleeping in their beds, removed from the public magazine in this city, and conveyed under an escort of marines on board one of his majesty's armed vessels lying at a ferry on James river.[1]

We beg leave to represent to your excellency, that as this magazine was erected at the public expence of this colony, and appropriated to the safe keeping of such munition as should be there lodged from time to time, for the protection and security of the country, by arming thereout such of the militia as might be necessary in case of invasion and insurrection, they humbly conceive it to be the only proper repository to be resorted to in times of imminent danger.

We further beg to inform your excellency, that from various reports at present prevailing in different parts of the country, we have too much reason to believe that some wicked and designing persons have instilled the most diabolical notions into the minds of our slaves, and that, therefore, the utmost attention to our internal security is become the more necessary.

The circumstances of this city, my lord, we consider as peculiar and critical. The inhabitants, from the situation of the magazine in the middle of their city, have for a long tract of time been exposed to all those dangers which have happened in many countries from explosions and other accidents. They have, from time to time, thought it incumbent on them to guard the magazine. For their security, they have for some time past judged it necessary to keep strong patrols on foot.[2] In their present circumstances, then, to have the chief and necessary means of their defence removed, cannot but be extremely alarming.

Considering ourselves as guardians of the city, we therefore humbly desire to be informed by your excellency upon what motives and for what particular purpose the powder has been carried off in such a manner; and we earnestly entreat your excellency to order it to be immediately returned to the magazine.

Virginia Gazette (Pinkney), 20 April 1775 [3]

Governor Dunmore to the Municipal Common Hall
An Oral Reply

⟨His Excellency answered⟩[4] That hearing of an insurrection in a neighbouring county, he had removed the powder from the magazine, where he did not think it secure, to a place where it would be in perfect security; and that, upon his word and honour, whenever it was wanted on any insurrection, it should be delivered in half an hour. That he had removed it in the night time to prevent any alarm; and that captain Collins ⟨Henry Colins⟩ had his express commands for the part he had acted. He was surprised to hear the people were under arms on this occasion, and that he should not think it prudent to put powder into their hands in such a situation.[5]

Ibid., 20 April 1775

Cumberland County Committee

The Committee Doth Cordially Approve and Much Resolve

At a Meeting for Cumberland County on Friday the [21st] [6] of April 1775. Present, George Carrington Chairman, Littlebury Mos⟨by, John⟩ Mayo,

Joseph Carrington, Carter Henry Harrison, Richard James, J⟨ame⟩s ⟨Plea⟩sants, George Carrington junr. William Smith, Robert Smith, B⟨enjamin⟩ Wilson, Maurice Langhorne, Richard Eggleston, Edward Carringto⟨n, John⟩ Woodson, John Hyde Saunders, Clerk,[7] and Charles Woodson junr.

The Chairman recommended that the Committee should take un[der con]sideration the Proceedings of the late Provincial Convention held at Richmond Town in the County of Henrico from Monday the [20th] of March to Monday the 27th: of the same. The Committee accordingly proceeded to the Consideration thereof and after maturest Deliberation came to the following Resolutions. Resolved unanimously that this Committee doth cordially approve the Proceedings and Resolution[s of] the late Provincial Convention and also recommend it in the strong[est] Terms to the Inhabitants of this County to observe them in every part[icu]lar, and that they use every means in their Power to carry them [into effect.]

Resolved unanimously, That the most cordial Thanks of this Committee and of all the Inhabitants of this County are justly due to the Honourable Peyton Randolph Esqr. and the rest of the worthy Delegates who represented this Colony in the late Provincial Convention, for their cheerful Undertaking and faithful Discharge of the Trust reposed in them, and for the Wisdom and Spirit displayed in their Proceedings.

Resolved, That in Compliance with the Recommendation of the late Provincial Convention for procuring Ammunition and other Articles of Military Preparation, the Sum of one Shilling and three pence be collected from the Inhabitants of this County for every tithable Person in it; an⟨d⟩ this Committee doth recommend it to the different Housekeepers and all other Persons in this County as speedily as possible to pay any Member of this Committee who shall apply for the same the Sum of one Shilling and three pence for every tithable Person which they listed or ought to have listed according to Law on the tenth of June last.[8]

Resolved, That to avoid any further Request of Money from the People on this Occasion, the Members of this Committee will take on themselves the Collection of the aforesaid Money; and that Mr. Mosby, Mr. Joseph Carrington, Mr. George Carrington jr. and Mr. Edward Carrington divide the County into twenty four Districts and allot to each Member his District for Collection.

Resolved, That the utmost Industry be used in collecting the said Money as soon as possible; and, although this Committee has the greatest Confidence in the Virtue and Spirit of the People of this County in general, yet knowing that in all Nations and Societies there are some who want Virtue, it is further resolved, that reports be made to this Committee of the few who shall refuse Payment and of their Reasons for refusing that proper Steps may be taken for publishing such Delinquents, in order that the Foes to the Cause of Free⟨dom⟩ may be known, if from the Circumstances of their Refu⟨sal⟩ such Publication shall seem proper.[9] ⟨Re⟩solved, That Mr. Chairman be appointed Treasurer and that ⟨each⟩ Member shall to him account for, and pay his, Collections. ⟨Resol⟩ved That some Part of the Ammunition and other Articles to be ⟨obtained⟩ for this County ought to be procured as soon as possible: ⟨And there⟩fore further resolved, that Mr. Mayo, Mr. Pleasants and ⟨Mr. Ch⟩arles Woodson junr. be a select Committee for the Purpose of ⟨procur⟩ing the same; that they as speedily as possible procure 500 ⟨lb. of⟩ powder, 1000 lb. of Lead and 2000 Flints; and that the Trea⟨surer⟩ out of the Fund to be lodged in his Hands furnish the said ⟨C⟩ommittee with as much Money as the aforesaid Articles, with ⟨ch⟩arges of Transportation, shall cost. Resolved, that Wednesday the 17th. day of May be appointed for the Election of Delegates to represent this County in Provincial ⟨C⟩onvention; that it be recommended to the Freeholders thereof to ⟨c⟩onvene at the Court House on that day for the Purpose of ⟨elec⟩ting the said Delegates.[10]

Resolved, That this Committee conceive the bestowing any Victuals or strong Liquors by Way of Treat on account of such Elections as a Species of Extravagance; and that it directly tends to lead the People into Dissipation; It is therefore further resolved, that no Candidate shall by himself or by means of any other Person either previous to, or after the day of Election, give or bestow any such Treat or make Preparation for or by any Means encourage an expectation of a Treat at his own House or else where.

Signed by
Geo. Carrington, Chairman
Teste, THOMAS MILLER, Cl. Com.

Committee MS journal, the whole, including Carrington's signature, in hand of Thomas Miller (Archives Division, Virginia State Library) [11]

1. Under its character of incorporation, 28 July 1722, the government of the city of Williamsburg assumed the aspect of a closed corporation. The 1st mayor, recorder (effectually the city attorney), and 6 aldermen were appointed by the Crown. They in turn chose 12 men to constitute the Common Council. All of these officials sitting together formed the Common Hall, with the power of enacting ordinances. Aldermen and common councilmen held office during good behavior and annually elected the mayor and the recorder from among the aldermen. Vacancies in the number of aldermen were filled by the Common Hall from among the councilmen, and among the councilmen from among worthy outsiders (Lyon Gardiner Tyler, *Williamsburg, the Old Colonial Capital* [Richmond, 1907], p. 26; *Statutes at Large*, IV, 138–39).

2. The citizens of Williamsburg had kept "strong patrols on foot" to guard the magazine for about a week previous to the removal of the gunpowder because of word spread by "an armourer employed by lord Dunmore" that His Excellency was having the locks removed from the arms in the arsenal and would probably take away the powder. But several nights of patrolling "the streets till day break" sufficed to quell fears. The guard grew "negligent" and was disbanded on Thursday, 20 Apr. (Burk, *Hist. of Va.*, III, 409 n.).

3. The date of Pinkney's newspaper discloses that he held the issue open until the protest of the Common Hall and the governor's reply could be printed.

4. The bracketed transition replaces the newspaper heading: *"To which Address His Excellency returned this verbal Answer:"*.

5. For responses to this pronouncement, see 26 Apr. 1775, Henrico Co. Committee; 29 Apr., Spotsylvania Council; 3 May, New Kent Co. Committee; 8 May, Sussex Co. Committee; 9 May, Hanover Co. Committee, Spotsylvania Co. Committee; 13 May, Mecklenburg Co. Committee; 19 May, Caroline Co. Committee; 22 May, Prince William Co. Committee; 23 May, Westmoreland Co. Committee; 26 May, Loudoun Co. Committee; 27 May, Frederick Co. Committee; 6 June, James City Co. Committee; 19 June, Prince Edward Co. Committee; 10 July, Fincastle Co. Committee.

6. The date and such words, syllables, and characters as are within regular brackets are taken from Peter Force, ed., *American Archives* . . . , 4th ser. (6 vols., Washington, D.C., 1837–46), II, col. 372, in which select parts of the document are printed. Words, syllables, and characters now illegible because of fading near the margins are supplied by the present editors and enclosed within angle brackets.

7. John Hyde Saunders was a "Clerk" in the sense of being a minister of the Gospel.

8. For the recommendation of the second Virginia Convention "for procuring Ammunition and other Articles of Military Preparation," see 8 Apr. 1775, n. 4. A standing statute of 1762 ("An Act for the Better and More Regular Collecting the Publick Taxes") obligated the justices of the peace (who rather obviously in the present instance were also members of the county committee of correspondence) to list the tithables within given districts, the clerk of the county court to consolidate the lists by 30 Nov., and the county high sheriff to collect the taxes assessed "on or before the tenth day" of each succeeding June. On 25 Aug. 1775 the third Virginia Convention would find that although the justices and the clerks were apparently discharging their duties, "several sheriffs" were taking advantage of the confusion of the time "in order to evade paying the money received on executions levied by them" (p. 490 below).

9. No "such Publication" reached the gazettes during the period of time covered within the present volume. It is possible, however, that a few souls wanting "Virtue" were posted in handbills or broadsides no longer extant.

10. The next recorded meeting of the Cumberland County committee was to be on 1 May. No mention of the election on 17 May 1775 would be made in the manuscript journal, but on that day William Fleming and John Mayo were reelected convention delegates.

11. For the provenance of the Cumberland County committee manuscript journal, see *Rev. Va.*, II, 292. The portions of the journal appearing within the present volume have previously been edited by H[enry] R. McIlwaine and printed in the *15th Annual Library Report*, pp. 9–17.

Monday, 24 April 1775

Third Virginia Convention

Election of Delegates in Middlesex County

At *a meeting of the freeholders of* Middlesex *county, convened at the court-house at* Urbanna, *on* Monday *the 24th of* April 1775, EDMUND BERKELEY, *and* JAMES MONTAGUE, *Gentlemen, were unanimously chosen delegates to represent the said county in convention, for one year.*[1]

Simon Fraser, clerk.

Virginia Gazette (Pinkney), 26 May 1775

Berkeley County Committee

Advertisement of Requests and an Order

The Gentlemen of the Committee for Berkeley are Requested to meet without fail at the Court house on the first day of May, next ensuing to take under consideration matters of the greatest Importance Respecting their existence as Freemen—It is wished the Gentlemen of the Vestry were appointed to meet the same day at the same place as their advice and concurrence is much desired.[2]

The second day of May is appointed for General Muster at the same place when all officers of the militia Volunteer Companies & others are ordered to attend as they wish well to themselves & Country.

The Freeholders are Requested to meet the same day to choose Delegates who are to continue for one year to represent them in Colony Convention.[3]

Adam Stephen.

> MS transcript in unidentified hand, enclosed in autograph document signed by Daniel Sturges on 23 May 1775, in loose papers of third Virginia Convention (Archives Division, Virginia State Library)

1. For the recommendation of the second convention that the Virginia constituencies elect convention delegates "for one year," see 13 Apr. 1775, n. 1.

2. The "Advertisement" (as on 23 May it would be labeled) is arbitrarily assigned the present date. Stephen was well positioned to issue this summons. He was chairman of the Berkeley County committee, commander of the county independent company, and a past delegate to the second Virginia Convention. In addition, he was county high sheriff and probably appointed a deputy to conduct the election in which he was himself a candidate. But the results of the balloting were not to go unchallenged, and the matter would be laid before the third Virginia Convention on 21 July 1775 (*Rev. Va.*, II, 336; William Thomas Doherty, *Berkeley County, U.S.A.: A Bicentennial History of a Virginia and West Virginia County, 1772–1972* [Parsons, W.Va., 1972], p. 383).

3. See 13 Apr. 1775, n. 1.

Tuesday, 25 April 1775

Bedford County Committee

Approval, Dissolution, and Recommendation

AT a meeting of the committee of the county of Bedford, at the courthouse of the said county, on Tuesday the 25th of April, 1775, John Talbot, gentleman, in the chair: The resolves of the convention held at the town of Richmond, the 20th of March, 1775, were read.

Resolved unanimously, that this committee will strictly observe and adhere to the several resolutions of the said convention, and will leave no means in their power unessayed to carry the same into effect.

On a motion made that this committee be dissolved,

Resolved unanimously, that this committee do consider their delegation as now at an end, and that it be recommended to the freeholders of this county to meet at the courthouse, on Tuesday the 23d of next month, for the purpose of electing delegates to represent them in colony convention for one year, and to elect another committee.[1]

Virginia Gazette (Pinkney), 8 June 1775

Gloucester County Committee

Premiums and a Forfeit of Title

Tuesday the 25th of April, 1775, the committee met according to adjournment, and came to the following resolves:

Resolved, that as an encouragement to the manufacturing GUNPOWDER in this colony, we will give a premium of 25 *l.* to any person who shall produce to the chairman of this committee, on or before the 25th of October next, 300 lbs. of good gunpowder made in Virginia, which we will purchase at the current price of that commodity; and if it shall be proved to be made wholly of the materials of this colony, we will give an additional premium of 10 *l.*[2]

Resolved, that we will give 50 *l.* to any person who shall produce to the chairman of this committee 60 pair of good WOOL and 60 pair of good COTTON CARDS, on or before the 25th of October next, with an authentick certificate of their having been made in this colony; and we will purchase the same at the usual price.[3]

The committee having received authentick information, that last Thursday night an officer of one of his Majesty's armed vessels, with a party of armed men, by express command of Lord Dunmore, privately removed the *gunpowder belonging to this colony* out of the magazine, it was unanimously resolved that the removal of the powder from the publick magazine, on board one of his Majesty's armed vessels, by order of the Governour, is exceedingly alarming at this time.

Resolved, that his Lordship's verbal answer to the address of the Mayor, Recorder, Aldermen, and Common Council of the city of Williamsburg, on that occasion, is unsatisfactory, disrespectful, and evasive.

Resolved, that his Lordship, by this and other parts of his conduct, which have lately transpired, has justly forfeited all title to the confidence of the good people of Virginia.

Resolved, that the powder ought immediately to be restored.[4]

Ordered, that the clerk send by express copies of these resolves to each of the printers, and they are desired to publish them in the next Gazettes.

Jasper Clayton, clerk.

Virginia Gazette (Purdie), 28 April 1775, supplement

1. The results of the respective elections, along with the transactions of other business, will be found under the date indicated. The present item consists of the first 4 paragraphs of a 7-paragraph notice. In dissolving itself, the Bedford County committee acted uniquely so far as surviving records indicate; but on 25 Aug. 1775 the third Virginia Convention would pass an ordinance ("for Regulating the Election of Committeemen in the Several Counties and Corporations within this Colony, and for Other Purposes Therein Mentioned") decreeing that members be elected annually in November, with the right of reelection implied (p. 489 below; *Statutes at Large*, IX, 58).

2. On 27 Mar. 1775 the second Virginia Convention had "Resolved unanimously that the making of Gun Powder be recommended" (*Rev. Va.*, II, 382).

3. See 7 Apr. 1775, n. 7.

4. See pp. 4–6 above; 21 Apr. 1775, The Capital.

Wednesday, 26 April 1775

Essex County Committee

Reports on Public Sales of Goods

And[1] at a committee, held for the said county of Essex, on Wednesday the 26th of April, 1775: John Brockenbrough and Thomas Strishley ⟨Streshley⟩, two of the gentleman appointed to sell the goods imported by Mr.

Archibald Ritchie, reported to the said committee that they had sold the said goods for £.47 15 2 three farthings, current money, being the amount of the cost and charges of the said goods.

. . . . .[2]

And at a meeting of the committee for the county of Essex, on the 26th of April, 1775, John Lee, Muscoe Garnett, and Henry Garnett, three of the gentlemen appointed to sell the goods imported by the said John Rowzee, returned a report of their proceedings to the committee, viz. Pursuant to the directions of the committee of Essex county, we have sold the goods imported by Mr. John Rowzee as stated below.

	Sterling.		
Amount of costs and charges, — — — — — — — —	£.9	4	6
In hand, for the suffering poor in Boston, — — —	0	4	6
	£.9	9	0

Amount of the sale, the whole purchase by the Importer, Nine Pounds Nine Shillings Sterling.

> John Lee,
> Muscoe Garnett,
> Henry Garnett.

Ordered, that the foregoing proceedings be published in the Virginia Gazette.

> By order of the committee.
> Jack Power, clerk of the committee.

Virginia Gazette (Pinkney), 1 June 1775

Henrico County Committee

Detestation and Abhorrence

In committee, Wednesday, April 26, 1775.

It appearing, from the Virginia Gazette of the 21st instant, that the powder in the publick magazine, in the city of Williamsburg, deposited there at the expense of the country, and for the use of the people in case of invasion, or insurrection, had been secretly removed, under the clouds of the night, by Captain Collins ⟨Henry Colins⟩, of the Magdalen sloop of war, and by order of the Governour; and the committee having taken into their consideration the address of the corporation of the city of Williamsburg, as also his Excellency's answer thereunto, came to the following resolutions: [3]

Resolved, that it is the opinion of this committee, that the removing the said gunpowder, in the manner, at the time, and for the reasons given for so doing, is an insult to every freeman in this country, a high reflection upon the respectable corporation of the city of Williamsburg, and to the last degree cruel, under their circumstances, being then threatened with an insurrection; that we consider the act itself as a determined step, tending towards establishing that tyranny we so much dread, and which the British Ministry, with unrelenting fury, have so long and are still endeavouring to effect: And farther, that we consider it as injurious to the same, and tending to destroy the pleasing idea, we had entertained, of his Excellency's regard for the happiness and true interests of this colony.

Resolved, that we think it incumbent upon us to avow our sentiments upon this occasion; and while we declare our detestation and abhorrence of the act, we will use our best endeavours to procure an immediate restitution of the said powder, to the magazine from whence it was taken.

Resolved, that as we cannot rest satisfied with his Excellency's answer to the address of the corporation of the city of Williamsburg, that it be an instruction to the committee of correspondence to write to the committee of the city of Williamsburg, or to the committees of York or James City counties, and procure the most authentick intelligence respecting the same, and report to this committee at their next meeting.[4]

By order of the committee,
John Beckley, clerk.

Virginia Gazette (Purdie), 28 April 1775, supplement

1. The present item begins with the 2d paragraph of a single notice. The public sales of goods reported this day had been ordered by the Essex County committee on 20 Feb. and 6 Apr. 1775 respectively (*Rev. Va.,* II, 296; 6 Apr. 1775 above). These are the last of such reports within the present volume.

2. The ellipsis deletes the paragraph relating the proceedings of the committee on 6 Apr. 1775.

3. For the background motivating the action of the Henrico County committee this day, see pp. 4–6 above; 21 Apr. 1775, The Capital.

4. Neither the letter ordered to be written nor the "authentick intelligence" received by the Henrico County committee has been found. For the answer to a query from Spotsylvania County, see 27 Apr. 1775 below.

Thursday, 27 April 1775

The Capital

Peyton Randolph to Mann Page, Jr., Lewis Willis,
and Benjamin Grymes, Jr., Esquires[1]

Gentlemen/   Williamsburg the 27th April 1775
In compliance with your request we give you a candid Relation of the Disturbance which happened last Week in this City about the removal of

the Powder from the Public Magazine. Early on Friday morning the Inhabitants were universally and much alarmed at the Report that the Powder had been removed the preceeding Night under an Escort of Marines and carried on board an Armed Vessel at Burwells Ferry. The Common Hall assembled and presented the address which we presume you have seen with the Governors Answer.[2] The Inhabitants were so much exasperated that they flew to their Arms; This incensed the Governor a good deal and from every thing we can learn was the principal Reason why his Answer was not more explicit and favourable. His Excellency has repeatedly assured several Respectable Gentlemen that his only motive in Removing the Powder was to secure it, as there had been an alarm from the County of Surry, which at first seem'd too well founded, 'tho it afterwards proved Groundless; besides what he has said in his Public Answer, he has given private assurances to Several Gentlemen, that the Powder shall be Return'd to the Magazine, 'tho he has not condescended to fix the Day for its Return. So far as we can Judge from a Comparison of all Circumstances, The Governor considers his Honor as at Stake; he thinks that he acted for the best and will not be *compell'd* to what we have abundant Reason to believe he would cheerfully do, were he left to himself. Frequent Messages have been sent from the Neighbouring Counties to enquire into the State of this unfortunate affair with the most friendly and Spirited offers of assistance and Protection. The City could not but hold themselves exceedingly obliged to those Gentlemen as they do to you Gentlemen, and the rest of our worthy Country Men, by whom we understand you are sent. We hope that you and the other Gentlemen can have no doubt of our paying the utmost attention to the Country's Interest as well as our own Security in particular. If we then may be permitted to advise, it is our opinion and most earnest request that Matters may be quieted for the present at least; we are firmly persuaded that perfect Tranquility will be speedily Returned; By pursuing this Course we foresee no Hazard or even inconvenience that can ensue; whereas we are apprehensive, and this we think on good Grounds, that violent measures may produce effects, which God only knows the consequences of.

We beg that our thanks and best Wishes may be presented to the several Gentlemen of this Country who have interested themselves in our Behalf and are Gent:

Yr. much oblige Hble Servts.

PEYTON RANDOLPH for self and the Corporation
of the City of Williamsburg

> MS letter in hand of Jacob Bruce, clerk, with Randolph's autograph signature (Lee Family Papers, Manuscripts Department, University of Virginia Library)

1. This letter is the reply to a query from the independent companies gathered in Fredericksburg as to what they should do about the seizure of the gunpowder.

That the letter was addressed to Mann Page, Jr., because he was present in Williamsburg to present the "request" of the independent companies needs no comment. Had Randolph in the same letter additionally addressed anyone in Fredericksburg, the addressee most logically would have been Hugh Mercer, who was masterminding the course of events there. But the letter's being addressed instead to the present trio indicates that, contrary to the long-accepted version, Page did not make the arduous rides between the county seat of Spotsylvania and the colonial capital alone but was accompanied by Willis and Grymes. Describing the scene to Lord Dartmouth, Dunmore wrote that "three gentlemen of principal families in the Country" had come down from Fredericksburg (P.R.O., C.O. 5/1353, fol. 138).

Lewis Willis, who lived at Willis Hill near Fredericksburg, was fairly prosperous and, as befitted a cousin of George Washington, was a veteran defender of American rights. He had signed the Westmoreland Association in opposition to the Stamp Act in 1766 and was at the present time a member of the Spotsylvania County committee. In his 41st year, he would soon be serving in the Continental Army ("The Willis Family," *Wm. and Mary Qtly.*, 1st ser., VI [Apr. 1898], 108–9; *Virginia Magazine of History and Biography*, X [July 1902], 109–10; *Rev. Va.*, I, 24, II, 197).

Benjamin Grymes, Jr., son of a former Spotsylvania County burgess and of a mother who was born a Fitzhugh, had not been so conspicuous in the cause. But then he was only 19 years of age ("Grymes Family," *Va. Mag. of Hist. and Biog.*, XXVIII [Apr. 1920], 118; ibid., VIII [Apr. 1900], 363). Why young Grymes went along, and though yet a minor was included among the "Esquires" raises a question; but he was of a family fond of racing and possessed of fast horses, and the triumvirate of couriers may have reached Williamsburg on mounts from the Grymes stables (W[illiam] G. S[tanard], ed., "Racing in Colonial Virginia," *Va. Mag. of Hist. and Biog.*, II [Jan. 1895], 302, 305).

2. See 21 Apr. 1775, The Capital.

Friday, 28 April 1775

Royal Chief Magistracy

Extract of a Letter from the Earl of Dunmore to the Earl of Dartmouth, Dated Williamsburg, December 24, 1775; Laid before the House of Commons, February 15, 1775, by Lord North.[1]

My necessary absence on the occasion of the Indian disturbances, will, I hope, account and excuse me for my not having acknowledged your Lordship's several letters in due time and order; and for not having regularly communicated accounts of the public affairs of the colony, to which some of them refer; and I wish I were now so fortunate as to have it in my power to make a representation of their appearing with a more favourable aspect, than when I last wrote upon those important concerns.

The associations, first, in part, entered into, recommended by the people of this colony, and adopted by what is called the continental congress, are now enforcing throughout this country, with the greatest rigour. A committee has been chosen in very county, whose business it is to carry the association of the congress into execution; which committee assumes an authority to inspect the books, invoices, and all other secrets of the trade and correspondence of merchants; to watch the conduct of every inhabitant, without distinction; and to send for all such as come under their suspicion into their presence, to interrogate them respecting all matters which, at their pleasure, they think fit objects of their inquiry; and to stigmatise, as they term it, such as they find transgressing, what they are now hardy enough to call the laws of the congress; which stagmatising is no other than inviting the vengance of an outrageous and lawless mob to be exercised upon the unhappy victims. Every county, besides, is now arming a company of men, whom they call an independent company, for the avowed purpose of protecting their committees, and to be employed against government, if occasion require. The committee of one county has proceeded so far as to swear the men of their independent company to execute all orders which shall be given them from the committee of their county.[2]

As to the power of government which your lordship, in your letter of November 11, directs should be exerted to counteract the dangerous measures pursuing here, I can assure your lordship that it is entirely disregarded, if not wholly overturned. There is not a justice of peace in Virginia that acts, except as a committee man. The abolishing the courts of justice was the first step taken, in which the men of fortune and pre-eminence joined equally with the lowest and meanest. The general court of judicature of the colony is much in the same predicament, for though there are at least a majority of his majesty's council who, with myself, are the judges of that court, that would steadily perform their duty, yet the lawyers have absolutely refused to attend, nor, indeed, would the people allow them to attend, or evidences to appear.[3] The reason commonly assigned for this proceeding is, the want of a fee-bill, which expired at the last session of assembly, and it is a popular argument here, that no power but the legislature can establish fees; and the fee-bill not having been renewed, it is attributed to the dissolution; but the true cause of so many persons joining in so opprobrious a measure, was to engage their English creditors, who are numerous, to join in the clamours of this country, and not a few to avoid paying the debts in which many of the principal people here are much involved.[4]

With regard to the encouraging of those, as your lordship likewise exhorts me, who appeared, in principle, averse to these proceedings, I hope your lordship will do me the justice to believe, I have left no means in my power unessayed to draw all the assistance possible from them to his majesty's government, but I presume your lordship will not think it very extraordinary that my persuasions should have been unavailing against the terrors which, on the other hand, are held out by the committee.

Independent companies, &c. so universally supported, who have set themselves up superior to all other authority, under the auspices of their congress, the laws of which they talk of in a stile of respect, and treat with marks of reverence, which they never bestowed on their legal government, or the laws proceeding from it, I can assure your lordship, that I have discovered no instance where the interposition of government, in the feeble state to which it is reduced, could serve any other purpose than to suffer the disgrace of a disappointment, and thereby afford matter of great exultation to its enemies, and encrease their influence over the minds of the people.

But, my lord, every step which has been taken by these infatuated people must inevitably defeat its own purpose. Their non-importation, non-exportation, &c. cannot fail, in a short time, to produce a scarcity, which will ruin thousands of families. The people indeed of fortune may supply themselves and their negroes for two or three years, but the middling and poorer sort, who live from hand to mouth, have not the means of doing so, and the produce of their lands will not purchase those necessaries (without which themselves and negroes must starve) of the merchants who may have goods to dispose of, because the merchants are prevented from turning such produce to any account. As to manufacturing for themselves, the people of Virginia are very far from being naturally industrious, and it is not by taking away the principal, if not the only encouragement to industry, that it can be excited; nor is it, in times of anarchy and confusion, that the foundation of such improvements can be laid. The lower class of people, too, will discover that they have been duped by the richer sort, who, for their part, elude the whole effects of the association, by which their poor neighbours perish. What then is to deter those from taking the shortest mode of supplying themselves, and, unrestrained as they are by laws, from taking whatever they want wherever they can find it?

The arbitrary proceedings of these committees, likewise, cannot fail of producing quarrels and dissensions, which will raise partisans of government; and, I am fully persuaded, that the colony, even by their own acts and deeds, must be brought to see the necessity of depending on its mother country, and of embracing its authority.[5]

Virginia Gazette (Pinkney), 28 April 1775

Virginia Committee

Maryland Committee to Virginia Committee via Fairfax County Committee

A true copy, received in *Annapolis, Friday, April* 28, 1775, half after nine o'clock, A.M., and forwarded at ten, per express.[6]

Mat. Tilghman,
Ch. Carroll, of *Carrollton*,
Charles Carroll,
J. Hall,
Thos. Johnson, Jun.
Samuel Chase
} Committee of Correspondence for Maryland [7]

Force, *American Archives*, 4th ser., II, col. 366

Fairfax County Committee to Prince William County Committee

Friday, Alexandria, Eight o'clock, P.M.
We received the enclosed from *Annapolis* at six o'clock; please forward it to *Fredericksburgh*. I am, for self and the Committee of Correspondence in this place, gentlemen, your humble servant,

Wm. Ramsay.[8]

Ibid., II, col. 366

1. After the presentation to the House of Commons of the extract of Lord Dunmore's letter, Arthur Lee obtained an attested copy from a member of Parliament and sent it to Peyton Randolph. William Lee also sent a copy to Robert Carter Nicholas. In all probability it was the attested copy that the speaker laid before the House of Burgesses on 15 June 1775; and either he gave a copy of the attested copy to John Pinkney, or the treasurer presented his own or another copy to the printer (Arthur Lee to Francis Lightfoot Lee, 25 Feb. 1775, Lee Papers, Houghton Library, Harvard University; William Lee to Robert Carter Nicholas, 6 Mar. 1775, in Worthington C. Ford, ed., *Letters of William Lee* [3 vols., New York, 1891; reprint, New York, 1968], I, 140; *JHB, 1773–1776*, p. 241).

With one alteration in paragraphing and minor changes in wording and punctuation, Pinkney followed the Commons version. In the 3d paragraph, however, he erred in printing "November 11." The original was "No. 11," indicating the 11th dispatch from Dartmouth to Dunmore, one of several to which the governor's present letter was the reply.

The unprinted portion of this very long letter contained 3 paragraphs presenting the governor's proposal for a total blockade of the Virginia coast, so that "Their Ports should be blocked up, and their Communications Cut off by Water even with their neighbouring Colonies." He would, further, "suspend" every function of legal government and cause all royal officials to be "withdrawn." These tactics followed, he predicted, confusion "would immediately reign" and the people, "Sensible" at last "from what Source their former happiness flowed," would hasten to "prostrate them Selves before the Power which they had so lately Considered as inimical, and treated with Contempt" (T[homas] C. Hansard, *The Parliamentary History of England, from the Earliest Period to the Year 1803* . . . [36 vols., London, 1806–20], XVIII, cols. 314–16; P.R.O., C.O. 5/1353, fols. 33–34). But this gratuitous counsel did not accord with Lord North's policy, which was to enforce the Coercive Acts, to await American response to the Conciliation Act, and in the meantime to let matters drift (Valentine, *Lord North*, I, 338–61).

2. See 11 Apr. 1775 above.

3. The "general court of judicature of the colony," the General Court, was composed of the governor (or his deputy) and the members of the governor's Council.

4. For the "fee-bill," the expiration of which had left county officials with no legal means of collecting emoluments for the performance of their duties, see *Rev. Va.*, I, 106, 172, 206, 280.

5. For observations on this extract, see 4 May 1775, Norfolk Co. Committee; 8 May, Sussex Co. Committee; 19 May, Caroline Co. Committee; 23 May, Westmoreland Co. Committee; 19 June, Prince Edward Co. Committee.

6. In Force the "true copy" is made to appear a letter, dated 24 Apr. at Wallingford, Conn., testifying to an "authenticated" but wholly inaccurate account of the British retreat from Concord (col. 365). On its face, however, the account was so unauthoritative as not to have caused couriers on foaming mounts to plunge down the length of the Atlantic seaboard to Charleston, S.C., where whatever was the "true copy" was received on 10 May (cols. 368–69). More likely that copy was one of extracts of 3 letters, one dated 19 Apr. and two 20 Apr., all at Boston, giving much more detailed and accurate narratives of the retreat (cols. 359–60), along with reports subsequently added by committees in New York. At least these were the items (although one only in part) that Pinkney printed in his *Va. Gazette* of 4 May, and Purdie in his of 5 May 1775.

7. The signatories are 6 of the 7 members of the colonial committee elected by the "meeting," or convention, of Maryland deputies on 12 Dec. 1774 (*Rev. Va.*, II, 118). In succession the abbreviations for given names stand for Matthew, Charles, John, and Thomas.

8. William Ramsay is known to have been a member of the Fairfax County committee at least by 19 Dec. 1774 (ibid., II, 203). The "enclosed" would reach Dumfries around 10:00 A.M., and Fredericksburg about 3:30 P.M. on 30 Apr. 1775.

Saturday, 29 April 1775

Albemarle County

Proceedings of the Independent Company of Volunteers [1]

On the company's receiving a letter [2] from Capt. Hugh Mercer, informing them that the Speaker and others advised that the companies assembled should be dismissed, they were at a loss what to do, and therefore put it to the vote of the volunteers. No committee could be had, members not attending. All present but John Coles and David Rodes voted for a march, on which it was the opinion of the Comp'y that they ought to be drum'd out of the company, as an example of that kind, from people of such conspicuous characters in the County, might be of dangerous consequence.[3]

> Autograph diary and Revolutionary memoranda of Dr. George Gilmer (Virginia Historical Society)

Caroline County Committee

Recommendation and Leave

AT A MEETING of the COMMITTEE 29th. of April 1775. Present 15. of the Committee

It is recommended to the Independent Company of Caroline to continue together till they see the Honl. Peyton Randolph Esqr. before they march to Wms.Burg or not[4]

The Independent Company has leave from this Committee to make use of the Powder in their possession on their intended expedition to Williams Burg

> Committee MS minutes in hand of Samuel Haws, Jr., clerk (Henry E. Huntington Library and Art Gallery of San Marino, Calif.)

Spotsylvania Council

Pledge of Readiness at a Moment's Warning

FREDERICKSBURG, Committee Chamber, *Saturday the 29th of April,* 1775.

AT a Council of one hundred and two members, Delegates of the Provincial Convention, officers and special deputies of fourteen companies of light horse, consisting of upwards of six hundred well armed and disciplined men, friends of constitutional liberty and America, now rendezvoused here in consequence of an alarm occasioned by the powder being removed from the country magazine in the city of Williamsburg, in the night of Thursday the 21st instant, and deposited on board an armed schooner by order of his Excellency the Governor:[5]

The Council having before them the several matters of intelligence respecting this transaction, and particularly a letter from the Hon. PEYTON

RANDOLPH, Esq; Speaker of the late House of Burgesses of Virginia, received here last night by an express despatched to Williamsburg for the purpose of gaining intelligence, informing that the Gentlemen of the city of Williamsburg and neighbourhood have had full assurances from his Excellency that this affair shall be accommodated, and advising that the Gentlemen assembled here should proceed no further at this time,[6] this Council came to the following determination, and offer the same as their advice to those public spirited Gentlemen, friends to BRITISH LIBERTY and AMERICA, who have honoured them by this appointment. Highly condemning the conduct of the Governor on this occasion, as impolitic, and justly alarming to the good people of this colony, tending to destroy all confidence in Government, and to widen the unhappy breach between Great Britain and her colonies, ill timed and totally unnecessary, consider this instance as a full proof that no opinion which may be formed of the good intentions of a Governor in private life can afford security to our injured and oppressed country, but that obedience to arbitrary, ministerial mandate, and the most oppressive and tyrannical system of Government, must be the fatal line of conduct to all his Majesty's present servants in America; at the same time justly dreading the horrors of a civil war, influenced by motives of the strongest affection to our fellow subjects of Great Britain, most ardently wishing to heal our mutual wounds, and therefore preferring peaceable measures whilst the least hope of reconciliation remains, do advise that the several companies now rendezvoused here do return to their respective homes. But considering the just rights and Liberty of America to be greatly endangered by the violent and hostile proceedings of an arbitrary Ministry, and being firmly resolved to resist such attempts at the utmost hazard of our lives and fortunes, do now pledge ourselves to each other to be in readiness, at a moment's warning, to re-assemble, and, by force of arms to defend the laws, the liberty, and rights of this, or any sister colony, from unjust and wicked invasion. Ordered that expresses be despatched to the troops assembled at the Bowling Green, and also to the companies from Frederick, Berkeley, Dunmore, and such other counties as are now on their march, to return them thanks for their cheerful offers of service, and to acquaint them with the determination now taken.

GOD SAVE THE LIBERTIES OF AMERICA.

The foregoing determination of Council having been read at the head of each company, was cordially and unanimously approved.

Virginia Gazette (Pinkney), 11 May 1775

1. Although George Gilmer did not date the item, Hugh Mercer's letter referred to herein could not have been written before the night of 28 Apr., and was probably not written until after the meeting of the Spotsylvania Council (below) on 29 Apr. Moreover, on this same day, Charles Lewis, George Gilmer, and John Marks wrote to Colonel Washington, indicating that the company would have "attended at Fredericksburgh in order to have proceeded to Williamsburgh," but Peyton Randolph's advice

via Hugh Mercer had reached the Albemarle officers before the "alarm" (George Washington Papers, Library of Congress).

2. Not found.

3. It is difficult to reconcile the "opinion of the Comp'y" with the resolution of the Albemarle County committee circa 11 Apr. that the unit "should not be led to duty without the voice of the committee," especially since "No committee"—or at least a quorum thereof—"could be had." Nor would it appear that under the "termes" of enlistment of circa 18 Apr. a volunteer could be justly accused of "falling" or "flying back" before an enemy simply because he supposed there was none to face. Again, voting not to accede to a nonexistent order hardly constitutes disobedience or necessarily presages disobedience should an authentic order be received. But if unhappy at having incurred the displeasure of their fellow volunteers, John Coles and David Rodes were probably otherwise unconcerned. Admittedly "conspicuous characters," they were themselves members of the county committee and in that capacity would conclude that their actions this day were justified (see 31 May 1775, Albemarle Co. Committee, 2 entries). Thus the picture of events for this day in Albemarle County is most to be remembered for its inconsistencies.

4. That the committee "recommended" instead of ordered the independent company to "continue together" is further proof that the governor's assertion that all the companies were under the control of their respective committees was an exaggeration (see 28 Apr. 1775, Royal Chief Magistracy).

Mr. Speaker had let it be known in time to appear in Purdie's *Va. Gazette* of 28 Apr. that he would meet the assembled volunteers as he passed through the region on his way to attend the second Continental Congress. He, Col. Benjamin Harrison, and Edmund Pendleton would counsel moderation when they met the Caroline County volunteers at Bowling Green on 4 May (*Va. Gazette* [Purdie], 12 May 1775, supplement; Jones and Girardin, *Hist. of Va.*, IV, 13 n.).

5. For the assembling of these troops, see pp. 4–7 above. The 2 recently reelected "Delegates" for Spotsylvania County were George Stubblefield and Mann Page, Jr. (20 Apr. 1775 above).

6. See 27 Apr. 1775 above.

Sunday, 30 April 1775

Virginia Committee

Editorial Note

On this date Alexander Purdie issued a broadside stating that "This Morning the Committee of Correspondence met, and have determined to send Expresses to the southward."

Rather obviously Purdie meant that only such members of the full committee as may have been in or near the capital at the time answered a summons to meet with the members of the select committee, of whom in turn only Robert Carter Nicholas and Dudley Digges could have been present, because Peyton Randolph was already on the road to Philadelphia. If John Tazewell, the committee clerk, was also present, he left no record of the meeting.

The decision of this rump committee was to transmit southward sparse but electrifying "advices" that units of the Massachusetts militia had clashed with British regulars and that at the time the despatches were penned, heavy fighting was continuing beyond Concord toward Boston. This intelligence had at an undesignated hour on 28 April reached Fredericksburg, where John Harrower, an indentured tutor, correctly noted that it contained "no particulars." The information was received in Williamsburg around 5:00 P.M. the same day. It was printed both in Pinkney's *Virginia Gazette* of 28 April (delayed in issuance by a day) and in that of Dixon and Hunter of 29 April 1775 (Noël Hume, *1775,* p. 155; Edward M. Riley, ed., *The Journal of John Harrower, an Indentured Servant in the Colony of Virginia, 1773–1776* [Williamsburg, 1963], p. 94; *Va. Gazette* [Purdie], 28 Apr., supplement; ibid. [Dixon and Hunter], 29 Apr. 1775). It was probably about the time the attenuated committee was reaching its decision that another rider, bearing later and more detailed accounts of the sanguinary events in Massachusetts, galloped into Dumfries.

Prince William County Committee to Virginia Committee via Stafford County and Spotsylvania County Committees [1]

Dumfries, April 30, *Sunday.*
GENTLEMEN: The enclosed came to hand this morning, about ten o'clock. In one hour I hired the bearer to convey it to your place to the different Committees. For self and the Committee of Correspondence in this place, I am, gentlemen, your most obedient servant,

William Carr. [2]

Force, *American Archives,* 4th ser., II, col. 366

Spotsylvania County Committee to Virginia Committee via Caroline County and King William County Committees

Fredericksburgh, Sunday evening, half past Four.
GENTLEMEN: The enclosed arrived here about an hour ago, and is forwarded to your Committee by your very humble servants,

Jas. Mercer,
Geo. Thornton, } Committee [3]
Mann Page, Jun.,
Hugh Mercer.

Ibid., 4th ser., II, col. 366

1. Although the covering note is addressed only "To the *Committee of Correspondence* at *Fredericksburgh*. By express.," the relative slowness with which the "enclosed" (for which see 28 Apr. 1775, Va. Committee, 1st entry) reached Williamsburg bespeaks at least a showing of the documents to members of intervening county committees.

Moreover, Carr's phrase "to your place to the different Committees," if not the last word in clarity, does hint at an amount of transcribing and of expresses crisscrossing the colony. This impression is given substance by the fact that on the same day that the documents reached the capital their contents were known in Surry County south of the James River.

2. Carr had been elected a member of the Prince William County committee on 19 Dec. 1774 (*Rev. Va.*, II, 204).

3. The "Committee" is but a handful of the 45 or more members elected on 14 Dec. 1774; but of the present signatories, only Mann Page, Jr., cannot be demonstrated to have been elected on that date (Ibid., II, 195 n. 2). The "enclosed" would reach Carter Braxton the next day.

Monday, 1 May 1775

Third Virginia Convention

Election and Subscription in King William County

At a meeting of the Freeholders of the County of *King William*, at the Court-House, on *Monday* the first of *May, Carter Braxton* and *William Aylett*, Esquires, were unanimously chosen their Delegates to represent them in Convention for one year, from the date hereof.[1]

A subscription being then opened for the relief of our brethren in *Massachusetts-Bay*, and it being thought highly necessary, at this important crisis, that supplies should be sent to them, and money being the only means by which the relief could be afforded with certainty, the sum of one hundred and seventy-five Pounds was immediately contributed, and it is expected that a much larger sum will be given, when collections are made from the whole County.[2]

Force, *American Archives*, 4th ser., II, cols. 450–51

Virginia Committee

King William County Committee to Virginia Committee via New Kent County Committee

King William, May 1, 1775.

Gentlemen: The enclosed arrived here to-day, and is forwarded to your Committee by your most obedient servant,

Carter Braxton.[3]

Ibid., 4th ser., II, col. 366

Cumberland County Committee

Evocation of Military Power

At a Meeting of the Committee for Cumberland County on Monday the first day of May 1775. Present, George Carrington, Chairman, William Fleming, Littlebury Mosby, John Mayo, Joseph Carrington, Richard James, Carter Henry Harrison, James Pleasants, John Netherland, Robert Smith, Frederick Hatcher, Edward Carrington, Richard Eggleston, John Woodson, Peter Stoner, Mr. ⟨John Hyde⟩ Saunders, Clerk, and Charles Woodson junr.

Mr. Chairman opened the Business of the day by laying before the Committee the Information received from the Northward respecting the Attack lately made by the British Troops on the Inhabitants of Massachusetts Bay, upon which the Committee after the maturest Deliberation came to the following Resolutions.

Resolved unanimously, That the Attack lately made by British Troops on our Brethren, the Inhabitants of Massachusetts Bay renders it absolutely necessary, both to secure ourselves against an Attack from the same Quarter and to enable us to afford them Assistance if requi[red,] that the Military Powers of this County be immediately collected an[d] put in the best Condition; It is therefore further resolved that Wednesday the 10th. of this Month be appointed for a general Muster of the [mili]tia of this County; and that all free Men be summoned agree[able] to the Militia Law, to appear at the Court House on that da[y e]quipped with whatever Arms and Ammunition they can pro[vide.] [4]

Resolved, That this Committee be adjourned to Wednesday [the 3rd.] day of this Instant.

> Signed by Geo. Carrington, Chairm[an]
> Teste Ed. Carrington Secretary
> Test, THOMAS MILLER, Cl[erk]

> Committee MS journal, the whole, including signatures of George and Edward Carrington, in hand of Thomas Miller (Archives Division, Virginia State Library)

Norfolk Borough Committee

William Davies to Prince George County Committee

A Charge was laid before the committee for Norfolk borough, that Mr. James Marsden had purchased of Capt. ⟨James⟩ Fazakerly one puncheon of linens, imported since the 1st of February, and that he had furnished him with 20 barrels of pork. Upon inquiry, it appeared that Mr. Marsden knew nothing about the linens, but furnished Capt. Fazakerly with the pork by order of Capt. Charles Alexander. As there may have been some foundation for the charge, I am directed by this committee to request you will please to enquire of Capt. Alexander, for what consideration he gave the order.[5]

Signed,   William Davies, Sec'ry.

Virginia Gazette (Dixon and Hunter), 28 October
1775

1. See 13 Apr. 1775, n. 1.

2. The subscription was taken up in response to a reading of the "enclosed" (for which see 28 Apr. 1775, n. 1; 30 Apr., Spotsylvania Co. Committee) in the item that follows.

3. Braxton's comment and signature afford the 1st documentary evidence found of the existence of the committee of correspondence in King William County. His covering note and the enclosures would reach Williamsburg on 3 May 1775.

4. In all probability this response to "the Attack lately made" was engendered by receipt and reading of Pinkney's delayed *Va. Gazette* of 28 Apr., with its supplement issued the following day, or of Dixon and Hunter's newspaper of 29 Apr. 1775 (30 Apr. 1775, Va. Committee, ed. n.). Otherwise, copies of the documents received by Braxton this day would have had also to be received at the Cumberland County courthouse, which at the time lay more than 50 miles due west of that of New Kent County.

The basic "Militia Law" of 1738, last extended in force by "An Act for Further Continuing an Act Intituled an Act for the Better Regulating and Disciplining the Militia," had expired on 20 July 1773 (*Rev. Va.*, I. 105). It was to compensate for the legal lack of military defense that independent companies of gentlemen volunteers had formed in many Virginia counties, including Cumberland, and exercised His Excellency. By effectually reviving a lapsed colonial statute within the area of its control, the Cumberland County committee was usurping a power both legislative and executive in nature; but it was doing so with the full authorization of the second Virginia Convention, which on 25 Mar. 1775 had "strongly recommended" recourse to this measure throughout the "Colony" (ibid., II, 374).

5. According to his own account, as related in a petition submitted to the second Virginia Convention on 25 Mar. 1775, Fazakerly was "master of the Ship Hodge." He sailed her from Liverpool on 10 Nov. 1774, with "a few packages of Medicines" and "a quantity of Salt sufficient for a winter's ballast and no more." Unhappily, he "met with very violent weather at sea" and after a "tedious" voyage exceeding 12 weeks limped into port at Norfolk, his craft "but little better than a wreck." Worse, this was after the deadline set by the second Continental Congress for the nonimportation of British goods. As a friend to Virginian "just rights and Privileges," he therefore "humbly" prayed that the convention would except his cargo and permit him to dispose "of so much as may be sufficient to discharge the necessary repairs and outfit of the same ship" and to grant "such other and further relief as to the wisdom of this Convention shall seem meet." But in its wisdom the convention summarily rejected the petition (*Rev. Va.*, II, 373–74).

By what transactions Captain Fazakerly came into title of a puncheon of linens is not disclosed, but neither for title nor exchange was he to be the object of censure. The interrogation of Charles Alexander, Prince George County merchant, by the committee of his county would take place on 8 May 1775.

The present item is the 2d paragraph of a 16-paragraph notice.

Tuesday, 2 May 1775

Royal Chief Magistracy

Governor Dunmore to His Council

Gentlemen.

COMMOTIONS and insurrections have suddenly been excited among the people, which threaten the very existence of his majesty's government in this colony; and no other cause is assigned for such dangerous measures than that the gunpowder which had, for some time past, been brought from on board one of the king's ships to which it belonged and was deposited in the magazine of this city, hath been removed, which, it is known, was done by my order, to whom, under the constitutional right of the crown which I represent, the custody and disposal of all public stores of arms and ammunition alone belong; and, whether I acted in this manner (as my indispensable duty required) to anticipate the malevolent designs of the enemies of order and government, or to prevent the attempts of any enterprizing Negroes, the powder being still as ready and convenient for being distributed for the defence of the country upon any emergency as it was before, which I have publicly engaged to do, the expediency of the step I have taken is equally manifest; and therefore it must be evident that the same head-strong and designing people who have already but too successfully employed their artifices in deluding his majesty's faithful subjects, and in seducing them from their duty and allegiance, have seized this entirely groundless subject of complaint, only to enflame afresh, and to precipitate as many as possible of the unwary into acts, which involving them in the same guilt, their corruptors think may bind them to the same plans and schemes which are unquestionably meditated in this colony, for subverting the present, and erecting a new form of government.[1]

Induced by an unaffected regard for the general welfare of the people, whom I have had the honour of governing, as well as actuated by duty and zeal in the service of his majesty, I call upon you, his council in this colony, for your advice upon this pressing occasion, and I submit to you, whether a proclamation should not issue conformable to what I have now suggested; and before our fellow subjects abandon themselves totally to extremities, which must inevitably draw down an accumulation of every human misery upon their unhappy country, to warn them of their danger, to remind them of the sacred oaths of allegiance which they have taken, and to call up in their breasts that loyalty and affection, which upon so many occasions have been professed by them to their king, their lawful sovereign; and farther, to urge and exhort, in particular, those whose criminal proceedings on this occasion have been, and are still, so alarming, to return to their duty, and a due obedience to the laws; and, in general, all persons whatsoever to rely upon the goodness and tenderness of our most gracious sovereign to all his subjects, equally, and upon the wisdom of his councils, for a redress of all their real grievances, which redress can only be obtained by constitutional applications; and, lastly, to enjoin all orders of people to submit, as becomes good subjects, to the legal authority of their government, in the protection of which their own happiness is most interested.[2]

Virginia Gazette (Pinkney), 4 May 1775

Virginia Committee

Williamsburg Committee to North Carolina Committee via Isle of Wight County Committee

Williamsburgh, May 2, 1775.

GENTLEMEN: The enclosed is this moment come to hand, and I forward it to you by express, with the request of the Committee of Williamsburgh that you will be pleased to forward the papers to the Southward, and disperse the material passages through all your parts.

I am, very respectfully, gentlemen, your most obedient servant,

Ro. C. Nicholas, *Chairman.*[3]

Force, *American Archives*, 4th ser., II, col. 367

Gloucester County Committee

Not a Single Hogshead

At a meeting of the committee of Gloucester, at the courthouse, on Tuesday the 2d day of May, 1775:

Resolved, that we will not ship a single hogshead of tobacco to Great Britain until the determination of the continental congress, respecting exportation, be known.[4]

Resolved, that we deem the resolution of our committee, last November, not to ship any tobacco in future to Mr. ⟨John⟩ Norton's house, as still obligatory; the ship Virginia having arrived without the concessions then required.[5]

Jasper Clayton, clerk.

Virginia Gazette (Pinkney), 4 May 1775

Surry County Committee

Committee to Undesignated Addressees

Surry County, May 2, 1775.

GENTLEMEN: The enclosed arrived here this evening, and is forwarded by your most obedient humble servant,[6]

Allen Cocke.

Force, *American Archives,* 4th ser., II, col. 366

1. For the background of the "gunpowder" affair, see pp. 4–6 above.

2. Pinkney follows this item with a paragraph stating that "The council thereupon acquainted his excellency, that as the matters he had been pleased to communicate to them were of the greatest consequence, they desired time to deliberate thereon till the next day." On 3 May 1775, the Council would respond with advice, and the governor take action accordingly.

3. There can be little doubt but that when it forwarded the "enclosed" on 28 Apr. 1775, the Maryland Committee of Correspondence also intended not only that the "material passages" be dispersed as widely as possible but that the original packet of documents be received by the Virginia Committee and be transmitted, with broadcasting of the contents while in route, to the Committee of North Carolina. Evidently on this date only Robert Carter Nicholas of the Virginia Select Committee was in Williamsburg, and rather than to delay on a technicality, he gathered a quorum of the town committee, to which he had been elected to 2d place (after Peyton Randolph) on 23 Dec. 1774 (*Rev. Va.,* II, 208) and fulfilled his role as acting "*Chairman.*"

4. The "determination of the continental congress" would be made known to the Gloucester County and other constituent committees at some time subsequent to 22 Aug., the date on which the third Virginia Convention was to receive a resolution secretly adopted at Philadelphia on 15 July 1775 (Procs. and n. 4).

5. The resolution of "last November" had been adopted on the 7th of that month in retaliation for the action of John Norton & Sons, commission merchants of London, in filling an order by John Prentis & Company of Williamsburg for 2 half chests of tea. When the members of the Gloucester County committee "repaired" to where the Norton merchantman *Virginia* lay moored, they found that their counterparts of the York County committee had already thrown the tea into the York River. On one matter of the present day, however, the Gloucester County committeemen were in error. The returning *Virginia* had brought the desired "concessions." Penned by Norton

on 5 Jan., with a postscript added on 16 Jan. 1775, they were first to appear in Dixon and Hunter's *Va. Gazette* of 6 May 1775 (*Rev. Va.*, II, 218–19, 238–39).

6. Although employing no address, by a positioning of notes of transmittal, Force makes it appear that on 1 May 1775 Carter Braxton forwarded the "enclosed" to the Surry County committee. It is highly improbable that Braxton did so, for from King William County the shortest route to Williamsburg lay through New Kent and James City counties. To have sent the documents meandering through Surry County would have placed them south of the James River, thereafter to necessitate their being boated upstream to the capital. The present item is, therefore, most acceptable as one standing in isolation, with no demonstrable point of cause or of destination, but as one affording proof that news of the fighting in Massachusetts was in fact being "dispersed."

Wednesday, 3 May 1775

Royal Chief Magistracy

Advice of His Council to Governor Dunmore and His Excellency's Resultant Proclamation

At a COUNCIL held at the PALACE May 3, 1775.
Present, his Excellency the Governor, Thomas Nelson⟨, Sr.⟩, Richard Corbin, William Byrd ⟨III⟩, Ralph Wormeley, junior, esquires, John Camm, clerk,[1] and John Page, esquires.[2]
The board, resuming the consideration of the subject laid before them yesterday by the governor, advised him to issue the following proclamation; and the same was ordered accordingly.[3]

By his EXCELLENCY *the right honourable* JOHN *Earl of* DUNMORE, *his Majesty's Lieutenant and Governor General of the Colony and Dominion of* VIRGINIA, *and Vice Admiral of the same.*

A PROCLAMATION.

VIRGINIA, to wit.
WHEREAS there is too much reason to suppose that some persons, in the different parts of this colony, are disaffected to his majesty's government, and by their weight and credit with the people are endeavouring to bring the country into such a situation as to afford them the fairest prospect of effecting a change in the form of it, covering their wicked designs under the specious appearance of defending their liberties, and have taken advantage of the unhappy ferment, which themselves have raised in the minds of their fellow subjects, in prosecution of their dangerous designs to oppose the most undoubted prerogative of the king, which in a late instance I thought it expedient to exert by removing on board his majesty's ship the Fowey, a small

quantity of gunpowder, belonging to his majesty, from the magazine in this city; I have thought fit, by advice of his majesty's council, to issue this my proclamation, with a view of undeceiving the deluded, and of exposing to the unwary the destruction into which they may be precipitated, if they suffer themselves to be longer guided by such infatuated counsels.

Although I consider myself, under the authority of the crown, the only constitutional judge, in what manner the munition, provided for the protection of the people of this government, is to be disposed of for that end; yet for effecting the salutary objects of this proclamation, and removing from the minds of his majesty's subjects the groundless suspicions they have imbibed, I think proper to declare that the apprehensions which seemed to prevail throughout this whole country of an intended insurrection of the slaves, who had been seen in large numbers, in the night time, about the magazine, and my knowledge of its being a very insecure depositary, were my inducement to that measure, and I chose the night as the properest season, because I knew the temper of the time, and the misinterpretations of my design which would be apt to prevail if the thing should be known. Acting under these motives, I certainly rather deserved the thanks of the country than their reproaches. But, whenever the present ferment shall subside, and it shall become necessary to put arms into the hands of the militia, for the defence of the people against a foreign enemy or intestine insurgents, I shall be as ready as on a late occasion to exert my best abilities in the service of the country.[4] In the mean time, as it is indispensably necessary to maintain order and the authority of the laws, and thereby the dignity of his majesty's government, I exhort and require, in his majesty's name, all his faithful subjects, to leave no expedient unessayed which may tend to that happy end. Such as are not to be influenced by the love of order for its own sake, and the blessings of this colony, as well as the dangers to which it is exposed from a savage enemy; who, from the most recent advices I have received from the frontier inhabitants, are ready to renew their hostilities against the people of this country. But, as on the one hand, nothing can justify men, without proper authority, in a rapid recurrence to arms, nothing excuse resistance to the executive power in the due enforcement of law, so on the other, nothing but such resistance and outrageous proceedings shall ever compel me to avail myself of any means that may carry the appearance of severity.

Anxious to restore peace and harmony to this distracted country, and to induce a firmer reliance on the goodness and tenderness of our most gracious sovereign to all his subjects equally, and on the wisdom of his councils for a redress of all their real grievances, which can only be obtained by loyal and constitutional applications, I again call upon and require all his majesty's liege subjects, and especially all magistrates and other officers, both civil and military, to exert themselves in removing the discontents, and suppressing the spirit of faction, which prevail among the people, that a dutiful submission to the laws of the land may be strictly observed, which shall ever be the rule of my conduct, as the interest and happiness of this dominion ever have been, and shall continue to be, the objects of my administration.

GIVEN *under my hand, and the seal of the colony, at* Williamsburg, *this 3d day of* May, 1775, *and in the 15th year of his majesty's reign.*

Dunmore.

GOD SAVE THE KING.[5]

Virginia Gazette (Pinkney), 4 May 1775

Virginia Committee

Isle of Wight County Committee to the *Committee* of the County of *Nansemond,* or any of them. An express from *Boston*

Smithfield, May 3, 1775, *Five o'clock in the morning.*
The enclosed [6] arrived here this morning, and is forwarded to your Committee of Correspondence by your humble servants,

Arthur Smith,
Nathaniel Burune.[7]

Force, *American Archives,* 4th ser., II, col. 367

Nansemond County Committee to *Committee* of *Chowan* County,
North-Carolina

GENTLEMEN: The enclosed is this moment come to hand and we forward it to you by express, with the request of the Committee of *Nansemond,* and you will be pleased to forward them to the Southward.
We are, gentlemen, your most obedient servants,

Willis Ridduh,
Willis Ceowper.[8]

Ibid., 4th ser., II, col. 367

Amelia County Committee

Preparations for Armed Conflict

At a meeting of the committee for the county of AMELIA, *at the courthouse thereof, on Wednesday the 3d of May,* 1775.
WILLIAM ARCHER, *Esq; was chosen chairman for the day.*

IT appearing to this committee, that the militia of this county, since the expiration of the late militia laws, hath been totally neglected; and it being indispensably necessary, for the internal security of the county, that the same be properly and regularly disciplined, and that patrollers in every neighbourhood be constantly kept on duty: [9]

Resolved, that application be made to the Lieutenant of this county, to direct forthwith a general muster of the militia of the county; that he do his utmost to carry into execution the law made in the year 1738, for embodying and disciplining the militia of this colony; that he give all the countenance and encouragement in his power to the officers who are recruiting or embodying independent companies, agreeable to the resolution of the Convention of the 25th day of March last.[10]

Resolved, that every member of this committee open a subscription for raising half a pound of gunpowder, and one pound of lead, by voluntary donation from each tithable person in this county, agreeable also to the said resolution of the 25th.[11]

Resolved, that JOHN TABB, and EVERARD MEADE, or either of those Gentlemen, be appointed immediately to purchase, for the use of this county, 800 lbs. of gunpowder, and 3200 lbs. of lead, at least; for which we, and every of us, oblige ourselves to pay.

Resolved, that every member of this committee have in readiness a stand of arms and ammunition, agreeable to the said resolution of the 25th.

Resolved, that the ammunition, when purchased, be lodged in the care of Mr. JOHN TABB, at his store, Mr. THOMAS G⟨RIFFIN⟩. PEACH⟨E⟩Y, Mr. SAMUEL SHERWIN, Mr. THOMAS WILLIAMS, Mr. GABRIEL FOWLKES, Mr. JOHN PRIDE, with each 100 lbs. of powder, and 400 lbs. of lead; and with Mr. JAMES SCOTT, at this courthouse, 200 lbs. of powder, and 800 lbs. of lead.

Resolved, that publick notice be given to the freeholders of this county to meet and choose DELEGATES at next court, to represent them in convention for one year.[12]

Resolved, that this committee be adjourned till the fourth Thursday in this month.[13]

John Pride, clerk.

Virginia Gazette (Purdie), 19 May 1775, supplement

Cumberland County Committee

Resolution, Complaint, and Thanks

At a Meeting of the Committee for Cumberland County on Wednesday the third day of May 1775. Present, George C[arring]ton, Chairman, William Fleming, Littlebury Mosby, John May[o], Joseph Carrington, Richard James, Carter Henry Harrison, James [Plea]sants, John Netherland, Robert

Smith, Edward Haskins, Benjam[in] Wilson, Edward Carrington, Richard Eggleston, John Woodson, Peter Stoner, Mr. ⟨John Hyde⟩ Saunders, Clerk,[14] Henry Macon and Charles Woo[d]son junr.

Resolved, That each Member of this Committee will pay the Money due for his own Tithables according to the Resolution of the 21st. of April on or before the 10th. day of this Month, and that Mr. Chairman write to the absent Members of this Resolution.[15]

A Complaint being made to this Committee by John Wily⟨,⟩ Collector of Mr. ⟨Maurice⟩ Langhorne's District, that Zachariah Hendrick refuseth to pay the Request of one Shilling and three Pence per Tithable, and otherwise misbehaves himself with respect to this Committee, it is resolved that Mr. Langhorne or his Collector summon the said Hendrick by Authority of an Attested Copy of this Resolution, to appear at the next Meeting of this Committee to answer the said Complaint.[16]

Resolved unanimously, That the Thanks of this Committee and of all the Inhabitants of this County are justly due to Captain Charles Scott and his Independent Company for their Spirited offers of their Services in defending this Colony against wicked Invaders; and their cheerful Appearance at this Place to day in readiness to march forward, on a late Alarm; and that this Committee in Behalf of themselves and of their Constituents do accordingly present to the said Captain Scott and his Independent Company, the most cordial Thanks as aforesaid.[17]

Resolved, That this committee be adjourned till Wednesday the 10th. of this Month.

Signed by Geo. Carrington, Chairman
Test. Ed. Carrington Secry.
Teste, THOMAS MILLER, Cl. Com.

> Committee MS journal, the whole, including George and Edward Carrington's signatures, in hand of Thomas Miller (Archives Division, Virginia State Library)

New Kent County Committee

To Act on Any Emergency

AT a meeting of the committee for NEW KENT county, at the courthouse, the 3d day of May, 1775.

Resolved unanimously, that Lord Dunmore's conduct, in removing the powder from the magazine of this colony, on board an armed vessel, at the time and in the manner it appears to have been done, was an ill advised and arbitrary step, tending to disquiet the minds and endanger the safety of his Majesty's loyal subjects of this colony in general, and of the inhabitants of the city of Williamsburg in particular.[18]

Resolved, that his Lordship's verbal answer to the address of the Mayor, Aldermen, and Common Council of the city of Williamsburg, was unsatisfactory and evasive, and that his Lordship's not returning the powder, agreable to their request, and the known desire of the people of this colony, is a sufficient proof that he was influenced by the worst motives.[19]

Resolved, that this, and other parts of his Lordship's conduct, which have lately transpired, evince him to be an enemy to liberty and the true interests of this colony, and a zealous supporter of tyranny and despotism over the people who have the unhappiness to live under his government; and that he has, thereby, forfeited all title to their confidence.[20]

Resolved, that the city of Williamsburg are entitled to the ready and cheerful assistance of this county, in case they should be in danger from any invasion or insurrection.

Resolved, that the thanks of this committee are due to the committee of Hanover, for communicating their order of the 2d instant; that this committee are sensible of the dangers that threaten us from the Governour's conduct, as well as from other quarters, and will co-operate with a majority of the counties of this colony in such measures as shall be adopted for their defence and preservation.[21]

It appearing to this committee, that a body of armed men, from the county of Hanover, have marched through this county, in order to make reprisals upon the King's property, to replace the gunpowder taken from the magazine.

Resolved, that such proceedings make it particularly necessary for the inhabitants of this county to prepare for their defence, against any dangers that may ensue in consequence of it, by keeping their arms in the best order, and the greatest readiness, to act on any occasion.

Resolved, that it be recommended to the inhabitants of this county immediately to form a company of volunteers, to be assembled at the lower part of this county, ready to act on any emergency, as may be found necessary.[22]

By order of the committee.

(A Copy.)   William Smith, clerk.

Virginia Gazette (Purdie), 19 May 1775, supplement

1. A "clerk" in the ministerial sense, Rev. John Camm, D.D., was commissary of the Church of England in Virginia and president of the College of William and Mary ([Lyon G. Tyler], ed., "Sketch of John Camm," *Wm. and Mary Qtly.*, 1st ser., XIX [July 1910], 30).

2. According to his own later testimony, of the 6 councilors present (they being a majority of 11 then living), John Page of Rosewell, Gloucester County, did not "advise" the governor to promulgate "the following proclamation." Appointed to the Council in June 1773, when only 30 years old, Page soon fell afoul of His Excellency by challenging the appointment of an additional visitor for the College of William and

Mary. The young man won, but the governor was a poor loser. "In the Council," reminisced Page, "I adhered to my former Whiggish principles"—or, according to Dunmore, panted after "popularity." When the governor summoned his Council in the present instance, Page rebuked him for having seized the powder and urged him to return it. Thereupon His Lordship "flew into an outrageous passion, smiting his fist on the table, saying, 'Mr. Page, I am astonished at you!'"

As the story came down to John Daly Burk, an embarrassed silence followed. Finally recovering, Dunmore resumed his "politeness." He arose and declared that he would absent himself and leave his advisors "to a free and unbiassed discussion." It was Wormeley who undertook to draft the proclamation, but he so couched it with inflammatory expressions that the others insisted these be softened. In its present form the document was presented to His Excellency, "who appeared to feel unusual pleasure in its perusal." Wormeley proposed that it be subscribed by all the members present, declaring that he would glory in seeing his name "handed down to posterity, as the strenuous opponent of a licentious multitude." But his colleagues demurred. And Page, it may be noted, was thereafter never summoned to attend a meeting of the Council (James LaVerne Anderson, "The Virginia Councillors and the American Revolution: The Demise of an Aristocratic Clique," *Va. Mag. of Hist. and Biog.*, LXXXII [Jan. 1974], 56–58, 63–66, 68; Page, "Memoir," *Va. Historical Register*, III [1850], 142–51; Burk, *Hist. of Va.*, III, 414).

3. For "the subject laid before" the Council "yesterday," see 2 May 1775, Royal Chief Magistracy.

4. The "late occasion" was Dunmore's War of 1774.

5. For observations on this proclamation, see 11 May 1775, New Kent Co. Committee; 12 May, Richmond Co. Committee; 19 May, Augusta Co. West Committee; 23 May, Westmoreland Co. Committee; 25 May, Lancaster Co. Committee; 26 May, Loudoun Co. Committee; 9 June, Unidentified County Committee; 10 July, Fincastle Co. Committee.

6. For the "enclosed," see 28 Apr. 1775, Va. Committee and n. 6, and 2 May, Va. Committee, above.

7. Arthur Smith and Nathaniel Burwell (in Virginia seldom "Burune") were elected members of the Isle of Wight County committee on 5 Jan. 1775 (*Rev. Va.*, II, 221).

8. Willis Riddick is known to have been a member of the Nansemond County committee by 6 Jan. 1775 (ibid., II, 225–26). The present item establishes the fact that Wills Cowper, if not also a member by that date, was elected at sometime during the succeeding four months.

9. For the "late militia laws," see 1 May 1775, n. 4, 2d para. The "patrollers" were select militiamen who, under the provisions of an act of 1766 amendatory to the basic militia law of 1738, at least once a month visited "all negro quarters and other places suspected of entertaining unlawful assemblies of slaves, servants, or other disorderly persons." The patrollers were also enjoined to apprehend slaves "strolling" between plantations without authentic passes. Apprehended misdemeanants were to be hailed before a justice of the peace, and he was empowered to impose up to 20 lashes "well laid on" to bared backs (*JHB, 1770–1772*, p. 140; *Statutes at Large*, VIII, 195–97, 503).

10. A gap in the court records for Amelia County makes it impossible to identify the county lieutenant commanding the militia at the time this resolution was adopted. The resolution adopted by the second Virginia Convention on 25 Mar. 1775 "strongly recommended" that each constituency "diligently" put into "Execution the Militia Law passed in the Year 1738" and that the "Inhabitants of the several Counties" form "one or more volunteer Companies of Infantry and Troops of Horse" (*Rev. Va.*, II, 374–75; 1 May 1775, n. 4).

11. For the "said resolution of the 25th.," see 13 Apr. 1775, n. 4.

12. See 13 Apr. 1775, n. 1.

13. The "fourth Thursday" in May 1775 was the 25th. No record of a meeting of the Amelia County committee on that day reached newsprint.

14. "Clerk" in the ministerial sense.

15. For the committee's "Resolution" see 21 Apr. 1775 and n. 8.

16. The journal for the "next Meeting of this Committee" contains no mention of the said Hendrick, suggesting that at sometime during the ensuing week he reconsidered his refusal and misbehavior and so avoided the necessity of appearing in order to answer the "said Complaint."

17. Capable Capt. Charles Scott will be found in Williamsburg by 19 July and elected lieutenant colonel of the 2d Virginia Regiment of Infantry on 17 Aug. 1775.

18. For the affair of the "powder," see pp. 4–6 above.

19. For His Lordship's "verbal answer," see 21 Apr. 1775, The Capital, 2d entry.

20. By adoption of this resolution the New Kent County committee disputed the resolution adopted on 25 Mar. 1775 by the second Virginia Convention that Dunmore's "People" were fortunate in their "happiness to live under his Administration" (*Rev. Va.*, II, 376); but such had been the direction of events in little more than 6 weeks that few, if any, of the delegates to that convention could have taken umbrage at the committee's resolution.

21. For the action of the Hanover County committee while convened at Newcastle on "the 2d instant," see 9 May 1775, Hanover Co. Committee.

22. In the brace of concluding resolutions there is a certain vagueness. Although in his march on Williamsburg Patrick Henry was reported to have been joined by "armed men" from New Kent County (*Va. Gazette* [Purdie], 5 May 1775, supplement), the resolutions imply that no independent company had yet therein been organized—a surprising matter in view of the exposed location of the county. On the other hand, there can be extrapolated from the resolutions the existence of 1 such company, with a call for the organization of a 2d for defense against a British thrust "at the lower part." But there is also a hint that Henry's "proceedings" had been as nerve-racking to the committee as would have been an enemy invasion, and that prudence dictated the presence of a force to counter one's friends should they on some future occasion get out of hand.

Thursday, 4 May 1775

Hanover County Committee

Patrick Henry to Richard Corbin: A Receipt [1]

Duncastle's ordinary, New Kent, May 4, 1775, received from the honourable Richard Corbin, esquire, his majesty's receiver general, 330 *l.* as a compensation for the gunpowder lately taken out of the public magazine by the governor's order; which money I promise to convey to the Virginia delegates at the general congress, to be, under their direction, laid out in gunpowder for the colony's use, and to be stored as they shall direct, until the next colony convention, or general assembly, unless it shall be necessary, in the mean time, to use the same in the defence of this colony. It is agreed, that in case the next convention shall determine that any part of the said money ought to be returned to his majsty's said receiver general, that the same shall be done accordingly.[2]

Patrick Henry, junior.

A true copy
Test Samuel Meredith, Parke Goodall.

Virginia Gazette (Pinkney), 11 May 1775

Patrick Henry to Robert Carter Nicholas: A Statement

Sir,   May 4, 1775.
THE affair of the powder is now settled, so as to produce satisfaction to me, and I earnestly wish to the colony in general. The people here have it in charge from the Hanover committee to tender their service to you, as a public officer, for the purpose of escorting the public treasury to any place in this colony where the money would be judged more safe than in the city of Williamsburg. The reprisal now made by the Hanover volunteers, though accomplished in a manner least liable to the imputation of violent extremity, may possibly be the cause of future injury to the treasury. If therefore you apprehend the least danger, a sufficient guard is at your service. I beg the return of the bearer may be instant, because the men wish to know the destination.[3]

With great regard, I am, sir, your most humble servant,

Patrick Henry, junior.

Teste, Samuel Meredith, Garland Anderson.

Ibid., 11 May 1775

Norfolk County Committee

Refutation of Defamatory and Atrocious Charge

At a meeting of the Committee of the county of NORFOLK, *at the courthouse of said county, on* Thursday, *the* 4th *of* MAY, 1775:
THE resolves of the Convention held at the town of Richmond, on the 20th of March last, were read, and unanimously approved.

Resolved, that the thanks of this Committee be presented to Thomas Newton, junior, and James Holt, Esquires, our worthy Delegates, for their faithful discharge of the important trust reposed in them.

Having heretofore placed the highest degree of confidence in the good intentions of our Chief Magistrate towards his Majesty's most loyal and faithful subjects, the good people of this dominion, over whom he presides, which we can safely affirm had gained him their universal esteem and respect, with equal surprise and sorrow we have seen, in our public gazettes, extracts of a letter said to be wrote by our said Chief Magistrate, on the 24th of December last, to the Earl of Dartmouth, one of his Majesty's principal Secretaries of State, most grossly misrepresenting all the good people of this colony, particularly the magistrates, and those whom the people have elected as committees to be the guardians of their inestimable rights and liberties; and as his Excellency has not thought proper to disavow being the author of such letter, we must take it for granted that the extract published is a faithful copy: [4] We therefore think it our indispensable duty, in justice to our own reputations, and that of our constituents, who have honoured us with such marks of their confidence and esteem, to refute so unjust and unmerited, so defamatory and atrocious a charge. First, then, we declare that we know of no instance wherein any committee in this or the neighbouring counties has assumed an authority to inspect the books, or any other secrets of the trade of merchants. We admit to have known of some instances where some merchants, being suspected of a breach of the association, have voluntarily offered some private letters and books to be inspected, in order to acquit themselves of such charge.

He next says, we stigmatize those we discover to have transgressed what we hardily call the laws of the Congress; which stigmatizing, to use the words in the said extract, "is no other than inviting the vengeance of an outrageous and lawless mob to be exercised on the unhappy victims." Several in this borough and county have been held up for public censure for breaches of the association, but no vengeance of any mob or individual has been inflicted on them, not even that fashionable one lately introduced by the troops under the command of General ⟨Thomas⟩ Gage; [5] and we could call upon sundry persons here, who were thus stigmatized, to justify this assertion.

We wish his Excellency had deigned to name the county where the committee had proceeded so far as to swear the men of their independent company to execute all orders which they should give them, as it is a piece of information entirely new to us, as well as that of every other county forming an independent company for the avowed purpose (as he says) of protecting their committees, and to be employed against Government, if occasion require. [6] We hope all the dark plots of our most secret or declared enemies will prove ineffectual in bringing matters to that unhappy issue; and we have so high an opinion of the virtue of our countrymen, that we look upon the solemnity of an oath altogether unnecessary to stimulate them to stand forth firm and intrepid [7] upon all just occasions in support of their civil and religious rights and liberties.

Whilst we were thus fondly flattering ourselves that we had, in his Excellency, a most powerful advocate in order to accommodate the unhappy disputes subsisting between Great Britain and the colonies, we leave the world to judge what poignant sorrow we must feel on the discovery that it was a vain delusion, and that, instead of the good offices we expected, he was all the time widening the breach by misrepresenting so greatly our conduct to those in power; and we now discover, from his Excellency's said letter, that his gentle and lenient conduct, which we were too ready to attribute to the regard he professed, and which we flattered ourselves he had, for his Government, proceeded only from his fears of the disgrace of a disappointment; and we find, as soon as it was known that letter would be made public, the mask was thrown off, and the first step taken to open the eyes of the people was the seizing of the gunpowder in the public magazine in the most secret manner: How far such a manoeuvre is justifiable is not our intention at present to inquire into, that being a point on which the public will undoubtedly undertake to judge for themselves; but we cannot help giving it as our opinion, that his Excellency's answer to the address of the respectable Corporation of the city of Williamsburg on that occasion is highly disrespectful and evasive.[8] And now, my countrymen, let us, by our steady perseverance in virtue and unanimity, convince his Excellency, when he says that every step we take must inevitably defeat its own purpose, that he (to use the phrase of our late truly worthy and noble Governor) has not augured right.[9]

We thought ourselves under the indispensable necessity of making the foregoing strictures on the above-mentioned letter, least [10] our silence might be construed by our countrymen, or others, into a tacit confession of our guilt; and now we submit to the public how far his Excellency merits the continuance of that unlimited confidence heretofore placed in him: The tribute of our respect we are still willing to pay him as our Chief Magistrate, and the representative of our most gracious Sovereign, to whom we shall always pay all due obedience.

Ordered, that the Clerk send a copy of these proceedings to Messrs. Dixon and Hunter, and Mr. John Hunter Holt, to be published; and they are desired to publish them in their next gazettes.[11]

Benjamin Crooker, Clerk.

Virginia Gazette (Dixon and Hunter), 13 May 1775

York County Committee

A Spirit of Cruelty Unprecedented in the Annals of Civilized Times

THE town of York being somewhat alarmed by a letter from Capt. Montague ⟨George Montagu⟩,[12] commander of his Majesty's ship the Fowey, addressed to the Hon. Thomas Nelson, ⟨Sr.⟩, Esq; President of his Majesty's Council in Virginia; and a copy of said letter being procured, a motion was made, that the copy should be laid before the committee, and considered. The copy was read, and is as follows:

"Sir,   Fowey, May 4, 1775.

I have this morning received certain information that his Excellency the Lord Dunmore, Governor of Virginia, is threatened with an attack at day break this morning, at his palace in Williamsburg, and have thought proper to send a detachment from his Majesty's ship under my command, to support his Excellency, therefore strongly pray you to make use of every endeavour to prevent the party from being molested and attacked, as in that case I must be under a necessity to fire upon this town.[13]

To the Hon. Thomas Nelson,   From
                                                        George Montague."

The committee, together with Capt. Montague's letter, taking into consideration the time of its being sent, which was too late to permit the President to use his influence, had the inhabitants been disposed to *molest and attack the detachment*; and further considering that Col. Nelson, who, had this threat been carried into execution, must have been a principal sufferer, was, at that very moment, exerting his utmost endeavours in behalf of Government and the safety of his Excellency's person, unanimously came to the following resolutions:[14]

Resolved, that Capt. Montague, in threatening to fire upon a defenceless town, in case of an attack upon the detachment, in which the town might not be concerned, has testified a spirit of cruelty unprecedented in the annals of civilized times; that, in his late notice to the President, he has added insult to cruelty; and that, considering the circumstances, already mentioned, of one of the most considerable inhabitants of said town, he has discovered the most hellish principles that can actuate a human mind.

Resolved, that it be recommended to the inhabitants of this town, and to the county in general, that they do not entertain or shew any other mark of civility to Capt. Montague, besides what common decency and absolute necessity require.[15]

Resolved, that the Clerk do transmit the above proceedings to the public printers to be inserted in the Virginia gazettes.

(A true copy.)
                                        William Russell, Clk. Com.

Virginia Gazette (Dixon and Hunter), 6 May 1775

1. For the background of this and the following letter, see pp. 4–10 above, and 9 May 1775, Hanover Co. Committee, by order of which the letters were transmitted to the printers.

2. The "330 *l*." was in the form of a bill of exchange (*Va. Gazette* [Purdie], 5 May 1775, supplement, which incorrectly records the sum as being £320).

If the king's officers had seized the colony's gunpowder, Patrick Henry must have reasoned, it was the king's money that should be taken in compensation. Assuming this to have been his thought, he sought out the receiver general, a crown official who collected the quitrents, land fees, navigation duties, and other revenues payable to the royal treasury. (The colonial treasurer, on the other hand, was an agent of the Gen-

eral Assembly, elected by and accountable to that body for the collection and disburse-
ment of income arising from taxes levied by itself for the use of the colony.) But to
whom did the gunpowder belong? This was a constitutional question complex with
niceties never clearly resolved. Certainly the colony was a part of His Majesty's dominions, and Lord Dunmore was his viceregent. Munitions placed in the public magazine were therefore under the governor's protection, and regardless of the source of
their procurement, he had a right and a duty to provide for their safety. Yet this posed
another question, resolvable by appeal to "natural law": provide for their safety against
whom?

The £330 would have been the approximate value of 20 barrels of gunpowder, which
initial reports indicated as the quantity that the governor had caused to be removed.
Henry took the bill to Philadelphia and met with a lukewarm response. "The Congress," observed Edmund Pendleton to William Woodford, "will not meddle with the
Subject, nor did the Deputies from Virginia choose to dispose of the money, but left
it to the Colony Assembly or convention." In the end it was to be the last-named assemblage that would take up "the Subject" on 10 Aug. 1775 and, in a reversal of judgment, dispose of it 15 days later (Mays, *Letters and Papers of Pendleton*, I, 103; pp. 412,
488 below).

3. Replying coolly, the treasurer said in effect that he "had no apprehension of the
necessity or propriety of the preferred service" (9 May 1775, Hanover Co. Committee). But the people of Williamsburg were less cool than he, and on the night of 4 May
1775 "Upwards of 100 of the citizens" patrolled the streets and guarded the treasury,
and if not entirely in fear of a coup by the governor, then perhaps by any armed
groups that might break from the discipline of the host (the numbers of which were
unknown) lying at Doncastle's Ordinary (*Va. Gazette* [Purdie], 5 May 1775, supplement). Two county committees, that of Spotsylvania on 9 May and that of Cumberland on 17 May 1775, would urge that the treasury be removed to a place of greater
security.

4. See 28 Apr. 1775, Royal Chief Magistracy.

5. The "fashionable" practice "lately introduced" by General Gage's troops in
Massachusetts was the application of tar and feathers. Some of the king's troops had
recently so decorated a certain Thomas Ditson, from the backcountry of Massachusetts, who had tried to persuade one of the soldiers in Boston to desert. A serious
threat of violence was averted even as the soldiers hauled their captive through the
city streets, because Gage, who was both commander in chief of British land forces in
North America and governor of Massachusetts, cooperated with Boston officials to
prevent the trouble from getting out of hand. A report of the incident, without mention of Gage's intervention, had appeared in the Norfolk newspaper 2 weeks before
(John Richard Alden, *General Gage in America* [Baton Rouge, La., 1948], pp. 222–23;
Va. Gazette, or the Norfolk Intelligencer, 20 Apr. 1775).

6. See 11 Apr. 1775, n. 2.

7. The printer set the word as "intripid."

8. See 21 Apr. 1775, The Capital, 2d entry.

9. The "late truly worthy and noble Governor" was Norborne Berkeley, Baron de
Botetourt, who had uttered a variation of this phrase in dissolving the General Assembly in 1769 (*Rev. Va.*, I, 70).

10. An archaic form of "lest," at the time still in usage.

11. The "next issue" of John Hunter Holt's *Va. Gazette, or the Norfolk Intelligencer*
was for 11 May 1775, but there are no extant copies for that date.

12. Destined for a long and distinguished career as a flag officer in His Majesty's

navy, Capt. GEORGE MONTAGU was the son of Adm. John Montagu, recent commander of the Royal Navy in North America. The captain, now only 24 years old, hailed from Wiltshire, had attended the Royal Naval Academy at Portsmouth, and had not to this point in his career been hindered by the fact that he was a member of the same family as the Earl of Sandwich, now first lord of the Admiralty. Captain Montagu had stood off Boston ready to receive Gage's beseiged forces before being ordered south to Virginia in 1774 in command of the *Fowey*, of 20 guns and 130 men. In January 1775, he and his men received the thanks of the people of Portsmouth, Va., for helping to extinguish an "alarming fire in that town" (John Marshall, *Royal Naval Biography* [4 vols., London, 1823–35], I, 39–43; William Laird Clowes et al., *The Royal Navy: A History from the Earliest Times to the Present* [7 vols., London, 1897–1903], IV, 192; Clark, *Naval Docs. of the Am. Rev.*, I, 47; *Va. Gazette* [Dixon and Hunter], 21 Jan. 1775).

13. These men, 43 in number, were hurrying to Williamsburg at the request of the governor to protect His Excellency and family from whatever damages might be caused if Patrick Henry and his men should descend on the capital (see pp. 7–11; *Va. Gazette* [Pinkney], 4 May 1775; ibid. [Purdie], 5 May 1775, supplement).

14. Precisely how the York County committee "procured" a copy of the letter is not clear. Presumably Nelson was either in Williamsburg, where he had attended a meeting of the Council the day before (the Council would meet again on the 6th, although there is no record of what members attended), or he was at Doncastle's Ordinary. Edmund Randolph recalled that Nelson had ridden out with Robert Carter Nicholas to meet Patrick Henry and persuade the captain not to march into Williamsburg (Randolph, *History of Va.*, p. 220). And while Nelson was thus "exerting his utmost endeavours" to preserve tranquillity, his handsome house in Yorktown, "the first object which struck the sight as you approached the town," was standing without its master, a prime target for naval guns ([Jean François], Marquis de Chastellux, *Travels in North America in the Years 1780, 1781 and 1782*, trans. and ed. Howard C. Rice, Jr. [2 vols., Chapel Hill, N.C., 1963], II, 385).

15. Too far removed to be able to refuse to "entertain or shew any other mark of civility" to Captain Montagu, the Caroline County committee would on 19 May 1775 content itself with expressing "abhorrence" at his letter.

Friday, 5 May 1775

Virginia Committee

Henry Remsen to The Committee of Correspondence, Williamsburgh, Virginia [1]

Gentlemen   New York May. 5. 1775.

At a time when the most vigorous exertions are absolutely necessary, for the Defence of American Liberty, against the Depridations of Ministerial

Power, and the Blood of our Brethren in the Massachusets has been Actually Shed, for daring to Maintain the rights of Englishmen; The inhabitants of this City and County have in the Most Explicit manner (as you may Perceive by the Inclos'd Association) resolved to Stand and fall with the Freedom of the Continent.[2]

We are Confident that our Constituents are Sincere in the Strong Assurances they have given us, that while we Continue in Office, they will be guided by our advice and Direction. We have thought it necessary to Advise the Witholding, Supplies from the British Fisheries, on the American Coasts, And to Cease all exports to those Colonies, which at this Alarming Juncture, refuse to Unite in the Common Cause: The Expediency is too evident to need any elucidation, and will Doubtless procure us many hearty Advocates in Britain; besides which we have resolved to withold all Provisions and Necessaries from the Army and Navy at Boston.

Our late Committees of Observation thought Proper to recommend the Appointment of a Provincial Congress; in Consequence of which our Constituents have Chosen 21. Deputies, to meet at this City on the 22nd. Inst. Those who may be appointed for that purpose in the other Counties of this Colony. for your farther Satisfaction on these Matters, we beg leave to Refer you to the Inclosed Papers. we Request you to Communicate the Substance of this Information to your next neighbours, and to Assure you that in our Department we shall Watch Incessantly for the publick Safety [3]

By Order of the Committee
I am Gentn. Your mo. obdt. & Hbl Srvt
HENRY REMSEN Dpy. Chairman [4]

Recipients' copy, MS letter, in unidentified clerical hand, with autograph signature (Archives Division, Virginia State Library)

[28 April 1775]

To the Freeholders and Freemen of the City and County of New-York:

We regret, gentlemen, the necessity we are under of addressing you upon this occasion, and perceive with anxiety the disorder and confusion into which this City has been unfortunately involved.

From cool and temperate counsels only, good consequences may be expected; nor can union (so essential to the success of our cause) be preserved, unless every member of society will consent to be governed by the sense of the majority, and join in having that sense fairly and candidly ascertained.

Conscious that the powers you conferred upon us were not adequate to the present exigency of affairs, we were unanimously of opinion that another Committee should be appointed; and well knowing that questions of the highest moment and the last importance would come under their consideration, and call for their determination, we thought it most advisable that it should consist of a large number, in order, by interesting many of weight and consequence in all publick measures, they might meet with the more advocates, receive less opposition, and be attended with more certain success.

The names of one hundred persons were mentioned by this Committee; you were left at liberty to approve or reject them, and appoint others in their room; and that your sense might be better taken, polls in each Ward were directed to be opened. What could be more fair?

By all means, gentlemen, let us avoid divisions; and instead of cherishing a spirit of animosity against one another, let us join in forwarding a reconciliation of all parties, and thereby strengthen the general cause.

Many, no doubt, have become objects of distrust and suspicion, and, perhaps, not without reason; you have now an opportunity of trying them. It surely never can be good policy to put it out of their power to join us heartily; it is time enough to reject them when they refuse us their aid. In short, gentlemen, consider that our contest is for liberty; and therefore we should be extremely cautious how we permit our struggles to hurry us into acts of violence and extravagance inconsistent with freedom.

Permit us to entreat you to consider these matters seriously, and act with temper as well as firmness; and, by all means, join in the appointment of some Committee, to whom you may resort for counsel, and who may rescue you from tumult, anarchy, and confusion.

We take the liberty, therefore, of recommending it to you to go to the usual places of election in each of your Wards, on *Monday* next [5] at nine o'clock in the morning, and then and there give your voices for a Committee of one hundred; to consist of such persons as you may think most worthy of confidence and most capable of the arduous task. Being also fully persuaded of the necessity of a Provincial Convention being summoned with all possible expedition, we recommend it to you, at the same time, to choose twenty Deputies to represent this City and County in such Convention, to meet here on the 22d day of *May* next.[6]

> By order of the Committee:
> Isaac Low, Chairman.[7]

Force, *American Archives*, 4th ser., II, cols., 427–28; original missing and contents not transcribed by John Tazewell in committee MS copybook

Committee for the City of New-York to the Several Counties in the Province.
Committee Chamber, New York, April 28, 1775.

GENTLEMEN: The distressed and alarming situation of our Country, occasioned by the sanguinary measures adopted by the *British* Ministry, (to enforce which the sword has actually been drawn against our brethren in the *Massachusetts,*) threatening to involve this Continent in all the horrours of a civil war, obliges us to call for the united aid and counsel of the Colony at this dangerous crisis.

Most of the Deputies who composed the late Provincial Congress held at this City, were only vested with powers to choose Delegates to represent the Province at the next Continental Congress, and the Convention having executed that trust, dissolved themselves.[8] It is therefore thought advisable by this Committee, that a Provincial Congress be immediately summoned to deliberate upon, and from time to time direct such measures as may be expedient for our common safety.

We persuade ourselves that no arguments can now be wanting to evince the necessity of a perfect union; and we know of no method in which the united sense of the people of the Province can be collected, but in the one now proposed. We therefore entreat your County heartily to unite in the choice of proper persons to represent them at a Provincial Congress to be held in this City on the 22d of *May* next. Twenty Deputies are proposed for this City, and in order to give greater weight and influence to the councils of the Congress, we could wish the number of Deputies from the Counties to be considerable.

We can assure you, that the appointment of a Provincial Congress, approved of by the inhabitants of this City in general, is the most proper and salutary measure that can be adopted in the present melancholy state of this Continent; and we shall be happy to find that our brethren in the different Counties concur with us in opinion.

By order of the Committee:
Isaac Low, *Chairman.*

Ibid., 4th ser., II, cols. 427–28; original missing and contents not transcribed by John Tazewell in committee MS copybook

The following association was set on foot here on Saturday the 29th[9] *instant, and on that day it was signed by above 1000 of our principal inhabitants.*[10] *It is to be transmitted to all the counties in the province, where we make no doubt it will be signed by all ranks of people.*

PERSUADED that the salvation of the rights and liberties of America depends, under God, on the firm union of its inhabitants, in a vigorous prosecution of the measures necessary for its safety, and convinced of the necessity of preventing the anarchy and confusion which attend a dissolution of the powers of government, we, the freemen, freeholders, and inhabitants, of the city and county of New York being greatly alarmed at the avowed design of the Ministry to raise a revenue in America; and shocked by the bloody Scene now acting in the Massachusetts Bay, do, in the most solemn manner, resolve never to become slaves; and do associate under all the ties of religion, honour, and love to our country, to adopt, and endeavour to carry into execution whatever measures may be recommended by the Continental Congress, or resolved upon by our Provincial Convention, for the purpose of preserving our constitution, and opposing the execution of the several and arbitrary and oppressive acts of the British Parliament, until a reconciliation between Great Britain and America, on constitutional principles (which we most ardently desire) can be obtained; and that we will, in all things, follow the advice of our general committee, respecting the purposes aforesaid, the preservation of peace, and good order, and the safety of individual, and private property.

Virginia Gazette (Dixon and Hunter), 30 June 1775

Third Virginia Convention

Election of Delegates in Henrico County

AT a meeting of the freeholders of Henrico county, at the courthouse, on Friday the 5th of May 1775, to elect delegates to represent them in Convention one year, agreeable to the recommendation of the late Convention, RICHARD ADAMS, and RICHARD RANDOLPH,[11] Esquires, were elected for the purpose.

John Beckley, clerk.

Virginia Gazette (Purdie), 26 May 1775

King William County Committee

Subscriptions for Northward Brethren

Yesterday there was a meeting of the committee of King William county, and part of the militia, when the contents of the second express from the Northward was communicated,[12] and it had such an effect on the minds of the people, that near 200 *l.* was immediately subscribed for the use of our brethren now fighting in the common cause. Most of the principal Gentlemen subscribed ten pounds each, and as not half of the county were present, there [13] is no doubt but that it will be nearly doubled.[14]

Virginia Gazette (Dixon and Hunter), 6 May 1775

Williamsburg

Anonymous to Alexander Purdie: A Public Query

Mr. Purdie.   Williamsburg, May 5.
PLEASE to inform the publick, that the Mary, Capt. James Miller, now loading in York river, is partly owned by Mr. John Wilkinson of London, who is likewise owner of two ships, the Lion and Brilliant, that formerly loaded in

Virginia; which two ships the said Mr. Wilkinson has let to the Ministry, to carry troops to Boston, to cut the throats of all the Americans.

Quere. Is it not incumbent on every friend of liberty, and his country, to refuse shipping a single hogshead of tobacco on board any ship belonging to such a blood-minded man as Mr. Wilkinson? Would it not be as proper to send the Mary back, in ballast,[15] as the Virginia?[16] Her being chartered by another person cannot be any good objection to sending her away in ballast, since the charterer must have known of Mr. Wilkinson's crime before the Mary left London, and therefore has made himself *particeps criminis*, an accessory to the guilt.[17]

Virginia Gazette (Purdie), 5 May 1775

1. On 7 Apr. the Virginia Select Committee of Correspondence posted letters to New York in a quest to ascertain whether the action of the Assembly of that colony had represented popular sentiment when it failed to endorse the work of the first Continental Congress and voted not to send delegates to the second. Remsen's letter and the enclosures are items nearest to a response of which there is record; but doubt that they were so intended is deepened by the request that the Virginia Committee "Communicate the Substance of this Information" to its North Carolina counterpart.

2. News of the shedding of "the Blood of our Brothers" in Massachusetts was received in New York City by express around 4:00 P.M. on 23 Apr. 1775. Almost immediately all semblance of royal authority vanished, and for a week thereafter the city was under control of the radical-led mob (Carl Lotus Becker, *The History of Political Parties in the Province of New York, 1760–1776* [Madison, Wis., 1909], p. 194).

3. If the Virginia Select Committee complied with this request, John Tazewell made no record that is extant.

4. A scion of a prominent Long Island family, HENRY REMSEN, JR., had been so extremely successful in New York City as an importer of dry goods that he was already retired at the age of 39. From business, that is. A pronounced whig, he was much engaged in politics, had performed yeoman service on the Committee of Fifty-one, and would perform more as deputy chairman of the Committee of One Hundred. Should the time come for New York to equip troops, there would be no need to rack brains in order to find the man for the job (Becker, *Hist. of Pol. Parties in the Prov. of N.Y.*, p. 8; John Austin Stevens, *Colonial Records of the New York Chamber of Commerce, 1768–1784, with Historical and Biographical Sketches* [New York, 1867], 2 pts., [2d pt.], p. 158).

5. "*Monday* next" was 1 May 1775.

6. This document and the 2 remaining enclosures disclose the influence of such practical conservatives as John Jay, James Duane, and Isaac Low. Having heretofore failed to contain the radical faction, they were now bent on joining and attempting to control it, with the hope that their own strength would be augmented by a successful appeal to the likeminded to follow. In this move the associates were acting with skill. Radical extremists saw the potential for their being pushed aside while more moderate heads assumed guidance of the Revolutionary movement in the colony, but the movement could not possibly succeed unless those heads, belonging as they did to men of talent and leadership, were united to the cause. On the other hand, it was now palpable that whether wavering conservatives wished the formation of the Committee of One Hundred or not, it would be formed; should they find the occasion propitious to participate in its formation (and the time when sides must be chosen was nigh), the invita-

tion to do so was extended; and whether or not they desired royal government to be superseded by that of a provincial convention, the succession of a new authority—or anarchy—seemed inevitable (Becker, *Hist. of Pol. Parties in the Prov. of N.Y.*, pp. 195–96).

7. Having left his native New Jersey as a youth, Isaac Low settled in New York City and, engaging in "General & Importing Business, Beaver Skins, &c.," acquired wealth. The Stamp Act threw him into politics, in which field even his friends found him extremely ambitious and opinionated and suspected him of leaning toward republicanism. After having been sent as a delegate to the Stamp Act Congress, he continued active in protesting the injuries to trade produced by British imperial regulations and taxes and in 1768 headed a committee of inspection to enforce nonimportation. In 1774 he served on the Committee of Fifty-one, subsequently to be elected chairman of the Committee of Sixty. But by then certain of his fervors were abating. Already by 1770 he had discarded the tactic of nonimportation as being counterproductive, and in 1773 he opposed forceful resistance to the landing of tea. A delegate to the first Continental Congress, he urged mild measures, "to provide ourselves with a retreat or a recourse," and he signed the Continental Association only reluctantly. John Adams, who breakfasted with the New Yorker at this time, described him as "a Gentleman of Fortune and in Trade" but was more prepared to admire Low's beautiful wife and his conspicuous opulence than his "Sincerity," which was being questioned. Although made chairman of the Committee of One Hundred, Low declined election to the New York Provincial Convention of 22 May 1775 and thereby rendered himself ineligible for membership in the second Continental Congress. Erelong he would part company with Jay and Duane and retire into the stiffly conservative precincts of the New York Chamber of Commerce, which he had helped found (ibid., pp. 107–8, 185–92; Jones, *Hist of N.Y. during the Rev. War*, I, 34–35, II, 296–306; Stevens, *Colonial Recs. of the N.Y. Chamber of Commerce*, [2d pt.], pp. 69–104; Arthur M. Schlesinger, *Colonial Merchants and the American Revolution* [new ed., New York, 1939], pp. 186, 225, 433–34; L[yman] H. Butterfield et al., eds., *The Adams Papers*, ser. I, *Diaries: Diary and Autobiography of John Adams* [4 vols. and supplement, Cambridge, Mass., 1961–66], II, 106, 108).

8. The first, or the "late Provincial Congress," had met in New York City on 20 Apr. 1775 and "dissolved" itself 2 days later (Becker, *Hist. of Pol. Parties in the Prov. of N.Y.*, pp. 191, 193).

9. Dixon and Hunter misprinted the date as the "1st."

10. It has been estimated that in 1775 the city and the county of New York contained a combined total population of 22,891 (Stella H. Sutherland, *Population Distribution in Colonial America* [New York, 1936], p. 69).

11. For the "recommendation of the late Convention," see 13 Apr. 1775, n. 1.

Richard Randolph lived in Henrico County, at the pleasant plantation home erected by his namesake father. As the son of a "Red Bolling" mother and the grandson of William Randolph II of Turkey Island, he was a descendant of Pocahontas and affiliated upon a numerous and worthy progeny. Uncles William and Peter Randolph had been members of the governor's Council. One first cousin was the mother of Thomas Jefferson, a 2d wife of John ("Potato Hole") Woodson of Goochland County, and a 3d the widow of long-time speaker-treasurer John Robinson. Richard's sister Jane was married to Anthony Walke of Princess Anne County, his sister Mary to short-tempered Archibald Cary, and his brother John would beget that singular genius John Randolph of Roanoke. Around 1750 he himself married Anne Meade, of a Nansemond County family with more than a little influence. And his eldest daughter would be taken to wife by a Harrison of the Berkeley branch. At least 45 years of age at this time, Randolph had served in many public capacities, including as a vestryman for Henrico Parish, a trustee for the Henrico towns of Richmond, Warwick, and Manchester, a justice of the peace and county high sheriff, and a burgess from 1766 to 1772. In the last-indicated year he was, as the result of an improperly conducted election, unseated in favor of Samuel Du Val. He had, meanwhile, signed the nonimportation associations of 1769 and 1770 and been elected a member of the county committee of correspondence in 1774. Why, in a reversal of outcome, he should have succeeded or displaced Du Val as a delegate to the third Virginia Convention no record states, but it is evident that from the viewpoint of the voters the county would be well served (Lucille Blanche Griffith, *The Virginia House of Burgesses, 1750–1774* [rev. ed., University, Ala., 1970], pp. 140–41; J[oshua] Staunton Moore, comp. and ed., *Annals of Henrico Parish . . .* [2 pts., *Richmond,* 1904], pt. 2, p. 81; *Statutes at Large,* VI, 281, VIII, 412, 422; Palmer *Cal. Va. State Papers,* I, 265; William G. and Mary Newton Stanard, comps., *The Colonial Virginia Register* [Albany, 1902], pp. 174, 176, 178, 181, 183, 188, 190–91; *JHB, 1770–1772,* pp. 175, 179, 195; *Rev. Va.,* I, 76, 83, II, 172 n. 3, 189).

12. The "second express from the Northward" bringing detailed accounts of the engagements at Lexington and Concord had arrived in King William County on 1 May and the accounts were now "communicated" to the committee and "part of the militia" (30 Apr. 1775, n. 1; 1 May 1775, King William Co. Committee). Purdie's *Va. Gazette* of 5 May 1775, supplement, reported that there were "armed men" from King William County with Patrick Henry at Doncastle's Ordinary on 4 May, but whether that contingent was "part of the militia" the printer did not record.

13. In the newspaper the adverb is misprinted as "their."

14. This apparently spontaneous "subscription for the use of our brethren now fighting in the common cause" may have been doubled by later contributions from the remainder of the county, but if so, no record is to be found among the extant newspapers.

15. In the newspaper the word in the first of 2 uses is printed as "balast."

16. For "the Virginia," the merchantman belonging to John Norton & Sons of London, see *Rev. Va.,* II, 163, 166, 218-19, 238–39, 279.

17. Captain Miller's animadversions on this notice to the "publick" are under the date heading of 12 May 1775, Williamsburg.

Saturday, 6 May 1775

Royal Chief Magistracy

By his Excellency the Right Hon. JOHN *Earl of* DUNMORE, *his Majesty's Lieutenant and Governor General of the Colony and Dominion of* VIRGINIA, *and Vice Admiral of the same:*

A PROCLAMATION.

VIRGINIA, to wit,

WHEREAS I have been informed, from undoubted Authority, that a certain *Patrick Henry,* of the County of *Hanover,* and a Number of deluded Followers, have taken up Arms, chosen their officers, and styling themselves an Independent Company, have marched out of their County, encamped, and put themselves in a Posture of War, and have written and despatched Letters to divers Parts of the Country, exciting the People to join in these outrageous and rebellious Practices, to the great Terrour of all his Majesty's faithful Subjects, and in open Defiance of Law and Government; and have committed other Acts of Violence, particularly in extorting from his Majesty's Receiver General the Sum of 330 *l.* under Pretence of replacing the Powder I thought proper to order from the Magazine;[1] whence it undeniably appears, that there is no longer the least Security for the Life or Property of any Man:[2] WHEREFORE I have thought proper, with the Advice of his Majesty's Council,[3] and in his Majesty's Name, to issue this my Proclamation, strictly charging all Persons, upon their Allegiance, not to aid, abet, or give Countenance to, the said *Patrick Henry*, or any other Persons concerned in such unwarrantable Combinations; but, on the Contrary, to oppose them and their Designs by every Means; which Designs must, otherwise, inevitably involve the whole Country in the most direful Calamity, as they will call for the Vengeance of offended Majesty and the insulted Laws, to be exerted here, to vindicate the constitutional Authority of Government.[4]

GIVEN *under my Hand, and the Seal of the Colony, at* Williamsburg, *this 6th Day of May,* 1775, *and in the* 15*th Year of his Majesty's Reign.*

Dunmore.

GOD SAVE THE KING.

Virginia Gazette (Dixon and Hunter), 13 May 1775

1. For differing interpretations of the removal of the gunpowder "from the Magazine," see pp. 4–8 above, and 9 May 1775, Hanover Co. Committee.

2. On 12 July 1775 Atty. Gen. John Randolph would feel constrained to deny an "industriously propagated" charge that he too was of the opinion that Henry's troops were a threat to private property (Williamsburg).

3. There is no surviving record to disclose which councilors were present this day to give their "Advice." Of the 6 who had met on 3 May, John Page was not now present, and Thomas Nelson, Sr., was sufficiently uneasy about the course of events that he may well have advised toning down the language of the proclamation. But the other 4—Richard Corbin, William Byrd III, Ralph Wormeley, Jr., and Rev. John Camm— no doubt approved or would have approved (see 3 May 1775, Royal Chief Magistracy and n. 2; Anderson, "The Virginia Councillors and the American Revolution," *Va. Mag. of Hist. and Biog.,* LXXXII [Jan. 1974], 57, 64–66, 69–70, 71). If Nelson and the 4 tories were the only members in Williamsburg, the governor was acting under his instruction with the minimum quorum desired by the Crown; if the number of councilors was fewer than 4, he was acting upon an "Extraordinary Emergency" ("The Aspinwall Papers," Pt. II, *Collections of the Massachusetts Historical Society,* 4th ser. [10 vols., Boston, 1852–71], X, 632).

4. But by this date, of course, Henry's men had dispersed, and there were no "unwarrantable Combinations" on the march for "all Persons, upon their Allegiance" to "oppose."

Students of this matter have ranged in contention from affirmation to denial that the governor's proclamation was a declaration of outlawry (e.g., Hamilton J. Eckenrode, *The Revolution in Virginia* [Boston, 1916; reprint, Hampden, Conn., 1964], p. 52; Noël Hume, *1775,* p. 138), but none of Henry's biographers has been so uncharitable to His Excellency as to charge him with trying to revive an unconstitutional executive practice, one proscribed by Article 39 of Magna Carta 5½ centuries .before (William Sharp McKechnie, *Magna Carta: A Commentary on the Great Charter of King John* [Glasgow, Scotland, 1914], pp. 384–85). In the form of judicial writs to compel attendance at court and in some instances involving treason, declarations of outlawry still persisted, but in the latter case (and then only when an accused was not on hand to stand trial), a writ of outlawry could not be issued until after procurement of an indictment of treason according to "the law of the land" or passage of an act of attainder. In no case was a stigmatized party condemned solely by the executive nor made fair game for such of His Majesty's faithful subjects as might be minded to essay that party's death (Trial of Treasons Act, 7 and 8 William III, *cap.* 3 (A.D. 1696), in W[illiam] C. Costin and J[ohn] Stephen Watson, eds., *The Law and the Working of the Constitution: Documents, 1660–1914* [2 vols., London, 1952], I, 81).

Had Henry in fact seized and "rebelliously kept or detained" the gunpowder for 6 days, he would have violated the Treason Act of 1534 (26 Henry VIII, *cap.* 13, in George Burton Adams and H[enry] Morse Stephens, eds., *Select Documents of English Constitutional History* [New York, 1902], pp. 240–42). Yet he still had placed himself in jeopardy by threatening to seize the powder and by impairing the dignity of the Crown. He had, moreover, endangered the person of Governor Dunmore, who was custodian of the king's munitions and "deputed" to secure the forts and arsenals "beyond the sea" in Virginia. Thus although His Lordship's proclamation has been called both "foolish" and "toothless," it was in effect a bill of particulars that, depending on the outcome of the evolving struggle, could easily lead to the passage of an act of attainder by a Parliament that more than once had discovered a disposition to sacrifice American lives in upholding its own presumed prerogatives (*Rev. Va.,* I, 70–71, 106, 117, 250).

Henry's actions were too fiery for moderates, but of the county committees that made public their sentiments there was only praise for the Hanover County militia captain, his men, and their heroics, and equivalent condemnation for the governor, his councilors, and their misdeeds (8 May 1775, Albemarle Co. Committee, Louisa Co. Committee; 9 May, Caroline and Culpeper Co. Committees, Hanover Co. Committee, Orange Co. Committee, Spotsylvania Co. Committee; 22 May, Prince William Co. Committee; 26 May, Loudoun Co. Committee; 6 June, James City Co. Committee; 19 June, Frederick Co. Committee, Prince Edward Co. Committee; 10 July, Fincastle Co. Committee).

Monday, 8 May 1775

Royal Chief Magistracy

Virginia, to wit
  By his Excellency the Right Hon. John Earl of Dunmore, his Majesty's Lieutenant and Governor of the Colony and Dominion of Virginia, and Vice-Admiral of the same:

A
Proclamation

Whereas upon Petitions of sundry Persons claiming and settled upon lands in the back Parts of this Colony, praying that the Grants made to the Officers and Soldiers under his Majesty's Proclamation in 1763 might not be located so as to interfere with their Claims, it was ordered, December the 16th, 1773, by the Governor and Council, that the Officers and Soldiers be at Liberty to locate their Grants wherever they should desire, so as not to interfere with legal Surveys or actual Settlements; that those should be deemed Settlers, who resided on any Tract of Land before October 1773, and continued to do so, having cleared some Part whereof,[1] whereby their Intention to reside was manifested; and that every Settler should have fifty Acres at least, and also for every three Acres of cleared Land fifty Acres more, and so in Proportion, which should be taken as Part of the Grant, to which the said Petitioners were entitled, when the Land Office should be open to them, unless such Settlers should choose to hold under the Officers or Soldiers aforesaid.[2]

And Whereas certain Surveyors in the County of Augusta have, without any Authority, prevailed upon Numbers of People to make Entries with them for the Lands which they choose to have surveyed, and have located several of them on Land which had been already settled, contrary to the above Order, taking Half a Crown from each the said People for such Entry, which they pretended was to entitle them to a Grant of four Hundred Acres of Land: [3]

I have thought fit to issue this my Proclamation for the Information of all Persons, that no Surveyor, or other Person, is entitled to take Entries for Land, it being contrary to the Regulations established by his Majesty for the granting of his vacant Lands; and I do hereby charge the said Surveyors forthwith to return the Money to the Persons from whom they have in the above recited improper Manner taken it.[4]

Given under my Hand, and the Seal of the Colony, at Williamsburg, this 8th Day of May, 1775, and in the 15th Year of his Majesty's Reign.

Dunmore.

God Save the King.

Benjamin J. Hillman, *Executive Journals of the Council of Colonial Virginia*, VI, 666–67

Albemarle County Committee

Editorial Note

In his *Virginia Gazette* of 19 May 1775, Alexander Purdie noted that eleven days before publication the Albemarle County committee delivered "thanks" to Captain Patrick Henry and the Hanover County volunteers for their conduct in procuring monetary recompense for the gunpowder removed in the morning of 21 April from the Williamsburg Magazine by order of Lord Dunmore. This notice is incorporated in a brief paragraph following the letter "presented" to Henry by the Orange County committee under the date heading of 9 May 1775. For the affair of the gunpowder, see pp. 4–11 above.

Louisa County Committee

Return of Most Hearty Thanks

At a committee held for the county of Louisa, *at the courthouse, the 8th day of May,* 1775.
THIS committee being fully sensible of the benefits that may redound to the community in general from the spirited behaviour of Captain PATRICK HENRY, and the other officers and Gentlemen soldiers of the volunteer company of Hanover, in procuring satisfaction for the gunpowder taken out of the colony's magazine, beg leave to return them our most hearty thanks.
Thomas Walker, William White, James Dabney, Charles Barret, Samuel Ragland, William Pettus, Waddy Thomson, Garritt Minor, Thomas Johnson, jun. Thomas Johnson, sen. Nathaniel Anderson, John Crutchfield, Robert Anderson, Charles Smith.
Signed by the whole committee, except one, who was absent.

Henry Garritt, clerk.

Virginia Gazette (Purdie), 19 May 1775

Mecklenburg County Committee

Election of Committee

AT a general meeting of the freeholders of Mecklenburg county, convened on Monday the eighth of May, 1775, at the courthouse of the said county, in order to elect a committee pursuant to a resolution of the American continental congress, the better to secure a due observation of the association entered by [5] the said congress; [6] the freeholders then proceeded to the choice of a committee, and elected into that office the following gentlemen, viz John Speed, Bennett Goode, William Lucas, Henry Speed, Francis Ruffin, Lewis Burwell, Robert Burton, Edmund Taylor, Clevereous (Cluverius) Coleman, Thacker Burwell, sir Peyton Skipwith, Benjamin Whitehead, George Baskerville, Reuben Vaughan, Joseph Speed, John Tabb, John Jones, William Leigh, Robert Ballard, Samuel Hopkins, junior, and John Ballard, junior.

JOHN SPEED, esquire, was unanimously chosen chairman, and Mr. ISAAC HOLMES clerk of this committee.

Resolved unanimously, that every member of this committee exert his endeavours to enlist volunteer soldiers agreeable to the resolution of the late provincial convention.[7]

It being too late in the day to proceed on business, the committee adjourned to Saturday the 13th of May 1775.[8]

Virginia Gazette (Pinkney), 1 June 1775

Prince George County Committee

Attendance, Confession, and Voluntary Agreement

At a committee held for the county of Prince George, the 8th of May 1775, present twenty of the members.

The following letter from the committee of the borough of Norfolk, to the Chairman of this committee, was read, viz.

. . . . .[9]

Capt. Charles Alexander, being requested, did attend the committee, and made the following confession, viz. That he had himself purchased the linens inadvertently, without considering the consequence of violating the resolutions of the Continental Congress,[10] to which he acknowledged he ought to have paid agreeable regard; and he is extremely sorry for having thus incurred the displeasure of the good people of America, and thereby forfeited that good opinion which he would be always happy to have, and those favours which he might otherwise have hoped to have enjoyed from them. He also confesses that Mr. ⟨James⟩ Marsden was acquainted with the circumstances of the said goods being imported contrary to the terms of the association, subsequent to the said Alexander's purchasing of them; and that the said Marsden paid the pork to the order above-mentioned, knowing that it was for part of the price of the said linens, and afterwards sent the said linens, and a parcel of shoes, with an invoice thereof, accompanied with a letter to Humphrey Richards, factor for the said Alexander in Blandford.

Signed,   Marsden, Maxwell, & Co.

And the said Alexander further says, that the order he gave on Mr. Marsden, to pay the pork to Captain ⟨James⟩ Fazakerly, was a conditional order, to pay Capt. Fazakerly in case the Convention then sitting should consent to the sale of the said goods, as there was then a petition before the Convention for that purpose.[11] Captain Alexander has further voluntarily agreed to re-ship the linens, and a parcel of shoes (under the same circumstances) remaining unsold at his own cost, or store them under the inspection of the committee; and that the profits arising upon such part thereof as are already sold, amounting to _____, shall be lodged in the hands of this committee for the use of, and forthwith to be sent to, the poor of Boston.

Signed,   Charles Alexander.[12]

Virginia Gazette (Dixon and Hunter), 28 October 1775

Certification and Intelligence

AT a meeting of the committee for Prince George county, held at Blandford, on Monday the 8th of May, 1775, the following resolutions were entered into, viz.

Resolved, nem⟨ine⟩. *con*⟨tradicente⟩. that every merchant, trader, or other person, importing any goods, wares, or merchandise, into this county, before he lands the same ought to produce, to the Chairman of this committee, a certificate from the Chairman of the committee of the county, town, or city from whence the said goods, wares, or merchandise, were re-shipped, that the same were imported into this colony before the first day of February.[13]

Resolved, that a committee of intelligence, consisting of Benjamin Harrison of Brandon, David Meade, Richard K⟨idder⟩. Meade, Hubbard Wyatt, Peter Eppes, James Cocke, Nathaniel Harrison, John Baird, Robert Boyd, William M'Whann, Richard Bland, jun. Theodorick Bland, jun. Nathaniel Raines⟨, Jr.⟩, Thomas Bonner, and John Raines, sen. be appointed to convey any alarm, as speedily as possible, to the adjacent counties, and that the same mode be recommended to every county in this colony.

Ordered, that a copy of the above resolutions be transmitted to the printer, and he is desired to publish them as soon as possible.

Signed by order of the committee.   Hartwell Raines, Sec'ry.

Virginia Gazette (Pinkney), 1 June 1775

Sussex County Committee

The Best Posture of Defence Possible

At a meeting of the committee for the county of Sussex, *at the courthouse, on Monday the 8th of May,* 1775.

PRESENT,

David Mason, Augustine Claiborne, Michael Blow, Henry Gee, John Cargill, William Nicholson, William Blunt, Robert James, John Peters, John Mason, junior, James Jones, George Rieves (Rives), *Richard Parker, and George Booth,* Gentlemen.

Resolved, THAT the thanks of this committee be given to the Rev. Mr. CAMPBELL, for his excellent prayer of this morning, prior to the committee entering upon business.

This committee taking into consideration a paragraph which appears in the publick newspapers, said to be extracted from a letter written to Lord Dartmouth, one of his Majesty's principal secretaries of state, by Lord Dunmore, Governour of Virginia, on the 24th day of December last,[14]

Resolved unanimously, as their opinion, that the said extracts (being fraught with calumny, falsehoods, and illiberal reflections against the good people of this colony in general, who are now, and for some time past have been, contending for their dearest rights, in the most decent and orderly manner) can be no other than a wicked and detestable forgery, or the work of some dirty ministerial sycophant, intending to widen our present unhappy differences with the mother country, and impress the people of this colony with unfavourable sentiments of a ruler who, they are unwilling to believe, would so meanly forfeit that general esteem he had, by a mild and pacifick administration, so generally acquired. With this opinion of the said extract, this committee cannot forbear, however reluctantly, to observe, that a late manoeuvre, in seizing the powder in the publick magazine of this colony, and privately conveying it away in the night, together with his evasive answer to the address of the corporation of the city of Williamsburg, presented to his Lordship upon that occasion,[15] but too plainly points out to this colony that the first magistrate has swerved from the line of conduct which has hitherto marked his administration, and impressed this committee with an idea that his private wishes are unfavourable to the welfare of this colony and the liberties of mankind. No other motives, we presume, could have actuated him to the commission of an act conceived in secrecy, and brought forth in darkness; the design of which was evidently to render (at least as far as in his power so to do) this colony defenceless, and lay it open to the attacks of a savage invasion, or a domestick foe, which a late proclamation threatens us with, and which his Excellency could not be ignorant of.[16]

Resolved unanimously, that it is absolutely necessary that this county be put into the best posture of defence possible; and, to that end, that a meeting of the people be convened at the following places, on the following respective days, that is to say: Those that muster under Captains ⟨Thomas?⟩ Moore, ⟨Gray⟩ Judkins, and ⟨John⟩ Mason, at Brown's Quarter, on Tuesday the 16th instant; those that muster under Captains ⟨Peter?⟩ Jones, ⟨Lawrence⟩ Smith, ⟨Green⟩ Hill, and ⟨Hartwell⟩ Marrable, at the High Hills, on the 17th; and those that muster under Captains ⟨John?⟩ Nicholson, ⟨Richard?⟩ Parker, Reeves ⟨George Rives⟩, ⟨John?⟩ Irby, and ⟨William⟩ Harrison, at the plantation lately belonging to Captain James Jones, on the 19th; and that they, and every of them, do bring with them, to the said several meetings, what arms they and every of them have. And this committee do earnestly request the field-officers and captains to attend the said several meetings, in order to animate the people, in the present time of danger, to compliance of the resolutions of the late Convention.[17]

Resolved unanimously, that we the members of this committee, now present, and every of us, will, in order to raise a sufficient sum of money to purchase ammunition, in this time of imminent danger, pay, by way of contribution for that purpose, the sum of 10 *l.* current money, on or before the first day of June next; and as we doubt not but the absent members of this committee will do the same for themselves, therefore Mess. John Cargill, James Jones, and George Reeves, are requested immediately[18] to purchase ammunition for the use of this county, to the amount of 200 *l.* current money, the present members engaging to indemnify them in such purchase, and that they make report of their proceedings to the next committee.[19]

Resolved unanimously, that a committee of intelligence and correspondence be appointed, of the following persons, that is to say: Mess. Blow, Peete, Nicholson, Cargill, Gee, David Mason, Claiborne, and Blunt; that upon they, or any one of them, receiving an alarm, he or they do forthwith fall upon the best methods in his or their power to give notice of such alarm, throughout this county, and also to some one or more of the committees of Southampton and Brunswick fixing upon the most convenient place for the people to rendezvous at, being guided therein by the quarter threatened most with an invasion, insurrection, or other attack.[20]

Ordered, that the proceedings of this day be transmitted by the chairman, as soon as may be convenient, to the press, in order to their publication.

Michael Blow, chairman.

Virginia Gazette (Purdie), 7 July 1775, supplement

1. In the original order of the Council, the word is "thereof" (Benjamin J. Hillman, *Exec. Journs. Coun. Col. Va.*, VI, 553).

2. The order was in compliance with instructions drafted in London and dated 7 Apr. 1773. It provided that officers and soldiers who had served in the French and Indian War could obtain land patents beyond the Proclamation Line of 1763. This permitted some settlement far west of the line, with the expectation of checkerboard mentalities in the British capital that all would proceed in orderly, predetermined fashion and the region not be reopened to chaotic speculation (Thomas Perkins Abernethy, *Western Lands and the American Revolution* [New York, 1937], p. 100).

3. The "certain Surveyors" were probably Willis Lee and Hancock Lee, who were engaged in platting the old claim of their employer, the Ohio Company of Virginia, and in doing so were charging well above the going rate. Thomas Lewis, the surveyor of Augusta County, in which part of the claim lay, may have registered some of the surveys brought in by William Crawford and Dorsey Pentecost, his entry agents, even though, strictly speaking, the lands were not opened. The uncertainty produced by frequent changes in regulations from London via Williamsburg was driving Lewis to distraction. Both the Ohio Company of Virginia (which included such personages as George Washington, George Mason, and James and George Mercer) and the Grand Ohio Company (in which members of His Majesty's cabinet were personally interested) cast covetous glances beyond the Blue Ridges, and their schemes had become deeply enmeshed in both Virginia and Pennsylvania politics. Governor Dunmore was decidedly not partisan to the Ohio Company of Virginia, the surveys of which he now enjoined. Or thought that he enjoined them, for the region was not known for the fastidiousness with which land claims were made therein. The whole West was overlaid with conflicting claims and occupancies—enormous private claims by Colonel Washington and the picturesque former deputy Indian agent George Croghan; legal patents granted to veterans of the French and Indian War; legal patents to some speculators; dubious ones to others; illegal ones to still others; and frequent possessions by pioneers who unceremoniously squatted where their eyes found the lands most fair. It was a picture at once tremendous and kaleidoscopic, beyond the ken of any mortal. How to safeguard the rights of those with valid claims (when and if determinable) and yet comply with the stream of requirements flowing from London? On whose word could one rely, Lewis begged to know, "In Cases where Justice & the Laws of the Land stand in Direct opposition to Ministerial mandate?" (Abernethy, *Western Lands and the Am. Rev.*, pp. 133–34; *Cal. Va. State Papers*, I, 282–83, III, 630–31; [Lyman Copeland] Draper MSS, State Historical Society of Wisconsin, microfilm in Va. State Library, 4QQ20).

4. For all of Lewis's problems in Augusta County, they were less aggravating than those of William Preston, his counterpart in Fincastle County (10 July 1775, Third Va. Convention, 2d and 3d entries).

Dunmore's proclamation would be presented to the third Virginia Convention which would ruminate but not resolve the western-land problems (19 July 1775, Procs. and n. 8).

5. In the newspaper the word is "dy."

6. For the "resolution" of the "said congress" to establish committees, see 8 Apr. 1775, n. 6.

7. For which see 18 Apr. 1775, n. 5.

8. The next proceedings of the Mecklenburg County committee will be found under the date heading indicated. The present item consists of the first 4 paragraphs of a 9-paragraph notice.

9. The ellipsis deletes the text of the letter dated 1 May 1775 from the Norfolk Borough committee requesting the Prince George County committee "please to enquire" why Capt. Charles Alexander had ordered James Marsden to exchange 20 barrels of pork for a puncheon of linens held by Captain James Fazakerly. The present item consists of a heading and 4 paragraphs of a 16-paragraph notice.

10. For the 10th article of the Continental Association, see 5 Apr. 1775, n. 1.

11. Captain Fazakerly's petition was rejected (1 May 1775, n. 6).

12. A report of the Norfolk Borough committee's examination of Captain Alexander is under the date heading of 22 May 1775.

13. The concept of further enforcing the provisions of the Continental Association by necessitating the certification of imported goods entering a county had previously been adopted, by the Richmond County committee on 7 Feb. and by the Prince William County committee on 20 Mar. 1775 (*Rev. Va.*, II, 282, 350).

14. The offending letter is under the date heading of 28 Apr. 1775, Royal Chief Magistracy; "a paragraph" refers to the entire "extract."

15. For the "address" and the "answer," see 21 Apr. 1775, The Capital.

16. The "attacks of a savage invasion, or a domestic foe" were those on which His Excellency had mysteriously touched in his proclamation of 3 May 1775.

17. In requesting the county militia to reconstitute itself as an independent organization, the committee was responding favorably to "the resolutions of the late Convention" adopted on 25 Mar. 1775 (1 May 1775, n. 4, 2d para.).

18. In the newspaper the word is misprinted "immediatey."

19. By this resolution the committee departed from the letter of the convention recommendation that committees collect the money from "their Constituents"; and in its sense that "imminent danger" did not permit adherence to the letter, the Sussex County committee was following the example set on 13 Apr. 1775 by that of Southampton Co.

20. Aside from its obvious purpose, the resolution can be interpreted as offering sanctuary to the inhabitants of the 2 adjoining counties. The offer of refuge would be more clearly stated by the committee of Cumberland Co. on 10 and 17 May 1775, by that of Buckingham Co. on 22 May, and by that of Bedford Co. on 27 June.

Tuesday, 9 May 1775

Caroline and Culpeper County Committees

Editorial Note

In a paragraph following the letter addressed this day by the Orange County committee to Patrick Henry and the "Gentlemen independents of Hanover," Alexander Purdie notes that on the same day "similar addresses of Thanks" were prepared by the committees of Caroline and Culpeper counties. For the events to which letter and addresses pertain, see pp. 7–11 above, and the entry next following.

Hanover County Committee

This Committee Do Approve

AT a committee appointed and held for Hanover county, at the courthouse, on Tuesday the 9th of May, 1775. Present, John Syme, Samuel Overton, William Craghead, Meriwether Skelton, Richard Morris, Benjamin Anderson, John Pendleton, John Robinson, Nelson Berkley, and George Dabney, junior.

AGREEABLE to a resolution of the committee held at Newcastle the 2d instant, setting forth, that they, being fully informed of the violent hostilities committed by the king's troops in America, and of the dangers arising to the colony by the loss of the public powder, and of the conduct of the governor, which threatens altogether calamities of the greatest magnitude, and most fatal consequences to this colony, and therefore recommending reprisals to be made upon the king's property sufficient to replace the gunpowder taken out of the magazine, it appears to this committee, that the volunteers who marched from Newcastle, to obtain satisfaction for the public powder, by reprisal, or otherwise, proceeded on that business as follows, to wit; that an officer with 16 men was detached to seize the king's receiver general,[1] with orders to detain him; and this, it was supposed, might be done without impeding the progress of the main body. The said receiver general not being apprehended, owing to his absence from home, the said detachment, according to orders, proceeded to join the main body on its march to Williamsburg; and the junction happened the 3d instant, at Duncastle's ordinary, about sun-set. A little after sun-rise next morning, the commanding officer being assured that proper satisfaction in money, should be instantly made, the volunteers halted, and the proposal being considered by them, was judged satisfactory as to that point; and the following receipt was given, to wit: . . . .[2]

It was then considered, that as a general congress would meet in a few days, and probably a colony convention would shortly assemble, and that the reprisal now made would amply replace the powder, with the charges of transportation, the commanding officer wrote the following letter, and sent it by express.

. . . . .[3]

To which an answer was received from the said Mr. ⟨Robert Carter⟩ Nicholas, importing, that he had no apprehension of the necessity or propriety of the proffered service.[4] For which reasons, and understanding, moreover, from others, that the private citizens of Williamsburg were in great measure quieted from their late apprehension for their persons and property, the volunteers judged it best to return home, and did so accordingly, in order to wait the farther directions of the general congress, or colony convention. It appears also to this committee, that before and on the march, strict orders were repeatedly given to the volunteers to avoid all violence, injury, and insult towards the persons and property of every private individual; and that in executing the plan of reprisal on the persons of the king's servants, and his property, bloodshed should be avoided, if possible; and that there is the strongest reason to believe that the foregoing orders, respecting private persons, and property, were strictly observed.

Resolved, that this committee do approve of the proceedings of the officers and soldiers of the volunteer company, and do return them their utmost sincere thanks for their services on the late expedition; and also, that the thanks of this committee be given to the many volunteers of the different counties who joined, and were marching, and ready, to co-operate with the volunteer company of this county.[5]

Ordered, that the clerk do transmit a copy of these proceedings to the printers, and desire that they will be pleased to publish the same in the gazettes as soon as possible. By order of this committee.

Bartlett Anderson, clerk.

Virginia Gazette (Pinkney), 11 May 1775

Orange County Committee

An Endorsement of Violence and Reprisal

THE committee for ORANGE county, met on Tuesday the 9th of May, taking into their consideration the removal of the powder from the publick magazine, and the compensation obtained by the independent company of Hanover; and observing also, that the receipt given by Capt. PATRICK HENRY, to his Majesty's Receiver General, refers the final disposal of the money to the next Colony Convention, came into the following resolutions:

1. That the Governour's removal of the powder lodged in the magazine, and set apart for the defence of the country, was fraudulent, unnecessary, and extremely provoking to the people of this colony.

2. That the resentment shewn by the Hanover volunteers, and the reprisal they have made on the King's property, highly merit the approbation of the publick, and the thanks of this committee.

3. That if any attempt should be made at the ensuing Convention to have the money returned to his Majesty's Receiver General, our delegates be, and they are hereby instructed, to exert all their influence in opposing such attempt, and in having the money laid out in gunpowder for the use of the colony.[6]

4. That the following address be presented to Capt. PATRICK HENRY, and the Gentlemen independents of Hanover.

GENTLEMEN,

WE the committee for the county of Orange, having been fully informed of your seasonable and spirited proceedings in procuring a compensation for the powder fraudulently taken from the county magazine by command of Lord Dunmore, and which it evidently appears his Lordship, not withstanding his assurances, had no intention to restore, entreat you to accept their cordial thanks for this testimony of your zeal for the honour and interest of your country. We take this occasion also to give it as our opinion, that the blow struck in the Massachusetts government is a hostile attack on this and every other colony, and a sufficient warrant to use violence and reprisal, in all cases where it may be expedient for our security and welfare.

James Madison, chairman, *James Taylor, Thomas Barbour, Zachariah Burnley, Rowland Thomas, James Madison, jun. William Moore, James Walker, Lawrence Taliaferro, Henry Scott, Thomas Bill.*[7]

Virginia Gazette (Purdie), 19 May 1775, supplement

Spotsylvania County Committee

Approval, Removal, and Request

At a committee for the county of SPOTSYLVANIA, *held at the courthouse in Fredericksburg, on Tuesday the 9th of May,* 1775, *present 26 members.* FIELDING LEWIS, *Esq: in the chair.*
THE committee having before them a copy of the proceedings of Capt. PATRICK HENRY, and other Gentlemen, officers and volunteers under his command, concerning the powder taken from the country magazine, cordially approve of the same, and unanimosuly vote them their thanks for their prudent, firm, and spirited conduct on that occasion.[8]

Resolved unanimously, that the easy acquisition of the powder from the country magazine, in the city of Williamsburg, by order of his Excellency the Governour, and the convenient situation of that city with respect to the navy, render it unsafe to continue the publick treasury at that place; and that it is the opinion of this committee that the same ought to be removed, to a place of greater safety.[9]

Resolved, that Mr. Chairman, Charles Dick, James Mercer, Charles Mortimer, and George Thornton, Gentlemen, do write to the Treasurer, requesting him to call a convention of the delegates for this colony as soon as possible.[10]

(A true copy.)

Alexander Dick, clerk.

Virginia Gazette (Purdie), 19 May 1775, supplement

1. The "officer" was Ens. Parke Goodall, the "king's receiver general," Richard Corbin.

2. The ellipsis deletes the text of the receipt, which is under the date heading of 4 May 1775, Hanover Co. Committee, 1st entry. The present item consists of the heading and 6 paragraphs of an 8-paragraph notice.

3. The ellipsis deletes the text of Patrick Henry's letter to Robert Carter Nicholas, under the date heading of 4 May 1775, Hanover Co. Committee, 2d entry.

4. No text is known to exist, but the gist of Nicholas's "answer" may be surmised by referring to the letter of 27 Apr. 1775 from his close political ally Peyton Randolph to Mann Page, Jr., and others.

5. Purdie's *Va. Gazette* of 5 May 1775 (supplement) reported "armed people" from New Kent and King William counties at Doncastle's Ordinary on 4 May. It would ap-

pear that volunteers from Albemarle County and perhaps from Orange County marched part way down the country and met the returning Hanoverians on 4 or 5 May (Philip Mazzei, *Memoirs of the Life and Peregrinations of the Florentine Philip Mazzei, 1730–1816,* trans. and ed., Howard R. Marraro [New York, 1942], pp. 210–11; Dumas Malone, *Jefferson and His Time* [Boston, 1948–], I, 198 n. 5; Irving Brant, *James Madison* [6 vols., Indianapolis, 1941–61], I, 177–78).

6. The delegates elected to the third Virginia Convention for Orange County were Thomas Barbour and probably James Taylor, but only Barbour would attend. His "influence" was not to be sufficient to keep a majority of the convention members on 25 Aug. 1775 from reaching a decision partly at variance with the intent of this instruction (Procs. and n. 7).

7. Because a copy of this letter is "among his papers, and in his own handwriting," William Cabell Rives entertained "no doubt" that the letter was the product of the pen of James Madison, Jr. (*History of the Life and Times of James Madison* [3 vols., Boston, 1859–68], I, 94–95); yet although the contents were in accord at the time with the sentiments of the future 4th president of the United States, there is no proof that he composed the letter. Perhaps accompanied by others, Madison may have presented the letter to Patrick Henry, who received it at Port Royal in Caroline County while on his way to Philadelphia to attend the second Continental Congress (Brant, *James Madison,* I, 177–78; William T. Hutchinson, William M. E. Rachal, et al., eds., *The Papers of James Madison* [Chicago, 1962–], I, 147 and n. 1). Henry's reply is under the date heading of 11 May 1775, Orange Co. Committee.

8. Ten days previously members of the Spotsylvania County committee had in all probability participated in the meeting of the Council of 102 when it met in the "Committee Chamber." They thereby acceded when, "preferring peaceable measures whilst the least hope of reconciliation remains," the council bowed to the advice of Peyton Randolph and abandoned the idea of an immediate march on Williamsburg (29 Apr. 1775, Spotsylvania Council). They may not now have been wholly consistent in applauding Henry's action; but they were confronted with a fait accompli, and it is not unlikely that they made their applause a matter of public record lest their prior stand be misinterpreted—a misinterpretation especially to be avoided following receipt around 3:30 A.M. on 30 Apr. 1775 of more detailed accounts of the fighting in Massachusetts (Spotsylvania Co. Committee to Va. Committee).

The "copy of the proceedings" of Henry's expeditionary force may have been the narrative account contained in the supplement of Purdie's *Va. Gazette* of 5 May 1775.

9. Cf. 17 May 1775, Cumberland Co. Committee, para. 5.

10. Whereas the first Virginia Convention of 1–6 Aug. 1774 had, in the event of Peyton Randolph's death, authorized Robert Carter Nicholas "to convene the several Delegates of this Colony, at such Time and Place as he may judge proper" (*Rev. Va.,* I, 234), the journal of the second, of 20–27 Mar. 1775, remains silent on this head. It seems to have been tacitly understood, however, that in event of Randolph's inability to act (and he was now absent in Philadelphia), his authority would devolve upon Mr. Treasurer, whose name next to that of the speaker-president was undoubtedly the most politically prestigious in the colony. In view of the "present alarming Situation of American Affairs," the committee of Cumberland also, on 17 May, would "recommend" that Nicholas convoke "a Colony Convention." In the end, Dunmore's proclamation for the House of Burgesses to convene on 1 June 1775 would bring Randolph back to Williamsburg, with his issuance of a summons for the third Virginia Convention following 25 days later.

Wednesday, 10 May 1775

Cumberland County Committee

Free Contribution, Gaming, and Protection

At a Meeting of the Committee for Cumberland County at the Court House on Wednesday the 10th. day of May 1775.[1]

Present, George Carrington, Chairman, William Fleming, Littlebury [M]osby, John Mayo, Joseph Carrington junr. William [Smi]th, Robert Smith, Benjamin Wilson, Joseph Calland, Fre[der]ick Hatcher, Edward Carrington, Richard Eggleston, John [Wood]son, Peter Stoner, Mr. ⟨John Hyde⟩ Saunders, Clerk, and Henry Ma[con.]

[Mr. C]hairman having informed the Committee, that he as Treasurer of [the s]ame had received one hundred fifty eight Pounds and [three][2] pence, a free Contribution of the Inhabitants of the County, for the [purp]ose of purchasing Ammunition &c. for their Use;[3] Resolved, [that] Mr. Edward Carrington be fully empowered to lay out the [m]oney so contributed in such Manner as to him in his Discret[ion] shall seem most proper for the Purpose aforesaid at the Countys Risque, and that Mr. Chairman pay him from Time to Time [w]hatever Money he may call for out of the Fund in his Hands, as Treasurer.

John Scruggs appearing before the Committee confessed that he had lately inprudently fallen into a Breach of the Continental Association, by Gaming, made Concessions, and exhibited such Marks of true Penitence, that it is resolved that the said Scruggs be again considered as a worthy Member of the Community.[4]

A Complaint being made to this Committee that Ray Moss and John Woodson junr. have within the Limits of this County made a Breach of the Continental Association by Gaming. Resolved, that John Scruggs summon the said Woodson and Moss, by authority of a Copy of this Resolution, attested by the Secretary, to appear before the Committee at the Court House on Wednesday the 17th. of this Instant to answer the said Complaint; and that the said Scruggs to attend as a Witness.[5]

Resolved, that this Committee in Behalf of themselves and their Constituents, doth offer Protection to the Inhabitants of the lower Parts of this Colony for their Families and Property in Case any Invasion shall be made there and that Mr. Harrison and Mr. Fleming do prepare an Address for the Purpose of inviting them in such Case to remove their Families and Property to us.[6]

Resolved, that the most cordial Thanks of this Committee are justly due to the Inhabitants of this County, for so cheerfully contributing the Money requested of them for the Purpose of procuring Ammunition &c.

Resolved, that this Committee be adjourned to Wednesday the 17th. day of this Instant.[7]

Test   Ed. Carrington Secrey.
Teste, THOMAS MILLER, Cl. Com.

Committee MS journal, the whole, including Car-
rington's signature, in hand of Thomas Miller
(Archives Division, Virginia State Library)

1. The last preceding meeting of the Cumberland County committee had been on 3 May 1775.

2. The word is torn from the document, but must have been legible in 1919 when Henry R. McIlwaine published the proceedings in the *15th Annual Library Report*, pp. 12–13. The sum collected, however, is not a multiple of the "one Shilling and three Pence" which the committee had directed on 21 Apr. 1775 be collected "from the Inhabitants of this County."

3. This fund was collected pursuant to the committee's resolution of 3 May 1775.

4. For the 8th article of the Continental Association, which discountenanced and discouraged "Gaming," see 13 Apr. 1775, n. 3.

5. A week later the journal was to note that Messrs. Moss and Woodson were "inhabitants of the County of Buckingham."

6. For the address prepared by the subcommittee, see 17 May 1775.

7. The further proceedings of the committee will be found under the date heading indicated.

Thursday, 11 May 1775

Caroline County Committee

Alternate Delegate, Imports, Grain, and Linen

AT A MEETING of the Committee May 11th. 1775 [1] Present thirteen members

The Committee recommended It to the freeholders here Present to choose some Person to day to represent this County as a Deligate in the absence of Colo. Edm⟨un⟩d. Pendleton. They therefore made choice of Capt. W⟨illia⟩m. Woodford in the absence of Colo. Pendleton.[2]

Robert Johnston produced before this Committee a memorandum of certain goods he had imported from Philadelphia agreable to the Association & he has leave from this Committee to dispose of them on the same terms that other merchants in this County have sold such for a year Preceding the Association [3]

William Woodford John Tennant James Taylor & Thomas Lomax Gent⟨lemen⟩. or any two of them are appointed to enquire into the quantity of grain Received for relief of the Bostonians & that they dispose of It as they shall think proper [4]

Anthony Thornton Wm. Woodford George Taylor James Taylor & John Tennant or any two of them are appointed by this Committee to consult with Gentlemen of other Committees about a Scheme for manufacturing Linnen &c. [5]

> Committee MS minutes in hand of Samuel Haws, Jr., clerk (Henry E. Huntington Library and Art Gallery of San Marino, Calif.)

Hanover County Committee

A True Patriot to John Pinkney: An Open Letter

MR. PINKEY:

As the gentlemen of Hanover, from misinformation, and their zeal in support ⟨of⟩ the great American cause, may have been precipitated into acts as pernicious in their consequences as they were intended to be salutary, it is ardently wished they would revise their proceedings, or lay them before a provincial or general congress, and if they are found derogatory to the line of conduct which ought religiously to have been adhered to, that there may be [6] made such concessions and reparation, for damages, as may be perfectly consistent with sound policy and the strictest justice. [7]

This, I think, the public have a right to expect, who, I suppose, will be held responsible for every inadvertency given into by individuals, should they not disapprove of, and endeavour at a redress of such grievances as they may occasion. There never was a time, sir, that required more prudence and circumspection than the present. All would do well to consider this, and govern themselves accordingly. Be assured that I am

A True Patriot. [8]

Virginia Gazette (Pinkney), 11 May 1775

New Kent County Committee

Unfeigned Loyalty and Opposition
to All Tyrannical Attempts

AT a meeting of the committee for NEW KENT county, at the courthouse, the 11th day of May, 1775.

The committee taking into consideration Lord Dunmore's proclamation dated the 3d day of this month, said to be issued with the advice of his Majesty's Council, wherein the inhabitants of this colony are indiscriminately charged, in general terms, with disaffection to his Majesty's government, and a design to effect a change in the form of it,[9] think it necessary, for themselves and their constituents, to declare their sentiments, and accordingly

Resolve unanimously, that unfeigned loyalty to his Majesty's person and government, as by law established, and a due obedience to the laws of our country,[10] are the ruling principles of the inhabitants of this county; and that the suggestion on which the said proclamation appears to be founded, so far as it respects the inhabitants of this county, is an injurious reflection upon them, and has no foundation in truth. At the same time, we are determined, for ourselves and posterity, to support and maintain the rights and privileges of British subjects, which we are entitled to, against all tyrannical attempts whatever.

Resolved, that the resolutions of this committee entered into on the 3d of this month, and the first resolution entered into this day, be sent to the printers, to be published.

By order of the committee.

(A Copy.)   William Smith, clerk.

> *Virginia Gazette* (Purdie), 19 May 1775, supplement

Orange County Committee

Patrick Henry to James Madison, Sr.

Sir.   Port Royal may 11th. 1775

I think myself & the Volunteers of Hanover peculiarly happy to find, that the Reprizal we have made for the purpose of compensating the Colony for the Loss of the Powder from the Magazine, has met with the Approbation of your Committee.[11]

Give me leave to assure you Sir, that nothing called us forth upon that Occasion, but Zeal for the public Good.

I can discover nothing improper for the public Eye in the several Votes & Resolutions sent me. The Gentm. who are now so kind as to escort me, wish it (together with similar Votes of three other Cotys recd. today), to be printed.[12]

Be pleased to present my best Compliments to the Committee & believe me to be Sir yr. mo. obedt. sert.

P. HENRY JR.

> Autograph letter, signed (Lloyd W. Smith Collection of the Morristown National Historical Park, Morristown, N.J.)

1. The last recorded preceding meeting of the Caroline County committee was that of 29 Apr.; but there must have been a subsequent meeting at which was composed the address of "Thanks" reported to have been written to Patrick Henry on 9 May 1775.

2. Edmund Pendleton was one of the Virginia deputies to the second Continental Congress and would necessarily be absent should there be an early summons for a third Virginia Convention. Although the fact would not be public knowledge until the issuance of Purdie's *Va. Gazette* of 19 May 1775, the committee of Spotsylvania County had already resolved on 9 May 1775 to request Robert Carter Nicholas to convoke a convention.

WILLIAM WOODFORD, JR., was born on his English-immigrant father's plantation, Windsor, on the Rappahannock River below Fredericksburg. Maj. William Woodford, Sr., married Anne Cocke, the daughter of the secretary of the colony, and served as the 1st sheriff of Caroline County. The younger William also married well, to Mary Thornton, a daughter of Col. John Thornton, a kinsman of the Washingtons. Woodford served as a justice of the peace and was an officer in the French and Indian War. The House of Burgesses voted him a year's pay in 1762 after he brought Cherokee Indian chiefs to Williamsburg in order to conclude a peace. On 10 Nov. 1774 he was elected to the Caroline County committee and thereafter inspected merchants's books and bought gunpowder for the volunteer company. His name would come prominently before the third convention on 3, 5, and 17 Aug. 1775, when the members were casting about for leaders to command the troops being raised. Woodford was 40 years old (Marshall Wingfield, *A History of Caroline County, Virginia* [Richmond, 1924], pp. 185–86; T[homas] E[lliott] Campbell, *Colonial Caroline: A History of Caroline County, Virginia* [Richmond, 1954], pp. 168–69; *Statutes at Large*, VII, 493; *Rev. Va.*, II, 168, 200–201, 210, 284, 317; pp. 393, 400–401, 457–58 below).

3. That is, according to the terms of the 9th article of the Continental Association (8 Apr. 1775, Norfolk Borough Committee).

4. The committee was continuing to discharge this function pursuant to a resolution of the second Virginia Convention on 24 Mar. (19 Apr. 1775, n. 2). That notwithstanding, it must have been clear by this date that the situation to the north had changed. More appropriately, the King William County committee had already on 1 and 5 May 1775 collected donations for "our brethren" in Massachusetts as a whole.

5. For the recommendation of the second Virginia Convention respecting "manufacturing Linnen &c.," see 7 Apr. 1775, n. 5.

6. In the newspaper the verbal is misprinted "me."

7. The third Virginia Convention would indeed consider Patrick Henry's expedition

(4 May 1775, Hanover Co. Committee; 25 Aug. 1775, Third Va. Convention, Procs. and n. 7).

8. That the Hanover County committee had on 9 May endorsed Henry's march was probably unknown to "A True Patriot," for the fact of endorsement was first revealed in the issue of Pinkney's newspaper that carried the "True Patriot's" admonition. On 1 June 1775 the patriotic author was to have the knuckles of his writing hand smartly rapped by "A Ranger."

9. For "Lord Dunmore's proclamation," see 3 May 1775, Royal Chief Magistracy.

10. In the newspaper the word is misprinted "county."

11. The reference is to the letter addressed to Patrick Henry and "the Gentlemen independents of Hanover" by the committee of Orange County on 9 May 1775. James Madison, Sr., was chairman of the committee.

12. The "Gentm." with Henry were "a number of respectable gentlemen Volunteers" from Hanover, King William, and Caroline counties, who escorted him to the Maryland border as he made his way north to attend the sessions of the second Continental Congress then meeting in Philadelphia (*Va. Gazette* [Purdie], 19 May 1775, supplement). The identity of the "three other" counties is unknown, but they probably were Caroline, Culpeper, and Spotsylvania. The first 2 are mentioned, and the letter of the Spotsylvania County committee is printed, along with that of the Orange County committee, in the supplement to Purdie's *Va. Gazette* of 19 May 1775.

Friday, 12 May 1775

Third Virginia Convention

Call for Election of Delegates Yet Unchosen and of Alternates for Those Also Now Serving in Congress

THE freeholders of those counties and corporations, who may not yet have chosen deputies to represent them in a General Convention, are desired to do it without loss of time; as it is judged necessary, by some respectable Gentlemen, that all the deputies should be prepared to meet on the shortest notice. It is the wish and desire of the worthy Delegates from this colony, who are now attending the General Congress, that others may be chosen to supply their place, during their necessary absence.[1]

Virginia Gazette (Purdie), 12 May 1775, supplement

Richmond County Committee

At the Hazard of Lives and Fortunes

At a committee elected for the county of RICHMOND, *meeting by adjourn-ment from the 10th of this instant, at the courthouse of this county, on the 12th of May, 1775.*

PRESENT.

LANDON CARTER, *Esq; chairman, and a very full bench of the members.*

THE committee appointed on the 10th instant, having brought in their report, according to the order of that day,[2] the same was received and read, and is as follows:

Your committee, taking into consideration, according to order, the late address of his Excellency the Governour to the Council, on the 2d of this instant, and the proclamation issued, in consequence of their advice on the 3d instant,[3] think themselves indispensably bound to their constituents to vindi-cate them from the groundless aspersions, and very unjust accusations, with which, as a part of this community, they are therein charged, and which are only calculated to induce a belief that the people of this country are medi-tating a plan to change the present form of government. They have therefore resolved,

1. That the late commotions in some parts of this country, alluded to in the address and proclamation, arose from a full conviction of a cruel and determined plan of administration to enslave these colonies, which has been manifested in various instances, and of which the late proceedings of his Excellency, in removing the powder from the magazine, with the several circumstances attending the same, appear to be a part.

2. That our repeated and dutiful applications for redress of grievances, our patient endurance under a long course of irritating and oppressive meas-ures, and our most solemn declarations, "That our utmost wish was a restitu-tion of the rights which we enjoyed until the year 1763," are a convincing proof of our attachment to the constitution, our loyalty to our sovereign, and our love of order.

3. That the whole of his Excellency's conduct, respecting the unhappy disputes between the colonies and the British ministry, especially the ground-less and injurious charges alledged against the people of this colony, in his address to the Council, and in his proclamation of the 3d of this instant May, are unjustifiable and inimical, and therefore he has justly forfeited the con-fidence of the people of this colony.

4. That the members of his Majesty's Council who advised the above men-tioned proclamation, acted inconsistently with that *wisdom, justice,* and *generosity,* which ought to characterise them as *legislators, judges,* and *natives* of the most distinguished rank in the colony; and we do declare, that we find ourselves deeply affected that those, who should be *mediators* between the

executive power and the people, should concur in fixing a stigma on their fellow subjects, so *unjust* and so *undeserved*.

5. That in order to remove these *atrocious* aspersions, and to convince the world of our *firm* attachment to the constitution, as it existed before the year 1763, we hereby solemnly pledge ourselves to support it, at the hazard of our *lives* and *fortunes*.

Every resolve contained in the foregoing report being distinctly read, and separately considered, was passed *nemine contradicente*.

Ordered, that these proceedings of this day, as soon as may be convenient, be transmitted to the press, for the satisfaction of the publick.

William Smith, clerk, *pro tempore*.

Virginia Gazette (Purdie), 19 May 1775, supplement

Williamsburg

Captain James Miller to Alexander Purdie: An Open Letter [4]

Mr Purdie,   Williamsburg, May 12, 1775
IT is an unpardonable crime in any man wantonly to rob his neighbour of his fortune and reputation, by a partial representation of facts. Your correspondent should have informed the publick that Mr. ⟨Samuel⟩ Gist is principal owner of the ship Mary, and has sole management of her himself; that he built her to accomodate his friends in Virginia with freight, in a good stout vessel; and that the small part Mr. ⟨John⟩ Wilkinson has in her was intended to promote that end, by his superintending the building of her in Yorkshire, where he resides. I hope the impartial publick will consider that Mr. Wilkinson's political principles did not appear at the time Mr. Gist became connected with him, that, in short, they do not now appear, as it is notorious that when ships are wanted for government service the King does not ask merchants whether they are willing or not to let them. If Mr. Wilkinson has voluntarily transgressed, I can pledge myself for Mr. Gist that he will resent it in such manner as is most agreeable to the Americans, and will conduce the most to promote the glorious cause in which they are embarked; His connexions with, and obligations he is under to Virginia are well known, and he is very ready to acknowledge them. Several Gentlemen, who are just arrived from England, can testify that he proved himself a zealous friend to American liberty on a late important occasion. The querist is respectfully acquainted, that it is possible to serve a friend without injuring the innocent.[5]

I am, Mr. Purdie, your's, the publick's, and especially Mr. Gist's friends, obedient humble servant, and, whenever it is requisite they shall be waited upon in person by

James Miller.

Virginia Gazette (Purdie), 12 May 1775, supplement

1. Almost beyond doubt this notice was published at the request of Robert Carter Nicholas. Because the governor on this very day issued a proclamation summoning the General Assembly to convene on 1 June 1775, no date was set for the convocation of the third Virginia Convention. The impending meeting of the House of Burgesses would necessitate the return to Williamsburg of Peyton Randolph. His would be the decision as to when a convention should meet. At the same time, it was important that the Virginia constituencies not neglect to elect delegates, for the need of a more nearly permanent and potent colonial authority would follow from a refusal by the House of Burgesses to accept Lord North's proffered Olive Branch. The terms of his offer were generally known, and already one assembly, that of Pennsylvania on 4 May, had rejected them (*Va. Gazette* [Purdie], 28 Apr., 26 May 1775; ibid. [Dixon and Hunter], 29 Apr. 1775).

During the initial weeks of session of the third convention an alternate would serve in the place of each of Virginia's "worthy Delegates" to the second Continental Congress. By the present time William Woodford had been elected the alternate for Edmund Pendleton (11 May 1775, Caroline Co. Committee).

2. The Richmond County committee published no account of its meeting "on the 10th instant," and the composition of the subcommittee submitting the report is unknown. One member only can be identified with certainty by noting that the subcommittee's draft of these resolutions is in the hand of Col. Landon Carter (Sabine Hall Papers, Manuscripts Department, University of Virginia Library).

3. See 2 May 1775, Royal Chief Magistracy; 3 May, same.

4. The item is a reply to the anonymous attack of 5 May 1775 (Williamsburg).

5. Samuel Gist was probably the British merchant of that name who for 26 years had lived in Virginia and accumulated "a Considerable Fortune" before returning to London to engage in trade. In the spring of 1775 he was having financial difficulties, and his plantations in Hanover and Goochland counties were in severe straits (P.R.O., Audit Office [hereafter A.O.], 13/30, fol. G II, unpaged). It seems probable that he had "proved himself a zealous friend to American liberty on a late important occasion" by subscribing to one, the other, or both of 2 petitions presented to the House of Commons in Jan. 1775 by leading London merchants. On 23 Jan. they prayed that the House would "enter into a full and immediate examination of that system of commercial policy" that had seen a once-brisk North Atlantic trade reduced to a state of "great stagnation" and then brought to a "total stop." The 2d petition, presented on 26 Jan. 1775, requested a hearing on the 1st (Hansard, *Parliamentary History*, XVIII, cols. 168–71, 184–85).

Saturday, 13 May 1775

Mecklenburg County Committee

Approval, Thanks, and Alarm

Saturday, the 13th of May 1775. The committee met according to adjournment,[1] and came to the following resolves.

The resolves of the convention held at the town of Richmond the 20th of March, 1775, were read, and unanimously approved of.

Resolved, that the thanks of this committee be presented to Robert Burton and Bennett Goode, esquires, our worthy delegates, for their faithful discharge of the important trust reposed in them.[2]

Resolved unanimously, that the removal of the gunpowder of the magazine, by express order of lord Dunmore, is truly alarming, and that by his answer for such conduct to the mayor, recorder, alderman, and common council, of the city of Williamsburg, on that important occasion, has highly forfeited all title to the confidence of the good people of Virginia.[3]

Ordered, that the clerk send copies of these resolves to each of the printers, in order to be published.

Isaac Holmes, clerk.

Virginia Gazette (Pinkney), 1 June 1775

1. According "to adjournment" on 8 May 1775. The present item consists of 5 paragraphs of a 9-paragraph notice.

2. If not already reelected, the "worthy delegates" would at some undisclosed date be so to the third Virginia Convention.

3. For the affair of the gunpowder, see pp. 4–6 above; for Dunmore's "answer" for his "conduct," 21 Apr. 1775, The Capital, 2d entry.

Monday, 15 May 1775

Royal Magistracy

The Governor's Council to the People of Virginia[1]

To all the good People *of* Virginia.

We his Majesty's faithful subjects, the council of this colony, deeply impressed with the most sincere regard for the prosperity of our country, and the welfare of all its inhabitants, and being desirous, by our example, and by every means in our power, to preserve the peace and good order of the community, can no longer forbear to express our abhorrence and detestation of that licentious and ungovernable spirit that is gone forth, and misleads, the once happy people of this country.

The council recommend it to all orders of men, to consider seriously what will be the probable consequences of such a conduct as hath been lately pursued, and whether a redress of the grievances complained of will not be more likely to be obtained by gentle, mild, and constitutional methods, than by such intemperate behaviour, which must tend to exasperate and inflame rather than to reconcile, the differences that now unhappily subsist.

The council wish, upon this occasion, that all odious distinctions may be laid aside, and that they may be considered not as a separate body of men, and having a distinct interest from the rest of their countrymen and fellow subjects, but in the light in which they have always regarded themselves, as the watchful guardians of the rights of the people, as well as of the prerogative of the crown. They are, most of them, natives of this country, they have families, they have property, and they trust they have integrity too; which are the best securities men can give to any society for the faithful discharge of their duty.

Let, then, their exhortations have proper weight and influence among the people; and they plight their faith that they will join heartily with them in the use of such means as shall be judged most salutary and conducive for enforcing obedience to the laws, and supporting the constitution of their country, under which it has flourished from its infancy, and for obtaining a happy and speedy conclusion to all our troubles.

As his excellency the governor hath issued his proclamation for the speedy meeting of the general assembly, the council are happy in finding an opportunity will be given the people of representing their grievances in the manner prescribed by the constitution.[2]

Signed by order of the members of the council.

John Blair, c. c.

Virginia Gazette (Pinkney), 18 May 1775

Third Virginia Convention

Brutus to His Undesignated Constituents: An Address

Editorial note. The following address by the pseudonymous "Brutus" might have been delivered by any one of dozens of second-magnitude men in Virginia public life. The speaker's grasp of British-colonial constitutional fact and theory, of the nature of royal statutes against which the colonists were protesting, and of

the basics of the quarrel between the mother country and her American offspring
is manifest, but it is not so extraordinary as to eliminate many burgesses or convention delegates (or, indeed, many who were neither) from consideration as
putative author. The speaker's defense of Patrick Henry's procuring a presumed
monetary equivalent for the allegedly purloined gunpowder does eliminate the
more conservative. In that sense the speaker in current phraseology occupied a
position to the left of center. On the other hand, his appeal to his auditors to
eschew "Rashness and violence" and to pursue a course of "Prudence and moderation" stamps him as having been no radical.

As much as it does anything else, the address provides a study in a phase of
colonial politico-sociology. If it evidences the patronizing wise in which a "cava-
lier" might speak to those of "the middling and lower classes," it is well to note
that his addressees were his patrons in turn; and at this time so few were the white
adult males too poor to qualify as freeholders that the percentage of voters in Virginia exceeded that of those even in "egalitarian" Massachusetts (Charles S.
Sydnor, *Gentlemen Freeholders: Political Practices in Washington's Virginia*
[Chapel Hill, N.C., 1952], p. 38).

Mr. Purdie,

THE following pages contain an address delivered to the inhabitants of a certain county in this colony, assembled for the purpose of choosing deputies to
represent them in colony convention. If it will not take up too much of your
time, or be attended with expense to you, the publication of it will give
satisfaction to many of your friends; as it is adapted to the understandings,
and intended for the information of, the middling and lower classes of people,
and may tend to reconcile the different opinions (if there be any now prevailing in this colony) respecting the necessity or propriety of resisting the
enemies of American liberty and the British constitution.

I am, Sir, your, &c.

Brutus.

Friends and Countrymen,
It is impossible that any people, impressed with the least sense of constitutional liberty, should ever patiently submit to the enormous grievances under
which we have already in some respects fallen, and with which we are likely
to be much more oppressed; and accordingly we find our brethren and fellow
subjects, in all the colonies, are pursuing such measures as are thought to be
most likely to recover and secure our lost rights and privileges. Shall the
people of this colony, heretofore active, particularly in the time of the detestable stamp act, to oppose all attempts to deprive them of their personal
security and private property, be now inactive, and silent? Forbid it liberty!
Humanity forbid it!

The several acts of parliament, made for ten years last past, relating to the
British colonies in North America, and their operation upon the property,
liberty, and lives, of the people in this country, and America in general, are
too well known, to many of you, to require any enumeration or explanation;
but many of you also have not the knowledge of these things, and are therefore ignorant of the danger in which you stand. To inform you of your un-

happy situation, and to open your minds to a just sense of the dangers which threaten you, is, principally, the design of this address.

From the first settlement of the colonies, till about the year 1763, we had but little reason to complain of the injustice of our fellow subjects in Great Britain. There were two or three instances, indeed, in which the colonies were oppressed, under the notion of right to regulate our trade, and make us serviceable in commerce to Great Britain. Amongst these was an act of parliament declaring that we should not erect any SLITTING MILLS for the purpose of making nails in these colonies, and we were forbidden to manufacture hats to be sold amongst ourselves under severe penalties.[3] At that time, my friends, we only complained of the hardship and injustice of such an act; and, wanting the protection of Britain, looking upon our fellow subjects there as friends and allies, we did not erect any more *slitting mills* for making nails, and hats were manufactured only by a few individuals, to a very small extent, and sold within the respective colonies. Thus did they attempt to restrain our manufacturers in the only instance wherein they thought us, at that time, likely to succeed, to the injury of the British manufacturer; intending thereby to compel us, through necessity, to apply to them for even the necessaries of life, and to pay them, by our labour, the prices they might think proper to lay on them.

Another instance of oppression was that of establishing a POST-OFFICE in these colonies, and thereby seizing, in effect, the private property of individuals here who had engaged in that business. By that act, all letters coming from Great Britain, or otherwise circulating through these colonies, are liable to be seized by the post-master appointed to that office, and subjected to a tax to be paid before the delivery of them; and part of the money arising from this tax is applied towards the support of the office, and the balance sent to Britain, to be disposed of by government there.

Although the effects of that act are not universally felt amongst you, yet it is an instance of oppression, which *all* are, more or less, subject to, who are concerned in trade, or have any intercourse with men at a distance from them; and I mention this, to show you that if you are not oppressed by this law, it is because your circumstances in life are such that you have but little to do with *letters*, and the officers are not generally so strict in the performance of their duty as the law requires them to be. But surely, my friends, you cannot be but sensible, that if, as in this instance, the *British parliament* have a right to make a law to seize your effects, and keep them from you, until you pay a tax to redeem them, you must be in a wretched condition, whenever parliament shall think it proper to extend this authority to things which may more essentially and more immediately affect all ranks and degrees of people in these colonies. That act has hitherto been suffered to be executed, because the people who are most affected by it are traders in some respects, and often receive an advantage in having speedy and regular intelligence from their various correspondents in different parts of the world; and they were unwilling to differ with their fellow subjects in *Britain*, concerning a thing which seemed to be intended for the benefit of both. The great inconvenience, therefore, of that act, is principally this, that it has taken out of the hands of the people in these colonies a business they were engaged in, and which might be carried on with the same advantages to commerce, whilst the money arising from that tax would be the property of people here, and not be applied to the purposes of government in *Britain;* and farther, that it is declaratory, in its consequences, of a right to take our property from us, whenever the people of Britain shall be inclined to do so.[4]

And let us, my fellow-subjects, consider the consequences which followed our submission to those acts, even in the manner above-mentioned. Not satisfied with the advantages they received from their trade with the American colonies, a trade so circumstanced that it was morally impossible for us to procure more than the mere necessaries of life by the produce of our labour exported to Britain, they no sooner found us in a condition to export a large proportion of grain, and other commodities, not requisite for the British markets, to foreign countries (which, if permitted, might be of advantage to Britain, by enabling us to pay for, and consequently to consume, more of their manufactures) than they indulged us with the liberty of carrying our grain, and some other articles, to particular markets, but with this restriction, that we should not import such goods as were to be had from Britain, and that we should carry whatever articles they did permit us to receive into Britain first, and pay a duty there. However, as this regulation amounted almost to a prohibition of such articles, and they were likely not to [5] receive such advantages as they at first expected, we were at length allowed to bring them immediately into these colonies, on paying to the officers of the customs here a very high duty, to be disposed of by government in Britain. Hence proceed the duties we pay at this day on wines, coffee, molasses,[6] &c. &c. all which duties are not applied to the support of government in these colonies, but increase the revenue of Great Britain, and enable them to maintain standing armies in America, to secure the execution of their laws, under the denomination of guards and garrisons to protect us and our property.[7]

Another instance of oppression is the extending the jurisdiction of the COURTS OF ADMIRALTY, with pains and penalties heretofore unknown. In this court, we are deprived of our trial by jury, and must submit to the decision of a dependent party-judge, whose emoluments of office arise from his condemnations; and although we may be released from the prosecution, we must still suffer the injury and oppression brought upon us by the iniquitous prosecutor, who is exempted from the damages we sustain by means of an unjust prosecution.[8]

The suspending the legislative power of New York, until their House of Burgesses rescinded or blotted out a vote they had passed, declaring their right to the same freedom which the people of Great Britain enjoy, and complied with an arbitrary requisition to provide for troops, is another capital instance of the tyrannical disposition of the British parliament towards America.[9] All these things, and many more, have we known; to convince us that the British parliament have not viewed us with the eye of brotherly love and affection, but with a determination to make us subservient to our fellow subjects in *Britain*, in all cases whatever, and our condition as wretched as that of slaves.

The detestable STAMP ACT furnished us with another memorable proof of the injustice and tyranny they had prepared for us; and I thank the God of heaven and earth, who permits the wicked sometimes to provide torments for themselves, that, of his gracious mercy to us, he suffered that act to be passed, which opened our eyes, and made us behold the *slavery* intended for three millions of people. Let us return thanks to HIM, my countrymen, for his great mercy; and let us look up to HIM for protection, in the day of our distress.

The consequences that would have attended a submission to that act you are better acquainted with than those which have arisen from all the other acts I have mentioned. The reason is plain: You were told by parliament, that you must pay a *tax* on every instrument of writing used in these colonies; that you must pay a *tax* on *painters colours*, oil, glass, and paper, which you were obliged to import from *Great Britain*. This was a doctrine none of us could misunderstand; by this *all* were affected, and so sensibly, too, that it was like drawing the vital blood from our veins. By that act, our *money* was demanded; and we were reduced to the necessity of paying, or resisting. We resisted: the happy effects of our opposition you cannot have forgotten, and our method of resistance must still be fresh in your memories. We shut up our courts, we associated, we refused to buy their goods: They took off the tax.[10] Was the parliament actuated in this respect by principles of justice and regard to us? No, my countrymen; they were not. They saw the impropriety of their conduct, not in having taxed us, but in the mode of taxing us. They perceived their inability, at that time, to enforce submission to a law against which they had not expected any opposition. They had attacked all ranks and degrees of men in these colonies, and had met with a sudden, unexpected, and violent opposition. The clamours of their merchants, tradesmen, and manufacturers, contributed also to the repeal of those duties, as they were immediately affected by the opposition. But let us examine this repeal a little farther: Did they take off all the duties upon British merchandise imported into these colonies? Did they relinquish the right of taxing us? No; we find that they reserved a duty on the article of *tea*, trifling indeed as to the sum, but fatal in its consequences to our liberty and property. We find at this time also they passed another act, declaring their *right* to tax us, to regulate our trade, to prevent our manufacturing, or, in their own words, "to bind us in all cases whatsoever."[11] What! shall we then receive our laws from people 3000 miles distance from us, ignorant of our situation and circumstances in life, and not bound by the same laws? Shall we, like poor abject slaves, tamely give up our liberty, which our forefathers handed down to us, and suffer our property to be taken from us, at the will and direction of a *British* parliament? Shall we subject ourselves and our posterity, to be driven, by our masters, to such employments as they shall allot for us? To have our *looms*, our *spinning-wheels* destroyed, whenever they shall think we manufacture too much cloth? I wait your answer. But methinks I see the blood of *true Britons* swelling in your veins, and hear you cry, with one voice, *We will be free.*

Let us consider then, my countrymen, what it is we are to do. You are told, that the present dispute between Great Britain and the colonies is concerning the duty on *tea*. It is so. Perhaps some of you may now tell me it is a dispute with which you have nothing to do, as you do not make use of that commodity, and the duty cannot affect you. But you will go farther perhaps, and tell me, that the *high-minded gentlemen* are the occasion of the present confusion, and are bringing you into difficulties to support their extravagance and ambition. Is it possible you can be so blind to your real interests as not to perceive the oppression daily coming upon you from Britain? Can you suppose the *gentlemen* of all *America* would be so mad as to risk their lives and fortunes merely to save a trifling duty of three pence per pound on tea? Are not the *gentlemen* made of the same materials as the lowest and poorest amongst you? And do you suppose they cannot—they would not—refrain[12] the use of that article if that would procure the safety of these colonies? Have you found, in the course of your observations, that the *gentlemen* (as they are styled) are so very frugal and saving of their money as to bring themselves into the smallest difficulties for so small an advantage? No, my countrymen, you have not. Deceive not yourselves then, nor let others deceive you; listen to no doctrines which may tend to divide us; but let us go hand in hand, as brothers, as fellow sufferers in the same cause, firmly united to defend our rights and liberty, and to preserve freedom to our posterity. Fortunes we may never leave them, but we shall be despicable indeed if we tamely suffer them to become *slaves*.[13]

But let us reflect again on the nature of this dispute. The British parliament, when they repealed the *stamp act*, did not give up the right of taxing us; they reserved the duty on tea, and declared, by an act, that they had a right to bind us "in all cases whatsoever." The plain meaning of this declaration is, that we must either submit to such impositions as they may hereafter think proper to burthen us with, or they will not suffer us to make use of our property. In this situation have we been unmindful of the necessary means of defence, whilst they have been preparing to execute their laws upon us.

Having reserved the duty on *tea*, the consumption of that article has been lessened near two thirds, to the great injury of the East India company of merchants in Great Britain. As parliament had been the cause of this injury, the minister was determined not only to redress them, but at the same time to carry the favourite plan of taxing America into execution. An advantage is then offered to the East India company, which by law they had not been entitled to, of sending their tea immediately to America. This measure being adopted by them, the minister vainly hoped to find us submitting openly to this tax; as, notwithstanding the duty, we should receive the tea on cheaper terms.[14] If this measure should not succeed, he was then prepared to carry the declaration of parliament into force, and procure such other oppressive laws to be made as might lay us in the deepest distress, and compel us to submit.

In this manner, my countrymen, were the distresses of the people of Boston brought upon them. The East India company sent ships loaded with *tea* to different parts of America; they sent *tea* to Boston. In all other parts, they suffered it to be landed and stored, or it was agreed to carry it back to Britain. At Boston, they refused to carry it back, and the people would not suffer it to be landed; well knowing that, if it was, the duty would be paid by the company's agents, and the tea sold, if not in New England, to the other colonies in America. They remonstrated against the landing of the tea, they waited many days patiently for a satisfactory determination; the officers of the customs refused to suffer the ship to return; the men of war determined it should not pass; and by these circumstances were they reduced to the necessity of throwing the tea into the water, as they attempted to land it.

Although the law of nature and self-defence, in all such cases, does justify their conduct, yet the dispute is not now about the price of the tea, but the duty on that tea. It is not the sum of 10,000 *l.* which was the value of the tea, that the people of *Boston,* and all *North America,* are contending with Great Britain for; but it is our right to freedom, to dispose of our property when we have acquired it. If paying for the tea was the condition on which our rights should be restored, and on which our property might remain secure, all *America* would not engage in this dispute. But this is not the case: Parliament will not be satisfied with that, but have determined that we shall submit to their laws and to their taxes. And let us now inquire what methods they have taken to oblige us to submit.

Punishments should always be proportioned to crimes; and, where the laws direct the punishment, no power can go beyond it. This is the security we boast under our free constitution of government, and it is our invaluable privilege to make these laws. The power that deprives us of this privilege makes us *slaves.* What then is the conduct of parliament towards us? They will not be satisfied with pay for the tea; but farther insist, that we shall submit to whatever laws they make. To compel us to do this, they dissolve our assemblies, suspend our legislatures, block up the town of Boston, deprive upwards of 30,000 inhabitants of the means of subsistence, seize their wharfs, &c. to the amount of two hundred thousand pounds; which, by the act, are never to be restored to them, although they should submit to all that is required by that law.[15] They have altered the *charter* of Massachusetts Bay, which is an agreement between the people of that province and the king, in writing, under his seal;[16] and passed an act empowering the governour to seize the persons of such as do not conform to all things required by their laws, and to send them where he shall think proper (*even to Britain*) to be tried for their supposed offences, where, destitute of friends and money, they will fall unhappy victims to the avarice of corrupted judges, and the rapaciousness of merciless tyrants.[17] Many more things, of like tendency, are they now preparing for all North America. To you then, my countrymen, to *all* of us, does it belong to take such measures as shall prevent their wicked designs, and secure our lives, our liberty, and property. On the virtue and courage of the people of these colonies does it depend whether we shall be happy or miserable in this world, and enjoy in peace and quietness, the fruits of our labour. Your representatives in General Congress have planned the measures of resistance; on your courage and virtue do they rely for support in the execution of them. Let us then, my countrymen, go hand in hand; let us have one voice; let us convince mankind, that we are, as *one man,* actuated by *one soul;* and that, if we are not, we still deserve to be, FREE.

The mode of opposition recommended to us is an union and association of the colonies to break off all commercial intercourse with Great Britain, unless our grievances shall be redressed.[18] And why is this plan recommended to us? Surely because it is, of all others, the most safe, speedy, and effectual, we can embrace, to restore that harmony to Britain and the colonies we profess to desire.

Rashness and violence can never avail us in the execution of this plan, and therefore we should avoid every conduct tending to so destructive an end; for how can this association be observed unless we establish arts and manufactures? How is it possible these should succeed without peace, order, and the security of our property? And how can these be preserved unless we discourage every kind of violence, by promoting a due respect for the laws of our country, as far as our unhappy circumstances will admit of it? [19]

The principles of the ever-glorious *revolution* will always justify a suspension of the laws under like circumstances, but we should never enforce those principles unless compelled thereto by *extreme necessity.*[20] Prudence and moderation will give great weight to our measures, whilst a contrary conduct will only serve to disunite us, and consequently to involve us in confusion. This is a doctrine which every friend to liberty and his country will inculcate, and on this will the success of our present undertakings chiefly depend. But whilst I recommend to you a temperate conduct, I would not have you to neglect that provision for your safety which the urgency of the case requires. On the contrary, I would advise you to look forward to every contingency, and be prepared for "*mournful* events."

Virginia Gazette (Purdie), 14 July 1775

Isle of Wight County Committee

Augmentation, Gunpowder, and Salt

At a Committee held for Isle of Wight County at the Court House of the said County on Monday the fifteenth day of May in the year of our Lord Christ one thousand seven hundred and seventy five [21] Present John Scarsbrook Wills Chairman, Josiah Parker, Brewer Godwin, Thomas Peirce, John Day, Richard Hardy, John Mallory, Arthur Smith, Goodrich Willson ⟨Wilson⟩, Tristram Norsworthy Junr., and Nathaniel Burwell⟨,⟩ Gent⟨lemen⟩.

The new Comm. men Chosen &c.	Pursuant to Order of Committee for electing an additional number of ten new members, Rich⟨ar⟩d. Hardy⟨,⟩ Gent. having been appointed to manage the election thereof this day reported that John Driver, Joseph Cutchin Junr., Joshua Council, Henry Pitt, Thomas Fearn, Jethro Gale, Mills Wilkinson, William Jordan, Edmund Godwin and Thomas Smith Gentlemen were chosen by the freeholders of this County for that purpose, Whereupon John Driver, Joseph Cutchin Junr. Henry Pitt, Jethro Gale and Edmund Godwin Gent. appeared and took their seats accordingly.
Thos. Peirce & a2: to wait on Thos. Nelson Esqr to buy Powder – – – –	Resolved that Thomas Peirce, Nathaniel Burwell and Arthur Smith, Gent. or any two or more of them do wait on Thomas Nelson junr. Esqr and enquire of him whether he can supply this County with one thousand two hundred pounds of Gun Powder (and if so) treat with him for the same and make report thereof to the next Committee to be held for this County.[22]
Assistance Offered to the Town of York in case of an Attack – – – – –	And further to inform him that should he have a reason to apprehend an attack to be made on the Town of York from any enemy to the libertys of North America that we will on the shortest notice assist to the utmost of our power and abilities in quelling such an attack.[23]
Notice to be given the members of Committee – –	Resolved that notice be given to the several members of the Committee to attend at the Court-House of this County in the Town of Smithfield on Monday next.[24]
John Sym's Certif. to Norfolk Borough – – – – – –	Upon a motion made in behalf of Mr. John Sym It is hereby Certified to the Committee of Norfolk Borough, that the said Sym lately kept a Store in the Town of Smithfield in this County and that he has removed his Merchandise from the Store, which goods this Committee believes were imported agreeable to the resolutions of the general Congress, but we cannot take upon us to say that the said Sym hath no other goods than those he had at the Town of Smithfield.[25]
Subscribers to attd. to pay in their Money for makg. Salt	Resolved that the Clerk of this Committee do advertise that all persons who have subscribed for the encouragement for making Salt in this Colony do attend on monday next in the Town of Smithfield at the Court-House in Order to pay in their subscription money.[26]
John Scb Wills &c. to wait on	Upon an Information made to the Committee that Messrs. Andrew and Richard Mackie have in their pos-

A & R Mackie for
Powder &c.

session one half barrel of Gun Powder, It is therefore
Resolved that John Scb Wills, Thomas Peirce, and Arthur Smith Gent. do wait on the said Mackie's and request them to deliver the said Powder for the use of the
said County, and it is also requested that the above said
Gent. pay for the same which we promise to repay, and
if the said Mackie's acknowledge they have the said
Powder in possession and should refuse to deliver the
same on a tender of Ample satisfaction, or the Gent.
have sufficient reasons to believe they have such Powder,
they are hereby directed to dispossess them of it by the
most eligible means in their power, and make report of
their proceedings herein to the next Committee to be
held for this County.

Nath. Burwell's
dissent &c

Nathaniel Burwell Gent. dissented to the last mentioned
Resolve.[27]

The minutes of these proceedings were signed
"John Scb Wills Chairman"

Committee MS minutes, the whole, including Wills's
signature, in hand of Francis Young, clerk (Office
of county clerk of Isle of Wight County)

1. A broadside of this address is in the John Carter Brown Library, Brown University. As news, the address first appeared in Pinkney's *Va. Gazette* of 18 May
1775. In Purdie's newspaper of the next day the text was preceded by a notice of the
departure of the sailors and marines who had been stationed in Williamsburg since
Patrick Henry's threatened descent on the capital. The detachment was stated to have
departed on "Monday last," and on "The same day a Council was held at the Capital,
after the breaking up of which the following address was made publick."

There is no record to identify the councilors present at the meeting, but if sentiments be a guide, the composition of the group was probably much the same as that
on 6 May 1775 (n. 3). For the Council to address the people directly in this fashion
was not entirely unprecedented, but it was most unusual.

2. The governor's proclamation setting the "speedy Meeting of the General Assembly" for the "first Thursday in the next Month," or 1 June, was dated 12 May
1775 (*Va. Gazette* [Dixon and Hunter], 13 May 1775). So far as newsprint exists,
the address of the Council was not widely commented upon, but for 3 views expressed thereon, none charitably, see 25 May 1775, Richmond Co. Committee; 9 June,
Unidentified County Committee; 19 June, Frederick Co. Committee.

3. For "An Act to Encourage the Importation of Pig and Bar Iron from His
Majesty's Colonies in America; and to Prevent the Erection of Any Mill or Other
Engine for Slitting or Rolling of Iron; or Any Plateing Forge to Work with a
Hammer; or Any Furnace for Making Steel in Any of the Said Colonies," 23 George
II, *cap.* 29 (A.D. 1750); and for "An Act to Prevent the Exportation of Hats out of
Any of His Majesty's Colonies or Plantations in America," 5 George II, *cap.* 22 (A.D.
1732), see *Rev. Va.*, I, 246 and n. 3, 247 and n. 4.

4. The American colonial postal service was based on articles, subsequently amended, in "An Act for Establishing a General Post Office for All Her Majesty's Dominions, and for Setting a Weekly Sum out of the Revenues Thereof for the Service of the War, and Other Her Majesty's Occasions," 9 Anne *cap.* 10 (A.D. 1711). The enforcement of this act was stoutly resisted in Virginia as bestowing a monopoly on postmasters general in London and levying a tax without the consent of the General Assembly. Not until 1732 was the colony embraced within the postal system, and then the regulations were rather routinely and oft ingeniously evaded. The appointment of Benjamin Franklin as deputy postmaster general for the American colonies in 1753 produced improvements and eventually, to the astonishment of London, a monetary profit. Although he was absent for years in Great Britain, his ideas were implemented by his associate deputy postmasters, William Hunter of Virginia until 1761, and John Foxcroft, successively of Virginia, Pennsylvania, and New York, until Franklin's dismissal from office in 1774.

At its best, however, the system was cumbersome. A letter sent from New York City to Charleston, S.C., might be borne overland (what with the impediment of poor roads, the chances of inclement weather, and the danger of highway robbery) to Suffolk, Va., to which town another rider would bring mail from the more southern colonies for exchange. Or the New York postmaster might place the letter aboard a mail packet bound for London, whence the missive would be brought back across the Atlantic to its intended destination. By 1775 the system was deteriorating, and for that and other obvious reasons no committee of correspondence would have entrusted a document to its care (William Smith, *The History of the Post Office in British North America, 1639–1870* [Cambridge, Eng., 1920], pp. 13, 19, 22–23, 26, 35–36; Kenneth Ellis, *The Post Office in the Eighteenth Century: A Study in Administrative History* [London, 1958], pp. 35, 44, 45).

5. In the newspaper the word is misprinted "ro."

6. In the newspaper the word is misprinted "molosses."

7. It is difficult to follow the speaker's reasoning in this paragraph. He appears to have been referring to a number of the so-called "trade acts" passed after 1750, for some of which see *Rev. Va.*, I, 248 and nn. 2, 9. These statutes were supportive of and occasionally in refinement of the "navigation acts" of 1660, 1663, and 1696. Hence the "consequences" that followed "submission" to provisions of acts of 1711 and 1750 could scarcely have been the enactment of statutes of an anterior century; yet it was those statutes that established the principle against which the speaker was inveighing. See Oliver M. Dickerson, *The Navigation Acts and the American Revolution* (Philadelphia, 1951), pp. 7–8, 10–11, 31–32, 64–66, 103–22, 200–201, 290–300.

8. Incorporated in "An Act for Granting Certain Duties in the British Colonies and Plantations in America . . . ," 4 George III, *cap.* 15 (A.D. 1764) were 3 articles (41, 43, and 45) that caused the statute to be dubbed in the colonies "the Black Act." By these articles the burden of proof was placed on the owner or the master of a seized vessel; even should the defendant be acquitted, the ruling of a judge that there had been "probable cause" for seizure threw on the acquitted the costs of the trial; prosecutors and informers were shielded from suits for false arrest; and a seized vessel might be taken for trial to the port where the judge of admiralty for all the American colonies should establish his court. (As it turned out, he did so in Sept. 1764 at Halifax, Nova Scotia.) Before he resigned as judge of the Virginia court of vice-admiralty in 1765, Peyton Randolph ruled that properly listed goods protected both vessel and cargo (Carl Ubbelohde, *The Vice-Admiralty Courts and the American Revolution* [Chapel Hill, N.C., 1960], pp. 44–54; *Rev. Va.* I, 269 n. 6). In that Virginia's shipping

was largely confined to small craft engaged in the coastal trade, the colony seems to have been little affected by the "Black Act." So much is attested by the brevity of the speaker's reference to it.

9. For "An Act for Restraining and Prohibiting the Governor, Council and House of Representatives, of the Province of New York, Until Provision Shall Have Been Made for Furnishing the King's Troops with All the Necessaries Required by Law, from Passing or Assenting to Any Act of Assembly, Vote or Resolution, for Any Other Purpose," 7 George III, *cap.* 59 (A.D. 1767), see *Rev. Va.*, I, 53, 190, 248 and n. 7.

10. For "An Act for Granting and Applying Certain Stamp Duties . . ." ("the Stamp Act"), 5 George III, *cap.* 12 (A.D. 1765), the Virginia reaction thereto, and the "taking off," see ibid., I, 15–51, 209, 217, 248, 262, 263, 286.

11. For "An Act for the Better Securing the Dependency of His Majesty's Dominions in America upon the Crown and Parliament of Great Britain" ("the Declaratory Act"), 6 George III, *cap.* 12 (A.D. 1766), see ibid., I, 49, 52, 263, II, 47 n. 1.

12. The speaker used "refrain" in the then current sense of "curb" or "check."

13. If the speaker was not seeking to preclude dissension along lines foreseeably possible, the conclusion must be that he was arguing against "doctrines" he knew already to be circulating.

14. For the attempt of "the minister," Lord Frederick North, to save the East India Company while threatening the ruin of many merchants long engaged in the tea trade, see *Rev. Va.*, I, 93.

15. Because Boston did not house over 17,000 dwellers before its decline in population in 1775 (Sutherland, *Population Distribution in Colonial America*, p. 38), it would seem that the speaker included among the "upwards of 30,000 inhabitants" others largely dependent upon the economy of the town.

16. For "An Act for the Better Regulating the Government of the Province of the Massachusetts Bay, in New England" ("the Massachusetts Government Act"), 14 George III, *cap.* 45 (A.D. 1774), see *Rev. Va.*, I, 106.

17. For "An Act for the Impartial Administration of Justice in Cases of Persons Questioned for Any Act Done by Them in the Execution of the Law . . ." ("the Murdering Act"), 14 George III, *cap.* 39 (A.D. 1774), see ibid., I, 106, 117, 250.

18. The reference is to the Continental Association adopted by the first Continental Congress on 20 Oct. 1774, for which see ibid., II, 104–5, 169 n. 5, 191 n. 7, 212 n. 5, 310 n. 6.

19. In the newspaper the interrogation point is missing.
The establishing of "arts and manufactures" would of course itself be in defiance of British colonial laws.

20. The "ever-glorious *revolution*," was that which is 1688–89 shook the English constitutional and political world to its foundations.

21. The last preceding meeting of the Isle of Wight County committee had been held on 17 Apr. 1775, when much of the business of the present day was put on the agenda. With minor variations in phraseology and punctuation, and with different marginal notes, the transactions of this day are repeated in the manuscript minute book under the date of 15 June 1775. "The theory is," wrote Henry Read McIlwaine, "that this duplication was merely the mistake of a careless copyist" (*15th Annual Library Report*, p. 6). The careless copyist of his own previous labor was Francis Young.

22. The resolution that the subcommittee "wait on" Thomas Nelson, Jr., was natural and logical. Not only was he a noted merchant but he was one of the 3-member

"General Committee" appointed on 25 Mar. 1775 by the second Virginia Convention to assist county committees in the procurment of munitions (13 Apr. 1775, Southampton Co. Committee and n. 7).

23. The "Assistance" was proferred in response to the threat dispatched to Nelson's uncle, Thomas Nelson, Sr., by Capt. George Montagu (4 May 1775, York Co. Committee).

24. "Monday next" was 22 May 1775, under which date heading the committee will be found reconvened.

25. If not returned with his "goods" to Smithfield by 27 July 1775, the said Sym would nevertheless be transacting in Isle of Wight County business of a nature to cause the committee to summon him to appear and "Answer Sundry complaints."

26. On 27 Mar. the second Virginia Convention had "Resolved unanimously, as Salt is a daily & indispensable Necessity of Life, & the making of it amongst ourselves must be deemed a valuable Acquisition, it is therefore recommended that the utmost Endeavours be used to establish Salt Works; and that proper Encouragement be given to Mr. James Tait, who hath made proposals and offered a Scheme to the public for so desirable a Purpose." On the same day the members of the convention agreed to forward £10 from their constituencies to Robert Carter Nicholas. The sum was contributory only, for Nicholas was already engaged to receive and disburse funds raised or to be raised by private subscription (*Rev. Va.*, II, 382, 383, 387 n. 5).

27. Nathaniel Burwell probably "dissented" on the ground that until cooperation had been sought or moral suasion tried, the committee should not endorse "means" the' eligibility of which might end in violence, bloodshed, or worse.

Tuesday, 16 May 1775

Augusta County West Committee

Activation, Resolutions, and Instructions

At a meeting of the inhabitants of that part of Augusta county that lies on the west side of the laurel Hill, at Pittsburg, the 16th day of May, 1775, the following gentlemen were chosen a committee for the said district, viz: George Croghan, John Campbell, Edward Ward, Thomas Smallman, John Cannon, John McCullaugh ⟨McCullough⟩, William Gee, George Valandingham ⟨Vallandigham⟩, John Gibson, Dorsey Penticost ⟨Pentecost⟩, Edward Cook, William Crawford, Devereux Smith, John Anderson, David Rodgers ⟨Rogers⟩, Jacob Vanmetre ⟨Vanmeter⟩, Henry Enoch, James Ennis ⟨Innes⟩, George Willson ⟨Wilson⟩, William Vance, David Shepherd, William Elliot⟨t⟩, Richard Willis, Samuel Sample ⟨Semple⟩, John Ormsbey ⟨Ormsby⟩, Richard McMaher, John Nevill⟨e⟩, and John Sweringer ⟨Swearingen⟩; the foregoing gentlemen met in committee, and resolved that John Campbell, John Ormsbey, Edward Ward, Thomas Smallman, Samuel Sample, John Anderson, and

Devereux Smith, or any four of them, be a standing committee, and shall have full power to meet at such times as they shall judge necessary, and in case of any emergency, to call the committee of this district together, and shall be vested with the same power and authority as the other standing committees and committees of correspondence are in the other counties within this colony.[1]

Resolved unanimously, That the cordial and most grateful thanks of this committee are a tribute due to John Harvie, esquire, our worthy representative in the late colonial convention held at Richmond, for his faithful discharge of that important trust reposed in him; and to John Nevill, esquire, our other worthy delegate, whom nothing but sickness prevented from representing us in that respectable assembly.

Resolved unanimously, that this committee have the highest sense of the spirited behaviour of their brethren in New England, and do most cordially approve of their opposing the invaders of American rights and privileges to the utmost extreme, and that each member of this committee, respectively, will animate and encourage their neighbourhood to follow the brave example.[2]

The imminent danger that threatens America in general, from ministerial and parliamentary denunciations of our ruin, and is now carrying into execution by open acts of unprovoked hostilities in our sister colony of Massachusetts, as well as the danger to be apprehended to this colony in particular from a domestic enemy, said to be prompted by the wicked minions of power to execute our ruin, added to the menaces of an Indian war, likewise said to be in contemplation, thereby thinking to engage our attention, and divert it from that still more interesting object of liberty and freedom, that deeply, and with so much justice, hath called forth the attention of all America; for the prevention of all, or any of those impending evils, it is *resolved*, that the recommendation of the Richmond convention, of the 20th of last March, relative to the embodying, arming, and disciplining the militia, be immediately carried into execution with the greatest diligence in this county, by the officers appointed for that end;[3] and that the recommendation of the said convention to the several committees of this colony, to collect from their constituents, in such manner as shall be most agreeable to them so much money as shall be sufficient to purchase half a pound of gunpowder, and one pound of lead, flints, and cartridge paper, for every tithable person in their county, be likewise carried into execution.[4]

This committee, therefore, out of the deepest sense of the expediency of this measure, most earnestly entreat that every member of this committee do collect from each tithable person in their several districts the sum of two shillings and six pence, which we deem no more than sufficient for the above purpose, and give proper receipts to all such as pay the same into their hands; and the sum so collected to be paid into the hands of Mr. John Campbell, who is to give proper security to this committee, or their successors, for the due and faithful application of the money so deposited with him for the above purpose, by or with the advice of this committee, or their successors; and this committee, as your representatives, and who are most ardently labouring for your preservation, call on you, our constituents, our friends, brethren, and fellow-sufferers, in the name of God, of every thing you hold sacred or valuable, for the sake of your wives, children, and unborn generations, that you will, every one of you, in your several stations, to the utmost of your power, assist in levying such sum, by not only paying yourselves, but by assisting those who are not at present in a condition to do so. We heartily lament the case of all such as have not this small sum at command in this day of necessity; to all such we recommend to tender security to such as providence has enabled to lend them so much; and this committee do pledge their faith and fortunes to you, their constituents, that we shall, without fee or reward, use our best endeavours to procure, with the money so collected, the ammunition our present exigencies have made so exceedingly necessary.

As this committee has reason to believe there is a quantity of ammunition destined for this place for the purpose of government, and as this country, on the west side of the Laurel Hill, is greatly distressed for want of ammunition, and deprived of the means of procuring it, by reason of its situation, as easy as the lower counties of this colony, they do earnestly request the committees of Frederick, Augusta, and Hampshire, that they will not suffer the ammunition to pass through their counties for the purposes of government, but will secure it for the use of this destitute country, and immediately inform this committee of their having done so.[5]

Resolved, That this committee do approve of the resolution of the committee of the other part of this county, relative to the cultivating a friendship with the Indians;[6] and if any person shall be so depraved as to take the life of any Indian that may come to us in a friendly manner, we will, as one man, use our utmost endeavours to bring such offender to condign punishment.

Ordered, That the standing committee be directed to secure such arms and ammunition as are not employed in actual service, or private property, and that they get the same repaired, and deliver them to such captains of independent companies as may make application for the same, and taking such captain's receipt for the arms so delivered.

Resolved, that the sum of fifteen pounds, current money, be raised by subscription, and that the same be transmitted to Robert Carter Nicholas, esquire, for the use of the deputies sent from this colony to the general congress, which sum of money was immediately paid by the committee then present.[7]

Mr. John Campbell reported, from the select committee for considering the grievances as instructions to the delegates, which he read in his place, and handed it to the clerk's table, where it was again read, and is as follows.

To JOHN HARVIE AND GEORGE ROOTES, ESQUIRES.

Gentlemen,

You being chosen to represent the people on the west side the Laurel Hill in the colonial congress for the ensuing year,[8] we, the committee for the people aforesaid, desire you will lay the grievances hereafter mentioned before the congress at their first meeting, as we conceive it highly necessary they should be redressed, to put us on a footing with the rest of our brethren in the colony.[9]

1st. That many of the inhabitants in this part of the county have expended large sums of money, and supplied the soldiers in the last Indian war with provisions and other necessaries, many of whom have expended all they had; and though, at the same time, we bear grateful remembrance of the good intentions of the late colonial congress, so feelingly and generously expressed in their resolves, yet the unhappy situation we are reduced to by the payment of those supplies being delayed, involves this new and flourishing country in extreme poverty.[10]

2d. That the maintaining a garrison at this place, when there is no other method used for supplying them with provisions, but by impressing from the inhabitants of the country, ought to be considered.[11]

3d. That this country, joining the Indian territory and the province of Quebec (which by its late change of constitution, is rendered inimical to liberty) [12] lies exposed to the inroads of the savages and the militia of that province. And should the ministry or their emmissaries be able to stir up either of them against the colonies, this country will be in need of support to enable them to provide against, and withstand any attempt that may be made on their civil or religious liberties.

4th. That for want of freeholders we cannot get legal grand jurors, which are necessary for the well government of the country.

5th. That the unsettled boundary between this colony and the province of Pennsylvania, is the occasion of many disputes.[13]

6th. That the collecting the duty on skins and furs, for which a commission hath lately been sent up here, will banish the Indian trade from this place and colony.[14]

Which Report being agreed to, *resolved unanimously*, that a fair copy be drawn off and delivered to our delegates as their instructions.[15]

Ordered, that the foregoing proceedings be certified by the clerk of this committee, and published in the Virginia gazette.

By order of the committee.   James Berwick, clerk.

Virginia Gazette (Pinkney), 6 July 1775

Petition to President and Gentlemen of the Continental Congress

⟨A⟩ Petition of several Persons in that part of the County of *Augusta*, which is on the West side of the *Allegany* Mountain . . .[16]

⟨Humbly sheweth⟩ that the Petitioners have grievously suffered by the devastations of the *Indians* in the late war; [17] that, to avoid Captivity by an Enemy so insidious cruel and savage many of the Petitioners having been obliged to desert their habitations, and retire to Forts, so that they could not till the Ground, now want bread, and support themselves chiefly by the spontaneous productions of the Earth; that the promising appearance of a plentiful Crop had encouraged them to bear these afflictions without repining, and to hope for better times; but that those fair prospects will probably be delusive, unless effectual Measures are pursued to avert the Calamities with which they are threatened; That lord *Dunmore*, after the expedition against the *Indians* promised to meet them at *Pittsburg* in the spring, and conclude a peace, and then restore the Hostages, delivered to him, and discharge the Captives; that the *Indians* have been uneasy for some time because the treaty was deferred; that the *Delawares* particularly are very much dissatisfied, and repent that they had not joined the *Shawanese* in the War, since they find the white People are not to be depended on; that the Commandant in this quarter for Government has instructions, as the Petitioners are informed, to assemble the *Indians* at this place, so soon as he can, when the hostages and prisoners will be delivered up,[18] and that the Petitioners, unable to discover the design of Government, apprehend every evil from the threats of it, to enfranchise the Slaves, on condition they will rebel against their Masters;[19] and therefore pray the Congress, to which application is made because it is thought the Provincial Assemblies can not provide adequate remedies early enough, to take the Case of the Petitioners into Consideration; and appoint commissioners from this Colony and *Pennsylvania* to attend the meeting of the *Indians*, and cooperate with Government for the public good, or, if the latter should fail to nominate Persons for that purpose, proceed without them in the treaty which is absolutely necessary⟨.⟩[20]

Kennedy, *Journals of the House of Burgesses of Virginia, 1773–1776*, p. 230.

1. For the 11th article of the Continental Association recommending the formation of county committees, see 8 Apr. 1775, n. 5. Although instructed to permit the creation of no new counties, Lord Dunmore and his Council edged around the prohibition by constituting the western part of Augusta County a "district" and appointing a superfluity of justices whose interests lay there. It was then arranged that the county court should adjourn from time to time at Staunton and sit at Fort Pitt. Acting in effect as the court of a separate county, the westerners held their 1st meeting at Fort Pitt on 21 Feb. 1775 (Abernethy, *Western Lands and the Am. Rev.*, pp. 83, 94, 136; Richard W. Lovelace, ed., *Records of the District of West Augusta, Ohio County, and Yohogania County, Virginia* [Columbus, Ohio, 1970], pp. 525–27).

On 6 Mar., protesting that men living a great distance from them could not, though "ever so worthy," properly represent them, the "Inhabitants" of the district elected John Harvie and John Neville to attend the second Virginia Convention. Harvie presented himself on 21 Mar. 1775 and was promptly seated as a delegate (*Rev. Va.*, II, 313–14, 353).

2. News of the fighting in Massachusetts had penetrated the mountains and reached Fort Pitt sometime during the 1st week of May (Edgar W. Hassler, *Old Westmoreland: A History of Western Pennsylvania during the Revolution* [Cleveland, 1900], p. 13).

3. For the resolution of the second Virginia Convention that the militia be revived in the form of independent companies, see 11 May 1775, n. 4.

4. For the resolution of the second convention that sums of money be collected by county committees for the purchase of munitions, see 13 Apr. 1775, Caroline Co. Committee, n. 4.

5. What was the result of this appeal is unknown. The frontiersmen may have been eyeing a quantity of "Indian goods," among which was gunpowder, rumored to be on the way west. The goods were consigned to George Croghan and had been designed for the buying of lands from the Indians for the Grand Ohio Company. The goods were sequestered in Maryland on the eve of Dunmore's War in the autumn of 1774 (Abernethy, *Western Lands and the Am. Rev.*, pp. 120–21).

6. No pertinent resolution "of the other part of this county," with its seat at Staunton, has been found.

7. For the resolution of the second Virginia Convention requesting the delegates to raise £15 in each of the counties and corporations of the colony for the support of the deputies to the second Continental Congress, see 8 Apr. 1775, n. 6. There is no record in Robert Carter Nicholas's account book of his having received the money so promptly subscribed in Augusta County West.

8. For the election of convention delegates for the "ensuing year," see 13 Apr. 1775, n. 1.

GEORGE ROOTES was the 4th son of the wealthy Maj. Philip Rootes of Rosewall, King and Queen County. The father thought that the boy might make a career of the sea, but if George undertook to do so, he found the allurement of salt water transitory. When the major died in 1756, his estate passed to his eldest son. George can be demonstrated to have been in King and Queen County 10 years later, but thereafter his name disappears from the records. Early in 1773 he resurfaces in Winchester, well enough versed in the law to be admitted to practice before the bench of Frederick County. Although not of the local squirearchy (he was never a justice of the peace), he was specially elected a delegate to the first Virginia Convention, then was displaced by Rev. Charles Mynn Thruston as a delegate to the second. Continuing to ride the legal circuits, Rootes appeared before and was admitted to practice in the District of West Augusta when the "reconvened" court held its 1st meeting at Fort Pitt in Feb. 1775. Why he should now have been elected to represent the district in the third convention poses a question not answered with certainty. If anything, he appears not to have been involved in the game of attempted land-grabbing and fortune-building. Perhaps that was in his favor, he being of no faction. And it is possible that rough frontiersmen saw in an easygoing, affable, experienced, polished native of the Tidewater an agent likely to impress favorably the gentry in Richmond. At this time Rootes was probably around 40 years of age (*Rev. Va.*, I, 135–36, 235, II, 358 n. 11; William Clayton-Torrence, *Rootes of Rosewall: An Account of Major Philip Rootes of "Rosewall," King and Queen County, Virginia, and Some of His Descendants* [n.p., n.d. (ca. 1906)], pp. 18–21, 30, 32; Beverley Fleet, comp., *Virginia Colonial Abstracts*, 1st ser. [34 vols., reproduced from typewritten copy, Richmond, 1937–51], XXXIII, 66, 73; *Va. Gazette* [Purdie and Dixon], 27 Nov. 1766; Frederick County Order Book No. 16, 1772–1778, microfilm in Va. State Library, p. 99; Lovelace, *Recs. of the Dist. of W. Augusta*, p. 526.

9. On 22 Aug. 1775 the third Virginia Convention would resolve that "in all Matters relating to keeping the peace and good Behavior and in all criminal Matters" the eastern and western portions of Augusta County proceed "as if they were distinct Counties" (Procs., 2d and 3d paras.).

10. The second Virginia Convention on 27 Mar. 1775 unanimously thanked the officers and men "who lately defended this Colony from the Savage Enemy" during Dunmore's War, offered condolences to the kinsfolk and friends of those slain, and assured "all who have rendered such important Services to this Colony, that so soon as Opportunity permits, we will most chearfully do every thing on our part to make them ample Satisfaction" (*Rev. Va.*, II, 630–31). With the General Assembly apparently prorogued until September, and they yet unknowing that His Excellency had summoned the Assembly to convene on 1 June 1775 (12 May 1775, n. 1), the west Augustans were now placing this piece of public business into the hands of an extra-legal assemblage expected soon to be convoked. As matters were to fall out, the subject of compensation would be taken up by the House of Burgesses, but fruitlessly, and would devolve on the convention (pp. 14, 21–22, 22–23 above; 25 July 1775, Third Va. Convention, Procs. and n. 7).

11. On 7 Aug. 1775 the convention would provide for the garrisoning of Fort Pitt (Procs., 2d para.).

12. The "late change" caused by passage of the Quebec Act ("An Act for Making More Effectual Provision for the Government of the Province of Quebec in North America," 14 George III, *cap.* 83 [A.D. 1774]) was assertion within the act of the supremacy of Parliament, provision for no Canadian legislative assembly, permission for Canadians to tax themselves only for limited purposes, authorization of the trial of civil cases without a jury, and placement of the Roman Catholic Church on a privileged basis (*Rev. Va.*, II, 351, 367).

13. Some of those "many disputes" were to obtrude themselves upon the business of this newly formed committee in little over 5 weeks (22 June 1775, Augusta Co. West Committee).

14. In June 1774 John Connolly had attempted to enforce the provisions of a proclamation issued by Governor Dunmore on 25 Apr. 1774 enjoining and requiring the inhabitants of Fort Pitt and vicinity "to pay his Majesty's Quitrents, and all public Dues, to such Officers as are or shall be appointed to collect the same" (*Exec. Journs. Coun. Col. Va.*, VI, 656; William Henry Smith, ed., *The St. Clair Papers* [2 vols., Cincinnati, 1882], I, 323). The new "commission" (to whom issued is unknown) was "sent up" for the collection of duties on "skins and furs," however or to wherever exported. These duties were imposed by "An Act for the Better Support of the College of William and Mary," 22 George II, *cap.* 35 (A.D. 1748) (*Statutes at Large*, VI, 91–94). By recourse to these measures, His Lordship incurred the risk of alienating many, whether white or red, whose interest it otherwise would be to support him. But it was a calculated risk. For by enforcement of Virginia law in an area to which the Penn family professed to hold title, Dunmore might strengthen the claims of the colony he represented. For a phase of the border controversy with Pennsylvania, see 22 June 1775, n. 1.

15. Despite the unanimity attained by the committee, the western reaches of Augusta County harbored many men who believed that the activities of the protestants were too vigorous, or who were confused, or who had hedged against the uncertain outcome of the developing contest. At about this time 20 of the leading citizens of Fort Pitt and its environs, along "with Several hundred Inhabitants of Transmontane Augusta," composed and signed a letter to the governor praising the fidelity with which he pursued his "duty as a faithful officer of the Crown." The signatories, most of them veterans of Dunmore's War, included John Connolly, Valentine Crawford, Simon Girty, and Alexander McKee (P.R.O., C.O. 5/1353, fols. 289–90).

Also on 16 May 1775, Pennsylvanians assembled at Hannastown to form a committee of correspondence for Westmoreland County. They adopted resolutions professing much loyalty to the king and much abhorrence of the politics of his ministers, and praying "only that things may be restored to, and go on in the same way as before the era of the Stamp Act, when *Boston* grew great, and *America* was happy" (Force, *American Archives*, 4th ser., II, cols. 615–16). "We have nothing but masters and committees all over the country," sighed Arthur St. Clair, one of the Pennsylvania committeemen, "and everything seems to be running into the wildest confusion" (W. H. Smith, *St. Clair Papers*, I, 355).

16. Through the transitional words supplied within angle brackets the source from which this item is drawn reads: "*Richard Bland*, esquire, one of the delegates from this Colony to the General Congress at *Philadelphia*, acquainted the House, that a Petition of several Persons in that part of the County of *Augusta*, which is on the West side of the *Alleghany* Mountain, addressed to the President and Gentlemen of the Continental Congress having been presented to them, setting forth. . . ." The petition is undated but is editorially assumed to have been prepared as part of the proceedings of this day. It could not have been prepared before, or if so, could not have been endorsed before this day, because it was presented to the second Continental Congress on 1 June as from "the Committee representing the people in that part of Augusta county, in the colony of Virginia, on the west side of the Allegeny Mountain" (*JCC*, II, 76). Nor could the document have been subscribed to much later than 16 May and have been received in Philadelphia before or on 1 June 1775.

Receipt of the petition presented to an unconstitutional body a problem fraught with constitutional niceties. These the Congress resolved by referring the document "to the delegates of the colonies of Virginia and Pennsylvania." The solution arrived at by those delegates is under the date heading of 25 July 1775, Third Va. Convention, Va. and Pa. Delegates in Congress. . . .

Bland placed the petition, a copy of it, or a summary of it before the House of Burgesses in Williamsburg on 14 June 1775; and on 24 June a committee of 6 was established to ratify a treaty with the Indians (*JHB, 1773–1776*, pp. 230, 283; p. 24 above).

The original document has not been found. The present item is printed from the abstract in the journal of the Burgesses, and verbs therein have been recast in order to accord with what they more likely were in the original.

17. Dunmore's War of 1774 (*Rev. Va.*, II, 105–8).

18. The "Commandant" was Maj. John Connolly, whose beginning of the execution of his "instructions" is under the date heading of 19 May 1775, Third Va. Convention.

19. The "Petitioners" were referring to rumors circulating, not without foundation, during the gunpowder "commotions" that the governor intended to free the slaves, arm them, and employ them in reducing the colony to "obedience" (p. 6 above).

20. The bracketed period replaces a colon that was followed by the record of the action taken by Congress as noted in n. 16 above. Appended to the description of the petition in the journal of the Continental Congress is the entry: "Also a resolve of the sd. committee in these words, viz. 'That the unsettled boundary between this colony and the province of Pennsylvania is the occasion of many disputes'" (cf. the 5th grievance in the letter above to John Harvie and George Rootes). This entry, undoubtedly under instructions, Charles Thomson, secretary of the Congress, deleted by lining out, lest the fact of dissension between 2 of the "united" colonies be made a matter of public record upon publication of the journal.

Wednesday, 17 May 1775

Cumberland County Committee

Alarm, Insecurity, Haven, and Continuing Complaint

At a Meeting of the Committee of Cumberland County Wednesday May 17th 1775,[1] Present, George Carrington, Chairman, William Fleming, Littlebury Mosby, Joseph Carrington, Richard James, James Pleasants, Carter Henry Harrison, George Carrington junr. William Smith, Robert Smith, Edward Carrington, John Woodson, The Rev. Mr. ⟨John Hyde⟩ Saunders and Charles Woodson junr.

Mr. Chairman opened the Business of the Day by laying before the Committee the Information lately received by Express from the Northward respecting the Government of New York, among which is a Resolution of the Maryland Provincial Convention for immediately s[us]pending all Exportations from that Province to Quebec, Nova S[cotia,] Georgia and Newfoundland, or any Parts of the fishing Coast [or fishi]ng Islands or to the Town of Boston until the Continental Con[gress] shall give further Directions therein;[2] Wherefore the Committee after the maturest Deliberation came to the following Resolution[s:]

Resolved unanimously that this Committee doth heartily approve [the] said Resolution of the Maryland Provincial Convention as well concerted upon a View of the present Conjuncture of Affairs, and do recommend it as a proper Rule of Conduct to all Men.

Resolved, that the present alarming Situation of American Affairs especially in the Province of New York[3] renders it absolutely necessary that a Colony Convention be immediately called, and this Committee doth recommend it to Robert Carter Nicholas Esquire in the most earnest Terms to call a Colony Convention as speedily as possible, provided the General Assembly now called to meet on the first Thursday in June, shall be prorogued to a further day.[4]

Resolved, that it is the Opinion of this Committee that the Public Treasury of this Colony is at this Time in an insecure Place; and this Committee doth in the most earnest and respectful Manner recommend it to Mr. Treasurer to remove it nearer the Center of the Colony where it will be more secure.[5]

The following Address to the Inhabitants of the lower Parts of Virginia was proposed and unanimously agreed to.[6]

Friends and Countrymen,

We, the Committee for the County of Cumberland, taking into our serious Consideration the unremitting Efforts of a despotic Administration to effect the total Subversion of American Liberty; aided by the wicked Tools of Corruption who are endeavouring by the basest Misrepresentations and Falsehoods to effect an unnatural Division between the Mother Country and her Colonies; covering their wicked Design under the specious Pretence of Duty and Attachment to our gracious Sovereign and the sacred Laws of the British Empire: And also the unhappy Situation to which you will be reduced in Case of an hostile Invasion of this Colony, do for ourselves and our Constituents (should such a distressing Circumstance take place) most cordially invite you to remove so many of your Wives and Children into this County as the Inhabitants thereof can conveniently entertain, where they will meet with the best Protection and Accommodations which we are able to afford them.[7]

Resolved unanimously, That Mr. James and Mr. Edward Carrington or either of them be fully empowered to lay out the Money contributed by the Inhabitants of this County for the Purpose of purchasing Ammunition and other Articles of Military Preparation, in such Manner as to them in their Discretion shall seem proper, at the Risque of the County, and that Mr. Chairman pay whatever Monies they or either of them, shall from Time to Time call for or direct, out of the Fund lodged in his hands as Treasurer of this Committee.[8]

Resolved, That Mr. Chairman, Mr. Joseph Carrington, Mr. James, Mr. Harrison, Mr. George Carrington junr. Mr. Edward Carrington and Mr. John Woodson, or any three of them, be a Select Committee, from Time to Time to select from the Proceedings of this Committee such Parts as may be proper for Publication, and direct them to be published accordingly.

A Complaint being made to this Committee, that Ray Moss and John Woodson junr. Inhabitants of the County of Buckingham, have lately within the Limits of this [C]ounty made a Breach of the Continental Association by Gaming: Re[solv]ed that Mr. Chairman do at any Time hereafter, when he shall appoint [a me]eting of this Committee, issue his Summons directed to any person, [orderin]g them to summon the said Moss and Woodson to appear before [this Com]mittee to answer the aforesaid Complaint: And that he in like [mann]er order any Witness which he shall be informed of to be summoned.[9]

> Signed by George Carrington Chairman.
> Test Ed. Carrington Secy.
> Teste. THO. MILLER, Cl. Com.

> Committee MS journal, the whole, including George and Edward Carrington's signatures, in hand of Thomas Miller (Archives Division, Virginia State Library)

1. The last preceding meeting of the Cumberland County committee had been on 10 May 1775.

2. The summary is almost identical in wording with the resolution unanimously adopted by the Maryland Convention on 1 May 1775. A copy of the resolution appeared

in Pinkney's *Va. Gazette* of 11 May 1775. Nearly the entire 1st page and part of the 2d of that issue were taken up by petitions that the General Assembly of New York on 25 Mar. addressed to "*the* KING's *most excellent* MAJESTY" and "*the right honourable* LORDS SPIRITUAL *and* TEMPORAL *of* GREAT BRITAIN, *in parliament assembled*." This no doubt was the "Information" with which the Maryland resolution shared a saddlebag on the trip to the printer's office in Williamsburg.

On this same day, 17 May 1775, deputies to the second Continental Congress unanimously agreed to prohibit trade with Quebec and other portions of the continent that displayed insufficient zeal in supporting the common cause (see 11 July 1775, In Congress, p. 283 below).

3. For the coalition of moderates and radicals forming to counter the "alarming Situation" in New York, see 5 May 1775, Va. Committee.

4. With one county committee already on record (9 May 1775, Spotsylvania Co. Committee and n. 10) and the judgment of "some respectable Gentlemen" offered (12 May 1775, Third Va. Convention), the pressure on Nicholas to summon a convention was increasing; but with the actual meeting of the General Assembly on 1 June 1775, Peyton Randolph would be in the capital and the need for a convention temporarily abated.

5. Although this was the 3d suggestion that the treasury be moved, there is no evidence that as yet Mr. Treasurer had any "apprehension of the necessity or propriety" of the measure proposed (4 May 1775, Hanover Co. Committee, 2d entry, and n. 3; 9 May, Spotsylvania Co. Committee).

6. In the meeting of 10 May 1775 the committee had resolved that the address be prepared by Carter Henry Harrison and William Fleming.

7. The subject of refuge had been touched upon by the committee of Sussex County (8 May 1775 and n. 20). The "Address" of the Cumberland County committee was printed in the supplement of Purdie's *Va. Gazette* of 7 July 1775. A more detailed offer of refuge would be made by the committee of Buckingham County on 22 May 1775.

8. The "Fund" was collected pursuant to the committee's resolution of 3 May 1775 (see also 10 May 1775, Cumberland Co. Committee).

9. No further mention of the "Complaint" or disposition thereof has been found. The next meeting of the Cumberland County committee is under the date heading of 30 June 1775.

Thursday, 18 May 1775

Caroline County Committee

Commutation for Inconvenience

AT A MEETING of the Committee the 18th. day of May 1775
Eleven Members Present

Such Persons as have subscribed Grain for relief of the Bostonians may discharge the Wheat they have subscribed at four shillings & six pence & corn at two shillings per Bushell If Its inconvenient to pay the grain

James Upshaw John Tennant & William Woodford are appointed to dispose of the Grain recd. for the relief of the Bostonians as they or either of them shall think best[1]

> Committee MS minutes in hand of Samuel Haws, Jr., clerk (Henry E. Huntington Library and Art Gallery of San Marino, Calif.)

1. In its last preceding meeting, on 11 May 1775, the committee had appointed a 4-man subcommittee to determine the quantity of grain received and to "dispose of It" as seemed proper. Tennant and Woodford were members of that subcommittee. Why the composition of the subcommittee should now be altered and the membership reduced is unknown. The next meeting of the Caroline County committee is under the date heading of the following day, 19 May 1775.

Friday, 19 May 1775

Third Virginia Convention

Augusta County West: John Connolly to the Chiefs of the Shawnee[1]

Bretheren

I am sorry that the Business which has for some time past employed the great Man of Virginia[2] should have prevented his Meeting you at this place agreeable to his promise made you when in your Country,[3] But as the great Business yet continues he desires some of the chiefs of the Shawanese to come up as soon as possible to the forks of the River[4] so that the Chain of Friendship may be brightened[5] and the Affairs that were not finally settled with you and the Mingoes may be adjusted to our mutual Satisfaction. It is possible the Great Man may be here to meet you, but if not, some Person will be appointed by him to speak to you which I hope will be sufficient to convince you his younger Bretheren the Shawanese that notwithstanding the great hurry of his Affairs he has not forgotten their Interest. Your friends who went with the great man I expect will meet you here.

Given under my hand and the seal this 19th. day of May 1775.

Signed John Connolly (LS) [6]

> MS transcript, the whole, including Connolly's signature, in hand of James Berwick, clerk of the committee of the District of West Augusta County; excerpted from a restored and bound folio volume consisting of 29 pages (12½″ × 7⅝″) and cover, in papers of third Virginia Convention (Archives Division, Virginia State Library)

Caroline County Committee

Ill Treatment and Diabolical Disposition

AT a committee for the county of Caroline, on Friday the 19th of May, 1775,[7] the committee having taken into their most serious consideration his Excellency Lord Dunmore's Letter, dated the 24th of December last, to Lord Dartmouth, his Majesty's Secretary of State for the American department; also his Lordship's proclamation, and a letter wrote by a certain Capt. Montague ⟨George Montagu⟩, to the Hon. Thomas Nelson⟨, Sr.⟩, Esq; [8] (which were severally published in the Gazettes) think it their indispensable duty to remonstrate against the illiberal aspersions which are most injuriously thrown out against our constituents, as part of the community; and also to declare our abhorrence of the brutal disposition that dictated the menaces contained in the said Montague's letter: Therefore *resolved*,

1st. That his Lordship's letter, if founded on the information of others, fully evinces to us their unfriendly and inimical disposition towards this country, and his wishes to perpetuate the unhappy dispute between Great Britain and America, which we so fervently and ardently desire to terminate on constitutional principles. We cannot forbear adverting to that part of his Lordship's letter, where he asserts, that armed companies in some counties are formed and *sworn to enforce the orders of the committees*, directly in open defiance of the Crown: Such proceedings as these, we are apprehensive, never had existence, or we should have had as early intelligence of them as his Lordship.[9]

2. That that part of his Lordship's proclamation wherein he charges some persons with being disaffected to his Majesty's government, and endeavouring to effect a change in it, under the appearance of defending their liberties, contains an accusation totally groundless, and cannot be merely applied to the people of this colony, who ever were, and in future wish to be, distinguished in their loyalty to our most gracious Sovereign, whom we sincerely

pray may ever enjoy his reign in peace, happiness, and glory. We think ourselves extremely ill treated by his Lordship, while we are aiming to preserve that liberty and freedom which the God of nature originally gave, and our ancestors have handed down to us, to be charged with disaffection to his Majesty's government. On a review of his Lordship's conduct, we cannot avoid suspecting his design in removing the gunpowder (more especially in the night) was rather to deprive this colony of it, than to be used for suppressing any insurrection.[10]

3d. That Capt. Montague's threat of firing upon the defenceless town of York bespeaks such a base, and diabolical disposition, that he ought to be contemned and despised by all men of spirit and humanity; We therefore recommend it to our constituents, not to shew the said Montague any mark of civility or respect whatsoever.[11]

Samuel Haws, jun. Clk.

Virginia Gazette (Dixon and Hunter), 10 June 1775

1. The Shawnee tribe was a branch of the southern Algonquin nation. Indeed, the name Shawnee means "southerners," for they had resided in the Cumberland and the Savannah valleys before moving in the 1670s northward, there to found their principal towns near the present-day municipalities of Winchester, Va., and Oldtown, Md. As the last of their numbers drifted north in the early years of the 18th century, they filtered into the Susquehanna and the Wyoming River valleys and thence, about the mid-1750s, into the upper Ohio River Valley, hunting on both sides of the stream but preferring the south bank. Bitterly resenting the white man's encroachments, which constantly forced them farther from their homelands, and oft at war with other Indian tribes, the Shawnee were much feared. They had sided with the French during the French and Indian War. Ably led by their principal chief, The Cornstalk, the Shawnee suffered humiliation at the Battle of Point Pleasant during Dunmore's War. For the nonce they were more awed by than belligerent toward the Virginians (Frederick Webb Hodge, ed., *Handbook of American Indians North of Mexico,* Smithsonian Institution, Bureau of American Ethnology, Bulletin 30 [2 pts., Washington, D.C., 1907–10], pt. 2, 530–38; Reuben Gold Thwaites and Louise Phelps Kellogg, eds., *Documentary History of Dunmore's War, 1774* [Madison, Wis., 1905], pp. 385–86).

2. The "great Man of Virginia" was Lord Dunmore, and he was truthfully much "employed."

3. In Oct. 1774, after the Battle of Point Pleasant, Lord Dunmore had negotiated but had not concluded a formal treaty with the worsted Indians. The talks at Camp Charlotte, in what is now south-central Ohio, he called the "Terms of our Reconciliation." These terms were "that the Indians should deliver up all prisoners without reserve; that they should restore all horses and other valuable effects which they had carried off; that they Should not hunt on our Side"—that is, the south bank of—"the Ohio, nor molest any Boats passing thereupon; That they Should promise to agree to such regulations, for their trade with our people, as Should be hereafter dictated by the Kings Instructions, and that they Should deliver into our hands certain Hostages, to be kept untill we were convinced of their Sincere intention to adhere to all these Articles." The Indians "gave the most Solemn assurances of their quiet and peaceable deportment for the future; and in return," the governor explained to Lord Dartmouth, "I have given them every promise of protection and good treatment on

our Side." Four hostages, Wissecapoway, Chenusaw, Newa, and Cutemwha, of the Shawnee tribe were taken to Williamsburg, and 12 Mingo hostages were held at Fort Pitt (*Rev. Va.*, II, 175; Thwaties and Kellogg, *Doc. Hist. of Dunmore's War*, pp. 304–5 n. 20, 386; Reuben Gold Thwaites and Louise Phelps Kellogg, eds., *The Revolution on the Upper Ohio, 1775–1777* [Madison, Wis., 1908], p. 18; *Va. Gazette* [Purdie and Dixon], 22 Dec. 1774; 20 May 1775, Third Va. Convention, 1st entry; 29 June, same, p. 239 below).

4. The "forks" were the confluence of the Monongahela and the Allegheny rivers, which formed the Ohio River. This was the location of Fort Pitt, in 1774 rebuilt and renamed Fort Dunmore by John Connolly.

5. An old Indian legend had it that nations in the region of Albany became fast friends with the English there, and to prevent their new friends from leaving, tied their ship to a shrub on the banks of the river. Perceiving that the shrub might be pulled out of the ground, the Indians fastened the craft by a rope to a tree; but fearing that the rope might rot or the tree die, they secured the vessel to a mountain peak by a chain of silver. Thus the chain came to represent their everlasting friendship. But silver and friendships being similar in that both will tarnish if neglected, the chain had to be brightened by periodic exchanges of gifts and mellifluous talks (Wilbur R. Jacobs, *Diplomacy and Indian Gifts: Anglo-French Rivalry along the Ohio and Northwest Frontiers, 1748–1763* [Stanford, Calif., 1950], p. 18).

6. Dr. JOHN CONNOLLY, a native Pennsylvanian of Scotch-Irish and English ancestry, was, in grade of major, "captain commandant of Pittsburg and its dependencies" by appointment of Governor Dunmore. An old sketch depicts Connolly with a high, sloping forehead, thin eyebrows, a splendid Roman nose, thin lips, and close-cropped hair. "Bred to physic," in his youth he sojourned briefly in Martinique, then returned to the West to act as a surgeon's assistant in 2 campaigns against the Indians. For this service, and discovering his temperament much in accordance with his own, Dunmore granted him 1,000 acres in the vicinity of present-day Lexington, Kentucky. Patrick Henry had thought Dr. Connolly "a chatty, Sensible man," and George Washington described him as "curious in his observations and sensible in his remarks." In fact, Connolly was volatile, unpredictable, and opportunistic and scandalized the frontiers with his rash and violent behavior. Nicholas Cresswell, a young English speculator who happened through the Fort Pitt region this spring, noted in his journal that Connolly was "a haughty, imperious man." A British army officer at the doctor-major's table perhaps discovered a reason why he should be. On first seeing his hostess (Susanna, a daughter of Fort Pitt lawyer Samuel Semple) he was shocked to find her "inifinitely ugly." Some women offset ugliness with personal warmth and charm. Mrs. Connolly did not. Her guest thought her temper "very diabolical," and he was uncomfortable under her serpentine gaze. Thus possibly with her hissings to encourage him, Major Connolly infuriated Pennsylvanians in the vicinity by clapping them or their friends into jail or packing them off to Staunton in irons on provocation of the slightest visibility. As a member of the court for the District of West Augusta and Dunmore's principal agent in the boundary controversy with the Penn family, he brooked neither questioning of the governor's rectitude nor strong opposition to the policies of the British ministry; and it was probably he who about this time instigated the gathering of veterans of Dunmore's War who diluted criticism of His Excellency (16 May 1775, n. 15). Hence, piling up debts and straining his friendships, this man would bear watching, whether by creditor or patriot (Clarence Monroe Burton, "John Connolly, a Tory of the Revolution," *Proceedings of the American Antiquarian Society*, new ser., XX [Oct. 1909], 70–86; Percy B. Caley, "The Life Adventures of

Lieutenant-Colonel John Connolly: The Story of a Tory," *Western Pennsylvania Historical Magazine*, XI [Jan. 1928], 10–49, [Apr. 1928], 76–101; John Connolly, "A Narrative of the Transactions, Imprisonments, and Sufferings of John Connolly, an American Loyalist and Lieut. Col. in His Majesty's Service," reprint in *Pa. Mag. of Hist. and Biog.* XII [July 1888], 310–16; reproduction of crayon portrait in James Alton James, ed., *George Rogers Clark Papers, 1771–1781* [*Collections of the Illinois State Historical Library*, gen. eds. Hiram W. Beckwith et al. (32 vols., Springfield, Ill., 1903–45)], VIII, facing p. 385; "Selections from the Letter-Books of Thomas Wharton of Philadelphia, 1773–1783," *Pa. Mag. of Hist. and Biog.*, XXXIII [Oct. 1909], 455; John C. Fitzpatrick, ed., *The Writings of George Washington from the Original Manuscript Sources, 1745–1799* [39 vols., Washington, D.C., 1931–44], III, 128; Wainwright, "Turmoil at Pittsburgh," *Pa. Mag. of Hist. and Biog.*, LXXXV [Apr. 1961], 138; *The Journal of Nicholas Cresswell, 1774–1777* [New York, 1924], p. 65; Abernethy, *Western Lands and the Am. Rev.*, pp. 87–88, 92–97, 102–14; Thwaites and Kellogg, *Doc. Hist. of Dunmore's War*, pp. 18–20, 35–38).

"LS" is *locus sigilli*, Latin for "place of the seal," a symbol for a seal that was not actually used.

7. The last preceding meeting of the Caroline County committee had been the day before, on 18 May 1775. The sparseness of the entries in the manuscript minute book, accompanied by the fact that the proceedings of the present day are not to be found therein, hints that Samuel Haws, Jr., did not expend the last full measure of devotion in his role as committee clerk.

8. For "his Excellency Lord Dunmore's Letter," see 28 Apr. 1775, Royal Chief Magistracy; for "his Lordship's proclamation," 3 May, same; and for "a letter wrote by a certain Capt. Montague," 4 May, York Co. Committee.

9. For the lack of "intelligence" on this subject, see 11 Apr. 1775, n. 2.

10. For the background of the affair of the gunpowder, see pp. 4–6 above.

11. The next recorded meeting of the Caroline County committee is under the date heading of 8 June 1775.

Saturday, 20 May 1775

Third Virginia Convention

Augusta County West: John Connolly to the Chiefs of the Mingoes [1]

Bretheren

The Great Man of Virginia [2] at this time being engaged in very Important Business which may probably prevent his coming as soon as he could wish or you might reasonably expect in Order to convince his Bretheren the Six Nations [3] that he is not however unmindful of the Situation of some of your friends who lately have imprudently offended against his People has given me Directions to call you together to this Place as soon as Possible in order to brighten the Antient Chain of Friendship [4] and to restore to you in health and Peace the young men of your Nation which have remained here with us this Winter.[5] Your Friend the great Man of Virginia will if possible meet you here, if not he will appoint some person for him to shake hands with his Bretheren the Mingoes and to renew that Friendship between your People ⟨and⟩ the Big Knife which he hopes may never again be shaken

    Given under my hand and seal at Fort Dunmore this 20th. May 1775.

        Signed John Connolly (LS)[6]

> MS transcript, the whole, including Connolly's signature, in hand of James Berwick, in papers of third Virginia Convention (Archives Division, Virginia State Library)

Augusta County West: Alexander McKee to the Chiefs of the Shawnee and the Mingoes

Bretheren   Pittsburgh May 20th. 1775

    As you have now received Messages from your Brother the Governor of Virginia to come to a meeting proposed to be held with you at this Place you will be able to satisfy the uneasiness of your People for their friends detained amongst us and as I hope there is a near Prospect of every thing relative to them and other matters between you and your Brother the Governor of Virginia being settled to your Mutual Satisfaction⟨;⟩ therefore your own anxiety will I make no doubt expedite a few of your chiefs speedily to attend upon this Occasion agreeable to the Invitation you have received and that you will not be Deter'd or pay regard to any Misrepresentations as you may hear

    A String[7]

        Alexr. McKee[8]

        Depy. Agent for Indian Affairs

> MS transcript, the whole, including McKee's signature, in hand of James Berwick (ibid.)

1. The Mingo Indians, one of the northern Iroquois family of tribes, had once resided in central Pennsylvania. To the Dutch they were Minquas; to the French, Andastes; to the English, Susquehannocks and sometimes Conestogas. The name Mingo means "stealthy" or "treacherous." Before the middle of the 18th century these Indians moved to the upper reaches of the Ohio River and, unlike their eastern brethren, remained hostile to the white man. By 1775 they had drifted downstream and established themselves at Mingo Town, near present-day Sandusky, Ohio. For their lack of numbers —estimated in 1766 to consist of 60 families—they compensated by valor in war and extreme savagery in victory (Hodge, *Handbook of Am. Indians*, pt. 1, 867–78; Thwaites and Kellogg, *Doc. Hist. of Dunmore's War*, p. 28 n. 47).

2. Lord Dunmore.

3. The Six Nations were the Cayuga, the Oneida, the Onondaga, the Mohawk, the Seneca, and the Tuscarora. The first 5 were members of the famous Five Nations of the

Iroquois League, which had waxed powerful in Canada and in New York a century before but were now reduced to but about half of their once proud population of 20,000. The Tuscaroras were given a voice in the councils of the league in 1772, after having migrated north following internecine war with the whites and other Indians in the Carolinas. Collectively the Six Nations were the nominal arbiters of all the Indians from the province of Quebec to the colony of Virginia, and from the Hudson River to Detroit (Hodge, *Handbook of Am. Indians*, pt. 1, 844–47; Lewis H. Morgan, *League of Ho-Dé-No-Sau-Nee, or Iroquois* [New York, 1851], pp. 3–29).

4. For the significance of "the Antient Chain of Friendship," see 19 May 1775, n. 5.

5. The "young men" were the hostages whose retention at Fort Pitt was agreed to by the "Terms of our Reconciliation" reached at Camp Charlotte in Oct. 1774 (19 May 1775, n. 3).

6. Fort Pitt, more pretentiously Pittsburgh, had been rebuilt and renamed Fort Dunmore by John Connolly in honor of his governor-patron (19 May 1775, n. 4).

"LS" is *locus sigilli*, Latin for "place of the seal," a symbol for a seal that was not actually used.

7. A leather "String" of wampum was sent with the letter. Wampum was currency among Indians and even among frontiersmen. It was of 2 sorts, white and purple. The white was handworked from large conches into perforated beads. The purple was made from mussel shells and though held to be of more value than the white, was considered less appropriate for use in ceremonies attesting to friendship. If in negotiations the recipient of a string could not return one of at least equal value, he was obliged to give back the one received. This was a practice entirely acceptable to the red men but disesteemed by the white, whence "Indian giving." For matters of great importance, the strings were woven together to form belts about the width of a man's hand.

In active negotiations a belt was given in order to signify the good faith of the speaker. According to Sir William Johnson, the gift of a belt was considered "a Sacred Engagement amongst the Indians," and the object was preserved as a memorandum. When treating, the speaker would usually rise, declaim gravely, and extend the hand in which he held the belt or the string. Upon concluding, he would toss the wampum toward the party addressed and sit down; or if continuing on another subject, he would do so with another belt or string in hand. Diplomatic etiquette dictated that receipt of a belt be acknowledged by the utterance of a whoop (Henry R. Schoolcraft, *Information respecting the History, Condition, and Prospects of the Indian Tribes of the United States* [5 parts, Philadelphia, 1851–55], pt. 3, 185 n. 1; Jacobs, *Diplomacy and Indian Gifts*, pp. 11–28; James Sullivan et al., eds., *The Papers of Sir William Johnson* [13 vols., Albany, 1921–62], II, 500; E[dmund] B. O'Callaghan, ed., *Documents Relative to the Colonial History of the State of New York* . . . [11 vols., Albany, 1856–61; hereafter *N.Y. Col. Docs.*], VI, 966–67).

8. ALEXANDER McKEE had considerable experience in dealing with Indians and may have been part Indian himself. For years he had served as assistant to George Croghan while the latter was deputy to Sir William Johnson, superintendent of Indian affairs of the Northern District. In 1763 Croghan pronounced "Young Mr. McKee" to be "Modist" and a dependable interpreter. Eleven years later, when McKee himself became deputy, Sir William adjudged him "next" to Croghan "not only best acquainted with" but as having the "most influence over these Inds." McKee served as a lieutenant in the French and Indian War, and in Dunmore's War he particularly distinguished himself at Point Pleasant by landing a catfish that weighed 57 pounds. Although McKee was a loyalist, the later claims by Connolly and Dunmore that they had plotted to raise the Indians against the patriots does not prove that he was privy to the alleged scheme. At

the time he signed the present letter, the "Depy. Agent" could hardly have been less than 35 (Thwaites and Kellogg, *Rev. on the Upper Ohio*, pp. 74–75 n. 3; Thwaites and Kellogg, *Doc. Hist. of Dunmore's War*, p. 364; Albert T. Volweiler, *George Croghan and the Westward Movement, 1741–1782* [Cleveland, 1926], pp. 143–44, 177–78, 181, 207, 219, 220, 231–32; Sylvester K. Stevens, Donald H. Kent, et al., eds., *Papers of Col. Henry Bouquet* . . . [mimeographed, Harrisburg, Pa., 1940—], ser. 21649, pt. 1, 82; Sullivan, *Papers of Sir Wm. Johnson*, VIII, 491; Thomas Lynch Montgomery, ed., *Pennsylvania Archives*, 5th ser. [8 vols., Harrisburg, Pa., 1906], I, 182; Connolly, "Narrative," *Pa. Mag. of Hist. and Biog.*, XII [1888], 315–16; P.R.O., A.O. 12/54, fol. 18).

Sunday, 21 May 1775

Third Virginia Convention

Augusta County West: John Connolly to the Chiefs of the Delawares [1]

Bretheren

The great hurry of Business which has for some time past engaged the great Man of Virginia,[2] may possibly prevent him from coming out at this time to see you, Yet mindful of the great friendship that was shewn to his People by his Bretheren the Delawares he has desired me to call in the Chiefs to this Place so that the Chain of Friendship may be brightened and that the regard which he has for his Bretheren the Delawares may be shewn to all Persons [3]

It may so happen that the Great Man may not have the Satisfaction of personally shaking hands with his Bretheren the Delawares But in case that should happen from the important Business in which he is now engaged he will appoint some person for him to assure them of his Steady Friendship and the Remembrance which he has of their Attachment to his people during the late Troubles

Given under my hand & seal at Fort Dunmore this 21st. May 1775.

Signed John Connolly (LS) [4]

> MS transcript, the whole, including Connolly's signature, in hand of James Berwick, in papers of third Virginia Convention (Archives Division, Virginia State Library)

1. A confederacy of 3 tribes belonging to the northern Algonquin stock, the Delawares were the most ancient known inhabitants of the Delaware River Valley, a precedence that entitled them to be called "grandfather" by other Indians in Pennsylvania. The Delaware name, Lenápe, or Leni-Lenápe, means "real men." Divided into

the Munsee (Wolf), Unami (Turtle), and Unalachtogo (Turkey) tribes, the Delawares in the 1720s and 1730s fell under the domination of the Iroquois. Early in the 1740s, such became the pressure of white encroachment on the lands of the Lenápe that they dismantled their wigwams and silently stole away. First they migrated to the Wyoming River Valley and gradually spread westward into the Muskingum River region. Then early in the 1770s they settled on the lands between the Ohio and White rivers in Indiana. Captain Pipe, chief of the Wolf tribe, was an inveterate supporter of lost causes, but of the other chiefs, Newcomer, White Eyes, and Captain Killbuck had preserved a shrewd, if precarious, neutrality during Dunmore's War (Hodge, *Handbook of Am. Indians,* pt. 1, 385–87; Thwaites and Kellogg, *Doc. Hist. of Dunmore's War,* pp. 380–84).

2. Lord Dunmore.

3. See 19 May 1775, n. 5.

4. "LS" is "*locus sigilli,*" Latin for "place of the seal," a symbol for a seal that was not actually used.

Monday, 22 May 1775

Buckingham County Committee

In the Impending Struggle for Dearest Rights

THE committee of the county of Buckingham desire it may be known to the inhabitants of the lower counties, that should any of them, in the impending struggle for our dearest rights, be driven from their habitations, that the people of Buckingham are disposed to give the most friendly reception to as many of the wives, children, and slaves, of those their brethren, as their situations severally will permit, as also, to join them with their whole strength, to restore them to the peaceable and quiet enjoyment of their possessions. Farther, that if any of their said brethren would choose, by way of precaution, to make settlements, and cultivate grain in Buckingham, that, coming with recommendations from their county committees, they may have lands assigned them, and continue on them as their own, until a cessation of the present troubles. Also, that their flocks shall be equally welcome to the woods and fields of the said county, except such part as may propagate the murrain; which, as endangering the common means of subsistence, may be equally fatal to all parties.[1] The committee of Buckingham do not doubt but their sentiments upon the matter in question will be general throughout the interiour counties.[2]

Published by order of the committee, held at the courthouse, the 22d of May, 1775.

Rolfe Eldridge, clerk.

Virginia Gazette (Purdie), 2 June 1775

Isle of Wight County Committee

Reports on a Fruitless Quest

At a Committee held for Isle of Wight County the twenty second day of May in the year of our Lord Christ one thousand seven hundred and seventy five.[3] Present John Scarsbrook Wills Chairman, Josiah Parker, Brewer Godwin, Richard Hardy, John Day, John Mallory, The Reverend Henry John Burges⟨s⟩, Tristram Norsworthy⟨, Jr.⟩, Arthur Smith, Thomas Peirce, Goodrich Willson ⟨Wilson⟩, William Davis, Nathaniel Burwell, John Driver, Henry Pitt, Edmund Godwin, and Jethro Gale Gentlemen.

Committee men appeared and took their seats – – – – – –

John Lawrence, Thomas Fearn, Mills Wilkinson, and Thomas Smith⟨,⟩ Gent., appeared in Committee agreeable to the late election of ten Committee men to be added to the Committee & took their seats accordingly.[4]

Commissioners report from Thos. Nelson Esqr. – – – – – –

Pursuant to a Resolve of this Committee held for this County bearing date the fifteenth day of this Instant, "We the subscribers agreeable thereto waited on Thomas Nelson Junr. Esqr. of the Town of York with the said resolve who directed us to inform the Committee that he could not supply this County with a quantity of Gun Powder whatever, but would advise us to furnish our selves with that Article from Baltimore in Maryland and that he would willingly join us in the adventure, and thanked us for our proffered service to defend the Town of York.⟨"⟩ Arthur Smith, Thomas Peirce, and Nathaniel Burwell.

Commissioners report from Messrs. Andrew & Richd. Mackie – – – – –

Pursuant to a resolve of the Committee for this County bearing date the fifteenth day of this Instant, "We the subscribers applied to Messrs. Andrew and Richard Mackie of this County for a quantity of Gun Powder said to be in their possession, and the said Andrew Mackie from his candid behaviour fully satisfied us that no quantity of that Article remained in his possession but was removed to Sackpoint in the County of Nansemond a few days before, but that he would use the utmost of his endeavors to procure it for us.⟨"⟩ John Sck Wills Thomas Peirce, and Arthur Smith.

Resolved that the Committee be adjourned till the first Saturday in June next.[5]

The Minutes of these proceedings were signed
"John Sck Wills Chairman"

Committee MS minutes, the whole, including Wills's signature, in hand of Francis Young, clerk (Office of county clerk of Isle of Wight County)

Middlesex County Committee

Condemnation of Thomas Haddin

⟨A⟩nd [6] it plainly appearing that he had been summoned, but that he not only refused to appear but expressed himself in terms of the highest contempt, both of the association and committee,

Resolved, therefore, that the said Thomas Haddin be held forth to the public as an enemy to American liberty.

Ordered, that a copy of the above be transmitted to the printer of the Virginia gazette, and that he be requested to print the same.

Lodowick Jones, clerk.

Virginia Gazette (Pinkney), 15 June 1775

Norfolk Borough Committee

William Davies to Prince George County Committee

GENTLEMEN,   NORFOLK, *May* 22, 1775.

As Captain ⟨Charles⟩ Alexander is within your jurisdiction,[7] the committee of this borough are clearly of opinion that they have no authority to take up the matter with respect to his conduct, but only as far as relates to Mr. ⟨James⟩ Marsden. It is therefore the request of this committee, that you will please to resume the consideration of Capt. Alexander's conduct, and take such steps therein as you may think proper. With respect to the part Mr. Marsden took in the matter, Capt. Alexander denies that he was in any wise concerned, and that the facts contained in your letter have been mistaken by you. His testimony here directly contradicts his testimony before you. We therefore send you his examination, taken in writing, and repeatedly read and assented to by him. We shall be glad to be favoured with your answer.

Signed,　　William Davies, Sec'ry.

Captain ALEXANDER's *examination at* NORFOLK *borough.*

Q. Did Mr. Marsden know of your purchasing the linens, &c. from Capt. ⟨James⟩ Fazakerly?

A. I cannot tell positively, but think he did not know of my purchase.

Q. Did Mr. Marsden pay the pork to your order, knowing that it was for part of the purchase of the said linens?

A. He did not.

Q. Did Mr. Marsden send the linens and a parcel of shoes, with an invoice thereof, accompanied with a letter to Mr. Humphrey Richards, signed Marsden, Maxwell, and Co. or not?

A. He did not, but there was a letter directed to me, written by Mr. Marsden's young man (John Elm) in their name.

Q. Was the condition respecting the consent of the Convention, for Capt. Fazakerly to sell his goods, expressed in the order, or not?

A. It was not, but was only agreed to verbally between the Captain and myself.[8]

Virginia Gazette (Dixon and Hunter), 28 October 1775

Prince William County Committee

A Proper and Spirited Conduct

AT a meeting of a special committee for the county of Prince William, held at the house of Thomas Young, in the town of Dumfries, on Monday the 22d of May, 1775.

Present, FOUSHEE TEBBS, *esquire, in the chair:*

William Grayson, Thomas Blackburn, Henry Lee, Andrew Leitch, Richard Graham, William Brent, John Brett, John McMillan, Henry Peyton, John Peyton, Hugh Brent, James Triplet⟨t⟩, Lynaugh Helm, William Tebbs, Thomas Atwell, William Carr, Jesse Ewell, and Cuthbert Harrison, gentlemen of the committee.

A PROCLAMATION by his excellency lord Dunmore, with the advice of his majesty's council, having appeared in the public papers, charging a certain Patrick Henry, and his followers, with rebellious practices, for extorting from the receiver general the sum of three hundred and thirty pounds, in satisfaction for the powder his lordship thought proper to remove from the public magazine in Williamsburg: This committee, having taken the said transaction into their serious consideration, and it appearing to them, from the address of the corporation of the city of Williamsburg, on the removal of the powder, wherein a claim is made, as restitution is required, and no right in government by his excellency at that time alledged, which we conceive he would naturally and necessarily have done if any such had existed, and having also been informed, from respectable authority, that assurances had been given to several gentlemen in Williamsburg by his lordship, that, if no disturbances were raised, the powder should be returned;[9] for these, and other reasons which might be given, they are of opinion, that the powder removed from the public magazine in Williamsburg did of right belong to this colony.

This committee being further of opinion, that the late violent and hostile proceedings of his majesty's troops in the Massachusetts Bay, in attempting to seize the military stores of that colony, would have justified reprisals of a much greater MAGNITUDE,

Resolved, therefore, unanimously, that the thanks of this committee are justly due to captain PATRICK HENRY, and the GENTLEMEN VOLUNTEERS who attended him, for their proper and spirited conduct on that alarming occasion.

Signed by order,   Evan Williams, clerk.

Virginia Gazette (Pinkney), 1 June 1775

1. Murrain is a broad classification for infectious diseases suffered by cattle. It includes anthrax, foot-and-mouth disease, and, as Revolutionary Virginians did not know, "Texas" fever. Ever since 1638 epidemics of this "infectious distemper" had periodically swept through the southern counties of the colony, occasionally to wipe out entire herds. Underbrush and grass were often burned from the forest floor in order to kill the ticks that spread the disease. In 1762 Virginia probably would have quarantined the North Carolina border, to which the plague had spread, had it not been for the intervention of Lt. Gov. Francis Fauquier. He disliked the presence of murrain, but he disliked stoppages of commerce even more (Lewis Cecil Gray, *History of Agriculture in the Southern United States to 1860* [2 vols., Washington, D.C., 1933], I, 146–47).

2. This offer is similar to, but more generous than, than made by the Cumberland County committee on 17 May, and that to be made by the Bedford County committee on 27 June; it would elicit the public thanks of the committee of Charles City County on 23 June 1775.

3. The last preceding meeting of the Isle of Wight County committee had been on 15 May 1775.

4. The "late election" had been ordered by the committee on 17 Apr. 1775.

5. The "first Saturday in June" 1775 was the 3d day, under which date heading the next proceedings of the Isle of Wight County committee will be found.

6. The item begins in the middle of a sentence in the 1st paragraph of a 3-paragraph notice. It was on 17 Apr. 1775 that the committee had summoned Haddin to appear before it on the present date.

7. Captain Alexander had been interrogated by the Prince George County com-

mittee on 8 May 1775. The present item consists of the 6th through the 14th paragraph of a 16-paragraph notice.

8. On 3 July 1775 the Prince George County committee would be pleased "to resume" its investigations of the captain's activities.

9. For the proclamation, see 6 May 1775; for the "address of the corporation of the city of Williamsburg," 21 Apr. 1775, The Capital; for an example of information from "respectable authority," 27 Apr. 1775.

Tuesday, 23 May 1775

Third Virginia Convention

Some Objections in Berkeley County

Mr. ⟨Jacob⟩ Hite having some Objections to the Method that was taken of Advertising the Election of Provincial Delegates for this County desir'd me to certify what I know of the Matter. I do therefore Certify that there never was any Advertisement given me to publish, tho' I have four places of divine Worship to attend in this County. The within Advertisement I saw at the Church Door on Sunday the 24th. Day of April last after I came out of Church, and was informed that it was set up before divine Service began & there I found it last Sunday, when I took it down: [1] Given under my hand this 23 Day of May 1775.

DANIEL STURGES,[2]
Rect⟨o⟩r. of Norborne Parish in Berkeley Co⟨un⟩ty.

> Autograph document, signed; in loose papers of third Virginia Convention (Archives Division, Virginia State Library)

Bedford County Committee

Elections, Reconstitution, and Premium

At which time [3] the said freeholders accordingly met, and unanimously made choice of John Talbot and Charles Lynch, esquires, for their delegates,[4] and the following gentlemen were duly elected for a committee (agreeable to the eleventh article of the general congress) [5] to wit, John Talbot, Charles Lynch, William Mead, Richard Stith, Guy Smith, John F. Patrick ⟨Fitz-

Patrick), James Gallaway, Gross Scruggs, David Rice, Edmund Winston, James Steptoe, John Ward, John Callaway, William Callaway, junior, John Quarles, Simon Miller, Haynes Morgan, William Leftwich, William Trigg, and George Stovall. Then the said committee immediately proceeded to business, and entered into the following resolves.

Resolved unanimously, that John Talbot, gentleman, be appointed chairman of this committee.

Resolved, that Robert Alexander be appointed clerk of this committee.

Resolved, that as gunpowder is much wanted in this county, and finding from experience that every article made use of in the manufacturing of it, except sulphur (of which we have not yet made trial) can be easily procured here, we will give a premium of TEN POUNDS current money to any person who shall first produce to this committee 25 pounds of good sulphur, with an authentic certificate that the same was refined from materials in this colony.[6]

Robert Alexander, clerk.

Virginia Gazette (Pinkney), 8 June 1775

To Call Upon John Hook

At a meeting of the Committee for Bedford County the 23d Day of May 1775.

John Talbot Gent. in the Chair.

Whereas it has been represented to this Committee from Undoubted Authority that John Hook Mercht. in the Town of New London hath lately conducted himself in such manner as this Committee think it their Indispensible Duty to call upon him to answer for the same; It is therefore resolved that James Steptoe Gent. do wait on him and inform of this Order to appear before this Committee at the next Meeting.[7]

A Copy.

ROBERT ALEXANDER Clk.

Autograph document, signed, John Hook Papers (Manuscripts Department, Duke University Library)

Westmoreland County Committee

Note on provenance. The fact that any other than scattered newspaper accounts of the proceedings of the Westmoreland Co. committee are now available for this period is a debt owed to the curiosity of the Philadelphia artist James Reid Lambdin. While supervising architectural repairs at Mount Vernon during the Civil War, he observed some workmen warming themselves at fires started by igniting leaves torn from a "quaint old book." The few remaining manuscript pages contained records of meetings of the county committee and of a meeting of the "commissioners nominated by the committee of the said county, and commissioned by the committee of safety of this colony." It is probable that the volume was once the possession of John Augustine Washington, the brother of the master of Mount Vernon and the father of Bushrod Washington, who later inherited the estate. The destruction of the greater part of the manuscript suggests the kindred fates of many other Virginia records of the Revolution. A portion of what Lambdin rescued is now in the Charles Allen Munn Collection in the Fordham University Library. In 1890 the records of the two committee meetings printed in the present volume were still in traceable private possession.

Censures, Orders, and Certification

At a committee held at Westmoreland Courthouse
The 23d day of May 1775.
Present: The Revd Tho⟨ma⟩s Smith, chairman, W⟨illia⟩m Bernard, Phil⟨ip⟩: ⟨S⟩mith, Jno. Aug⟨ustine⟩: Washington, Richard Parker, Tho⟨ma⟩s Chilton, Rich⟨ar⟩d. Buckner, Rich⟨ar⟩d. Lee, W⟨illia⟩m Peirce ⟨Pierce⟩, Jos⟨eph⟩: Pierce, John Ashton, Fleet Cox, Sam⟨ue⟩l Rust, John Turbenville ⟨Turberville⟩, Edw⟨ar⟩d Sanford, James Davenport.

This committee having taken into considn the address of the citizens of Wmsburg presented to his excelly the govr on the 21st day of April last past and his excelly's verbal ansr thereto, as also his speech to the council of the 2d of may & the porcl: on the next day in consequence of the advice given him by a majority of the said council, look upon themselves as indispens'bly bound to declare their sentiments thereon, as well as to expose the inimical measures of men in high office, for a long time steadily pursued against the just rights of a loyal people and to take off the odium they have endeavoured by some late proceedings to fix upon this colony.[8]

The seizing upon the powder [9] confessedly placed in the magazine for the defence and protection of this colony by order of his excelly the govr was a step by no means to be justified, even upon the supposition of its being lodged there from on board of a man-of-war, as his lordship in his procl: asserted, although in his verbal ansr to the address of the citizens of Wmsbrg, he has tacitly acknowledged the powder to belong to the country, by agreeing to deliver it up, that is the same powder they demand as the country's; and we have been informed that the country had powder in the magazine wh cannot now be found there. We therefore consider the removing the powder privately, and when that part of the country was, as his address confesses, in a very critical situation, to be part of that cruel and determined plan of a wicked _____,[10] to enslave the colonies by first depriving them of the means of resistance, and DO [11] RESOLVE,

1st That the dissatisfaction discovered by the people of this country, and the late commotions raised in some parts thereof, proceeded, not as his address in his procol: has injuriously and inimically charged, from a disaffection to his Majesty's Government, or to a design of changing the form thereof, but from a well grounded alarm, occasioned altogether by the governor's late conduct which clearly evinced his steady pursuit of the beforementioned ministerial plan to enslave us.

2nd That so much of his excelly's procl: which declares "the real grievances of the colony can only be obtained by loyal and constitutional application" is an insult to the understanding of mankind, inasmuch as it is notorious, that this, and the other colonies upon this continent, have repeatedly heretofore, made those applications which have ever been treated with contumely, and as his lordship since the late unhappy differences between G. Britain and the colonies have subsisted, hath deprived us of the constitutional mode of application by refusing to have an assembly.[12]

3d That so far from endeavoring or desiring to subvert our ancient, and to erect a new form of government, we will, at the risque of our lives and fortunes support and defend it as it exists and was exercised until the year 1763 and that his lordship by misrepresenting the good people of this colony as well in his letters to the British minister,[13] as in his late Procl: hath justly forfeited this confidence.

4th That his Majesty's council who advised the procl: beforementioned have not acted as they were bound to do from their station in government, which ought to have led them to be Mediators between the first Magistrate and the people, rather than to join in fixing an unjust and cruel stigma on their fellow subjects.

5th That the thanks of this com: are justly due to the delegates of the late continental congress, and to the delegates from the colony particularly, for their purdent, wise and active conduct in asserting the liberties of America: and that the design of government which in some instances we are informed, has already been carried into execution to deprive them of their offices, civil and military, tends manifestly to disturb the minds of the people in general, and that we consider every person advising such a measure, or who shall accept of any office or preferment of which any of the noble assertors of American liberty have been deprived, as an Enemy to his country.[14]

Ordered that the foregoing RESOLUTIONS be forthwith sent to the printer to be published in the *Gazette*.[15]

Fleet Cox, Gent: is appointed Treasurer to this committee.

A claim of Daniel Marmaduke for riding to summon the committee of 20/

Also a claim of Job Shadrick for the same service 20/

Also a claim of same for another service of same kind 6/

Ordered that the Treasurer pay the above claim out of the money in his hands.

Ordered that the Treasurer out of the money in his hands pay James Muse his account of £2.9–for his expenses in furnishing the guards appointed to guard the powder lately purchased for the use of this committee.[16]

Resolved That every merchant or factor[17] who shall import European goods into this country from any other colony or district, shall before he be permitted to sell such goods produce to the chairman or anyone of this committee, a certificate from the Committee of the Colony county or district from whence such goods were purchased of their having been imported agreeable to the terms of the association of the continental congress.[18]

Thos Smith[19]

Magazine of American History with Notes and Queries, XXIII (Apr. 1890), 339–41

1. The "Advertisement" is under the date heading of 24 Apr. 1775, Third Va. Convention, Berkeley, and was an enclosure in the present document. "Mr. Hite" and 103 other men "having some Objections" framed and signed a petition to the convention praying for a new election, for which see 7 June 1775.

2. Little is known of Rev. DANIEL STURGES, except that at this time, when he was perhaps 30 years of age, he was 4 years into his 1st pastorate. He was to serve Norborne Parish for a total of 15 years, and according to that earnest church chronicler Bishop Meade, "tradition" would speak "well of him" ([William] Meade, *Old Churches, Ministers and Families of Virginia* [2 vols., Philadelphia, 1861], II, 297).

3. The present item consists of part of the 4th and the whole of the 5th through the 7th paragraph of a 7-paragraph notice. The portion immediately preceding contains the proceedings of the Bedford County committee on 25 Apr. 1775.

4. See 13 Apr. 1775, n. 1.

5. That is, the "eleventh article" of the Continental Association, for which see 8 Apr. 1775, n. 5.

6. For the recommendation of the second Virginia Convention that the manufacture of gunpowder be encouraged, see 25 Apr. 1775, n. 2.

7. The "next Meeting" of the Bedford County committee was to be on 27 June 1775. Hook would complain that "the Particular charges exhibited" against him had not been "fully expressed in the summons" and ask that details be given him "expressly in writing," that he could make his "Innocence appear" (17 June 1775, Bedford Co. Committee).

8. The "address of the citizens of Wmsburg" and "his excelly's verbal answr thereto" are under the date heading indicated, The Capital. The governor's "speech to the council" and his "procl: on the next day" are also under the date headings respectively indicated, Royal Chief Magistracy. It is perhaps worth noting that although Dunmore's proclamation of 3 May was announced as having resulted from the advice of his Council, and although John Page was listed as then being present, the Westmoreland County committee may have used "majority" not in the sense of a majority of the whole Council but of a majority of those attending. It is highly possible that Page's adherence to "Whiggish principles" was well known. At least his patriotism would be so well established by 17 Aug. 1775 that 70 members of the third Virginia Convention would unite to vote him 3d place on the Virginia Committee of Safety (Procs. and n. 7, 4th para.).

9. For the "seizing upon the powder," see pp. 4–6 above.

10. Why James Davenport, who served as the clerk of the committee, should have at this point left a space blank (assuming that he did and the transcription is accurate) is unclear. In the *Va. Gazette* (Pinkney) of 1 June 1775, the blank is filled by the word "administration," a noun scarcely offensive to good taste.

11. In the source the verbal is printed as a meaningless infinitive, "TO RESOLVE." It is here rendered as Pinkney printed it on 1 June 1775.

12. His Lordship had on 12 May (Third Va. Convention, n. 1) summoned the General Assembly to convene on 1 June 1775. The reference is therefore to the fact that the Assembly had not met since 26 May 1774, when it was suddenly dissolved, nor productively (and then only during a brief session) since 15 Mar. 1773.

13. For published extracts of Dunmore's letter of 24 Dec. 1774 to Lord Dartmouth, see 28 Apr. 1775, Royal Chief Magistracy.

14. The basis of this information is unknown. It was in fact rather a mild "design" when compared to others described according to the most "unquestionable authority." In the supplement of Pinkney's *Va. Gazette* of 28 Apr. 1775 and in Dixon and Hunter's newspaper of the day following, there was an announcement under a London dateline that the British ministry had dispatched to Gen. Thomas Gage a "Black List" of designated "rebel" leaders; that he had been empowered to bring them to trial and execution; and that among them was Peyton Randolph. Then on 5 May 1775 the supplement of Purdie's gazette contained the statement that from declarations made in Parliament, it was certain that the consequences of submission to Great Britain would be "execution of all those who stood forth for the people, and a confiscation of their estates." Thomas Jefferson also believed himself to have received the "honor" of having his name "enrolled in a bill of attainder" that was "suppressed in embryo by the hasty step of events" (P. L. Ford, *Works of Jefferson*, I, 16–17). The only clear fact attending this subject is that the propaganda was itself credited as factual.

15. In Pinkney's *Va. Gazette* of 1 June 1775 the contents of the 2d through the 8th paragraphs were printed; in Purdie's supplement of 22 July 1775 the final resolution was printed.

16. The gunpowder (representing one of the few successful purchases by a county committee) was acquired pursuant to a resolution of the second Virginia Convention (13 Apr. 1775, n. 4).

17. In the present source the word is "tractor," which in its lone usage in 1775 meant "one who or that which draws or pulls."

18. For previous examples of the certification of imports imposed by county committees, see 8 May 1775, Prince George Co. Committee and n. 13.

19. The excerpts in the *Va. Gazette* (Pinkney), 1 June, and ibid. (Purdie), 2 June 1775, supplement, as well as the one resolution in ibid. (Purdie), 22 July 1775, appear over the signature of James Davenport, member and clerk of the committee.

Thursday, 25 May 1775

Lancaster County Committee

Evidence of Attachment to Once Happy Constitution

THE committee of Lancaster county, on the 25th day of May, 1775, taking into consideration his Excellency Lord Dunmore's address to the Council, and their recommendation and proclamation issued in consequence thereof,[1] hold they are necessarily bound to justify themselves and their constituents from such cruel imputations and assertions, and that such proclamation must tend to excite a belief of an intention to change the government, or raise convulsions in the state.

That the behaviour of some of the people in this colony, alluded to, originated in a full assurance of the determined bloody plan to enslave the colonies, manifested in various instances and ungracious encroachments, and more particularly and immediately in his Excellency's clandestine removal of the powder from the public magazine of the colony.[2]

That his Excellency's ill-founded and injurious charge, to criminate the body of people in this colony, is hostile, and cannot be justified; therefore, he has forfeited the confidence of the inhabitants of this country.

That those members of his Majesty's Council who recommended and assisted in such proclamation, and also since gave their advice to the good people of this country, prefaced with cruel and indecent allegations, manifestly implying seditious and rebellious actions, tending to raise bitter dissentions and animosities, acted without prudence, policy, moderation, or generosity; and we are most sensibly aggrieved, that those whose duty and high department should warm them to every mode of reconciliation, should not only countenance, but themselves become incendiaries to fix, by their publication, a stigma by such an unmerited stricture on their brethren and fellow sufferers.[3]

That our application for redress of grievances, so justly founded, so often and vainly repeated, our long sufferance and forbearance under such unfellow-feeling, unrelented measures, and our ardent wishes and endeavours for a reconciliation, by the restitution of our just rights and privileges as we enjoyed them in the year 1763, evinces our attachment to our once happy constitution, and our allegiance to our gracious Sovereign.

We, in order to exculpate ourselves and our constituents from such heinous maledictions, and to convince the world of our upright intentions, pledge ourselves to support the constitution, and his Majesty King George III. in all his just rights and prerogatives, with our lives and fortunes.

Published by order of the committee.

Virginia Gazette (Dixon and Hunter), 10 June 1775

Norfolk Borough Town Meeting

A Determination to Give No Encouragement

To The Public.

The inhabitants of the borough of Norfolk, in town meeting assembled, being informed that captain Collins ⟨Henry Colins⟩, of the Magdalen armed schooner, is endeavouring to dispose of a sloop seized by him lately belonging to John Bowdoin, esquire, of the Eastern shore; and being also further informed, that the said Collins has made application to some persons for the purchase of a pilot boat, probably with an intention to convert her into a tender, to distress the trade of this or some other colony: [4] The inhabitants of this borough are therefore determined to give no encouragement to him, or any such men, nor purchase any of their prizes from them, nor in the least contribute to their emolument by bidding for the plunder of our countrymen; nor will we sell any pilot boat or any other vessel to them for their hostile purposes, nor in any respect have any kind of dealings with them. And the inhabitants of this borough, assembled as aforesaid, do further resolve, to have no dealing with any person that, in spite of the ties of duty and attachment to his country, shall counteract these our resolutions, by granting any assistance for the destruction of our rights and properties, or of any other of the good people of the confederated colonies. And we invite all persons to accede to this resolution.

May 25, 1775.   Test. William Davies, secretary.

Virginia Gazette (Pinkney), 1 June 1775

Richmond County Committee

Industrious Circulation of an Address, together with a Proposition

RICHMOND *County, May 25, 1775.*

In Committee, LANDON CARTER, *Esq; in the Chair.*

As his Majesty's Council have judged it proper to publish an admonitory address to the community at large, we should think ourselves wanting in respect to the deliberations of that Honourable Board not to consider it with the strictest attention.[5] We have done so accordingly; and as we find that the matter of the address is not only exceptionable, but are farther informed, that it is industriously circulated among the people, together with a proposition lately made in the House of Commons by Lord North, which covers the most insidious and dangerous views, under an artful guise of wisdom, humanity, and peace, we should be wanting in a much higher duty to ourselves, and our constituents, should we fail to animadvert on both with freedom and decency.[6] We cannot, then, but think,

1. That the mild professions of regard for the prosperity and welfare of this country, in the first part of the address, are inconsistent with the passionate expressions of detestation and abhorrence for the spirit in the people by which alone the liberties of this country can be secured. We confess we are entire strangers to any licentious and ungovernable spirit prevailing. If the Honourable Gentlemen mean to brand the late commotions with these appel-

lations, we are compelled to observe, that no person can so unjustly and uncharitably construe them, unless he entirely turn aside from the violent and provoking measures which justify them; for it cannot be expected that the people should continue quiet when every violence is offered to their privileges and prosperity, or that they should tamely suffer the foundation of their constitution to be overturned by a too scrupulous adherence to its form.

2. That their inviting and exhorting us to mild and constitutional modes of application clearly implies, that they esteem our former proceedings in this respect violent and irregular. The justice of this charge we leave to be decided by the world; who are in possession, and who have given ample testimony in favour of the many suppliant, wise, and firm applications, which have been addressed to the several branches of the British legislature.

3. We allow all due weight to the pledges of their friendship, which the Honourable Council have among us; and we hope that their integrity may ever be an effectual antidote to the influence of that servile and baneful spirit which we are authorized (by the explicit declarations of many independent and respectable members of both Houses of Parliament) to say, prevail extremely in this age, with men in office.

With respect to the proposition of Lord North above-mentioned, insultingly called, by *ministerial tools*, the OLIVE BRANCH, we are of opinion that it offers no kind of redress (even if the colonies should submit) of any one of the many grievances under which they now labour; for in the only instance in which a seeming redress is proposed (that of taxation) the Parliament of Great Britain is to settle the *quantum* to be raised by each colony, and the application thereof, the colonies determining only on the mode of levying.

This by no means is a relief to them, but in fact puts them in a worse situation than ever, as they thereby will fully acknowledge the absolute power of the British Parliament, and we are still to have the sword hang over our heads, ready to fall on such as shall in any instance disoblige the minister, or refuse to obey his dictates. Lord North himself declared his intention was only to divide the colonies, and thereby the more easily subdue them.[7] The selecting out Governor ⟨Thomas⟩ Pownal⟨l⟩'s speech alone, approving the motion, when so many excellent speeches were made exposing the measure, and setting its treachery and absurdity in a clear and evident light, is a certain proof of the design in the King's officers here to mislead the good people of this colony.[8]

By order of the committee.
Le Roy Peachy, clerk.

Virginia Gazette (Purdie), 2 June 1775, supplement

Williamsburg Independent Company

Proffer of Life and Fortune

At a meeting of the WILLIAMSBURG VOLUNTEER COMPANY, held the 25th day of May 1775

Resolved, that every member of this company *oblige themselves*, by the ties of honour and duty to their country, to march, on the smallest warning, to any part of the continent, where the general cause of American liberty may demand their attendance, provided that they do not by such step leave their own country in a defenseless state.

Resolved, that it is the opinion of this company, that the landing of any foreign troops in this country will be, at the present critical juncture of affairs, a most dangerous attack on the liberties of this country; and that this company will, therefore, keep the most watchful eye on any movement from this quarter, that they will consult their fellow countrymen in the different parts of this province on this head, and, should they find an unanimity of sentiment to prevail throughout this country respecting that particular, they are determined, with the aid and assistance of their fellow subjects, to resist all such arbitrary measures, at the expence of life and fortune.[9]

John Brown, clerk.

Virginia Gazette (Pinkney), 25 May 1775

1. For His Excellency's "address" to his "Council, and their recommendation and proclamation issued in consequence thereof," see 2 May, 3 May 1775, Royal Chief Magistracy.

2. For the "clandestine removal of the powder," see pp. 4–6 above.

3. The "advice" of the Council is under the date heading of 15 May 1775, Royal Magistracy.

4. Lieutenant Colins was plying the waters between and at the mouths of the James and York rivers in attempted enforcement of the navigation and the trade acts (Clark, *Naval Docs. of the Am. Rev.*, I, 122–23, 138, 500; 15 May 1775, Third Va. Convention and nn. 7, 8).

5. The "admonitory address" is under the date heading of 15 May 1775, Royal Magistracy. Because the address was being "industriously circulated" by broadside, the committee, with equal industry, caused to be struck off a broadside of its own (a copy of which is in the John Carter Brown Library) identical in contents with the present source.

6. The "proposition lately made" was that contained in Lord North's Olive Branch, the terms and some of the debates attending which were made public in the *Va. Gazette* (Purdie), 28 Apr. 1775, supplement, and ibid. (Dixon and Hunter) of 29 Apr. 1775, supplement, 20 May 1775.

7. In the *Va. Gazette* (Purdie), 28 Apr. 1775, supplement, Lord North was reported

as admitting "that he rather imagined this proposition would not be to the *taste* of the Americans, and would not be complied with by several of the colonies. However, if but ONE of them submitted, that ONE link of the chain would be broken; and if so, the whole would inevitably fall to pieces. This separation would restore our empire, and *divide et impera* ⟨'divide and rule'⟩ was a maxim never held unfair or unwise in government."

8. In Purdie's *Va. Gazette* of 28 Apr. 1775, supplement, several speeches were reported as being made by the opposition. In the Dixon and Hunter issue of 20 May 1775 there was printed only the speech delivered in the House of Commons by former Massachusetts governor Pownall. He declared that he had "always been an advocate for the colonies, and the rights of the British subjects in America," but that when he saw "that the Americans are actually resisting" the authority of the government, he felt compelled to seize upon North's proposal as offering the last chance to "open a door to reconciliation upon such terms as shall establish the authority of this country, and give security to the rights and liberty of America."

Just how the Richmond County committee accounted for the "selecting out" by the "King's officers" of a single speech to be printed by Dixon and Hunter poses a question not easily answered; but if there was a warning here that does not meet the editorial eye, it possibly met that of William Hunter, whose tory bent may have been suspected by his contemporaries (Lorenzo Sabine, *Biographical Sketches of Loyalists of the American Revolution, with an Historical Essay* [2 vols., Boston, 1864], I, 557).

At the same time, it is to be noted that in taking a stand in opposition to the adoption of the provisions of the Olive Branch even before its official presentation to the General Assembly, the committee was in effect instructing the Richmond County burgesses—Robert Wormeley Carter and Francis Lightfoot Lee—as to their expected deportment on that subject. On 27 May 1775 the committee of Frederick County will be discovered taking a like stand and instructing the county burgesses outright.

9. How widely the Williamsburg independent company "consulted" their fellow countrymen is not demonstrable. There are extant only 4 responses that reached print: those of the Albemarle County committee, on 31 May; the Albemarle independent company, on 1 June (qq.v. below); the Hanover County volunteer company, on 8 June; and the Lancaster County volunteer company, on 9 June 1775 (*Va. Gazette* [Dixon and Hunter], 17 June 1775; ibid. [Pinkney], 19 June 1775).

If the volunteers in the capital city had "consulted" with those in Botetourt County, the former would have found the latter cool to this suggestion—at least according to the rumors abroad in Bedford County "someti[me] in the month of May" (26 June 1775, Bedford Co. Committee).

Friday, 26 May 1775

Loudoun County Committee

To Hazard All the Blessings of This Life

At a meeting of the committee of Loudoun county, held at Leesburg on Friday, May 26, 1775.

Present, Francis Peyton, esquire, Josias Clapham, Thomas Lewis, Anthony Russell, John Thomas, George Johnston, Thomas Shore, James Lane, Jacob Reed, Leven Powell, William Smith, Robert Jamison, Hardage Lane, and John Lewis, gentlemen.

THE committee taking into consideration the conduct of the governor relative to the powder, which was by his express orders taken secretly out of the public magazine, belonging to this colony, in the night of the 20th ult. and carried on board the Magdalin schooner,[1]

Resolved, *nemine contradicente*, that his lordship, by this and other parts of his conduct, which have lately transpired, has not only forfeited the confidence of the good people of this colony, but that he may be justly esteemed an enemy to America; and that as well his excuse published in his proclamation of the 4th instant, as his verbal answer to the address presented him on that occasion by the city of Williamsburg,[2] are unsatisfactory, and evasive, and reflect, in our opinion, great dishonour on the general assembly and inhabitants of this colony, as from the latter a suspicion may be easily deduced that the representatives of the people are not competent judges of the place wherein arms and ammunition, intended for the defense of the colony, may be safely lodged, and that the inhabitants (unlike other subjects) cannot, *in prudence*, be trusted with the means necessary for their protection from insurrections, or even invasions; so in the former a very heavy charge is exhibited against the best men among us *of seducing their fellow subjects from their duty and allegiance;* a charge we are confident, not founded in reality, and which, we believe, is construed out of the discharge of that duty, which every good man is under, to point out to his weaker countrymen, in the day of public trial, the part they should act, and explain, on constitutional principles, the nature of their allegiance, the ground of which, we fervently pray, may never be removed, whose force we desire may never with reason be relaxed, but yet may be subservient to considerations of superior regard.

The committee being informed by some of the officers who commanded the troops of this county, that marched on the above occasion, that the reason of their marching no farther than Fredericksburg was their having received repeated requests from the honourable Peyton Randolph, esquire, to return home, assuring them that the *peaceable* citizens of Williamsburg were under no apprehension of danger, either in their persons or properties, that the public treasury and records were perfectly safe, and that there was no necessity for their proceeding and farther, three of the other delegates appointed to the continental congress, the only civil power we know of in this great struggle for liberty, being of the same opinion.[3]

Resolved, *nemine contradicente*, that we cordially approve the conduct of our countrymen, captain Patrick Henry, and the other volunteers of Hanover county, who marched under him, in making reprisals on the king's property for the trespass committed as aforesaid; and that we are determined to hazard all the blessings of this life rather than suffer the smallest injury offered to their persons or estates, on this account, to pass unrewarded with its equal punishment.[4]

Resolved, *nemine contradicente*, that it be recommended to the representatives of this county, as the opinion of this committee, that they by no means agree to the reprisals, taken as aforesaid, being returned.[5]

Ordered, that the clerk transmit immediately a copy of the preceding resolves to the printers of the Virginia and Pennsylvania gazettes, to be published.[6] By order of the committee.

George Johnston, clerk.

Virginia Gazette (Pinkney), 1 June 1775

Richmond County Committee

Landon Carter to Alexander Purdie: An Open Letter [7]

MR. PURDIE,

ALTHOUGH it may certainly seem beneath any sensible Gentleman, who has lived to an extreme great age,[8] preserving an unexceptionable character, as well in his publick capacity as in his private life, to take notice of any of the flirts [9] thrown out against him in print, yet there seem to be some creatures in the world who require a just reprehension, lest they become too *impertinent* for the society they live in. Of this sort is a certain JOHN FOWLER, who, in John Pinkney's paper of the 18th of May,[10] seems purposely designed to level some malice against me, for what cause (I thank God) I know not, unless he should be the same John Fowler who many years ago disputed my right to my own land, by making a short cut through it to a ferry to which he was going. First when I met him, I asked him if he had not mistaken his road, and was with great pertness answered, I had no right to ask that question in the King's highway; on which I endeavoured to convince him of my right, and upon his submission I let him go, desiring he would never more take that liberty.

His performance in Pinkney suggests a matter handed to you on the 17th of last February, as from the chairman of a respectable committee.[11] Would it not be reasonable for a man really *fearful* of purchasing displeasure from that *respectable body to* be fearful of *purchasing* it at the expense of truth? Such therefore must his atrocious intention be against me, in my private character, that he would not forbear taking that opportunity of wounding me in the capacity of chairman of that committee, if he could. Therefore, he represents the proceedings of that committee as being the transaction of the *chairman* alone; but as Fowler was not present, would not a little decency, if not common sense, have instructed him that his information must be base, as it is very remarkable it was in this particular instance? [12]

The complaint against the apprentice selling his goods from his vessel, against the ninth article of the association, was made by one of the members of the committee; and as the evidences were present, the committee immediately went into the inquiry, and finding cause to examine further, sent their messenger to summon this apprentice, and the skipper of the vessel (rendered before obnoxious to the committee of Gloucester for the same proceedings within their precinct) to appear before the committee the next day. Accordingly they did appear; and the chairman, only out of duty, acquainted them with the charge. Upon examination of the evidences before them, the whole committee (pretty numerous), came to those resolutions sent to your press under the hand of Richard Parker clerk *pro tempore;* but during the examination, as chairman, I dare challenge any man to say that I entered farther into the matter than to move their lenity to the apprentice.

However, Fowler has thought proper to suggest, that the determination, though pacifick, was no fault of the chairman, because he proposed to resolve that if his vessel was not removed out of the river in 24 hours that any one should be at liberty to set her on fire and burn her. Worthless indeed! and abandoned against the truth, must such a confident mortal be to assert and propagate so scandalous a report, which the whole committee and persons (very numerous) present, can declare, upon oath, had not the least foundation, in one word or sentiment. How stupid then must his appeal be upon the rigid proceedings of the chairman, when it was only the invention of his own malicious brain? [13]

Sabine Hall, May 26, 1775.   Landon Carter.

Virginia Gazette (Purdie), 30 June 1775, supplement

Attached Certification

Having attended the whole of the above mentioned examination, I can with confidence assure the publick, that no motion to burn the vessel, as charged by Mr. Fowler, was made to the committee, either by the chairman or any other person; and I think the proposal for treating Mr. ⟨John⟩ Blatt⟨, Jr.⟩ the said Fowler's apprentice, on account of his youth, with lenity, came from the chair. And I do farther certify, that the same day, when said Fowler came to the courthouse, I shewed him the proceedings of the committee, as sent to the committee of Fairfax, who were requested to take cognizance of the matter, as he lived in that county, and therefore he had a very early knowledge of the determination of the Richmond committee.

Richard Parker.[14]

Ibid., 30 June 1775, supplement

1. For the "conduct of the governor relative to the powder," see pp. 4–6 above.

2. His Lordship's proclamation is under the date heading of 4 May 1775, Royal Chief Magistracy, his "verbal answer" to the Williamsburg Common Hall under that of 21 Apr. 1775, The Capital, 2d entry.

3. For "the reason of their marching," see pp. 6–7 above, and for the "requests from the honourable Peyton Randolph, esquire," 27 Apr. 1775, The Capital. According to

the contemporary observation of James Madison, Jr., the 3 other delegates "of the same opinion" were George Washington, Richard Henry Lee, and Edmund Pendleton (Hutchinson and Rachal, *Papers of Madison*, I, 144). For the second Continental Congress to be the "only civil power" the committeemen of Loudoun County recognized "in this great struggle for liberty" may have been also their issuance of an oblique invitation to the House of Burgesses, upon its being convened on 1 June 1775, to fill the colonial void, or should the House be dissolved or unseasonably prorogued, to the third Virginia Convention not to resolve and recommend but to resolve and ordain.

4. For the "conduct" of Captain Henry "and the other volunteers of Hanover county," see pp. 7–11 above; 9 May 1775, Hanover Co. Committee.

5. What efforts Clapham and Peyton, the delegates for Loudoun County, made to forward the "opinion of this committee" is not evident in the journal of the convention of 17 July–26 Aug. 1775; but on 25 Aug. the majority of that assemblage would order part of the "reprisals" returned (Procs. and n. 7).

6. A copy of these proceedings appeared in the *Pennsylvania Gazette* of 14 June 1775.

7. The present editors have taken the freedom of resetting Colonel Carter's single-paragraph letter in 4 paragraphs.

8. The "extreme great age" of the writer was 64 years (Greene, *Diary of Colonel Landon Carter*, I, 3).

9. Beside its more familiar signification, in the 17th and 18th centuries a "flirt" connoted a sharp rap or blow by finger or fist, or a stroke of wit delivered either as a jest or a jeer, in which last sense Carter used the noun.

10. See 17 Apr. 1775, Richmond Co. Committee.

11. For the background of this "matter," see *Rev. Va.*, II, 234–35, 279, 280–81.

12. In the newspaper the interrogative sentence is ended by a period.

13. If to this blast John Fowler conjured up a reply from the depths of his "own malicious brain," it is not to be found among Colonel Carter's extant papers or in any public print.

14. The subscriber was probably Richard Parker, Jr., the son of Carter's old friend Richard Parker of Westmoreland County. The younger man had been serving as clerk pro tempore to the Richmond County committee since 6 Feb. 1775 (Greene, *Diary of Colonel Landon Carter*, I, 583 and n. 23; *Rev. Va.*, II, 279, 282).

Saturday, 27 May 1775

Frederick County Committee

Unanimity and a Twisting of the Olive Branch

Frederick county committee, May 27, 1775.
Resolved unanimously, THAT the thanks of this committee be presented to the Rev. Charles Minn ⟨Mynn⟩ Thruston, and Col. Isaac Zane⟨, Jr.⟩, who

represented this county in the late Convention, from a just sensibility of a faithful discharge of the trust reposed in them.[1]

Resolved unanimously, that this committee do recommend to the representatives of this county to use their influence, in the ensuing session of Assembly, to procure adequate satisfaction to the officers and soldiers who bravely ventured their lives, in defence of their country, in the late expedition against the Indians; and also to those who advanced their property, on the credit of the publick, for the support of the army.[2]

Whereas it is expected that proposals will be made to the Assembly, on behalf of administration, to levy a certain sum of money annually, disposable by Parliament, it is therefore earnestly recommended to our representatives to oppose such proposal to the utmost of their abilities, and to express their determined resolution to reject any proposition whatever, which may be offered, while an armed force remains on this continent, for the purpose of compelling submission to parliamentary mandates; and every requisition for levying money on their constituents, coming through any other channel than the official servants of the crown; the uses to which such monies are to be applied being always expressed in such requisitions. And we would have it understood, as the sense of this committee, that no measures with administration, which may affect the liberties of America, ought to be agreed to, on behalf of this colony, without the concurrence of our sister colonies.[3]

Resolved unanimously, that the several arbitrary and illegal proclamations lately issued by Lord Dunmore, *his* seizure of the colony powder, and his gross misrepresentations of the state of this colony to the ministry, render it highly necessary to regard with *peculiar* attention whatever comes through *his* hands.[4]

Ordered, that the clerk transmit a copy of the above to the publick printer.

William Heth, clerk.

Virginia Gazette (Purdie), 7 June 1775, supplement

1. The "late Convention" was that held in Richmond, 20–27 Mar. 1775.

2. The "late expedition against the Indians" was Dunmore's War of 1774, for which see *Rev. Va.*, II, 105–7. For the effort "to procure adequate satisfaction" for the veterans and their dependent survivors, see 16 May 1775, Augusta Co. West Committee and n. 10.

3. The proposals expected to be made to the General Assembly "on behalf of administration" were those contained in Lord North's Olive Branch (for which see pp. 11–12 above). The "representatives of this county" in the House of Burgesses were James Wood and Isaac Zane, Jr. Rather obviously, the "concurrence of our sister colonies" respecting any "measures" of the British ministry would best be left to the colonies as in second Continental Congress assembled, which was not quite what Lord North was reported as intending (25 May 1775, Richmond Co. Committee and n. 7).

4. The "proclamations lately issued" were those under the date headings of 3 and 6 May 1775, Royal Chief Magistracy. For Dunmore's "seizure of the colony powder," see pp. 4–6 above; for his "gross misrepresentations," 28 Apr. 1775, Royal Chef Magistracy.

Wednesday, 31 May 1775

Albemarle County Committee

They Had Not Broke the Resolves

At a Committee, held on 31st May, it was agreed they had not, by their not marching, broke the resolves of the Committee.[1]

> Autograph diary and Revolutionary memoranda of
> Dr. George Gilmer (Virginia Historical Society)

Committee to the Gentlemen Volunteers of the
Williamsburg Independent Company

Gentlemen,

THE committee, for the county of Albemarle, rejoice at the spirit shewn by the independent company of Williamsburg, and they are determined, with them, to look on the landing of armed force, in this colony, not only as a dangerous attack, but as an open declaration of war, and will, with all their might, at all events, endeavour to oppose it, and every arbitrary proceeding; and we think it would be proper to fix on some general, and certain method, of communicating an alarm.[2]

We hope that all apostates to the American cause will be properly stigmatized by the assembly.[3]

With great respect, we remain, gentlemen, your very humble servants,

Isaac Davis, Charles Lewis, John Coles, William Sims, Nicholas Lewis, David Rodes, James Quarles, George Gilmer, John Henderson, junior.[4]

At a committee, held on the 31st of May 1775, at Charlottesville, for the county of Albemarle, the above letter was directed to be transmitted to the independent company of Williamsburg.[5]

> Tucker Woodson, c. c.

Virginia Gazette (Pinkney), 6 July 1775

Williamsburg

The Gentlemen Volunteers of the Independent Company to Peyton Randolph: An Open Letter [6]

SIR,

WE, the members of the volunteer company in Williamsburg, embodied, to support the constitutional rights and liberties of America, are exceedingly alarmed to hear, from report, that the same malevolent daemons, from which have originated all the evils of America, are now exerting their utmost treachery to ensnare your life and safety. The friends of liberty and mankind have never escaped the fury of arbitrary despots. No wonder, then, that you should be selected, as a Proper victim, to be sacrificed to the malice of the present administration.[7]

Permit us, therefore, attached to you by the noble ties of gratitude and fellow citizens, to entreat you, in the warmest manner, to be particularly attentive to your own safety, as you regard the interests of this country. We now proffer to you our services, to be exerted at the expence of every thing a freeman ought to hold dear, as you may think most expedient, in the defence of your person, and constitutional liberty, and will most chearfully hazard our lives in the protection of one who has so often encountered every danger and difficulty in the service of his countrymen. MAY HEAVEN GRANT YOU LONG TO LIVE THE FATHER OF YOUR COUNTRY, AND THE FRIEND TO FREEDOM AND HUMANITY![8]

Virginia Gazette (Pinkney), 1 June 1775

Peyton Randolph to the Gentlemen Volunteers of the Independent Company: An Open Letter

GENTLEMEN,

THE affection you have expressed for me demands the warmest returns of gratitude. I feel very sensibly the happiness resulting from the kind attention of my worthy fellow citizens to my security and welfare. Your apprehensions for my personal safety arise from reports, which I hope have no foundation. Such unjust and arbitrary proceedings would bring on the authors of them the resentment and indignation of every honest man in the British empire. I shall endeavour to deserve the esteem you have expressed on this occasion, and shall think it the greatest misfortune that can attend me if ever my future conduct should give you any reason to be displeased with the testimony you have now offered of your approbation.

Ibid., 1 June 1775

1. The "they" who had "by their not marching" brought this issue before the Albemarle County committee were John Coles and David Rodes (29 Apr. 1775, Albemarle Co. Committee). Whether because of their "vote" not to march, or for another reason no longer evident, the company did not march at all. There is evidence, however, that it did respond 3 or 4 days later when Patrick Henry launched his thrust toward Williamsburg (9 May 1775, n. 5). Now, as judges of the accused, Coles and Rodes voted for their own acquittal. But they must have been supported by others, some of whom perhaps arrived at a decision shaped by second thoughts. Of the signatories of the letter next following, only Nicholas Lewis is not known to have been an officer or an enlisted man in the county's 1st independent company of volunteers.

2. The present item is the only known response by a county committee to the resolutions adopted by the Williamsburg volunteers 6 days before (25 May 1775, Williamsburg Independent Company).

3. That is, by the General Assembly, scheduled to convene on the next day, 1 June 1775.

4. The chairman of the Albemarle County committee, Thomas Jefferson, and the next ranking member, John Walker, were, if not already in Williamsburg, en route thither to attend the sessions of the General Assembly.

5. The present letter, along with another composed by the Albemarle County independent company on 1 June, would be read aloud to the Williamsburg company at a muster in the capital on 1 July 1775 (*Va. Gazette* [Pinkney], 6 July 1775).

6. On Monday morning, 29 May, 36 mounted Williamsburg gentlemen volunteers rode north to meet Peyton Randolph, who had vacated the presidency of the second Continental Congress in order inevitably to resume the speakership of the House of Burgesses. At about noon on Tuesday, 30 May, the cavalry encountered Randolph in the company of Carter Braxton at Ruffin's Ferry. Despite very unpleasant weather, this group was greeted in turn by the remaining local volunteers some 3 miles north of Williamsburg, which they thereafter reached around 5:00 P.M. The entry into the city was notable. Bells rang. The "inhabitants" cheered. And Randolph was escorted to his home in triumph. Then the volunteers and "other respectable Gentlemen" repaired to the Raleigh Tavern and "spent an hour or two in harmony and cheerfulness, and drank several patriotic toasts." As early the next morning as the occurrences of the previous evening would permit, the volunteers reassembled before Randolph's house, delivered the message below, and received the reply it evoked (*Va. Gazette* [Pinkney], 1 June 1775; ibid. [Purdie], 2 June 1775, supplement; ibid. [Dixon and Hunter], 3 June 1775).

7. For the reported drawing up by the "same malevolent daemons" of a "Black List" that included Randolph's name, see 23 May 1775, n. 14.

8. Although the addressee's friendliness for freedom and humanity might have been all-encompassing, the "country" to which the gentlemen volunteers assigned him paternity was limited to the colony of Virginia.

Thursday, 1 June 1775

Albemarle County Independent Company

Gentlemen Volunteers to Those of Williamsburg

GENTLEMEN,

THE first company of independents for the county of Albemarle are highly pleased with the resolves of the gentlemen volunteers in Williamsburg, and have been truly alarmed at the late arbitrary proceedings carried on in that city.[1] We think that every apostate to the American cause should be properly stigmatized. We coincide with you in opinion, that the landing any armed force in this colony, will not only be a dangerous attack, but a sufficient cause to justify us, with our countrymen, in any opposition; and we are determined, at all events, to act on that occasion as men of spirit ought to do, in defence of their natural rights and country's cause. With great respect we remain, gentlemen, your humble servants,

> Charles Lewis, captain
> George Gilmer, ⎫
> John Marks,   ⎬ lieutenants.
>   ⎭

CHARLOTTESVILLE,
June 1, 1775.

Virginia Gazette (Pinkney), 6 July 1775

Hanover County Committee

A Ranger to A True Patriot: An Open but Rather Anonymous Letter [2]

PROFESSIONS, however great and pompous, will never give a right to the character assumed; nor can merit, taken on one-self, receive any additional value from being published in a newspaper. A bad heart, and a weak head, are exposed by such vanity. The want of a complete knowledge of mankind is shewn by the latter, as is a consciousness of not being justly entitled to a character assumed proved by the former. Under which of these to consider *the True Patriot* (or whom I take to be the same person, *a Real Associator*)

I neither know, nor is it very material to the world that it should be determined with precision.[3]

Strange that any gentleman can *now* even privately condemn an action which is agreed by a vast majority of, if not all the colony, to be at worst, but the ebullition of patriotism; disapproved by the snarling wretch only, whose soul envies the honour of being the agent! Be it known unto ye, Mr. *True Patriot*, that it is dangerous at this time to damp the spirit prevailing in the back counties, or circumscribe their actions within the line of meer prudence and circumspection. Are the lower counties (for I suppose you live below) able, independent of any aid from the frontiers to resist any invasion that may be made? If you are not, and I verily believe you are not, your disapprobation of the Hanover volunteers conduct on the late alarm will teach us, that no confidence is to be placed in any alarm, and may probably induce us to leave you to your fate; and how *you* may stand the fiery trial (if you stand it at all) I have not sufficient knowledge of you to determine. Did you ever hear this observation doubted, "that the man who has not a native worth sufficient to raise his fame thereon must, from the very nature of his constitution, aim at its establishment, by reducing characters of a superior worth to a level with his own?" The former must be considered as the *True Patriot*, and abhorred; the latter we all know and admire.

To talk of prudence and circumspection, when the wounded honour of our country calls aloud for resolute activity, is [4] the language of cowardice, and only flows [5] from the lips that lately opposed the putting this colony into a posture of defence, and endeavoured in an elaborate speech to prove that Virginia was not immediately interested in the fate of Boston.[6]

But why need I canvass this *True Patriot?* I cannot wish the Ethiop white. His breast, not animated with one spark of sterling patriotic fire, but an humble slave to prudence, that cold monitor, and adhering to its kindred earth, is too confined to admit such feelings as warmed the Hanover volunteers. Their march was not dictated by the prudence and circumspection of this *True Patriot;* their conduct therefore must naturally be condemned by the man, whose ideas of *sound policy and the strictest justice* accord sweetly with the temper of the times, as the noise of a tingling cymbol with the delicate feelings of an Italian eunuch. Be under no apprehension, good sir, that you will be *held responsible for this inadvertency given into by individuals;* you have disapproved it, though by it clearly the undoubted right you have to your signature. At the worst, should the general assembly or convention *not disapprove of, and endeavour at a redress of such grievances as this inadvertency may occasion,* you may be relieved from danger by those *horrida bella* ("dreadful wars"), which you seem so much to dread, by removing to the westward of the Blue Ridge, where you may rest in perfect security, and possibly be pardoned for your publication on a sincere repentence: Of which however the honest hunters must have some infallible proof; such as a generous contribution towards purchasing arms and ammunition: Here is their touch-stone of patriotism. An acknowledgement in the gazette will not satisfy them; they judge of a man by his actions, not his professions; and will certainly conclude with me that there can be no little sincerity in a repentance of the latter sort, as truth in your assumed character.[7]

A Ranger.

Virginia Gazette (Pinkney), 1 June 1775

Middlesex County Committee

Absolute Refusal of One Parsons

HAVING received a letter from a member of the committee of this county, dated, I believe, the 29th of May last, informing me that one ⟨John⟩ Parsons, a ship-builder, then at Urbanna, had reported that goods to a considerable amount had been landed at Urbanna, on Thursday the 25th of the aforesaid month, and put into the store of mess. James Mills and co. and being desired to call a committee to inquire into the truth of the report, I immediately repaired to Urbanna, and summoned the aforesaid Parsons to appear before the committee, to make good the report he had propagated; but he absolutely refused to attend the meeting of the committee, yet nevertheless was willing, and very much insisted, upon making oath before a magistrate, that he was not the author of such report, and moreover, that he had never seen any goods landed and put into mr. Mills's store, or any other persons whatever, contrary to the association of the Continental Congress. Upon which I told him, that in all probability his deposition would not satisfy the committee; that his personal appearance was necessary; and, if he failed to appear, the committee would be obliged to hold him forth to the publick as a propagator of falsehoods.[8]

Virginia Gazette (Purdie), 22 July 1775, supplement

1. For the "resolves of the gentlemen volunteers in Williamsburg," see 25 May 1775, Williamsburg Independent Company; for the "arbitrary proceedings carried on in that city," pp. 4–6 above.

2. For the letter by the "True Patriot," to which the present item is a reply, see 11 May 1775, Hanover Co. Committee.

3. On 29 Dec. 1774 the "Real Associator" had in effect accused the Norfolk Borough committee of negligence in enforcing the 9th article of the Continental Association (for which see 8 Apr. 1775, Norfolk Borough Committee), in this instance in respect to the sale of salt. For that accusation he had been sharply rebuked by William Davies, secretary of the committee (*Rev. Va.*, II, 211–12, 227–28). It would appear that the "Ranger" concluded that the original accusation and the appeal of 11 May 1775 for the exercise of "prudence and circumspection" were of a common seed and sown for the purpose of spreading discord.

4. In the newspaper the verb is missing.

5. In the newspaper the verb is printed "flow."

6. The "lips" that were parted to oppose placing the colony into "a posture of defense" and "endeavoured in an elaborate speech to prove that Virginia was not immediately interested in the fate of Boston" may have been those of Robert Carter Nicholas. It was he who on 24 May 1774 had introduced the resolution by which the House of Burgesses, in reaction to "the hostile invasion of *Boston*," set aside 1 June 1774 as a day to be spend in fasting, humiliation, and prayer (*Rev. Va.*, I, 93–95). Almost certainly Nicholas supported adoption of the resolution with declamation, later to be referred to by James Parker of Norfolk as the treasurer's "Hostile invasion Speech." But though in Parker's judgment this speech "first set fire to the train" of events that followed, Nicholas recoiled when in the second Virginia Convention on 23 Mar. 1775, Patrick Henry moved that "this Colony be immediately put into a posture of Defence," for, declared the treasurer, his only "intention" was "to have errours rectified, & not to alter or destroy the Constitution" (James Parker to Charles Steuart, 6 Apr. 1775, in Steuart Papers, National Library of Scotland; *Rev. Va.*, II, 368 n. 8).

It is also to be noted that steeped in the thought and terminology of Aristotelian logic, as were the educated men of his day, Nicholas (and the "Ranger," if reporting accurately) would have used the adverb "immediately" in the sense of an event's occurring without the agency of an intermediate event; and hence, whatever British power might effect in Boston, Virginia would not be directly affected thereby but at worst would be so "not immediately," or only after the occurrence of an intermediate event or events. Thus there would be time to arm at a later date, should there prove any need to arm at all.

Nicholas's prime candidacy for the role of being the individual who "lately opposed" Henry's resolutions is further underlined by Thomas Jefferson's assertion that even Peyton Randolph, the treasurer's close political ally, had by the present date concluded or was shortly thereafter to conclude that his ally's "mind was not yet up to the mark of the times" (P. L. Ford, *Works of Jefferson*, I, 17).

7. Undaunted by the "Ranger's" vitriolic attack, the "True Patriot" would on 9 June 1775 reply and, in doing so, partly lift the mask of his anonymity.

8. The narrator of the events related in the present item, which consists of the 1st paragraph of a 3-paragraph notice, was the chairman of the Middlesex County committee, Rev. Samuel Klug. For the action of the committee following Parson's failure to appear before it, see 6 June 1775.

Friday, 2 June 1775

Westmoreland County Committee

Acquittal of a Certain Dr. Thomas Thomson

At a meeting of the committee of Westmoreland county on the 2nd day of June 1775, pursuant to a special summons for that purpose.[1]

Present The Revd Mr Tho⟨ma⟩s Smith, chairman, J⟨ohn⟩. A⟨ugustine⟩. Washington, Rich⟨ar⟩d Parker, Burdett Ashton, W⟨illia⟩m Nelson, Phil⟨ip⟩ Smith, Tho⟨ma⟩s Chilton, Richd. Buckner, Dan⟨ie⟩l Tibbs ⟨Tebbs⟩, Ben⟨jamin⟩: Weeks, Edw⟨ar⟩d Sanford, Jos⟨eph⟩: Peirce ⟨Pierce⟩, James Davenport.

A certain doctor Thos Thomson having been duly summoned before the committee to ansr a complaint for killing Lamb unseasonably and contrary to the resolutions of the colony convention on that head[2]—the said Thomson appeared and the whole matter was fully heard on Evidence, and the question being put it is the opinion of the committee that the said Thomson hath acted contrary to the sense of the said convention, and that the said Thomson having said that he has acted as he did without considering the Recommendation of the colony convention with respect to the not killing of Lamb as a prohibition, and that he should have acted in that respect conformable to the sentiments of this committee, he is acquitted of any further censure on that account.[3]

Thos Smith

Magazine of American History with Notes and Queries, XXIII (Apr. 1890), 341

1. The last preceding recorded meeting of the Westmoreland County committee had been on 23 May 1775.

2. On its last day of session, 27 Mar. 1775, the "colony," or second Virginia, "convention," as one of several measures designed to promote the domestic manufacture of cloth, "Resolved unanimously that from & after the first Day of May next no Person or Persons whatever ought to use, in his[, her,] or their families, unless in Case of Necessity, & on no Account sell to Butchers or kill for Market any Sheep under four years old; and where there is a necessity for using any Mutton in his, her or their families, it is recommended to kill such only as are least profitable to be kept" (*Rev. Va.*, II, 382).

3. No other record of a meeting of or an action by the Westmoreland County committee during the remaining period of time encompassed within the present volume has been found.

Saturday, 3 June 1775

Isle of Wight County Committee

To Make Dispatch Therein and Make Report Thereof

At a Committee held for the County of Isle of Wight at the Court house of the said County on the third day of June in the year of our Lord Christ one thousand seven hundred and seventy five.[1]

Present Josiah Parker, Brewer Godwin, Richard Hardy, Arthur Smith, Henry John Burges⟨s,⟩ Clerk,[2] Thomas Peirce, John Mallory, Goodrich Willson ⟨Wilson⟩, William Davis, Thomas Fearn, Jethro Gale, Edmund Godwin, and Thomas Smith⟨,⟩ Gent⟨lemen⟩.

Smith Arthur money collected by him &c. – – – –

Arthur Smith Gent. one of the Captain's of the militia of this County this day returned an account of three pounds eleven shillings and nine pence by him collected from the Company under his command for the purpose of purchasing Gun Powder for the use of this County pursuant to a former Resolve of this Committee[3]

Subscriptions to be by Sundry Capts. collected &c. – – – – – – –

Sundry subscriptions were this day returned by the several Captains of the militia of this County amounting to eight pounds four shillings and four pence for the purpose of purchasing Gun Powder for the use of this County which several subscriptions are to be by the said Captains collected as soon as possible who are hereby Ordered to account with the Committee for the same.

Circular letters to be sent to the different Comms.

The present state of this County renders it highly necessary that a sufficient quantity of Gun Powder be immediately procured for the protection and the defence thereof, and as we have too much reason to fear that the Neibouring County's are in the like situation – Resolved that circular letters be Wrote to the different Committees of the County's of Southampton, Surry, Sussex, York and nansemond informing them that we have good reasons to believe that no considerable quantity of Gun Powder can be had but by Importation which we have reasons to apprehend may be done on good Terms provided they will Joine us in the Interprise.

Henry Jno. Burges &o's: to Write & prepare Circular letters &c.

Resolved that Henry John Burges Clerk, Brewer Godwin, Thomas Peirce, Arthur Smith, and Josiah Parker Gent. be appointed a Sub. Committee to Write and prepare circular letters to the different Committees of the County's of Southampton, Surry, Sussex, York, and Nansemond and to make dispatch there in and make report thereof to the Committee.[4]

Money to be collected from the several Membs. &c. – – –

Resolved that the above Gent. be appointed to receive from Members of this Committee three pounds for the purpose of purchasing Gun Powder for the use of this County which said sum the respective Members of this Committee have already subscribed for the purpose aforesaid, and that they do endeavour to collect the same by the nineteenth day of this Instant.[5]

Committee Adjourned till the nineteenth Instant.[6]

The minutes of these proceedings were signed
                    Henry John Burges Chairman Pro: temp

> Committee MS minutes, the whole, including Burgess's signature, in hand of Francis Young, clerk (Office of county clerk of Isle of Wight County)

Norfolk Borough Committee

A Determination to Turn Away

Norfolk borough, Committee Chamber, June 3, 1775.[7]

Present Mr. Chairman and 20 members.[8]
The Committee being informed that the ship Molly⟨,⟩ Capt. ⟨Samuel⟩ Mitcheson⟨,⟩ has lately arrived from Great-Britain laden with a large quantity of goods for Messrs. ⟨Jonathan⟩ Eilbeck, ⟨David⟩ Ross & Co. and the circumstances of the importation appearing very suspicious, and inducing this Committee to believe there was an intention thereby to counteract the Association,[9] RESOLVED therefore that agreeably to the said Association, the said ship ought on or before Tuesday morning next to return directly back with the said goods; and that a copy of the invoice ought to be delivered to the sub-committee hereafter mentioned; and that a certificate, properly authenticated, that the said goods have been actually relanded in Great-Britain, ought also to be procured to this Committee by the said Eilbeck, Ross and Co. as soon as the said certificate can be procured and transmitted to their hands.

RESOLVED that Capt. ⟨John⟩ Selden, Mr. Matthews ⟨Thomas Mathews⟩ and Mr. Christopher Calvert be a sub-committee to go on board said ship, and examine whether any goods have been landed from the same; and to ascertain by invoice or other lawful means, what quantity were shipped from Great-Britain on board the said ship.[10]
Ordered that the above resolutions be published.

> *Virginia Gazette, or the Norfolk Intelligencer*, 15 June 1775

1. The last preceding meeting of the Isle of Wight County committee had been on 22 May 1775, when adjournment was set to the present day.
2. Henry John Burgess was a "Clerk" in the ministerial sense.

3. The "former Resolve of this Committee," pursuant to which this fund was collected and the funds mentioned in the immediately succeeding minute were to be collected was that adopted on 17 Apr. 1775.

4. What response the committee procured from the "circular letters" after they were "Wrote" is not evident from any entries in the manuscript minute book or from any other surviving records.

5. The committee made such collections pursuant to a recommendation adopted by the second Virginia Convention on 25 Mar. 1775 (13 Apr. 1775, n. 4).

6. The minute book contains no record of any meeting on 19 June, so evidencing the continued absence of Francis Young, the regular clerk, and his subsequent inability to find any loose paper(s) outlining the proceedings of that day. The next recorded meeting of the committee is that of 27 July 1775.

7. The present item consists of the first 4 paragraphs of a single 13-paragraph notice.

8. "Mr. Chairman" was Matthew Phripp.

9. That is, to violate the nonimportation stipulations of article 10 of the Continental Association (5 Apr. 1775, n. 1).

10. For the inconclusive report of the nonboarding "sub-committee," see 4 June 1775.

Sunday, 4 June 1775

Norfolk Borough Committee

Search for the Good Ship *Molly* [1]

Present Mr. Chairman and 22 members.[2]
The sub-committee appointed yesterday to go on board the ship Molly, reported, that they had not been able to discover where the ship was, but that they had been credibly informed by several pilots and others who well knew the ship, that she went up the James river yesterday afternoon.[3]

A letter was delivered in at the table from Messrs. ⟨Jonathan⟩ Eilbeck, ⟨David⟩ Ross & Co. and Mr. Eilbeck and Mr. Ross attending and a thorough and impartial enquiry being made into the circumstances of the arrival of the Molly with goods, it was thereupon RESOLVED that the resolution of yesterday, with respect to the said ship be strictly adhered to.

Upon motion RESOLVED, that it be published at the same time with the resolutions of yesterday, that Mr. Eilbeck and Mr. Ross did this day attend before the Committee, and produced their invoice of goods on board the ship Molly, and that it did not appear that the said goods were shipped by their order but on their account by Mr. Chambers ⟨Walter Chambre⟩ of Whitehaven.

RESOLVED that the sub-committee appointed yesterday to go on board the said ship Molly, be directed to ascertain the quantity of goods shipped from

Great-Britain in her, and comply with the other directions contained in the resolution for their appointment.[4]

Virginia Gazette, or the Norfolk Intelligencer, 15 June 1775

1. The present item consists of the 5th through the 9th paragraph of a single 13-paragraph notice.
    2. "Mr. Chairman" was Matthew Phripp.
    3. For the appointment of and instructions to the "sub-committee," see the proceedings of the previous day, 3 June 1775.
    4. For the further report of the "sub-committee," see the proceedings of 6 June 1775. On that same day the reported presence in the James River of the *Molly* would stimulate the James City County committee to undertake preventive action.

Tuesday, 6 June 1775

James City County Committee

Information, Resolutions, and Thanks

AT a committee held for James City county, on Tuesday the 6th day of June 1775.[1]

The committee being informed that Capt. ⟨Samuel⟩ Mitcheson, of the Molly, from Whitehaven, consigned to Mess. ⟨Jonathan⟩ Eilbeck and ⟨David⟩ Ross, merchants at Norfolk and Petersburg, had lately arrived in James river with a large quantity of merchandise, and it being represented to them that there was great reason to suspect an attempt would be made to land some of the articles, either in this or other counties,[2] the committee came to the following resolutions:

Resolved, that it be earnestly recommended to the several select committees, who were formerly appointed by this committee for such purpose,[3] that they exert their utmost vigilance and endeavours to prevent any part of the cargo from being landed or disposed of within this county, and if they shall discover an attempt of the sort, that they immediately give notice thereof to the chairman.

Resolved, that it be also recommended to the committees of the several counties to use their endeavours to frustrate an attempt to commit so flagrant a breach of the resolutions of the Continental Congress; and particularly to the committee of the county of Dinwiddie to inquire strictly into the conduct of Mess. Eilbeck and Ross, and that they would prevent any of the said goods from being landed or disposed of within their counties.[4]

The committee took into consideration the late expedition of Patrick Henry, Esq; and the Gentlemen volunteers from Hanover and several other counties, in order to obtain satisfaction for the gunpowder removed from the publick magazine by order of the Governor; and resolved, that their thanks be presented to all those Gentlemen, for rendering this country so essential a service.[5] And it was ordered, that these resolutions should be published in the Gazette.

Virginia Gazette (Purdie), 16 June 1775, supplement

Middlesex County Committee

False and Groundless Report [6]

On the 6th of June the committee met;[7] and the said ⟨John⟩ Parsons not appearing before them, they, after the strictest inquiry, and by the testimony of capt. ⟨William⟩ Boyce (being first sworn) who had the keys of the warehouse belonging to the company that very night on which the said Parsons had said the goods were landed, I say, it appearing fully to the satisfaction of the committee, that no goods for or belonging to the company had been landed and put into their warehouse or store, from capt. ⟨Moses⟩ Robertson's ship, the committee thought it their duty to advertise the publick, that the report so maliciously propagated by the said Parsons was false and groundless.

To what I have above asserted I am ready to make oath, whenever called upon for that purpose.[8]

Samuel Klug.

Virginia Gazette (Purdie), 22 July 1775, supplement

As Elsewhere Reported

AT a meeting of the committee for the county of Middlesex, on the 6th of June, 1775, present ten members. It having been reported by one John Parsons, a ship-builder, that goods to a considerable amount, contrary to the association of the Continental Congress, had been landed at Urbanna, on Thursday the 25th ult. and put into the store of Mess. James Mills and co. the committee convened, and after inquiry, and the testimony of a witness being first sworn, it appeared that the report had not the least foundation. To the end therefore, that the public may not be imposed on by such false and groundless reports, the committee think it their duty to declare, that the Gentlemen concerned in said store, have never, as far as they know or believe, been guilty of the smallest breach of the association; but on the contrary, have adhered to the same with a scrupulosity becoming the friends of American liberty.

Ordered, that a copy of the above be sent to the printers of the Virginia gazette, and they are desired to print the same.

Samuel Klug, Chairman.

Virginia Gazette (Dixon and Hunter), 17 June 1775

Norfolk Borough Committee

No Reconsideration of the Matter [9]

Committee Chamber, June 6, 1775.

Present the Deputy chairman and 17 members.[10]

Captain ⟨John⟩ Selden and Mr. Matthews ⟨Thomas Mathews⟩ not being able to go on board the ship Molly as by a former order they were directed,[11] Mr. Christopher Calvert reported that Major ⟨Stephen⟩ Tankard and himself had examined the hold of said ship, and that it did not appear to them from any thing they could discover, that any goods had been taken from on board the said ship.[12]

The ship Molly being unable as yet, on account of contrary winds, to proceed to sea as directed by this Committee, Mr. ⟨David⟩ Ross applied for the consent of this Committee, to reship on board the Jenny now about to sail, the goods imported in the Molly, and that the Molly may take in a cargo of tobacco. It was thereupon RESOLVED, that this Committee would not enter into a reconsideration of the matter.[13]

ORDERED that the proceedings of this Committee relative to the ship Molly be published in the Gazette.

Extract from the minutes.
William Davies, sec'ry

Virginia Gazette, or the Norfolk Intelligencer, 15 June 1775

1. The present proceedings are the 1st of which record has been found for the James City County committee since its meeting on 13 Feb. 1775. The committee chairmanship was held by Robert Carter Nicholas, in addition to his holding the vice-chairmanship of the Williamsburg City committee. But since he and the vice-chairman of the James City County committee, William Norvell, were on this day attending the House of Burgesses, the present meeting was possibly presided over by Col. Philip Johnson, on 25 Nov. 1774 elected to 3d place (*Rev. Va.*, II, 177, 287–88; 2 May 1775, n. 3; *JHB*, 1773–1776, pp. 189, 196).

2. The *Molly*, which was already under search by a "sub-committee" of the Norfolk Borough committee (4 May 1775), was on this same day discovered—though no man

stated precisely where—and boarded by Christopher Calvert, a committee member, and Stephen Tankard, who may have been one.

3. The personnel of the "several select committees" must remain unknown because of the nearly 4-months' hiatus in the committee records.

4. This is the first indication that a committee had been formed in Dinwiddie County, wherein lay Petersburg, the town of David Ross's residence.

5. For Patrick Henry's "late expedition," see pp. 7–11 above; 4, 9 May 1775, Hanover Co. Committee. Of all surviving resolutions respecting "so essential a service," this one of the James City County committee is least effusive, probably in respect to the well-known views of the absent chairman.

6. The present item consists of the 2d and 3d paragraphs of a 3-paragraph notice.

7. For the purpose for which the Middlesex County committee met on this date, see the committee proceedings of 1 June 1775.

8. On 10 July 1775 John Parsons would undertake an ill-advised vindication of his conduct; but he would not be so careless as to attempt refutation of any statement of fact on which the present signatory was "ready to take oath," for Chairman Samuel Klug was a reverend man of God.

9. The present item consists of the 10th through the final paragraph of a single 13-paragraph notice.

10. The "Deputy chairman" of the Norfolk Borough committee probably was Dr. James Taylor (*Rev. Va.*, II, 261 n. 3, 278).

11. The directive was that laid down by the committee on 3 June 1775 and fruitlessly undertaken by Selden, Mathews, and Christopher Calvert on the following day.

12. At an undisclosed subsequent date John Hunter Holt was to "hear" that with better luck, "the sub-committee appointed for the purpose have obtained copies of the cockets and the necessary parts of the invoices of the goods shipped in the Molly" (*Va. Gazette, or the Norfolk Intelligencer*, 15 June 1775).

13. With a change in the winds, the *Molly* sailed for England on Thursday morning, 8 June (ibid., 15 June 1775). On 23 Aug. 1775, the committee will be found making a final disposition of the case of the craft and her cargo.

Wednesday, 7 June 1775

Third Virginia Convention

Protest against a Scheme Alleged to Have Been Laid in Berkeley County [1]

To the Honourable the Moderator and the Delegates of the [Colony of Virginia in Convention assembled:] [2]

The Petition of [the Freeh]olders of the County of Berkeley Humbly sheweth That it being represented to the Inhabitants of the Colony by the late Convention that the State of publick affairs rendered it indispensably necessary for each County in the Colony to Elect two Delegates to represent

them the ensuing year with full powers to make all such Regulations for the
Co[n]duct of the Colony from time to time as might be found expedient.[3]
That your Petitioners conceive at a Time when the greatest Dangers seem to
threaten the whole Continent with the total Destruction of whatever ought
to be esteemed in Life it behoves the [Inha]bitants of each County [to be
particularly at]tentive to the Choice they make of [pe]rsons who are to guide
and direct their Councils in times of such Difficulty and Distress, To which
End they apprehend the most publick Notice of the time and place of Election ought to be given to the Inhabitants of each County that the whole
Inhabitants might be apprized of a Transaction of such Consequence to them
and further that such a Period should be fixed for the Election from the time
of Notice that they might have it in their Power to canvass and consider
the merits and abilities o[f su]ch persons as might be proposed for their
Choice That an entire Disregard to those two essential points (by which a
person altogether improper at this time has been returned to represent this
County) oblige your Petitioners to trouble your H[o]nor[s] with a state of
the Transactions upon the Occasion.

That Colo. Adam Stephen without consulting any person in the County
as far as your Petitioners have been able to learn arrogated to himself the
sole power of appointing the time of Election and notifying it to the public That the time fixed upon by him for the Election succeeded so quickly
to the Notification and the Notification was given in so partial and private
[a] manner that a great Number of the Freeholders did not hear of the Election untill it was over and many of those who did attend were not acquainted
with it till the very day of the Election.

That many of your Petitioners who were present could view those measures in no other [Lig]ht than a Scheme laid by that Gent to procure himself
to be elected again[st the ge]neral Sense of the County which they openly
declared and requested that another day might be appointed for the purpose
or if that should not be judged expedient that the Poll might be kept open
till a succeeding day that proper Notice might be conveyed to those who
were as yet unapprized of the Election a Proposal which your Petitioners
conceived no person of Candour could make the least Objection to However,
Colo. Stephen refused to adopt either of the Measures and imperiously declared that he viewed himself as duly elected and whatever might be the
Opinion of the County [was determined to attend whenever a Convention
should be summoned which induced many to submit to the Proceedings of
the Day.

That your Petitioners conceive this to be a most daring and violent attack
upon their Liberty of Suffrage at a time when the publick Voice in all matters referred to them ought to] be collected in the most free open and un-
biassed manner and therefore hope that you'll take the same under your
Consideration and refuse the said Colo. Stephen a Seat among you untill a
free and open Election may be procured in the said County.

And your Petitioners shall pray, &c.[4]

Jacob Hite [5]
Joseph Barny
John West
John Rion
Horatio Gates
Peter Burr
William Lucas
Mickel Ingel ⟨Engel⟩
Danl. Hendrix
Philip Engle
Timothy Sewel
Martin Wolford
James Morris
Walter Baker
Samuel Kerchevall
William Morgan
Edward Lucas Jun [6]
William Darke
Daniel [Sti?]saubly
Cornelius Thompson
George Cloak
Andrew McCarmick
John Strode
Wm Vestall
Henry Schultz
Heinrick Fink
Michael Hentzal
Mardin Endler
Adam Endler
John Taylor
Samuel Ta[y]lor
[Gerry Smid]
[Adam Birker]
George Bishop
Thomas Hart Senr

Thomas Hart Junr
Jeremiah Stillwell
Michael Billmires
Robert Lemen
  Junior
Nicodemus Perck
  Dull
Thos Pearce
Henry Hanes
Melzer Pope
Thomas Worly
Levi Jamyson
Adrian Wynkoop
Benjamin Blackford
Michael Bedinger
Jacob W[re]n
Michael Eng[l]e
Mychael Welsh
Joseph Swearingen
Benoni Swearingen
Wm. Brown
Abel Morgan
Van Swear[in]gen
John Now[lan]d
Henry Ett[er][s?]
Wm. Morgan
Thos. Swearingen
William Hall
John Gantt
Ja Keith [7]
John Jann[uste]
[Anthony
  Gholson] [8]
Mic[hae]l Blane
Robert Lonery
Edward Lucas
  Sener [9]
Adam Moler
Caspar Pettles

Wm Morgan Capn [10]
Andreas Hieronymus
Gorg Fögals
James Hendricks
Moses Tullis
Gorg Fant
Jacob Coons
Heinrich Endler
Henry Strup
Thomas Nelson
Thomas Hall
Ird[rin?] Sirrt⟨?⟩ [11]
George Maret
William Strup
Caspar Seiver
John Smith
Jacob Miller
John N Alvin
Jonathan Britton
William Right
John Sewell
Thomas Crow
Philip Thyts
Peter Wals
Jacob Israel
Isaac Israel
Nicholas Hain
Ulrich Nachmann
Samuel Roberts
George Ludwig
  Rosenberger
Thos. Rutherford
John Hite Junr.
Joseph Hite
  his
Wm. X Coyle
  mark

MS document in unidentified clerical hand, with autograph signatures and one illiterate's mark, in loose papers of third Virginia Convention (Archives Division, Virginia State Library)

Election of Alternate Delegate in Charles City County

BENJAMIN HARRISON, jun, esq; of Berkeley, is chosen one of the delegates
for Charles City county, in convention, in case of the absence of his father,
Col. Benjamin Harrison, now at the General Congress.[12]

Virginia Gazette (Purdie), 23 June 1775, supplement

1. The date heading of the present document is arbitrary. It is here positioned to
follow by 15 days the certification of Rev. Daniel Sturges supportive of the statements
herein contained (23 May 1775, Third Va. Convention) and to precede by one week
the petition of some members of the Berkeley County committee in defense of the
procedures followed in the election of delegates (14 June 1775, Third Va. Convention).

2. The document, now in places more torn or deteriorated than seems to have been
the case in the early years of the 20th century, has previously been edited by William G. Stanard and printed in the *Va. Mag. of Hist. and Biog.*, XII (Apr. 1906),
412–15. It is from that source that bracketed words, syllables, and letters in the text
have been drawn; but a comparison of signatures in the present item with those in the
Stanard rendition will disclose a number of variations, for the augmentation in genealogical data of more recent years has had the double effect of decreasing uncertainty
in certain instances while increasing it in others.

3. For the election of convention delegates for one-year terms, see 13 Apr. 1775, n. 1.

4. This petition, together with that of the Berkeley County committee, would be
presented to the third Virginia Convention on 21 July 1775.

5. JACOB HITE, a son of Joist Hite, one of the earliest settlers in Frederick County
and a staunch contestant in disputing full title of Thomas Fairfax, 6th Baron Fairfax,
to the "Northern Neck Proprietary" as then constituted, was the instigator of this petition. Jacob Hite patented lands in Frederick County as early as 1734 and reportedly
made a trip to Ireland late in the 1730s to stir up interest in settlement in the Shenandoah Valley. A noted and unrestrained speculator, he in 1770 forged a letter from the
Cherokee chief Oconestoto to Norborne Berkeley, Baron de Botetourt, then governor,
in the unrealized hope of opening additional Indian lands. "Mr. Hite," recalled Samuel
Kerchevall, "kept a large retail store, and dealt largely with the Creek and Cherokee
nations." Hite owned lands as far south as South Carolina. In the spring of 1775 he was
continuing with Adam Stephen a feud begun in 1772, when they bitterly contended for
the location of the county seat of Berkeley County, then formed from Frederick
County. Stephen won that round. But now in an unrelated business matter, each would
soon be accusing the other of malfeasances ranging from mere peculation to genuine
misconduct. At this time Hite was probably in his early 60s (Samuel Kerchevall, *A
History of the Valley of Virginia* [2d ed., rev. and enlarged, Woodstock, 1850; 4th ed.,
duopage reproduction, Strasburg, 1925], pp. 50, 180; William Couper, *History of the
Shenandoah Valley* [3 vols., New York, 1952], I, 248–49; John Richard Alden, *John
Stuart and the Southern Colonial Frontier* [Ann Arbor, Mich., 1944], p. 279; *Rev. Va.*,
II, 362 n. 1; *Va. Gazette* [Pinkney], 6 July 1775; ibid. [Dixon and Hunter], 30 Sept.
1775).

Although for spatial reasons the following signatures are printed in 3 columns, in the
manuscript they are entered in 2. The 1st column of the initial page ends with the
name of Samuel Taylor, but from the bottom of that page is torn a portion sufficient

for 1 or 2 other signatures. Here the present editors have within regular brackets inserted the names of Gerry Smid and Adam Birker, as those names nowhere else appear in the manuscript but are included in the Stanard version. The 2d column on the 1st page begins with the name of George Bishop and ends with that of Michael Blane. The 1st column of the 2d page begins with the name of Robert Lonery and ends with that of Nicholas Hain. The 2d column of the 2d page begins with the name of Ulrich Nachmann and ends with the mark of William Coyle.

6. Edward Lucas, Jr.

7. Given name probably James.

8. Here the manuscript is torn and the name drawn from Stanard.

9. Edward Lucas, Sr.

10. Capt. William Morgan probably added his militia rank in order to distinguish himself from his 2 namesakes, whose signatures, as here printed, occur in the 1st and 2d columns respectively.

11. Signature, perhaps forgiveably, overlooked by Stanard.

12. The date is arbitrary. The election would not be widely noticed until publication of the source quoted. But the "first Wednesday" of the month had been court day for Charles City County since 1748 (*Statutes at Large*, V, 490), and it is probable that when the freeholders gathered to conduct other business, they chose an alternate convention delegate.

Because Colonel Harrison had found himself a poor manager of his own financial affairs and disrelishing the fruits of his ineptitude, he early banished from the mind of his son BENJAMIN HARRISON, JR., any thoughts of frittering time away on a college education. Instead, the youngster was sent to Philadelphia, where apprenticed to the mercantile firm of Thomas Willing and Robert Morris, he was inducted into the mysteries of commerce and trade. Eventually he went to Europe to cultivate acquaintances with the heads of commercial houses there, and returning to Virginia in mid-1773, reembraced the patriot cause—he had already subscribed to the nonimportation association of 22 June 1770; and in Dec. 1774 he was elected a member of the committee of correspondence for his native county. He may have joined with Patrick Henry in the march on Williamsburg in May 1775. He was a capable man, of unshakable loyalties, handsome of person, and free of the excess body weight that encumbered his father's movements without slackening the bluntness of his speech. The younger Harrison was at this time about 33 years of age but as yet was unwed (W[illiam] G. Stanard, "Harrison of James River," *Va. Mag. of Hist. and Biog.*, XXXV [Jan. 1927], 89–92; [Mrs. Frank L. Harris et al.], comps. and eds., *DAR Patriot Index* [Washington, D.C., 1966], p. 307; *Rev. Va.*, I, 83, II, 38 n. 1, 201; Hugh Blair Grigsby, *The History of the Virginia Federal Convention of 1788*, ed. R[obert] A. Brock [2 vols., Richmond, 1891; reprint, 2 vols. in 1, New York, 1969], I, 249).

Thursday, 8 June 1775

Royal Chief Magistracy

Extract of Another Letter from the Earl of DUNMORE, *to the Earl of* DARTMOUTH, *Dated* WILLIAMSBURG, *6th June*, 1774 [1]

My Lord,

SINCE the dissolution of the assembly of Virginia, but before all the members of the house of burgesses had quitted this city, there arrived an express dispatched from Boston to the committee of correspondence here; as I learn, has likewise been done to all the other colonies, to excite and encourage the whole to shut up the courts of justice against all English creditors, to join in a general association against the importing any British manufactures, or even exporting any of their own produce to Great Britain, and proposing a congress of deputies from all the colonies forthwith. [2]

I am really unable to suggest to your lordship to what lengths the people of this colony will be induced to proceed, further than what they have already made manifest by the order of the house of burgesses and subsequent association, the copies of which I have already transmitted to your lordship; [3] but the part of the late burgesses remaining in town at the arrival of the Boston messenger, having taken upon themselves to receive his dispatches, and to enter into a consideration of their contents, and then to summon the inhabitants all above the age of twenty one to appear at an hour they chuse to appoint, and to propose to them to agree to all those violent measures above mentioned, which that they may be more solemnly entered into and more generally adopted, they have deferred the execution of to a further consideration on the first day of August next, when all the members that composed the late house of burgesses are required to attend; [4] these circumstances give too much cause to apprehend that the prudent views, and the regard to justice and equity, as well as loyalty and affection, which is publicly declared by many of the families of distinction here, will avail little against the turbulence and prejudice which prevails throughout the country; it is, however, at present quiet. [5]

In the order of the house of burgesses, which I before transmitted, your lordship will observe, that the reverend Mr. Thomas Gwatkin, who was the professor of mathematics and natural philosophy in this college, and is now the principal master of the grammar school, and who is of the most exemplary good character and great literary abilities, is appointed to preach the sermon on that occasion; in justice to which gentleman, I think it necessary to let your lordship know, that his name was made use of entirely without his knowledge; and that he civilly, but with firmness, declined being employed for such a purpose, and which proved no little mortification to the party who dictated the measure.[6]

I am your lordship's most obedient humble servant,

                                                             Dunmore.

P.S. The paper which is herewith enclosed is just come out of the printing office, and contains resolutions which the city of Annapolis have entered into, and are the same which I have already mentioned to your lordship are proposed for this colony to join in; but the time that has been set for the consideration of them may possibly be sufficient to cool the heat of the party, which is now so strenuously endeavouring to establish them.[7]

                                                             D.

Virginia Gazette (Pinkney), 8 June 1775

Caroline County Committee

One Thousand Pounds of Powder

At a meeting of the Committee – June the eight⟨h⟩ 1775
Twelve Members Present

William Woodford or John Tennant is appointed to engage 1000 pounds of Powder & hire a person for that purpose & pay him out of the money collected for ammunition &c.[8]

> Committee MS minutes in hand of Samuel Haws, Jr., clerk (Henry E. Huntington Library and Art Gallery of San Marino, Calif.)

Williamsburg

An Astonishing Duplicity

It is astonishing with what duplicity the ch——n[9] of a certain noble lord is capable of acting; for though he made a merit to his noble patron of refusing to preach the *fast sermon* last year, at the request of the house of burgesses, yet it is an undoubted fact that he boasted he wrote the identical sermon that was preached on that occasion.

It is imagined that the above reverend gentleman will soon be promoted to a bishopric, and it is confidently believed that he will be collated to the see of *Saint Asaph,* in order to break the charm it has long since been under of being filled with patriotic clergymen, as it is supposed the above gentleman will be proof against any foolish suggestions or impulses of the *spirit* of liberty.[10]

Virginia Gazette (Pinkney), 8 June 1775 [11]

1. The "extract" is in fact the complete text of His Lordship's letter (P.R.O., C.O. 5/1352, fols. 108–10). Pinkney printed the document directly below an extract of a letter, dated 29 May 1774, also from the governor to Lord Dartmouth, secretary of state for the colonies. The 2 dispatches, describing the meeting of the General Assembly in May 1774 and the immediate aftermath of its dissolution, had been laid before the House of Commons on 19 Jan. 1775 (Hansard, *Parliamentary Hist.,* XVIII, cols. 136–38) and may have reached Pinkney through a chain of events similar to the one preceding his publication of Dunmore's letter of 24 Dec. 1774 (28 Apr. 1775, n. 1). Except for minor changes in punctuation, spelling, and capitalization, the original of the present letter and the copy are almost indistinguishable. The postscript (in which Pinkney amended 2 verbs) may not have been presented to the Commons. For the events to which the letter refers, see *Rev. Va.,* I, 93–104, II, 71–75.

2. For the contents of the letters borne by the "express," see *Rev. Va.,* II, 71–73, 75–77, 79–81. The proposal to "shut up the courts of justice against all English creditors" came from the Annapolis Committee of Correspondence (ibid., II, 81).

3. For the "order" of 24 May by the House of Burgesses setting aside 1 June as a day of "Fasting, Humiliation and Prayer" and the "subsequent association" signed by 89 former members of the dissolved House on 27 May 1774, see ibid., I, 91–95, 96–98.

4. For the linkage of events by which the "members that composed the late house of burgesses" were summoned to reconvene in the first Virginia Convention, see ibid., I, 99–102.

5. His Excellency performed a disservice to history by neglecting to place on the written record at least a partial list of the "many families of distinction" in Williamsburg reckless enough "publicly" to announce a holding of "prudent" views.

6. No "little mortification" was on this same day to be shifted from the shoulders of the "party who dictated the measure" to those of others, for which readjustment see under the heading of Williamsburg.

7. The "paper" to which the governor referred in his postscript came from the press of Clementina Rind and contained a copy of the resolves of the "inhabitants of the city of ANNAPOLIS, on *Wednesday* the 25th of *May,* 1774" (P.R.O., C.O. 5/1352, fol. 111). The resolves were incorporated in the letter written by the Annapolis committee and laid before and read by the Virginia Committee on 31 May 1774 (*Rev. Va.,* II, 80–81, 90).

8. The "money" was collected pursuant to a resolution adopted by the committee on 13 Apr. 1775. The next recorded meeting of the Caroline County committee was to be on 29 Aug. 1775, a date not encompassed within the present volume.

9. In addition to his professorial duties described by the governor on this same date (Royal Chief Magistracy), Rev. Thomas Gwatkin had recently assumed those attendant on being His Lordship's private chaplain. Unless the testimony of Edmund Randolph was biased, success in this particular chaplaincy would indeed add a star, for the conduct of the "coarse and depraved" Dunmore was not "regulated by one ingredient of religion" (*Va. Gazette* [Dixon and Hunter], 18 Feb. 1775; Randolph, *Hist. of Va.,* ed. Shaffer, p. 197).

10. The implication that the bishopric of St. Asaph in Wales had "long since" provided an unbroken succession of "patriotic clergymen" is difficult to sustain. The Right Reverend Jonathan Shipley, bishop since 1769, was a favorite object of toasting by the colonists because of his opposition to ministerial policies. Otherwise, it was necessary to glance back to the holding of the see by the Most Reverend Robert Hay Drummond, bishop from 1748 to 1761; he was at the present time archbishop of York and little minded to move politically, owing to his disgust with the course of tory administration.

11. In this same issue of Pinkney's newspaper there is printed an open letter by a pseudonymous "Philo Virginius" that is a completely scurrilous, personal attack on Gwatkin. In it the reverend target is charged with being of "pitiful" character, of only "pretended zeal for religion," of "pusillanimous hypocrisy," and of harboring a soul of "genuine deformity." The scattering of Dunmore's letter, the present item, and the attack by "Philo Virginius" through separate pages of the same gazette imparts the appearance of casualness. The odds against such chances are so great, however, that it seems probable that withholding knowledge until its revelation should be most pertinently pointed, Pinkney himself was "Philo Virginius."

At any rate, with a matter the complete truth of which had probably been known to only 2 men now being bruited about, Rev. Thomas Price felt obligated to come forward and publish a type of confession (15 June 1775, Williamsburg).

Friday, 9 June 1775

Hanover County Committee

A True Patriot to A Ranger: An Open and Less Anonymous Letter [1]

The person alluded to in Mr. Pinkney's last paper, as the author of an address under the signature of "A True Patriot," presents his compliments to the RANGER, and assures him that he has entirely missed his aim; as that person does not, to this moment, know who was the author or publisher.

The Ranger is a total stranger to the principles of the man he vainly attempts to censure; nor has he done justice to the active, though *perhaps prudent* part, that person hath taken in our present unhappy political struggles. The distinction of *upper* and *lower* counties is odious; it is rather to be wished that this wide-extended country *could* be considered as one large entire family, and that we should one and all embrace as friends. The threats thrown out by the Ranger have fallen equally short of their mark. If he expected to *intimidate* or *deter* the person for whom they were intended from doing whatever he conceives to be his duty, he has entirely mistaken his man. The rights and privileges we contend for are common to all. *Freedom* of sentiment, and *liberty* of speech, surely are most essential parts of our GRAND CHARTER: [2] If two men differ in opinions, is not the diversity equal on each side? Does *A*, in such a case, differ more from *B* than *B* from *A*? Why then should there be any ill humours amongst us?

It would seem that every subject, especially of great importance, should be open to a *decent, candid,* and *free* discussion. From a collision of opinions, truths, and the most essential interests of the community, are in the fairest track of promotion. When, indeed, the publick voice hath *fixed* the *decision,* the acquiescence of individuals, and a *proper exertion* in the common cause, becomes a duty. These are genuine sentiments, and not to be departed from by

R. A.[3]

Virginia Gazette (Purdie), 9 June 1775, supplement

Unidentified County Committee

Most Unfriendly Strictures and Unfavourable Insinuations [4]

This Committee having been Presented with an Address of his Majesty's Council to the Good People of Virginia; [5] And having deliberately considered the same; and finding it built wholly on some most Unfriendly Strictures and unfavourable insinuations agst the People of this Colony do now in behalf of themselves, their Constituents and others in this County agree to the following Resolve (to wit)

Resolved nemine Contradicente that they cannot but look upon an address in so late a Period of the Present Unhappy disputes begun at first by many arbitrary and Oppressive measures through the machinations of a despotic Ministry in G. Britain tending to enslave America: As inimical rather than in the least friendly to the cause of freedom; and Therefore the committee judges it highly expedient, that their Sentiments as a part of this Community should be made known to the Colony as well as to the American World, by an Address To those members of the Council whoever they were that chose in this late day to exhort the People of this Colony in the manner they have done; and that   be requested to Prepare and bring in the same for the immediate consideration of this Committee.

The said Address being accordingly brought in and unanimously agreed to, Ordered that the same be sent with all convenient dispatch to be struck off in   [6] hand bills and also to be inserted in Mr. ⟨Alexander⟩ Purdie's Gazette.[7]

MS document in unknown hand, on verso of broadside of 15 May 1775 by governor's Council To all the good PEOPLE of VIRGINIA (John Carter Brown Library, Brown University; photocopy in Virginia State Library)

1. For the anonymous open letter to which the present item is the rejoinder, see 1 June 1775, Hanover Co. Committee.

2. The writer was using the term "GRAND CHARTER" in a generic sense to describe the rights of free Britons. Neither *"Freedom* of sentiment" nor *"liberty* of speech" is guaranteed by Magna Carta, the instructions of 18 Nov. 1618 (the "Great Charter") of the London Company to Governor-designate Sir George Yeardley, any of the charters of Virginia, or the Bill of Rights of 1689. If as a justice of the peace "A True Patriot" had recently purchased a copy of Sir William Blackstone's *Commentaries on the Laws of England,* he may in the 4th volume have read that the "liberty of the press is indeed essential to the nature of a free state" and that "Every freeman has an undoubted right to lay what sentiments he pleases before the public." Notwithstanding these liberal assertions, the author-jurist approved of the restrictions in Great Britain then imposed upon freedom of expression and so unwittingly lent the weight of his prestige to guaranteeing the existence there of what a later generation would call an "underground press" (William Blackstone, *Commentaries on the Laws of England* . . . [4 vols., London, 1765–69], IV, 151–52).

In the colonies the case of the New York printer John Peter Zenger, adjudicated in 1735, had given a broader scope to freedom of the press than was true in the mother country ("For what Notions," defense counsel had inquired with pointed effectiveness, "can be entertained of Slavery, without the Liberty of complaining?"), and the record of that cause célèbre had gone through several editions. It is true that time had been when colonial printers carefully skirted a "freedom" that might be construed as an endorsement of sedition. But by June 1775 what constituted disloyalty was definable by one's own politics, and while continuing to pay deference to His Majesty's presumed virtues, many an American printer was at last busily and happily exploring beyond the erstwhile ultima Thule of scurrility (Livingston Rutherford, *John Peter Zenger: His Press, His Trial and a Bibliography of Zenger Imprints* [New York, 1941], p. 106; Zechariah Chaffee, Jr., *Free Speech in the United States* [Cambridge, Mass., 1942], p. 21; *Rev. Va.,* I, 17).

The "True Patriot" was confining his apologia to a finer concept of freedom and growing body of tradition. Yet by the very fact that he felt compelled to vindicate his position, it was evident that among more hotheaded patriots, "prudence" was becoming a dirty word.

3. Although the identity of "R. A." is not demonstrable, there comes readily to mind the name of Richard Adams, former burgess, chairman of the Henrico County committee of correspondence, delegate to the first 2 Virginia conventions, and already elected a delegate to the third (*Rev. Va.,* I, 221, II, 171, 171–72 n. 2, 310, 337; 5 May 1775, Third Va. Convention).

4. The date for this item is arbitrarily assigned, and the county committee that unanimously adopted the sentiments expressed below unknown. The present editors have been unable to identify the hand that penned the document.

5. See 15 May 1775, Royal Magistracy.

6. Space was here left to indicate the number of handbills. If ever "struck off," none appears to have survived the vicissitudes of time.

7. No copy of the "said Address" has been found in any extant issue of "Mr. Purdie's Gazette."

Wednesday, 14 June 1775

Third Virginia Convention

Defense of Election of Adam Stephen in Berkeley County
as Very Proper

At a meeting of the Committee for the County of Berkeley at the Court
house on the second Wednesday in June 1775 According to Adjournment[1]
    Present 18 Members.
A Copy of a petition to the Colony Convention which this Committee were
Informed was Prompted by Jacob Hite and Thomas Hite[2] seting forth, that
there was "not proper Notice given to the freeholders for an Election of
Delegates to represent this County in the said Convention for one year, and
that Colo. Adam Stephen had appointed the day for the same in an Arrogant
manner &c" being read, Resolved, that (upon enquiry,) It appears to this
Committee, That the sd. Adam Stephen, in appointing the day for the said
Election acted by the advice of Several members of this Committee.
    Resolved that, It is the Opinion of this Committee that the day appointed
for the said Election was very proper for the same it being the day appointed
for a General Muster of the Militia and the next Succeeding day after the
seting of the Committee & Vestry and that by reason of the publick Notoriety
thereof a Numerous and Respectfull body of the freeholders appeared and
Voted on the said Election. And this Committee further Considering that the
Subject of this Petition upon a motion made to the Committee on the day of
Election (who were then Sitting,) by the sd. Jacob Hite & Thomas Hite by
the Consent of all the Candidates had been twice Referred and as often determined, by a Majority to be a fair Election. Therefore we cannot help thinking That the said Petition is groundless and only tends to Create Jealousies
and Divisions in the County.[3]

                    A Copy.   PHIL. PENDLETON Clk Comm.

                    Autograph document, signed, in loose papers of
                    third Virginia Convention (Archives Division, Vir-
                    ginia State Library)

    1. This is the 1st account of the proceedings (in which Philip Pendleton's orthogra-
phy is left in its original purity) of the Berkeley County committee of which there
is record. The "Advertisement" arbitrarily placed under the date heading of 24 Apr.
1775 called for a meeting of the committee, which presumably convened, on "the first
day of May," but whether that meeting or a later one adjourned to "the second
Wednesday in June" is indeterminable.

2. It is probable that Thomas Hite, now approximately 25 years of age, did join his father, Jacob Hite, in "Prompting" the drawing up and the signing of the petition arbitrarily placed under the date heading of 7 June 1775 (Third Va. Convention). It is equally probable that in order to maneuver the committee into appearing as though it was conjuring up a chimera, he did not himself sign the document.

3. Along with the petition to which it is the attempted refutation, this copy of the proceedings would be laid before the third Virginia Convention on 21 July 1775.

Thursday, 15 June 1775

Third Virginia Convention

Election of Delegates in Warwick County

WILLIAM HARWOOD and WILLIAM LANGHORNE, Esqrs. are chosen delegates to represent the county of Warwick, for one year, agreeable to the directions of the late Convention at Richmond.[1]

Virginia Gazette (Purdie), 16 June 1775

Norfolk Borough Committee

Sly-Boots, Jr., to John Hunter Holt: An Open Letter

Mr. Holt,

As a friend to the good people of this Borough, I can no longer, in silence, hear the unjust imputations of witlings and snarlers, that we are destitute of Genius, Learning, Wits and Politicians. At present I shall content myself with adducing one instance as a specimen to disprove this malicious aspersion.—It is a truth, not to be denied, that there is in being, and now actually residing in this borough of Norfolk, a person, who for the display of his political Knowledge, his profound Learning, his universal Genius and vast Comprehension, deserves most justly to be celebrated, and who (to the emolument of this place) resigned his absolute government of a wooden world, to become a fellow-citizen with us. He is a strenuous asserter of the supreme legislative power of the British Parliament, an EXACT PENMAN, POWERFUL in his Arguments, ELEGANT in his Address, and POLITE in his Conversation; in short he is a very Beau of a Politician, and so completely skill'd in all the finesse requisite for a professed courtier, that he can whip you the devil around a stump; import a cargo of goods contrary to a solemn association sign'd with his own hand; and can shew you how a vessel may bring in ninety bales of osnibrigs and seven hundred pieces of linen, and carry out only six bales of the former, and about eighty pieces of the latter, and yet not leave a single bale or piece behind! And what is surely a MASTER STROKE in Policy, he has not only escaped a severe whipping (the smallest punishment due to such flagrant insults) but he has convinced the good people of this town, that he is an HONEST MAN; and strictly adheres to the Association.— I hope, Mr. Printer, this will convince the public that Norfolk is not altogether so unfruitful as has been insinuated in the production of those whom you may call Gentlemen of uncommon Abilities.[2]

I am Mr. Printer, Yours, &c.[3]

Sly-Boots, junior.

Virginia Gazette, or the Norfolk Intelligencer, 15 June 1775

Williamsburg

The Reverend Thomas Price to the Public, Anonymously through John Pinkney [4]

As your paper last week contained a charge against a certain reverend gentleman for writing (though he refused to preach) the FAST SERMON, at the request of the honourable House of Burgesses on the first of June 1774, we are now authorized to confirm that assertion.[5] The necessary duties of a parish, joined with those of the office of chaplain to the House of Burgesses, together with the short time allowed for the composition, were strong inducements with the gentleman that *preached* that sermon to request the assistance of a friend. To these, if the great estimation in which Mr. G—— was at that time held by the House of Burgesses, and the request of that respectable assembly that he would preach the sermon of that occasion, be added, it will not appear strange that Mr. —— should accept of his good offices at such a juncture. He would, however, by no means have permitted the sermon to have been printed in his own name, but as the publication was requested by the honourable House of Burgesses, and the author was bound by the sacred ties of honour and inviolable secrecy, he flatters himself he shall be considered more excusable in the eyes of the public than if an inclination to indulge the emotions of vanity had suggested such a step.[6]

Virginia Gazette (Pinkney), 15 June 1775

1. For the "directions of the late Convention," see 13 Apr. 1775, n. 1. As was true of the second convention, to which both Langhorne and Harwood were elected delegates, the former would be in attendance at the third, the latter would not.

2. As with 2 separate cryptic epistles from a "Sly Boots" (Senior?) that had appeared in the *Va. Gazette, or the Norfolk Intelligencer* of 7 July and 8 Sept. 1774, the present letter, penned if not by the same writer, then by a spiritual and perhaps biological son, is replete with arcana probably decipherable only by local contemporaries. It is, however, the supposition of the present editors that the subject of the innuendoes was Jonathan Eilbeck (pron. Eel'beck), who had arrived in Norfolk from Whitehaven, England, in 1767. Although occasionally returning to the mother country, he became a Norfolk "fellow-citizen," domiciled in a handsome brick house, held a part interest in a ropewalk, and only in the month last past had married Mary Talbot (American Loyalists: Transcript of Manuscript Books and Papers of the Commission of Enquiry into the Losses and Services of American Loyalists . . . from the Public Record Office, London, New York Public Library, microfilm in Va. State Library, LIX, 187–94; Edward Wilson James, ed., *The Lower Norfolk County Virginia Antiquary* [5 vols., Baltimore, 1895–1906], IV, 173).

Eilbeck's "resignation" of the "absolute government of a wooden world" of merchantmen was more apparent than real, for despite his settling in the colony, this partner in the firm of Eilbeck, Chambre, Ross, & Co. continued to act as shipping manager, a position "for which few men were, by education, practice, and perseverence, so well qualified" (William Hutchinson, *The History of Cumberland, and Some Places Adjacent, from the Earliest to the Present Time . . .* [2 vols., Carlisle, Eng., 1794], II, 85). Eilbeck and David Ross had recently been involved in the affair of the ship *Molly* (3, 4 June 1775, Norfolk Borough Committee), but for Walter Chambre there was reserved a future day for attaining the distinction of being denounced as "an enemy to American liberty" (23 Aug. 1775, Norfolk Borough Committee).

3. Unamused by this letter, lest it make them appear remiss in the discharge of their functions, some members of the committee would wait on the "gentleman" writing as "Sly-Boots, jun." and procure from him a word of explanation (22 June 1775, Norfolk Borough Committee).

4. The namesake son of a former Middlesex County burgess and himself chaplain of the House of Burgesses since 1764, Rev. Thomas Price, in lieu of Rev. Thomas Gwatkin, who had "civilly, but with firmness, declined," delivered in the Bruton Parish Church the sermon "suitable to the important occasion" on the "Day of Fasting, Humiliation and Prayer" (George Maclaren Brydon, "Addendum to Goodwin's List of Colonial Clergy of the Established Church" [carbon typescript, Richmond, 1933, in Va. State Library], pp. 63–64; *JHB, 1761–1765*, p. 229; *Rev. Va.*, I, 95, 103–4).

5. See 8 June 1775, Williamsburg.

6. This, then, is the explanation as to why the sermon delivered on an historic occasion never found its way into print. Public acknowledgment of the true authorship was doubtlessly embarrassing to the Rev. Mr. Price, was probably so even to the "boastful" Rev. Mr. Gwatkin, and was possibly so to the governor. Yet although Gwatkin felt that he could not endorse the political postures assumed by dissident former burgesses and others by delivering the sermon personally, he was not necessarily inconsistent in composing words that might have been spoken with as little offense to a congregation in London as to one in Williamsburg.

Friday, 16 June 1775

Second Virginia Convention

Robert Carter Nicholas to William Goodrich [1]

Sir

Herewith you will receive five thousand pounds sterling in Bills of Exchange to lay out in Powder which I make no doubt of your best endeavours to do, as youre well acquainted with our great want of it.[2] I wou'd recommend to you to communicate this scheme to your Brother [3] for fear of any accidents happening to you to prevent your transacting the business. we must rely altogether for your endeavours for the best as it is impossible for me to say what is the [bes]t method to take in the Islands[; I] therefore leave it to you to transact this matter as you think [best] for the good of the voyage. Youl have some letters to the merchants in Antigua [4] particularly to Mr. Jno Taylor & Mr. Harvey to whom you'l please to refer any one that shou'd doubt the Credit of the bills. Mr. ⟨Matthew⟩ Phripp has also wrote Mr. Wan Dam ⟨Isaac Van Dam⟩ & Mr. Jenings ⟨Richard Downing Jennings⟩ of Statie [5] that I hope you'l meet with no difficulty in passing the Bills. should it please God that you readily meet with the Gun powder you'l please to write to your father what time we may expect you on the Coast that we may keep a look out to warn you of any danger, but I would advise you to slip into Carolina if you meet with a favorable opportunity & inform us over Land where to meet you that we may provide assistance. Let me beg of you to be as expeditious as possible for I know not how soon it may be wanted. I am wishing you a good voyage.[6]

Y'r H'ble Servt.

P.S. the two letters to ⟨John⟩ Norton & Sons you'l give to the purchasers of the bills being Letters of advice—

> Autograph letter, unsigned, in hand of Robert Carter Nicholas, loose papers of fourth Virginia Convention (Archives Division, Virginia State Library)

1. This item, which was probably an enclosure in a petition John Goodrich, Sr., presented to the fourth Virginia Convention on 10 Jan. 1776, is undated. On 31 Oct. 1775 the recipient identified himself to Lord Dunmore and explained that "on the 14th. of June 1775 or thereabouts he was Spoke to" by Thomas Newton, Jr., burgess-delegate from Norfolk County, "who informed him that the Treasurer"—Robert Carter Nicholas—"wished to Speak with him on some business." Goodrich and New-

ton "a day or two thereafter" waited upon the treasurer in the capital and the following document is the "business" transacted (P.R.O., C.O. 5/1353, fol. 352).

2. Nicholas's authority to contract for the importation of gunpowder from either the British or Dutch West Indies—in violation of royal edict—was derived from a resolution adopted on 25 Mar. 1775 by the second Virginia Convention appointing him chairman of a 3-member committee to procure munitions for the colony (see 13 Apr. 1775, n. 7).

Nicholas undoubtedly selected William Goodrich, 1 of the 5 sons of Portsmouth-based merchant John Goodrich, Sr., because he believed that the family's patriotism was made of sterner stuff than would later prove to be the case. The patriarch, proprietor of extensive properties in Norfolk, Isle of Wight, and Nansemond counties, was an affluent merchant with wide connections. He had been a member of the Norfolk Borough–Portsmouth Town joint committee formed on 30 May 1774, but since that time his name has not appeared on any patriot document known to the present editors. The surname was often written "Gutrick" by contemporaries, giving a clue as to its pronunciation. Mr. Treasurer, however, had no clue to forewarn him how tangled would become this net he cast abroad for ammunition (P.R.O., A.O. 13/30, folder G IV; Fairfax Harrison, "The Goodriches of Isle of Wight County, Virginia," *Tyler's Quarterly Historical and Genealogical Magazine*, II [Oct. 1920], 130; Sabine, *Biog. Sketches of Loyalists*, I, 80–81; *Rev. Va.*, II, 89).

3. The "Brother" was probably John Goodrich, Jr., of Portsmouth.

4. Antigua, one of the Leeward Islands, British West Indies.

5. St. Eustatia, an island in the Dutch West Indies.

6. William Goodrich's voyage would not be altogether "good." It would be the beginning of October before he returned, as requested via North Carolina, but shortly thereafter to fall into Lord Dunmore's hands.

Saturday, 17 June 1775

Bedford County Committee

John Hook to Committee

Sir   New London June 17th, 1775.
 When I heard I was Cited to appear before the Committee, I was in hopes the Particular charges exhibited against me would have been fully expressed in the summons given me to attend, it cannot be supposed that I can recollect, the instant the charges come against me, what to say in justification, or who to call upon to make my Innocence appear, in case the Charges being groundless, I hope therefor to be excused for not attending the Committee till after the charges are given me expressly in writing.[1]

J. H.

Autograph draft letter, initialed (John Hook Papers, Manuscripts Department, William R. Perkins Library, Duke University)

1. For the summons to which this is the reply, see 23 May 1775, Bedford Co. Committee, 2d entry. The identity of the addressee is not evident. It may have been James Steptoe, the committee member designated to deliver the summons; or it could have been Charles Lynch, who was committee chairman pro tempore during the absence of John Talbot, attending the House of Burgesses in Williamsburg.

The "Particular charges" would be "exhibited" by the committee in a letter to Hook which the accused received on 26 June 1775 (Bedford Co. Committee).

Monday, 19 June 1775

Third Virginia Convention

Augusta County West: A Minute of Arrival

Fort Dunmore [1] June 19th. 1775.
A Number of Six Nation Chiefs arrived in consequence of a Message sent them to attend a treaty to be held with the Western Indians by the Earl of Dunmore on behalf of the Colony of Virginia [2]

> MS transcript in hand of James Berwick, in papers of third Virginia Convention (Archives Division, Virginia State Library)

Frederick County Committee

Commendations and Condemnations

COMMITTEE CHAMBER, FREDERICK county, *June* 19, 1775.
THE late conduct of Patrick Henry, Esq; relative to his making reprisals from the king's receiver-general, for the powder so clandestinely taken from the colony magazine, being laid before this committee,[3] they took the same into consideration; when it was

Resolved unanimously, that an express be immediately dispatched to Williamsburg, with the following address to the printer.

Mr. PURDIE,
SIR.
WE should blush to be thus late in our commendations of, and thanks to, PATRICK HENRY, Esq; for his patriotick and spirited behaviour in making

reprisals for the powder so unconstitutionally (not to use a term more harsh, which perhaps it deserves) taken from the public magazine, could we have entertained a thought that any part of the colony would have condemned a measure calculated for the benefit of the whole; but as we are informed this is the case,[4] we beg leave, through the channel of your paper, to assure that Gentleman that we did from the first, and still do, most cordially approve, and commend, his conduct in that affair. The good people of this county will never fail to approve and support him, to the utmost of their power, in every action derived from so rich a source as the LOVE of his COUNTRY.

We heartily thank him for stepping forth to convince the tools of despotism that free-born men are not to be intimidated, by any form of danger, to submit to the arbitrary acts of their rulers; and hope he knows *us* better than to suppose any proclamated distinctions, respecting the property of the powder, can ever make us condemn activities so worthily atchieved, or forsake the atchievers.[5]

And, more fully to express our sentiments, we cannot but wish he had proceeded to secure what arms and ammunition might remain after the plunder of the magazine.

An address from the Council to the good people of this colony, being laid before the committee,[6] it was, after mature deliberation,

Resolved unanimously, that the following be transmitted to the publick printer, in answer thereto.

This committee, considering the very extraordinary powers assumed, and exercised, by the Council of this colony, are induced the more attentively to investigate their conduct on this alarming crisis, and to express their *abhorrence* and *detestation* of having the generous struggles for liberty branded with the opprobrious terms of *licentious* and *ungovernable.*

The peace and good order of the community in their county (and they have been informed it is general through the colony) they will venture to say, has been preserved inviolate, and the people as *governable* as in times of the most profound tranquility, unless frequent meetings to perfect themselves in MILITARY EXERCISES, and a steady resolution to oppose, to the last extremity, all invaders of their just rights and liberties, be deemed *a licentious and ungovernable spirit.* THEN, INDEED, they must glory such a spirit has gone forth, and pledge their faith to their countrymen that nothing but death shall rob them of *their* part of it.[7]

This committee has seriously considered, according to the recommendation of the Council, the probable consequences of the conduct which hath been lately pursued, and are of opinion it is the only method to obtain a redress of their grievances. Every lenient measure, they think, has already been tried, without success (a circumstance with which their HONOURS *would* seem to be unacquainted) and they have nothing left but tamely to submit, or resolutely oppose, of which two, they hope, the latter will be the choice of every *American.*

This committee would have wished not to doubt the integrity of the

Council, nor to make any *odious distinctions*, from the important place they hold in the state; but when such *odious* epithets as LICENTIOUS and UNGOVERNABLE are made use of to stigmatise men labouring in the glorious cause of liberty, the conduct of a man to whom they hold themselves, and the whole colony, much obliged, for his patriotick behaviour, they conceive it their duty to speak their minds without disguise, to any man, or set of men, under heaven.

(A copy from the minutes.)

William Heth, clerk.

Virginia Gazette (Purdie), 7 July 1775, supplement

Prince Edward County Committee

Disengenious, Illiberal, and Vitiously Subtle
Misrepresentations

At a meeting of the COMMITTEE *for the county of* PRINCE EDWARD, *at the courthouse, June* 19, 1775: [8]

PRESENT, Col. JOHN NASH, junior, Chairman for the day; John Morton, Robert Lawson, William Booker, Francis Watkins, Obediah Woodson, Thomas Flourney, James Allen, senior, and Thomas Haskins, committeemen.

THE committee taking under their consideration his Excellency Lord Dunmore's conduct, in the removal of the powder from the public magazine in the city of Williamsburg,[9] after the most mature deliberation, came to the following resolutions.

I. That, for ourselves and our constituents, we do hereby publickly avow our unfeigned attachment, and affectionate loyalty, to the sacred person of our most gracious King, George III. and that we ardently pray for nothing more than a speedy pacification between Great Britain and her American colonies, upon permanent, constitutional, and generous principles, as the only probable means of preserving to us our inherent, legal, and just rights and privileges; rights and privileges which his Majesty's subjects of Great Britain have ever had claim to, and have received the ample enjoyment of; and, deprived of which inestimable blessings, the Americans must, of necessity, cease to be a free, happy, and flourishing people.

II. Under these sentiments, and when exerting every human effort to effect a reconciliation between us and the parent State upon the grounds aforesaid, we can but lament, that his Excellency Lord Dunmore, as representative of our Sovereign here, whose duty it was to have given a fair and impartial state, to the Ministry, of the people committed to his care and government, should, on the contrary, delight, by disingenious, illiberal, and vitiously subtle misrepresentations, to keep up the unhappy ferment between us and them. The truth of which charge against his Lordship appears but too clearly in his letter to the Earl of Dartmouth, of the 24th of December last, as published in the different gazettes on this continent; the authenticity of which said letter his Lordship (as far as we know) has never, as yet, thought proper to disavow.[10]

III. That his Lordship's conduct in the removal of the powder from the public magazine, in the city of Williamsburg, under the covert of the night, in the manner it appears to have been done, at that critical juncture of affairs, was as despotic, cruel, and unwarrantable, as his verbal answer to the address of the Mayor, Aldermen, and Common Council of Williamsburg, was unmanly, evasive, and affrontive; and that, in conjunction with some other parts of his conduct, it was a clear declaration of his inimical and hostile designs against this country; and thereby he has forfeited all claim to the further confidence and respect of the good people thereof.[11]

IV. We, therefore, under the above circumstances, and having before us the proceedings of Capt. Patrick Henry, do approve of the same, and unanimously vote him, and the volunteers under his command, our cordial thanks, for their firm, prudent, and spirited conduct, in obtaining an equivalent for the powder, so unjustly removed out of the public magazine.[12]

Ordered, that the clerk do transmit a copy hereof to Mess. Dixon and Hunter, and entreat them to publish the same in their gazette.

Ben⟨jamin⟩: Lawson, Clk. Com.

Virginia Gazette (Dixon and Hunter), 29 July 1775

1. Fort Pitt (see 19 May 1775, n. 4).

2. The "Six Nations Chiefs" who arrived this day were probably the same 5 who, along with 4 warriors, would be listed by James Berwick in the journal for 29 June 1775.

3. For the "repraisals," see pp. 7–11 above. By this date the episode had been thoroughly exploited in the gazettes, but the report that was probably "laid before this committee" as being most authoritative was that "ordered" published by the Hanover County committee on 9 May 1775.

4. The committee may have been "informed" of the lack of unanimity by a reading of the animadversions of "A True Patriot" and the ensuing exchange between him and "A Ranger," whose western biases almost certainly reflected those held by patriots in Frederick County (11 May, 1 June, 9 June 1775, Hanover Co. Committee). Or the committee may by now have heard rumors of the unpublished commendation of Governor Dunmore's conduct by "Several hundred Inhabitants of Transmontane Augusta" (16 May, n. 15). Or, again, the committee may have come by later intelligence of which no record has been found.

5. The "proclamated distinctions" were the aspersions cast in 2 of the governor's proclamations upon the leaders of the "commotions" that had followed his seizure of the gunpowder (3, 6 May 1775, Royal Chief Magistracy).

6. For the "address from the Council," see 15 May 1775, Royal Magistracy.

7. For "frequent meetings" in which patriots sought "to perfect themselves in MILITARY EXERCISES," see 1 May 1775, n. 4.

8. The present item offers the 1st documentary evidence of the existence of a committee of correspondence in Prince Edward County.

9. See pp. 4–6 above.

10. The extract of His Lordship's letter is under the date heading of 28 Apr. 1775, Royal Chief Magistracy.

11. For His Excellency's unmanly, evasive, and affrontive "verbal answer to the address," see 21 Apr. 1775, The Capital, 2d entry.

12. The "proceedings of Capt. Patrick Henry" were probably the same viewed with pleasure this same day by the Frederick County committee (n. 3 above).

Tuesday, 20 June 1775

Accomack County Committee

Certification in Estoppage of Evil Consequences

At a meeting of the committee held in Accomack county, on Tuesday the 20th of June, 1775.

JAMES HENRY, *Esq; in the chair.*[1]

WHEREAS the trade carried on in small vessels, in any of the rivers or creeks in this county, or goods imported by any of the merchants or traders here from any port or place in America, may be productive of very evil consequences, if not under proper regulations: For remedy whereof,

Resolved unanimously, that every master or owner of a vessel having any goods on board for sale, or any merchant or trader residing here having imported any goods, wares, or merchandise, from any part of America, shall not sell any such goods or merchandise, or part with the same in exchange for any commodity whatever, unless they produce a certificate, from the committee of the county from whence they were brought, to this committee, that the same were imported into America agreeable to the terms of the association of the General Congress.[2]

Ordered, that the resolution be published in the Virginia gazette.

John Powell, clerk.

Virginia Gazette (Purdie), 22 July 1775, supplement

1. These proceedings are the 1st extant since the formation of the committee on 23 Dec. 1774 (*Rev. Va.*, II, 208). James Henry was chairman pro tempore. On 27 June 1775 Southy Simpson would again be "in the chair."

2. For other examples of the certification of imported goods being required by county committees, see 8 May 1775, Prince George Co. Committee and n. 13; 23 May, Westmoreland Co. Committee and n. 18.

Wednesday, 21 June 1775

Third Virginia Convention

Augusta County West: Preliminaries to Good Talks

June 21st.

The above Chiefs [1] met ⟨John⟩ Connolly at Col. ⟨George⟩ Croghans [2] where they performed those Ceremonies of Wiping the tears away and cleaning their Ears with removing every uneasiness from the heart; [3] after which they informed him that they would wait upon him next day at the fort and speak further to him. [4]

> MS transcript in hand of James Berwick, in papers of third Virginia Convention (Archives Division, Virginia State Library)

1. See 19 June 1775, n. 2.

2. No portrait or birth record exists for GEORGE CROGHAN, who on 16 May 1775 had been elected chairman of the Augusta County West committee. That is not to state that contemporary descriptions of the "fat old trader" (who pronounced his name "Crawn") are so lacking as to leave him without suppositional image or known character. He had immigrated to Pennsylvania from Dublin in 1741, the master of a diction peculiarly his own. Shrewd, resourceful, and intensely ambitious, he moved to the West, where among the "Ingans" he learned several dialects of their "languidge," gained their confidence, and by 1750 was "the most considerable Indian trader" in the sunset reaches of Pennsylvania. For a time deputy to northern Indian agent Sir William Johnson, the transplanted Irishman traded, bargained, and explored. He was with Gen. Edward Braddock on the latter's disastrous expedition and caused the army nearly to starve by his inability to deliver transport horses and flour for which he had contracted. Yet in the French and Indian War his talents were not wasted, for "onst a Month" he provided a "kag" of liquor to the Indians living near his Fort Pitt home for a "frolick," and by that and other timely strategems warmed the heart of many a red man for the British cause. In 1765 and 1766 he made two expeditions to the Illinois country, met there with his old friend "Pondiac," and concluded a peace. Descending the Mississippi River in the latter year to New Orleans, he found reason to reiterate his opinion, formed on a visit to London 2 years before, that the royal Board of Trade was "imensly ignerant" of American western affairs. Early in the 1770s he embarked on gigantic land speculations in New York and western Virginia. But although his dreams outran his abilities, his dragging down colleagues in his scheme was grandly impartial, because he went down too. By turns ruined and wealthy, he spoke (and one almost suspects wrote) with a thick brogue, consumed potent distillates with unfeigned enthusiasm, when in funds dressed with gaudy splendor, and living

"in greet harmony" with assortments of squaws, sired tawny offspring for whose numbers there are no accounts. "Mr. Croghan," observed an associate, "may be led, but can not be drove." This was true, except as it involved nature, for the very force that does create, lead, and drive, may also decelerate, and by the date the aging colonel played host to the "above Chiefs" and Major Connolly, he was gouty and rheumatic (Volwiler, *George Croghan*, passim; Nicholas B. Wainwright, *George Croghan, Wilderness Diplomat* [Chapel Hill, N.C., 1959], passim; Abernethy, *Western Lands and the Am. Rev.*, pp. 6, 23–24, 45, 118–19).

3. The performance of these "Ceremonies" was metaphorical and was accompanied by an exchange of wampum and other gifts. For the ceremonies that were to begin the formal negotiations, see 29 June 1775, Augusta Co. West.

4. Although the chiefs would duly "wait upon" Major Connolly the "next day at the fort," a surprising occurrence was to prevent their speaking "further to him" at that time (22 June 1775, Third Va. Convention and n. 2).

Thursday, 22 June 1775

Third Virginia Convention

Augusta County West: Disappointment and Meeting with Principal Inhabitants

June 22d.

The Six Nations being arrived here in order to have a Meeting with Major ⟨John⟩ Connolly agreeable to their Engagement yesterday[1] were disappointed; This Gentleman having been carried off the Evening before by a number of armed men and taken toward Ligonier[2] the Indians therefore informed me that they would be glad to speak to the principal Inhabitants here and desired that I[3] would be present.

At a Meeting of the Principal Inhabitants of this place, the Six Nations Spoke as follows
Bretheren
Yesterday we spoke to our Brother Major Connolly who represented the Big-knife, Coll. ⟨George⟩ Croghan and Keyashuta. We wiped the tears from their Eyes, opened their Ears and cleared their throats that what we might say to the White People might have a due Impression on their minds, but when we came to this place to day to speak again to our Brother the Big-knife, were surprised to find nothing but his bed, himself not to be found⟨.⟩ we are at a loss to account for the reason, but we look back to the Council of our wise forefathers our hearts continue to retain the Same good Sentiments towards you. Brothers, You know you sent to our Town this Belt and that you allowed us to come here to the Council Fire.[4] we are now come as you

see us agreeable to your Invitation to listen to every thing that is good which has been of so long continuation between us.

A Belt.

Bretheren

Our Brother the Big Knife and Mr. ⟨Alexander⟩ McKee sent this speech to us last Summer advising us in what manner to conduct ourselves in the Troubles at that time that as we had no Chiefs among us in the town we lived in we were to be pitied. Therefore you desired us not to take any Notice of the foolish part that Some people were acting at that time. Brothers, tho' we are young we took your advice and recommended the Same to our young men and have now met you this day in Council.

A String.

Bretheren

The Big Knife and Coll Croghan sent us up a Speech desiring us to be in readiness to come down to a little Council fire and to bring two of each tribe along with us as the times were hard on account of the scarsity of Provisions; We are now come as you see us with sincere friendship toward you and we hope yours is the Same to us [5]

A Belt.

Bretheren

This is all we have to say at this time and we want to know at what time we shall have an answer

to which the following reply was made

Bretheren

We return you thanks for the kind professions of Friendship you have made to us by your Speeches & will thoroughly consider them and give you an answer as soon as possible [6]

A String.

MS transcript in hand of James Berwick, in papers of third Virginia Convention (Archives Division, Virginia State Library)

Norfolk Borough Committee

Inquiry and Disclamation

Norfolk borough, Committee Chamber, June 22, 1775.
THE Committee being apprehensive that some misconstruction to the prejudice of this Committee may be made in consequence of a publication in the Norfolk Gazette of June 15, under the signature of Sly-Boots, jun.,[7] has enquired of the gentleman that handed the letter to the press, who utterly disclaimed all intention of reflecting upon the conduct of this Committee, and

further declared that the author does not know that any goods have been landed from on board the ship addressed to the person pointed at in the said publication.

By order of the Committee.

William Davies, sec'ry.

Virginia Gazette, or the Norfolk Intelligencer, 28 June 1775

1. Q.v.

2. The abduction of Major Connolly resulted from his being Governor Dunmore's overly vigorous agent in the Virginia boundary dispute with Pennsylvania. Because of imprecision and outright overlapping in the charter grants of the 2 colonies, the authorities of each laid claims to Fort Pitt and its adjacent lands, on which by the early 1770s many more Virginians than Pennsylvanians had settled. The Virginia claim was legally no more firm (nor any less shaky) than the Pennsylvania. But for years Virginians had defended the area against the French and Indians, while the Quaker-dominated Assembly in Philadelphia behaved as though it wished that, except for fur-trade profits, the region would go away. For these reasons, by 1775 some of the western Pennsylvanians, conspicuously among them George Croghan, were disaffected. Determined to protect the settlers from the "aspiring and encroaching spirit of the princely Proprietor," Lord Dunmore waged epistolary war with Gov. John Penn, and discharging batteries of proclamations across Mason and Dixon's Line, the 2 chief magistrates demeaned each other in their dispatches to London (Percy B. Caley, "Lord Dunmore and the Pennsylvania-Virginia Boundary Dispute," *Western Pa. Hist. Mag.,* XXII [June 1939], 87–93; John E. Potter, "The Pennsylvania and Virginia Boundary Controversy," *Pa. Mag. of Hist. and Biog.,* XXXVIII [Oct. 1914], 407–11).

Early in 1774 in enforcement of Virginia's claims, Connolly and some 200 men broke up a meeting of the Pennsylvania court of Westmoreland County and arrested 3 of the magistrates. Catching him off guard, the Pennsylvanians arrested him in turn, and he was at the same time rebuked by his governor-patron for having allowed "intemperate heat" to guide his conduct. But just as Dunmore refused to yield a jot of Virginia's pretensions, so did Connolly, following his release, refuse to surrender an iota, and he did so with such vehemence that he forced Colonel Croghan back into the proprietary camp (Caley, "Lord Dunmore and the Pennsylvania-Virginia Boundary Dispute," *Western Pa. Hist. Mag.,* XXII [June 1939], 93–95).

In the spring of 1775 the major again arrested a number of Pennsylvania magistrates and with abusive remarks oversaw the plundering of their property by his armed bullies. If short on dignity, the frontier was long on the lex talionis, and respect to themselves forced the opposition to adhere to the demands of their code. Thus once more Connolly was seized, on this occasion to be hauled from Fort Pitt for some 45 miles east-southeastward to Fort Ligonier, where he was incarcerated under the custody of Arthur St. Clair (ibid., pp. 95–99; *Pa. Archives,* 1st ser., IV, 476–95, 526–30, 541–42, 564–68). It was a cause of "Elarm" to the Indians and their Virginian hosts at Fort Pitt, Valentine Crawford reported to General Washington, that "our grate Man wase Stole," for "Now other person was So able to Setle bisness with them as him" (Stanislaus Murray Hamilton, ed., *Letters to Washington and Accompanying Papers* [5 vols., Boston, 1898–1909], V, 178–79).

The Connolly drama will be found continued on 26 June 1775, Third Va. Convention, Augusta Co. West, 2d entry.

3. The ego appears to be that of James Berwick, whose presence was probably desired that these remarks might be made a matter of record.

4. A "Belt" of wampum (for which see 20 May 1775, n. 7) seems to have accompanied a letter of invitation that Connolly sent, probably around 19 or 20 May 1775, when he had addressed the chiefs of the Shawnee and Mingoes respectively.

5. Unfortunately, no "Speech," or letter, sent by "Coll Croghan" has been found.

6. It was probably Croghan who delivered the "reply."

7. Q.v. under Norfolk Borough Committee. Either the identity of "Sly-Boots, jun." was known to the committee, or it was quickly established by a visit to John Hunter Holt. Once before the committee had been nettled by the observations of an anonymous newspaper contributor (*Rev. Va.*, II, 211–12, 227–28). Despite his disclaimers, "Sly-Boots, jun." had in fact accused "the person pointed at" of having caused goods to be "landed from on board the ship," by which he probably meant the *Molly*.

Friday, 23 June 1775

Charles City County Committee

Subcommittee to Buckingham County Committee and Freeholders: An Open Letter [1]

To the Gentlemen of the committee and freeholders of Buckingham *county.*

GENTLEMEN.

BEING fully sensible of the obligations we are under to you, by your generosity and humanity in offering us an asylum in the bosom of your friendship, at a time when all the evils of a civil war are precipitately approaching, and knowing we must be involved, by our situation, in much greater difficulties than you, how can we longer restrain the spring of gratitude within the compass of our own breasts?

We observe, Gentlemen, in our papers, an address from you to the people in the lower parts of the country, inviting them to make use of your plantations for the safety and refuge of their wives and little ones, with all things they think fit to carry with them for their support. Such an instance of tender and brotherly feeling must convey an idea of the noblest disposition, and unequalled affection in you; and such an example, who would not, in every situation of life, anxiously endeavour to follow!

Permit us then, Gentlemen, in the fulness of our gratitude, to inform you how much we are obliged to you; and that, if the unhappy differences between us and our parent state should so increase as to compel us to the necessity of accepting your offer, we shall, with the risk of our lives, endeavour to secure your region from the tyranny now threatening: So shall *yours*, and *ours*, enjoy the same blessings—one safety—till our gracious sovereign is again pleased to communicate to all his people the generous language of unity and peace!

That you may long enjoy every blessing this little life can give, and that the impending dangers Almighty God may yet vouchsafe to avert, is the ardent and daily prayer of, Gentlemen, your much obliged and most affectionate countrymen.

By order of the committee of Charles City county.

William G. Munford.[2]
Samuel Harwood.
John Tyler.

June 23, 1775.

Virginia Gazette (Purdie), 30 June 1775, supplement

Williamsburg

To Guard against Any Surprise

Last Friday there was a very full meeting of the inhabitants of this city at the courthouse, convened there by desire of our representative, the Hon. Peyton Randolph, Esq; to consider the expedience of stationing a number of men here for the publick safety, as well as to assist the citizens in their nightly watches, to guard against any surprise from our enemies; when it was unanimously agreed (until the General Convention meets, who no doubt will provide against every contingency) [3] to invite down, from a number of counties, to the amount of 250 men, who are expected in a very few days.[4]

Virginia Gazette (Purdie), 30 June 1775, supplement

1. The letter is in response to that under the date heading of 22 May 1775, Buckingham Co. Committee.

2. William Green Munford.

3. In 3 days more "the Hon. Peyton Randolph, Esq;" would issue a summons for the "General Convention" to meet. Despite its qualified offer of 25 May "to march, on the smallest warning, to any part of the continent," the Williamsburg independent company was finding more business demanding its attention at home than its limited manpower permitted it, unaided, to discharge. By the time the third convention would be in session, it was to find that the guarding of the capital was under control, but the real problem was that of controlling the guards.

4. On 27 June the inhabitants would again assemble in order to cogitate the matter of their security.

Volunteers from James City and New Kent counties reinforced the Williamsburg company during the following week and were to be joined before the convention met by others from the Tidewater and from the more distant counties of Albemarle, Goochland, Louisa, and Spotsylvania (*Va. Gazette* [Purdie], 30 June 1775, supplement, 7, 14 July 1775; ibid. [Pinkney], 6 July 1775; ibid. [Dixon and Hunter], 15 July 1775).

Saturday, 24 June 1775

Third Virginia Convention

Oconestoto to the Delegates in Convention

Dr: Friends & Brothers—   June 24th 1775.

Now I am going to let you know what has happened since I went to see our Brothers the white people at long Cain & Mr. Cammeron.[1] That some Two Ill disposed Malicious of our men has Kill'd Two of your men, which Accident we are all very sorry for and as there is some Evil minded people amoungst the whites that will not adhear to the Whites law, but according to their own Malicious Suggestions Commit murder or any Mischiefs they see Cause in Spite Thereof.[2] We Therefore are in hopes the whites our Brothers will rest fully Assured & satisfy'd That we utterly abhor & disallow all such proceedings, & as it is our Ardent desire to live in Perpetual Peace & friendship with our Brothers the whites, we shall use all Assiduous means we Can to bring the perpetrators of so unnatural & attrocious a Crime to Condign punishment as soon as possible, in Consequence of which we are in hopes Our Brothers the Whites will lay aside all Thoughts of revenge & Bury the remembrance of the late Transaction in Oblivion. & we humbly request the favour of you, our Brothers to send us an answer by the first oppy. while we remain your loving Friends & Brothers &c &c &c. Chotah[3]

The Great Warrior[4]

PS. & in a further Token of our love & desire of Peace, we will send the little Carpenter[5] in soon to aver the Truth Thereof.

Oconestoto

> MS transcript in unidentified hand, in loose papers of third Virginia Convention (Archives Division, Virginia State Library)

1. Alexander Cameron was deputy to John Stuart, Indian agent for the Southern Department. Cameron's home was near the Long Canes River, a tributary of the Little River, in present-day Abbeville County, S.C. (Alden, *John Stuart*, pp. 187 n. 34, 279 n. 71).

2. The 2 men "Kill'd" by "some Two Ill disposed Malicious" Indians were probably those of Daniel Boone's party slain in a surprise night attack while the pioneer and

his group were returning to Harrodsburg (in the present state of Kentucky) after having participated in negotiating a "treaty" at Sycamore Shoals. It was at the shoals that Judge Richard (less formally, "Carolina Dick") Henderson had "purchased" a great extent of western Fincastle County from the Cherokees (10 July 1775, n. 8; John Bakeless, *Daniel Boone: Master of the Wilderness* [New York, 1939], pp. 87–88). The "Accident" had occurred late in March. The delay in writing the present letter may be explained by the currency of Oconestoto's intelligence. He may have imagined that the second Virginia Convention had superseded the royal government in Virginia. Or he may have intended the letter to be delivered to the House of Burgesses. But it was to be the third convention that on 27 July 1775 would receive the letter and merge it in a larger consideration of Indian affairs (Procs. and nn. 3, 9).

3. Chotah (or Chote) was the principal town of the Overhill Cherokees. It was located on the Little Tennessee River a few miles above Fort Loudoun in present Monroe County, Tenn.

4. Aged, wrinkled, and bitterly resentful of white encroachments on his tribal hunting grounds, OCONESTOTO was known to his people as "The Great Warrior," and to many whites as "The Emperor." One veteran settler described him as of "heavy and dul countenance, somewhat corpulent and weighed 180. he did not speak any english but the traders who could converse with him, said that he was very dul in point of interlect." A fierce and sometimes headstrong warrior, "The Emperor" was paid homage by Indians from the Ohio River to the Gulf of Mexico. According to his grasp of the white man's quarrel, he was already beginning to see the lesser evil in supporting the British (Hodge, *Handbook of Am. Indians*, pt. 2, 105–6; John Redd, "Reminiscences of Western Virginia, 1770–1790," *Va. Mag. of Hist. and Biog.*, VII [July 1899], 5).

5. The LITTLE CARPENTER, so-called by the British because of his dexterity in joining and inlaying treaties, had visited England in 1729–30 and caught the message of irresistible power. The consequence was that it was he who frequently dissuaded Oconestoto from taking to the warpath. Of extremely small physical stature but a giant in diplomacy, Attakullaculla—for such was his Indian name—was by now very old, and it may have been for that (or a more subtle) reason that he did not soon or later come "in" to Virginia "to aver the Truth" of anything (Hodge, *Handbook of Am. Indians*, pt. 1, 115; Alden, *John Stuart*, passim, esp. pp. 32–33, 62, 78–80, 86–87, 118–20, 120–21, 127, 129–32).

Part Two   A Hand on the East, an Eye to the West

Saturday, 24 June–Saturday, 26 August 1775

Saturday, 24 June–Saturday, 26 August 1775

An Introductory Note

With the self-prorogation of the House of Burgesses on Saturday, 24 June, to "*the twelfth day of* October *next*," Peyton Randolph was not only free but was compelled by exigency to convoke a third colonial convention. This he proceeded to do on the following Monday, stating that as with the second, so would the third be convened in the "town of Richmond," on 17 July 1775.[1]

It would not be until the third week in August that His gracious Majesty would proclaim his subjects in the English-speaking provinces of the North American mainland to be in a state of rebellion. The signing of such a proclamation would be in effect a declaration of war. But that act would hardly evoke gasps of disbelief by those against whom it was directed. For the fact of war was already evident, and Lexington and Concord were, as Bunker Hill soon would be, place-names even to Virginians who would be lost fifty miles from home.[2]

How war might come to Virginia in the fullness of its fury no man could foretell. Had the departed governor possessed the power to strike, there can be no doubt that he would have struck quickly and hard. But as matters stood, war was momentarily only a breaking off of communications between a fled chief magistrate and decamping burgesses—purely a mental state based on years of irritation festering into hatred and scorn.

That is not to say that there was no noise or movement. To the contrary, and the Virginians moved first, in an incident that produced no heroes but did produce weapons. On the night of that Saturday when the burgesses rose, "a considerable body of men" raided the governor's Palace. Despite any objections that may have been offered by the remaining staff, a group of them entered by breaking in a window, and they then admitted the others by forcing open "the principal door." And when the whole group left, it was with "all the Arms they could find," possibly as many as 300 stand, pilfered from the hall, and a number of muskets and other arms, His Lordship's "own Property."[3]

Who would move next, and with what effect, became an all-absorbing question. Governor and rebels circled warily. Alexander Purdie reported on 30 June that "Early yesterday morning" the "Magdalen schooner" had sailed from Yorktown, bound directly for England with Lady Dunmore, "the rest of the "Governour's family," and the unholy Reverend Thomas Gwatkin. The *Fowey*, Purdie "heard," was at the same time bearing His Lordship and the crafty Captain Edward Foy to Boston "on a visit to General Gage." Not quite so, countered John Dixon and William Hunter the next day. They had "heard" that although "the Magdalen will proceed to England," the *Fowey* "is to return to York with the Governor, after having convoyed the schooner as far as the capes." Amendment accepted, nodded Purdie: On Sunday, 2 July, "the Fowey man of war returned to her moorings before York town, with Lord Dunmore and Captain Foy on board." [4] These sailings were admittedly not blows. But they did give the aspect of clearing decks for action, and the capital was on edge with assertions and denials of blows soon to be struck.

Still lacking manpower, however, Dunmore at best could only employ a spy service to give him an ear to the stirrings in Williamsburg. Rebel independent companies, he informed Lord Dartmouth, had "flocked" to the town and "made a Barrack of the Capitol." Their cavalry units had taken possession of the palace gardens and were "wantonly" butchering the governor's cattle. Then a few days after the arrival of "these Gentry," on 6 July, they too broke into the Palace, smashed the locks of doors to all the rooms, cabinets, and "private places," and walked off with what remained of His Excellency's personal collection of weapons. This looting was committed "in the face of day" under the very nose of a son of Robert Carter Nicholas, and since Mr. Treasurer and Peyton Randolph were in town at the time, anyone could see that they countenanced, if they had not suggested, the "infamous robbery." [5]

The day after commission of the infamy, 7 July, Dunmore and Captain George Montagu decided to combine business with pleasure. The *Fowey* needed a new mast, and the governor, aboard ship since the date of his flight, was in a mind to relax his sea legs and to enjoy such a dinner as to which in more cheerful days he had been no stranger. Captain and chief magistrate thus climbed into the ship's boat, or "Barge," with a crew and two carpenters, and set out for Dunmore's "Farm" at Porto Bello, "about twelve miles above the Town of York where the Ship lay." With an imprudence surpassing understanding, they pulled away, also "in the face of day," as though supposing that not having the strength to attack the patriots, the latter would suspend hostilities while their enemies indulged in a leisurely repast. But the patriots viewed the matter in a different light. The barge was observed from the town, its destination "easily conjectured," and an express sent galloping to Williamsburg.

His Excellency did not later advise Lord Dartmouth whether the servants at Porto Bello were pleased to see their master. Undoubtedly the most of them were, existing as they had been in a twilight of belligerency, not taken captives to date but uncertain of what tomorrow might bring. At least they were assured that their master had not forgotten them. And so it was probably with the best of service that, once seated, governor and captain guest ate their fill, savored their wine, and drank consternation and worse to all rebels.

No sooner had they "done dinner," however, than servants hurried into the house, to announce that a "body of men in Arms" was advancing through the woods. Host and guest went outside to see for themselves. The servants were correct. The picture that follows is not one in the more sedate traditions of peerage and royal naval service—a confusion of shouts and a scramble for the barge, oarsmen pulling lustily downstream, and some of the intruders taking pot-shots at a servant frantically paddling a canoe in the wake of the barge.

Nor did Captain Montagu come away with his mast. The two carpenters, who had been working some distance from the house, were "Seized by these people," upon the governor's "own land!"; and the last he heard of the poor fellows, they were in Williamsburg "under a guard." But Dixon and Hunter, who, being on the spot, spoke with better authority, declared that when brought into the capital that same evening, the carpenters were "greatly satisfied in being removed from so disagreeable a situation as theirs was on board the man of war." [6]

Three days later, on 10 July, the *Mercury* (20 guns), Captain John Macartney, arrived in the York to relieve the larger *Fowey*, which having "being Stationed" in Virginia waters for "Some time," was ordered returned to Boston. A rebel pilot boat detected the approach of the relieving craft and notified Wilson Miles Cary, naval officer of the Lower District of the James River. In His Lordship's opinion Cary was also "one of the most active and virulent of the Enemies of Government." In support of this opinion, Cary immediately dispatched expresses to "allarm the Country," by giving it out that the *Mercury* was bringing British troops. This in turn inspired Peyton Randolph and Robert Carter Nicholas—the true rulers of the colony—"gladly" to seize upon the fiction in order to infuse "fresh apprehensions of threatening danger" and for "enviting" more independent companies down to the capital. That evening when the *Mercury* dropped anchor off Yorktown, a detachment arrived from Williamsburg to reinforce the local independent company, and "these People" set up camp behind the town a half-cannon shot from the two men-of-war. The rebels were "Continually parading in arms" along the shore, and when His Excellency sought nightly repose, he heard the soft lapping of waves against the *Fowey's* hull mixed with challenges shouted by the independents to "every boat or person that approaches them." His servants were by this means "prevented from passing with provisions," and his only recourse to sustain himself was to send armed parties to unguarded parts where necessities could be seized.[7] Most evidently, the governor was compelled to find a base more secure and congenial for future operations.

Prematurely Purdie reported the departure of the *Fowey* as of 13 July—she would not leave until the twenty-first. But he was correct in stating that one of her passengers would be Captain Foy. This was a stunning parting: it was Machiavelli abandoning Cesare Borgia. Purdie imagined that the captain had accepted command of General Gage's artillery, but in fact, as Foy marked out his itinerary for Ralph Wormeley, Jr., it was to "take a peep at the *Manoeuvres* at Boston and at the end of the summer to go to England."[8]

On 15 July, at 5:00 A.M., Lord Dunmore was boated from the *Fowey* to H.M. Schooner *Otter*, Captain Matthew Squire, which three hours later dropped anchor off Norfolk. On the seventeenth, one week having sufficed to give him his fill, His Lordship sat down and composed a letter in which while praising Captain Montagu for his "Zeal and Assiduity," he assailed Captain Macartney for seeming "to be actuated altogether by Principles totally different, and to have principally at heart the making Friends among his Majesty's greatest Enemies in this Country"—or, there could now be no further talk of compromise, and His Lordship having predicted that the colonists sought independence, they must be either crushed or driven to achieve according to his prediction. At 12:30 P.M. there was penned in the Otter's journal: "loosed sails to dry, and got out part of Lord Dunmore's bagage on board the Tender with his servants to go to Norfolk." Half an hour later there was written in the journal of the *Fowey*, which had dropped down to the Elizabeth River: "anchored with the Best Bower in 4 fathom Water off Sprowls Wharf to protect the *William* Merchant Ship taken into Government service by Lord Dunmore."[9]

In all probability His Lordship's mind on 17 July 1775 was not occupied exclusively by thoughts of Captain Montagu's zeal and assiduity, Captain Macartney's principles and heart, his own baggage and servants, or the seizure of private vessels. Almost certainly with the bitterness that frustration engenders in a mind of restricted compass, his thoughts were also on the meeting of many of his most inveterate enemies in the Anglican Town Church on Richmond Hill some sixty-odd air-miles to the northwest. For this was the day on which the third Virginia Convention was called to order.

If His Lordship was confronted by the problem of finding means to reimpose a now-collapsed status, his enemies were confronted by the problem of finding means to direct meaningfully a status in evolution. He had not the strength to reimpose, at least for the time being; they did have the strength to direct, again for the time being. With strength, reimposition, though with a bloodbath, would have been the easier task, for the route was known and could further be straightened by the application of vengeful power. Direction of an evolution was more difficult, for except that with necessary modifications it be traced along the known route, the way was wholly unexplored.

To patriots revolting without intent of revolution it was clear that during the interregnum a substitute executive authority must be erected. It was clear that the executive should be left to exercise its delegated powers when the present or a successor convention should not be in session. And it was clear that to avoid the peril of one-man dictatorship the executive should be plural, and to avoid the peril of plural tyranny the executive should be limited in tenure, regulated, and held accountable. Otherwise would be to trade a corrupt and corrupting authority for another potentially as venal and degrading.

It was also clear that once constituted, executive and legislature (for the latter the convention was to make itself) must be defended, as indeed insofar as possible the whole colony must be defended. That fact necessitated the creation of a unified military command—a colonial "army"—and what with a revived militia as a reserve, something more effective—and controllable—than were the independent companies which, even as the convention would be sitting, were to reveal that ardor and wisdom are not needfully identical twins.[10]

If the colony as a whole was to be defended, there was utmost obligation to keep an eye steadily on the West, that the hell of war be not compounded and that those long rifles in the use of which the hardy frontiersmen were amazingly skillful be released to further the military education of the enemy in the East. For this accomplishment skills not of marksmanship but of diplomacy would be demanded, because the Indian tribes were reportedly restless that Lord Dunmore had not reappeared in their midst to negotiate and, placating with gifts, conclude a final peace. With these considerations in mind, the House of Burgesses and the Council had on 24 June elected commissioners to take His Lordship's place. All but one of the six commissioners were unable to act immediately or to act at all. That one, James Wood, still technically a burgess, set out toward the end of June on a mission that was essentially a holding action designed to restrain the natives until they should be assembled at Fort Pitt on or about 10 September for a conclusive treaty; and since there was no longer a General Assembly to which he could report, he was instead to disclose his progress to the convention.[11]

Closely related to conditions on the frontiers were those arising from Dunmore's War of 1774 and from the assertion by the king that the right to grant vacant lands lay exclusively in his hands. As for the situation arising from the war, the governor had affirmed that the relief of unpaid officers and enlisted men was a matter deserving the "Attention" of the burgesses; but then on technical grounds he had refused to sign a bill providing relief, and crying needs would now be for the convention to assuage. As for the king's alleged ownership of vacant lands, any pronouncement of a Virginia position was left in abeyance by the fact that a committee to investigate and report had been appointed only on the last day of session of the second convention. Neither would a new committee report to the third. But the subject was to resurface with such vigor that the third would be compelled to deal with it.[12]

Establishing and supporting an interim executive, raising an army and a militia reserve, treating with Indian headmen, and compensating the convention delegates for their services (itself a matter no longer to be put off) presupposed adequate financing. The technicalities on which Lord Dunmore had refused to assent to the militia-payments bill were that it provided for an emission of paper money and contained no suspension clause by which it would remain ineffective until the royal pleasure, and then perhaps with disallowance, should be known. Yet how else could the funds be provided? Though without intrinsic value, a paper currency could be given worth by being made receivable in payment of taxes, by being made to represent given amounts of tobacco or other kind, or by being made to signify ownership of so many acres of land—provided they were not the king's—and by being retired at specified dates.[13]

Fully as consequential as the will to erect, treat, finance, and fight was acquisition of the munitions with which to fight. Gone was the time when a convention could content itself with "recommending" that local committees look into the matter of producing commodities basic to military supply. The appointment of Robert Carter Nicholas, Thomas Nelson, Jr., and Thomas Whiting as a munitions-advisory committee had thus far accomplished nothing beyond sending out an agent to purchase "Powder" in the West Indies. An Isle of Wight County subcommittee had asked Nelson where it might procure powder, and he replied that he supposed some might be had at Baltimore and offered to join in the "adventure." And apparently the limits of Whiting's accomplishments had been reached when he joined the other members of the Gloucester County committee in offering a premium to anyone who would produce "good gunpowder made in America." [14]

By 17 July 1775 the work of the delegates to the third Virginia Convention was cut out for them. And they dared not fail. But before many days should have passed, fear of failure must have risen high, for the evidence is that the practiced hand that had guided the House of Burgesses smoothly through its final session was observed to tremble. And the certainty is that erelong the proceedings of the convention were confounded.

1. See p. 24 above; 26 June 1775, Third Va. Convention.

2. The 1st printed notice of the Battle of Bunker Hill appeared in the *Va. Gazette* (Dixon and Hunter) of 6 July 1775.

3. P.R.O., C.O. 5/1353, fol. 168.

4. *Va. Gazette* (Purdie), 30 June 1775, supplement, 7 July 1775, supplement; ibid. (Dixon and Hunter), 1 July 1775.

5. P.R.O., C.O. 5/1353, fols. 227–28.

6. Ibid., fol. 228; *Va. Gazette* (Dixon and Hunter), 8 July 1775.

7. P.R.O., C.O. 5/1353, fols. 228–29.

8. *Va. Gazette* (Purdie), 14 July 1775; Noël Hume, *1775*, p. 267.

9. Clark, *Naval Docs. of the Am. Rev.*, I, 893, 903–4, 904.

10. See 26 July 1775, Third Va. Convention; 28 July, same, Procs. and nn. 7–8, Randolph to Officers and nn. 12–13; 29 July, same, Procs. of Officers and nn. 13–14, Corbin to Officers and nn. 15–16; 1 Aug., same, Procs. of Officers and nn. 17–21, Officers to President and Gentlemen and nn. 22–26; 5 Aug., same, Procs. and n. 12; 9

Aug., same, Duncan to President and Members and nn. 10–14; 10 Aug., same, Procs. and nn. 5–6; 11 Aug., same, Procs. and n. 5.

11. See pp. 19, 24 above; Thwaites and Kellogg, *Rev. on the Upper Ohio,* p. 35; 9 July 1775, Third Va. Convention, Wood to Randolph; 18 Aug., same, Wood to Randolph.

12. See pp. 14, 21–22, 22–23, 103–4 above; *Rev. Va.,* II, 383–84; 10 July 1775, Third Va. Convention, Fincastle Co. Committee, William Preston.

13. *Rev. Va.,* I, 1–8, II, 239, 240–41 n. 3; Jack P. Greene, "The Currency Act of 1764 in Imperial-Colonial Relations, 1764–1776," *Wm. and Mary Qtly.,* 3d ser., XVIII (Oct. 1965), 33–74; Joseph Albert Ernst, "Genesis of the Currency Act of 1764: Virginia Paper Money and the Protection of British Investment," ibid., 3d ser., XXV (Jan. 1968), 177–211.

14. *Rev. Va.,* II, 375–76; 16 June 1775, Second Va. Convention; 22 May 1775, Isle of Wight Co. Committee; 25 Apr. 1775, Gloucester Co. Committee.

Monday, 26 June 1775

Third Virginia Convention

Summons to Assemble

JUNE, 26, 1775.
THE delegates appointed by the counties and corporations of the colony are desired to meet at the town of *Richmond*, in the county of *Henrico*, on *Monday* the 17th of *July* next.[1]

Peyton Randolph, President.

Virginia Gazette (Purdie), 30 June 1775

Augusta County West: Request and Assurance

June 26th.
A Message to the Six Nations

Bretheren, Chiefs of the Six Nations
    As Some Chiefs of our Bretheren the Delawares are expected here this day; We request that you would also remove and encamp near them opposite to this place as you will then be more convenient when we are ready to speak to you which we hope will be very soon; and we desire you will not be uneasy on that account untill those of our friends necessary to be present are collected together[2]

A String.

MS transcript in hand of James Berwick, in papers of third Virginia Convention (Archives Division, Virginia State Library)

Augusta County West Committee: Thanks to Brave and Spirited Captain, with Qualification

June 26th: 1775

In Committee of the Western Waters of Augusta County
Resolved that the thanks of this Committee be given to Capt. George Gibson

who upon hearing of Major ⟨John⟩ Connollys being illegally carried off by the Sheriff of Pennsylvania[3] and prevented by that means from executing the trust reposed in him by Government did in a brave and Spirited manner take Possession of the Fort and Arms submitting his Conduct to the directions of this Committee.

Resolved that the taking of Messrs. ⟨Joseph⟩ Spear, ⟨George⟩ Wilson and ⟨Devereux⟩ Smith without authority from the Civil Majestrates was illegal and this Committee do give their Instructions to Captain Gibson to have those Gentlemen brought before a Justice of the Peace to be dealt with as the Law directs.[4]

> A Copy from the Minutes
> JAMES BERWICK
> Clerk to the Committee

> Autograph document, signed, loose papers of third Virginia Convention (Archives Division, Virginia State Library)

Bedford County Committee

The Committee Desire the "Atendance" of Mr. John Hook[5]

This committee are in[for]med by Mr. Charles Lynch, that someti[me] in the month of May in conversation with Mr. John Hook, at Samuel Crockets, about an Independent Company in Bottetourt, entering of their protest about going out of the Colony;[6] the sd. Lynch told the sd. Hook they had men enough to the Northward; yes, sd. the sd. Hook & swore there were too many, the sd. Lynch answered, yes, too many by all the Regular Troops, the sd. Hook then expressed himself in the warmest manner, & swore by God, there never will be peace till the Americans get well Floged, the sd. Lynch then reproached the sd. Hook with being an unworthy member of Society, & accused him with dispersing a number of Pamphlets wrote against the American cause with an intention of raising divitions among the People, which he did not deny but; endeavoured to justify, by saying that a majority of the Country was of his Opinion, at least he was certai[n] a majority of the People of Bedford were. Whereupon the Committee ordered that James Steptoe & Haynes Morgan Gent. do wait upon the sd. Mr. Hook with the above Charge & desire his Atendance before the Committee tomorrow at Ten O'C[loc]k to answer it.[7]

> Recipient's copy, MS document, unsigned, in unidentified hand, John Hook Papers (Manuscripts Department, William R. Perkins Library, Duke University)

1. At last the speaker-president had dropped the other shoe. The reasons for selecting Richmond as the site for the third convention were now even more compulsive
than when the town had been designated as the meeting place for the second (*Rev.
Va.*, II, 253).

2. This message was probably sent either by George Croghan, chairman of the
district committee, or by John Campbell, "Vice President." Major Connolly's inability
as the governor's agent to procure supplies because of the "Unhappy disputes of the
Times," forced the committee itself to stretch local resources for the provision of
gifts and sustenance (12 July 1775, Third Va. Convention, John Campbell . . .). The
matter thus appears to have involved a convenience in distribution.

3. The sheriff of Westmoreland County, Pa., was John Carnaghan (Hassler, *Old
Westmoreland*, p. 15).

4. For Connolly's abduction, see 22 June 1775, Third Va. Convention and n. 2. Capt.
GEORGE GIBSON was the brother of John Gibson, elected to the district committee on
16 May 1775. Fluent in several languages and Indian dialects and a failure in as many
business ventures, George was a native Pennsylvanian who had sided with the Virginians in the border dispute. He had seen action as a 2d lieutenant in the Battle of
Point Pleasant, was at this time 28 years old, and could assuage lonelier moments by
playing the fife (Thwaites and Kellogg, *Rev. on the Upper Ohio*, p. 144 n. 51).

Judging 1 Virgina militia major the equivalent of 3 Pennsylvania justices of the
peace, young Gibson descended with "a Mobb or Sett of Conely's friends" and seized
the persons of Spear (a trader with a store at Kittanning), Wilson (whose land at the
mouth of Georges Creek was "in the heart of Virginianism"), and Smith (a trader at
Fort Pitt) and bore them off in a leaky flatboat to Fort Fincastle at Wheeling. There,
if Arthur St. Clair's information be credited, the captives were "exposed to every
species of insult and abuse," and to add to the outrage, "An attempt" was also made
"to carry off the sheriff, but miscarried."

This much wrought, the members of the Augusta County West committee, according to Valentine Crawford, "wrote a verey Sperited Letter to the gentlemen of pen
Cometee to demand Conely Back and all Signd and Sent it with an express on the receipt of which they amedently sent Majer Conely Back." The 3 insulted and abused
prisoners were then released (Hamilton, *Letters to Washington*, V, 178; Hassler, *Old
Westmoreland*, pp. 10, 15, 25; W. H. Smith, *St. Clair Papers*, I, 375).

That Smith and Wilson were members of the Virginia committee (16 May 1775,
Augusta Co. West Committee) illustrates not that these occurrences were clashes between zealous patriots and dedicated loyalists, but that in a region of uncertain jurisdictions confusion was regnant.

5. The following document is itself not dated. It is here entered under the date of
receipt as docketed by Hook: "recd. June 26 1775 of Jas Steptoe one of the Committee
for Bedford County." The committee's reference in the last sentence to its meeting
"to morrow," indicates that the letter was written on 26 June, for the committee met
on 27 June 1775.

6. There is no other record attesting the proceedings of "an independent company
in Bottetourt" County in protest against being, or the possibility of being, called to
serve outside the confines of Virginia. It may have been that the protest was known
to members of the third Virginia Convention. Almost certainly it was known to John
Bowyer, the single Botetourt delegate to attend. But a protest like this was not the
stuff from which patriot propaganda could be made. Propaganda could properly be
made out of a pledge of service such as had been proferred by the Williamsburg independent company on 25 May 1775—and even that pledge had been hedged by the

stipulation that the men not depart from the colony should doing so leave "their own country in a defenceless state," according to whose judgment being unstated. Thus was there hard necessity, as George Mason would express it, to "melt down all the volunteers and independent companies" into one "great establishment," for only if so reorganized could units and individuals be controlled (19 July 1775, n. 5).

7. Hook's response is under the date heading of 27 June 1775, Bedford Co. Committee, 2d entry.

Tuesday, 27 June 1775

Third Virginia Convention

Williamsburg Representation on Late Alarming Report

At a meeting of the inhabitants, last Tuesday, at the Court-house, it was agreed upon to represent to the Delegates in Convention the expediency of reinforcement of men from the adjacent counties, to be stationed here with the city company, on account of the late alarming report of troops being destined for this colony, from Great Britain.[1] The number thought requisite at present is 250. It is generally believed this measure will be approved of by the Convention, and that the towns below this will be provided in like manner;[2] so that, in case of emergency, the whole can unite upon the shortest notice, and act in opposition to any attempt that may be made by British troops towards the destruction of public liberty in this colony.[3]

Virginia Gazette (Dixon and Hunter), 1 July 1775

Accomack County Committee

A Navigation Chart and a Flaxen Rope

At a meeting of the committee of Accomack *county, at the courthouse, the 27th of June* 1775.[4]

SOUTHY SIMPSON, *Esq; in the chair.*

A COMPLAINT having been made, that *James Arbuckle*, a member of this committee, had drawn a map of the Eastern Shore, and that the sea coast was delineated therein, so as to furnish information to vessels to explore our harbours, and that the same had been delivered to his Excellency the Governour for that purpose.

The said *Arbuckle* appeared voluntarily before the committee, and acknowledged that he had drawn a draught, or map, of the internal part of the Eastern Shore, but denied that he had illustrated any of the harbours, or marked any of the soundings or shoals, which he had delivered to mr. Andrew Sprowle of Gosport.[5]

Sundry witnesses were then called in, and duly sworn; and, by their testimony, it appeared that the said *Arbuckle* had shewn the said map publickly to many of the inhabitants of this county, before he parted with it; that he had drawn the same at the request of the custom-house officers, and, so far as relates to this county, from an old draught which he had made some years ago; and that the use the said officers told him they designed to make of it was to excuse themselves to his Excellency the Governour from a suspicion of neglect in office.[6] And it also appeared, that there were none of the harbours laid down with such exactness as to give any new insight to any person to come into them; and it appeared, that the governour is in possession of the said map. And it appearing farther, that the said *James Arbuckle* has, as well heretofore, as before this committee, expressed great uneasiness that he should have been so imprudent as to have done any thing to alarm his country at this time.

Resolved unanimously, that it is the opinion of this committee that the said *James Arbuckle* is not intentionally guilty of any offence against *American* liberty.

A complaint having also been made against *John Sherlock*, of this county, that he has expressed himself in such manner as to prove him an enemy to the liberties of this country, and he being called upon to attend the committee this day, refused, but wrote them an abusive and insulting letter.[7]

Several witnesses were then called upon, and sworn; and, by their evidence, it appeared that he had, at sundry different conversations, declared, in substance, "that such people as oppose the ministerial measures with America are rebels; that he shall be employed hereafter in hanging them; and that if no hemp can be got, he has plenty of flax growing." It is therefore *unanimously resolved*, that we hold the said JOHN SHERLOCK to be *an enemy to American liberty;* and that we are determined, immediately, to break off all dealings and intercourse with him, and with every person who shall have any connection with him, until he shall make such proper acknowledgments, and show such genuine marks of repentance and reformation, as shall be satisfactory to a majority of the committee.[8]

Resolved, that these proceedings be immediately printed in the Virginia gazette.

John Powell, clerk.

Virginia Gazette (Purdie), 22 July 1775, supplement

Bedford County Committee

The Most Cordial Reception

AT a meeting of the committee for the county of Bedford, the 27th day of June, 1775. The committee being apprehensive that the inhabitants of the lower parts of this colony may, possibly (in the course of the present unhappy dispute between Great Britain and her American colonies) be compelled to quit their habitations, wish it to be known to them, that the inhabitants of this county will cheerfully give them, and whatever they may think proper to remove among us, the most cordial reception, afford them every possible assistance, and that they shall freely participate of any thing we possess.[9]

Ordered, that the clerk of this committee do transmit a copy of this resolution to the printer, to be inserted in the Virginia gazette.

Robert Alexander, clerk.

Virginia Gazette (Purdie), 22 July 1775, supplement

Pledge to "Conceil" Sentiments Disagreeable to Committee

Gentmn

In Answer to your Summons and Memorandum of charges exhibited against me by Mr. Charles Lynch, I beg leave to reply as follows: [10]

If I said there never would be Peace 'till the Americans get well flog'd, I meant to say the Bostonians; I am loth to Contradict Mr. Lynch but think he must be mistaken as to the word Americans, it has allways been my oppinion since the beginning of this unhappy dispute, the Bostonians did not behave well in distroying the Tea [11] and that it is wrong to take a Brothers Part under those circumstances; it was on this Principle that I wished them a scurging and not from any Enmity to the Liberties of America. I cannot allow by not gainsaying Mr. Lynchs Accusation "of dispersing a number of Pamphlets wrote against the American cause, with an intention to raise devisions amongst the People," to be construed an acknowledgment of the charge, or sufficient Evidence to Prove it; I show'd the Pamphlets here spoke of, but to a very few of my acquaintance, I do not recollect of there ever being dispersed by me to any one, except two or three of the inhabitants of this Town and one of lending them to Mr. Robt. Cowan which he had a sight of at Mr. ⟨James⟩ Donald's without my knowledge and afterwards wrote to me for the loan of the same; I beg leave to observe to this Committee that amongst the Pamphlets here spoke of there was some for as well as against the present Measures, that I never conceiled those for or exposed those against the American cause which may be supposed I would have done, If I had any design of making devisions amongst the People as is alledged; I assure this Committee that I had no kind of design in bringing those Pamphlets to this County, more then to inform my Self both sides of the question.

From the intercourse I have lately had amongst the People of this County (which on recollection I find to be only a small part of them), I was led to beleve that there was a Majority against the Present violent Measures, but from Present appearances, I now think otherwise; I think Mr. Lynch is wrong in saying that I was Certain a Majority of the People of Bedford disapproved of the Present Proceedings, I only gave it as my opinion.

Since I find my Political sentiments disagreeable to this Committee which I wish ever to live in Friendship with, I assure them that in time to come I will conceil them, and as to the Pamphlets I will deliver them up to the Committee to be delt with as they please.[12]

When I Assure this Committee that I wish the Liberty and Prosperity of this Countrey as sincerely as any of them possibly can do, I hope a difference in oppinion as to the mode of Attaining the same, will not be judged sufficient grounds for declaring one of such Sentiments an enemy to American Liberty.[13]

> Autograph letter draft, unsigned, John Hook Papers (Manuscripts Department, William R. Perkins Library, Duke University)

1. Following the meeting of 23 June, that of the present day appears to have been triggered by a "late alarming report" printed in Purdie's *Va. Gazette* of 24 June 1775 that "parties" of 2,000 men each were to be "detached" from the royal troops at Boston, with missions of striking at "South Carolina, Virginia, and such of the provinces as are deemed the most refractory."

2. Under this concept, in the same wise that Williamsburg would provide a shield for the third convention or for any executive authority that it might establish to sit in Richmond or elsewhere, presumably above the Tidewater, "the towns below"—Yorktown, Hampton, and Portsmouth—would provide a shield for Williamsburg.

3. If the meeting prepared a petition to the convention or an "instruction" to the city delegate, Peyton Randolph, it has not been found. At best Randolph may have discussed the matter informally with other delegates, for one of the very 1st considerations of the convention was to be the raising of "a sufficient armed Force" for the "Defence and protection" of the colony as a whole (19 July 1775, Third Va. Convention).

4. The last preceding recorded meeting of the Accomack County committee had been a week earlier, on 20 June 1775.

5. Mr. Sprowle was a prominent Gosport merchant whose name erelong would further be newsworthy (9, 12, 14, 16 Aug., 1775, Norfolk Borough; 16 Aug., Norfolk Co. Committee).

6. The collector at the port town of Accomac (the spelling of which does not contain the terminal *k* dignifying that of the county) was Walter Hatton; the naval officer assisting, David Bowman. The comptroller had died in the previous spring, and his position was probably still vacant (*Exec. Journs. Coun. Col. Va.*, VI, 388; *Va. Gazette* [Dixon and Hunter], 14 Apr. 1774). The port was a minor one, and collec-

tions on commodities exported from there to Great Britain could not be expected to be large. But since Oct. 1771 until almost the end of 1774 His Majesty had realized only some £35 in revenue from the custom house at Accomac. During that same period of time none of the houses of the 5 other ports of entry reported less than £12,000, and most of them considerably more (P.R.O., C.O. 5/1350, fol. 180; C.O. 5/1351, fols. 22, 42; C.O. 5/1352, fols. 40, 126; C.O. 5/1353, fol. 99). A map of such general character as Arbuckle described might have been of little use to a pilot, but it could have been employed to show how the broken, cove-riddled, island-concealing Eastern Shore, especially on the Atlantic side, would necessitate the presence of flotillas of revenue cutters to be kept from being a smuggler's paradise.

7. The "abusive and insulting letter" has not been found.

8. For the "calm reflection" that would lead John Sherlock to revise his convictions, see 28 June 1775.

9. Bedford was the 3d county of record to offer haven to potential refugees (10, 17 May 1775, Cumberland Co. Committee; 22 May, Buckingham Co. Committee).

10. The "memorandum" to which the present item is John Hook's reply is under the date heading of 26 June 1775, Bedford Co. Committee.

The present item is undated and is arbitrarily assigned on the supposition that Hook prepared it for presentation to the committee on the present date. That the committee met is demonstrated by the immediately preceding entry.

11. On the night of 16 Dec. 1773 (*Rev. Va.*, I, 93).

12. This offer varies wholly from that futilely made by Rev. John Wingate in Orange County 3 months earlier (ibid., II, 377–78, 386).

13. The disposition of this case is unknown, but apparently the committee judged that there was not evidence concrete enough to justify proceedings against Hook as "an enemy to American Liberty." Still suspected, he was later mobbed and in Oct. 1777 forced to sign a loyalty oath. Then after the war he would have immortality of sorts thrust upon him in a trial involving his attempt to collect on a warrant owed him by the Commonwealth of Virginia for 2 steers taken for the Continental Army. Patrick Henry, opposing counsel, convulsed the courtroom with a ludicrous and implausible tale of a mercenary Hook at Yorktown "hoarsely bawling through the American camp, '*beef! beef! beef!*'" (Audrey K. Spence, "John Hook, Loyalist," *Va. Mag. of Hist. and Biog.*, XXXIV [Apr. 1926], 149–50; Wirt, *Patrick Henry* (9th ed.), pp. 389–91).

Wednesday, 28 June 1775

Accomack County Independent Company

Free and Voluntary Recantation of
John Sherlock beneath Liberty Pole

Mr. Pinkney, at a meeting of the Committee of Accomack county, held at the court house on Tuesday last,[1] it was found necessary to hold up to public contempt a certain John Sherlock, of the said county, for having expressed himself, at sundry times, in the most daring and insulting manner against the good people who have proved themselves, by their behaviour, friends to American liberty. Mr. Sherlock, instead of appearing before the committee, agreeable to summons, wrote them an abusive, insulting letter; whereupon the day next after the committee had proceeded against him agreeable to the rules of the association (the proceedings of which will be in Purdie's paper) [2] part of the Independent Company of this county went to his house, took, and carried him to the court house, and, after a solemn trial, received from him, under the Liberty Pole, his recantation; a copy whereof you have enclosed. Mr. Sherlock, at the Company's approach, took shelter in an upper room of his house, with two loaded guns, but was prudent enough to decline making use of them.

WHEREAS I the subscriber have thoughtlessly and imprudently at sundry times, expressed myself to the following purpose: that such people as oppose the present ministerial measures respecting America, are rebels, and that I expect to be employed at a future day in hanging them, and if no hemp could be had I had flax enough, and that I wanted no greater bondage, under the banner of liberty, than to be bound by the association; and I have also expressed myself very imprudently in calling the Independent Company of this County an unlawful mob, and many other idle and foolish words; I do hereby, in the most solemn and serious manner, declare that at those times, when I have held such language, I did not mean as much as I said, and I do hereby declare my most unfeigned sorrow for what I have done or said, and in the most humble manner ask the pardon of the said Independent Company, (which was accordingly done by application being made to each member of the said Company respectively) and I declare I look upon the said Company as a very respectable body of men, and, upon the most calm reflection, I declare my opinion to be altered. I most heartily wish success to this my native country in her present honest struggle for liberty with the mother country, and do here promise to do all in my power to retrieve my character with my countrymen. This acknowledgment and confession I make freely and voluntarily, and desire the same may be published in the public papers.

John Sherlock.

Virginia Gazette (Pinkney), 20 July 1775

1. That is, on the preceding day, 27 June 1775.

2. The "rules" by which the committee had "proceeded" were those of article 11 providing for the publication of the names of violators of the Continental Association (8 Apr. 1775, n. 5). The "proceedings" were printed in the supplement to Purdie's "paper" of 22 July 1775, but since the present narrative and Sherlock's declaration appeared in Pinkney's gazette of 2 days earlier, the public learned of the result of the proceedings before it could read the formal statement of their cause.

Thursday, 29 June 1775

Third Virginia Convention

Augusta County West: Sweat, Dust, Ears, and Tears

At a Meeting held with the Indians at Fort Dunmore [1] June 29th. 1775 on behalf of the Colony of VIRGINIA

Present.

Major John Connolly,[2] Alexr. McKee Esqr. Depy. Agent
Coll George Croghan
Majors William Crawford
Edward Ward
Thomas Smal⟨l⟩man
John McCullough
Captains Stephenson ⟨John Stevenson⟩
⟨Dorsey⟩ Pentecost
⟨Caleb⟩ Graydon

John Campbell ⎫
John Cannon   ⎬ Gent Justices of the Peace
Alexr. Ross   ⎪
John Gibson   ⎭

The Revd. Mr. ⟨Alexander⟩ Balmain⟨e⟩, Mr. Charles Simms ⟨Sims⟩ Atty at Law, with a number of other Gentlemen principal Inhabitants of the Country.

Indians.

Six Nations	Delawares
Keyashota	Custaloga
Enyouyouda	New Comer
Chauchauchauteda	Capt. White-eyes
Sonowois	Capt. Pipe
Sirewhoane	Capt. Killbuck
Warriors	Seapichili
Concuyendau	Esheeaunechowet
Cughsauego	Metechamin
Togashswegauent	
Canechtowne	

Major Connolly spoke as follows.[3]
Bretheren
Chiefs of the several Nations present
I am glad to see so many of you met together on my Invitation, and I take

this opportunity of bidding you hearty welcome; agreeable to Custom, Bretheren, I wipe the sweat and dust off your bodies which the Fatigue of your Long Journey hither may have occasioned.[4]

A String [5] to each Nation

Bretheren

I next clean your Ears of every false and evil report that may have entered them on your way and that may [6] be prejudicial to the occasion we are now met upon that you may be the better able distincly to comprehend what may be said to you

A String to each Nation

Bretheren

I now wipe the Tears from your Eyes which hath been shed for the losses you have sustained in the death of any of your family since we last saw each other in Council; [7] and I likewise remove any Grief from your hearts which may continue to give you Trouble on this account, that your minds may be at ease and Tranquility to receive the good speeches that is to be delivered to you with Satisfaction

A String to each Nation

Bretheren

Chiefs of the Six Nations present.

It gives me pleasure to see so many of you here who have shewn your Wisdom by a strict adherence to the peace of this Country during the last Summer, and that I have an opportunity of restoring into your hands those of your Emigrants who have been heretofore led astray who we hope for the future will have the benefit of your wise advice and I would be glad to convince you that it was the sole design of your Brother the Big-knife in ordering them to be brought to this Place and that we had nothing more at heart than the general good of the whole which I make no doubt you will be fully convinced of and that you will chearfully join with us in establishing a lasting friendship.[8]

A Belt.

Bretheren

Chiefs of the Mingo Prisoners

As we now return you into your former Situation in the chain of friendship [9] we are to expect that you will be strong in promoting good and that you will ever for the future have a due regard to the Advice and Councils of the wise Chiefs of the Six Nations whom you will always find so strictly united in friendship with their Bretheren the English as not to be shaken and they are the only People who study your real Welfare. Therefore we make no doubt from the friendship and brotherly treatment you have met with amongst us, that it is our greatest desire to live in peace and Amity not only with you but all our Indian Bretheren, in promoting of which from your Knowledge now of our kindness you will have it greatly in your power to promote and to enable you to this good end We deliver this belt.

A Belt.

Bretheren
    Chiefs of the Several Nations
    As our younger Bretheren the Shawanese are not yet arrived and we have
finished the necessary Ceremonies usual upon such Occasions between us
who are present, We think it best to wait a few days for the Shawanese as it
is probable we may in that time see or hear from them; This will convince
them we were not unmindful of them.[10]

A String

This is all Bretheren the Bigknife has to say to you at Present.
    The Answer of the Six Nations to the speech requesting their Opinion
whether the Treaty is to be delay'd for the coming of the Shawanese
Brother the Big Knife [11]
    We like well to hear what you say concerning our younger Bretheren the
Shawanese which will convince them they were not forgot by either of us,
but as our situation here is well known to both of us with respect to the
Scarsity of Provisions,[12] time cannot be delayed long⟨;⟩ however we are willing to stay three days and if we do not hear from them in that time we shall
then be better able to judge how to proceed at our meeting

A String

    The Delawares Answer to the same [13]
Bretheren
    We return you thanks for what we have heard to day. we are glad to see
from what has passed that our friendship bears so good an aspect. what the
Six Nations have agreed to with regard to the Shawanese we are satisfied
with.[14]

> MS transcript in hand of James Berwick, in papers
> of third Virginia Convention (Archives Division,
> Virginia State Library)

Augusta County West: John Proctor to the Committee

Gentlemen
    We have this Day met and Consulted our Brethren in Committee for our
County concerning the Present dangerous Disputes subsisting this long time
between the Colonies of Virginia and Pennsylvania, and as we Repose Con-
fidence in the Gentlemen members of your Committee that you will Maturely
Deliberately and honestly consider the Injuries that daily Arise from these
Disputes to Every Inhabitant of this young and once Peaceable Unanimous
and very Prosperous County, We have thought it prudent in order to have
Annimosities and Feuds of every Kind as well as Jealousies Hostilities and
Violent proceedings Entirely Removed to propose to your Honourable
Chamber A Treaty of Peace and Reconciliation by Settling a Temporary
Line or Boundary as Soon as Possible.
    We have appointed Mr. James Kinkead [15] a member of our Committee to

attend on your Honors And will Expect the Sence of your Chamber by him at his Return. next Tuesday we meet to Receive your Answer, And will Proceed farther Agreeable thereto.[16]

Westmoreland County ⎫   Signed by Order of the Committee
Committee Chamber   ⎬   John Proctor [17] Chairman
29th June 1775.   ⎭   A Copy

                                        JAMES BERWICK
                                        Clk to the Comtee. of the
                                           West Waters.

                                                                     Ibid.

1. That is, Fort Pitt (19 May 1775, n. 4).

2. For the return of Major Connolly, see 26 June 1775, n. 4.

3. When Connolly rose and spoke, the actual treaty negotiations were begun.

4. What was "agreeable to Custom" was a metaphorical saving of time; it was also an elusion of what might have been an extreme physical difficulty in removing "any Grief" from human "hearts."

5. Of wampum (20 May 1775, n. 7).

6. James Berwick miscopied the word as "me."

7. The "last" council at which Major Connolly had been the spokesman for Virginia was held early in May 1774 at Fort Pitt before the outbreak of Dunmore's War. The Shawnee, then present, had been frank enough to brand his promises possible "lies" (Randolph C. Downes, *Council Fires on the Upper Ohio* [Pittsburgh, 1940], p. 167).

8. Those of the "Emigrants" restored were the 12 Mingo hostages held at the fort through the previous winter. The Mingo were emigrants from central Pennsylvania (19 May 1775, n. 3; 20 May, n. 1).

9. See 19 May 1775, n. 5.

10. The Shawnee were the "younger Bretheren" of the Delawares, who in the later years of the 17th and the earlier of the 18th century had invited them to settle in Pennsylvania; hence they were also the "second sons," or grandsons, of the Six Nations, which claimed suzerainty in the lands of the Old Northwest (Hodge, *Handbook of Am. Indians*, pt. 2, 533; 20 May 1775, n. 3).

11. The spokesman for the Six Nations may have been Keyashota, 1st-named chief in the journal.

12. For the "Scarsity of Provisions," see 26 June 1775, n. 2.

13. The spokesman for the Delawares may have been Custaloga.

14. The negotiations would be resumed on 3 July 1775.

15. The spelling of the surname of James Kinkead was susceptible to a number of variations, especially on the frontier.

16. For the sorts of "Jealousies Hostilities and Violent proceedings" that the Pennsylvania committeemen were professedly eager to see "Entirely Removed," see 22 June 1775, n. 3 and 26 June, n. 5. The Virginia committee would reply to this proposition on 3 July 1775.

17. JOHN PROCTOR, an orthographer of horrendous attainments, signed but could not have written this letter. Notwithstanding the nature of his compositions (for an example of which see Draper MSS, 1U129, State Hist. Soc. of Wis.), he had been sheriff of Bedford County, Pa., and of Westmoreland when the latter county was

carved from the former in 1773. For at least 6 years a resident in the West, he was now about 35 years of age and had been engaged during the past month in raising a militia regiment (Charles Dahlinger, "Fort Pitt," *Western Pa. Hist. Mag.*, V [Jan. 1922], 40; Hassler, *Old Westmoreland*, p. 15; Thwaites and Kellogg, *Rev. on the Upper Ohio*, p. 200 n. 37).

Friday, 30 June 1775

Cumberland County Committee

Munitions and an Address [1]

[At] [2] a Meeting of the Committee for Cumberland County June 30th, 1775.
[Pre]sent, Mr. Chairman ⟨George Carrington⟩, Mr. ⟨William⟩ Fleming, Mr. ⟨Littlebury⟩ Mosby, Mr. ⟨John⟩ Mayo, Mr. Joseph Car⟨rin⟩gton, Mr. ⟨Richard⟩ James, Mr. George Carrington junr. Mr. William Smith, Mr. Robert [S]mith, Mr. ⟨Benjamin⟩ Wilson, Mr. ⟨Frederick⟩ Hatcher, Mr. Edward Carrington, Mr. John Woodson and Mr. Charles Woodson junr.

Mr. James and Mr. Edward Carrington informed the Committee, that their most careful Endeavours to procure Gun Powder in America had proved ineffectual; and desiring to be advised whether they should risque the Money put into their Hands for that Purpose upon a Plan proposed by Robert Carter Nicholas Esqr. for importing that Article from foreign Parts; Resolved that it is the Opinion of this Committee that Mr. James and Mr. Carrington continue their Endeavours to procure Gun Powder and other Articles of Ammunition in America; but that the Attempt to procure it from foreign Parts be suspended till the Resolution of the ensuing Convention in that Respect be known.[3]

Resolved, that Application be made to the several Committees of Amelia, Chesterfield, Buckingham and Prince Edward, requesting them to join this Committee by Way of Subscription in erecting a Powder Mill, with six Beaters on each side; and that Mr. ⟨Richard⟩ Eggleston and Geo. Carrington junr. or either of them, apply to Amelia, Mr. Mayo to Chesterfield, Mr. Fleming to Goochland, Mr. Ed. Carrington to Buckingham and Prince Edward.

Resolved, that Mr. Fleming and Mr. Edward Carrington, draw a Scheme for the Purpose aforesaid and furnish Copies to the Members aforesaid, also each Member of this Committee that they may apply for Subscriptions.[4]

The following Address to the Inhabitants of this County was proposed and unanimously agreed to.

Dear Country Men,

In Contemplation of securing your dearest Rights and Liberties against the Oppression of Great Britain, you, some Months ago, by your free and un-biassed Suffrages, elected us, subordinate to those august Bodies, the Continental Congress and Provincial Convention, Guardians of these invaluable Blessings.[5] At an early Period, after receiving this Honour, we convened ourselves for the Purpose of discharging the important Trusts so reposed in us, and have from Time to Time devised such Measures towards a happy Event of your important Contest, as the maturest Deliberation could suggest; in return you have ever paid us the grateful Tribute of entire Confidence, testified by the most implicit Acquiescence and Concurrence in whatever we recommended. We with pleasure bear in Mind a very recent Instance of your Confidence, that of the speedy and cheerful Contribution of Monies requested of [you] for the Purpose of making Military Preparation; and this [con]tribution you may depend that no Means shall be untried fo[r] laying out to the best Advantage. We however find that you can still contribute much to this Preparation by immediately applying with Diligence to the making of Salt Petre; this is an Article n[ow] wanted as an Ingredient for Gun Powder; your Tobacco Houses and Stable Floors are Foundations from which it may be produced, with but little Trouble, in great Abundance and Perfection: [We] therefore most earnestly request, that you obtain the most short an[d] ready Process, and lose no Time in making this necessary, but easy procured Article.[6]

We have been attentive to the Movements of the cursed instruments of your Troubles, and, had any Prospects of an Accommodation with the parent State come within our View, should gladly have laid them before you; such an Event however we have till lately hoped for, but must now tell you it cannot be expected at all[.] Your Enemies seem implacable in their Determinations to ruin American Liberty, and for effecting that diabolical Purpose, suffer no Engine to ly still, that can be put in Motion, by any Manouvre, however mean, cowardly and detestable: For Instances we need only refer you to the late Conduct of that MERCENARY, MINISTERIAL TOOL, LORD DUN-MORE, within your own Colony, and be assured that many such Hirelings are employed, and will be as long as Means can be supplied for paying them.[7] In short believe us, when we say, that Nothing can be expected for your Relief from the Virtue of a British Ministry or Parliament; although there are some Members in both Houses of the latter, who, ashamed of the black Deeds of their Body, daily, to their lasting Honour, hold out their Names as Dissentients; yet, unhappily for Britain, and America too, they are but few. You may indeed consider yourselves as in a State of War with Great Britain, for several Engagements have been between her Troops and the Inhabitants of your Sister Colony of Massachusetts Bay, and each Power still stands in opposite Military Array. All the American Colonies have long since united in opposing British Oppression, a Blow, therefore, struck alone, must be considered as struck at all; You may daily look for the Invaders in your own Colony, or should the whole Force of the Enemy be bent on that, or any other Province, your Assistance must not be denied. In your Arms, under divine Providence, rests your Security. We entreat you therefore by that Regard you have for the Safety of your own Persons; for your Liberties, civil and religious; for every Thing which can render your Being on Earth happy; for what is of more weighty Consideration, the Happiness of yr. Posterity for endless Ages to come; under Sanction of that Confidence you repose in us; that, without delay, you take up your Arms; put them in the best Condition; get acquainted with the Military Discipline; and stand in readiness for actual Service, upon the first Sound of the Trumpet of War. Suppress every Animosity among yourselves; pay Obedience to officers properly ap[po]inted; let no discontents on Account of their Advancement in[ter]rupt the necessary Preparations; let Harmony dwell a[mo]ngst you: — Remember the old Proverb, "United, we stand; Divided, we fall." Preserve what Ammunition you have by you; do not expend it on any Occasion whatever, except in the greatest Necessity, for more will be wanted for your Protection than can shortly be procured. Observe these En[tr]eaties, and fear not; your American Brethren are firm; you have many Friends in Great Britain and Ireland; and [i]n the Justness of your Cause, you may, with Confidence, look up to Heaven for Assistance: In Compliance with the Appointment of the Grand Continental Congress, devote Thursday the twentieth Day of July to publick Humiliation, Fasting and Prayer.[8]

Resolved, that the foregoing Address from the Committee to the Inhabitants of Cumberland County, be read by the several Ministers to their Congregations; that it be sent to Mr. ⟨Alexander⟩ Purdie to be printed and that he also be requested to furnish the Chairman with a Number of Handbills thereof for the Benefit of this County.[9]

Signed Geo. Carrington, Chairman
Teste, THOMAS MILLER, Cl. Com.

> Committee MS journal, the whole, including Carrington's signature, in hand of Thomas Miller (Archives Division, Virginia State Library)

To March and to Support

At a Meeting of the Committee for the County of Cumberland the same 30th. day of June 1775. Present, the same Members as before, Mr. ⟨Frederick⟩ Hatcher excepted.

Mr. Chairman laid before the Committee a Letter dated the 27th. Instant, requesting that twenty five Men should march from this County to join a Body for the Protection of Williamsburgh, and it's Neighbourhood, against Violence apprehended from British Troops.[10]

Resolved, that Captain Charles Scott be in the most respectful Manner requested to detach that Number from his Company of Volunteers for the Purpose aforesaid.[11]

Resolved, that each Member of this Committee will pay his Proportion of five Pounds advanced by the Representative of this County as a further Contribution for the Support of the Delegates in behalf of this Colony, now sitting at Philadelphia.[12]

Signed, Geo. Carrington, Ch.Man
Teste, THOMAS MILLER, Cl. Com.

Ibid.

1. The last preceding meeting of the Cumberland County committee had been on 17 May 1775.

2. Letters and one punctuation mark placed within regular brackets in the present item are those torn from the left margin and borrowed from the printed copy in McIlwaine, *15th Annual Library Report*, pp. 14–16.

3. The "most careful Endeavours" were those undertaken pursuant to the committee order of 21 Apr. 1775 (pp. 56–57 above). The "Plan" of Robert Carter Nicholas may have been made in consultation with Thomas Nelson, Jr., or Thomas Whiting, or both, they being the other members of the committee elected by the second Virginia Convention to procure munitions for the colony (13 Apr. 1775, n. 7). For what was probably part of the "Plan," see 16 June 1775.

4. Implementation of the "Scheme" would be reported on 28 Aug. 1775, a date not encompassed within the present volume.

5. For the 11th article of the Continental Association in which the first Continental Congress in effect directed the counties to form committees of correspondence, see 8 Apr. 1775, n. 5. The irony of subordination to an "august" provincial convention arose from the fact that the convention was an integer devised by the freeholders and "Inhabitants" of many parts—counties and corporations—that were themselves the creatures of royal authority.

6. For the "cheerful Contribution of Monies" made by the inhabitants of the county, see the proceedings of 10 May 1775. On its last day of session, 27 Mar. 1775, the second Virginia Convention had "Resolved unanimously that Salt Petre & Sulphur being Articles of great & necessary use the making, collecting & refining them to the utmost extent be recommended, the Convention being of Opinion that it may be done to great Advantage" (*Rev. Va.*, II, 382).

7. For examples of "the late Conduct" of Lord Dunmore, see pp. 4–11 above. If a tool be mercenary, his services must be performed for a recompense not a reward in heaven. His Excellency, however, was not doing well otherwise. By establishing an export tax on tobacco in "An Act for Raising a Publique Revenue for the Better Support of the Government of This His Majesties Colony," Virginia since 1680 had provided a salary for "the maintenance of the governor," which income was supplemented by perquisites and occasional legislative donations. But Dunmore now found the tobacco "Fund" withering, to cease altogether after the nonexportation provision of the Continental Association should go into effect on 10 Sept. 1775; and for 2 years past he had "received little or no perquisites," because collectors could not "be brought to account." He trusted, therefore, that Lord Dartmouth would be good enough to instruct him as to how, let alone uphold the dignity of the Crown, he might even

"Subsist" (*Statutes at Large*, II, 466–69; *Rev. Va.*, II, 105; P.R.O., C.O. 5/1353, fol. 229).

8. On 12 June 1775 the "Grand Continental Congress" had recommended that "Thursday, the 20th day of July next," be set aside "as a day of public humiliation, fasting and prayer" in "all the English colonies on this continent"; that prayer be offered to "the all-wise, omnipotent, and merciful Disposer of all events" to "inspire" the king "with wisdom to discern and pursue the true interest of all his subjects, that a speedy end may be put to the civil discord between Great Britain and the American colonies, without further effusion of blood"; that "the divine blessing may descend and rest upon all our civil rulers, and upon the representatives of the people, in their several assemblies and conventions, that they may be directed to wise and effectual measures for preserving the union, and securing the just rights and privileges of the colonies"; and that Christians of all denominations "assemble for public worship" and "abstain from servile labour and recreation on the said day" (*JCC*, II, 87–88). Virginians read this resolution in the *Va. Gazette* (Pinkney) of 22 June 1775.

9. The "Address" was printed in Purdie's *Va. Gazette* of 14 July 1775, but no "Handbills" that he may have furnished have been found.

10. Although the missing "Letter" bears the same date as that on which the "inhabitants" of Williamsburg met for a 2d time to consider the best method of defending their city, the document appears to have been written in compliance with the decision reached at the 1st meeting (27 June 1775, Third Va. Convention).

11. If Captain Scott did not himself lead the volunteers detached from his company, he soon afterward joined them (19 July 1775, Norfolk Borough Committee).

12. For the resolution of the second Virginia Convention to assess the counties and the municipalities of Norfolk and Williamsburg £15 each to pay the expenses of the colony's deputies to the second Continental Congress, see 8 Apr. 1775, n. 6. On the day after the convention adjourned, William Fleming, a delegate, handed Robert Carter Nicholas £15 on behalf of Cumberland County; and on 10 June 1775, John Mayo, the other Cumberland County delegate, added a "further Contribution" of £5, so swelling to £315 the purse with which Thomas Jefferson on the next day set out for Philadelphia (Cash Book, Treasurer's MS Item no. 16, Archives Division, Va. State Library, unpaged; Malone, *Jefferson and His Time*, I, 202).

Saturday, 1 July 1775

Third Virginia Convention

Augusta County West: Two Messages to the Shawnee

Inquiry being made after two remaining Prisoners, the following Message was sent by the Six Nations and Delawares to the Shawanese –

Bretheren the Shawanese

As your Brother the big Knife and we are now in Council strengthening the Chain of Friendship [1] and your Brother the Big Knife makes a request to us that you will send up as soon as possible, two Prisoners who are yet in your Custody; [2] We desire you to be strong and to comply with it and also perform every other promise you have made to the Big Knife at Camp Charlotte last Fall,[3] as they have now complied with our request to them in delivering up our flesh and blood at this Time.[4]

A Message to the Shawanese by David Duncan [5]
Bretheren of the Shawanese

As there has now some considerable time past,[6] since that appointed for you to meet in Council and that the Chiefs from the Six Nations and Delaware are and have been waiting for you; I therefore take this opportunity by David Duncan to inform you of those things and that we have also heard that some French Men who have been amongst you had called you to a Council;[7] If this is the real Cause of your delay I would be glad you would inform me of it as I cannot Possibly remain here much Longer and those nations now met here are desirous of returning home.

Given under my hand & Seal this 1st. day of July 1775.

Signed John Connolly (LS) [8]

To the Chiefs of the Shawanese

> MS transcript in hand of James Berwick, in papers of third Virginia Convention (Archives Division, Virginia State Library)

1. See 19 May 1775, n. 5.

2. The identities of the "two Prisoners" taken captive anterior to or during Dunmore's War are unknown. A Shawnee problem was forcing the delivery of men who, having come to prefer the Indian way of life, did not wish to be returned to the confinement of civilization (Downes, *Council Fires on the Upper Ohio*, p. 107).

3. For promises made at Camp Charlotte, see *Rev. Va.*, II, 107–8; 19 May 1775, n. 3.

4. For the "delivering up" of "our flesh and blood"—or, more accurately, that of the Mingo hostages—see 29 June 1775 and n. 9.

5. That is, the written "Message" was to be carried by David Duncan, a prominent trader in western Pennsylvania (Thwaites and Kellogg, *Rev. on the Upper Ohio*, p. 61 n. 89).

6. In the 18th century "past" was an acceptable form for preterit and perfect tenses of the verb "to pass."

7. The British commander at Detroit, aided by 1 or 2 Frenchmen, had recently urged the Indians to avoid negotiating with the Virginians, alleging that the Big Knife's true objective was to dispossess the native of his hunting grounds (ibid., p. xiii; 23 July 1775, Third Va. Convention). In this wise, commandant and Lord Dunmore's agent seemed to be at cross-purposes; but winning the red man's friendship, coupled with a shift in circumstance (for could the white American for long accept restraints imposed on his westering?), they might soon be playing the same game.

8. "LS" stands for *locus sigilii*, Latin for "place of the seal," a letter symbol for a seal not actually used.

Monday, 3 July 1775

Third Virginia Convention

Augusta County West: Three Strings and Two Belts

At a meeting held with the Indians at Fort ⟨Dunmore⟩ [1] the 3d. day of July
1775 in behalf of the Government of Virginia—
Present.
Major John Connolly A⟨lexande⟩r. McKee Esqr. Depy Agent Col George
Croghan and the rest of the Gentlemen as before
Indians
The same Chiefs and Warriors of both Nations as before—
   The Six Nations spoke as follows— [2]
Bretheren
   A few days ago when we met together in Council, you then performed the
Ceremonies usual on such Occasions and also delivered up our flesh and blood
for which we are extreamly thankful and we can assure you when we report
it to the Council of the Six nations it will afford them singular Satisfaction [3]
   When you delivered them up you desired them to listen to their own
Chiefs; We have told them to be strong and to turn their Eyes towards us
which they have promised to do for the future

                                                          A String. [4]

Bretheren
   Our Flesh and Blood whom you have delivered up to us, are very thankful
for what you have done for them as well as us, and we now accompany the
belt you gave them with this String to the heads of those scattering Mingoes
upon Scioto and recommend it to them in Conjunction with you to observe
the Advice which you gave them on your Part and we now desire them to
look towards the Chiefs of the Six Nations for the Government of their
future Conduct. [5]

                                    Shew'd a Belt and a String.

Bretheren
   As We cannot well do without a person who understands the Language of
the Six Nations, We therefore desire that Simon Girty [6] should be appointed
to interpret any matters we may have to say to you hereafter upon Public
Business; and if it agreable to you we desire that your String may accompany
ours to the Six Nations upon this Subject to let them know of such Agreement
Bretheren
   I have no more to say now but to return you thanks once more for your

good Speeches and the Delivery of our Flesh and Blood into our Possession Bretheren

When you first invited us to this Council here, We expected that Business would not be delayed⟨.⟩ We have now waited the three days for our Younger Bretheren the Shawanese,[7] and we would be glad ⟨to learn⟩ how soon any further Business you may have with us could be finished.

A String.

From the Delawares to the Six Nations, spoke by Capt White Eyes[8]

Uncles the Six Nations— [9]

It gave us your Nephews great Pleasure to hear you and your Bretheren the White People relate over Matters relative to the friendship which has been established between us at Sir William Johnstons[10] and we congratulate you upon the restoration of your friends and we are obliged to our Bretheren the White People for the good Advice which they have given them And we not only desire them to be strong and turn their Eyes towards the chiefs of the six Nations; but we desire that scattered Mingoes will remove and settle themselves under the Eyes of their Chiefs⟨;⟩ this will be the right method of taking Pity on your Women and Children and preventing disturbances for the future.

A Belt sent to the Stragling Mingoes on Scioto.

Major Connolly told the several Nations that he was glad they appeared so well satisfied and requested they would be ready tomorrow to appear in Council when they were sent for and that he would then speak further to them[11]

MS transcript in hand of James Berwick, in papers of third Virginia Convention (Archives Division, Virginia State Library)

Augusta County West: John Campbell to
the Committee at Hannahs Town

Gentlemen

We are now to acknowledge the receipt of your Letter of the 29th: of June by Mr. Kinkhaid ⟨James Kinkead⟩, and we are very Sensible of the distress'd and unhappy situation of the People on this side of the Laurell hill arising from the causes which you have mentioned.[12] We have considered the subject with that mature deliberation which a matter of so much consequence deserves, and are earnestly desirous of contributing every thing in our Power, to restore peace and Tranquility, to this unfortunate Country.

But We are fully convinced the mode that you prescribe for that purpose by striking a Temporary line far exceeds the power of a Committee, and can only be effected by the Executive powers of both Governments. Therefore the only method in our power to accomplish so desirable an end, must be by a Joint Petition sign'd without distinction by all the Inhabitants to the Westward of the Laurel Hill, to the Governors of Virginia and Pennsylvania, beseeching them to have a Temporary line drawn as soon as possible, and as We have Resolved on this mode of proceeding if agreeable to you be assured We will use every endeavour & Influence to expedite the Petition and promote it's success.

As no Community can subsist without a due submission to the civil Laws the people residing within the Limits ascertained by Lord Dunmores Proclamation, must untill the prayers of the Petition is obtain'd be amainable to the Laws of Virginia, The civil Majestrates of which Colony we are fully determined to support in the Execution of their Offices, as the only security for the Welfare of the People.[13]

This to every disinterested and unprejudiced person must appear to be the most probable means of restoring Harmony and Tranquility to the Country, for whilst the two Governments are contending for the Jurisdiction, daily outrages will be committed, the Rights of the Persons and the property of the people violated: as evidently appears from some recent instances.[14]

You can not but be sensible that his Majesty has the undoubted Authority & Dominion, over all his Territory and a Right to all quit rents &c where it does not appear that he has precluded himself by his Royal Grant. Therefore untill the proprietors of Pennsylvania make it Evidently appear in a Legal & Judicial manner that their Grant doth include this Country the Inhabitants ought not to be Subject to the Laws &c of that Government. To remove every doubt of our Sincere intentions for the Public good We herewith send You two Resolves the first of which proves at least that we have not been wanting in that particular and the latter impowers each District, or Township to send Members to represent them in this committee.[15]

We are Gentlemen

> Signed John Campbell [16] &c
> July 3d. 1775.[17]
> A Copy
>   JAMES BERWICK
>   Clk to the Comtee.
>   of the Western Waters

Ibid.

Augusta County West: James Kinkead to the Committee at Pittsburgh

Gentlemen   Hannahs Town July 3d. 1775
Your Letter without date in Answer to ours of the 29th. Ulto. by Mr Kinkaid we have received⟨.⟩[18] The Subject of that Letter certainly deserves that mature deliberation you are pleased to say you have bestowed upon it as the peace & Tranquility of the Country are intimately connected with it.

We did not mean to lead you into a discussion of the powers of Committees⟨;⟩ it would be difficult perhaps to Ascertain them⟨.⟩ You Gentlemen we supposed were the representatives of the People West of Laurel Hill who acknowledge the Jurisdiction and wish to live under the Laws of Virginia⟨.⟩ We are the representatives of those who submit to the Government of Pennsylvania⟨.⟩ in that Capacity we conceived there would be no impropriety in our consulting upon and fixing some boundary line convenient for both on the several sides of Which the respective Laws and forms of Government to which our several constituents had been accustomed might have operated and by that means the great Objects to our uniting in the common Cause of Liberty been removed.

Gentlemen we have not forgot the first rise of the dispute that now subsists between the Colonys of Virginia & Pennsylvania nor are we afraid of being charged with want of candour when We say that it was owing to the Avarice of some Individuals and to the Villiany of others with which we make no doubt some of your Committee are very well acquainted – That their Designs unhappily coincided with the passions & prejudices of a Weak Governor and the Vices of an incidious and Wicked Ministry inimical to the rights of Mankind and of America in particular and ever has been our opinion that that Dispute was set on foot on purpose to forward their Views and by involving two Great Colonys in a Quarrel about Territory detach them from the common Cause or at least prevent their giving their proper Attention to it [19]

A joint Petition to the different Governors to establish a temporary line signed without distinction by all the Inhabitants Westward of the Laurel Hill we think an Absurdity⟨.⟩ [20] Petitions would probably produce no effect as we know the Governor of Virginia has repeatedly rejected such a proposal from the Governor of Pennsylvania. [21]

The positive institutions of every Society are certainly binding upon the members of that Society and a power to compel obedience is necessaryly incident but how Lord Dunmores Proclamation is to give Authority from this position or how his intrusion into the possessions or Seizing the Government of a Society which never made any compact with him nor owes him obedience are to be justifyed by it we do not discover⟨.⟩ the Jurisdiction of Pennsylvania in this Quarter of the Country has been confirmed by the highest Authority and cannot be suppressed by any Act of the Subordinate nor Will Ten Thousand Proclamations alter the Nature of the Case or render one Inhabitant amenable to the Courts of Virginia. [22]

We intreat you to reflect upon the cause which has calld all America into Arms⟨.⟩ part of it certainly is the wanton Abrogation of Established constitutions that had been entered into by the Mutual consent of the Crown and the People⟨.⟩ America is now Bound to procure the restitution of the Antient Form of Government in the Massachusetts Bay and we pray you to believe whilst we are ready to Assist that Colony in repelling Incroachments of the Crown we will not suffer another to Obtrude their Government upon us⟨.⟩ The Majestrates of every Country ought to be supported in the execution of their very important Office and We shall not be behind Hand in affording those of our Government every Necessary Countenance.

The Bounds of a Letter (nor indeed the design of this) will not Allow us to enter into the Questions of Procedence or how far the granting of it to Virginia might contribute to restore Harmony and Tranquility to this Country

The Kings Authority & Dominion over all his territorys and His Right to Quit rents are distinct in themselves and Arise from very different considerations⟨.⟩ Why they are classed in your Letter or Why introduced at all we can not imagine nor is it easy to understand the sequel of that paragraph⟨.⟩ The Crown has not Charged the Proprietors of Pennsylvania with Incroachments⟨.⟩ When it does there is no Doubt that they will make it evidently appear in a Legal & Judicial Manner that they have not extended the Laws &c of their Government beyond their just limits and that consequently the People owe neither Obedience nor Quit rent to Virginia.

When your resolves have consistency that may possibly convince us that you suppose we have common sence but whilst they are evidently otherwise⟨,⟩ whilst a Vote of thanks to such a paracide [23] as George Gibson for an Action Acknowledged by himself to be contrary to the Laws of His Country disgrace your Minutes, you will hardly persuade Us of your sincere Intentions for the Publick Good [24]

Your Letter with a Copy of this Answer we shall immediately transmit to the Continental Congress.[25]

We are Gentlemen Your Very Humble Servants
Signed by Order of the Committee
James Kinkead Clerk

To the Committee at Pittsburgh

A Copy.
JAMES BERWICK
Clerk to the Comtee. of Augusta West of
the Laurel Hill

Ibid.

Dunmore County Committee

William Clarke to Committee

Note on provenance. The present document and its sequel of 5 July 1775 are the only items found for the Dunmore County committee within this volume. Both items, together with·twenty-two other Revolutionary period papers from the county, came into the possession of Abraham Bird, elected a member of the committee on 10 January 1775 (*Rev. Va.*, II, 229) and reposed for several generations at his home, Birdwood, in Woodstock (today in Shenandoah County, formed in 1777, then as "Shanando" County; *Statutes at Large*, IX, 424). They were discovered at Birdwood by Colonel Bird's descendant the Reverend Dr. William Twyman Williams. Through Bernard Samuels of New York City, Dr. Williams presented the collection to the Virginia Historical Society in 1936. The selections appearing within the present volume have been previously edited and published in *Wm. and Mary Qtly.*, 2d ser., XV (Jan. 1935), 78.

Gentm. I have this moment received a summons to appear before your grand Tribunal which (considering my duty to my Sovereign) I cannot comply with for Gentm. permit me to tell you that so long as you remain refractory and yield no submission to the Mandates of the King, I shall pay no obedience to the summons of an Illegal Assembly combin'd in the most unjustifiable Manner and Having [26] under their Consideration the most treasonable proceedings—Therefore you have my free Consent to make what conjectures you think proper with regard to my conduct, and I assure you, I feel with the most perfect indifference what they are or the consequence of them [27]

Autograph letter, unsigned (Dunmore County Committee Papers, Virginia Historical Society)

Prince George County Committee

Condemnation of Captain Alexander

⟨T⟩he [28] following letter from the committee of the said borough ⟨of Norfolk⟩, directed to the Chairman of the committee of Prince George, was laid before the said committee of Prince George the 3d day of July 1775, when 24 of the members were present, Richard Bland, Esq; in the chair.
. . . . . [29]
The said Charles Alexander having had proper notice, and failing to attend, and the committee taking into their consideration the aforesaid letter and examination,

Resolved unanimously, that the said Charles Alexander has infringed the 10th article of the Continental Congress, and that he be held up to the public as inimical to America, agreeable to the 11th article of the continental association; and it is recommended to the good people of America to break off all dealings with the said Charles Alexander, his factors, or agents.[30]

By order of the committee
Heartwell Raines, Sec'ry.[31]

Virginia Gazette (Dixon and Hunter), 28 October 1775

1. That is, Fort Pitt (19 May 1775, n. 4). In this instance James Berwick wrote only "at Fort."

The last preceding "meeting with the Indians" had been on 29 June 1775.

2. The spokesman for the Six Nations may have been Keyashota, 1st-named of the chiefs in the journal for 29 June 1775.

3. The "council of the Six nations" was composed of the principal chiefs of the confederated tribes and established the overall policies by which each tribe did or was supposed to abide (Hodge, *Handbook of Am. Indians*, pt. 1, 617–18).

4. Of wampum (20 May 1775, n. 7).

5. The "scattering Mingoes" on the Scioto River have been described as "a mongrel race, chiefly wanderers from the New York Iroquois stock." Like the Shawnee, they had been hostile to the Virginians in 1774, but after the Battle of Point Pleasant they refused to accede to Lord Dunmore's terms of "Reconciliation." The governor then deemed it essential to compel adherence, and a punitive force under Maj. William Crawford looted and destroyed one of their towns and took a number of captives. It may have been these prisoners who were the total or among the 12 "flesh and blood" held at the fort the past winter (Thwaites and Kellogg, *Doc. Hist. of Dunmore's War*, p. 28 n. 47; 19 May 1775, n. 3 and 20 May, n. 1).

6. Having spent nearly half his 34 years among Indians, Pennsylvania-born Simon Girty was indeed fluent in the "Language of the Six Nations." He was yet to display those politics and that character which would combine to earn him the unenviable epithets of "the Great Renegade" and "the White Savage" (Consul Willshire Butterfield, *History of the Girtys* . . . [Cincinnati, 1890], pp. 1–2, 13–34; 16 May 1775, Augusta Co. West Committee, n. 15).

7. The Shawnee were "Younger Bretheren" because they occupied lands of which the Six Nations claimed overlordship (20 May 1775, n. 3).

8. WHITE EYES, whose Indian name, Kequethagechton, may be translated "One Who Keeps Open Correspondence between His Tribe and Others," was among the most steadfast allies of the white man. Brave and of exemplary character, he befriended the Moravian missionaries who came into his country, and although he himself never found cause to undergo conversion, he urged his people to look well into the matter of Christianity. For years chief of the Turtle tribe of Delawares, he kept his people strictly neutral during Dunmore's War and won from the governor high praise for his "faithfulness, firmness, and remarkable good understanding" (Hodge, *Handbook of Am. Indians*, pt. 2, 994; John C. Heckewelder, *History, Manners, and Customs of the Indian Nations Who Once Inhabited Pennsylvania and the Neighboring States*, ed. William C. Reichel [*Memoirs of the Historical Society of Pennsylvania* (14 vols., Philadelphia, 1864–95)], XII, 153; Thwaites and Kellogg, *Doc. Hist. of Dunmore's War*, pp. 29, 384).

9. For the poetical degrees of kinship of the Delaware to the Shawnee, and of both to the Six Nations, see 29 June 1775, n. 10.

10. The late Sir William Johnson, Indian agent for the Northern Department, had called the Six Nations into council at Onondaga, N.Y., in the summer of 1774. Although he died before the work of the council was completed, he was nevertheless able to persuade the Six Nations to eschew joining the Shawnee and the latter's group of confederates (Downes, *Council Fires on the Upper Ohio*, pp. 170–71, 172–73).

11. For the council of "tomorrow," see 4 July 1775, Third Va. Convention.

12. The letter is under the date heading indicated, 2d entry.

13. "Lord Dunmores Proclamation" of 14 Sept. 1774, issued at Fort Pitt, had "ascertained" no precise "Limits" to the Virginia land claims "on the west Side of the Allegheny Mountains." The document had been designed to thwart "the Proprietors of Pennsylvania in Prosecution of their wild Claim" that their colony extended as far

southwest as the fort. His Lordship "strictly" prohibited the "Execution of any Act of Authority, on behalf of the Province of Pennsylvania" in the contested area, and enjoined "a due Regard, and entire Obedience, to the Laws of his Majesty's Colony of Virginia" therein (*Exec. Journs. Coun. Col. Va.*, VI, 657–58; *Rev. Va.*, II, 316 n. 2). For the border dispute, see 22 June 1775, n. 2.

14. For a "recent" instance, see 22 June 1775, n. 2; 26 June, n. 4.

15. This letter was to be laid before the third Virginia Convention on 21 July 1775 (Procs. and n. 3) and to evoke a sympathetic hearing and response. But there must have been convention members who objected to the thought expressed in the final paragraph that "his Majesty has the undoubted Authority & Dominion, over all his Territory," a "Right" to any quitrents not authorized by a colonial assembly, or power to make any "Royal Grant" of land whatsoever. Such members would be converts to the premises set forth in Thomas Jefferson's *A Summary View of the Rights of British America* that all American lands belonged not to the king but to the people "within the limits which any particular society has circumscribed around itself" (*Rev. Va.*, I, 254–55, II, 378–88 n. 9).

The "two Resolves" mentioned in the paragraph have not been found. For the response of the committee at Hannastown, see the item immediately following.

16. JOHN CAMPBELL of Fort Pitt was a native of Ireland whose age was possibly known only to himself. He had appeared in western Pennsylvania at some time before 1764, when he surveyed a town site at what is now the heart of Pittsburgh. He was for several years surveyor and clerk for George Croghan and by the 1770s had inherited much of the latter's profitable fur trade. A friend of John Connolly, Campbell journeyed with him to the Falls of the Ohio during the spring of 1774 (they both owned land there) and since October of that year had been serving with the contentious major on the western district court of Augusta County. On 16 May 1775 Campbell was elected to 2d place on the district committee and was its efficient acting chairman, or "Vice President," on such increasingly frequent days as Croghan's gout was acting up (Volweiler, *George Croghan*, pp. 289, 296, 301, 307; *Exec. Journs. Coun. Col. Va.*, VI, 543; 16 May 1775, Augusta Co. West Committee).

17. Although James Berwick dated the copy of the letter, in replying apparently on the same day, the Westmoreland, Pa., County committee referred to the original as being "without date." It may be, then, that Berwick forgot to date the original; that though he forgot, he dated the present copy correctly; or that forgetting, he dated the copy also as of that of the Westmoreland reply. In fact, the original may have been written earlier, on, say, 1 July 1775, 2 days after the 1st Westmoreland letter, and 2 days before the 2d, was penned. On the other hand, it may be that the Pennsylvanians misdated their 2d letter, for on 29 June they had stated that they would reconvene on "next Tuesday," the 4th of July, "to Receive your Answer." A last reasonable possibility is that although the trip would be onerous, James Kinkead, having been handed the Virginia letter in the morning of 3 July 1775, rode with it to Hannastown (lying about 30 air miles from Fort Pitt) and inscribed the reply for the hastily reassembled Westmoreland committee before retiring that night.

18. See 29 June 1775, Third Va. Convention, Augusta Co. West, 2d entry. The "Letter without date" is the item immediately preceding the present one.

19. For recent evidence that the "dispute" was enlivened by "passions & prejudices," see 22 June 1775, n. 2; 26 June, n. 4. The myth that a "Weak Governor" and an "incidious and Wicked Ministry" were conniving to involve "two Great Colonys" in a boundary dispute in order to divert attention from more important issues was one not credited by Pennsylvanians alone (*Rev. Va.*, II, 379–80 n. 17).

20. At this point the letter becomes a study in how to influence people without winning friends.

21. The statement was factual. In June 1774, for example, Gov. John Penn had sent 2 high-ranking Pennsylvania officials to Williamsburg to propose the running of a provisional boundary line subject to final ruling by the Crown. Lord Dunmore exchanged a lengthy correspondence on the subject but flatly refused to countenance the proposition. By that refusal he (and his Council) did not, however, display so much willful obstructionism as conviction that the Virginia position was legally correct (P.R.O., C.O. 5/1352, fols. 92–93, 94–97, 98–101). His instructions from Lord Dartmouth were that he "should continue to exercise the Authority of the Government of Virginia in the District" (ibid., fol. 48). But still unsure of what to do, the secretary of state for the colonies also rebuked him for using too much force to "exercise" that authority (ibid., fol. 90).

The Board of Trade had by now decided to strike a temporary boundary between the 2 colonies by extending Mason and Dixon's Line westward to the Monongahela River and thence north "until it touches the Ohio River above Fort Pitt" (ibid., C.O. 5/1353, fol. 136). This probably approximated the idea of the Westmoreland County committee, except that the line would have left the fort in Virginia possession. And anyone living in the area would have known that it was impossible to complete such a line, because the Ohio begins at Pittsburgh.

22. "Lord Dunmores Proclamation" was that of 14 Sept. 1774 (n. 3 above). The nearest thing to a written "compact" that the Pennsylvanians possessed was the "Charter of Privileges Granted by William Penn, Esq. to the Inhabitants of Pennsylvania and Territories" in 1701 (*Rev. Va.*, II, 43 n. 1), but a grant is not a compact arrived at by common assent of governor and governed, save as the governed concur in abiding by its provisions. The ultimate governor, then, was the king himself as through the Penn charter he had compacted to safeguard the rights of his subjects. The rest of the paragraph is arguable, and were it not, there would have been no occasion to write the present letter.

23. This word is smeared in the middle and may have been "parasite." If so, the intention may have been to classify Gibson as one who would draw sustenance from any convenient body, however illegal, with perhaps a hint of his having failed in a number of business enterprises. If the word is "paracide," it may be construed as indicating an assassin of his parent colony.

24. The "Vote of thanks" is under the date heading of 26 June 1775, 2d entry.

25. Neither the "Letter" nor a "Copy of this Answer" has been found in the papers of the Continental Congress. Each was received, however, and coupled with the petition of 16 May 1775 (Augusta Co. West Committee, 2d entry), referred to the delegates in Congress for Pennsylvania and Virginia. But it was to be to the subject of the border controversy that the delegates would address themselves (25 July 1775, Va. and Pa. Delegates to Congress . . .), for on 6 July negotiations with the Six Nations and the Delawares were successfully concluded, and there was no pressing need to comment or act upon that subject.

26. Clarke wrote the verb as "Have."

27. The date for the present item is arbitrarily assigned. On a date more certain, 5 July 1775, William Clarke would discover his "indifference" to be imperfect.

28. The present item consists of part of the 4th and all of the 2 concluding paragraphs of a 16-paragraph notice. The deleted portion immediately preceding reads, "The above examination was transmitted to the committee of the borough of Norfolk, in consequence of which. . . ." The "examination" is under the date heading of 8 May 1775, Prince George Co. Committee.

29. The ellipsis deletes the letter of transmittal and the attached "examination" (22 May 1775, Norfolk Borough Committee).

30. For the respective texts of the 10th and 11th articles of the Continental Association, see 5 Apr. 1775, n. 1; 8 Apr., n. 5. On 10 Feb. 1776 Alexander would cause to be printed in the *Va. Gazette* (Dixon and Hunter) a brief announcement understood not only by his creditors and debtors but also by patriots: "I INTEND TO LEAVE THE COLONY."

31. Hartwell Raines.

Tuesday, 4 July 1775

Third Virginia Convention

Augusta County West: Major Connolly Speaks

At a Council held at Fort Dunmore on the 4th. day of July 1775.
Present
Major John Connolly, Alex⟨ande⟩r. McKee Esqr. Dep Agent, Coll George Croghan with the same Gentlemen as before
Indians same as before— [1]
Major Connolly spoke to the Different Nations as follows
Bretheren
   Chiefs of the Six Nations Present.
   As you appeared yesterday in Council anxious of returning home and no certain Accounts when the Shawanese are to be expected ⟨have been received⟩, therefore at your desire we now proceed to finish the Business that we met upon

A String [2] to each Nation

Bretheren
   We have hitherto spoke of Matters which ⟨have⟩ been always considered at [3] meetings by our wise men; We next by these Belts collect all the bones of our deceased friends who have unfortunately fallen into the late disturbances by the rash Conduct of foolish People instigated by the evil Spirit and after burying them deep in the Earth We transplant the tree of Peace over them that every Remembrance of them may for ever hereafter be buryed in a future Enjoyment of a lasting Friendship. [4]

A Belt to each Nation

Bretheren
   As some foolish People of both sides have found means of getting into their possession Warlike Weapons with which they have destroyed one another We now take them out of their hands in behalf of the great man of Virginia [5] who proceeded into your Country last year with this design and

after thus convincing them of their folly, he then buried them deep in the earth. With this Belt we press the Earth close upon them that they may never rise again.

A Belt to each Nation

Bretheren

As we have buried the bones and Weapons which our Young People held in their hands and used against each other; by this Belt we now remove the Thorns and Briars which have grown up in the Path towards the Sun setting during the late disturbances which we now deliver to our Bretheren the Delawares to be handed thro' them to the Shawanese, Wyandots [6] and other Western Nations being best situated for the Purpose and that they may now inform our Western Bretheren that the Road is again opened and may now be travelled towards this Council fire with Ease & safety, that they may be assured that from hence towards our great People and the Six Nations the Road has never been obstructed but has been and yet remains plain and open as ordered by our wise men.

A Road Belt.[7]

Bretheren

As we now have the Pleasure once more of entering into our antient Council house, by this Wampum as usual on such Occasions I sweep it clean of all Dust which it has contracted since we last met in it, and I wipe away all those spotts which may have fallen upon it that no stain of Discontent may remain to trouble us, but when we are seated in it with ease and tranquility we may be enabled to look around us and see every thing appear clear and fair to our view

A Bunch of White Wampum to each Nation.

Bretheren

Chiefs and Warriors of the Several Nations here present.

Listen with Attention to what we are now going to say to you. I rejoice Bretheren that it has pleased God to permit so many of you to meet here this day at your old Council fire. It gives me pleasure to see you come with a good design of giving your Assistance to repair it and adding such fuel to it that the Blaze will again be beheld by all Nations in friendship with us, and that notwithstanding the bad Spirit had got so far the better of some foolish people to disturb it, we have still been able to guard it and preserve it from being totally extinguished by their rash inconsiderate Conduct which we now earnestly desire may be eternally forgot and buried in oblivion so that nothing may remain to interrupt us at this time from renewing the Friendship Covenant made and maintained long by our wise forefathers and that this fire which they have kindled for our mutual Advantage may by our Prudence burn bright to our latest Posterity

Bretheren.

From the Confidence we have all reason to Place in the Wisdom of our Bretheren the Delawares as well as their regard for the Peace of their Country which they have manifested in many Instances of their Conduct during the late troubles Therefore as a testimony of our Sincerity on this occasion We deliver into their hands this Belt of Friendship desiring that they would not only hold it up to the View of all here present but to all those linked in the great chain of Friendship with us, that what now has passed between us may be held in constant Remembrance

A Large Belt representing
The Chain of Friendship.[8]

Bretheren.

As we have now finished every material matter and brightened the Chain of Friendship, I have to inform you that your Brother the Big Knife is desirous that you should acquaint your People to refrain from hunting amongst his People who are now settling in great numbers on the South Side of the Ohio untill he may have an opportunity of regulating their Settlements least any Accidents prejudicial to the Peace now established should happen [9]

A Belt.

Bretheren.

With respect to the Speech you delivered yesterday desiring the Continuance of an Interpreter I shall forward it to Colonel Johnson who no doubt will consider the Necessity of allowing one to be continued and as soon as I am favoured with his directions I shall acquaint you of it [10]

A String

MS transcript in hand of James Berwick, in papers of third Virginia Convention (Archives Division, Virginia State Library)

1. The "same Gentlemen" and "Indians" as "before" were those listed on 29 June 1775.

2. See 20 May 1775, n. 7.

3. In Berwick's transcription the word is an unintended "as."

4. The collection of "all the bones," the transplantation of "the tree of Peace," and other improbable actions are to be understood in a metaphorical sense. The "late disturbance" was Dunmore's War, the "rash Conduct of foolish People" the raids of the Shawnee and other groups of tribesmen that precipitated the conflict.

5. The "great man of Virginia" was Lord Dunmore.

6. Heretofore unmentioned, the Wyandots (earlier known as Hurons) after generations of tribulations that in no wise mellowed their dispositions, had moved from the Valley of the St. Lawrence River and other parts of Canada to the Ohio Valley. Although their traditional foes, the Six Nations, claimed possession of the lands of the Old Northwest, the Wyandots dominated the greater part of the present state of Ohio and insisted on the right to light the fires of all intertribal councils held therein. Like the temporarily overawed Shawnee and the vengeance-thirsting Mingoes, the Wyandots were resolutely anticolonist (Hodge, *Handbook of Am. Indians*, pt. 1, 584–90).

7. A road belt was one specifically woven to signify the existence of friendship along a designated route (Jacobs, *Diplomacy and Indian Gifts*, pp. 21–22).

8. See 19 May 1775, n. 5.

9. Who should be master of the lands of Kentucky, "on the South Side of the

Ohio"—white man or red—had been the very point at issue in Dunmore's War; and that the master should be white pretty clearly fitted in with the personal plans of both Lord Dunmore and Major Connolly (*Rev. Va.*, II, 105; 3 July 1775, n. 16).

10. Nephew, son-in-law, and successor to the late northern Indian agent, Sir William Johnson, Col. Guy Johnson had business more pressing to "consider" than the "Continuance of an Interpreter." The colonel had just escaped into Canada, hotly pursued by New York patriots (*N.Y. Col. Docs.*, VIII, 658).

Wednesday, 5 July 1775

Third Virginia Convention

Augusta County West: Speech, Reply and Desire

At a Council held at Fort Dunmore [1] the 5th. July 1775.
Present
Major John Connolly Alex⟨ande⟩r. McKee Esqr. Dep Agent, and the same Gentlemen as before.
Also the same Indians of each Nation. [2]
    The Chief Warriors of the Senecas [3] in presence of the Six Nations spoke as follows—
    Bretheren the Big Knife
    You invited us to a small Council Fire at this place to which we readily repaired and we are extreamly glad to hear the good Speeches which you have now delivered us; We are now fully convinced that you are our sincere friends and that you are determined finally to settle the late disturbances which happened in this Country. We desire you to be strong and always continue in the same way of thinking. The Warriors and the Women are particularly thankful for this agreable circumstance and return you their hearty thanks. During the late disturbances the Chiefs of the Six Nations were at a loss how to judge of the matter from appearances but they are now heartily satisfied with your conduct and friendly disposition towards them and return you their hearty thanks also

A Belt [4]

    Bretheren the Big Knife
    We are very much obliged to you for calling to our recollection the good speeches which have passed between our forefathers and from what you have said now there remains no doubt of a lasting Friendship. As the Communication from all Quarters is now open to this Council Fire [5] which you have now Prepared we would gladly remind you of one thing which is That you would appoint a Smith to mend our Guns and Tom Hawks as usual when we passed up and down the River; And farther, that there may be a Person appointed for

the regulation of trade at this Place as it would be very agreable to all Nations and prevent Impositions on us in our Dealings with you; and as Amunition is so dear and Game become so scarce that it is out of our Power to provide ourselves with that Article, We therefore desire you to take Pity upon Us and consider of this Matter [6]

A String

Major Connolly made then the following Answer
Bretheren the Chiefs and Warriors of the Six Nations

I would be extreamly glad to do every thing in my power to Comply with your Request touching the Regulation of Trade, but as the Great Man of Virginia is much engaged in Business of Importance at this present time and that being a matter of Consequence can not be directly complied with, but I make no doubt as soon as circumstances will permit, the Great Man will consider of that Matter and will do every thing necessary to satisfy you upon that head.[7] As to the Smith that being a Business immediately under the direction of Colonel Johnson, Capt. McKee will write to him upon that Subject and you will do well to transmit a speech to him signifying the same Request [8]

A String

Capt. White Eyes then desired the Attendance of his Uncles the Six Nations and his Bretheren the Big Knife at the Council House tomorrow morning as he had something to say to them [9]

> MS transcript in hand of James Berwick, in papers of third Virginia Convention (Archives Division, Virginia State Library)

Dunmore County Committee

A Change of Tune

Dunmore County Sc.[10]

I William Clarke of the sd. County, do hereby declare on the holy Evangelist of Almighty God, that from henceforth I will not either publickly or privately hold any Correspondance with any person whatsoever who shall speak disrespectfully of the Continental Congress, or any Committee of any County, or their proceedings, and I hereby declare that the Americans are Justly intitled to those priviledges for which they are Contending, and further that I will depart from The Town of Woodstock within Ten Minutes from this time, and from the County of Dunmore before tomorrow night, and not return therein for the space of One Year, Given under my hand this fifth day of July 1775

WM. CLARKE [11]

> Autograph document, signed (Dunmore County Committee Papers, Virginia Historical Society)

1. That is, Fort Pitt (19 May 1775, n. 4).

2. The "same Gentlemen" and the "same Indians" were those noted as being present on 29 June 1775.

3. The Senecas had once been the most numerous of the Iroquois confederacy in New York. Their numbers declining, during the 18th century they drifted south and west and became so intermingled with the Mingoes along the Ohio River that it was frequently difficult to distinguish the one from the other. Some few of the Senecas had joined the Shawnee in the "late disturbances" prior to and during Dunmore's War (Hodge, *Handbook of Am. Indians*, pt. 1, 867, pt. 2, 502–7; *Rev. Va.*, II, 105–7). Which of the "Chief Warriors" at the council represented the Senecas is indeterminable.

4. Of wampum (20 May 1775, n. 7).

5. For the opening of the "Communication" to Fort Pitt, see 4 July 1775 and n. 7.

6. That the "regulation of trade" between the Indians and the Big Knife would be by dictation of the latter was provided by an article in the terms of "Reconciliation" reached at Camp Charlotte in Oct. 1774 (19 May 1775, n. 3). With "Amunition" costly even to the whites at Fort Pitt, and provisions of all kinds very scarce, the situation for the red man promised to become better only after it should have been worse (16 May 1775, n. 5; Augusta Co. West Committee, 2d entry; 26 June, Third Va. Convention and n. 2). It was his inability to manufacture or to repair superior metal weapons that made the Indian at once dependent on the Caucasian and unable to outlast him in sustained warfare (Morris Talpalar, *The Sociology of Colonial Virginia* [New York, 1960; 2d rev. ed., New York, 1968], p. 95).

7. Although the "Great Man of Virginia," Governor Dunmore, in sooth was "much engaged in Business of Importance," it is doubtful that at this time Connolly could more than guess what the business was (cf. 1 Aug. 1775, Third Va. Convention, Connolly to Rootes).

8. For the improbability that Col. Guy Johnson, now Indian agent for the Northern Department, had much time to reflect on the "Business" of a smith, see 4 July 1775, n. 10.

9. For what Captain White Eyes had to "say," see 6 July 1775.

10. Abbreviation of Latin *scilicet*, meaning "to wit" or "that is to say."

11. For this startlingly abrupt change of sentiments, see the signatory's convictions as previously couched (3 July 1775, Dunmore Co. Committee).

Thursday, 6 July 1775

Third Virginia Convention

Augusta County West: Conclusion of Good Speeches

July 6th 1775.
The Council met according to appointment [1] when Capt. White Eyes in behalf of the Delawares spoke as follows—
Bretheren the White People and Uncles of the Six Nations— [2]

As it was Proposed Yesterday we have met again in the Council House which has been cleaned and made white;[3] We have reason to thank God for allowing us to meet this day and we hope he will be a Witness to what passes between us⟨.⟩ As you have given us the Chain of Friendship[4] to hold forth to all Nations you may be assured we shall be so particular in that circumstance, that if a Tomhawk was to be struck into our head it should not disengage our hands from the fast hold which we have taken of that Belt; and that you may depend upon it that our utmost attention shall be constantly employed in reflecting upon the good speeches which have now passed between us, and in strengthening and Promoting the Friendship as directed by our wise forefathers

> Two Strings[5] one to the
> White People and the other
> to the Six Nations

Bretheren the White People and Uncles the Six Nations

It gives us particular Pleasure that you call upon God to witness our Transactions as he is present upon all Occasions and by his Assistance We hope what now passes between us may have a lasting Effect—That what has been said on your Part comes sincerely from your hearts as you may be assured that what you now hear from your Bretheren the Delawares is intirely so and that our Women and Children may hereafter have reason to rejoice at our present transactions

> A Belt to the White People
> and another to the Six Nations.

Bretheren the White People and Uncles the Six Nations

As you have sweeped out the Council house of your Antient forefathers and lighted up the Council Fire We look upon it ⟨as⟩ incumbent upon us to afford You our best Assistance in the good work⟨.⟩ therefore on our Parts up on this belt we wipe clean those Council Seats and that when who are young People are sitting in it, it may call to our minds, and consider the Prudent Conduct of our wise People formerly, with ease and satisfaction and you may depend upon it that we shall always govern our young People in such a manner as never to disturb the good business which is now so happily brought to a conclusion

> Two belts delivered as before

Uncles the Six Nations

Listen to what I am now going to say to my Brother the Big-Knife

Bretheren the White People

As you have now put the Chain of Friendship into my possession in the presence of my Uncles the Six Nations I now inform you that I take fast hold of it with both my hands: I am glad you have now told us that God will look down upon what passes between us and this is our desire⟨.⟩ it puts us in mind of the friendship cultivated by our Forefathers when they first met at the Shore side of the great Water and we were so fond of continuing that Friendship then cultivated that we removed back to give you room to settle as you grew more numerous as we then always understood you were one People

and governed by one King; We now desire the Big Knife to put one End of
this Belt into the hands of King George our mutual Father and acquaint him
we are setled at Quisoching where we hold fast by the other End being the
Centre of a tract of Country given to us by our Uncles the Wyandots [6]
where we are ready to hear from our great Father the King of England and
as we were first told that you were one people and had but one King We
hope that since we now have become one people, that matters may continue
upon the same peaceable footing as we conceived them to be at that same
time and that one King shall continue to govern us. [7]

A Belt.

Capt. White Eyes then addressed his Uncles the Six Nations and desired
them to look to the place above mentioned when they had any thing to say
to their Nephews the Delawares, after which he made the following Speech
to their Bretheren of Pennsylvania –
Brother The Governor of Pennsylvania

As I have informed my Brother the Big-Knife that I am now setled at
Quisoching I take the same Opportunity of informing you my Brother of
Pennsylvania of our Situation; that you may also acquaint our Brother King
George of it and that you will put the one end of this belt into his hands
and assure him that altho that antient Friendship which was first made by our
Forefathers and yours on their arrival into our Country from the other side
of the great Water was for some time disturbed Yet no sooner did we recollect that antient friendship and had our Eyes opened and saw our Bretheren,
than we determined to hold fast by that antient chain as made by them which
has been strengthened at this time and as the first white People acquainted
our forefathers that they were all one and governed by one great King we
now hope that the same Order may still continue as we are deeply interested
in that matter from friendship and that the King also would do every⟨thing⟩
in his power to promote good amongst all his People. We have delivered
you this Belt that what you say may correspond with what we have said to
our Brother the Big Knife upon the same Subject. [8]

A Large Belt.

Bretheren the White People and Uncles the Six Nations

You have heard what I have said to you and as I have been busily imployed
last Fall in bringing about the good that we are now engaged in as well as
last Spring, We have no⟨w⟩ a prospect of every thing being happily concluded

A String

Capt. Kilbuck then address'd the Big Knife in behalf of the Delawares [9]
Brother the Big Knife

We are glad to hear what you said Yesterday concerning our young
Peoples hunting on your side the Ohio⟨.⟩ You may be assured we shall comply
with it and we shall inform our young People at the Wabash to refrain from
hunting there untill such time as they hear from this Place [10]

A String

Brother

You have mentioned that the Trade at this place shall be regulated⟨.⟩ We would be very glad you would consider of that matter as soon as possible as our young men may as well sit down and not fatigue themselves to hunt whilst goods are so unreasonable

A String

Keyoshota [11] in behalf of the Six Nations present holding the several Belts and Strings which had been delivered in Council to them, returned thanks for the good Speeches which had been delivered upon them and said that it gave them the greatest Satisfaction to find that We had taken so much pity on them and that as none of the very heads of the Six Nations were present that We would be friendly enough to excuse their not speaking to you so fully as you might have expected upon this Occasion⟨.⟩ Be Assured that we do heartily join with you in every thing that has passed at this meeting and we shall Transmit every thing that has been said with the greatest dispatch to the head Council of the Six Nations and no Doubt you will hear soon from them of these Matters. [12]

Brother.

As you have been appointed by the great Man of Virginia [13] to desire to prevent our Young People from hunting on your side of the River Ohio as there are a great many of the White People setling there now which as you rightly Judge may occasion disturbances, we shall comply with ⟨your wish.⟩ As you have given the chain of Friendship to be kept by the Delawares we now recommend it to them to be strong and prevent all the young People from crossing to your side of the river

A String to the Delawares to
inforce this Recommendation

Major Connolly then answered the Delawares as follows—

Bretheren the Delawares

It has given us great Pleasure this day to hear such friendly Sentiments from our good Bretheren and we make no doubt of a Confirmation of Friendship in this Country and of your Assistance in promoting it and you may be Assured that the Belt which you have given me to be extended to the hands of our great and good King who as you rightly judge governs us all as one People shall be conveyed to him as expeditiously as possible and I am convinced he will be highly satisfied with the Friendship his Bretheren the Delawares have so warmly expressed for him⟨;⟩ and there is no doubt that as he has a sincere love for all his White as well as his Indian Friends that he will exert himself to procure happiness to them one and all and as you have by that Belt acquainted him with the Place of your intended residence you may shortly expect to hear from him in Answer to your friendly Speech

A Large Belt

Bretheren

With respect to what you mention about the Trade at this place we desire you would advert to what we said to our Bretheren the Six Nations Yesterday on this head and that is a matter that does more properly lay before our Great Men⟨.⟩ [14] We shall not fail to represent to them what you have said and we make no doubt but they will consider the matter properly

A String.

Keyashota then spoke as follows—
Bretheren—

We are glad to hear the good Speeches which we have before told you we shall forward them directly to the six Nations and you may look towards us for an Answer from them in about two months

A String of Black Wampum

Bretheren—

We have setled every thing now upon a good footing which gives great Satisfaction, But one thing you seem to have forgot which is a little Powder and Lead for our Young men to kill Provisions on their way home

A String of the Same Sort

Major Connolly told them he would consider them before he set off— [15]
A Speech from the Committee of Augusta County on the West side of the Laurell Hill
Bretheren [16]

I⟨t⟩ has given us your Bretheren and near Neighbours the greatest Satisfaction to have heard and Seen at this Meeting the unhappy differences for some time past subsisting between some of your People and us happily Ended⟨.⟩ We have heard what the Officer directed by the Earl of Dunmore has said to you on the Occasion and we flatter ourselves it will be sufficient to convince you that he means no other than to maintain that Tranquility which alone can make us both happy⟨.⟩ [17] We now assure you that we shall on our Parts take every Measure and do every thing in our Power to Preserve and obtain these desirable Ends.
Bretheren.

We consider you in the same Circumstances with ourselves⟨;⟩ the great Creator of all things made us both a free People and we are determined with all the Powers he hath given us to preserve our Lives our Liberties and our Propertys against every one who shall attempt to deprive us of them⟨.⟩ Be assured Bretheren that we will also exert ourselves to maintain you in undisturbed Possession of your natural rights and we expect the same brotherly friendship from you by your not interfering in any of our disputes⟨.⟩ In Testimony of our sincere dispositions and Intentions to cultivate a good Understanding and a friendly intercourse with you our Bretheren we Present you with this Belt. [18]

A Belt.

MS transcript in hand of James Berwick, in papers of third Virginia Convention (Archives Division, Virginia State Library)

1. The "appointment" had been made at the request of Captain White Eyes, "who had something to say" (5 July 1775, Third Va. Convention, final para.).

2. For the avuncular kinship of the Six Nations to the Delawares, see 29 June 1775, Third Va. Convention, 1st entry and n. 10.

3. The cleaning and whitening of the council house, along with other physical activities described below, is to be taken in a metaphorical sense.

4. See 19 May 1775, n. 5.

5. Of wampum (20 May 1775, n. 7).

6. The Delawares had probably negotiated their first, the "Great Treaty," in 1682 with William Penn on the "Shore side" of the Delaware River at Shackamaxon, their town lying approximately in the present-day Kensington section of Philadelphia (Catherine Owens Peare, *William Penn: A Biography* [Philadelphia and New York, 1957], pp. 252–56). "Quisoching" was Berwick's rendition of Coshocton, the main town of White Eyes's Turtle Delawares near the center of the country between the Ohio and White rivers where they had been settled for about 5 years (Hodge, *Handbook of Am. Indians*, pt. 1, 351, 385). For "our Uncles the Wyandots," see 4 July 1775, n. 6.

7. In possession of this "talk," Lord Dunmore in Aug. 1775 would attempt to send a letter to White Eyes pleading with that chief to ignore the "foolish" and "imprudent" deportment of the frontier patriots and to let whatever they might say in future negotiations "pass in at one ear and out at the other." A month later His Excellency was to enclose a copy of White Eyes's speeches in a packet of documents London-bound and express a fear that the Indians would, "if not immediately employed in His Majesty's Service, take part with the Rebellion" (*Va. Gazette* [Purdie], 10 Nov. 1775; P.R.O., C.O. 5/1353, fols. 296–97). Virginians entertained a contrary fear. His Majesty's place in the evolving scheme of things, meanwhile, could not but be puzzling to the Indians. So much James Wood was to discover on his western odyssey, and in addition he would be disturbed to find that the red man tended to believe that the Virginian Big Knife was not united with the other colonists (27 July 1775, Third Va. Convention, Augusta Co. West; 18 Aug., same, Wood to Randolph).

8. No evidence has been found that either a copy of this "Speech" or the "Large Belt" was forwarded to Gov. John Penn, and from a Virginian point of view, whether royal or "with the Rebellion," there was every reason that neither should be.

9. Gelelemend was his Indian name. It meant "Leader." But to the English-speaking white man he was Captain John Killbuck. Born about 1722, Killbuck was the son of a father who was among the best-educated Indians of his day, and in the view of Rev. David Jones, who met him in 1773, the son himself was "sensible." During the wars of the 1750s and 1760s Killbuck had exhibited a notable antipathy toward the colonials. A medicine man and a shrewd councilor, he was by this date a power in the upper Ohio Valley and would succeed White Eyes as chief of the Turtle Delawares in 1778. Late in life (he was to live until 1811) he would manifest a sincere friendship for old adversaries and be baptized William Henry. His speech on the present occasion needed no interpreter, for he spoke "good English" (Hodge, *Handbook of Am. Indians*, pt. 1, 489; *Pa. Mag. of Hist. and Biog.*, X [Jan. 1886], 116–17; David Jones, *A Journal of Two Visits Made to Some Nations of Indians on the West Side of the River Ohio, in the Years 1772 and 1773* [Burlington, N.J., 1774; reprint, New York, 1865], pp. 97–98).

10. That is, after the "large council," which it was hoped would meet later in the year.

11. Keyashota was one of the principal chiefs of the mixed Mingo-Seneca tribes on the Ohio River. Convinced that the only good paleface was a dead paleface, he had been enemy to the greater of 2 evils and opposed the British during the French and Indian War, whereafter, in 1763, he had been a participant in Pontiac's "conspiracy."

In the next year, however, he signed a treaty at Tuscarawas with Col. Henry Bouquet and buried the hatchet with the words, "Now we have thrown every thing bad away & nothing remains in our Hearts but Good." These words the chief took with utmost seriousness; he did not participate in Dunmore's War and seems to have gone to the Illinois country in order to urge keeping the peace. For all that, he continued suspicious of whites and during the autumn of 1775 would attempt to breathe new life into the defensive alliance of the Six Nations (Hodge, *Handbook of Am. Indians*, pt. 1, 682; Thwaites and Kellogg, *Rev. on the Upper Ohio*, pp. 38–39 n. 65, 108–10; Stevens, Kent, et al., *Papers of Bouquet*, ser. 21654, pp. 235–37; "Selections from the Letter-Books of Thomas Wharton," *Pa. Mag. of Hist. Biog.*, XXXIII [Oct. 1909], 450).

12. For the "very heads" of the "Council of the Six Nations," see 3 July 1775, n. 3.

13. The "great Man of Virginia" was Governor Dunmore.

14. In the sense that Connolly intended, "our Great Men" were the governor, his Council, and the House of Burgesses.

15. Before he "set off," Connolly lingered on at Fort Pitt at least until 18 July. Thereafter, leaving his sibilant spouse to provide for her own passage eastward (she would be in Philadelphia by the following spring), he passed through Warm Springs and arrived at Winchester on 31 July (18 July 1775, Third Va. Convention, Augusta Co. West; 1 Aug., same, Connolly to Rootes).

16. In place of the ailing George Croghan, John Campbell, "Vice President," probably delivered the "Speech from the Committee."

17. In a community sure of itself only in its desire for peace with the Indians, the speaker was forced to perform an oral balancing act. Thus what he gave away in the present paragraph he offset in the next.

18. With the presentation of this belt, the Connolly-inspired negotiations with the Indians were ended. In 3 days, however, on 9 July 1775, Capt. James Wood, deputized by the House of Burgesses but to relate his activities to the third convention, would arrive and undertake measures for the holding of a more inclusive council.

Friday, 7 July 1775

Third Virginia Convention

Richard Bland to Samuel Sheild: An Open Letter

To the Reverend Mr. SHEILD.

SIR,

YOU must not be surprised to find me addressing you, in this publick manner. I am a stranger to your person and place of residence, and can think of no way more proper to apply to you, in a case extremely interesting to myself. I understand that you are a native of this country, lately returned from England, in holy orders; that, upon your arrival here, in my absence from the colony, you declared, with much confidence, I had solicited, by letter, some person in administration for a pecuniary appointment under government; that, in return for such a favour, I had promised to exert myself to carry into execution the ministerial measures against the rights and liberties of America; and that you had seen a letter to this purpose, subscribed with my name.

A young clergyman, who is just entering into publick life, would, I suppose, be very cautious of flinging out reports which reflect upon the characters of other men, unless he was certain of the truth of them. I now, therefore, call upon you to make good your charge; or to make a publick atonement to me, for the high insult you have offered my character.

I have been honoured, for more than thirty years, with the affection and confidence of the county I live in, as their first representative in General Assembly; and I have received, from the representative body of my country, the pleasing approbation of my publick conduct, by their twice appointing me one of their delegates at the General Continental Congress.[1] You, Sir, have attempted to deprive me of this honour, and this confidence; and to load me with publick contempt and infamy, which I most justly merit, if your charge is true.[2]

If, therefore, you refuse to comply with my reasonable demand, you may rest assured that I will take another method to vindicate myself from the infamous and invidious falsehood you have so industriously and boldly propagated against me.[3] I am, Sir, your humble servant,

Richard Bland.

Virginia Gazette (Purdie), 7 July 1775

1. Bland had been elected to the "General Continental Congress" by the first Virginia Convention on 5 Aug. 1774, and by the second on 26 Mar. 1775 (*Rev. Va.,* I, 225, 228, 229, II, 376, 377).

2. Although not a word of the Sheild charge against Bland, who was "Commonly called Spectacle Dick" (if the word of the unfriendly James Parker be accepted) had appeared in any of the Virginia newspapers, the rumor of the weak-eyed colonel's defection was evidently widespread. James Madison, Jr., had heard it and commented that "Bland is in needy circumstances & we all know age is no stranger to avarice"; and even the judicious Edmund Pendleton, who had served with Bland in 2 sessions of Congress, gave the rumor some credit and thought that should it be proven true, his old colleague might best be sent "to slink in infamous Obscurity" (Parker to Charles Steuart, 14 Aug. 1774, Steuart Papers, National Library of Scotland; Hutchinson and Rachal, *Papers of Madison,* I, 151–52; Mays, *Letters and Papers of Pendleton,* I, 109).

3. Had Bland written this paragraph at a later day, his promise of seeking vindication by "another method" might have been construed as resorting to the code duello. Such, however, was not Bland's intention. Not only would the myopic colonel have been at a disadvantage in fingering pistol or wielding épée, but dueling was not to become a fashion—as it would particularly among the gentry of the southern states—until introduced by British and French officers during the war (Ben C. Truman, *The Field of Honor* . . . [New York, 1884], p. 81). What Bland did mean was that he would submit his case to the third Virginia Convention. First, however, he must await

Sheild's reply. It would be forthcoming on 12 July 1775 (Third Va. Convention, 2d entry).

Sunday, 9 July 1775

Third Virginia Convention

Augusta County West: Journal of Captain James Wood

Note on provenance. On Saturday, 24 June 1775, the last day on which a quorum of the House of Burgesses ever assembled, that body and the Council elected George Washington, Dr. Thomas Walker, James Wood, Andrew Lewis, John Walker, and Adam Stephen commissioners "to meet the Chiefs or head Men" of the northwestern Indians "as soon as the same can be done, at such place, as they shall find most proper, to ratify and confirm" a treaty such as would allay reported native unrest (*JHB, 1773–1776,* p. 282). For obvious reasons, Washington found no time to participate, and Dr. Walker thereby became the commission chairman. The Walkers, father and son, and Stephen (the last-named under a charge of irregularity) were also elected to and attended the third Virginia Convention. Lewis was probably elected but did not attend. Thus, with Charles Mynn Thruston and Isaac Zane, Jr., reelected to represent his home county, Frederick, Wood alone was free and of a disposition to initiate the work for which the commission had been formed.

Captain Wood kept a journal of his travels and interviews with Indian notables. Since he forwarded what he considered pertinent parts of the journal to the convention, they should be among the papers of that assemblage, but they are not. The journal as a whole was later copied by the commissioners' clerk in their "Proceedings" as the negotiators-designate waited at Fort Pitt in September 1775 for the arrival of the Indians with whom they were to treat. This copyist was John Madison, Jr., who though a son of the clerk of Augusta County, had obstinately fought and triumphed over his father's more literate concepts of spelling and punctuation. The younger Madison's version of the Wood journal is disputably faithful, but it is all that is now extant. The entire "Proceedings," containing the butchered journal, in the early years of the twentieth century were in the private possession of Walker's descendant Dr. William C. Rives, of Washington, D.C. With what appears to have been great care, Dr. Rives transcribed or superintended the transcribing of the "Proceedings" and sent the completed transcript to Reuben Gold Thwaites, at the time secretary of the State Historical Society of Wisconsin; and the latter and his assistant, Louise Phelps Kellogg, in turn edited the transcript with the excellence comporting with their reputations and incorporated it in *The Revolution on the Upper Ohio, 1775–1777* (Madison, Wis., 1908), pp. 25–127.

The Rives transcript no longer exists. Dr. Josephine L. Harper, reference archivist of the State Historical Society of Wisconsin, informs the present editors that according to the editorial practices of his time, Dr. Thwaites considered his final approval of page proof warranty of a reliable printed record, and hence saw no purpose in retaining either transcripts or working papers.

The portions of Wood's journal that are reproduced within the present volume are included in the Thwaites and Kellogg work from page 34 to page 67, both inclusive. But not all those pages are herein reprinted, for although the captain understood that the members of the third convention would be interested in the gist of his parleys with "Chiefs or head Men," it is highly probable that he did not believe that they would care to hear or read about the routes he took or the miles he traveled to reach the sites where the parleys were conducted. This probability is underscored by the nature of the information that he passed on to the committee for the District of West Augusta County. That information, stripped to its essentials, consisted of events and talks for selected days between 22 July and 2 Aug. 1775. It was published in Philadelphia on 11 Sept. in *Dunlap's Pennsylvania Packet, or, the General Advertiser,* as from "*the Committee of Pittsburg, August* 10." Peter Force also printed the accounts, with uncharacteristic accuracy, in *American Archives,* 4th ser., III, cols. 76–78.

9th July I Arrived at Fort Pitt where I received Information that the Cheifs of the Delawares and a few of the Mingoes had lately been Treating with Major ⟨John⟩ Connolly agreeable to Instructions from Lord Dunmore and that Shawanese had not come to the Treaty Agreable to their Appointment⟨.⟩ [1] upon Examining the Proceedings with the Delawares and Mingoes I found that they had been given assurances that a General Treaty would be soon held with all the Ohio Indians upon which I thought it Adviseable to dispatch an Express to the Convention with the following Letter directed to the Honorable Peyton Randolph Esqr

Sir – On my Arrival at this Place I found that Majr Connolly had finished a Treaty with the Delaware and Mingo Cheifs who had assembled agreable to Lord Dunmores Appointment and were returned well satisfied with Assurances that a General Treaty would be soon held with them and the Other Ohio Tribes⟨.⟩ It seems from the Governors Instructions to Majr Connolly that he only intended a few of the Cheifs should be called together in order to make them easy till a treaty could be properly negotiated with them⟨.⟩ [2] I am now waiting to see the Cornstalk who is on his way and is Expected here tomorrow or the next day⟨.⟩ [3] the Reason that the Shawanese did not Attend at the Treaty lately held is not known but generally beleived to be owing to Two French Men who were at their Towns and desired to speak to the Cheifs of that Nation in Council⟨.⟩ [4] as soon as I see the Cornstalk I purpose setting off for the Shawanese Towns in hopes of being able to Counteract any diabolical Schems formed by the Enemies of this Country to remove any bad Impressions which may have been made on the Minds of these Savages and to Satisfy them concerning their Hostages⟨.⟩ from thence I shall proceed to the Wyandots Towns where it is said the same Frenchmen have lately been in Council with that Nation and to return by way of the Delaware and Mingo Towns

I find that the Indians have been led to expect a General Treaty and that they would as Usual receive Presents upon a Compliance with the Terms imposed by Lord Dunmore so that I am realy Apprehensive we shall not be able from the Sum Allowed by the Assembly to make the different tribes a Present that will Answer their Expectations Considering the Excessive dearness of Provisions in this part of the Country and the high Advance we must Necessarily pay for Goods from the Great Scarcity now in the Country⟨.⟩ from these Considerations I would beg the Gentlemen of the Convention to consider whether It would not be adviseable to direct the whole Sum of Two Thousand Pounds allowed by the Resolve of the House should not be laid Out to the best Advantage for this Necessary purpose⟨.⟩ [5] I am well Assured it will have an Exceeding good Effect and that a lasting peace may be Established with all the Ohio Indians

By the same Express that brings this the Committee of West Augusta purpose sending to their Delegates the Proceedings of the late Treaty held with the Delawares and Mingoes together with a Copy of thir Resolves prior to the Treaty⟨.⟩ [6] In Justice to the Committee (among whom are Many respectable Characters) I must beg leave to Observe that they have been Attentive to the Interest of their Country on this important Occasion⟨.⟩ as no kind of provision was made by Government towards providing Necessaries for the Indians who were Called to a Council by the Governor the Committee at a Considerable Expence provided a Quantity of Provisions with a present in Goods which were distributed Among the Indians and which I beleive gave them General Satisfaction⟨.⟩ on the other hand if they had not thus taken up the Matter the Certain Consequence must have been that the Indians would have returned dissatisfied and a General discontent would have prevaled among the different Tribes

The Committee as well as Major Connollys most inveterate Enemies all agree that he Conducted this Affair in the Most Open and Candid Manner that it was transacted in the presence of the Committee and that he laid the Governors Instructions on this Occasion before them⟨.⟩ [7] I shall be Extremely happy if my poor Endeavours on this or any future Occasion should in the smallest Degree Contribute to the Service of my Country⟨.⟩ I have the honor to be &c [8]

as soon as I dispatched my Letter I sent for White Eyes and Killbuck Chiefs of the Delawares and Kyashota [9] and the White Mingo Cheifs of the Mingoes and delivered the following Speech sent by Thomas Walker and Andrew Lewis Esqr two of the Commissioners to the Cheifs and Warriors of the Shawanese Wyandots Delaware and Mingo Nations.

Brothers we are Appointed by your elder Brothers of Virginia to meet you in Council to finish the treaty began by Lord Dunmore last Year⟨.⟩ [10] we hope to put an End to all differences between your People and ours so effectually that your Children and ours may live in the Strictest friendship till the Sun Shall shine no more or the Waters run in the Ohio

Brothers your Freind Capn James Wood who is Appointed one of the Commissioners on this Important Occasion will deliver you this talk by whom you will be informed of the Imprudent Behaviour of your Brother Chenusaw who we hope has got safe to you before this⟨.⟩ the Manner in which he went from us gives us reason to fear he may give you some alarming Accounts but we hope Capn Wood will satisfy you that we are your freinds and have been kind to your people⟨.⟩ the Wolf and Newau will come with us to the Treaty at Fort Pitt where we hope to meet you on the tenth day of September to Compleat this great Work and must request you to give Notice to all your Neighbouring Nations that are Concerned⟨.⟩ we desire you will bring with you all the Prisoners and be fully prepared in every respect to fulfill your agreement with Lord Dunmore⟨.⟩ [11] to which White Eyes Answered

Brother I return you as well as our two Brothers that sent it thanks for the good talk you have now delivered us and you may depend I will make it my business to send the String now delivered to me to all my freinds and make no doubt but they will receive it in the same freindly and thankful Manner I do⟨.⟩ [12] The White Mingo [13] then Spoke as follows *Brother* I am very thankful to you and your two Brothers in Virginia for your good talk and String now delivered⟨.⟩ I am certain It will give all my freinds the same Pleasure which it gives me to meet you at the time Appointed for holding the treaty at this place and you may be assured they shall be told of it

Thwaites and Kellogg, *Revolution on the Upper Ohio, 1775–1777*, pp. 35–40

1. That "a few of the Mingoes" were accounted for by James Berwick as "Six Nations" (29 June 1775, Third Va. Convention, 1st entry) attests to a confusing tribal demography. For example, Keyashota, who spoke for the Six Nations, was chief of the Seneca and Mingo tribes (6 July 1775, n. 11).

2. "It seems," rather, that governor and major bent to necessity when only "a few of the Cheifs" appeared and politics perforce altered His Lordship's proposed western itinerary. The original intention of holding a "General Treaty" at which the governor should have been present is implicit in Connolly's and Alexander McKee's letters to the Shawnee (19 May 1775, Third Va. Convention; 20 May, same, 2d entry; 1 July, same). Nor does the observation on 5 July 1775 of the "Chief Warriors of the Senecas" that the Big Knife had invited the conferees "to a small Council Fire at this place" necessarily mean other than that the invitation was issued after it had been determined that the "Council Fire" was not to be "General."

3. For "the Cornstalk," the Shawnee chief Keightughqua, see *Rev. Va.*, II, 105, 106–7.

4. For the "Two French Men," see 1 July 1775, Third Va. Convention and n. 7.

5. For the "Excessive dearness of Provisions in this part of the Country," see 12 July 1775, Third Va. Convention, 1st entry, p. 293 below. In the same resolution in which the House of Burgesses on 24 July 1775 had constituted the commission to treat with the Indians, provision was made that all "expences" and "charges" incurred in negotiations should not "exceed the sum of two thousand Pounds" (*JHB, 1773–1776*, p. 282).

6. The "Proceedings of the late Treaty" were those begun on 19 May 1775, Third Va. Convention, Augusta Co. West, and terminated on 6 July, same. The "Resolves" of the committee "prior to the Treaty" were those of 16 May 1775, 1st entry.

7. The "Governors Instructions" have not been found.

8. As the 1st order of business on 21 July 1775 Wood's letter was to be laid before the third convention, "read and ordered to lie on the Table for the perusal of the Members."

Capt. JAMES WOOD is often confused with his father, Col. James Wood, the founder of Winchester and George Washington's proxy when the last-named was first elected to the House of Burgesses, for Frederick County, in 1758. Colonel Wood, an Oxford University alumnus, saw to it that his son was properly educated. The younger Wood wrote with a fine, precise hand and was highly literate. He probably would have experienced an attack of 18th-century "vapours" ("blues" is in more current usage) had he seen what mutilation was wrought in copying his journal. Captain Wood was first elected a burgess in 1766, a fact rather arguing against the contention of some that he was born in 1750. January 1741 seems more probable. In 1770 he was seated on the Frederick County court and the next year bought one of the 1st sets of Blackstone's *Commentaries* seen in that part of the colony. In 1773 he went to west Florida as an agent for Washington, who wrote that he was "a Gentlemen well esteemed in Virginia" and "perswaded" himself that he "would not disgrace any little Civilities you might please to show him." In Dunmore's War Captain Wood escaped death in an ambush by the timely arrival of Daniel Morgan. Well acquainted with the West and having been all the way to the Mississippi River, Wood was well qualified for the present mission (Freeman, *George Washington*, II, 318–21; Katherine Glass Greene, *Winchester, Virginia, and Its Beginnings, 1743–1814* [Strasburg, 1926], pp. 133–35, 161; *Col. Va. Reg.*, p. 174; *Cal. Va. State Papers*, I, 263; *Wm. and Mary Qtly.*, 2d ser., I [July 1921], 185; Fitzpatrick, *Writings of Washington*, III, 124–29, 151, 184; Thwaites and Kellogg, *Doc. Hist. of Dunmore's War*, p. 241; North Callahan, *Daniel Morgan: Ranger of the Revolution* [New York, 1961], pp. 40–41).

9. Keyashota.

10. See 19 May 1775, Third Va. Convention and n. 3.

11. Wissecapoway, one of the Shawnee hostages carried to Williamsburg, had been returned to his people by Lord Dunmore. Chenusaw had been "Imprudent" enough to escape. The Wolf (Cutemwha) and Newa remained. For Wood's further explanation, see 18 July 1775, Third Va. Convention, Augusta Co. West.

12. It would seem that although Wood did not record the fact, as he was later to do (e.g., 18 July 1775, Third Va. Convention, Augusta Co. West), he nevertheless considered these initial "good" talks sufficiently formal to dignify them by presenting strings of wampum.

13. The WHITE MINGO (Kanaghragait or Canigaat) was already a leader of significance before he settled in 1759 in the vicinity of Fort Pitt, presumably within walking distance of George Croghan's "kag." Charges that he aided and abetted Pontiac were unsubstantiated, and during Dunmore's War he appears to have been the very exemplar of quiescence. It is true that he was not above stealing horses, even from members of his own tribe, but such lapses must have been infrequent or else held as evidencing mere puckishness, for we have Colonel Croghan's word for it that he "behaved himself well." His age is lost to history, but at this time the chief must have been at least from 45 to 50 years old (Charles A. Hanna, *The Wilderness Trail, or The Ventures and Adventures of the Pennsylvania Traders on the Allegheny Path* . . . [2 vols., New York, 1911], I, 203, 246; *Colonial Records of Pennsylvania* . . . [16 vols., Harrisburg, 1838–53], VI, 784; Nicholas B. Wainwright, ed., "George Croghan's Journal, 1759–63," *Pa. Mag. of Hist. and Biog.* LXXI [Oct. 1947], 406–7 and n. 182, 408).

Monday, 10 July 1775

Third Virginia Convention

Augusta County West: Journal of Captain James Wood

10th July White Eyes came with an Interpreter to my Lodgings⟨.⟩ he informed me he was desirous of going to Williamsburg with Major Connolly to see Lord Dunmore who had promised him his Interest in procuring a Grant from the King for the Lands claimed by the Delawares⟨;⟩ that they were all desirous of living as the White People do and under their Laws and Protection⟨;⟩ that Lord Dunmore had engaged to make him some Satisfaction for his Trouble in going several times to the Shawanese Towns and serving with him on Campaign and likewise the damage he has sustained by some of our Men Plundering and destroying his Effects⟨;⟩ that he was a very poor Man and had Neglected to raise Corn by endeavouring to serve us and that his wife and Childern were now almost starving for Bread⟨.⟩ he told me he hoped I would advise him whether It was proper for him to go or not

I was then Under the Necessity of Acquainting him with the disputes subsisting between Lord Dunmore and the People of Virginia and engaged whenever the Assembly met that I would go with him to Williamsburg and represent his Case to the Assembly and made no doubt they would Amply reward him for his Services and damages sustained⟨.⟩ he was very thankful and Appeared perfectly satisfied with the promise I made him [1]

> Thwaites and Kellogg, *Revolution on the Upper Ohio, 1775–1777*, pp. 40–41

Fincastle County: Petition of William Preston to President and Delegates [2]

To the Honourable Mr. Chairman and the Delegates from the several Counties and Borroughs in the Colony of Virginia met in Convention.

The Petition of William Preston Surveyor of Fincastle County humbly sheweth

That some time early in April last your Petr. received Instructions from Lord Dunmore to Survey Lands in the uninhabited parts of this County agreeable to a Proclamation his Lordship had Just then Issued; and which was under Consideration of the Convention then sitting. And as there was nothing said, nor no Resolution entered into by the Convention relative to Surveying those

Lands, Your Petr. therefore Apprehended that the same was tacitly allowed of to prevint Disputes amongst the first Adventurers who might Settle in that Country. But as his Assistants were then going to the Ohio to finish the Business they had left undone the preceding Year, they were Supplyed with a Copy of the Governors instructions, and had Verbal Directions to Survey a small District each, untill it could be known what Report the Committee appointed by the Convention might make on this Subject.[3]

Notwithstanding, your Petr. hath on all Occasions given the Strongest Assurances that he will not return a Single Survey under the aforsd. Instructions without the Approbation of the Honourable the House of Burgesses, or this Honourable Convention ⟨if⟩ first had; and tho' by the last accounts recd. from his Assistants they had not Surveyed any Lands under the sd. Instructions; yet he finds that many People are displeased with his Conduct, not knowing the Motives from which he has Acted.[4]

Your Petitioner therefore Prays that this Honourable Convention would be pleased to take this Matter once more under their Serious Consideration, and that they will Condescend to give such Order, or Directions therein, as they in their Wisdom may think proper; to which their Petr. will pay the most ready and cheerful Observance; as nothing is further from his Heart, or Intention, than to give the Smallest Assistance, to put any Ministerial Instructions into Execution, that may appear to be Contrary to the Ancient Charters, or the true and real Interest of his Country; let the Consequence be what it will to his Family, or Private Emolument.

And your Petr. as in Duty Bound shall every Pray &c.[5]

> Autograph document, unsigned, in loose papers of third Virginia Convention (Archives Division, Virginia State Library)

Fincastle County Committee to President and Delegates:
A Petition [6]

To the honourable, the President and Gentlemen of the Convention.

The Petition of the Committee of Fincastle County in behalf of themselves and the Inhabitants thereof.

In March last, Lord Dunmore issued a Proclamation, for locating the vacant Lands in this County, which were afterward to be put up at publick Auction, subject to an additional Quit-rent and other Innovations, contrary to established usages, which we deem hard & burthensome.[7]

It did not a little lessen our Apprehensions to observe in your Proceedings in Convention, about the same time, wherein it was recommended to the good People of this Colony, not to purchase, or be otherwise concerned in the Sale or accepting any Grants under the said Proclamation: But sorry are we now to observe that the force of your salutary Advice may not have its full intended Effect; Because in consequence of written Instructions from Lord Dunmore to the Surveyor of this County Surveyors have gone out to survey under the said Proclamation, who we are informed also undertake to mark out Lands to private Adventurers, which we conceive will have an evil and injurious tendency by its being reserved for private purposes, & waiting for Contingencies to validate unfair Monopolies; by which means Adventurers as Settlers are at a loss to distinguish the Officers Lands from those that are privately survey'd; which proceedings we apprehend will be productive of such Confusion and Litigation as may be extremely prejudicial to the Prosperity of those, who may settle in that extensive and most fertile Country.[8]

To these Grievances your Petitioners humbly request the honorable the Convention's immediate attention; and that you would give such Advice or Redress to your Petitioners, as to you may seem most Advisable. And your Petitioners shall every pray &c.[9]

> MS transcript in unidentified hand, in loose papers of third Virginia Convention (Archives Division, Virginia State Library)

Fincastle County Committee

In Defence of Just and Reasonable Rights and Liberties

At a committee held for Fincastle *county, July* 10, 1775.

WILLIAM CHRISTIAN, esq; chairman.

THE committee taking into their consideration the clandestine removal of the gunpowder from the magazine of this colony, by order of our governour, are clearly and unanimously of opinion that his lordship's conduct reflects much dishonour on himself, and that he very justly deserves the censure so universally bestowed on him.[10]

Resolved, that the spirited and meritorious conduct of PATRICK HENRY, esq; and the rest of the gentlemen volunteers attending him on the occasion of the removal of the powder out of the magazine in Williamsburg, very justly merits the hearty approbation of this committee; for which we return them our thanks, with an assurance, that we will, at the risk of our lives and fortunes, support and justify them with regard to the reprisal they made.[11]

Resolved, that the council of this colony, in advising and co-operating with Lord Dunmore in issuing a proclamation of the 3d of May last, charging the people of this colony with an ungovernable spirit, and licentious practices, is contrary to many known matters of fact, and but too justly intimates to us that those who ought to be mediators, and guardians of our liberties, are become the abject tools of a detested administration.[12]

Resolved, that it is the opinion of this committee, that the late sanguinary attempt and preparations of the king's troops in the colony of Massachusetts Bay is truly alarming and irritating, and loudly calls upon all, even the most distant and interiour parts of the colonies, to prepare and be ready for the extreme event, by fixed resolution, and a firm and manly opposition, to avert ministerial cruelty, in defence of our just and reasonable rights and liberties.[13]

Virginia Gazette (Purdie), 22 July 1775, supplement

Frederick County Committee

Charles Mynn Thruston to Chairman and Gentlemen of the Committee of the Borough of Lancaster, Pennsylvania

Frederick County Virginia 10th July 1775
Gentlemen   In Committee
We have employed Mr. Andrew Cox to purchase Two hundred Rifles for the Use of this County. We request you will give him your Countenance and assistance to expedite this Matter, which to the General Cause and to us in particular, is of great Importance. We pledge the faith of this Committee; and you may rest assured, that the money shall be paid as soon as the Guns are delivered—
We further request, that if those Guns cannot be Speedily procured in your Town, You will communicate this Letter to such of the Neighbouring Committees as may be most likely to assist in this Urgent Business—Signed by Order and on behalf of the Committee [14]

CHARLES MYNN THRUSTON
Ch. F. C.

Recipients' copy, autograph letter, signed (Peter Force Collection, ser. 9, Library of Congress)

Middlesex County Committee

A Vindication of Character

In consequence of a resolution of the committee of Middlesex, entered into on the 6th of June,[15] respecting some goods taken from on board captain Moses Robinson ⟨Robertson⟩ by Mess. Mills and company, in vindication of my own character, I am induced to inform the public, that being at Urbanna, where I went to deliver a vessel to those gentlemen, I saw boats pass divers times in the night to and from captain Robinson's ship; at the same time a gentleman of that company stood on the shore, where we saw parcels landed, which appeared to be goods. This we are ready to make oath to whenever required.

> John Parsons,
> William Degge,
> John Degge,
> William Hudgin.

Virginia Gazette (Pinkney), 13 July 1775

And a Variant Thereof

Gloucester, *July* 10, 1775.

IN consequence of the resolution of the committee of *Middlesex* county, entered into on the 6th of last month, respecting some goods taken from on board capt. *Moses Robertson*, by mess. *Mills* & co. in vindication of our characters, we are induced to inform the publick, that being at *Urbanna*, in order to deliver a vessel to those gentlemen, we saw boats pass, divers times, in the night, to and from a ship which we were told was capt. *Robertson;* at the same time, a gentleman of that company stood on the shore, where we saw parcels landed, which appeared to us to be goods. This we are ready to make oath to, when required.[16]

> John Parsons.
> William Degge.
> John Degge.
> William Hudgin.

Virginia Gazette (Purdie), 14 July 1775

1. While holding Connolly under arrest in June 1775, Arthur St. Clair had plied his guest with "a cheerful glass" and heard a variation on this theme. The prisoner asserted that he intended going to "England with White Eyes and some other Delaware chiefs, to solicit for them a confirmation of the country where they now live in" and that Lord Dunmore would support the appeal "with all his interest" (22 June 1775, Third Va. Convention and n. 2; W. H. Smith, *St. Clair Papers,* I, 358). It is possible that White Eyes was not as "perfectly satisfied" as Wood imagined and that he was one of the "three Indian Chiefs" on whom Connolly "prevailed" to travel with him on his journey from Fort Pitt to see the governor. With Dunmore's proclamation of 21 Mar. 1775 in hand, Connolly could have been persuasive, for in that document His Lordship in effect had announced that all lands to which legal title was not already held were "vacant" and belonged to and were exclusively assignable by the Crown (*Rev. Va.,* II, 383–84, 387–88 n. 9). And although there were "disputes subsisting between Lord Dunmore and the People of Virginia," it was obvious that the very "Assembly" from which the chief might expect compensation for his losses could be convoked only by the authority of the governor.

In his later "Narrative" Connolly alleged that he used the Indians as a cover against patriot suspicions of his loyalty, and that at Winchester he informed the chiefs that he "must now part with them" (*Pa. Mag. of Hist. and Biog.*, XII [1888], 321, 323). Be that as it may, when Wood on 22 July was to ride by "White Eyes' Town about 10 o'Clock" in the morning, he would not stop to pay his respects, so implying that the chief still was absent (Thwaites and Kellogg, *Rev. on the Upper Ohio*, p. 45).

For a further word on "the vacant lands," see the 2 items immediately following.

2. The document is not dated and is arbitrarily placed here next a related petition from the Fincastle County committee. That Preston drew up his petition previous to this date is obvious from his letter to William Christian, apparently written on the night of 12 July 1775 (Draper MSS, 4QQ32, State Hist. Soc. of Wis.). It is possible that Preston indited this document after receipt on an undisclosed date of a letter from Thomas Lewis dated 19 June 1775 detailing events in the Tidewater which bore on the subject of western lands (ibid., 4QQ20).

Col. WILLIAM PRESTON, born in Londonderry on Christmas Day, 1729, and brought to Virginia late in the 1730s, was an impressive, ruddy-faced Irishman with fair hair and hazel eyes. He stood nearly 6 feet tall and though by this date somewhat rotund, was physically powerful, of easy and graceful address, and of a taste for poetry. He had sired 11 children and now lived at his plantation, Smithfield (site of the later town of Blacksburg, Montgomery County). Once sheriff and a burgess for Augusta County, a member of the 1st court of Botetourt when that county was formed in 1770, and a surveyor and justice of the peace for Fincastle since its creation in 1773, he was one of those intrepid pioneers who persistently pushed back the frontier. An old Indian fighter (a captain under Andrew Lewis in 1755–56 and a colonel in Dunmore's War), he had taken up the cause of the patriots and was made a member of the Fincastle County committee on the day of its formation, 20 Jan. 1775 (Rumsey Bissell Marston, "Colonel William Preston," *The John P. Branch Historical Papers of Randolph-Macon College*, 1st ser., IV [June 1915], 257–73; J[ohn] Lewis Peyton, *History of Augusta County, Virginia* [Staunton, Va., 1882], p. 142; Lewis Preston Summers, *Annals of Southwest Virginia, 1769–1800* [Abingdon, Va., 1929], pp. 58–59, 66, 588; *Rev. Va.*, II, 255).

3. Lord Dunmore's "Instructions" to Colonel Preston were dated 21 Mar. 1775 (Draper MSS, 4QQ9), the same day His Lordship "Issued" a "Proclamation" for the surveying and sale of "vacant lands" in the colony, a document that incensed the delegates to the second Virginia Convention "then sitting" in Richmond. The convention appointed a committee to study and make recommendations for the future, and for the time being adopted a resolution recommending to "all persons whatever to forbear purchasing or accepting grants of lands on the conditions" prescribed by the governor (*Rev. Va.*, II, 383–84, 387–88 n. 9).

4. Preston and his "Assistants" (James Douglas, John Floyd, and Isaac Hite) sympathized with the desire of the governor to throw the West open to settlement. But at least one of the deputy surveyors was carrying his zeal too far, which, as the next following item indicates, made "many People" more than a little "displeased" (Draper MSS, 4QQ7, 4QQ32; *Cal. Va. State Papers*, I, 308–10). As evidence of his good faith, Preston had already sent word to his deputies to cease surveying (Draper MSS, 4QQ32).

5. Although Preston sent a copy of this petition to William Christian, a delegate for Fincastle County to the third convention, and another to Archibald Cary of Chesterfield County, it seems most probable that yet another copy, by this time already dispatched to Thomas Lewis of Augusta County, was the one placed before the convention on 18 July 1775, for of the 3 recipients, Lewis would report to Preston most

particularly upon the reception of the petition and had the strongest personal reasons for desiring a resolution of these complexities (ibid., 4QQ32, 4QQ29; 8 May 1775, n. 3).

6. The document is not dated, but writing on 12 July 1775 to explain the circumstances under which it was prepared, William Christian indicated that it was agreed to at the committee meeting of "monday last" (Draper MSS, 4QQ25), on which day, as is demonstrated by the item next following, the committee did meet.

7. See n. 3 above.

8. For the "Proceedings in Convention," the "said Proclamation," and the "written Instructions from Lord Dunmore," see n. 3 above.

By the time Preston's deputies reached the Kentucky River, they found already encamped on Virginia soil a party of North Carolinians under the leadership of Judge Richard Henderson, the life and spirit of the unchartered Transylvania Company. Disregarding inconvenient laws and proclamations, these "private Adventurers" had bargained with the Cherokee Indians at Sycamore Shoals in Mar. 1775 for rights to settle a "great and Valluable Country below the Kentucky," some of which was within, some of which was beyond, the Proclamation Line of 1763, and some of which consisted of "Officers Lands" set aside for veterans of Dunmore's War. Cherokee competence to bargain away any "rights" whatever was very questionable; but the undaunted Henderson and his followers in the region of Boonesborough established a "legislature" and treated Virginia claims with such disregard as to threaten fulfillment of Preston's fears that an "independent Government" would be erected in the wilderness (24 June 1775, n. 2; Draper MSS, 4QQ32; Bakeless, *Daniel Boone*, pp. 83–102; George W. Ranke, *Boonesborough: Its Founding, Pioneer Struggles, Indian Experiences, Transylvania Days, and Revolutionary Annals*, Filson Club Publications, no. 16 [Louisville, Ky., 1902], pp. 22–31; Hamilton, *Letters to Washington*, V, 152–53).

With promises of free land, Henderson soon wooed Floyd from his responsibilities, and it was not long before the deputy surveyor of a chartered colony was acting as "Entry Clerk" for an illegal company (Archibald Henderson, "Richard Henderson's Occupation of Kentucky, 1775," *Mississippi Valley Historical Review*, I [Dec. 1914], 358–60; Ranke, *Boonesborough*, pp. 174–75, 190; *Cal. Va. State Papers*, I, 309). Floyd's extracurricular activities, along with Preston's having sent out survey parties in the first place, roused strong opposition and resulted in the initiation and signing of the present petition (Draper MSS, 4QQ25).

9. The Fincastle County petition would be presented to the third Virginia Convention on 18 July 1775, along with the petition from William Preston.

10. For "his lordship's conduct," see pp. 4–6 above.

11. For the "spirited and meritorious conduct" of Henry and the "gentlemen volunteers attending him," see pp. 7–11 above; 9 May 1775, Hanover County Committee.

12. The proclamation is under the date heading indicated, Royal Chief Magistracy.

13. For the diffusion of the news of "the late sanguinary attempt" in Massachusetts, see 28 Apr. 1775, Va. Committee and n. 6; 30 Apr., same, ed. n. and n. 2; 2 May, Surry Co. Committee and n. 6. By this time "preparations of the king's"—not, it may be worth noting, the "ministerial"—troops had been richly documented in the 4 Virginia newspapers; but if intelligence of the affair at Bunker Hill had reached the isolated Fincastle County committee, it almost certainly consisted of the fragmentary reports contained in Pinkney's *Va. Gazette* of 6 July 1775.

14. The committee's search for "two hundred Rifles" was undertaken in order to provide the county's gentlemen volunteers with the "good Rifle if to be had, or otherwise with a Common Firelock" and accoutrements recommended by the second Vir-

ginia Convention on 25 Mar. 1775 (*Rev. Va.*, II, 375). Among the numerous extant manuscripts of the Lancaster Borough committee and its parent body, the Lancaster County committee, is no other record relating to this request from Virginia. The present letter was simply docketed by its recipients, "July 10th.—Letter from the Committee of Fredk. Coty. Virginia." But whether from the assistance of the addressees or from help rendered by "such of the Neighbouring Committees" as might have been enlisted in the search for arms, the inquiry was apparently successful. On 12 Aug. 1775 the "Members from the County of Frederick" in the third Virginia Convention would inform the other members "that some Gentlemen in their County had purchased a Number of Rifles & a Quantity of Gun Powder at a low rate," which they then offered "for the Use of the Public" at cost (Procs. and n. 13).

15. Q.v.

16. For a categorical denial of these allegations, see 13 July 1775, Middlesex Co. Committee, and for fatal defects in John Parson's attempted "vindication," 22 July 1775, same.

Tuesday, 11 July 1775

Third Virginia Convention

Virginia Delegates in Congress to Peyton Randolph

Sir   Philadelphia, July 11, 1775
The continued sitting of Congress prevents us from attending our colony Convention; but, directed by a sense of duty, we transmit to the Convention such determinations of the Congress as they have directed to be made public. The papers speak for themselves, and require no comment from us. A petition to the king is already sent away, earnestly entreating the royal interposition to prevent the further progress of civil contention by redressing American grievances; but we are prevented from transmitting a copy of it, because a publick communication, before it has been presented, may be improper.[1] —The Convention, we hope, will pardon us for venturing our sentiments on the following subjects, which we submit to their superior wisdom.—The continuance and the extent of this conflict we consider as among the secrets of providence; but we also reflect on the propriety of being prepared for the worst events, and, so far as human foresight can provide, to be guarded against probable evils at least. Military skill we are certainly not so well provided with as military violence opposed to us may render necessary. Will not this deficiency be supplied by sending at the publick expence a few gentlemen of genius and spirit to the military school before Boston to learn that necessary art, which in these days of rapine can only be relied upon for public safety⟨?⟩ [2]

The present crisis is so full of danger and incertainty that opinions here are various. Some think a continued sitting of Congress necessary, whilst others are of opinion that an adjournment to the Fall will answer as well. We conclude that our powers go not to the latter, but that a Fall Congress will be indispensible, with adjourning powers given to your delegates that they may be prepared to meet contingencies. The Convention will therefore see the propriety of proceeding to a new choice of delegates and being explicit about the time they chuse to limit the continuance of their delegation.[3]—It is expected that at the next Congress the delegates from the respective colonies come provided with an exact account of the number of people of all ages and sexes, including slaves. The Convention will provide for this.[4]

It is with singular pleasure that we can congratulate you on the success with which providence has been pleased to favor our righteous cause by giving success to the operations in defence of American liberty.[5] We are, Sir, Your most humble servants.[6]

> P. HENRY JR.
> RICHARD HENRY LEE
> EDMD PENDLETON
> BENJA. HARRISON
> TH: JEFFERSON

> MS letter in hand of Thomas Jefferson, with autograph signatures (Simon Gratz Autograph Collection, Historical Society of Pennsylvania)

In Congress [7]

Wednesday May 17. 1775

Resolved unanimously That all exportations to Quebec, Nova Scotia the island of St. Johns, Newfoundland, Georgia except the Parish of St. Johns, & to East and West Florida immediately cease & that no provisions of any kind or other Necessaries be furnished to the British Fisheries on the American coast until it be otherwise determined by the Congress.[8]

Friday May 26. 1775

Resolved Unanimously

1. That his Majestys Most faithful subjects in these colonies are reduced to a dangerous & critical situation by the attempts of the British Ministry to carry into execution by force of Arms several unconstitutional and oppressive acts of the British Parliament for levying taxes in America, to enforce the collection of those taxes, and for altering & changing the constitution and internal police of these colonies, in violation of the natural and civil rights of the colonists.

2. Hostilities being actually commenced in the Massachusetts bay by the

British troops under the command of General ⟨Thomas⟩ Gage and the lives of a number of the inhabitants of that colony destroyed⟨,⟩ the town of Boston having not only been long occupied as a garrisoned town in an enemys country, but the inhabitants thereof treated with a severity and cruelty not to be justifyed even towards declared enemies; large re-inforcements too being ordered and soon expected for the declared purpose of compelling these colonies to submit to the operation of the sd: Acts, resolved therefore that for the purpose of securing and defending these colonies and preserving them in safety against all attempts to carry the sd. Acts into execution by force of Arms, these colonies be immediately put into a state of defence.[9]

Saturday May 27. 1775

Resolved, That where any Person hath been or shall be adjudged by a committee to have violated the continental association & such offender shall satisfy the convention of the colony where the offence was or shall be committed or the committee of the Parish of St. John's in the colony of Georgia if the offence be committed there, of his contrition for his offence & sincere resolution to conform to the association for the future, the sd. convention or committee of the Parish of St. Johns aforesaid may settle the terms upon which he may be restored to the favour and forgiveness of the public and that the terms be published.[10]

Monday May 29. 1775

Resolved That no provisions or necessaries of any kind be exported to the island of Nantucket except from the colony of Massachusetts bay, the convention of which colony is desired to take measures for effectually providing the sd. island, upon their application to purchase the same, with as much provisions as shall be necessary for its internal use and no more.

The Congress deeming it of great importance to North America that the British Fishery should not be furnished with Provisions from this continent thro Nantucket earnestly recommend a vigilant execution of this resolve to all committees.[11]

Friday June 2. 1775

Resolved, That no Bill of Exchange draught or Order of any officer in the army or navy their agents or contractors be received or negotiated or any money supplied to them by any persons in America. That no provisions or necessaries of any kind be furnished or supplied to or for the use of the British Army or Navy in the colony of Massachusetts bay and That no Vessel employed in transporting British troops to America or from one part of America to another, or warlike stores or provisions, for said troops be freighted or furnished with provisions or any necessaries, until farther orders from this Congress.[12]

Friday June 9. 1775

Resolved, That no obedience being due to the act of parliament for altering the charter of the colony of Massachusetts bay nor to a Govr. & Lieutenant Govr. who will not observe the directions of but endeavour to subvert that charter,[13] the Govr. and Lieutenant Govr. of that colony are to be considered as absent & these offices vacant; and as there is no council there and the inconveniences arising from the suspension of the powers of government are intolerable especially at a time when Gen: Gage hath actually levied war and is carrying on hostilities against his Majesty's peaceable & loyal subjects of that colony; that in order to conform as near as may be to the spirit & substance of the Charter it be recommended to the provincial Congress to write letters to the inhabitants of the several places, which are entitled to representatives in Assembly, requesting them to chuse such representatives, and that the assembly when chosen should elect Counsellors, which assembly & council should exercise the powers of Government until a Governor of his Majesty's appointment will consent to govern the colony according to its charter.[14]

Saturday June 10. 1775

Resolved, That it be recommended to the conventions and committees of the colonies of Virginia, North Carolina, & South Carolina, that they without delay collect the Salt Petre & Sulphur in their respective colonies and procure these articles to be manufactured as soon as possible into GunPowder for the use of the continent.[15]

Resolved, That it be recommended to the several inhabitants of the colonies, who are possessed of Salt Petre & Sulphur for their own use to dispose of them for the purpose of manufacturing GunPowder.

Resolved, That the Salt Petre & Sulphur to be collected in consequence of the resolves of Congress for that purpose be paid for out of the continental fund.

Wednesday June 14th. 1775

Resolved, That six companies of expert riflemen be immediately raised in Pennsylvania, two in Maryland & two in Virginia, that each company as soon as compleated shall march and join the army near Boston to be there employed as light infantry under the command of the chief officer of that army, that the pay of the officers and privates be as follows

a Captain @ 20 dollars per month
a Lieutenant @ 13⅓ dollars per month
a Serjeant @ 8 dollars per month
Corporal @ 7⅓ dollars per month
Drummer @ 7⅓ dollars per month
Privates @ 6⅔ dollars per month
⟨; they⟩ to find their own Arms and cloaths.

That each Company consist of a Captain, three lieutenants, four serjeants, four corporals, a drummer, or   , and sixty eight privates.[16]

That the form of enlistment be in the following Words.

I have this day voluntarily inlisted myself as a soldier in the American Continental Army for one Year unless sooner discharged and do bind myself to conform in all instances to such rules and regulations as are or shall be established for the government of the said Army.

Thursday June 15. 1775

Resolved, That a General be appointed to command all the continental forces raised or to be raised for the defense of American liberty.

That five hundred dollars per month be allowed for his pay and expenses.

The Congress then proceeded to the choice of a General, when George Washington Esqr. was unanimously elected.[17]

Friday June 16. 1775

Resolved, That four[18] Major Generals be appointed for the American Army.

That the pay of each Major General be one hundred forty six Dollars[19] per month.

That when any of these act in a separate department he be allowed for his pay and expence three hundred and thirty two dollars per month.

That there be eight Brigadiers General ⟨and⟩ that the pay of each be one hundred and twenty five dollars per month.

That there be one Quarter Master General for the Grand Army and a deputy under him for the separate army: That the pay of the Quarter Master General be eighty dollars per month, that of the deputy forty dollars per month.

That there be a Pay Master general and a deputy Pay Master general under him for the Army in a separate department; that the pay for himself be one hundred dollars per Month, and for the deputy Paymaster under him fifty dollars per month.

That two assistants be employed under him, that their pay be twenty dollars per month each.

That there be a chief Engineer for the Army in a separate department and two assistants under him, that the pay of the Chief Engineer be sixty dollars per month & the pay of the assistants twenty dollars per month each.

That there be three Aid de camps, & their pay thirty three dollars per month each.

That there be a secretary to the General & his pay sixty six dollars per month.

That there be a secretary to the Major General When acting in a separate department and that his pay be thirty three dollars per month.

That there be a Commissary of the Musters & his pay twenty dollars per month.

Saturday June 17. 1775

The Congress then proceeded to the choice of the Officers of the Army When Artemas Ward was chosen Major General & second in command. Horatio Gates Esqr. was unanimously chosen Adjutant General.

Resolved, That Mr Gates shall rank as a Brigadier General.

Charles Lee Esqr. was chosen second Major General to be third in command.

Monday June 19. 1775

Philip ⟨John⟩ Schuyler Esqr. was chosen third Major General & Israel Putnam Esqr. was unanimously chosen 4th Major General.

⟨Thursday June 22. 1775⟩ [20]

Resolved That the number of Brigadiers General be augmented to eight.
The Congress then proceeded to the choice of the Brigadiers viz.
Seth Pomeroy Esqr. first
Rich⟨ar⟩d. Montgomery Esqr. second
David Worster ⟨Wooster⟩ Esqr. third
W⟨illia⟩m. Heath Esqr. fourth
Joseph Spencer Esqr. fifth
John Thomas Esqr. sixth
John Sullivan Esqr. seventh
Nathaniel Green ⟨Nathanael Greene⟩ Esqr. eighth

Resolved, That the troops including the Volunteers be furnished wth. Camp equipage and Blankets Where necessary at the Continental expence.

Resolved, That the Officers now in the Army receive their Commissions from the general.

Resolved, That a sum not exceeding two Millions of Spanish Milled dollars be emitted by the Congress in bills of Credit for the defence of America.[21]

Resolved, That the pay of the Aids de camp of the Majors General be encreased to thirty three dollars per month.

⟨Friday June 23. 1775⟩ [22]

Resolved, That the number and denomination of the Bills to be emitted be as follows vizt.

49,000 bills of	8 dollars ea.	392,000
49,000 do.	7 do.	343,000
49,000 do.	6 do.	294,000
49,000 do.	5 do.	245,000
49,000 do.	4 do.	196,000
49,000 do.	3 do.	147,000
49,000 do.	2 do.	98,000
49,000 do.	1 do.	49,000
11,800 do.	20 do.	236,000
403,800		2,000,000

Resolved, That the form of the Bills be as follows
Continental Currency
No.

This Bill entitles the bearer to receive . . . . . Spanish Milled Dollars or the value thereof in gold or silver according to the resolutions of the Congress held at Philadelphia on the 10th day of May 1775.[23]

Monday June 26. 1775

Whereas it is represented to this Congress that the enemies of the liberties of America are preparing Measures to divide the good people of the colony of North Carolina & to defeat the American association

Resolved, that it be recommended to all in that colony who wish well to the liberties of America to associate for the defence of American liberty & to embody themselves as Militia under proper officers.

Resolved, That in Case the Assembly or Convention of that colony shall think it absolutely necessary for the support of the American association & safety of the colony to raise a body of forces not exceeding one thousand Men, this Congress will consider them as an American Army & provide for their pay.[24]

Tuesday July 4. 1775.

Resolved, That the two acts passed in the first Session of the present Parliament, the one entitled "An act to restrain the trade and commerce of the Province of Massachusetts bay & New-hampshire, and colonies of Connecticut & Rhode-island & providence plantations in North America, to Great Britain, Ireland and the British islands in the West indies; and to prohibit such provinces and Colonies from carrying on any fishing on The banks of Newfoundland or other places therein mentioned, under certain conditions and limitations⟨,⟩" [25] The other entitled "An act to restrain the trade and commerce of the colonies of New Jersey, Pennsylvania, Maryland, Virginia & South Carolina to Great Britain Ireland and the British islands in the West indies under certain conditions & limitations" [26] are unconstitutional oppressive and cruel, and that the commercial opposition of these colonies to certain acts enumerated in the association of the last Congress ought to be made against these, until they are repealed.[27]

> Autograph documentary excerpts from journal of second Continental Congress, in hand of Charles Thomson, secretary, in papers of third Virginia Convention (Archives Division, Virginia State Library)

1. The "petition to the king" was penned by John Dickinson and although with general "disgust," was adopted in order to mollify him and such moderates as still thought one more "humble" plea for His Majesty's gracious intervention an application meet and seemly. Delighted with the adoption, Dickinson rose and said, "There is but one word, Mr. President, in the paper of which I disapprove, and that is the word *Congress*."

Then up rose "Ben" Harrison and said, "There is but one word in the paper, Mr. President, of which I approve, and that is the word *Congress*" (*JCC*, II, 158–62; P. L. Ford, *Works of Jefferson*, I, 19).

The text of the petition first appeared in a Virginia newspaper with the issuance of Dixon and Hunter's *Va. Gazette* of 2 Sept. 1775. That was the very day that Arthur Lee in London learned that the king had treated the document with studied contempt (Memorandum of interview with Lord Dartmouth and draft of letter to Congress, autograph document, much mutilated, in hand of Arthur Lee, Lee Papers, Harvard Univ.).

2. In a letter to Washington on 21 July 1775 Benjamin Harrison made clear that by the phrase "military school" the Virginia delegation in Congress did not mean anything as formal as a corps of cadets organized in a paleo-officers candidate school. Though for some time a rumor persisted that "60 young gentlemen" would be sent to Boston at "public expence," the third convention would on 26 Aug. 1775 subsidize only one

cadetship, for Otway Byrd, and not limit his apprenticeship to what could be learned at the site of the siege (Edmund C. Burnett, ed., *Letters of Members of the Continental Congress* [8 vols., Washington, D.C., 1921–36; hereafter *Letters Cont. Cong.*], I, 170; *Va. Gazette* [Purdie], 28 July 1775).

3. This the "Convention" would do on 11 Aug. 1775 (Procs. and nn. 9–13).

4. The first Continental Congress had agreed that each colony should have but one vote, "The Congress not being possess'd of, or at present able to procure proper materials for ascertaining the importance of each Colony" by population (*Rev. Va.*, II, 108). The "Convention" would on 25 Aug. 1775 undertake to "provide for" a colony-wide census (p. 488 below).

5. The "success" the delegates had in mind was probably that centering in the northern colonies, with the capture of Fort Ticonderoga and its "Noble Train of Artillery" and a number of skirmishes near Boston, where despite their Pyrrhic victory at Bunker Hill, the British were effectively pinned down (Richard Frothingham, *History of the Siege of Boston . . .* [Boston, 1848; 6th ed., Boston, 1903; reprint of 6th ed., New York, 1970], pp. 224–25).

6. This letter, together with the following enclosure, would be "laid before the Convention" by Peyton Randolph on 24 July 1775.

7. In transcribing from the manuscript journal of the second Continental Congress, Charles Thomson, the secretary, introduced a few inconsequential modifications in capitalization, spelling, punctuation, and syntax. Since he had only one clerical assistant, he may have been hard-pressed and eye-weary (*JCC*, II, 49).

8. The resolution was adopted pursuant to article 14 of the Continental Association which bound adherents to "have no trade, commerce, dealings or intercourse whatsoever, with any colony or province, in North-America, which shall not accede to, or which shall hereafter violate this association" (ibid., I, 79). Virginians attentive to their newspapers would have read the resolution in the *Va. Gazette* (Dixon and Hunter) of 10 June 1775. On 19 June 1775 Richard Bland, former member of the first congress, presented this and 2 other resolutions to the House of Burgesses, which approved of them and "recommended it to the several Committees within this Colony, for carrying into execution the Continental Association, to be vigilant in seeing the said Resolutions strictly complied with" (*JHB, 1773–1776*, p. 252). The "Parish of St. Johns" represented a unique case. Riven since the first general congress was proposed in the summer of 1774, the Georgia colonial convention in August of that year voted down a motion offered by the representatives of St. John's to send deputies to Philadelphia. Persisting, the patriots even set on foot a futile design to secede and present their parish to patriotic South Carolina. A 2d Georgia convention (boycotted by St. John's) finally acceded to the association, but with reservations, and elected 3 deputies to attend the second congress. Because they would not represent the entire colony, the deputies-elect refused to go. The people of St. John's then chose Dr. Lyman Hall to represent them and sent him north with upward of 200 barrels or rice and £50 for the relief of Boston. Since he had not been chosen by the whole colony, the doctor in turn declined to vote and sat silently while only the domain of his steadfast constituents was exempted from the proscription laid on Georgia (Kenneth Coleman, *The American Revolution in Georgia, 1763–1789* [Athens, Ga., 1958], pp. 39–50; *Rev. Va.*, II, 157–58, 159 n. 1; *JCC*, II, 44–48, 49–50).

9. For 11 days previous to the adoption of this resolution, Congress had sat almost continuously in Committee of the Whole debating "the state of America." On the next day, 27 May 1775, George Washington was appointed chairman of a committee of 6 "to consider ways and means to supply these colonies with Ammunition and military

stores." At least inwardly, Patrick Henry must have smiled. It was only 65 days since he had encountered bitter opposition in moving that Virginia "immediately be put into a posture of Defence" (Edmund Cody Burnett, *The Continental Congress* [New York, 1941], pp. 69–70; *JCC*, II, 64–65, 67; *Rev. Va.*, II, 366–67, 368–69 n. 8). The vote in Congress was unanimous.

10. This resolution, printed in *Dunlap's Pa. Packet* the day of adoption, was the 1st act of the second congress to be made public (*JCC*, II, 68 n. 1). In Virginia the resolution could have been read in the *Va. Gazette* (Purdie) of 16 June 1775. It was adopted for the relief of 2 New York merchants who having tried to evade the Continental Association, became repentant when "published" by the committee of Elizabeth Town, N.J. (William A. Whitehead et al., eds., *Documents Relating to the Colonial*[, *Revolutionary and Post-Revolutionary*] *History of the State of New Jersey* [1st ser., 42 vols., Newark, N.J., 1880–1949], X, 561–69).

11. Introduced from the floor, probably by a member from Massachusetts, this injunction was adopted in retaliation for the recent passage of the parliamentary "Act to Restrain the Trade and Commerce of the Provinces of *Massachusett's Bay*, and *New Hampshire*, and Colonies of *Connecticut*, and *Rhode Island* and *Providence Plantation*, in *North America*, to *Great Britain, Ireland* and the *British* Islands in the *West Indies*, and to prohibit such Provinces and Colonies from carrying on any Fishery on the Banks of *Newfoundland*, or other Places therein mentioned, under certain Conditions and Limitations," 15 George III, *cap.* 10 (A.D. 1775), commonly called "the New England Fisheries Act." One of the "Limitations" of the act was the specific exclusion of the island of Nantucket, the Quaker inhabitants of which had balked at joining their protesting fellow subjects but who, without exemption, would be forced to depend for sustenance entirely upon the rebels of the mainland (Hansard, *Parliamentary History*, XVIII, cols. 298–300, 383–85, 423–25, 433, 434, 446). On 11 May the debates on the bill were extensively reported in the *Pa. Gazette* and doubtless read by members of Congress.

On 7 July the Massachusetts Provincial Congress prohibited all commerce with Nantucket until its residents should give adequate assurances that they were carrying on no trade in violation of the Continental Association (William Lincoln, ed., *The Journals of the Provincial Congress of Massachusetts in 1774 and 1775, and the Committee of Safety* . . . [Boston, 1838], p. 470). Virginians read the resolution in the *Va. Gazette* (Purdie) of 16 June 1775, and the resolution was the 2d of the 3 presented to the House of Burgesses by Richard Bland 3 days later (*JHB, 1773–1776*, p. 252); but Virginia had no special need to be "vigilant" in respect to unauthorized trade with Nantucket.

12. This resolution was printed in the *Va. Gazette* (Purdie) on 16 June 1775 and was the last of the 3 presented to the House of Burgesses by Richard Bland 3 days later (*JHB, 1773–1776* p. 252). It was redolent of the thought expressed (though in the case he chose, ineffectually) by the anonymous writer who on 5 May stated that penalties should be visited on shipowners who "let to the Ministry, to carry troops to Boston, to cut the throats of all the Americans" (Williamsburg). Although predating the resolution, a more current application of the principle on which it was based was that of 25 May 1775 by the Norfolk Borough committee against Capt. Henry Colins.

13. For the "Massachusetts Government Act," see *Rev. Va.*, I, 106.

14. The resolution was adopted in response to a request of 16 May 1775 by the Massachusetts Provincial Congress for "most explicit advice, respecting the taking up and exercising the powers of civil government" (Lincoln, *Journs. of the Prov. Cong. of Mass.*, pp. 229–31).

15. The second Virginia Convention had already taken steps toward the "making, collecting & refining" of saltpeter (30 June 1775, n. 6). But this was not to end the matter. The third convention would hear more on the subject from the second Continental Congress (15 July 1775, Third Va. Convention; 28 July 1775, same); would adopt a resolution for the preservation of "Trash Tobacco" in making saltpeter (29 July 1775, same); would appoint a committee to prepare an ordinance to encourage the making of saltpeter (12 Aug. 1775, same); and would pass the ordinance as its final act of session (26 Aug. 1775, same, pp. 503–4 below).

16. The missing word is "trumpeter." Thomson apparently was transcribing from the rough journal of the Continental Congress (MS document, in hand of Thomson, National Archives, Washington, D.C., microfilm in Va. State Library), in which the word was later entered above a caret. As "light infantry," the riflemen, who were marksmen such as most Britons had never seen, would move rapidly, with few impedimenta. Raising these companies was not to be a work of the third convention but was that of the county committees. By the time the convention met, Daniel Morgan was already on the way to Boston from Frederick County with the 1st company, and Hugh Stephenson from Berkeley County with the 2d (Don Higginbotham, *Daniel Morgan, Revolutionary Rifleman* [Chapel Hill, N.C., 1961], p. 22).

17. On 16 May the Massachusetts Provincial Congress also requested Congress to assume "direction" of the intercolonial forces before Boston. On 14 June, John Adams urged "adoption" of the American army there and declared that it would also be well to think of a commander. He then spoke warmly in behalf of a "gentleman from Virginia." President John Hancock, who had expected his fellow deputy to nominate him, sat in stunned silence. Washington hurried from the chamber. The hours following sufficed to mitigate the apprehensions of Edmund Pendleton and others who questioned the propriety of setting a southern man over northern soldiers. Thus on the 15th, as Adams informed his wife, Congress "made Choice of the modest and virtuous, the amiable, generous and brave George Washington Esqr., to be the General of the American Army" (Freeman, *George Washington*, III, 433–38; L. H. Butterfield, *Adams Papers*, ser. II, *Adams Family Correspondence* [Cambridge, Mass., 1963–], I, 215).

18. The resolution as reported from the Committee of the Whole on 16 June provided for 3 major generals, but was amended to 4, then to 2. On 19 June, Congress "*Resolved*, That there be four Major generals" (*JCC*, II, 93 n. 1, 99).

19. Thomson erred. The sum ordered was "one hundred sixty six dollars" (ibid., II, 93).

20. Again Thomson's eye or pen slipped as he failed to insert the proper date (ibid., II, 103).

21. It might have been of more interest to the members of the third convention had Thomson, instead of following with a resolution respecting the wages of aides-de-camp, inserted the resolution that follows in the journal: "That the twelve confederated colonies be pledged for the redemption of the bills of credit, now directed to be emitted" (ibid., II, 103).

22. Once more Thomson's attention lapsed.

23. That is, of the Congress that convened "on the 10th day of May 1775." But what was the value of a Spanish milled dollar? Since the paper emissions of the colonies varied as pegged to the British pound sterling, a committee of Congress was eventually to be appointed for the purpose of reducing chaos to a semblance of order. This task it would fulfill in Sept. 1776 by reporting that a dollar equaled 0.444 ad infinitum of a pound sterling, or more simply, two-ninths of a dollar equaled one shilling (A[lonzo]

Barton Hepburn, *A History of Currency in the United States* . . . [New York, 1915], pp. 33–34).

24. The offer to embody 1,000 select militiamen as "an American Army" was less motivated by any robust challenge to patriot control in North Carolina (Gov. Josiah Martin was holed up in Fort Johnston near the mouth of the Cape Fear River) than by a desire to jar patriotism into greater activity. The trade of the colony had been exempted by Parliament from restraints laid on that of other colonies. To the North Carolina delegates in Congress, the reason was clear—without the naval stores of their colony, the British Royal Navy would be hard pressed. Therefore on 19 June 1775 those delegates wrote to the county and town committees of their colony urging strictest application of nonexportation resolutions of Congress and the formation of a "Militia" (Hugh T. Lefler and William S. Powell, *Colonial North Carolina: A History* [New York, 1973], pp. 269–70).

25. This is 15 George III, *cap.* 10 (A.D. 1775), "the New England Fisheries Act," as in n. 11 above.

26. The act is 15 George III, *cap.* 18 (A.D. 1775), commonly called one of the "Restraining Acts."

27. This resolution first reached public attention in Virginia when printed in the *Va. Gazette* (Dixon and Hunter) of 22 July 1775.

Wednesday, 12 July 1775

Third Virginia Convention

John Campbell to John Harvie and George Rootes

Gentlemen   Fort Dunmore [1] July 12th: 1775

We now take this Oppertunity of informing you that a Treaty has been heald here with the Chiefs of the Six Nations and Dellawares in Consequence of an Invitation from Major John Connolly by order of the Earl of Dunmore and that the Shawneys are now on the way and Expetted here the day after tomorrow⟨.⟩ as we wish to Justify our Conduct in this as well as every other Publick matter we now inclose you a Coppy of the Proceedings of the Treaty together with the Resolves of this Committee relative thereto as well as some others which we think necessary for your inspection and which we begg leave to refer you [2]

you will Please observe that the Indians Coming here in Consequence of Major Connollys invitation and he being disappointed by the Unhappy disputes of the Times of Supplies which he expected made it absolutely necessary for this Committee to use their utmost endeavours to procure Provisions and their necessaries [3] in order to Satisfy them and to acquire their friendship so essential ⟨to the⟩ welfare of this distressed Country and as we have acted in

this Particular from no other motive than the Publick good we flatter ourselves that we shall meet with the approbation of the Colonial Convention.
We are astonished to hear from undoubted authority that reports have been
propagated so much to the Prejudice of the Principal Inhabitants here without the smallest Foundation and to Major Connolly in Particular⟨.⟩ [4] in
Justice to that Gentleman we begg leave to assure you that from what we
have seen of his Conduct in this Conference or treaty with the Indians
nothing of the same nature could be Conducted with greater Candour and
honesty nor tend more to the Welfare of the Country in General which was
no small inducement for us to give him all the aid and assistance in our power
and we have now the Satisfaction to assure you that they were purfectly
Satisfied with the treatment they received during their Stay here. The Resolves of this Committee herewith sent you we request you with the Proceedings of the Treaty hitherto Carried on ⟨to⟩ lay before the Colonial Convention
which we hope will Convince them that to promote the publick good and
Prosperity of the Country in General are the only motives by which we have
been actuated, as we have . . . [5] everything to apprehend from Ministerial
influence and the Particular Zeal and assiduity of General Carlton [6] who
would humbly beg leave to recommend to the Consideration of the Convention the defenceless Situation of this Country and unless this Post is kept
by being Properly Garrisoned we leave it to them to Judge how easy it
would be for the Enemies of our Country to Possess themselves of this very
Important Post and by that means have it in their power to Alienate the
affections of the natives from us, and not only oppulate [7] this Flourishing
Country but likewise put it in their Power to harrass and molest the interior
Parts of the Continent [8]

We likewise request you to represent to the Convention that the Inhabitants of this infant Country not only labour under the Calamities
Common to their fellow Countrymen but are greatly distressed by the incroachments of the Proprietors of Pennsylvania whose officers seem to be
determined to enforce the Laws of that Province here and to commit every
outrage on all those who will not Conform to them so that their Libertys
and Propertys are very Precarious and insecure as evidently appears from a
recent instance on the Person of Major Connolly at a time it was Generally
known he was to meet the Indians and to Conclude a peace with them and
some of the Six nation Chiefs had actually arrived⟨.⟩ the pretended Sheriff of
Westmoreland with a number of armed men came the night of the 21st. June
and violently dragged him out of his Bed and hurried him off to Legonier
(55 miles distance from this Place) without Informing him for what he was
taken⟨.⟩ after Confining him Six days his Inlargment was procured⟨.⟩ [9] as we
are determined to be guided by the directions of the members of the Convention we most Earnestly begg that they would instruct us in what manner
to proceed and Such instructions are at this time the more necessary as it is
industriously propagated by those whose Interest it is that the Laws of
Pennsylvania should be Established here that the extending of the Laws of
Virginia was a ministerial Scheme Set on foot to divide the two Govern-

ments⟨.⟩ in order to put a period to the dispute and Restore peace and Tranquility to the People we proposed the only method which we thought would bring about so desirable an end as will appear by our Letter to them their answer to which now inclosed you will Show you how much they were disposed too reconciliation⟨.⟩ [10] depending on your particular attention to these matters we expect that you will advise us by Express of the Sentiments of the Convention upon them and that you will by every oppertunity inform us of every interesting account

      we are Gentlemen yrs

Signed by John Campbell Vice President to John Harvie and George Rootes as Representatives of the Inhabitants on the west of Laurel Hill to be presented in the Colonial Convention at Richmond the 20th. July 1775. [11]

Letter MS transcript in unidentified hand (Manuscripts Department, University of Virginia Library)

The Reverend Samuel Sheild to Richard Bland:
An Open Letter [12]

Sir,

Publick addresses considered as essential to fair and candid inquiries, and expressed in terms of decency, become less disagreeable in proportion as they are more necessary, and generally are received with a suitable degree of deference and respect; but when, instead of establishing truth, they are intended to fix upon persons to whom they are addressed the most opprobrious appelations; when, instead of modest and rational language, they abound with invective and illiberal abuse; they are not only unpleasing, but excite that just indignation which every man of sensibility, when injured, must feel. Should a harsh expression, therefore, drop from my pen, the impartial publick, I hope, will not consider it as the effect of inclination, but what the exigency of the case requires.

You say, "that, during your absence from the colony, I had, with much confidence, declared, you had solicited by letter some person in administration for a pecuniary appointment under government; that, in return for such a favour, you had promised to exert yourself to carry into execution the ministerial measures against the rights and liberties of America; and that I had seen a letter to that purpose, subscribed with your name." I deny the charge. Had the same degree of temper and candour directed your inquiry, and my relation of a conversation which happened in England, you probably, by being better informed, would not have been betrayed into that excessive virulence of expression which equally disgraces your abilities and age. The low arts of slander and calumny I abhor, and resign them to those ignoble beings, who, like yourself, set a value upon no one's character but their own. Believe me, I have never been so great an enemy to virtue as not to behold the character of every one in the most sacred light: I have always considered integrity as an essential ingredient to complete the happiness of man, and therefore was well aware of the delicacy with which subjects of such a nature ought to be treated.

"A young clergyman, who is just entering into publick life, would, you suppose, be very cautious of flinging out reports which reflect upon the character of other men, unless he was certain of the truth of them." This argument, viewed in a proper and reasonable light, might also have induced you to put a milder construction upon my conduct, which you have censured in terms most odious and severe; for what could have more strongly indicated an infatuated mind than an attempt, at my first entrance into publick office, to cut off all prospect of future advantage therefrom, by at once declaring myself a rebel to virtue and the happiness of mankind? This was to act against the known rules of prudence. What more certain proof could I have given of baseness and folly, than wantonly to have endeavoured to strip those laurels from another's head which I was certain could never encircle my own? Besides, sir, in society, I believe there are reciprocal duties. If I, as a clergyman, am bound to observe a more circumscribed and uniform conduct than others, as a clergyman, I am fully entitled to receive the degree of respect which that character has always thought to deserve. I cannot but wish that you had enlivened your *instructive* lesson by a corresponding example. I am really sorry that those thirty years, wherein "honours have been blushing thick" upon you, should have been so illy employed, that you are now found altogether destitute of propriety and good manners. It is easy enough to point out the proper line of duty to others; but how difficult it is to pursue it ourselves, you have sufficiently demonstrated.

In what light to consider the last paragraph of your letter, I am indeed at a loss. That, a stranger to my person and character too, you would treat me so like the most degenerate of mankind, as peremptorily to pronounce that "I had boldly and industriously propagated an infamous and invidious falsehood," I cannot believe, unless you expected, by the clamours of guilt, to stifle the gentle rebuke of conscience, and, under the appearance of an enraged zeal for your character, to transfer upon me, as a liar, the odium which you were likely to incur from being a traitor. Whether this be the case, or an habitual practice in scurrility and abuse have rendered you callous to every generous sentiment, and insensible of the distinction between things that are decent and those that are opprobrious, I shall gladly appear before the tribunal you last mention (your own person I suppose is meant) to be informed.[13] With however great care you may endeavour to preserve inviolate those honours which have accrued to you from being the *first* representative of a county for thirty years past, with however great pleasure you may reflect on your appointment to represent this country in the Grand Continental Congress, be assured, that I shall watch over my character not only as a clergyman, but as one who acts upon the principles of honesty and truth with no less jealous eye, and that the proper discharge of my duty will be attended with reflections equally agreeable as that of yours can be.

Not to make atonement for an insult which I have not offered, but to vindicate my character, and to inform the publick whence your malicious accusations have originated, I shall relate part of a conversation, which happened the night before my departure from Gravesend, between a gentleman and myself; who, from the best information I could get, was a person of considerable property, and an unblemished character. This gentleman, in the presence of three others (one or two of whom is in the country at present, and I doubt not ready to attest what I shall say [14]) asked me, "what I should think of the matter if he was to inform me that one of the delegates of Virginia had applied to lord North for the office of tax-gatherer upon the duties of tea." I, of course, expressed astonishment at such a question. He, however, pledged his word and honour "that he had seen a petition from one of the delegates to that purpose; that the correspondent of the delegate through whose hands it passed had not any interest, nor even personal acquaintance, with the minister; that, in consequence thereof, the correspondent was obliged to get it delivered through the medium of a friend; that the last mentioned gentleman shewed it to him, while it was in his possession; that the delegate therein assured the minister, it had been in his power to inflame the minds of some of the people, that he could compose them at will, and only waited an opportunity to distinguish himself on behalf of government." This relation naturally excited our curiosity to know the person, and conjectures were accordingly made. The names of several were mentioned, whom he declared to be innocent; when the name of Mr. Bland was mentioned, he said that he did not choose to discover the person at all. Thus was the matter in substance related to me, and thus have I invariably related it since my arrival in Virginia. How far this account corresponds with the representation that you have made, it rests with the impartial publick to determine. To have suppressed an information, which at the same time it contained matter of the greatest importance to the publick weal, bore the most evident mark of truth, might have been well deemed a sanction given by me to secret villainy. Any disguised enemy I have always considered as dangerous, but when one, to whom the supreme direction of the affairs of the state is intrusted, took upon himself that character, I thought it my duty, if possible, to drag him from his obscurity, and expose him to the publick view, not only as a dangerous but truely formidable foe. That in this business, however, I proceeded with the greatest caution, and did not, in one circumstance, exceed the limit which either truth or my information prescribed to me, I can with *much confidence* affirm. A modest application, at any time would have induced me to stand forth the advocate of justice and truth, and declare what I now do, as thereby the innocent might have had an opportunity of clearing themselves of suspicion; but you, sir, in an unmanly and ungenerous manner, have extorted it from me, by the most base and false accusations; and, instead of leading a young man into the perplexing wilds of controversy with that moderation becoming your character and age, have, with rancorous malice, hurried me before the publick eye, under the most unfavourable appearances.

I do therefore call upon you, in the most solemn manner, to deliver up your author, either in private or publick manner; or, be assured, that it shall rest with you to make good the allegations in your letter.

I am, sir, your humble servant,

CAROLINE, *July* 12, 1775.   Samuel Sheild

Virginia Gazette (Purdie), 21 July 1775, supplement

Williamsburg

Denial of Industriously Propagated Allegation

WILLIAMSBURG, *July* 12, 1775.

IT having been asserted, and industriously propagated, that some little time before the late meeting of the merchants, in conversation with a person at my own house, I said that the merchants would not meet, because they were afraid of being robbed of their money by *Patrick Henry* and his followers: I take this opportunity to declare, upon my honour, that I never said or thought any such thing, and that the person who charges me with uttering such expressions must have mistaken my words, or inferred from them a meaning never intended by

John Randolph.[15]

Virginia Gazette (Purdie), 14 July 1775

1. That is, Fort Pitt (19 May 1775, n. 4).

2. The "Coppy of the Proceedings of the Treaty" was James Berwick's transcript, beginning with the entry of 19 May and ending with that of 6 July 1775 (Third Va. Convention, Augusta Co. West). The "Resolves of this Committee relative thereto" may have included those adopted on 26 June 1775 (same, 2d entry). The papers designated as "some others" were probably those specified by Campbell in his final paragraph.

3. For the shortage of "Supplies" and the problem of distribution, see 26 June 1775, n. 2; 29 June 1775, Third Va. Convention, Augusta Co. West and no. 12.

4. The "reports" probably called into question the loyalty of some of the "Principal Inhabitants" and of "Major Connolly in Particular" (see 16 May 1775, n. 15). Connolly's servant was later to testify that when his master quitted Fort Pitt, he did so "fearing some Injury from the Inhabitants, who suspected him of being an Enemy of his Country" (Deposition of William Cowley, 12 Oct. 1775, copy enclosed in George Washington to John Hancock, same date, Papers of the Continental Congress, National Archives, Washington, D.C., microfilm in Va. State Library). It would be interesting to know whether the "Inhabitants" who suspected the major were among those of the "Principal" sort who were themselves suspected.

5. In the transcript there is written between "have" and "everything" the verbal "been," inclusion of which renders meaningless a sentence already sufficiently freighted.

6. Maj. Gen. Guy Carleton, since Sept. 1774 governor of the Province of Quebec, had recently declared martial law, but despite the persistence of rumors that he was plotting to set the Indians loose upon the rebel frontiersmen, the red men watched him warily, and the thought of employing tomahawk and scalping knife was repugnant to him (Hilda Neatby, *Quebec: The Revolutionary Age, 1760–1791* [London, Eng., 1966], pp. 142–47; O'Callaghan, *N.Y. Col. Docs.*, VIII, 636).

7. That is, "oppilate," to stop, block, or obstruct.

8. The third Virginia Convention on 7 Aug. 1775 would take steps to secure "this very Important Post."

9. For the violence visited on "the Person of Major Connolly" and his subsequent "Inlargment," see 22 June 1775, Third Va. Convention, Augusta Co. West and n. 2; 26 June, same and n. 4. The estimation of the distance from Fort Pitt to Fort Ligonier may have been exaggerated as the crow flies but not as a man traveled over mountainous terrain.

10. Our "Letter" and "their answer" are under the date heading of 3 July 1775, Third Va. Convention, Augusta Co. West, 2d and 3d entries.

11. If the date of presentation to the "Colonial Convention" was not an exercise in directive precognition by Campbell, it was (as seems far more likely) a notation by the unknown transcriber of intent on the part of Harvie and Rootes. But on 19 July the convention would adjourn to the 21st in order that the delegates might properly observe the day of public humiliation, fasting and prayer recommended by Congress (30 June 1775, n. 8). It would, then, not be until 21 July 1775 that the letter and its enclosures should be "laid before the Convention and read" as companion pieces to James Wood's letter of 9 July 1775 to Peyton Randolph (Third Va. Convention).

12. The item is a reply to Bland's open letter of 7 July 1775.

SAMUEL SHEILD, a native Virginian of York County, had earned high marks and a medal for "Classical Learning" at the College of William and Mary before embarking for England to prepare himself for holy orders in the established church. Shortly after his return in the spring of 1775 he was, despite some "Clamours," elected by the vestry to serve as pastor for established souls in Drysdale Parish, Caroline County. With an income assured, the young minister took to wife Miss Molly Hansford, sister-in-law of the Rev. John Camm, the marriage being somewhat ironically noticed in a newspaper column adjacent to the one containing Colonel Bland's airing of Sheild's alleged libels. Sheild, who must have been in his mid-20s, was a vigorous expounder of the Gospel, the tenor of the present letter giving some hint as to why one of his parishioners later averred that he preached so much death and damnation on Sunday mornings that it took her the rest of the day just to cool off ([Lyon G. Tyler], "The Sheild Family," *Wm. and Mary Qtly.*, 1st ser., III [Apr. 1895], 270–71; Brydon, "Addendum to Goodwin's List of the Colonial Clergy of the Established Church," p. 70; Mays, *Letters and Papers of Pendleton*, I, 109; *Va. Gazette* [Purdie], 7 July 1775).

13. The "tribunal" to which Bland would appeal, as he did on 22 July 1775 as the 1st order of business for the day, was the third Virginia Convention.

14. One of the auditors "in the country at present" may have been Rev. John Hurt, who had received his license for the Virginia Anglican ministry on the same day as had Sheild. It is likely that the 2 youthful clerics sailed the Atlantic together, Hurt then being en route to Norborne Parish, Berkeley County (Edward Lewis Goodwin, *The Colonial Church in Virginia* [Milwaukee, 1927], pp. 281, 306). At any rate, Hurt on Saturday, 22 July 1775, would be summoned to appear before the convention on the Friday following.

15. The "meeting of the merchants" to which the attorney general refers was probably the semiannual convocation of the colony's leading vendors, a body combining features of a present-day state chamber of commerce and retail merchants association. Andrew Sprowle of Gosport was the chairman. The "late" meeting may have been around 12 June, when many of the more prominent members were in Williamsburg (Noël Hume, *1775*, pp. 232–33). The allusion to *"Patrick Henry* and his followers" would seem to establish Randolph's alleged "uttering such expressions" as early in May, during or shortly after Captain Henry's march toward the capital (pp. 7–11 above). In the following week Randolph would find his veracity challenged (19 July 1775, Williamsburg).

Thursday, 13 July 1775

Middlesex County

Moses Robertson to John Dixon and William Hunter: An Open Letter [1]

To *Mess*. DIXON & HUNTER.
 Ruffin's Ferry, *July* 13, 1775.
  Gentlemen.
I AM this day informed, by a friend, that a very extraordinary publication is to appear in your gazette this week, stigmatising Mess. ⟨James⟩ Mills and ⟨George⟩ Lorimer, and myself, in the most unjustifiable manner, in regard to a quantity of goods which four men of Gloucester county supposed I had brought in from London for the above-mentioned gentlemen, and landed at Urbanna.[2] I shall, without hesitation, take upon me to say, that I did not bring any goods for *them*, or any other person, and am ready to make oath to this assertion, whenever I may be called upon for that purpose; and my chief mate, and other officers, will attest the same. The conduct of these men is highly reprehensible and malicious, as they have endeavoured to fix a heavy charge upon me, without having proper grounds to support it. As to those

gentlemen whose characters have been aspersed, as well as my own, they will, I make no doubt, be able to confute every thing their accusers have charged them with.[3]

I am, Gentlemen, Your humble servant,

Moses Rorinson.[4]

Virginia Gazette (Purdie), 14 July 1775, supplement

1. Although this letter is addressed to Dixon and Hunter and appeared in their *Va. Gazette* of 15 July 1775, it found its way into the supplement of Purdie's newspaper dated one day earlier. How Purdie came by a copy of the letter is unknown.

2. The "very extraordinary publication" was also printed by Purdie. It had already appeared in Pinkney's gazette of 13 July 1775; and it was printed in Dixon and Hunter's of 15 July 1775 directly above Robertson's letter (10 July 1775, Middlesex Co. Committee).

3. Letters and statements in support of Captain Robertson were to pour into the printing offices during the ensuing week. The 1st of these documents is under the date heading of 18 July 1775, Middlesex Co. Committee.

4. A man seeking to protect his good name probably would prefer that the whole of it be spelled correctly. In their *Va. Gazette* of 22 July 1775 Dixon and Hunter would bring forth the captain's surname as "Robinson."

Saturday, 15 July 1775

Continental Congress

Secret Resolution of Continental Congress respecting Exception to Continental Association

Agreeable to the order of yesterday,[1] the motion made by Mr. F ⟨Benjamin Franklin⟩ was taken into consideration, and after some debate they came to the following Resolution: —

Whereas, the government of Great Britain hath prohibited the exportation of arms and ammunition to any of the plantations, and endeavoured to prevent other nations from supplying us: [2]

Resolved, That for the better furnishing these colonies with the necessary means of defending their rights, every vessel importing Gun powder, Salt petre, Sulphur, provided they bring with the sulphur four times as much salt petre, brass field-pieces, or good muskets fitted with Bayonets, within nine Months from the date of this resolution, shall be permitted to load and export the produce of these colonies, to the value of such powder and stores aforesd, the non-exportation agreement notwithstanding; [3] and it is recommended to the committees of the several provinces to inspect the military stores so imported, and to estimate a generous price for the same, according to their goodness, and permit the importer of such powder and other military stores aforesaid, to export the value thereof and no more, in produce of any kind.

Ordered, That a copy of the above be delivered to the delegates of the Colony of Pennsylvania, who are desired to request the committee of this city to forward the same in hand bills to the West Indies and such places as they think proper, taking care that it be not published in the news papers. [4]

W. C. Ford, *Journals of the Continental Congress*,
II, 184–85

1. That is, of Friday, 14 July 1775, when toward the end of the session "Doct. Franklin" moved this resolution, consideration of which was postponed until "to Morrow morning" as the 1st order of the day when Congress sat again "at 8 o'Clock" (*JCC*, II, 184).

2. On 19 Oct. 1774 Lord Dartmouth addressed a circular letter to the governors of the North American colonies informing them that the king that day had signed a proclamation prohibiting the exportation of "Gunpowder, or any sort of arms or ammunition" from the ports of Great Britain to the colonies (O'Callaghan, *N.Y. Col. Docs.*, VIII, 509). The Virginia reading public had been aware of the order at least since the publication of the supplement to the *Va. Gazette* (Purdie and Dixon) of 8 Dec. 1774.

3. Within the limitations imposed by the resolution, exceptions were made to the enforcement of parts of articles 1, 5, 6, and 14 of the Continental Association (*JCC*, I, 77–80).

4. The object of keeping the resolution from "the news papers" was that implementation might be affected clandestinely as long as possible by colonial conventions, congresses, and subordinate committees. The "committee of this city" caused broadsides to be struck off by the printing firm of William and Thomas Bradford (ibid., III, 510); but it is doubtful that what was "*Ordered*" in the final paragraph was included in the copy of the resolution as laid before the third Virginia Convention on 22 Aug. 1775.

Sunday, 16 July 1775

Third Virginia Convention

Augusta County West: Journal of Captain James Wood

16th July the Cornstalk[1] Nimwha Wryneck Blue Jacket Silver Heels and about fifteen other Shawnese arrived⟨.⟩ they immediately got drunk and Continued in that situation for two days[2]

Thwaites and Kellogg, *Revolution on the Upper Ohio, 1775–1777*, p. 41

1. For "the Cornstalk," see *Rev. Va.*, II, 105, 106, 107.
2. It is obvious that Wood did not make this entry before 18 July, the date on which he would undertake personal negotiations with the Shawnee (Third Va. Convention, Augusta Co. West). It seems also reasonably clear that despite the paucity of "Supplies" at Fort Pitt as related by John Campbell in his letter of 12 July 1775 to John Harvie and George Rootes (Third Va. Convention, 1st entry), the committee of the District of West Augusta County contrived, before serious business should be undertaken, to gather "necessaries" sufficient to permit its Indian guests a measure of relaxation.

Monday, 17 July–Saturday, 26 August 1775

Editorial Note

When the third Virginia Convention rallied in the Anglican Town Church in Richmond on 17 July 1775, the membership ideally would have totaled 128. Sixty-one counties and the District of West Augusta County were entitled to 2 delegates each, and the 4 corporations—the ghost "city" of Jamestown, the borough of Norfolk, the city of Williamsburg, and the College of William and Mary—to 1 apiece. It appears in fact that there were eventually to be present at one time or another 114, of whom 109 were full-fledged delegates and 5 were alternates for deputies still sitting in the Continental Congress. These figures are arrived at by drawing on Alexander Purdie's printed journal. Handed or permitted by John Tazewell to examine a roll (which no longer exists in manuscript) of the members, the printer once again listed every delegate (alternates excepted) who attended the convention at any time as being "Present" on the opening day of session. Yet not only was that attendance manifestly an impossibility but according to the testimony of Jonathan Clark, representing Dunmore County, he was not in Richmond until the second day of session (Autograph Diary of Jonathan Clark, Filson Club Docs., 2 vols., unpaged, photocopy in Va. State Library, I, entry for 18 July 1775); and although from one particular it is unsafe to induce a generality, the established disinclination of many burgesses and conventioneers to be among the first to appear at an elective assemblage strongly suggests that Clark's case was not unique.

Also for the first time Tazewell included in the pertinent daily proceedings the fact of initial attendance by some delegates who necessarily or otherwise arrived late: Patrick Henry, Edmund Pendleton, Benjamin Harrison, and Thomas Jefferson, returned from Congress, on 9 August; Henry Pendleton of Culpeper County and Lewis Burwell of Gloucester County, presenting themselves on 10 August; and Richard Henry Lee, returned from Congress, on 11 August 1775. Thus the membership, at its fullest reaching the total of 109, represented 85.1% of potential representation.

Even though no delegate had been chosen by "the College," representation in the second convention stood at 93.7% of the potential. In this wise, in the third convention there was, under the same set of circumstances, a falling off of 8.6%. Or put another way, attendance at the third was but 90.8% of that of the second. Yet now royal authority, although still uncontestably "legal," was being directed against the colonial commonweal and was therefore factual piracy and banditry. Now real power lay in hands that, although uncontestably "extralegal" (and by the king's proclamation on 23 August would be outlawed), alone could establish enforceable rules and maintain social order. Now it was a patriotic, categorical imperative to exercise that power for the establishment of a government de facto. And that being the case, it was evident that the problems confronting the members of the third convention would not be only 90.8% as momentous or perplexing as those that had confronted the members of the second.

But for those delegates-elect who did not attend the third, absence surely was less induced by indifference or by misconstruing public need than it was imposed by personal necessity. For example, John Bowdoin of Northampton County would on 30 July 1775 inform Peyton Randolph that his nonattendance was obliged by illness in his family, as was also the case with Bowdoin's Northampton colleague, John Burton. Nor can a second possibility impelling absence be overlooked. On 4 March 1775 the voters of Hanover County had resolved that "it is just and reasonable that the Delegates that attend colony conventions should be reimbursed their expences."[1] But if broached at the second convention, the subject seems not to have emerged from the vestments room. In palmier days men might at their own expense travel to and from Williamsburg or Richmond, supporting themselves with reasonable ease during sessions that lasted a week or scarcely more, and still have in pocket money for the support of the colony's delegates to Congress.[2] But times had changed. Hard money, never plentiful, was now scarcer. And to maintain themselves in Richmond for a convention that promised to be of considerable duration (and which was in truth to extend for 33 sessions held over the course of 41 days) was very probably beyond the means of some of the 18 delegates-elect who did not present their credentials.

Of the 5 alternate delegates, none had legislative or conventional experience. Otherwise, Peyton Randolph presided over an assemblage composed substantially of veterans. Of the 109 delegates, 86, or 78.8%, had served as burgesses; 79, or 72.4%, had sat in the first convention; 94, or 86.2%, had sat in the second; and 78, or 71.5%, had sat in both.

Of all the delegates the most prestigious and influential undoubtedly were in succession Randolph himself, Robert Carter Nicholas, Richard Bland, and Benjamin Harrison. On 16 August the president accepting an invitation to conserve his health by quitting the chair, Mr. Treasurer the next day was elected in his stead. Nicholas, who had been chairman of the Committee on the State of the Colony and of the Committee of the Whole, was succeeded in those positions by Bland. And Bland (physical debility probably necessitating a less active role) was on 18 August succeeded by Harrison in turn.

What 10 delegates among the remaining 105 were most influential, or at least most called upon to exercise their talents, is roughly determinable. Of all 105 only 56 were assigned membership on a committee, but some of them were assigned several. If a committee chairmanship be weighted at 5 points and a membership at 1, first place goes to Edmund Pendleton, with 16 points. Second goes to Archibald Cary, with 14. Tied for third place are Paul Carrington and George Mason, with 9 each. Fifth is John Banister, with 8. Sixth is Richard Henry Lee, with 7. And tied for seventh are Richard Adams, Dudley Digges, Patrick Henry, and Isaac Zane, Jr., with 6 each. Since he was not present in the convention until the eighteenth day of session, the positioning speaks most eloquently of the rising stature of Pendleton.

Following is a list of all the delegates probably elected to this convention. The names of those who were present at any time are in capital letters. The names of those who were elected or probably elected but did not attend are, except for beginning capitals, set in lowercase.

Accomack County. Southy Simpson (probably elected); Isaac Smith (probably elected).

Albemarle County. THOMAS JEFFERSON (seated 9 Aug.; given leave 16 Aug.); CHARLES LEWIS (alternate for Jefferson 17 July–9 Aug.);[3] JOHN WALKER (given leave 11 Aug.).

Amelia County. JOHN TABB; JOHN WINN.

Amherst County. JOSEPH CABELL; WILLIAM CABELL, JR.

Augusta County. THOMAS LEWIS; SAMUEL MCDOWELL.

Augusta County West. JOHN HARVIE (given leave 17 Aug.); GEORGE ROOTES.

Bedford County. CHARLES LYNCH; JOHN TALBOT.

Berkeley County. ROBERT RUTHERFORD (disqualified 27 July); ADAM STEPHEN (disqualified 27 July).

Botetourt County. JOHN BOWYER; Andrew Lewis (probably elected; would attend next session).

Brunswick County. FREDERICK MACLIN; HENRY TAZEWELL.

Buckingham County. ROBERT BOLLING (died 21 July);[4] JOHN NICHOLAS.

Caroline County. EDMUND PENDLETON (seated 9 Aug.); JAMES TAYLOR; WILLIAM WOODFORD (alternate for Pendleton 17 July–9 Aug.).

Charles City County. WILLIAM ACRILL; BENJAMIN HARRISON (seated 9 Aug.); BENJAMIN HARRISON, JR. (alternate for father 17 July–9 Aug.).

Charlotte County. PAUL CARRINGTON; ISAAC READ.

Chesterfield County. ARCHIBALD CARY; BENJAMIN WATKINS.

Culpeper County. HENRY FIELD, JR.; HENRY PENDLETON (seated 10 Aug.).

Cumberland County. WILLIAM FLEMING; JOHN MAYO.

Dinwiddie County. JOHN BANISTER; JOHN RUFFIN.[5]

Dunmore County. JONATHAN CLARK (seated 18 July; absent 19–26 Aug.); John Peter Gabriel Muhlenberg (elected; would attend next session).

Elizabeth City County. HENRY KING; WORLICH WESTWOOD.

Essex County. MERIWETHER SMITH; James Edmondson (probably elected; would attend next session).

Fairfax County. CHARLES BROADWATER; GEORGE MASON.[6]

Fauquier County. THOMAS MARSHALL; JAMES SCOTT.

Fincastle County. WILLIAM CHRISTIAN; STEPHEN TRIGG.[7]

Frederick County. CHARLES MYNN THRUSTON; ISAAC ZANE, JR. (given leave 21 Aug.).

Gloucester County. LEWIS BURWELL (seated 10 Aug.); Thomas Whiting (probably elected; would attend next session).

Goochland County. THOMAS MANN RANDOLPH; JOHN WOODSON.

Halifax County. MICAJAH WATKINS; Nathaniel Terry (probably elected; would attend next session).

Hampshire County. JAMES MERCER; Joseph Neville (probably elected; would attend next session).

Hanover County. PATRICK HENRY (seated 9 Aug.); JOHN SYME; GARLAND ANDERSON (alternate for Henry 17 July–9 Aug.).[8]

Henrico County. RICHARD ADAMS; RICHARD RANDOLPH.

Isle of Wight County. JOSIAH PARKER; JOHN SCARSBROOK WILLS.

James City County. ROBERT CARTER NICHOLAS; WILLIAM NORVELL.

Jamestown City. CHAMPION TRAVIS.

King and Queen County. GEORGE BROOKE; GEORGE LYNE (given leave 23 Aug.).

King George County. WILLIAM FITZHUGH; JOSEPH JONES.

King William County. WILLIAM AYLETT; CARTER BRAXTON.

Lancaster County. CHARLES CARTER; JAMES SELDEN.

Loudoun County. JOSIAS CLAPHAM (given leave 22 Aug.); FRANCIS PEYTON (given leave 22 Aug.).

Louisa County. THOMAS JOHNSON; THOMAS WALKER (given leave 11 Aug.).

Lunenburg County. DAVID GARLAND; THOMAS TABB.[9]

Mecklenburg County. ROBERT BURTON; BENNETT GOODE.

Middlesex County. JAMES MONTAGUE;[10] Edmund Berkeley (probably elected; would attend next session).

Nansemond County. ANDREW MEADE; JAMES MURDAUGH.[11]

New Kent County. BURWELL BASSETT (given leave 23 Aug.); BARTHOLOMEW DANDRIDGE.

Norfolk Borough. JOSEPH HUTCHINGS.

Norfolk County. JAMES HOLT; THOMAS NEWTON, JR.

Northampton County. John Bowdoin (elected); John Burton (elected).

Northumberland County. RODHAM KENNER; PETER PRESLEY THORNTON (given leave 17 Aug.).[12]

Orange County. THOMAS BARBOUR; James Taylor (probably elected; would attend next session).

Pittsylvania County. Benjamin Lankford (probably elected; would attend next session); Peter Perkins (probably elected; would attend next session).

Prince Edward County. WILLIAM BIBB;[13] ROBERT LAWSON.

Prince George County. RICHARD BLAND; PETER POYTHRESS.

Prince William County. THOMAS BLACKBURN (given leave 22 Aug.); HENRY LEE (given leave 22 Aug.).

Princess Anne County. WILLIAM ROBINSON; Christopher Wright (probably elected; would attend next session).

Richmond County. ROBERT WORMELEY CARTER; Francis Lightfoot Lee (elected).

Southampton County. EDWIN GRAY (given leave 19 Aug.); Henry Taylor (probably elected; would attend next session).

Spotsylvania County. MANN PAGE, JR.; GEORGE STUBBLEFIELD (probably absent *ca.* 24 July–2 Aug.).

Stafford County. CHARLES CARTER; THOMAS LUDWELL LEE.[14]

Surry County. ALLEN COCKE; NICHOLAS FAULCON, JR.

Sussex County. HENRY GEE; DAVID MASON.

Warwick County. WILLIAM LANGHORNE; William Harwood (elected; would attend next session).

Westmoreland County. RICHARD LEE (given leave 22 Aug.); RICHARD HENRY LEE (seated 11 Aug.); JOHN AUGUSTINE WASHINGTON (alternate for R. H. Lee 17 July–11 Aug.).[15]

William and Mary College. (No delegate elected).

Williamsburg City. PEYTON RANDOLPH (given leave 16 Aug.).

York County. DUDLEY DIGGES; THOMAS NELSON, JR. (given leave 14 Aug.).

1. *Rev. Va.,* II, 312.

2. Ibid., II, 384–85, 388 n. 10.

3. Elected Jefferson's alternate within the month past, CHARLES LEWIS of North Garden was a member of the Albemarle County committee and commander of the county's 1st company of gentlemen volunteers. He was a son of Robert Lewis of Belvoir, who had been county lieutenant of Louisa and had represented that county in the Burgesses 3 decades earlier. To the confusion of future genealogists, Charles of

North Garden married a daughter of his father's cousin, Charles Lewis, Jr., of Buck-eyeland (or Buck Island), Albemarle County, who in turn was the son of Charles Lewis of Goochland County. The captain's mother-in-law was Mary Randolph Lewis, a daughter of Isham Randolph and a sister of Jefferson's mother. Within the year Charles's older brother William had been presented with a manchild, Meriwether, "of whom," history would say, "more later." The Lewis coat of arms was inscribed with the motto *Omne Solum Forti Patria Est* ("Every Soil Is Homeland to the Brave")—a fitting maxim, according to Philip Mazzei, who served briefly with the Albemarle volunteers, for Charles Lewis of North Garden was valiant and, beyond leading a company, was "capable of commanding even a regiment." At this time Lewis was probably in or near his 36th year ([Lyon G. Tyler], "The Lewis Family," *Wm. and Mary Qtly.*, 1st ser., XI [July 1902], 46; Sarah Travers Lewis (Scott) Anderson, *Lewises, Meriwethers and Their Kin* . . . [Richmond, 1938], pp. 61–62, 93; Rosalind Williamson Lewis, *Lewis* [n.p., 1969], p. 9; Mary M. Sullivan, "The Gentry and the Association in Albemarle County, 1774–1775," *Magazine of Albemarle County History*, XXIII [1964–65], 137; Boyd, *Papers of Jefferson*, I, 238; Mazzei, *Memoirs*, trans. and ed. Marraro, p. 209; 18 Apr. 1775, Albemarle Co. Committee; 31 May 1775, same, 2d entry above).

4. ROBERT BOLLING of Chellowe formerly appended "Jr." to his name to distinguish himself from his distant, recently deceased cousin, Col. Robert Bolling, sometime burgess for Dinwiddie County, signatory to the nonimportation association of 1769, and a delegate to the first Virginia Convention. Robert of Chellowe was a 5th-generation descendant of John Rolfe and Pocahontas, hence of the "Red Bollings" in contradistinction to the "White Bollings" of a collateral branch. Robert's father had been a burgess from 1744 to 1757, first for Henrico County, then for Chesterfield County; and he himself had been one of the 1st burgesses for newly formed Bucking-ham County from 1761 to 1765, when he became sheriff. Though he "blushed" to do so, he admitted that he had been "an accomplished youth." Precocious and witty, he had studied languages with much success at Wakefield, in Yorkshire, England, and a little law with Benjamin Waller in Williamsburg. Young Bolling, scribbled John Randolph of Roanoke on the back of a translation of his family genealogy that the former had penned in French, "wrote equally well in latin, French and Italian." At Chellowe, Robert Bolling busied himself in reviving an old Anglo-colonial dream by writing letters, pamphlets, and articles urging the establishment of viniculture in Virginia and arguing that "we shall become a more hardy and manly Race of People, when our Constitutions are no longer jaundiced nor our Juices vitiated by abominable West Indian Distillations, rendered still more detestable by our own fraudulent Mixtures," besides which Virginia could also produce "Raisins, an Article of Commerce far from despicable." In 1773 he persuaded the House of Burgesses to grant him a subvention of £450 for the importation of vines—local grapes, he asserted, "want Fire." But while attending the third convention, Robert Bolling, then aged 37, died. "Poor Bob. Bolling," sighed George Gilmer, "adieu to Burgundy" (Robert Bolling, *A Memoir of a Portion of the Bolling Family in England and Virginia*, trans. from French by John Robertson, Jr., ed. Thomas H. Wynne [Richmond, 1868]; Wyndham Robertson and Robert A. Brock, *Pocahontas, Alias Matoaka, and Her Descendants* . . . [Richmond, 1887], pp. 31–32, 61–62; *Col. Va. Reg.*, pp. 116–42 passim, 154–68 passim; *Rev. Va.*, I, 76, 122, 220, 235; *JHB*, 1773–1776, pp. 16–17; *Va. Gazette* [Dixon and Hunter], 25 Feb., 29 July 1773; *Exec. Journs. Coun. Col. Va.*, VI, 449; Boyd, *Papers of Jefferson*, I, 238).

5. A new arrival on the colonywide scene, JOHN RUFFIN had recently been elected

to the Burgesses for Dinwiddie County in the stead of Col. Robert Bolling, deceased, but not in time to participate in the final historic sessions in June 1775. He bore a name with which older legislative heads were acquainted. With one brief interruption, his grandfather had sat for Surry County from 1738 to 1755, and his father for Dinwiddie County from 1758 through 1760. Now, at some undisclosed date, John had also replaced William Watkins as a delegate to the convention. The newcomer was a kinsman of the wealthy and numerous Ruffins of Rich Neck, Surry County; and although his age at this time is uncertain (let us call it about 22), he no doubt was born at a seemly interval after the death in the summer of 1751 of his mother's 1st husband. She came into a considerable property, and while serving as "Administrator" of her estate, Robert Ruffin chanced to observe the attractiveness of the widow whose it was. Although youthful, John Ruffin probably was already a justice of the peace, for not long past he had purchased a set of Blackstone's *Commentaries* (*Wm. and Mary Qtly.*, 1st ser., XII [Apr. 1904], 207–8; [Lyon G. Tyler], "Ruffin Family," ibid., 1st ser., XVIII [Apr. 1910], 251–52; ibid., 2d ser., I [July 1921], 185; *Col. Va. Reg.*, pp. 111–23 passim, 131–39 passim, 146, 150, 152; *JHB, 1773–1776*, pp. 163, 164).

6. In appearance swarthy GEORGE MASON of Gunston Hall was striking. He was handsome; his rich, dark brown hair flowed almost to his shoulders; his eyes pierced. And his sense of justice was so innate that it seemed part of his physical being. He walked into his century directly from the pages of Plutarch—earnest without austerity, learned without pedantry, energetic without bustle, congenial without sham, and honorable without proclamation. After his father had drowned in the Potomac River, the youth fell under the guardianship of his uncle John Mercer, in whose excellent library he began an education such as no college could fully have provided. "He was," in the words of Edmund Randolph, "behind none of the sons of Virginia in knowledge of her history and interest." But his astuteness came not from books; "At a glance he saw to the bottom of every proposition which affected" the colony. Strongly civic-minded, he served as vestryman of Truro Parish, as justice of the peace for Fairfax County, as trustee of the town of Alexandria, and for one term extending from 1758 to 1761 as burgess. But the glacial majesty with which the House was wont to act, coupled with wordy wastages and favor-exchanging, chilled any enthusiasm that the master of well-managed Gunston Hall might otherwise have roused for a legislative career. Likewise, because of ill health frequently attended by incapacitating attacks of gout, and because of a preference for domestic felicity, Mason was dissuaded from playing on a larger stage. Yet though himself avoiding footlights, he was an expert prompter, and his opposition to the Stamp Act and the Declaratory Act in the mid-1760s was, however indirect, vigorous. When the king in 1773 revoked the charter of the Ohio Company of Virginia, of which Mason was treasurer, the Virginian's response was a product of his study, a pamphlet titled *Extracts from the Virginia Charters, with Some Remarks upon Them*—a statement of colonial rights set forth with a cogency and an asserted faith in constitutional processes that was the trademark of a life. Although the confidant of George Washington (whom in this convention he was succeeding) in forwarding politico-economic strategy, and although on 18 July 1774 elected a member of a Fairfax County committee "to Concert & Adopt such Measures as may be thought most expedient and Necessary" to implement that strategy, Mason to date had been much less conspicuous than his younger brother, Thomson Mason. Yet equally with Thomson, he was on the highroad to revolution and was known well and widely enough that he would attend the convention as a respected figure. A widower (Anne Eilbeck Mason, natively of Charles County, Md., had died in 1773), Mason was now 50 years old (Kate Rowland Mason, *The Life of*

George Mason, 1725–1792 [2 vols., New York, 1892], I, 1–197; Helen Hill, *George Mason, Constitutionalist* [Cambridge, Mass., 1938], pp. 3–122; Robert A. Rutland, *George Mason, Reluctant Statesman* [Williamsburg, 1961], pp. 3–45; Randolph, *Hist. of Va.*, ed. Shaffer, p. 192; Rutland, *Papers of Mason*, I, 163–85; *Col. Va. Reg.*, pp. 146, 148, 150, 152; *Rev. Va.*, I, 72, 78, 93, 110, 133, 153).

7. When William Trigg died in Bedford County near the end of 1772, he bequeathed his oldest son, STEPHEN TRIGG, "the place Called Pole catt Mountain" and a "Negro Wench." But the son was already doing sufficiently well that he could have managed without either. The keeper of an ordinary, or tavern, he was of a popularity and stature that in 1770 he became a justice of the peace for Botetourt County, and for Fincastle when the latter county was formed in 1772. He was elected to the Burgesses for the session of May 1774, and thereby made eligible to attend the first Virginia Convention, but he absented himself from both assemblages to serve as a captain in Dunmore's War. On 20 Jan. 1775 he was present and elected a member of the Fincastle County committee, and subsequently he was probably elected a delegate to the second Virginia Convention, but if so, he was again among the absentees. Notwithstanding this record, he retained the confidence of his neighbors, who reelected him to the House of Burgesses for the session of 1 June 1775. At last he presented himself, though apparently 12 days late. He also attended the third convention, the evidence being that on this occasion he was present on the day of initial session. If his influence was to be felt, however, it was by the exercise of means invisible from any action occurring on the floor. Now 33 years of age and the brother-in-law of William Christian, he may have been interested in policy determined at the Fall Line chiefly as it affected the West. At least, within 3 years, sustained by a strong faith in Christ, he would move on to Kentucky (Bedford County, Va., Will Book No. 1, with Inventories and Accounts, 1763–87, microfilm in Va. State Library, pp. 167–69; Robert Douthat Stoner, *A Seed-Bed of the Republic: A Study of the Pioneers in the Upper (Southern) Valley of Virginia* [Roanoke, 1962], pp. 29, 44; Summers, *Annals of Southwest Va.*, I, 69, II, 588; Thwaites and Kellogg, *Doc. Hist. of Dunmore's War*, p. 44 n. 79; *Rev. Va.*, I, 255, II, 295 n. 4; *JHB, 1773–1776*, pp. 162, 217; *DAR Patriot Index*, p. 687; Draper MSS, 4QQ176, State Hist. Soc. of Wis).

8. GARLAND ANDERSON, the son of a Hanover County attorney, owned land in the upper part of St. Martin's Parish, as well as across the North Anna River in Caroline County. He was a merchant and the owner of a gristmill or two, and as a religious, civic, and dissident subject of His Majesty, was a vestryman of St. Martin's, a justice of the peace, and a past colleague in Patrick Henry's demonstration toward Williamsburg. At this time Anderson was probably 33 years of age (Eugenia G. Glazebrook and Preston G. Glazebrook, comps., *Virginia Migrants: Hanover County, 1743–1781* [Richmond, 1940], p. 477; Rosewell Page, *Hanover County: Its History and Legends* [Richmond, 1926], p. 114; 4 May 1775, Hanover Co. Committee, 2d entry).

9. The immigrant ancestor of THOMAS TABB of Lunenburg County had landed in Virginia over 100 years past. The given name Thomas was a favorite among his proliferating descendants. Only distantly related to John Tabb, also present in the third convention, Thomas of Lunenburg was a gentleman planter in comfortable circumstances. He was now replacing the ailing Richard Claiborne, and for that succession he had undergone the traditional training—justice of the peace from 1757 to 1770, sheriff for the interim, justice again from 1772 to the present, and county lieutenant commanding the militia when a militia there was. But as a conventioner, he was undergoing his novitiate, and the journal marks his silence by its own. At this time, Tabb was 45 ([Lyon G. Tyler], "The Tabb Family," *Wm. and Mary Qtly.*,

1st ser., XIII [Oct. 1904], 123, XIV [Jan. 1906], 153; Landon C. Bell, *The Old Free State: A Contribution to the History of Lunenburg County and Southside Virginia* [2 vols., Richmond, 1927], I, 333, II, 70; *Exec. Journs. Coun. Col. Va.*, VI, 332).

10. When he served in the House of Burgesses, for Nansemond County in 1652–53, and for Lancaster County in 1657–58, planter Peter Montague did not exactly establish a family tradition. Not for 115 years would a clerk of the House intone the name of a Montague, and when a clerk again did so in 1773, it was that of JAMES MONTAGUE, Peter's planter great-great-grandson. The public career of the 1st legislator Montague had been animated. That of his legislator descendant was made in even more stirring days. James Montague subscribed to the association of 27 May 1774. He and his fellow delegate, Edmund Berkeley of Barn Elms, were instructed by the freeholders of Middlesex County on 15 July 1774 on what postures to assume in the first Virginia Convention, which they both attended. But they ignored those instructions and went home to face their constituents. So doing, they on 11 Mar. 1775 procured election to the second convention (which Montague did not attend) without apparent difficulty. Possibly the couching of the terms of the Virginia Association of 6 Aug. 1774 (for which see *Rev. Va.*, I, 230–35) wrought disembarrassment. But evidence warrants the belief that Montague and Berkeley were in command of political sentiment in their county; and this would have been in the face of tradition (if true) that freedom-lover though he was, Montague loved freedom only for proper persons, among whom he did not count religious dissenters. At the time the third convention met, he was 34 (George William Montague, comp., *History and Genealogy of Peter Montague of Nansemond and Lancaster Counties, Virginia, and His Descendants* [Amherst, Mass., 1894], pp. 49–58, 59–62, 63–64, 66–67, 70, 84–85; *Col. Va. Reg.*, pp. 69, 70, 73, 191, 194, 196, 199; *JHB, 1619–1658/59*, pp. xxi, xxii, xxiii; *Rev. Va.*, I, 98, 221, II, 162, 325, 327 n. 4, 337; 24 Apr. 1775, Third Va. Convention).

11. The representation for Nansemond County alone can conclusively be shown to have been changed as the result of elections held following the rising of the second convention. For the 1st time in 39 years the surname Riddick disappears from rolls as either burgess or delegate. In all probability Lemuel Riddick, nearing the age of 64, declined to stand a poll. Along with another member, he had already resigned from the vestry of the county Upper Parish, in his own case "on account of age and infirmities," and 1 of the successors of the 2 was Andrew Meade. As for Willis Riddick, it was more likely that the voters were once more pleased to ease him into one of those declivities marking his undulant political career (Wilmer L. Hall, ed., *The Vestry Book of the Upper Parish, Nansemond County, Virginia, 1743–1793* [Richmond, 1949], p. 224; W. Meade, *Old Churches, Ministers and Families of Va.*, I, 290).

ANDREW MEADE, of a propertied family, was a grandson of a former governor of North Carolina and of Col. Andrew Meade, who had been a conspicuously important settler in Virginia in the early days of the century. The younger Andrew was administrator of the spacious estates with which his family was blessed in 2 colonies; was probably a member of the Nansemond County committee; and was not least of all the husband of Susannah Stith Meade, "a most estimable woman." At this time, he was aged approximately 23 (David Meade, "Meade Family History," *Wm. and Mary Qtly.*, 1st ser., XIII [Oct. 1904], 89, 101; ibid., 1st ser., XX [Jan. 1912], 200).

JAMES MURDAUGH, a 3d-generation Virginian, was a past student of the College of William and Mary, a lawyer, and a planter. Himself probably a member thereof, he on 6 Mar. 1775 appeared before the Nansemond County committee as a witness respecting the outrageously loyalist "behaviour" of Rev. John Agnew. Murdaugh would soon become the captain of such a company of minute men as were to be "ordained" into being by the third convention on 21 Aug. 1775. His wife was Mary ("Molly") Walke, in the winning of whose hand he had extended his own into Princess Anne County. At sometime during 1775 he would be 32 years old (Robert Armistead Stewart, ed., *The Researcher* [2 vols., Richmond, 1926–28], I, 46–47; *Wm. and Mary Qtly.*, 1st ser., II [July 1893], 73; *Rev. Va.*, II, 314).

12. Enormously wealthy planter PETER PRESLEY THORNTON, like his father (late of the governor's Council), placed race horses high among his loves and had proved the point by importing blooded mounts from England. A justice of the peace and a burgess since 1771, on the death of his father the younger Thornton assumed manage-ment of the family estates, with their main seat at Northumberland House, which lay on the Potomac River in sight of Chesapeake Bay. He attended the first Virginia Convention, was replaced by Thomas Jones for the second, was a member of the county committee, and now was returned as a delegate to the third convention. Thornton was of course well espoused, to Sally Throckmorton Thornton, late of Gloucester County, but his marriage seems to have been childless; and his influence notwithstanding, he experienced domestic difficulty, for soon his otherwise-minded, widowed mother would remove to England with his 3 half brothers. When the third convention came to order, Thornton was just a week past his 25th birthday (W. G. S[tanard], "Racing in Colonial Virginia," *Va. Mag. of Hist. and Biog.*, II [Jan. 1895], 302; *Exec. Journs. Coun. Col. Va.* VI, 405; W[illiam] G. Stanard, "The Thornton Family," *Wm. and Mary Qtly.*, 1st ser., IV [Oct. 1895], 163–64, V [Jan. 1897], 198; *Va. Mag. of Hist. and Biog.*, XXII [Apr. 1914], 203–7; *Va. Col. Reg.*, pp. 188, 191, 194, 196, 200; *Rev. Va.*, I, 221, 235, II, 264, 360 n. 18).

13. WILLIAM BIBB was the son of one John Bibb, described as a Huguenot from Wales. William lived to middle age in Hanover County. About 1774, perhaps shortly after the death of his 1st wife, he betook himself and children to Prince Edward County. There the freeholders, espying worth, promptly sent him as a delegate to the first Virginia Convention, and although not returning him to the second, chose him a burgess to the last House, and elected him to the present convention. He is less remembered for subsequent services in Virginia (militia captain, member of the re-publican House of Delegates, and county sheriff) than he is for the fruit of his loins by his 2d marriage. In 1779 he would wed Sally Wyatt (a descendant of Gov. Sir Francis Wyatt and a kinswoman of Martha Washington), a lady of some wealth and more beauty, and father another and remarkable family. A brace of sons by this marriage were to be the first 2 governors of Alabama, whither in 1791, leaving his shrievalty accounts in a certain disarray, he would move. In 1775 he was 40 years old (Herbert Clarence Bradshaw, *History of Prince Edward County, Virginia, from Its Earliest Settlement through Its Establishment in 1754 to Its Bicentennial Year* [Rich-mond, 1955], passim, esp. p. 632; John Edmonds Saunders and Elizabeth Saunders Blair Stubbs, *Early Settlers of Alabama* . . . [New Orleans, 1899], pp. 434–36; *Rev. Va.*, I, 221, 235, II, 345–46 n. 2; *Col. Va. Reg.*, p. 200). It is yet to be determined what at the time in the soil and air of Prince Edward County (or was it at another time and in those of Wales?) produced 2 future governors of Alabama, and in Abner Nash one of North Carolina (*Rev. Va.*, II, 360 n. 19).

14. When in Philadelphia, George Wythe told John Adams that THOMAS LUDWELL LEE "was the delight of the eyes of Virginia and by far the most popular man they had." Thomas Ludwell was the oldest living of the brothers Lee "of Stratford Hall" (albeit it cannot be proved that he was born there), among whom the others in descent of age were Richard Henry, Francis Lightfoot, William, and Arthur. Thomas

Ludwell had shot ducks with his friend of Mount Vernon, invested with him in the
grandiose schemes of the Ohio Company, and was married to Mary Aylett Lee, a
near relative of his friend's lady. Lee's formal education was completed in England,
where it included the study of law at the Inner Temple. After his return to Virginia,
he established his seat at Bellview, from whence he was sent to represent Stafford
County in the Burgesses for the 7 years from 1758 to 1765. In the following year, on
27 Feb. 1766, he signed the Westmoreland Association in open defiance of the Stamp
Act, and in 1774 he was elected a member of the Stafford County committee formed
to enforce such policies as should be agreed to by the members of the first Virginia
Convention. The politics were clear, but for a handsome man whose kinsfolk and
friends were legion, whose disposition (in contrast to his brother Arthur's) was
temperate, and whose bearing charmed by its modesty, something was lacking. What
was lacking (and here he was in harmony with Francis Lightfoot) was a taste for
public life. Brother William thought him a bit indolent and dilatory. Edmund
Randolph remembered him for a "sensibility" that petrified him when essaying to address an assembly. "But when the formality of a public body did not agitate him, he
was a real orator. He enraptured with his grace every private society. In the subordinate committees he struck the point with a promptness which excited a wonder
how he could ever be destitute of confidence in himself. By fair reasoning out of the
house, he satisfied political skeptics and fortified the wavering." Lured out of Bellview
once again when elected to replace the deceased John Alexander, Thomas Ludwell
Lee, although only 45, would go to the third convention and therein be treated much
like an elder statesman (L. H. Butterfield, *Diary and Autobiography of John Adams*,
III, 367–68; Burton L. Hendrick, *The Lees of Virginia: Biography of a Family* [Boston
and New York, 1935], pp. 85–87, 110–111; Cazenove Gardner Lee, *Lee Chronicle:
Studies of the Early Generations of the Lees of Virginia*, comp. and ed. Dorothy Mills
Parker [New York, 1957], pp. 72–73, 220, 267–68; *Col. Va. Reg.*, pp. 147–70 passim;
Rev. Va., I, 24, 161; Randolph, *Hist. of Va.*, ed. Shaffer, p. 192).

    15. "Jack," as George Washington described his younger brother JOHN AUGUSTINE
WASHINGTON, was "the intimate companion of my youth, and the friend of my ripened
years." The brothers were much alike in appearance. So to a degree were their homes,
Jack's plantation house, Bushfield near the mouth of Nomini Creek in Westmoreland
County, having some of the features of Mount Vernon. While Major and Colonel
Washington had been away bearing messages, losing battles, and winning fame preceding and during the French and Indian War, John Augustine (though during the
earlier years still in his nonage) remained in the Tidewater tending Mount Vernon.
Unlike many of George Washington's relatives who accumulated debts in confidence
that he would discharge them, Jack was a prudent manager; so much his will in 1787
would prove. John Augustine had engaged in no legislative life, but within his home
county he was a man of stature. He had subscribed to the Westmoreland Association
of 1766 and in January 9 years later was elected a member of the newly formed county
committee. He made the complex Washington family tree more knotty in 1756, when
he married Hannah Bushrod and so entangled the genealogy with the even more involved permutations of Bushrods and Corbins. But if this bothered him, he left no
evidence of his disquietude, and of that union the most notable offspring would be the
future United States Supreme Court justice Bushrod Washington, the general-
president's favorite nephew and himself master-to-be of Mount Vernon. At this time,
John Augustine Washington was 39 (Fitzpatrick, *Writings of Washington*, XXIX,
209; Freeman, *George Washington*, I, 53 n. 31, 339, II, 19; Augusta B. Fothergill, *Wills
of Westmoreland County, Virginia, 1654–1800* [Richmond, 1925], p. 188; *Rev. Va.*,
I, 25, II, 272).

Monday, 17 July 1775

Third Virginia Convention

Note on provenance. What exists in the Virginia State Library of the manuscript journal of the third Virginia Convention is the lengthiest of the journals of the Revolutionary conventions held in the colony to the time. That still leaves something to be said respecting imperfections.

The journal is not bound. It consists, rather, of 48 folios of various sizes. Before lamination and restoration in recent years the daily proceedings appear to have been folded, along with their respective minutes, so that they could be stored as a packet or packets. John Tazewell, clerk of the convention, or after 4 August, he or John Ruffin, a youthful delegate for Dinwiddie County, numbered a page either of the journal or of the minutes to indicate the proper sequence of the daily proceedings. The manuscript journal for 26 August 1775 was therefore probably numbered "33" —Tazewell docketed the minutes for that day only by date. The last numbered day, "29," is that of Tuesday, 22 August 1775. For two days, 23 and 24 August, no manuscript journal or minutes exist; thus, as with certain transactions of the second convention, on those days we are forced to resort to Alexander Purdie's printed journal. For 25 and 26 August dependence is only partial, because for those days Tazewell's minutes are available, and on both they disclose an order of proceedings greatly at variance from what Purdie prints.

Tazewell's methods of constructing a journal are easily ascertained. Although a primitive science of English shorthand was already in use, none of its forms was known to Tazewell, or if known, was employed by him for present purposes. Instead, as the transactions of a given day progressed, he minuted them, frequently by recourse to standard or personal abbreviations and symbols. Thereafter probably not the most tenacious memory could have expanded his jottings into an intelligible record. But he had at hand resolutions and orders penned either by himself or others and retained in possession or else handed to him by the president or delegates during the course of the day. So provided, he was able to recapture events and words that otherwise would have been lost in time.

Even then, however, Tazewell did not resort to that intermediate step taken by Charles Thomson, secretary of the Continental Congress, of composing a rough journal and from it inditing a more elegant, official journal consisting of such parts as could be made public knowledge. The Virginia clerk instead inscribed the official convention journal from his minutes and accompanying papers—and oft with results that were untidy, cryptic, and inaccurate. There can be little doubt that he was himself confused by the proceedings of an assemblage that for "some Weeks" transacted business in an atmosphere of perplexity and about-faces until, in the words of George Mason, "the Bablers were pretty well silenced" and "a few weighty Members began to take the Lead" (Rutland, *Papers of Mason*, I, 255).

Nor can there be little doubt that by omissions and transpositions Tazewell deliberately falsified the record. In the context of the time, this was forgivable, for by its nature the journal was a war document and as such an instrument of propaganda;

and one propagandizes ill when he paints for his people a picture of their leaders in disarray. Yet for two centuries the seeker after light who has depended on Purdie, or since 1816 on the reprint by the Richmond firm of Ritchie, Truehart & Du-Val, has quested through a source that frequently obscures almost as much as it illumes.

Proceedings of First Day of Session

At a Convention of Delegates from the Counties and Corporations in the Colony of Virginia, at the Town of Richmond, in the County of Henrico, on Monday the 17th. of July 1775.[1]

The honorable Peyton Randolph Esq: was unanimously elected President of this Convention, and John Tazewell clerk thereof.

[Members called &c][2]

Resolved, that this Convention will observe in their Debates & Proceedings, the same Rules and Orders as are established in the house of Burgesses of this Colony.

Resolved, that the revd. Miles Selden be appointed Chaplain to this Convention, and that he be desired to read prayers every Morning at 8. oClock, and also to preach a Sermon on thursday next, being the Day recommended by the General Congress to be kept as a solemn Fast.[3]

Adjourned till Tomorrow 9. oClock.

> Convention MS journal in hand of John Tazewell
> (Archives Division, Virginia State Library)[4]

1. In the printed journal Purdie follows this heading with a list of names of all the delegates present during any day of session.

2. The bracketed notation concerning the roll call of members-elect, a transaction performed alphabetically by counties and then by corporations (undoubtedly excluding the tory-dominated, unrepresented College of William and Mary) is taken from Tazewell's minutes for this day. The notation follows the entry "J. Tazewell Clerk" and precedes the entry "Same Rules established as in the House of Burgesses." At the most, but that improbably, 106 delegates presented their credentials to the clerk.

3. Rev. Miles Selden, pastor of the Anglican Town Church, had been chaplain of the second convention, at which he had performed the same function "every Morng.," but an hour later, "9 oClock" (*Rev. Va.*, II, 348, 351 n. 3). For the "Day recommended by the General Congress to be kept as a solemn Fast," see 30 June 1775, n. 8. But on Wednesday "next" the Rev. Mr. Selden would be "indisposed" and another desired to act in his stead (19 July 1775, Third Va. Convention, Procs., 1st para.).

4. Tazewell wrote "Nos. 1. & 2" edgewise on the bottom of the 4th of 4 pages on which he entered the journal for this day and that for 18 July 1775.

Tuesday, 18 July 1775

Third Virginia Convention

Proceedings of Second Day of Session[1]

On a Motion made,

Resolved, that this Convention will immediately resolve itself into a Committee to take under their Consideration the State of the Colony.

[Declaration of the Congress referred thereto.] [2]

Mr. President ⟨Peyton Randolph⟩ left the Chair.

Mr. ⟨Richard⟩ Bland took the Chair of the Committee.

Mr. President resumed the Chair.

Mr. Bland reported from the Committee, that they had had under their Consideration the State of the Colony, but not having time to go through the same, had directed him to move for Leave to sit again.

Resolved that this Convention will Tomorrow again resolve itself into a Committee, to take under their further Consideration, the State of the Colony.

A Petition of William Preston gent: Surveyor of Fincastle County, setting forth, that, early in the month of April last, he had received Instructions from Lord Dunmore, to survey Lands in the uninhabited parts of this Colony, agreable to a Proclamation his Lordship had just then issued, and which was under the Consideration of the late Convention; but that as there was then no final Determination respecting it, he apprehended the same was tacitly allowed to prevent disputes among the first Settlers of such Lands. That he gave Directions to his Assistants to survey a small District of Land each, until it could be known what Report the Committee appointed by the late Convention would make.[3] That he hath given the strongest Assurances, no Survey should be returned under the said Instructions without the approbation of the house of Burgesses or this Convention, yet that many persons were displeased with his Conduct, not knowing the Motives on which he acted, and praying that this Convention will take the same under their most serious Consideration, as nothing is farther from his Intentions than to carry into execution any ministerial Instructions contrary to the chartered Rights or real Interest of his Country, let the Consequence be what it will to his family or private Emolument.[4]

Also, a Petition from the Committee of Fincastle County complaining that Surveys had been made in consequence of Lord Dunmore's proclamation and Instructions contrary to the ancient Usage of taking up Lands in this Colony, which were likely to be the Occasion of much Confusion & Litigation, and praying the Advice of this Convention in the premises, were severally presented to the Convention and read.[5]

Ordered, that the said Petitions be referred to R⟨obert⟩. C⟨arter⟩. Nicholas, R⟨ichard⟩. Bland, A⟨rchibald⟩. Cary, James Mercer, Thomas Lewis, Jos⟨eph⟩: Jones, Paul Carrington, George Rootes & Thomas Walker Esqs.; that they inquire into the Allegations thereof, and report the same with their Opinion thereon, to the Convention.[6]

Adjourned till tomorrow 9. oClock.

> Convention MS journal in hand of John Tazewell
> (Archives Division, Virginia State Library)[7]

Augusta County West: Journal of Captain James Wood

18th The Shawanese being assembled[8] I made The following Speech to them⟨:⟩ *Brothers the Shawanese* I am now on my way to your towns by directions of the great Council of Virginia⟨.⟩[9] my Business is to give the Cheifs of your Nation an Invitation to meet Commissioners Appointed by them in general Council at Fort Pitt in 53 days from this time in order fully to Confirm the peace agreed upon last year with Lord Dunmore⟨.⟩[10] your Brothers Cuttemwha and Newau are well and you may depend upon seeing them at the time Appointed for your Meeting⟨.⟩ about forty days ago Chenusaw left us without any provocation that we know of⟨.⟩ as soon as we found he was gone we dispatched many Men on horseback with Writen papers directing all our People to treat him kindley and to let him Pass to you without receiveing any hurt⟨.⟩ your Brother Cuttemwha desired me to tell you to be Strong and to come at the time which I Appoint⟨.⟩[11] *A String of White Wampum*[12]

I then delivered Messrs ⟨Thomas⟩ Walker and ⟨Andrew⟩ Lewis's speech[13] with a String of Wampum soon after which Cornstalk made the following Answer⟨:⟩ *Brothers the Big-knife* I am greatly oblidged to you as well as to all my Elder Brothers of Virginia for their good talks and Intentions towards their Younger Brothers the Shawanese⟨.⟩ I look upon what you have said in the Manner as if delivered by your great Council and am as happy in seeing you as if they were all present⟨.⟩ I shall deliver your talks to the Cheifs on my return and make no doubt but they will meet you at the time Appointed

The Cornstalk after delivering the speech told me he thought it would be best for me to go to the Shawanese Towns least Chenusaw should return and make any bad reports⟨.⟩ he then informed me that some of the Shawanese were desirous of going to Winchester in order to meet their freinds Cuttenwha and Neawau and to talk with our trading People and desired I would write to my friends to treat them kindly⟨.⟩ I then wrote the following letter to the Committee of Frederick

GENTLEMEN—You will receive this by Major ⟨John⟩ Connolly⟨.⟩ with him three of the Shawanese Cheifs purpose going to Winchester in Order to see their Freinds and to talk with some of our Tradeing people⟨.⟩ if the Hostages should not yet have Arrived I would beg leave to Recommend that an Express be immediately dispatched to Doctor Walkers to bring them up as the treatment these Indians receive will be taken particular Notice of as well by them as the Whole Nation⟨.⟩ I beg the Attention of the Committee on this Occasion⟨.⟩ [14] I am &c

Thwaites and Kellogg, *Revolution on the Upper Ohio, 1775–1777*, pp. 41–43

Middlesex County Committee

Statement of Hugh Walker

Urbanna, *July* 18, 1775.

Upon hearing that John Parsons, ship-builder in Gloucester, should say, there was a large quantity of goods landed at Urbanna for mess. ⟨James⟩ Mills and co. I taxed him about it the night before he left Urbanna; but he denied to me he ever had said such a thing, and said he had or would go before doctor ⟨Robert⟩ Spratt to make oath of the same, as he was summoned by the rev. Samuel Klug to appear before our committee, and asked me if that would not be sufficient to the said committee. I told him, he ought to appear in person.[15]—I was on board Capt. ⟨Moses⟩ Robertson's ship, who told me he was afraid of bringing even common necessaries for himself, for fear he should give offence.[16] I am at any time ready to make oath to this.

Hugh Walker.

Virginia Gazette (Purdie), 22 July 1775, supplement

1. If all who possibly presented their credentials to Tazewell on the previous day were present on this, the membership stood at 107, for although the journal does not so record, Jonathan Clark of Dunmore County took his seat for the 1st time in the "Convention sitting at Richmond" (Autograph diary of Jonathan Clark, Filson Club Docs., 2 vols., unpaged, I, entry for 18 July 1775).

2. The bracketed phrase, indicating the nature of the "Consideration" on the "State of the Colony," is taken from Tazewell's minutes for this day. The phrase follows the entry "Resolved into a Committee of the whole on the State of the Colony" and precedes the entry "Committee to rise & move for Leave to sit again." From the determination of the committee and the convention on 19 July, it is evident that the "Declaration of the Congress" was that of 26 May 1775 stating in the 1st paragraph that "his Majestys Most faithful subjects" were "reduced to a dangerous & critical situation," and in the 2d that hostilities having already begun, "these colonies" should "be immediately put into a state of defence."

But these were the resolutions that, along with others, the Virginia delegates in

Congress addressed to Peyton Randolph on 11 July and which he would not lay before the convention until 24 July 1775. It is obvious, therefore, that the "Declaration" reached the convention sooner by other means—that either one or more of the Virginia deputies in Philadelphia sent it separately by express, or (as is more likely) that Charles Thomson, the secretary of Congress, or his assistant, Timothy Matlack, did so.

3. The "late Convention" was the second, that of 20–27 Mar. 1775. The "Committee" was appointed on the last day of session and had no time to report (*Rev. Va.*, II, 383–84).

4. For the "Petition of William Preston gent:" see 10 July 1775, Third Va. Convention, Fincastle Co.

5. For the "Petition from the Committee," see 10 July 1775, Third Va. Convention, Fincastle Co. Committee.

6. The next mention of this subject will be on 19 July 1775, with referral to the committee of the governor's proclamation on which Preston based his authorization to survey (Third Va. Convention, Procs., final para.).

7. Tazewell wrote "Nos. 1. & 2" edgewise on the bottom of the 4th of 4 pages on which he combined the journal for this day with that for 17 July 1775.

8. "The Shawanese" were enumerated by Captain Wood in his journal for 16 July 1775.

9. The "great Council of Virginia" was composed of the House of Burgesses and the Council, but it was to be to the convention that Wood's report was sent (9 July 1775, Third Va. Convention; 18 Aug. 1775, same, Wood to Randolph).

10. Fifty-three days hence would be 9 Sept., but as he indicated successively to Delaware, apparently to Seneca and Mingo, to Wyandot and Tawa (or Ottawa), and to Shawnee leaders on 22, 25, and 27 July, and on 2 Aug. (Third Va. Convention, Augusta Co. West), Captain Wood set the date from 10 to 12 Sept. 1775. Possibly he meant to stagger the times of arrival of the different chiefs at Fort Pitt, but a spread of 20 days would have done as well, for as he knew, Indian negotiators seldom synchronized watches or moved out at *H*-hour. For the "peace agreed upon last year with Lord Dunmore," see 19 May 1775, n. 3.

11. The "Brothers" Cutemwha, Newa, and Chenusaw were 3 of the Shawnee hostages taken by Governor Dunmore to Williamsburg following the negotiations at Camp Charlotte in 1774 (19 May 1775, n. 3). On the day of his appointment by the General Assembly, Wood recorded in his journal the fact of Chenusaw's leavetaking and the thought that one of the responsibilities of the "Commissioners" would be "to remove any bad impressions" that the escapee might have spread among his people (Thwaites and Kellogg, *Rev. on the Upper Ohio*, p. 34).

12. See 20 May 1775, n. 7.

13. For "Messrs Walker and Lewis's speech," see 9 July 1775, Third Va. Convention.

14. Evidence from Connolly's own hand will place him and 3 Indians in Winchester on 1 Aug. 1775 (Third Va. Convention, Connolly to Rootes), but one of the accompanying trio may have been the Delaware chief White Eyes (10 July 1775, Third Va. Convention, Augusta Co. West and n. 1). Wood's next journal entry is under the date heading of 20 July 1775.

15. Dr. Spratt was sheriff of Middlesex County (*Exec. Journs. Coun. Col. Va.*, VI, 546). He will be found taking 2 depositions on 22 July 1775.

16. How on or about 25 May, Captain Robertson managed to dine George Lorimer and "some ladies and gentlemen" aboard his ship yet was afraid to provide himself even with "common necessaries," invites pondering (1 June 1775, Middlesex Co. Committee; 19 July 1775, same, 4th entry). But it was not the captain who was now on the

defensive. For additional testimony even less helpful to Parsons, see 19, 22 July 1775, Middlesex Co. Committee.

Wednesday, 19 July 1775

Third Virginia Convention

Proceedings of Third Day of Session [1]

Resolved, that the revd. Charles Mynn Thruston be desired to read prayers to this Convention & to preach Tomorrow in the Room of the revd. Miles Selden, who is at present indisposed.[2]

The Order of the Day being read,[3] the Convention resolved itself into a Committee to take into their further Consideration, the state of the Colony and after sometime spent therein, Mr. President ⟨Peyton Randolph⟩ resumed the Chair, and Mr. ⟨Richard⟩ Bland reported that the Committee had had the same under their Consideration, and had come to a Resolution thereon, which he read in his Place, and then delivered in at the Table, where the same was again read and agreed to, as follows.

Resolved, that a sufficient armed Force be immediately raised and embodyed, under proper Officers for the Defence and protection of this Colony.[4]

Ordered, that Richard Bland, Robert Carter Nicholas, James Mercer, Joseph Jones, George Mason,[5] George Rootes, Adam Stevens ⟨Stephen⟩, Isaac Zane⟨, Jr.⟩, John Banister, Thomas Blackburn, Charles Mynn Thruston, Thomas Ludwell Lee, Carter Braxton, Thomas Nelson⟨, Jr.⟩, William Woodford, Henry Lee, and William Christion ⟨Christian⟩ do prepare and bring in an Ordinance pursuant to the said Resolution.[6]

Resolved, that this Convention will again resolve itself into a Committee on Friday next to take into their further Consideration, the State of the Colony.[7]

The Govr's proclm. refd. to same Com. as formerly appointed.[8]

Convention MS journal in hand of John Tazewell
(Archives Division, Virginia State Library) [9]

Middlesex County Committee

Request and Certification

Mr. PURDIE,

BE pleased to insert in your gazette, that as the publishment in your last of the 15th, of mess. John Parsons, John and William Degge, and William Hudgin, can creditably be proved notorious falsehoods, that I think it is making them and their abetters of too much consequence to take any other notice than to advise the publick to beware of such men.[10]

URBANNA, *July* 19, 1775   James Mills.

THIS is to certify all whom it may concern, that capt. Moses Robertson, of the ship London, from London, entered at Port Rappahannock the 24th of May last, with ballast only.

Given under my hand, the 19th of July 1775.

Zachariah Shackleford,
Deputy naval officer.[11]

Virginia Gazette (Purdie), 22 July 1775, supplement

Statement by Robert Brown

URBANNA, *July* 19, 1775.

I REPEATEDLY heard John Parsons, ship-builder in Gloucester, say, that he saw upwards of 1000 *l.* worth of goods landed and put into one of James Mills and co. warehouses; likewise that said goods came from on board the ship London, capt. Moses Robertson. A few days afterwards, the rev. Samuel Klug summoned the said John Parsons to appear before the committee of this county; but he absolutely refused to attend, swearing he never saw one farthing's worth of goods landed. He also said, if it would be satisfactory to the committee, he would willingly go before any magistrate and make oath that he was not the propagator of such a report.

I am ready to make oath to the above, whenever called on.

Robert Brown.

Ibid. (Purdie), 22 July 1775, supplement

Statement by James Ross

THE above-mentioned John Parsons told me, he was determined not to appear before the committee; but, if he thought it would be satisfactory to go before a magistrate in his own county (Gloucester) and take his oath that he never saw any goods landed, he would willingly do it, and send it up. The above I will make oath to, when called on.

J. Ross.

Ibid. (Purdie), 22 July 1775, supplement

Letter of and Statement by George Lorimer

URBANNA, *July* 19, 1775.

Mr. PURDIE,

IN vindication of my own character, and in justice to Mr. ⟨John⟩ Norton and capt. ⟨Moses⟩ Robertson, I must beg you to publish the enclosed in your paper; that the publick may be convinced how little regard ought to be paid to the reports of John Parsons, and his apprentices.

I am, sir, your very humble servant,

George Lorimer.

WHILE John Parsons was delivering me a vessel at Urbanna, my own property, and not belonging to Mills and co. as he sets forth in his advertisement, capt. Robertson arrived from London. By invitation, I dined on board his ship, with some ladies and gentlemen, when he obligingly spared me a pair of pistols, and a coateau de chasse,[12] which he had brought for his own use, and not for sale; I bought no other goods of him. Indeed, I verily believe he had not a shilling's worth on board; for I never saw such a clear ship. I never corresponded with mr. Norton, or received goods from that house; nor did ever James Mills and co. correspond or receive goods from those gentlemen; nor had they any goods by that ship, or by any other from Britain, since last November.[13] While capt. Robertson lay at Urbanna, capt. ⟨Alexander⟩ Massenburg, a trader from Norfolk to this river, came up late one evening with passengers, whose trunks were landed here, as well as some muscovado sugar [14] for James Mills and co. and two casks of wine and sugar for mr. Benjamin Browne; which last goods were landed in the night (as capt. Massenburg would not wait till the morning, the wind being fair) and deposited in one of the warehouses of James Mills and co. by capt. William Boyce, who had the keys thereof. This is what gave occasion to the report which Parsons and his apprentices, have so industriously propagated. The above I am ready to swear to, whenever called on.

George Lorimer.

N.B. It may be necessary to observe, that it must have been the apparition of one of the company which Parsons saw on the bank; for I was seven miles from Urbanna, mr. Mills spent the evening at Mr. ⟨James⟩ Gregory's with company, and Mr. ⟨Charles⟩ Colby was at Gloucester.[15]

Ibid. (Purdie), 22 July 1775, supplement

Norfolk Borough Committee

Officers of Independent Companies of Gentlemen Volunteers at Williamsburg to Norfolk Borough Committee

19 July 1775

To the Committee at Norfolk

Gentlemen/

We Judge you are sensible it requires no extraordinary Genius to divide, & true wisdom despises the infamous task⟨.⟩ you have hitherto shewen the diffusive spirit of benevolence to our cause, in your strictures on Lord Dunmores letters⟨.⟩ [16] we are therefore the more truly alarmed at a report which gives us too much grounds to fear you are some of you desserting the Glorious Cause, being informed that there are Volunteers recruiting in opposition to the Continental plan⟨.⟩ [17] our desire is that you inform us of the virity of this report that we may assist the proper side with all our force, as soon as we obtain proper authority from the Convention which is at present sitting, before whom we shall not fail to lay the whole state of your Case.[18]

from the officers of the difft. Independent Companies now in W*msbgh*

Chs Scott [19]	Thos. Ruffin Pgeo [20]
John Fleming	James Ennis [21] Wmsbg
Richd. K. Mead	Wm Finnie Wmsbg
—— Blunt	Geo Gilmer Albe
Henry Taylor	Benj. Temple Kg Wm
George Nicholas Wmsbgh	John Taliaferro Kg G
W*m* Duvall. Henrico	F. Eppes

MS transcript in autograph diary and Revolutionary memoranda of Dr. George Gilmer (Virginia Historical Society)

Williamsburg

William Eaton to Alexander Purdie: A Public Deposition

Mr. Purdie,

As I have the greatest reason to believe that I am the person whom the attorney-general supposed has made use of so much industry to propagate a conversation that passed between us, at his own house relative to Mr. Patrick Henry (which I see he has denied in your last paper) [22] I have sent you a true state of that conversation, sworn before Mr. Graves, which I shall be much obliged to you to publish.

I happened at the attorney-general's, I believe some time in May; and after some conversation, I asked him what time he thought the merchants would meet. He replied, "Do you think the merchants will be such fools as to come to Williamsburg, with money in their pockets, when Patrick Henry, or any other set of men, might come and take their money from them?" I asked the attorney-general, whether he thought Mr. Henry would take any man's private property from him; his answer was, "He might as well do it as to have extorted the money in the manner he did from the receiver-general." [23]

William Eaton.[24]

The above was sworn to before me, by William Eaton.

William Graves.[25] July 19, 1775.

Virginia Gazette (Purdie), 21 July 1775, supplement

1. If all the delegates who possibly had presented their credentials on the 1st and 2d days of session were present on this, their number stood at 107. Although unmarked in either journal or minutes, on this day George Mason "gave notice in Convention" that whereas by terms of the Continental Association certain commodities were prohibited from exportation on and after 10 Sept., he "on Monday," 24 July, would move that in Virginia the date be set forward to 5 Aug. 1775 (*Rev. Va.*, II, 105; Rutland, *Papers of Mason*, I, 241).

2. "Revd. Miles Selden" had been appointed "Chaplain" on the 1st day of session, 17 July. He had also been "desired" to "preach a Sermon" on 20 July 1775, "being the Day recommended by the General Congress to be kept as a solemn Fast." In the absence of Rev. Peter Muhlenberg of Dunmore County, "the revd." Mr. Thruston was the only delegate present who was an ordained minister.

3. The "Order of the Day" was consideration of the "Declaration" of Congress, laid before the convention on the previous day, that the colonies "be immediately put into a state of defence."

4. In the printed journal, p. 7, Purdie substitutes "*Resolved,* That it is the opinion of this committee, that. . . ." More than the adoption of this one-paragraph resolution was debated. Richard Bland evidently believed that the resolution should be prefaced by a justificatory paragraph. In the convention loose papers there is an incomplete preface in his hand. Taking up pen, Tazewell, with minor amendments, wrote the paragraph in full:

"Whereas his Excellency the Earl of Dunmore Governor of this Colony, by withdrawing himself from the Seat of Government on Board the Fowey one of his Majesty's Ships of War; by declaring that he will set fire to the City of Williamsburg, lay Waste the Country and emancipate our Slaves, several or whom have already been received and detained on Board the said Ship, hath plainly demonstrated the most hostile & inimical Designs against the good people of this Colony, and thereby compelled us for the Security and Preservation of our Lives, Liberties & Estates, to take the most effectual Measures to defeat such his wicked intentions,"

The resolution in the journal next follows.

Tazewell then continued, "Resolved, that the Forces so to be raised be put under proper Regulations & Restrictions.

"Resolved, that a sum of Money not exceeding   be raised, for maintaining and supporting the said Forces."

The prefatory paragraph and the 2d and 3d resolutions were either withdrawn or defeated. Flagellating His Lordship's conduct was an exercise to be assigned employment in "A Declaration *of the* Delegates" on the final day of session (pp. 500–502 below). Drawing up articles of war was properly the business of a separate committee, which would be appointed and return its ordinance on 21 Aug. (Procs. and nn. 2, 4, 6–8), and monetarily undergirding the armed forces the business of another, appointed on 25 July 1775 (Procs. and n. 10).

5. "The committee," wrote Mason 3 days after his appointment, "meet every morning at seven o'clock," work until 9:00 A.M., when "the Convention meets, which seldom rises before five in the afternoon, and immediately after dinner and a little refreshment sits again till nine or ten at night." It was "hard duty," true, but little to be "wondered at when the extent and importance" of the subject was considered—"to raise forces for the immediate service," to remodel "the whole militia," to render approximately a 5th of it "fit for the field at the shortest warning," and to "melt down all the volunteers and independent companies into this great establishment" (Rutland, *Papers of Mason,* I, 241).

6. Since the House of Burgesses was still a constitutional entity, the convention could not pass an "act" without admitting to a usurpation. Hence "an Ordinance," which, though of statutory force, was a synonym undoubtedly soothing to the sensibilities of the more doctrinaire delegates. "Every Ordinance," explained Mason, "goes thro all the Formalities of a Bill in the House of Burgesses has three readings &c. before it is passed, & in every respect wears the Face of Law. Resolves or Recommendations being no longer trusted in Matters of Importance" (ibid., I, 252).

7. After several deferments, "this Convention" would "resolve itself into a Committee" to consider "the State of the Colony" only on 1 Aug. 1775, the 12th day of session.

8. Purdie does not print this entry. Tazewell jotted it down in a hand hastier than that in which he inscribed the rest of the journal for this day, as though minuting an afterthought, that he might be reminded in whose possession the "Govr's proclm." was. The proclamation was Dunmore's of 8 May 1775 (Royal Chief Magistracy). The "same" committee was that appointed on 18 July 1775 (Third Va. Convention, Procs. final para.).

9. Edgewise on the bottom of the 2d of 2 pages on which Tazewell entered this day's journal he wrote "No. 3."

10. The "publishment" was Parson's attempted "vindication" of his crumbling "character" (10 July 1775, Middlesex Co. Committee), triggered by the action of the county committee in condemning his behavior (1, 6 June 1775, same). For other challenges to the shipbuilder's veracity, see 13, 18 July 1775, same. The present and the 3 items following concern the same incident.

11. A deputy naval officer assisted, often to the point of doing all the work of, a naval officer. Whether or not a sinecurist, a naval officer was legally responsible for the maintenance of records of all ships clearing through his port, noting their respective owners, masters, ports of origin, destinations, and cargoes. Charles Neilson was the naval officer at Urbanna, the port for the Rappahannock District; but it may have been deemed best to procure this certificate from Shackelford, because Neilson had of late orally wished ill to the patriot troops before Boston, for which sentiment he would offer a "concession" to the Middlesex County committee on 28 Aug. 1775 (*Exec. Journs. Coun. Col. Va.,* VI, 465; *Va. Gazette* [Purdie], 15 Sept. 1775, supplement).

12. That is, *couteau de chasse,* a hunting knife.

13. That the *London* was a merchantman owned by John Norton & Sons, English commission merchants, with their Virginia offices on the York River, especially obligated Lorimer, Mills, and Robertson to set the record straight. Involved as a principal in a "tea party" in Nov. 1774, when 2 half chests of tea were thrown from one of his ships into the York River, John Norton only in May 1775 had reached the Virginia public with protestations of his and his firm's innocence of any intent to flout colonial rights (*Rev. Va.*, II, 23 n. 1, 163–67, 175–76, 214, 217 n. 8, 218–19, 223–24 nn. 1–3, 238–39).

14. Muscovado is raw or unrefined sugar.

15. With 2 additional items under the date heading of 22 July 1775, Middlesex Co. Committee, this particular Parson's cause will be found definitively closed.

16. For "strictures on Lord Dunmores letters," see 4 May 1775, Norfolk Co. Committee. If the officers were not mistaken in the identity of the committee, and the borough committee had published separate "strictures" on Dunmore's letters of 24 Dec. and 6 June 1774 (for which see respectively 28 Apr. 1775, 8 June 1775, Royal Chief Magistracy), neither item has been found.

17. What was meant by "the Continental plan" is indeterminable. It is possible that rumors were abroad that denizens of Norfolk, the lifeblood of which was trade, were arming to resist further application of the Continental Association. It is possible that the supposed arming was conceived to be directed against visitation by elements of the Continental Army, the "plan" for which began to assume shape when Congress on 14 June resolved that "six companies of expert riflemen be immediately raised," 2 of them in Virginia (11 July 1775, Third Va. Convention, In Congress and n. 16). But the resolutions embodying this 2d "plan" were laid before the convention only on 18 July 1775, and there is no evidence that their contents were public knowledge in the Tidewater.

18. William Davies would present a "state" of the Norfolk Borough committee's "Case" on 21 July 1775.

19. Officers lacking elements of identification by name or home county are respectively Charles Scott, Cumberland; Fleming, Goochland; Richard Kidder Meade, Prince George; Benjamin Blunt, Southampton; Taylor, Southampton (probably the delegate of his name absent from the convention); and Francis ("Frank") Eppes, Dinwiddie.

20. "Pgeo" was Gilmer's abbreviation for Prince George.

21. Innes.

22. For Mr. Purdie's "last paper," see 12 July 1775, Williamsburg.

23. For Henry's "extortion" of money from Receiver General Richard Corbin, see pp. 7–11 above. John Randolph would find the present item in the newspaper when he returned from Norfolk, whither he had gone on 18 July and "waited upon his Excellency the Governor" (*Va. Gazette, or the Norfolk Intelligencer*, 19 July 1775). As to Eaton's deposition, the attorney general remained silent. But this in no wise diminished criticism. On 27 July, for example, Pinkney's *Va. Gazette* carried a letter from "A Surry Volunteer" to "J——n R——ph, *esquire*," advising that "If your principles are incorrigible, if you are rooted in wrong, pray abscond yourself, push for some remote corner of the globe, where the imprecations of your countrymen, and the invectives of a much injured people, cannot assail your adamantine ears."

For the nonce "J——n R——ph" appeared to be holding his own against such abuse, but in little more than a month he would announce that in intending to "leave the colony for a few months," he was authorizing the sale of his "estate, both real and personal" (*Va. Gazette* [Purdie], 25 Aug. 1775).

"The Attorney General," Lord Dunmore explained to Lord Dartmouth, "has been very unpopular in this, his native, Country, ever Since the Stamp Act," the enforcement of which he had refused to oppose; and "though he is Confessedly the best Lawyer in the Colony, he has been employed upon very few occasions, and therefore has been deprived of any other means of living than his office." Moreover, "The Fund for the Support of Government" would cease with the effectuation of the terms of the Continental Association on 10 Sept. 1775, "when we shall be all destitute; but the Attorney General, who has little or no private fortune, will be entirely ruined" (P.R.O., C.O. 5/1353, fol. 222).

24. Of a numerous family which had settled in the lower Tidewater a century before and spread upstream into several other counties, William Eaton was a resident of York County (perhaps also of Williamsburg), a vestryman of Bruton Parish, and a gentleman consequential enough that his death would be noticed in a Richmond newspaper 12 years hence (*Va. Mag. of Hist. and Biog.*, XXXVI [July 1928], 230 n. 11; W[illiam] A. R. Goodwin, *Historical Sketch of Bruton Church, Williamsburg, Virginia* [Petersburg, 1903], p. 119; *Va. Independent Chronicle* [Richmond], 20 June 1787).

25. Also of an old tidewater family, William Graves was a fellow vestryman of William Eaton and since 1773 had served as a justice of the peace for York County, so being a very proper person before whom to swear one's word (Goodwin, *Historical Sketch of Bruton Church*, p. 119; York County Records, Judgments and Orders, no. 2, 1770–1772, microfilm in Va. State Library, p. 476).

Thursday, 20 July 1775

Third Virginia Convention

Augusta County West: Journal of Captain James Wood

20th Started very Early⟨;⟩ [1] met Garret Pendergrass⟨, Jr.⟩ about 9 o'Clock who informed us that he left the Delaware Towns two days before⟨;⟩ [2] that the Delawares were just returned from the Wiandots Towns [3] where they had been at a Great Council with the French and English Officer and the Wyandots⟨;⟩ that Monseur Baubee and the English Officer told them to be upon their Guard⟨;⟩ that the White People intended to strike them very soon⟨;⟩ that tho' their fathers the French were thrown down the last War by the English they were now got up again and much stronger than ever and would Assist their Children (the Indians) as they formerly did⟨;⟩ [4] about two days after met two Delaware Squas who upon interrogations gave the same Account

Thwaites and Kellogg, *Revolution on the Upper Ohio, 1775–1777*, pp. 43–44

Deposition of Garret Pendergrass, Jr., before John Gibson

Augusta County Ss.[5]

Personally appeared before me John Gibson One of his Majesties justices for the County of Augusta, Garret Pendergrass, who Being sworn on the Holy Evangelists of Almighty God, Deposeth and saith, that he left the Delaware towns, on Muskingham on Monday last, that he was informed there By some of the Delawares that a Number of their People had lately come from Detroit, that one Baubee,[6] a french Trader had held a Council with them, and that he desired them immediately to strike the white people, that the Wiandots and all other tribes would join, that he woud furnish them and at the same time Offered them Ammunition for that purpose. He also told them, the White people were now quite Round them and Intended soon to fall on the Indians. that they told Babee they coud not join in any thing of the kind, as their head men had made a firm peace with their Brethren the English and refused Receiving any Ammunition from him. and further Saith not.[7] Sworn and Subscribed this 20th. July at Logs town.[8] Garret Pendergrass Junr[9] Before me

JNO. GIBSON[10]

Recipients' copy, autograph document, signed, in loose papers of third Virginia Convention (Archives Division, Virginia State Library)[11]

Norfolk County Committee

Election of New Committee

WE the Subscribers, appointed to superintend the election of a committee for Norfolk County, do declare the following persons duly elected agreeably to the ballots.[12]

| PAUL LOYAL⟨L⟩, | JOHN WILSON, |
| BASSETT MOSEL⟨E⟩Y, | WILLIAM DAVIES, |

July 20, 1775.

George Veal⟨e⟩, James Webb, John Portlock, Arthur Boush, Bassett Mosel⟨e⟩y, Edward Archer, John Willoughby, sen., Stephen Wright, James Nic⟨h⟩olson, Charles Mayle, John Wilson, Matthew Godfrey, Edward Strong, Thomas Creech, Abraham Wormington, Caleb Herbert, David Porter, William Smith, Thomas Nash, jun., James Grymes (Western Branch),[13] Goodrich Boush, Malachi Wilson, jun., Cornelius Calvert, Alexander Skinner, Patrick Mackey, John Brickell, jun., Paul Proby, William

Bressi⟨e⟩, Benjamin Crooker, Malachi Maund, George Kelly, Samuel Portlock, John Willoughby, jun. Henry Bressi⟨e⟩, Daniel Sandford ⟨Sanford⟩.

Virginia Gazette, or the Norfolk Intelligencer, 26
July 1775

1. Accompanied by Simon Girty, who would serve as "Interpreter" for the remainder of his western journey, Captain Wood left Fort Pitt "at 5 o'Clock" in the
evening of 18 July 1775 and traveled approximately 10 miles before encamping. On
the 19th, having started "before Sunrise," he and his companion "travelled about 45
Miles this day the Course nearly West" (Thwaites and Kellogg, *Rev. on the Upper
Ohio,* p. 43; C. W. Butterfield, *Hist. of the Girtys,* p. 35).

2. The "Delaware Towns" clustered about Coshocton, for which see 6 July 1775,
n. 6.

3. The Wyandots (for whom see 4 July 1775, n. 6) were living along the Sandusky
River in present-day east-central Ohio (Thwaites and Kellogg, *Rev. on the Upper
Ohio,* p. 36 n. 62).

4. The French having been "thrown down" in the "last," or the French and Indian,
War, Duperon Baby long since had cast his lot with the British. That he pursued an
anti-American policy by being equally anti-English is manifestly untrue. This mis-
understanding arose from the Indian's own confusion as to the identity of the "White
people" with whom they had dealt or were to deal—whether they represented the
British interest, white colonials in general, or the Virginia Big Knife only (23 July,
27 July, 2 Aug. 1775, Augusta Co. West; 18 Aug., Third Va. Convention, Wood to
Randolph).

5. An abbreviation for the Latin *scilicet,* meaning "to wit," or "that is to say."

6. Duperon Baby (n. 4 above).

7. The "firm peace" which the Delawares had made with "their Brethren the
English" was that negotiated by Maj. John Connolly at Fort Pitt (29 June, 1, 3, 4, 5,
6 July 1775, Third Va. Convention, Augusta Co. West).

8. Logstown, where John Gibson was maintaining his trading post, was on the
west bank of the Ohio River 18 miles below Fort Pitt. The post had once been a
major gathering place for Indian and white but was rapidly declining in importance
and within another decade would be abandoned (Thwaites and Kellogg, *Rev. on the
Upper Ohio,* pp. 26–27 n. 52).

9. A Garret Pendergrass had been in the upper Ohio Valley as early as 1738 and
was probably the man of that name who founded Raystown (now Bedford) in
Pennsylvania in the 1750s. There he kept a convivial public house to which George
Croghan occasionally repaired. GARRET PENDERGRASS, JR., of uncertain age, was the
son of this publican. Going west in 1770, he was granted "full leave and liberty" by
the Six Nations "to settle on a tract of land on the north side of the Aligania River
opposite to Fort Pitt, in a form of a Cemi Circle from said landing." As with others,
his name appears in the record of the 1st court held when Westmoreland County, Pa.,
was erected in the wilds—but not as a magistrate; he was arraigned for "Forcible
entry" and saw fit not to appear. Tax lists indicate that he still lived in western
Pennsylvania as late as 1786, so it was probably his father or another namesake who
was parted from his scalp in Kentucky in 1777 (*Cal. Va. State Papers,* I, 232; Hanna,
Wilderness Trail, I, 52; Alexander S. Guffey, "The First Courts in Western Pennsylvania," *Western Pa. Hist. Mag.,* VII [July 1924], 153–54; Henry M. Egle, ed., *Pennsyl-*

vania Archives, 3d ser. [26 vols. and gen. index, Harrisburg, 1894–97], XXII, 24, 496;
cf. Thwaites and Kellogg, *Rev. on the Upper Ohio,* p. 43 n. 69).

10. Like Capt. John Smith, JOHN GIBSON had been captured by Indians and would
have been otherwise disposed of had Cupid not interceded. And Gibson, whose
narrow escape had occurred during the French and Indian War, lived to wed a different squaw, a sister of the Mingo chief Logan, but only to have her slain by raid-
ing whites. Gibson had for long kept a store near Fort Pitt, and because he was
accomplished in Indian tongues, had been Lord Dunmore's official interpreter in 1774.
Although a native of Lancaster County, Pa., he was now a justice of the peace for
the District of West Augusta and since 16 May 1775 had been serving on the county's
western committee. His major accomplishment to date was to have audited and preserved (and perhaps improved on) a famous speech in which Logan, burying the
hatchet, justified his murderous retaliations on the whites for the loss of his family.
Armed with a classical education as well as an earnest desire to restore and maintain
peace between red man and white, Gibson was a man "of respectability and good
sense" and widely trusted. At this time he was 35 years old (John B. Gibson, "General
John Gibson," *Western Pa. Hist. Mag.,* V [Oct. 1922], 298–304; "Memoirs of
Brigadier-General John Lacy, of Pennsylvania," *Pa. Mag. of Hist. and Biog.* XXV
[Jan. 1901], 6; David I. Bushnell, Jr., "Virginia Frontier in History—1778," *Va. Mag.
of Hist. and Biog.,* XXIV [Apr. 1916], 175–76; *Exec. Journs. Coun. Col. Va.,* VI, 543;
16 May 1775, Augusta Co. West Committee).

11. This deposition would be laid before the convention on 5 Aug. 1775 (Procs.
and n. 10).

12. It can be shown that a committee was in operation in Norfolk County no later
than 23 Jan. 1775 (*Rev. Va.,* II, 260). It seems most probable that the reconstitution
of the committee according to the 11th article of the Continental Association (8 Apr.
1775, n. 5) and the extension of its area of functions to include the town of Portsmouth
was intended as a step in the direction of efficiency and vigor. Among those "appointed to superintend the election" were 2 who may have been brought in as neutrals
—Paul Loyall, mayor of the borough, and William Davies, secretary of the borough
committee.

But so merged were the interests of those living principally in either borough or
county that there could have been "brought in" hardly an intelligent man innocent of
a knowledge of county personalities. In proof of this coalescence of interests, the
Norfolk urban committee will on 28 July 1775 "instruct" not only Joseph Hutchings,
the borough delegate to the third Virginia Convention, but also James Holt and
Thomas Newton, Jr., those for the county.

A large gathering probably was present, this being the date set aside by Congress
to "assemble for public worship" during the day of "public humiliation, fasting and
prayer" (30 June 1775, n. 8).

13. The members whose names follow "(Western Branch)" were those to whom
was assigned control of the region of the West Branch of the Elizabeth River, an
area including the town of Portsmouth. This method of dividing the county was
logical, corresponding as it did roughly with the division of the area into 2 parishes
(*Statutes at Large,* VII, 416). In addition to Portsmouth and the agricultural lands
lying immediately to the south of the town, most of Portsmouth Parish encompassed
the eerie wastes of the Dismal Swamp.

Friday, 21 July 1775

Third Virginia Convention

Proceedings of Fourth Day of Session [1]

The President ⟨Peyton Randolph⟩ laid before the Convention a letter from James Wood Esquire on the subject of Indian Affairs, which was read and ordered to lie on the Table for the perusal of the Members.[2]

The proceedings at a Treaty lately concluded with the Indians at Fort-Pitt together with several Resolutions of the Committee for the County of Augusta were laid before the Convention and read.[3]

Ordered, that the said proceedings and Resolutions be referred to the Committee appointed to draw up and report an Ordinance for raising and embodying a sufficient force for the Defence and protection of this Colony.[4]

A Petition of sundry persons Freeholders of the County of Berk⟨e⟩ley complaining of an undue Election and Return of Adam Stephen Esq: to serve in this Convention for the County of Berkley, and also the Proceedings of the Committee of the said County relating thereto, were presented to the Convention and read.[5]

Ordered that the said Petition & proceedings be referred to Dudley Digges, Robert Carter Nicholas, Richard Bland, Archibald Cary, Joseph Jones, Carter Braxton, William Fitzhugh, Charles Carter, of Lancaster, Charles Carter of Stafford, Paul Carrington, Thomas Nelson⟨, Jr.⟩, David Mason, Burwell Bassett, Bartholomew Dandridge, James Holt, Richard Lee, Henry Lee, James Mercer, William Fleming, Mann Page⟨, Jr.⟩ & Samuel McDowell, Esqs and they are to examine the Matter thereof & report the same together with their Opinion thereon to the Convention.[6]

Resolved that eleven of the said Committee be a sufficient Number to proceed on Business.

Resolved, that it be an Instruction to the Committee appointed to draw up & report an Ordinance for raising and embodying a sufficient Force for the Defence and Protection of this Colony, that they receive a Clause or Clauses for the pay and Support of the Forces to be raised.[7]

Ordered, that Thomas Marshall, Bartholomew Dandridge and Robert Rutherford, Esquires be added to the said Committee.[8]

Adjourned till to Morrow 9. oClock.[9]

Convention MS journal in hand of John Tazewell
(Archives Division, Virginia State Library) [10]

Norfolk Borough Committee

William Davies to Officers of Gentlemen Volunteers of Independent Companies at Williamsburg

Gentlemen: Norfolk 21 July 1775

We are happy in every Expression of your Attachment to the common Interest of your Country, & are glad we can inform you there is not the least Foundation for the Fears you have declared for our safety, upon an ill-grounded Report that any among us are deserting the cause of their country & enlisting against it.[11]

It is a report, we can assure you that is totally devoid of Truth. You may depend we would not sit still, as indifferent Spectators of such hostile Measures. The time may come when we may stand in need of your Assistance, surrounded as we are by armed vessels, & some suspected inhabitants.[12] We trust we shall then receive it. And should the Convention, hereafter, think it necessary to quarter any of you among us, you may rest assured we shall wellcome you with willing hearts and open arms.[13]

We are Gentlemen, your humble Servants,
By order of the Committee.[14] Wm. Davies Secy.

> MS transcript in autograph diary and Revolutionary memoranda of Dr. George Gilmer (Virginia Historical Society)

Resolution Respecting Pilots

Norfolk borough, Committee Chamber, July 21.
PRESENT
Mr. Chairman and 21 members.[15]

UPON motion RESOLVED, that no pilot ought to give any assistance to the ships and other vessels, that are expected to arrive from Great-Britain with cargoes contrary to the Association, upon penalty of being published to the world for such misconduct.[16]

Published by order,
William Davies, sec'ry.

> *Virginia Gazette, or the Norfolk Intelligencer*, 26 July 1775

1. With the death this day of Robert Bolling, the possible active membership was reduced to 106.

For a reason long lost, John Tazewell preceded his date entry, "Friday July 21. 1775.," with a quotation mark and placed a closing quotation mark at the end of the 3d paragraph of text.

2. For the "letter from James Wood Esquire," see 9 July 1775, Augusta Co. West.

3. For the "proceedings at a Treaty," see 19 May, 21, 22, 26, 29 June, 1, 3, 4, 5, 6 July 1775, Third Va. Convention, Augusta Co. West. The "several Resolutions" may have included those adopted on 26 June 1775 (same, 2d entry). Definitely included in the papers was the correspondence with the committee of Westmoreland County, Pa. (29 June 1775, Third Va. Convention, 2d entry; 3 July 1775, 2d and 3d entries). These documents were enclosures in John Campbell's letter of 12 July 1775 to John Harvie and George Rootes.

4. The committee, of which Richard Bland was chairman, had been appointed on 19 July 1775.

5. For the complainants' "Petition" and related documents, see Berkeley County entries under the date headings of 24 Apr., 23 May, and 7 June 1775; for the "Proceedings of the Committee of the said County," 14 June 1775.

6. Purdie in the printed journal, p. 8, transposes the names of the 2 Charles Carters and of Richard and Henry Lee. In his minutes for this day Tazewell labeled the committee one "of privileges & Elections," as it would have been designated in the House of Burgesses. The committee would report on 27 July 1775.

7. In his minutes for the day Tazewell wrote, "Instructions to the Com: for raising men that they provide the ways & Means." Provision of the ways and means would be a duty silently transferred to a committee initially named on 25 July 1775 and augmented 4 days later to prepare an ordinance for compensating the veterans and sufferers of Dunmore's War (25 Aug. 1775, Procs. and n. 10; 29 July, same and n. 6; 12 Aug., same and n. 16; 24 Aug., same and n. 2).

8. With the addition of the 3 delegates named, the number of members comprising the committee for defense and protection was raised to 20, with no quorum established.

9. In the manuscript journal Tazewell lined through "to Morrow" with ink and above the words wrote "Monday." Because the convention did meet on Saturday, and because in his minutes for this day Tazewell entered no note respecting the day to which the convention was adjourned, one can only speculate as to why he left standing the error that Purdie corrects in the printed journal, p. 8. It may have been that a motion was passed to adjourn on Saturday in respect to the memory of Robert Bolling, and it was later learned that memorial services were planned to be held in the Town Church on Sunday. Getting the word around that Mr. President thought it best to reconvene on Saturday would not have been overly difficult with a group not exceeding 106 in number and housed in a small town or its environs.

10. Edgewise on the top of the 4th of 4 pages (the 2d and 3d pages being blank) on which Tazewell kept the minutes for this day he wrote "No. 4." The journal occupies all of the recto and most of the verso of a separate sheet of paper.

11. The letter is in reply to that of the officers dated 19 July 1775, Williamsburg. In Purdie's *Va. Gazette* of 28 July 1775 it is stated that the letter from the officers was borne from the capital to Norfolk on 20 July by "one of the Dinwiddie volunteers," and that the reply was taken to Williamsburg by the same courier on 22 July.

12. Of "suspected inhabitants" in and around Norfolk there were to be enough that from their ranks the governor would raise a loyalist regiment in November (Thomas J. Wertenbaker, *Norfolk, Historic Southern Port*, ed. Marvin W. Schlegel [2d ed., Durham, N.C., 1962], p. 56). At present His Excellency was residing at or near Andrew Sprowle's establishment at Gosport, from which 2 men-of-war could be

seen riding offshore (*Va. Gazette, or the Norfolk Intelligencer,* 12, 19 July 1775; *Va. Gazette* [Dixon and Hunter], 15, 22 July 1775). Sprowle's proximity to His Lordship's person would yet confront the former with a difficulty (9 Aug. 1775, Norfolk Co. Committee).

13. The convention would on 4 Aug. 1775 order "five hundred effective Men" to Norfolk (Procs. and n. 9).

14. Davies's reassuring words were not what armed young men, bored with spit-and-polish routine, had hoped to read or hear, in demonstration whereof they would within 4 days commit a patriotic nuisance and be enabled to address the members of the convention after all (26 July 1775, Third Va. Convention).

15. "Mr. Chairman" was probably still Matthew Phripp (*Rev. Va.,* II, 308).

16. Near the end of June 1775, a Liverpool merchantman that "appeared very deep in the water" with cargo had entered Chesapeake Bay, but her captain fearing that he would meet "with a disagreeable reception" if he attempted to unload his goods, put about and sailed for home. Reporting the incident, John Hunter Holt noted that "there is reason to expect the speedy arrival of the others laden with goods from Great-Britain" (*Va. Gazette, or the Norfolk Intelligencer,* 5 July 1775). Article 10 of the Continental Association required that any imports arriving after 1 Feb. 1775 "be sent back, without breaking any of the packages thereof" (5 Apr. 1775, n. 1).

Saturday, 22 July 1775

Third Virginia Convention

Proceedings of Fifth Day of Session [1]

Richard Bland Esquire, a Member of this Convention, and one of the Deputies appointed to represent this Colony in General Congress, informed the Convention that certain false and scandalous Reports highly reflecting on him in his publick Character, had been propagated; to wit, that he had made Application to the Earl of Dartmouth or some of the ministry for an Appointment to collect the Taxes imposed on America by Parliament, and that as an Inducement to them to grant the same had promised to promote the Designs of the Ministry against this Country; and also that his Conduct in general Congress had been such, that he was obliged suddenly to decamp from the City of Philadelphia.[2]

That he had served as a Member of the General Assembly for upwards of thirty Years and should hope, that the part he had always publickly taken, would have secured him in his Age, from an Imputation so injurious to his Character. – That he earnestly requested that a full and publick Inquiry should be made into the Truth of the said Reports, and that the revd. Samuel Shield ⟨Sheild⟩ and ⟨the Rev.⟩ John Hurt, Samuel Overton and Joseph Smith, who, he understood, had propagated the said Reports, should be summoned to attend the said Inquiry, and that every other person who had heard any thing of the said Reports would also attend, that the fullest Examination might be made into the Truth thereof.

Resolved, that this Convention will on Friday next, examine into the Truth of the Reports mentioned in the said Information.[3]

Ordered that Mr. Thomas Claiborne be appointed Messenger to this Convention, and that he summon the revd. Samuel Shield & John Hurt, and Samuel Overton & Joseph Smith to attend this Convention on Friday next.

Ordered, that Champion Travis Esq: be added to the Committee appointed to draw up and report an Ordinance for raising and embodying a sufficient force for the Defence of this Colony.[4]

Adjourned till Monday 9 oClock.[5]

> Convention MS journal in hand of John Tazewell
> (Archives Division, Virginia State Library) [6]

Augusta County West: Journal of Captain James Wood

22d July Arrived at Koshocktin at 1 O'Clock⟨.⟩[7] taken to the Council House⟨,⟩ found Many of the Indians drunk and King New Comer a Sleep⟨.⟩ waked the King at Dark and Delivered the following speech to him in the Presence of Winganum Young Killbuck and a Number of other Warriours: *Brothers the Delawares* your Elder Brothers in Virginia in their Great Council have Appointed me to come to this Place in Order to Assure you that their hearts are good towards you⟨,⟩ that they are desirous of brightning the Antient Chain of Freindship[8] between you and them and for which they have Appointed Commissioners to meet you and the other Nations in a General Council at Fort Pitt in 50[9] days from this time when they will be glad to meet the Cheifs of your Nation and will use their best Endeavours to give you a hearty Welcome[10]

Brothers I have heard with great Concern that you have lately been in Council with the French and Wyandots and that you have received a Speech from the French and a belt and String of Black Wampum⟨;⟩ as there has long subsisted the Greatest Freindship between you and us I desire and insist that you will make me Acquainted with any thing which may have been said to you by the French or any others to the Prejudice of your Elder Brothers of Virginia *A String of White Wampum*[11]

> Thwaites and Kellogg, *Revolution on the Upper Ohio, 1775–1777*, pp. 45–47

As Related to Augusta County West Committee

Mr. Wood informs the Committee that at Cushocton, a Delaware Town, on the 22d of July, he delivered a speech to the Chiefs of that place, inviting them to a treaty to be held at Pittsburgh the 10th of September; likewise he informed them that he understood that the Windots and French had lately been to council with them, that they made a speech, and delivered a belt to them, and that he expected from the friendship that has for a long time subsisted between them and their elder brothers, the Virginians, that they would inform him what had passed between them.[12]

> *Dunlap's Pennsylvania Packet, or, the General Advertiser* (Philadelphia), 11 September 1775

Middlesex County Committee

Oath of William Hudgin before Robert Spratt

MIDDLESEX, to wit.
THIS day William Hudgin came before me, and made oath on the Holy Evangelists that John Parsons never had his consent to advertise that James Mills and company had landed any goods from the ship London, Moses Robertson; so far from it, he now deposes that he never saw any thing like goods. All that he told Parsons was, that he saw a flat go out of the creek, but he did not know to what vessel; and further, he deposes, that John Degge[13] was out in the country that night, seven miles, getting sparrs for the schooner Hannah. And further he saith not. Certified this 22d day of July, 1775.

Robert Spratt.[14]

> *Virginia Gazette* (Pinkney), 27 July 1775

And of Gabriel Hudgin

MIDDLESEX, to wit.
THIS day Gabriel Hudgin came before me, and made oath on the Holy Evangelists that he was in the town of Urbanna the 27th day of May, when captain Moses Robertson's ship lay off that harbour, and that he never saw any goods landed from that ship, or any other, by James Mills and company, or any body else. Further, he deposes, that John Degge that night was out in the country, getting sparrs for the schooner Hannah. And further he saith not. Certified this 22d day of July, 1775.[15]

Robert Spratt.

> Ibid., 27 July 1775

1. With the decease of Robert Bolling on the previous day, the number of delegates attending could not have exceeded 106, but because this may have been a "called" session, the number could have been considerably fewer.

2. For the "false and scandalous Reports," see 7 July 1775, and for the attempted justification of them by a propagator, see 12 July 1775, Third Va. Convention, Sheild to Bland. A coloring of truth could be imparted to the picture of Bland's being forced "suddenly to decamp," for he had left Philadelphia and returned to Williamsburg in time to be appointed to several committees of the House of Burgesses on 14 June 1775 (*JHB, 1773–1776*, p. 227). The exact date of his leaving the Congress is not certain. His name does not appear on the journal after 11 May 1775, but it would seem from the date of his arrival in Williamsburg that he stayed until about the 1st of June.

3. "Friday next" was 28 July 1775.

4. With the addition of Travis, the membership of the committee for defense and protection, created on 19 July 1775, with Richard Bland as chairman, was increased to 21, no quorum yet being established.

5. Here again Tazewell blundered. He first wrote "to Morrow," then lined the word through with ink and above it wrote "Monday."

6. Edgewise on the top of the 4th of 4 pages (the 3d of which is blank) Tazewell wrote "No. 5."

7. On 21 July 1775 Captain Wood and Simon Girty resumed their journey "very Early in the Morning." At 1:00 P.M. they arrived at "the Moravian Indian Town," probably Schoenbrunn, and "Examined the Minister (a Dutchman)," perhaps Rev. David Zeisberger. He "Confirmed the Accounts" about the powwow between the Delawares and "the French" (20 July 1775, Third Va. Convention, 2 entries). Six miles farther on Wood and Girty "Passed a small Delaware Town." A Delaware brave joined and rode with them to "New Comers Town," where they encamped, "having travelled about 30 Miles."

On the present day Wood and Girty "set off Early in the Morning" for "Koschoctin," or Coshocton, "the Cheif Town of the Delawares." They "Passed" the presumably absent "White Eyes' Town about 10 O'Clock" (Thwaites and Kellogg, *Rev. on the Upper Ohio*, pp. 44–45).

8. See 19 May 1775, n. 5.

9. The numerals are supplied where Wood left a space blank. In the item next following he set the date for "a treaty" at 10 Sept. 1775 (see 18 July 1775, n. 10).

10. The "Great Council" of Virginia was the Council and House of Burgesses; for the appointment of Wood and the other "Commissioners," see p. 24 above; 9 July 1775, Third Va. Convention, n. on provenance.

11. When Wood referred to a string of "Black" wampum, he meant "purple," the giving of which indicated that the "French and Wyandots" had not yet engaged in conclusive negotiations (20 May 1775, n. 7).

12. The "Answer" of the "King and Cheifs of the Delawares" in the "Council House" would be made the next day, 23 July 1775.

13. William Hudgin and John Degge had gratuitously been designated as signatories to John Parsons's "vindication" of his "character" on 10 July 1775 (Middlesex Co. Committee).

14. Dr. Spratt was sheriff of Middlesex County (18 July 1775, Middlesex Co. Committee, n. 15).

15. Unaware that with this issue of Pinkney's gazette, the last of Parsons's props would walk or be deposed away, the Gloucester County committee on 24 July 1775 was to announce suspension of judgment concerning his charges.

Sunday, 23 July 1775

Third Virginia Convention

Augusta County West: Journal of Captain James Wood

23d of July the King and Cheifs of the Delawares met in the Council House and delivered the following Answer to my Speech of Yesterday⟨:⟩ [1] *Brothers the Bigknife* your Brothers the Delawares are very thankful to you for your good talk to them Yesterday and are glad to find their Brothers hearts are good towards them and that they will be joyfull in meeting them at the time and place you Mention⟨.⟩ Brother in Order to Convince our Elder Brothers of Virginia that we desire to live in freindship with them I now deliver you this Belt and String⟨.⟩[2] they were sent to us by an English Man and French Man at Fort Detroit with a Message that the People of Virginia were determined to strike us⟨,⟩ that they would come upon us two different Ways⟨,⟩ the one by the Way of the Lakes and the other by the Ohio and that the Virginians were determined to drive us off and take our Lands⟨;⟩ that we must be constantly on our Guard and not to give any Credit to whatever you said as you were a people not to be depended upon⟨;⟩ that the Virginians would invite Us to a treaty but we must not go at any rate and to take particular Notice of the Advice they gave which proceeded from Motives of real Freindship and nothing else [3] *Delivers the Belt and String* [4]

> Thwaites and Kellogg, *Revolution on the Upper Ohio, 1775–1777*, pp. 47–48

As Related to Augusta County West Committee

On the 23d of July, Newcomer and some other Delaware Chiefs, delivered him a speech or answer to his of yesterday, in substance as follows:

"Thanking him for his speech, and that they would cheerfully meet the Virginians at the treaty; and to convince their brothers that they desire to live in the strictest friendship with them, they delivered to him a belt and string that was sent to them by an Englishman and a Frenchman from Detroit, with a message informing them, that the people of Virginia are determined to strike them, and that they would come on them two ways, the one by way of the Lakes, and the other by the Ohio, and that the Virginians are determined to drive them off and take their lands from them; and that they must constantly be on their guard, and not pay any regard to what the

Virginians would say to them, as they were a people not to be depended upon; and that the Virginians would invite them to a treaty, that they must not go by any means, and to take particular notice of the advice which they gave."

Dunlap's Pennsylvania Packet, or, the General Advertiser (Philadelphia), 11 September 1775

1. For Captain Wood's "Speech of Yesterday," see 22 July 1775, Third Va. Convention, Augusta Co. West, 2 entries.

The spokesman for the "Cheifs of the Delawares" was probably the "King," Noatwhelama, or NEWCOMER, who had succeeded The Beaver as principal chief of the Delaware tribes in 1772 and was by now a very old man. He had once lived on the banks of the Susquehanna River but in the 1760s had gone with his people, first to the Cuyahoga, then to the Tuscarawas, where he established himself at the town that still bears his English name. That is not to say that he had love for the English. On the contrary, in 1763 he accused them of aspiring to become "too Strong for God himself." But Newcomer was a realist, and he had also to be "Strong," for only by strength and skill could he keep White Eyes and Captain Pipe from plunging the Delawares into an intratribal war over the question of whether to take to the warpath against the whites. If Newcomer had been thus far successful in keeping the peace, it may be attributed to the experience gained in treaty negotiations, for he had attended each of the important ones held on the western waters for the past 15 years (21 May 1775, n. 1; Hodge, *Handbook of Am. Indians*, pt. 2, 65; "Journal of James Kenny, 1761–1763," *Pa. Mag. of Hist. and Biog.*, XXXVII [Apr. 1913], 187; Thwaites and Kellogg, *Rev. on the Upper Ohio*, p. 46 n. 75).

2. Of wampum (20 May 1775, n. 7).

3. The "English Man" remains unidentified. The "French Man" was Duperon Baby (20 July 1775, n. 4). The advice to abstain from further negotiations with the "Virginians" is much in line with that which Lord Dunmore would soon attempt to transmit to White Eyes (6 July 1775, n. 7).

4. The next extract from Wood's journal is under the date heading of 25 July 1775.

Monday, 24 July 1775

Third Virginia Convention

Proceedings of Sixth Day of Session [1]

The President ⟨Peyton Randolph⟩ laid before the Convention a Letter just received from the Deputies appointed to represent this Colony in General Congress inclosing several Resolutions and proceedings of the General Congress which were read and ordered to lie on the Table.[2]

[Resolved, that this Convention will, Tomorrow, proceed to the appointment of a Delegate to represent this Colony in General Congress during the necessary Absence of his Excellency General Washington.

Resolved, that this Convention will proceed, by Ballot in all Appointments.] [3]

Resolved, that no Flour, Wheat or other Grain, or Provisions of any kind be exported from this Colony to any part of the world, from and after the fifth Day of August next, until the Convention or Assembly, or the honorable the Continental Congress, shall order otherwise; that no Quantities of the said Articles more than are necessary for the Use of the Inhabitants be brought to, collected, or stored in the Towns or other Places upon or near the navigable Waters; and that the respective County Committees be directed to take Care that this Resolve be effectually carried into Execution; and that all Contracts made for the Sale and Delivery of any such Article for Exportation between this Time and the tenth Day of September next be considered as null and void. [4]

[Resolved also, that it be recommended to the Inhabitants of this Colony, within five Miles of Tide-Water, not to thresh out more of their Wheat than may from Time to Time be wanted for Home-Consumption; unless the same be imediately removed at least five Miles from any Landing.] [5]

Ordered, that Thomas Walker Esquire be added to the Committee appointed to prepare and report an ordinance for raising and embodying a sufficient force for the Defence & Protection of this Colony. [6]

adjourned til' tomorrow 9. oClock

Convention MS journal in hand of John Tazewell
(Archives Division, Virginia State Library) [7]

Chesterfield County Committee: A Memorial [8]

To the Honorable the Delegates of the Several Counties and Corporations of the Colony and Dominion of Virginia, met in Convention at Richmond.

The Memorial of the Committee of and for the County of Chesterfield
SHEWETH,

That it hath been doubted, whether the company of Volunteers raised for the defense of the Colony in the Several Counties are under the command of the officers of the Militia; and if they are not, it is to be feared, that many inconveniencies may follow, not only from the distinct powers of the two orders, but from one of them assuming an authority independent of any Military Controul by Law established; and that your memorialists have the more reason to apprehend some such inconveniencies, from a late transaction in this County, where a dispute of this kind produced Some disorderly behaviour in a muster-field. [9]

Your memorialists therefore hope that the Convention will take the matter into Consideration and make such regulations therein, as to them in their Wisdom, shall seem meet.

> Signed by order, and in behalf of the Committee for the County of Chesterfield
> BERNARD MARKHAM Chairman, P⟨ro⟩ T⟨empore⟩.[10]

> Recipients' copy, MS document in hand of Jerman Baker, clerk, with Markham's autograph signature, in papers of third Virginia Convention (Archives Division, Virginia State Library)

Gloucester County Committee

Thanks and Suspension of Judgment

AT a meeting of the committee of the county of Gloucester, on monday the 24th of July, it was

Resolved, that the readiness shewn by the volunteers, who marched to the assistance of the lower counties on the late alarms, merits our warmest thanks; and we assure them we should have cheerfully cooperated with them, had it been requisite.[11]

Resolved, that the most cordial thanks of the people of Gloucester county are justly due to the worthy inhabitants of those counties who have generously offered their houses as a retreat to our wives and children, in case they should be obliged to abandon their habitations here below.[12]

Resolved, that the information of John Parsons, John Degge, William Degge, and William Hudgin, was sufficient to induce a suspicion that goods had been landed at Urbanna contrary to the association, and that the vigilance of the gentleman who brought that affair before our committee is highly to be recommended; but as Parsons informs us the material evidences are out of the country at present, we must suspend our judgment till their arrival.[13]

> John Perrin, clerk.

Virginia Gazette (Purdie), 4 August 1775

1. A full attendance by all living delegates who had by this date presumably presented their credentials would establish their number as 106. It is positive, however, that even though no leave of absence is noted in the journals, Spotsylvania County delegate George Stubblefield would within 2 days be serving in his other capacity as captain of a company of volunteers in Williamsburg (MS diary and Revolutionary memoranda of Dr. George Gilmer, Va. Hist. Soc.). The date of his departure from the convention is unknown, but it could scarcely have been later than the present day.

2. For the "Letter" and the "several Resolutions" enclosed, see 11 July 1775. The resolutions enclosed under the heading of "Friday May 26. 1775" had already been received and laid before the convention on 18 July (Procs. and n. 2).

3. The bracketed resolutions were first entered by Tazewell in the manuscript journal and then deleted by running loops of ink through the written lines. The resolutions comport with his entry in the minutes of the day:

"To proceed to choose Delegates tomorrow by ballot in the Room of Genl. Washington

"To proceed in Choice in all Cases by Ballot."

Why Tazewell should have elected to delete from the public record a resolution that was a transaction of this day is indeterminable, but he apparently did so on or after 25 July 1775, when his minutes show the resolution to be "discharged" (Procs. and n. 5).

4. The resolution was one that George Mason on 19 July 1775 had promised to introduce this day (Procs. and n. 1).

5. Withheld, withdrawn, or defeated was Mason's 2d resolution, here bracketed, which, along with the 1st, is in his autograph in the convention loose papers. But passage of only the 1st resolution was itself enough to stir up a storm of protest, the initial blast of which would emanate from the chamber of the Norfolk Borough committee on 28 July 1775.

The "reason of this sudden stoppage," explained an observer to a correspondent in Antigua, "is owing to some of our Scotch Enemys who under the Cloak of clearing for the West Indies have supply'd Gage with provision" (William Reynolds to George Goosley, 28 July 1775, William Reynolds Letter Book, Libr. of Cong., microfilm in Va. State Library).

6. Walker's appointment to the committee created on 19 July 1775, Richard Bland, chairman, raised the membership to 22, with no quorum yet established.

7. Edgewise on the top of the 4th of 4 pages (the 3d of which is blank) Tazewell wrote "No. 6."

8. The "Memorial" is arbitrarily placed. It would be laid before the convention on the next day, 25 July 1775 (Procs., 2d para.).

9. For the lapsing of the militia act and the subsequent embodiment of "Volunteers," see 1 May 1775, n. 4. The committee for Amelia County had suggested that the county lieutenant, erstwhile commander of the county militia, reconstitute the defunct force through cooperation with gentlemen volunteers (3 May 1775 and n. 10). There are available no details respecting "disorderly behaviour in a muster-field" in Chesterfield County. Previously a protest of the Botetourt independent company against "going out of the Colony" had not been allowed to reach public print (26 June 1775, Bedford Co. Committee and n. 6). For obvious reasons, news of the difficulties in Chesterfield County was likewise apparently suppressed; but in view of the fact that on 20 Aug. 1775 certain "Freeholders and Inhabitants" of the latter county would petition the convention in derogation of the unrepresentative nature of the county committee, the "disorderly behaviour" may have had political overtones as well as those of command.

10. The chairman of the Chesterfield County committee was Archibald Cary, this day probably in attendance at the convention.

11. The "late alarms" in the "lower counties" had resulted in pleas for military assistance issued by inhabitants of Williamsburg on 23 and 27 June 1775.

12. The "worthy inhabitants" who through their respective county committees had offered haven to refugees from invasion were those of Cumberland, Buckingham, and Bedford (respectively 17, 22 May, 27 June 1775).

13. For what had already happened to Parson's "material evidences," see 22 July 1775, Middlesex Co. Committee. Any last underpinnings of his allegations was pulled

away with the issuance of Pinkney's *Va. Gazette* of 27 July 1775, which newspaper was unavailable to the members of the Gloucester County committee until 3 days after the present date. Since their resolutions appear in Purdie's paper of 4 Aug. 1775, it is evident that John Perrin forwarded the resolutions on or about the 27th and neglected, or for some reason was unable, to recall them in time. What action the committee took in respect to the discredited Parsons goes unrecorded. In attempted exculpation, he may have sought the last refuge of a scoundrel. But whatever his success or failure before the committee, to Captain Robertson he remained starkly "a Villain of Gloster County" (Frances Norton Mason, ed., *John Norton & Sons, Merchants of London and Virginia: Being the Papers of Their Counting House for the Years 1750 to 1795* [Richmond, 1937], p. 382).

Tuesday, 25 July 1775

Third Virginia Convention

Proceedings of Seventh Day of Session [1]

Ordered, that Archibald Cary, William Cabell⟨, Jr.⟩, Burwell Bassett, John Harvey ⟨Harvie⟩, Jonathan Clarke ⟨Clark⟩, Charles Lewis, Francis Peyton, John Nicholas and Paul Carrington⟨, Esquires,⟩ be added to the Committee appointed to draw up and report an Ordinance for raising and embodying a sufficient Force for the Defence and Protection of this Colony.[2]

A memorial of the Committee for the County of Chesterfield was presented to the Convention and read, setting forth that Doubts had arisen whether the Voluntiers raised for the Defence of this Colony were under the Command of the Officers of the Militia, which were likely to be productive of many Inconveniences, and praying that the same may be taken into Consideration & that such Regulations may be made therein, as will best answer the Design of the Convention in raising the said Voluntiers.[3]

Ordered, that the said Memorial be referred to the Consideration of the Committee appointed to draw up and report an Ordinance for raising and embodying a sufficient force for the Defence & protection of this Colony.[4]

[Order of the Day for choosing a Delegate discharged.] [5]

The Committee to whom the late Treaty with the different Tribes of Indians at pittsburg together with several Resolutions of the Committee on the Western Waters of Augusta County were referred, reported that they had had the same under their Consideration & come to the following Resolutions.[6]

Resolved, that it is the Opinion of this Committee, that the Committee of the County of Augusta have acted with the greatest propriety and prudence, and that the Expences of the Treaty and the Money advanced in Presents to the Indians, ought to be reimbursed by the Public.[7]

Resolved, that it is the Opinion of this Committee, that two Companies of one hundred Men each, besides Officers, ought, with all convenient Speed, to be stationed at Pittsburg, one other Company of one hundred men at Point-Pleasant, twenty five Men at Fort Fincastle, at the Mouth of the W⟨h⟩eeling and that one hundred men be stationed at proper Posts in the County of Fincastle for the protection of the Inhabitants on the southwestern Frontiers exclusive of the Troops to be raised for the Defence of the lower parts of the Country.[8]

Resolved, that the Thanks of this Convention be presented to the Committee on the Western Waters of Augusta for their great Prudence in conducting the Treaty with the Indians and securing the important Fort at Pittsburg.

Ordered, that Patrick Kirk be paid as a publick Express for bringing down the Treaty with the Indians & other proceedings relating thereto, to this Convention.

Resolved, that eleven of the Committee appointed to draw up and report an Ordinance for raising and embodying a sufficient force for the Defence and Protection of this Colony, be a sufficient Number to proceed on Business.[9]

Ordered, that Leave to given to bring in an Ordinance to make Provision for defraying the Expences of the Militia lately drawn out into actual Service and for paying the same, and that Mr. ⟨Isaac⟩ Zane⟨, Jr.⟩ do prepare and bring in the same.[10]

Ordered, that Leave be given to bring in an Ordinance for Regulating the Elections of Delegates & Committees for the several Counties & Corporations in this Colony, and that, Mr. ⟨Archibald⟩ Cary, Mr. ⟨Dudley⟩ Digges, Mr. ⟨Benjamin⟩ Watkins, Mr. ⟨Robert⟩ Lawson, Mr. ⟨John⟩ Ruffin & Mr. ⟨John⟩ Banister do prepare and bring in the same.[11]

Ordered, that Mr. William Dandridge Junr. be appointed Clerk to the Committee appointed to draw up and report an Ordinance for raising and embodying a sufficient force for the Defence and protection of this Colony.[12]

adjourned till Thursday next[13]

Convention MS journal in hand of John Tazewell
(Archives Division, Virginia State Library)[14]

Augusta County West: Journal of Captain James Wood

25th we Arrived at the Seneca Town[15] where we found Logan The Snake the Big Appletree with Several of the Mingoes who were lately Prisoners at Fort Pitt⟨.⟩[16] they all Appeared to be Pretty Much in Liquor and very inquisitive to know my Business⟨;⟩ called them together and made the same speech to them which I had before made to the Delawares⟨.⟩[17] they made no other Answer but they would Acquaint the rest of their Nation with what I had said and discovered that the Indians were very Angry [18]

> Thwaites and Kellogg, *Revolution on the Upper Ohio, 1775–1777*, pp. 48–49

As Related to Augusta County West Committee

That he arrived at a Seneca town the 25th of July, and found Logan there, with some of the Mingoes that were prisoners at Fort Pitt. They all appeared very desirous to know his business, he called them together, and made the same speech to them that he did to the Delawares; they made no other answer than that they would acquaint the rest of the nation with what he had said. These Indians appeared very angry, and behaved with great insolence to him.

> *Dunlap's Pennsylvania Packet, or, the General Advertiser* (Philadelphia), 11 September 1775

Virginia and Pennsylvania Delegates in Congress to Inhabitants on West Side of Laurel Hill

FRIENDS AND COUNTRYMEN   Philadelphia 25 July 1775

It gives us much concern to find that disturbances have arisen and still continue among you concerning the boundaries of our colonies.[19] In the character in which we now address you, it is unnecessary to enquire into the origin of those unhappy disputes, and it would be improper for us to express our approbation or censure on either side: But as representatives of two of the colonies united, among many others, for the defence of the liberties of America, we think it our duty to remove, as far as lies in our power, every obstacle that may prevent her sons from co-operating as vigorously as they would wish to do towards the attainment of this great and important end. Influenced solely by this motive, our joint and our earnest request to you is, that all animosities, which have heretofore subsisted among you as inhabitants of distinct colonies may now give place to generous and concurring efforts for the preservation of every thing that can make our common country dear to us.

We are fully persuaded that you, as well as we, wish to see your differences terminate in this happy issue. For this desireable purpose, we recommend it to you, that all bodies of armed men kept up under either province be dismissed, that all those, who, on either side, are in confinement or under bail for taking a part in the contest be discharged; and that until the dispute be decided every person be permitted to retain his possessions unmolested.[20] By observing these directions the public tranquility will be secured without injury to the titles on either side. The period we flatter ourselves, will soon arrive when this unfortunate dispute, which has produced much mischief, and, as far as we can learn, no good, will be peaceably and constitutionally determined.[21]

We are Your Friends & Countrymen [22]

P. HENRY JR.	JOHN DICKINSON
RICHARD HENRY LEE	GEO: ROSS
BENJA: HARRISON	B. FRANKLIN
TH: JEFFERSON	CHA: HUMPHREYS

> Recipients' copy, MS letter in unidentified hand, with autograph signatures (Peter Force Collection, ser. 9, Library of Congress)

1. With George Stubblefield in Williamsburg (24 July 1775, n. 1), the membership this day could not have exceeded 105 in number.

2. The addition of these 8 members to the committee for defense and protection, established on 19 July 1775 with Richard Bland as chairman, brought the total to 31. Later during this same day (4th para. from end) a quorum would at last be fixed. Unwontedly, Tazewell did not add "Esquires" to the list of new members. Nor in the printed journal does Purdie amend Tazewell, for there, p. 10, the surname of each appointee is preceded by "mr." and the given names of Cabell and Nicholas alone are printed, this to distinguish them from Joseph Cabell and Robert Carter Nicholas respectively.

3. For the "memorial," see 24 July 1775, Third Va. Convention, Chesterfield Co. Committee.

4. To obviate such issues as those raised by the Chesterfield memorial was precisely one of the objectives of the committee in seeking "to melt down" all of the Virginia military land forces into one "great establishment" (19 July 1775, n. 5).

5. The bracketed entry is from Tazewell's minutes for this day. It follows the entry "A Memorial from the County Committee of Chesterfield read & referred to above Com:" and precedes the entry "Resolutions respecting the Treaty & Augusta County read and agreed to." The "Order of the Day" refers to the 2 bracketed resolutions that constitute the 2d and 3d paragraphs of the proceedings of 24 July 1775. The reason for Tazewell's deletion of the paragraphs originally entered on the 24th must remain unknown, except that they were on the present day "discharged."

The reasons for discharge are more easily surmised. With a delegation of 5 deputies left to represent Virginia in Congress, there was no pressing need to elect a replacement for General Washington. The deputies now present in Congress might at any time join the convention and had already pointed out the "propriety of proceeding to a new choice of delegates" (11 July 1775). And combined with these considerations was another, that rules of eligibility for future membership in Congress should be laid down. The devising of such rules would be the 1st order of business on 5 Aug. 1775.

6. The committee to which "the late Treaty" and the "several Resolutions" were referred was that for defense and protection. Probably Richard Bland, the committee chairman, "reported." For the documents in question, see 21 July 1775 and n. 3.

7. A list of claims certified by the Augusta County West committee would be examined by the Committee of Safety on 11 Mar. 1776 and paid in the amount of £565 1s. 2d. (*Cal. Va. State Papers*, VIII, 117).

8. The phrase "the lower parts of the Country" was not intended to designate the

more southern counties but, by moving eastward from mountainous terrain, those counties composing the Piedmont and the Tidewater.

9. That only 11 of a committee of 31 should constitute a "sufficient Number to proceed on Business" is perhaps the 1st hint that all of the delegates who had presumably presented their credentials were not uniformly in attendance. So much would be manifest within 10 days more when on 5 Aug. there would be adopted the "Order" that the roll of members be called on "Wednesday next," or 9 Aug. 1775 (Procs. and n. 4).

10. The "Militia lately drawn out into actual Service" were those units and individuals participants in Dunmore's War of 1774. The failure of the General Assembly to provide for the payment of claims made no less pressing the demands of creditors, of incapacitated soldiers and their dependents, or of necessitous widows and orphans. In the convention loose papers the original manuscript motion begins with "Leave to bring" and concludes with "paying the same." It appears to be in the hand of William Fitzhugh of King George County.

But most certainly Isaac Zane, Jr., emphatically instructed on 27 May 1775 by the Frederick County committee to exert his "influence" toward procuring "adequate satisfaction" from the "Assembly," had continued his exertions in the convention. His appointment was therefore natural. On 29 July 1775 3 colleagues would be appointed to assist him in preparing an ordinance (Procs. and n. 6).

11. In the ordinance ultimately passed on 25 Aug. 1775 (p. 489 below), the time for elections was definitely set "in the month of April annually, on the several days appointed by law for the holding of the county or corporation courts respectively" (*Statutes at Large*, IX, 54). In this fashion was forfended such an election as had been held and challenged in Berkeley County, where Adam Stephen had set the date and the time to accord with his own interests. It may have been of significance that of the committee now appointed Cary and Digges were also members of the committee "of priviledges & Elections" (21 July 1775, Procs. and n. 6). It was probably Cary who introduced the proposed "Ordinance" on 12 Aug. 1775 (Procs. and nn. 8, 9).

12. Dandridge was the only committee clerk "appointed" by the convention.

13. The setting of adjournment "till Thursday next," 27 July 1775, undoubtedly resulted from the desirability of giving the committees, of which 5 were now sitting, more time for their labors.

14. Edgewise at the bottom of the 4th of 4 pages Tazewell wrote "No. 7."

15. Captain Wood and Simon Girty arrived around 5:00 P.M. this day at the "Seneca Town" following 3 days of hard riding on a westerly course well in excess of 100 miles. For the Senecas and their intermingling with the Mingoes, see 5 July 1775, n. 3. Exact location of the town is not possible, but it appears to have been on the trail between Wapatomica and Upper Sandusky in present-day Hardin County, Ohio (Thwaites and Kellogg, *Rev. on the Upper Ohio*, pp. 48–49 n. 77; Draper MSS, 2BB2–3, State Hist. Soc. of Wis.).

16. For the Indians "lately Prisoners at Fort Pitt," see 19 May 1775, n. 3. They had been "delivered up" by Maj. John Connolly at the fort on 29 June 1775 (Third Va. Convention and n. 8).

17. For the "same Speech," see 22 July 1775, Third Va. Convention, Augusta Co. West.

18. So "Angry" were some of them that they painted themselves black, the symbol of death, and plotted the assassination of the white emissaries. Warned "privately" by a squaw, Wood and Girty spent the hours before dawn hiding in the forest. Early the next morning they returned to meet Logan, who gave them assurances of safety and

related how in 1773 his family had been murdered and he had exacted revenge. This tale of woe the chief "repeated in Plain English" as he "wept and Sung Alternately" (Thwaites and Kellogg, *Rev. on the Upper Ohio*, pp. 49–50). Wood and Girty then left for the Wyandot villages. The next extract from the journal is under the date heading of 27 July 1775, Third Va. Convention, Augusta Co. West.

19. For the background of the Virginia-Pennsylvania boundary dispute and the most recent of many "disturbances" that had "arisen" therefrom, see 22 June 1775, n. 2. For a rancorous exchange of letters between the Augusta County West committee and that of Westmoreland County, Pa., see 29 June 1775, Third Va. Convention, Augusta Co. West, 2d entry; 3 July, same, 2d and 3d entries. Copies of those letters supposedly had been forwarded by the Pennsylvanians "to the Continental Congress," but whether the letters arrived or, if so, arrived in time for consideration by the "Delegates" preparatory to the writing of the present letter is uncertain.

What the delegates are known to have considered, and what was ostensibly the cause for the dispatch of the present item, was a petition from "several Persons in that part of the County of *Augusta*, which is on the West side of the *Allegany* Mountain." This document Congress received on 1 June 1775 and referred to "the delegates of the colonies of Virginia and Pennsylvania" (16 May 1775, Augusta Co. West Committee, Petition; *JCC*, II, 76).

20. For the very purpose of preserving "public tranquility," the Virginia Convention in less than 2 weeks (7 Aug. 1775) would direct that a company of 100 men take possession of Fort Pitt. And John Proctor the while would continue to march his regiment of Westmoreland County volunteers under a banner on which was emblazoned a rattlesnake and the motto "Don't Tread on Me" (Hassler, *Old Westmoreland*, pp. 15–16). There is no evidence that anyone "on either side" was at this time in confinement, but though for the nonce on the frontier there was a reign of peace, none could predict its duration.

21. How the controversy might be "constitutionally determined," except by the reestablishment of royal authority on a basis acceptable to the colonists posed a question not immediately answerable. John Randolph in July 1774 had laid a finger on the problem. There was only one British imperial constitution, and colonial border disputes could be properly adjudicated if the "Mother Country" alone exercised the "controuling Power." Left to themselves, the colonies might well be precipitated "into Hostilities," and the "transmontane Inhabitants," who were generally "a robust hardy Set of Men, used to Arms, and not very passive in their Tempers," were most likely to set off such conflicts (*Rev. Va.* II, 210–11). There was no American intercolonial constitution. Nor could there be one until time, custom, and precedents should combine to form one, or men write and the colonies adopt one. As matters stood, the colonies were thrown into a loose confederation of embassies met in a Congress that exercised no power beyond that of moral suasion. In instances the suasion might gather great force, but hardly enough to soar beyond the top of "the *Allegany* Mountain."

22. Approximately a half of the regular delegates from each of the 2 colonies signed the present letter. Peyton Randolph (with Jefferson his substitute) and Richard Bland were in Richmond. George Washington was at "the military school before Boston." Edmund Pendleton had left Philadelphia for Virginia on 22 July (Burnett, *Letters Cont. Cong.*, I, 171). Of the Pennsylvanians, both Edward Biddle and John Morton during this week were seriously ill; Thomas Mifflin had forsaken the senate for the battlefield; and Thomas Willing, later to be described as a "Constant attendant on Congress," appears on this particular day to have been unconstant (ibid., I, 154, 175, 199).

Wednesday, 26 July 1775

Third Virginia Convention

Officers of Gentlemen Volunteers of Independent Companies in
Williamsburg to President and Gentlemen of Convention
An Address, with Enclosure

Williamsburg July 26. 1775.

Mr President and Gentlemen of the Convention:

We the Officers of the several Volunteer Companies here assembled, beg leave to inform you, that this day on Mature deliberation, it was resolved in Council immediately to secure all the publick Monies, in the hands of the Receiver General, Naval Officers, and other Collectors for his Majesty. Mr Robert Prentis in consequence of our requisition, hath rendered an Account on Oath, by which there Appears to be in his Hands £317.14.2½. as Clerk to the Receiver General; and has engaged on Oath, that he will neither directly, or indirectly, pay away any part thereof, or any sum that he may hereafter Collect without your direction. And that, you may be fully informed of our proceedings, we have thought proper, to inclose you, a Copy of his Affidavit, together with Copies of what Instructions to the Officers of the several Detachments, who are ordered to wait on the Receiver General, Naval Officers, and other Collectors, to secure the Monies of the Crown in their Hands; till we could receive an answer from you relative thereto.[1]

This Step would not have been taken, without first obtaining your Concurrence, could we have thought the Circumstances of the case did not require an immediate procedure; but when we acquaint you, that this day we received Intelligence, that J. Earnshaw[2] one of his Majestys Comptrollers, has lately sent a very considerable sum of the Publick Money, on board the Fowey; that from the best information, we think it more than probable, the other Crown Officers, would soon follow his example, and believe any kind of delay, would be dangerous, and tend to defeat our purpose for these reasons, we hope to meet with your Approbation, and do assure you shall readily submit to your determination of this, and every other matter where you shall interpose.[3]

We are very respectfully Gent.

Your most obedient Servants

PS. Since writing the above we are informed   CHAS SCOTT[4]
that a Vessell belonging to a Man of War has   FRANK EPPES
lately carried off from the Naval Office at   RICHD K MEADE
Hampton all the Money in that Office   HUM: HARWOOD

amounting to upwards of Nine hundred Pounds which is sent to Boston. From want of time we can not give you our whole proceedings at present as intended.

HENRY TAYLOR
SA HARWOOD
GEORGE GILMER
WILIM. DUVALL
BEN. BLUNT
O. TOWLES
HENRY WESTBROOKE

> Recipients' copy, MS letter in hand of Francis Eppes, with autograph signatures, in loose papers of third Virginia Convention (Archives Division, Virginia State Library)

I Robert Prentis do hereby most solemnly swear before God & on the Sacred Evangelist that the Sum of three hundred seventeen Pounds fourteen Shillings & 2½ is all the Publick Money that I have on Hand as clerk to the Honble. Richard Corbin Esqr. Receiver General, & that I will not directly or indirectly pay away any Sum that I have at present by me or may hereafter collect, but to such purposes as shall be directed by the convention on pain of confiscation of my whole Estate & being treated as a Traytor to this Continent.

Sworn to by Robt. Prentis [5] before me this 26. Day of July

Copy   JOSEPH HORNSBY [6]

> Document MS transcript in hand of Joseph Hornsby, in loose papers of third Virginia Convention (Archives Division, Virginia State Library)

1. No copies of the "Instructions" are among the convention loose papers. In light of the postscript to the present letter, it is probable that copies were not forwarded with the other "proceedings."

2. Since Feb. 1769 John Earnshaw had been "Collector of the Duties on Skins and Furs" (*Exec. Journs. Coun. Col. Va.*, VI, 313).

3. Newspaper accounts of these events suggest that the actions were taken in response to "Information" received this day that "a man of war's people carried off a sum of money from the custom-house at Hampton" (e.g., *Va. Gazette* [Dixon and Hunter], 29 July 1775). But as the postscript to the present letter indicates, the news of that action reached the officers after they had commenced execution of their plans. And the plans were formulated and adopted because of the monotony shared with Lt. George Gilmer, who was champing at the bit after 2 weeks of remaining "totally inactive" at the bivouac in Waller's Grove just east of Williamsburg. "We appear rather invited to feast than to fight," he grumbled, and to remedy the ennui of a campaign "without action," he suggested "laying hands on all his Majesties money immediately which proposal was readily agreed to" (MS diary and Revolutionary memoranda of Dr. George Gilmer, Va. Hist. Soc.).

On receipt of this letter and its enclosure, the convention on 28 July 1775 would "immediately resolve itself into a Committee to take the said Letter into their Consideration" (Procs. and nn. 7–8).

4. Signatories not heretofore identified as to place of residence are Humphrey Harwood of Williamsburg, Samuel Harwood of Charles City County, Oliver Towles of Spotsylvania County, and Henry Westbrooke, probably of Southampton County.

5. Clerk to Receiver General Richard Corbin for at least 2 years, Prentis was less reluctant than would be his superior in cooperating with the gentlemen volunteers (see 29 July 1775, Third Va. Convention, 2d and 3d entries). Prentis's family ties permitted him to accommodate his views to patriotism with easy grace; his cousin Joseph Prentis, for example, would represent Williamsburg as an alternate delegate in the fourth Virginia convention, of 1 Dec. 1775–20 Jan. 1776. And in proof of the regard in which he was held by patriot worthies, Robert Prentis would in an ordinance passed by the third convention be designated an "overlooker of the press" in the emission of "treasury notes," and erelong by the court of York County an appraiser "in Current Money" of "the Slaves and Personal Estate of Peyton Randolph Esqr." (*Exec. Journs. Coun. Col. Va.*, VI, 525; *Col. Va. Reg.*, p. 207; *Statutes at Large*, IX, 68; York County, Va. Records, Order Book no. 4, 1774–84, microfilm in Va. State Library, p. 110).

6. Joseph Hornsby, a Williamsburg merchant, had been a justice of the peace for York County since Jan. 1774 (York County, Va. Records, Judgments and Orders, 1772–74, microfilm in Va. State Library, p. 473).

Thursday, 27 July 1775

Third Virginia Convention

Proceedings of Eighth Day of Session [1]

Resolved, that this Convention will tomorrow resolve itself into a Committe to take under Consideration the State of the Colony.[2]

[A Letter from Oconestoto the great Indian Warrior was laid before the Convention and read. Ordered that the said Letter be referred to the Committee appointed to draw up & report an Ordinance for raising and embodying a sufficient force for the Defence & protection of this Colony.][3]

[President to transmit Copies of the Resoln. respectg: Provisions &c to Maryland, No. Carolina & the Genl. Congress & to printers.][4]

Ordered that the Letter from the Deputies appointed to represent this Colony in General Congress together with the papers inclosed therein be referred to the Committee appointed to take under Consideration the State of the Colony.[5]

The Committee to whom the Petition of sundry Inhabitants of the County of Berk⟨e⟩ley was referred reported,[6] that they had had the same under their Consideration agreed upon a Report and come to a Resolution thereupon, which was read, and afterwards delivered in at the Clerk's Table, where the same was again read & agreed to by the Convention, as follows.

It appears to your Committee, that Colonel Adam Stephen with the Approbation of some of the Committee, of the County of Berkley, caused Notice to be given, appointed a Day for the Election of Delegates to represent the said County in General Convention, and that such Notice was published about ten Days before the Day of Election, but was not generally known by the Inhabitants of the said County, it appearing to your Committee that the Inhabitants of two Precincts of the said County were almost wholly unacquainted therewith, and therefore did not attend on the Day of Election; it also appears to your Committee, that Colo. Adam Stephen who was Commander in Chief of the said County, had previous to his appointing the Day of Election of Delegates, ordered a general Muster of the Militia on the same Day, at which a considerable Number of People attended, and were exercised, and kept under Arms for several hours, and were then marched directly to the Courthouse, and proceeded immediately to vote for Delegates to represent the said County in General Convention.

Resolved, that it is the Opinion of this Committee, that the Election of Delegates for the County of Berkley was irregular, and that the Freeholders of the said County after due and regular Notice being publicly given, ought to proceed to a new Election of Delegates to represent them in General Convention.[7]

[adjourned till 9 oClock tomorrow.] [8]

"A Letter from Oconestoto the great Indian Warrior was laid before the Convention & read.

Ordered, that the said Letter together with the other Papers relative to Indian Affairs be referred to the Committee appointed to take into Consideration the State of the Colony." [9]

adjourned

Convention MS journal in hand of John Tazewell
(Archives Division, Virginia State Library) [10]

Peyton Randolph to Delegates of
Maryland Provincial Convention [11]

Gent.   Richmond in Virga. July 27. 1775.

The Convention of Delegates for this Colony now sitting, have almost unanimously, come to the inclosed Resolution for stopping the Exportation of all kinds of Provisions after the 5th day of next month.

At this Time when the most secret Arts are practising to furnish our Enemies with the means of protracting the unhappy Dispute with the Mother Country, the Necessity of adopting this Measure appeared so evident, that this Colony have chearfully sacrificed a very considerable part of its property by agreeing to this Resolution.

I am directed to transmit the Resolution to you as early as possible, & have no doubt but you will as chearfully come to a similar one.[12]

> I am, with great Respect, Yr mo: obt St.
> PEYTON RANDOLPH
> President of the Convention

Recipients' copy, MS letter, in hand of John Tazewell, with Randolph's autograph signature (Red Book, X, 2, Maryland Hall of Records)

Augusta County West: Journal of Captain James Wood

27th July [13] at One O'Clock the Wyandots sent to my Camp to Inform me the Cheifs were Arrived and ready at their Council House to hear what I had to say to them and that two of the Tawaas [14] were there and would be ready to Carry my speech to their Nation⟨.⟩ went to the Council House and delivered the following Speech to the Wyandots and Tawaas

Brothers the Wyandots and Tawaas your Brothers of Virginia in their great Council [15] desirous of brightening the Chain of Freindship [16] between you and them have Appointed Commissioners to meet the Cheifs of the different Nations of Indians on the Ohio and Lakes at Fort Pitt in forty six days from this time and have ordered me to come to this place to Assure you that their Hearts are good towards you and that they hope to agree upon a peace with all the Indians⟨,⟩ so their children and ours may hereafter live in Greatest Friendship⟨,⟩ to give you a kind Invitation to their Council fire and that they will Endeavor to give you a hearty welcome⟨.⟩ *Brothers* It is with Great Concern I have lately heard that some people who I consider to be enemies as well to you as to us have endeavoured to make your Nations believe that the People of Virginia intended to strike you⟨.⟩ [17] this you may be Assured is the Greatest falsity as I can with truth assure you that they desire to live in Strict Freindship with all Indians while they continue peaceable with us

Brothers the Tawaas It is with great pleasure I have the Opportunity in the name of my Countrymen to return you thanks for the kind Treatment given by your Nation to one of our young Brothers who was delivered into your hands last Summer by the Shawanese and to Assure you that if any of your people should ever fall into our hands they will meet with the same freindly treatment [18] *A String of White Wampum Each* [19]

The War Post [20] then Answered *Brother the Big Knife* We have heard what you have said and desire time till to Morrow afternoon to consider it when we will meet you again in the Council house [21]

In the afternoon War Post and five or six other Indians came to my Camp⟨.⟩ they said that they always Understood that the English had but one King who lived over the Great Water⟨,⟩ that they were Much Surprized to hear that we were at War with ourselves and that there had been several

Engagements at Boston in which a great Number of Men were killed on both sides⟨,⟩ that as he had been told many different Stories they would be glad to know the Cause of the dispute or whether we Expected or desired their Assistance⟨.⟩ I then began and gave them a true and just Account from the beginning of the disputes with Great Britain and Assured them that we did not stand in need of or desire any Assistance from them or any other Nation but that we wished them to Continue in peace and freindliness with us by Observing a Strict neutrality as we had not the least doubt that all differences between ourselves would be soon Accomodated⟨.⟩ at the same time I made them Acquainted with the great Unanimity among the Americans and that they were now become so strong as not to fear any power on the face of the Earth⟨.⟩ In this Conversation I discovered that the Huron Indians [22] had been led to beleive that the People of Virginia were a different and distinct Nation from the other Colonies and that by going to War with us they need not fear the Interposition of the other Colonies⟨.⟩ this I think I Effectually removed by making them Acquainted with the Proceedings of the Continental Congress and that the Colonies were bound and Obliged to defend each other against Attacks from Whatever Quarter they might come⟨.⟩ these Questions were likewise put to me at other times by the Shawanese Delawares Mingoes and Tawaas and Answered in the same Manner

> Thwaites and Kellogg, *Revolution on the Upper Ohio, 1775–1777*, pp. 50–52

As Related to Augusta County West Committee

That on the 27th he delivered a speech to the Indians at the Windots town, which was as follows:

"Brothers, the Windots and Tawaas,

"Your brothers of Virginia, in their great council, are desirous of brightening the chain of friendship between you and them; they have appointed commissioners to meet the chiefs of the different nations of Indians on the Ohio and the Lakes, at Fort Pitt, in forty-six days from this time; and have ordered me to come to this place, to assure you that their hearts are good towards you, and that they hope to agree upon a peace with all the Indians, so that their children and ours may hereafter be in the greatest friendship, to give you a kind invitation to their council fire, and they will give you a hearty welcome. Brothers, it is with great concern I have lately heard that some people, whom I consider to be enemies as well to you as to us, have endeavoured to make you believe that the people of Virginia intend to strike your nation; this you may depend upon is the greatest falsity, as I can, with truth assure you, that they desire to live in strict friendship with all Indians, while they continue to live peaceable with us."

"Brothers the Tawaas,

"It is with great pleasure I take this opportunity of speaking to you in the name of my countrymen, to return you thanks for the kind treatment given by your nation to one of our young brothers, who was delivered into your hands, last summer, by the Shawanese, and to assure you that if any of your people should ever fall into our hands, they will meet with friendly treatment."

To which the War Post returned the following answer:

"Brothers, the Big Knife,

"We have heard what you have said, and desire time till to-morrow afternoon to consider of it, when we will meet you in the Council House at the time mentioned."

The War Post, with six others, came to his camp. They told him they came to talk with him as friends; that they always understood the English had but one King, who lived over the great river, that they were much surprised lately to hear that we were at war with ourselves, and that we had several engagements at Boston, where a great many men were killed on both sides; and as they had heard many different stories, they would be glad to hear and know the truth. Captain Wood then explained to them the nature of the disputes, and acquainted them of the general union of all the Colonies, and undeceived them in an error he found the Wiondots had been led into, viz. that the Virginians were a people distinct from the other Colonies.

> *Dunlap's Pennsylvania Packet, or, the General Advertiser* (Philadelphia), 11 September 1775

Isle of Wight County Committee

Tar, Feathers, Depositions, and Recantation

At a Committee held for Isle of Wight County the twenty seventh day of July in the year of our Lord Christ One thousand seven hundred and seventy five.[23] PRESENT The Reverend Henry John Burges⟨s⟩ in the Chair,[24] Brewer Godwin, Richard Hardy, Thomas Peirce, John Day, John Mallory, Goodrich Willson ⟨Wilson⟩, Arthur Smith, Nathaniel Burwell, Timothy Tynes, John Driver, Henry Pitt, Edmund Godwin, Jethro Gale, and Thomas Smith, Gent.

George Purdie Gent. Summnd. before the Committee &c.

George Purdie Merchant in the Town of Smithfield in this County having been charged at a former meeting of this Committee with violating the continental association and being Summoned to appear here this day to Answer the said charges, he informed the Committee by Letter[25] that he would willingly attend, but had been informed that he was to be Tarred and Feathered

Guilty or not Guilty, for which reasons he beged the protection of the Committee as the only power he could appeal to. Whereupon the Committee appointed three of their Members to wait on Mr. Purdie with the following Messuage, to wit, The Committee of the County of Isle of Wight grant Protection to Mr. Purdie provided he appears innocent, and would be glad of his personal attendance, if not they request him to give up the Author of the report refered to in his letter, that the people of this County would Tarr and feather him Guilty or not Guilty; In Answer to which Mr. Purdie begs the Committee will excuse his personal attendance at present and would be glad to know the particular charges alledged against him; In Answer to their request to be informed of the Author or Authors of the report attended in his letter he informs the Committee that Mrs. Purdie acquainted him with it from some of her acquaintants.

Gabriel Gibbs's Depsn. – – – – – –

The deposition of Gabriel Gibbs of full Age taken concerning a charge exhibited against Mr. George Purdie, being first Sworn on the Holy Evangelists of Almighty God deposeth and saith that he purchased of the said Purdie three or four yards of Crown Roles [26] for which he gave him one Shilling Current money of Virginia per yard, and further saith not.

James Peden's Deposition – – – –

The deposition of James Peden of full Age concerning a charge exhibited against Mr. George Purdie, being first Sworn on the Holy Evangelists of Almighty God deposeth and saith that he purchased of the said Purdie two yards of Crown Roles for which he gave one shilling current money per yard, and that he also purchased of the said Purdie three Scanes [27] of thread for which he gave one shilling current money and further saith not.

Wm. Flake's Depo: – – – – – –

The deposition of William Flake of full Age taken concerning a charge exhibited against Mr. George Purdie, being first Sworn on the Holy Evangelist of Almighty God deposeth and saith that he heard the said Purdie say that every person who signed the Continental association would be sent for to England and hanged, that he the said Purdie would never signe the said association unless compelled by force, thereto, for that he had known a number of people hanged at home for signing associations, whereupon this deponent refused to sign the association for some time 'till at length he was applyed to by John Scarsbrook Wills, Gent. who informed him this deponent that no danger could happen to him for signing the said association, that the said Wills would venture to be hanged for him this deponent if he was ever called upon for signing as aforesaid and thereupon this deponent did signe the said association, and further saith not.

The Depo: of John Driver	The deposition of John Driver of full Age taken concerning a charge exhibited against Mr. George Purdie, being first Sworn on the Holy Evangelists of Almighty God deposeth and saith that he was some time ago in Mr. Purdie's Store and that he saw a Lady (who he does not now recollect) purchase some pins in the said Store for which she gave one shilling and six pence or three shillings per paper Current money and at the same time he this deponent purchased the same kind of pins for seven pence halfpenny per paper current money, and further saith not.
The Depo: of Richd. Hardy Gent. ------	The deposition of Richard Hardy Gent. of full Age taken concerning a charge exhibited against Mr. George Purdie, being first Sworn on the Holy Evangelists of Almighty God deposeth and saith that the said Purdie acknowledged that he had violated the continental association by selling Needles at a double price, and further saith not.
Geor: Purdie & a o2. to be Sumd. &c. --------	Resolved that Brewer Godwin, Thomas Peirce, Thomas Smith, Arthur Smith and Jethro Gale or any one of them do Summon George Purdie, Robert Tynes, and John Sym to appear at the next Committee then and there to Answer Sundry complaints lodged against them.[28]
John Sterling [to] be Sumd. &c.	Resolved that the above mentioned Gent. or any one of them do Summon John Sterling to appear at the next Committee then and there to answer Sundry complaints lodged against him.
John Armstrong's Recantation	John Armstrong personally appeared in committee this day and made his recantation, which is in the words following, to wit, "Having made use of expressions inimical to the Interest of North America, I take this method publickly to declare that the said Words were spoke without consideration, and that I should think my self guilty of the greatest ingratitude in acting against a Country, in which I have been treated with the greatest Humanity and obtained a livelihood by the generosity of the Inhabitants. I am sincerely sorry that I have forfeited the esteme of the good people of this Country and

hope that my future behaviour will be such as to gain their good opinion. John Armstrong." Whereupon the said John Armstrong signed the Continental association.

Ordered that the Committee be adjourned 'till the 7th. day of August next at 10. o.Clock.[29]

The Minutes of these proceedings were signed.[30]

> Committee MS minutes in hand of Francis Young, clerk (Office of county clerk of Isle of Wight County)

1. With George Stubblefield probably still in Williamsburg (24 July 1775, n. 1), attendance this day could not have exceeded 105.

2. The convention had resolved on 19 July 1775 to sit on "Friday next," 21 July, as a committee to consider the "State of the Colony," but although the order of the day had since that time been constantly "put off," John Tazewell made no notation of the fact in either manuscript journal or minutes.

3. The bracketed paragraph was entered by Tazewell in the manuscript journal, then lined through with ink. Although he thereby deleted from the public record a genuine transaction, transference of Oconestoto's "Letter" toward the end of the day to the Committee on the State of the Colony evidently decided the clerk against making repetitious entries.

4. This 2d bracketed entry is drawn from Tazewell's minutes for this day. It follows the entry "Com: on State of Colony revived & Letter & Incd. papers from Delegates referred thereto—tomorrow." and precedes the entry "Letter from Indians &c. refd. to Committee of the whole." In his extremely sparse minutes for 27 July 1775 Tazewell did not even notice the report of the committee "of priviledges & Elections" on affairs in Berkeley County. The "Resoln." in question was George Mason's of 24 July 1775 (q.v.). For the president's covering letter transmitting a copy of the resolution, see the item next following.

5. The "Letter" with its enclosures had been "received" and "read and ordered to lie on the Table" at the opening of the 6th day of session, 24 July 1775.

6. The committee had been constituted on 21 July 1775. It was probably Dudley Digges, the committee chairman, who "reported," but the manuscript from which he read (the same being now in the convention loose papers) may be in the hand of Charles Carter of Lancaster County.

7. The committee resolution was "agreed to by the Convention," after having been "again twice read," Purdie in the printed journal, p. 12, correcting Tazewell's omission of one step in the parliamentary process. When Stephen went down, he took with him his colleague, Robert Rutherford, whose connivance in the irregularity of the Berkeley County election had never been asserted (he would be back at the next session of the convention, his record vindicated). The unseating of these 2 delegates reduced to 104 the number of those who could be present at any one time. There would be no more work for a committee "of priviledges & Elections" during the remainder of the session.

8. Tazewell penned in the journal the entry here bracketed, then drew a line of ink through the words. Toward the end of the session a resolution was evidently successfully offered from the floor that the "Letter from Oconestoto" and "the other

Papers relative to Indian Affairs" be transferred to the Committee on the State of the Colony.

9. Tazewell may have enclosed the 2 paragraphs within quotation marks as containing business of a repetitious nature, but is it fairly obvious that there was no need that Ononestoto's letter should again have been "read." In the printed journal, p. 13, Purdie does not reproduce the quotation marks and concludes with the notation "Adjourned till to-morrow, 9 o'clock." As an "order of the day," consideration of Indian affairs was not to be taken up until 11 Aug. 1775.

10. At the top of the 4th of 4 pages Tazewell wrote "No. 8."

11. Randolph signed the present letter in compliance with the 2d bracketed entry above.

12. Randolph was also directed to forward copies of the Mason nonexportation resolution to "No. Carolina & the Gen. Congress," but those letters have not been found. A copy of the resolve in the hand of Tazewell, with Randolph's autograph signature, is filed with the present letter, and another, which may have been that sent to Congress, is in the Simon Gratz Autograph Collection in the Historical Society of Pennsylvania. For the less-than-cheering reply to the present letter, see 1 Aug. 1775, Third Va. Convention, Tilghman to Convention.

13. Having left Logan "at 9 O'Clock in the Morning" of 26 July 1775, Captain Wood and Simon Girty "travelled very fast and Constant" until at 7:00 P.M. they reached the Wyandot town at Upper Sandusky and from there "sent off Runners to the Cheifs who were distant about twenty Miles" (Thwaites and Kellogg, *Rev. on the Upper Ohio*, p. 50).

14. Sometimes called Tawaas, these Indians of the Algonquin family were more correctly Ottawas. They were intertribal traders in the upper St. Lawrence River Valley and around the Great Lakes. They had been and continued friendly to the French, who reciprocated because it was the diplomatic and safe thing to do. In actuality the French thought the Ottawas rude, cruel, barbaric, and probably cannibalistic. Pontiac had been the Ottawas' last great leader. On the morrow Wood was to designate the 2 Tawaas by name—Ninnis and Mangagata—but neither on the present day nor the next did he record whether, as was the Ottawa custom in warm weather, they came naked to the council house (Hodge, *Handbook of Am. Indians*, pt. 2, 167–71).

15. The "Brothers of Virginia in their great Council" were the members of the governor's Council and House of Burgesses.

16. See 19 May 1775, n. 5.

17. Wood had several times heard of the machinations of the British commandant at Fort Detroit, most "lately" on 23 July 1775 from the "King and Cheifs of the Delawares."

18. One "of our young Brothers" was probably Ezekiel Field (Thwaites and Kellogg, *Rev. on the Upper Ohio*, p. 51 n. 81).

19. See 20 May 1775, n. 7.

20. THE WAR POST was the title of Chief Orontony, also called Rowtundee. He held what appears to have been a hereditary position of war chief of the Porcupine tribe of Wyandots. Of uncertain age, he was yet young enough to be restive under the stern discipline of the powerful Half King, Petawontakas (who would speak at the treaty at Fort Pitt in the following September), for The War Post was probably already suspicious of the "smooth Tongued" Virginians (Draper MSS, 11U34-36, State Hist. Soc. of Wis.; Louise Phelps Kellogg, ed., *Frontier Advance on the Upper Ohio, 1778–1779* [Madison, Wis., 1916], pp. 192 and n. 7, 200).

21. Q.v.

22. The Huron name had earlier been given to the Wyandots by the French (4 July 1775, n. 7).

23. The last recorded meeting of the Isle of Wight County committee had been on 3 June 1775, at which time adjournment was set to 19 June. But of that intermediate meeting there is no extant record, and it may be presumed that the proceedings alluded to in the minutes of the present day as having taken place at "a former meeting" were those of the 19th.

24. The committee chairman was John Scarsbrook Wills, absent to attend the convention in Richmond.

25. Not found.

26. Probably "Rolls."

27. "Scane" is an obsolete form of "skein," which is approximately 117 inches in length. Hence Peden purchased a little under 10 yards.

28. There being no minutes for the meeting of the "next Committee," recourse must be had to other records to determine Purdie's fate. To all appearances he was acquitted, for he continued to be a merchant of consequence in the county, remained a justice of the peace, and in Feb. and Mar. 1776 would be selling small quantities of supplies to the patriot armed forces ([Lyon G. Tyler], ed., "Isle of Wight County Records," *Wm. and Mary Qtly.*, 1st ser., VII [Apr. 1899], 269, 272, 280; *Cal. Va. State Papers*, VIII, 100, 103).

29. With the minutes for this day the manuscript records of the Isle of Wight County committee end. That is not to say that lethargy hereafter blanketed the county. To the contrary. John Pinkney in less than a month would "hear" that "a number of respectable inhabitants of Isle of Wight" had cooperated vigorously with the committee of Nansemond County, for the reporting of which cooperation see 24 Aug. 1775, Isle of Wight Co.

30. Contrary to his custom, Francis Young did not copy below the word "signed" the signature of the presiding officer for the day.

Friday, 28 July 1775

Continental Congress

Resolutions of Continental Congress respecting Manufacture of Saltpeter

Whereas the safety and freedom of every community depends upon having the means of defence in its own power, and that the United Colonies may not, during the continuance of their present important contest for Liberty, nor in any future time, be under the expensive, uncertain and dangerous necessity of relying on foreign importations for Gun Powder: And it being very certain from observation and experiment, that Salt Petre is to be obtained in great abundance from most parts of this Northern Continent; that the surface of the earth, in long used tobacco warehouses and their yards, or of common tobacco houses, is particularly and strongly impregnated with Nitre.

Resolved, That it be recommended to the Provincial Conventions of the tobacco Colonies, that as quickly as may be, they appoint one or more manufactories on each river, contiguous to the great inspections, and under the direction of persons qualified by their skill and diligence to bring this important business to a speedy and successful issue.

To the Assemblies and Conventions of the other Colonies, it is recommended immediately to put in practice such other mode of making Salt Petre, as may be found best adapted to their respective circumstances.

That all persons may be encouraged to apply themselves to the manufacture of Salt Petre, it is recommended to the several Assemblies and Conventions, to buy up, on account of the United Colonies, all the good and merchantable Salt Petre at *half a dollar* for each pound, that is, or shall be made in their respective Colonies before the first day of October, 1776.

It is recommended that the collecting Sulphur be encouraged: – And it is recommended to the several Provincial Conventions, to grant such premiums, for the refining of Sulphur in their respective Provinces, as may be judged proper.

And it is further recommended to the several Assemblies and Conventions, that they cause mills to be erected, and skilful persons to be procured and employed for making Gun Powder.

As Salt Petre is an article so necessary for defence, and in other respects, so extensively useful, it is an object that not only requires the public patronage, but demands the attention of individuals: – The following systems or methods of making Salt-Petre, suited to different circumstances and different materials, is recommended to the attention of the good people of the United Colonies.[1]

W. C. Ford, *Journals of the Continental Congress,
1774–1789*, II, 218–19 and n. 1

Third Virginia Convention

Proceedings of Ninth Day of Session [2]

Ordered, that David Mason & Isaac Reade ⟨Read⟩ be added to the Committee appointed to draw up and report a Plan for raising and embodying a sufficient Force for the Defence and Protection of this Colony.[3]

The Convention then, according to the Order of the Day [4] went into an Examination of the Reports said to have been propagated to the Prejudice of Richard Bland Esqr: a Member of this Convention and one of the Deputies appointed to represent this Colony in General Congress; and after the Examination of the revd. Samuel Shield ⟨Sheild⟩ the revd. John Hurt and many other Witnesses and a full Inquiry into the same do find the said Reports to be utterly false and groundless and tending not only to injure the said Richard Bland in his publick Character but to prejudice the glorious Cause in which America is now embarked.

Resolved unanimously, that this Convention do consider it as their Duty, to bear to the World, their Testimony, that the said Richard Bland hath manifested himself the Friend of his Country, and uniformly stood forth an able Assertor [5] of her Rights & Liberties.

Ordered, that the President ⟨Peyton Randolph⟩ be desired to transmit a Copy of the proceedings of this Convention relative to the said Inquiry to the General Congress.

Ordered, that it be an Instruction to the Committee of Correspondence, that they also transmit a Copy of the said Proceedings to Arthur Lee Esquire in London, and request him to make strict Inquiry for the Authors & Propagators of the said Reports in England.[6]

The President laid before the Convention a Letter from the Officers of the voluntier Companies in Williamsburg, informing the Convention that they had resolved, immediately to secure all the publick Monies in the hands of the Receiver General, Naval Officers and other Collectors for his Majesty, that they had sent out Detachments for that Purpose, and desiring the Opinion of the Convention relative thereto, as they should chearfully submit to their Determination on the Subject.[7]

Resolved, that this Convention will immediately resolve itself into a Committee to take the said Letter into Consideration.

The Convention accordingly resolved itself into a Committee and after sometime spent therein, Mr. President resumed the Chair and Mr. ⟨Richard⟩ Bland reported, that the Committee had had the Letter from the Officers of the voluntier Companies in Williamsburg under their Consideration and had come to a Resolution thereupon which he read in his Place and delivered in at the Clerk's Table, where the same was again twice read and agreed to as follows.

Resolved, that it is the Opinion of this Committee, that the Proceedings of the Officers of the voluntier Companies in Williamsburg mentioned in their Letter to the Convention, though they arose from the best Motives,[8] cannot be approved, and that they be required to desist from carrying their Resolutions into Execution.

The Order of the Day for the Convention to resolve itself into a Committee on the State of the Colony being read,[9]

Resolved, that this Convention will tomorrow resolve into a Committee to take into Consideration the State of the Colony.

[Resold. that Mr. ⟨Robert⟩ Prentis should be discharged from his Obligation.] [10]

adjourned till tomorrow 9. oClock.

Convention MS journal in hand of John Tazewell (Archives Division, Virginia State Library)[11]

Peyton Randolph to Officers of Gentlemen Volunteers
of Independent Companies in Williamsburg

Gent.   Richmond Town July 28. 1775.
I have just Time to enclose you a Copy of the Resolution, entered into by
the Convention on the Subject of yr Letter, which I immediately laid before
the Delegates.[12] During the Debates on the matter, I have the pleasure to
inform you no Censure was passed on yr Conduct, & that they considered the
steps you have taken as arising from very laudable motives.

It was the sense of the Convention that Mr ⟨Robert⟩ Prentis's affidavit
should be delivered up & he discharged from the obligation thereof.

I am, Gent., yr obliged humble Svt.

                                                         Peyton Randolph Pres.[13]

                            Letter MS transcript in hand of George Gilmer, in
                            autograph diary and Revolutionary memoranda of
                            Dr. George Gilmer (Virginia Historical Society)

Augusta County West: Journal of Captain James Wood

28th July went to the Council house at two O'Clock agreable to the Appointment of the Wyandots when Rotunda or the War Post in the Presence
of Coronyatte Surrahawa Aughunta and other Warriors of the Wyandots,
and Ninnis and Mangagata of the Tawaas delivered the following Answer to
my speech of Yesterday⟨:⟩ [14] *Brothers the Bigknife* you tell us you were sent
to our Towns by the Great Men of Virginia [15] to let us know that there is
now a large Council fire kindling at Fort Pitt that it would be ready in forty
six days and we should hear every thing that was good⟨.⟩ *Brother* we have
listned to what you have said with great Attention and Considered it well⟨.⟩
we think it is good and will immediately send it Over the Lakes to our Cheifs
and will be ruled by them in our determinations⟨.⟩ *Brother* I have nothing
farther to say but that it is always a Custom with us that Whatever News we
hear we immediately send it to our head Men as we shall on this Occasion.[16]
after delivering the Answer Rotunda told me that he heard the People of
Virginia were now building a Fort on Kentucke and intended to drive off all
the Indians and take Possession of their Lands⟨.⟩ [17] I told him that I never
heard of any Fort being built on Kentucke but that our People were settling
very fast in that Country which they had an Undoubted right to do⟨.⟩ the
whole Country to the Eastward of the Ohio as low down as the Cherokee
River was purchased from the Six Nations at the Treaty at Fort Stanwix
and that since which the People of Virginia had purchased the Pretended
right of the Cherokees that we should be able to make them sensible of this
at the Treaty to be held at Fort Pitt and that they might rest Assured that
we had no thoughts of encroaching any farther than we had already pur-

chased and honestly paid for⟨.⟩ [18] he then enquired after news and desired to
know whether we intended to take Fort Detroit from the Regulars⟨.⟩ this
I told them I knew not but beleived the Americans looked upon it to be a
place of no Consequence to them and that they would not Concern with it⟨.⟩
here I took an Opportunity of telling them that we had already taken Ty-
conderoga and Crown Point without any loss and that we had beaten the
Regulars in every Engagement with very Considerable loss on their sides and
very inconsiderable on ours⟨.⟩ [19] I then told him I was well Acquainted with
the Steps taken by the Officer Commanding at Fort D'Troit and Moneieur
Baubee ⟨Duperon Baby⟩ to prejudice them against the Americans in General
and Virginia in particular⟨.⟩ I then produced the Belt and String delivered to
me by the Delawares and asked him if he knew them⟨.⟩ here they all appeared
to be much Surprised but Acknowledged that they did upon which I proceeded to repeat what was said when they were delivered⟨,⟩ all of which they
Acknowledged⟨.⟩ Except that the French were concerned in it they said
Monsieur Baubee was present but that he did not interfere but added that
the Englishmen told them that the Virginians would take the whole Country
if they did not all join together against them⟨.⟩ I told War Post that I was
well Acquainted with the whole Matter⟨,⟩ that I had got it out at the different
Towns by degrees⟨,⟩ first from the Squaws and then from the Men⟨.⟩ [20] he
then desired me to give him a Copy of the Speech which I made in the Council Yesterday that no part of it might be forgot⟨.⟩ this I readily complied with
and we parted in the most freindly Manner⟨.⟩ I then sent Messages by the
Tawaas to the Tawixtawees, Picks and other Nations inhabiting the Mimamis
and Wabash Rivers with Invitations to meet at the Treaty [21]

Thwaites and Kellogg, *Revolution on the Upper
Ohio, 1775–1777*, pp. 52–56

As Related to Augusta County West Committee

At the appointed time the War Post delivered the following answer to
Capt. Wood's speech of yesterday.

"Brothers, the Big Knife,

"You tell us you were sent to our towns by the great men of Virginia, to
let us know there is now a large council fire kindling at Fort-Pitt; that it
would be ready in forty-six days, and that we should hear then and there
every thing that was good. Brothers, we have listened to every thing you have
said, with great attention, and consider it well. We think it is good, and will
immediately send over the lakes to our Chiefs, and will be ruled in our determination by them. Brothers, I have nothing farther to say, than that it has
always been a custom with us that whatever news we hear, we immediately
send it to our Head men, as we shall on this occasion."

*Dunlap's Pennsylvania Packet, or, the General Ad-
vertiser* (Philadelphia), 11 September 1775

Norfolk Borough Committee to Thomas Newton, Jr.,
James Holt, and Joseph Hutchings, Esquires [22]

Norfolk Borough Committee Chamber July 28. 1775.

The Committee, being informed that a Resolution passed the Honorable Convention of this Colony, restricting the exportation of provisions after the fifth day of August next,[23] and being fully sensible of the exceeding gre[at] [24] hardships, to which many of our constituents will be thereby subjected, do inst[ruct] the members of this Committee, who are members of the Convention, to exer[t] their utmost endeavors to procure a reconsideration of the said Resolution, as bearing very heavily upon the merchants, who, reposing full confidence [in] the latitude for exportation granted by the General Congress, have made large contracts for the articles so prohibited, and have now on hand cons[ider]able quantities of those perishable commodities,— have chartered vessels in foreign parts and regulated the voyages of their own shipping, so as to suit [the] continental regulations, without any expectation, or reason to expect a[ny] such provincial restriction. The said members are also hereby further instru[cted] to point out the peculiar hardships arising from the short notice bet[ween] the passing the said Resolution and the said fifth day of August, when it i[s] to take effect: by which means the merchants, unapprized of any such intent [and] unprepared for any such event, have had no opportunity to regulate their tra[de] agreeably to this unexpected resolve, but are suddenly prohibited from commerce in the midst of their engagements and to the very great prejudice of thei[r] concerns. And further to inform the Convention that we fear this meas[ure] will be productive of great disputes between buyers and sellers, as well as betwee[n] committees and their constituents; and that for our parts we are really un[der] some apprehension that so chearful an obedience will not be paid to this distres[sing] injunction, as our constituents are desirous to pay to all the decisions o[f] that honorable body; and that we humbly request that the said Resolution m[ay] be repealed, at least so far as to give time for vessels that are now loading to ta[ke] in their cargoes, and to allow the merchant some opportunity to order his affairs in the best manner he can to blunt the edge of this sudden calamity.

Ordered that the Secretary transmit a copy of these instructions to Thomas Newton junr. James Holt and Joseph Hutchings Es*qrs.* to be laid before the Convent[ion.] [25]

Extract from the minutes
WILLIAM DAVIES Secy.

Recipients' copy, autograph document, signed, in loose papers of third Virginia Convention (Archives Division, Virginia State Library)

Merchants and Traders of Norfolk Borough and Portsmouth
Town to Delegates in Convention [26]

To the Honorable the Convention of Virginia.
The Petition of the Merchants and Traders of the Borough of Norfolk and
Town of Portsmouth,
    Humbly Sheweth,
    That your Petitioners are greatly interested in the trade of this colo[ny]
and chiefly depend upon it for support—that we shall be most sensibly af-
f[ected] by the stoppage of exportation, as directed by the General Congress, but are still willing to make this great sacrifice to obtain the restoration
of our rights an[d] liberties—that your petitioners have been taught to place
the fullest confidenc[e] and dependance upon that respectable [27] Assembly,
for all measures intended to operate upon the commercial interests of the
United Colonies, sensible that any step of that nature adopted by one province and not by another must be [in]effectual and nugatory—that your
petitioners, both from reason and information have been fully satisfied that
no stoppage to exportation prior to the tenth of September is intended by the
Continental Congress—that upon this f[ai]th we have made large contracts
for grain and other provisions, with the planters and others in this colony,
and have now upon hand great quantities of those commodities ready for
exportation in a very short time—that your petitioners have many vessels now
at sea, and their voyages so ordered, that they may return a sufficient time
before the tenth of September to carry out other carg[oes] of the produce of
this colony—that some of your petitioners have chartered vessels in foreign
parts for the purpose abovementioned; which vessels are now at sea, and will
shortly arrive to take in their cargoes before the stoppage of exportation in
September—and that your petitioners have made [use] of every precaution in
our power to suit our trade to that period so as [to] avoid every possibility
of interfering with the Continental Association.
    Judge therefore with how great astonishment your petitioners were made
acquainted with a resolution of your honorable body, to restrict the exportation of all kinds of provisions after the fifth day of August now just commencing: a resolution, which we humbly conceive was adopted with great
haste, and without even allowing time or opportunity for the trading in-
teres[t] of the colony to know that such a measure was in agitation, much
less to lay their objections before the Convention.
    Your petitioners therefore do humbly beg leave to remonstrate to your
honorable body, against a step so ruinous to many individuals; and to represent to you that by this sudden stop to our commerce the great quantities of
grain and other provisions now upon hand will perish in our possession—
th[at] all our contracts, instead of being advantageous to us, will prove our
destruction[—]that our own vessels, whose arrival we daily expect in fruitless expectation of cargoes, to be exported from hence, will return upon us

useless and out of employ, [a]nd without any previous opportunity being allowed us to direct their voyage to other parts—that vessels, which we have chartered abroad for the prosecution of our lawful trade under the protection of the General Congress and of such advantage to the country, will soon arrive as the expensive mementos of our unexpected misfortunes, and without any possibility on our part of employing them to our advantage.

Your petitioners do also further represent, that we conceive it is a measure that gives an unnecessary preference in trade to the other colonies; and without an advantage to the common interests of America so long as the rest of the continent continue their exports—that we have no expectation that the [o]ther provinces will adopt this measure; in which opinion we are th[e] more confirmed from the example of New York, which city did for a short tim[e] stop its exports; but finding the great damage sustained by individuals th[ro'?] this measure and being strongly opposed in it by the city of Philadelphia, they opened their trade again by taking off the restrictions[28]—that if the other colonies should chuse to adopt the measure in consequence of your example, yet some time will elapse before they can be informed of it; a still longer time will be required to assemble their respective conventions, or to give such previous notice to their constituents as to guard against those inconveniencies of which we now complain; which will approach so near the [t]ime prescribed by the General Congress, as to render such a resolution unnecessary.

Your petitioners do also further beg leave humbly to represent tha[t] we conceive it to be a measure tending in its nature to destroy all confidence in the representatives of the people at this alarming crisis, when the most pe[r]fect union is so necessary—that it will reduce numbers to great straits, perhaps to bankruptcy, by which we shall be rendered utterly incapable to fulfill our engagements, to discharge our debts and make the payments due to the merchants and planters in the country—In fine your petitioners cannot [but believe?] that if no notice is to be given to parties when matters of the greatest moment to them are under consideration; if no regard is to be pai[d] to assurances from our own Delegates in Congress as well as others; if provincial conventions undertake the regulation of continental concern[s,] and that too during a session of the Congress itself, the only choice we have left to us is to lament the violation of the public faith and order, and flattered as we have been into deceitful expectations, to sit down the melancholy spectators of our own destruction.

Your Petitioners therefore do humbly pray th[at] your honorable body will take the premisses into your most serious consideration, and either repeal the said resolution altogether, or give such further latitude as may enable your petitioners so to order our concerns as to render the measure less ruinous and destructive,—and to grant such other and further relief as to your honorable body shall seem fit.

And your Petitioners, as in duty bound, shall ever pray &c.

PHRIPP & BOWDOIN[29]   JOHN MACKAY
CORNELIUS CALVERT   ROBERT GRAY

ARCHD CAMPBELL
GREENWOOD, RITSON, & MARSH
GILCHRIST & TAYLOR
EDWARD ARCHER
SAMUEL INGLIS & CO
JOHN PEW
THOS MATHEWS
PHRIPP TAYLOR & CO.
JOHN BEGG
WILLIAM FARRER
WILIM. NORTH
HENRY FLEMING & CO.
LOGAN, GILMOUR & CO

THOMAS WALKER
THOS HEPBURN
NEIL JAMIESON & CO.
HODGYARD & ALLASON
JOHN LAURENCE & CO.
CHARLES THOMAS.
DANIEL BARRAUD
THOMAS NEWTON SENR.
LEWIS HANSFORD
WILLIM. HOLT.

Recipients' copy, MS document in unidentified hand, with autograph signatures, in loose papers of third Virginia Convention (Archives Division, Virginia State Library)

1. Preamble, resolution, and recommendation appear in neither manuscript nor printed journals of Congress. In editing the 2d volume of the *Journals of the Continental Congress*, Worthington C. Ford borrowed all that is here included from a 12-page, octavo pamphlet issued by the Philadelphia printers William and Thomas Bradford for distribution through the colonies (II, 218–19, 219 n. 1; see also III, 511). "The following systems or methods of making Salt-Petre" comprised the greater part of the pamphlet, a copy of which (though now missing from the records of the third Va. Convention) was laid before that assemblage on 14 Aug. 1775.

The making of saltpeter had been "recommended" by the second convention on 27 Mar. (*Rev. Va.*, II, 383), but only the Cumberland County committee has left record of a serious attempt to comply with the recommendation, in an appeal to its "Dear Country Men" on 30 June 1775. On its own initiative the third convention would the next day, 29 July 1775, begin fumbling in the direction of a greater procurement of the commodity.

2. With the absence of George Stubblefield and the unseating of Adam Stephen and Robert Rutherford on 27 July 1775, the number of members attending the convention could not have exceeded 103.

3. Mason and Read replacing Stephen and Rutherford, the number of members on the committee continued at 31.

4. The "Order of the Day" was voted on 22 July 1775 (Procs. and n. 2).

5. Tazewell wrote the word as "Assestor."

6. Neither the presidential letter transmitting a "Copy of the proceedings" nor the committee's covering letter directed to Arthur Lee has been found.

7. For the "Letter," see 26 July 1775.

8. In the convention loose papers a draft of the resolution is in Tazewell's hand. Between the words "Convention" and "cannot" he inserted a caret and above it wrote, "tho' they arose from the best motives." Although Peyton Randolph in the item next following skirts the issue by stating, "no Censure was passed," the 7-word phrase may have been offered from the floor as an amendment designed to soften what in fact was a rebuke. Some delegates mistrusted the wisdom of Patrick Henry's actions in the

gunpowder affair, but he at least had exchanged what at the time seemed an equivalent. Seizure of revenues against which there were no just claims from a king to whom the convention still pledged allegiance was another matter.

9. The "Order of the Day," voted on 27 July, was that "the Letter from the Deputies appointed to represent this Colony in General Congress together with the papers inclosed therein" and the "Letter from Oconestoto," together "with the other Papers relative to Indian Affairs" be taken under consideration (Procs. and nn. 8–9).

10. The bracketed resolution is taken from Tazewell's minutes for this day. It is the last entry and directly follows "Order of the Day put off." The resolution appears to have been offered from the floor in clarification of the position taken on the actions of the "Officers of the voluntier Companies in Williamsburg." That the resolution was passed is clear from Peyton Randolph's final paragraph in the item next following.

11. Edgewise on the bottom of the 4th of 4 pages Tazewell wrote "No. 9."

12. See the preceding item and nn. 7, 8, 10.

13. The officers in Williamsburg would receive Randolph's letter on 1 Aug. 1775.

14. For Wood's "speech of Yesterday" and the "Appointment" to hear the reply thereto, see Third Va. Convention, Augusta Co. West, and nn. 18–20.

15. The "Great Men of Virginia" were the Council and House of Burgesses.

16. The principal towns of the Wyandots were north of Lake Erie opposite Fort Detroit (Thwaites and Kellogg, *Rev. on the Upper Ohio*, p. 53 n. 82).

17. The War Post appears to have heard of Judge Richard Henderson's colonization of the Kentucky River Valley. A stockade at Boonesborough was then building (10 July 1775, n. 8; Ranke, *Boonesborough*, pp. 25–26).

18. The "Treaty at Fort Stanwix" in upper New York in 1768—at which Virginia had been represented by Dr. Thomas Walker—was negotiated by Sir William Johnson. The "Sachems & Cheifs of the Six confederated Nations, and of the Shawanese, Delawares, Mingoes of Ohio and other Dependent Tribes" ceded to His Majesty "a considerable Tract of Country" in New York, western Pennsylvania, and to the high dudgeon of the Shawnee, all of the hunting grounds south of the Ohio River (O'Callaghan, *N.Y. Col. Docs.*, VIII, 111–37; Downes, *Council Fires on the Upper Ohio*, pp. 141–45, 148). The exclusion of the Six Nations from the lands south of the Ohio was reiterated during John Connolly's negotiations at Fort Pitt on 4 and 6 July 1775 (Third Va. Convention). The purchase of "the Pretended right of the Cherokees" to part of the same territory proved a matter of 2 installments. At the Treaty of Hard Labor in 1768 a line was drawn roughly south by southeast from the mouth of the Kanawha River to Fort Chiswell, erected in that portion of Fincastle County that is today Wythe County. Then in 1770, using "the confluence of the great Canaway & Ohio rivers" as a pivot, the negotiators at the Treaty of Lochaber swung the line west, so that it struck the Virginia–North Carolina "dividing line" at a point near the Holston River and encompassed most of what is now the state of West Virginia (*Va. Mag. of Hist. and Biog.*, IX [Apr. 1920], 360–64; Abernethy, *Western Lands and the Am. Rev.*, pp. 62–73).

19. Fort Ticonderoga and nearby Crown Point, both on the western shore of Lake Champlain, had fallen without loss on 10 and 12 May 1775 respectively to troops under the joint command of Col. Ethan Allen and Benedict Arnold (Allen French, *The First Year of the American Revolution* [Boston, 1934], pp. 151–52). Before he left Fort Pitt on 18 July, Wood may have seen issues of the *Pa. Gazette* for 28 June and 5 July 1775 containing accounts of the Battle of Bunker Hill. In the 1st issue one correspondent reported that the "Loss of the King's Troops must be very considerable," and another estimated the "killed and wounded" among the "Ministerial Troops" to

have been 1,000. In the 2d issue the indication was that the patriots had suffered about 50 killed and fewer than 100 wounded, with the combined British casualties reaching "upwards of fourteen hundred."

20. The "Belt and String" Wood had received from "the King and Cheifs of the Delawares" on 23 July 1775, at which time he heard the most complete account of the "Steps taken by the Officer Commanding Fort D'Troit." Unknown to Wood, the Detroit commandant, Capt. Richard Berenger Lernoult, shortly thereafter sent for the Wyandots and again tried to dissuade them from treating with the Big Knives. Wood's friend John Dodge, a Connecticut trader at Sandusky, prevailed upon the Indians to accept the Virginia emissary's invitation to negotiate (Thwaites and Kellogg, *Rev. on the Upper Ohio*, p. 55 n. 83).

21. The Tawixtawees, or Tightwees, were the Algonquin Miamis who early in the 18th century had wandered from Upper Canada down through Michigan and settled on the Miami River (Hodge, *Handbook of Am. Indians*, pt. 1, 852–53). The "Picks" were a group of Shawnee living in the same region and taking their English designation from their settlement Pickawillany, near what is now Piqua, Ohio (Thwaites and Kellogg, *Rev. on the Upper Ohio*, p. 15 n. 30).

Under the date heading of 31 July 1775, Captain Wood will be found talking with The Hardman at "the Shawanese Towns" (Third Va. Convention, Augusta Co. West).

22. The first 2 of the addresses were convention delegates for Norfolk County, the 3d the delegate for the borough, so indicating the interlinkage of interests of the 2 jurisdictions (20 July 1775, Third Va. Convention, Norfolk Borough Committee, and n. 12).

23. The "Resolution" was that offered by George Mason on 24 July 1775. The Norfolk newspaper was issued too early during the week of 23–29 July for the committee to have learned of "this sudden calamity" from its pages. The members may have seen Purdie's *Va. Gazette* of the present date carrying the notice that "*The General Convention of this colony has prohibited the exportation of grain, and all sorts of provisions, after saturday the 5th of August next.*" It is more likely, however, that one or more of the present addressees had written for instructions.

24. Bracketed words, syllables, and letters are borrowed from the transcription (the document then being less deteriorated) in the *Va. Mag. of Hist. and Biog.*, XIV (July 1906), 51–52.

25. The petition would "be laid before the Convention" on 1 Aug. 1775.

26. The document is not dated, but one Norfolk merchant "imagin'd" that the local merchants would "not abide to the Order of the Convention," and recorded on the present date that "A meeting" was "Now Call'd on the Occasion" (John Schaw to Robert Carter, 28 July 1775, Carter Papers, Va. Hist. Soc.). This "Petition" and the "Instructions" of the Norfolk Borough committee were to be laid before the convention on the same day.

27. As penned, the word is "respectably."

28. Here the subscribers were harkening back to events of nearly 5 years past. On 9 July 1770 the merchants of New York City had abandoned the nonimportation system initially erected against enforcement of the Townshend Acts. On 12 Sept. 1770 the merchants of Philadelphia followed suit, and thereafter what remained of the inter-colonial united front gradually collapsed (Schlesinger, *Col. Merchants and the Am. Rev.*, pp. 226–27; *Rev. Va.*, I, 84).

29. Of the firm of Matthew Phripp and John Bowdoin, the 2d-named partner, who was chairman of the Northampton County committee, will on 29 July 1775 be observed signing a petition of similar import.

Saturday, 29 July 1775

Third Virginia Convention

Proceedings of Tenth Day of Session [1]

The Order of the Day for the Convention to resolve itself into a Committee on the State of the Colony, being read,

Resolved, that this Convention will, on Monday next, resolve itself into a Committee to take into Consideration the State of the Colony. [2]

On a Motion made,

Resolved, that the several Inspectors of this Colony be directed to preserve the Trash Tobacco, at their respective Inspections, for the purpose of making Saltpetre, and that they deliver the same when required to such person or persons as may be appointed for that purpose by the Committee of the County. [3]

Resolved, that the several Inspectors of the publick Warehouses in this Colony do, sometime before the last of August next, and after advertizing the same in the publick Papers, at the Warehouses and at the Courthouses of their respective Counties, sell for ready Money all Transfer & other Tobacco which may have laid one Year in their respective Warehouses, and pay the Money arising from such Sale as the Law directs. [4]

Resolved, that the Chairmen of the Committees of the several Counties do, without Delay, procure all the Saltpetre and Sulphur which may be had, and that the same be paid for by the Public. And it is earnestly recommended to all Persons in this Colony to be assisting in procuring those necessary Articles, and cheerfully to deliver to the said Chairmen, what they may have in their Families, except so much as may be necessary for medicinal Pruposes. [5]

[Mr. Jos⟨eph⟩: Jones, Mr. John Nicholas & Mr. ⟨John⟩ Ruffin added to Com: appd. to draw Ordinance for Pay.] [6]

adjourned till Monday 9. oClock

Convention MS journal in hand of John Tazewell
(Archives Division, Virginia State Library) [7]

Northampton County Committee to The Honble. Peyton Randolph
Esqr. president of the Convention now sitting at Richmond.
per Express

To the Honorable the President and Delegates of the people of Virginia now
assembled in Convention in the Town of Richmond in the County of Henrico—the humble petition of the Committee of Northampton County in behalf of themselves & their Constituents

Humbly Sheweth

That the people of this County have ever been zealous in support of the
Common Cause and have inviolably observed those regulations established by
the General Congress for maintaining the Liberties of America. fully Convinced that those regulations would be strictly adhered to by all Ranks and
orders of men our Constituents have formed many engagements and entered
into Various Contracts in which they have considered themselves as under
the Faith and protection of the Country whilst they walked within the line
prescribed them by the united Voice of all America. amongst other things
they have in all their engagements had a particular Eye to that very material
Clause which prohibits the Exportation of all merchandize from this Country
to Great Britain or the West Indies after the tenth Day of September next
and have taken their measures in such manner as may be as little burthensome
to themselves as possible and at the same time with a full determination
strictly to perform that clause of the Continental Association.[8] it is therefor
with the utmost Sorrow we are informed that the Convention of this Colony
has directed that a total Stop be put to the export of Grain and provisions
from and after the fifth Day of August next a measure which if strictly en-
forced will bring the greatest Distress upon many merchants and private
families in this place and which we fear may tend to disturb that unanimity
which hath hitherto subsisted amongst us whilst the Determinations of the
Congress were received as an invariable rule of Conduct in those points which
that very respectable Body have taken under their Consideration.[9] Your petitioners beg leave to represent to the Convention that the people of this place
raise very large quantities of Indian Corn which is generally unsold late in
the Summer and altho we believe there is not so much now on hand as is
usual at this Season yet there are such quantities as to ruin many persons who
have made Contracts respecting the same if the ports are immediately stopped.
Your petitioners therefor in behalf of themselves & the other Inhabitants of
this place pray that the exports to the West Indies may be kept open till the
10th. of September next and we beg leave to assure the Convention that the
greatest Care will be taken by this Comittee to prevent the exportation of any
provisions to the Northward when there may be the least Danger of their
falling into the hands of the Army [10] and that it will be our Constant Study
to enforce within the limits of our appointment those regulations of the general Congress or Convention of this Colony which are now entered into or
may hereafter be adopted in Support of the Common Cause.[11]

Northampton County. 29th. July 1775.   Isaac Avery
John Bowdoin Chairman[12]   John Respass
John Burton   John Kendall
Mich Christian   John S. Harmanson
John Harmanson Sr.   Geo: Savage
Nathaniel L: Savage   Griffin Stith
John Wilkins   William Ronald

> Recipients' copy, MS document in unidentified hand, with autograph signatures, in papers of third Virginia Convention (Archives Division, Virginia State Library)

Proceedings of Officers of Gentlemen Volunteers of Independent Companies in Williamsburg

It is the opinion of the Gent. officers now in Wm*bgh*. that Capt. Oliver Towles and Thos. Booth[13] shd. wait on the hon. Rd. Corbin Esq & demand a state of his public acts⟨;⟩ that the balance on hand be delivered up on their receipts or that the said R. Corbin bind his whole Estate as Security that none of the publick money shall be applied to other use than the Convention shall direct. On the Receiver genls refusing to comply that the sd. Towles & Booth call all the Volunteers in reach to assist in bringing him to the Incampment in Wm*bgh* or send an express for assistance if it should be necessary.[14]

Chas. Scott

> Document MS transcript in autograph diary and Revolutionary memoranda of Dr. George Gilmer (Virginia Historical Society)

Richard Corbin to Officers of Gentlemen Volunteers of Independent Companies in Williamsburg

Gentlemen   Laneville July 29. 75

I am honor'd with your letter by Capt. Towles & Capt. Booth, to whom I have given all the satisfaction it is in my power to give them. I can do nothing myself as Receiver General without the advice & direction of the Council who are the stated Guardians of his Maj. Revenues. I shall therefore take the first opportunity of laying yr letter before them⟨.⟩ in the mean time if any quit rent money should be paid it shall not be remitted by me or any body for me.

Believe me Gentn. my attacht. to the Welfare of this my native Country is founded on the best inclina. My wife, my Children my property is here fixed & dispersed amongst you & I will at all times & upon all occasions contribute my best endeavors in support of its true interest, & most cordially Join in every necessary measure to effect so desirable a purpose.[15]

I am, Gentn, yr obd. Svt.

Rd. Corbin.[16]

Letter MS transcript (ibid.)

Williamsburg

Editorial note. In Force, *American Archives,* 4th ser., II, col. 1750, there is printed a letter from Robert Washington "To the Members of the Convention of Virginia." It appeared in Dixon and Hunter's *Virginia Gazette* of 29 July 1775, from which Force copied accurately, except that the letter was addressed "To the Printers."

1. Delegate George Stubblefield was undoubtedly still in Williamsburg, where, as the 3d and 4th items below indicate, much was occurring. The number of members present, then, could not have exceeded 103.

2. The "Order of the Day," voted on 27 July, was that "the Letter from the Deputies appointed to represent this Colony in General Congress together with the papers inclosed therein" and the "Letter from Oconestoto," together "with the other Papers relative to Indian Affairs" be taken under consideration. On 28 July the order was voted to be observed on the present day.

3. In 1686 the General Assembly defined "Trash Tobacco" as consisting of "seconds, slips and late planted tobaccoes, not having sufficient time to come to full maturity" and being characterized by "greenness, thinness and other ill qualities." A statue of 1765 imposed a heavy monetary penalty and possible prosecution "as in case of wilful and corrupt perjury" on anyone who under oath tried to slip hogsheads or casks of such "Trash" into a public warehouse (*Statutes at Large,* III, 34, VIII, 76–77). Now, under altered circumstances, yesterday's villain was offered opportunity to become today's hero. The present resolution represented an attempt to invigorate a resolution respecting saltpeter adopted by the second convention on 27 Mar. 1775 (*Rev. Va.,* II, 382). In Tazewell's hand, a copy of the present resolution, which was offered from the floor, is in the convention loose papers.

4. Although the beginnings of "Transfer Tobacco" may be glimpsed as early as 1691, the term seems not to have found its way into law until 1734. A statute of 1769 provided that when owing to wastage a hogshead or cask should weigh less than 1,000 pounds, the leaf in one such underweight container would be transferred to another in order to bring the 2d to legal weight, and a "transfer note" would be given to the owner who otherwise would have sustained loss. It usually occurred that there remained in warehouses amounts of tobacco not transferred, and following compensation to the owner, "the Law" directed that they be annually auctioned by the county courts and the proceeds remitted to the colonial treasurer (*Statutes at Large,* III, 48–49, IV, 388, VIII, 324, 325; see also [George] Melvin Herndon, *William Tatham and the Culture of Tobacco* [Coral Gables, Fla., 1969], pp. 84–86). Offered from the floor, a copy of this resolution is in Tazewell's hand in the convention loose papers. It was submitted in supplement to the 1st and to broaden invigoration of the resolution of 27 Mar. 1775.

5. Likewise offered from the floor and coupled to the first 2 resolutions, this 3d would see a kindred subsequent history. A copy of the resolution in Tazewell's hand is in the convention loose papers.

6. The bracketed notation is drawn from Tazewell's minutes for this day. Therein it follows the entry "Resn. abt. Tobo. for Salt petre aged. to." By "Pay" is meant the committee on war claims, to which Isaac Zane, Jr. (who by these additions became chairman), had been solely appointed on 25 July 1775 (Procs. and n. 10).

7. Tazewell wrote "No. 10 & 11" edgewise on the bottom of the 4th of 4 pages (the 3d of which is blank) on which he entered the journal for this day and that for 31 July 1775.

8. The "very material Clause" was the 4th article of the Continental Association, which read: "The earnest desire we have, not to injure our fellow-subjects in Great-Britain, Ireland, or the West-Indies, induces us to suspend a non-exportation, until the tenth day of September, 1775; at which time, if the said acts and parts of acts of the British parliament herein mentioned are not repealed, we will not, directly, or indirectly, export any merchandise or commodity whatsoever to Great-Britain, Ireland, or the West-Indies, except rice to Europe" (*JCC*, I, 77).

9. The "measure" threatening to disturb "unanimity" was George Mason's non-exportation resolution, adopted by the convention on 24 July 1775.

10. The "Army" meant was the British, confined to Boston under the command of Gen. Thomas Gage.

11. John Bowdoin would write a covering letter for this petition on the following day, 30 July 1775.

12. After the Huguenot Pierre Baudoine had emigrated from Boston, Mass., to settle in Northampton County, Va., in 1689, he found life good there and as a merchant prospered. And there his mercantile descendants (the family surname Anglicized and, according to Bishop Meade, at least by the 19th century pronounced "Bo'den") prospered likewise and intermarried with others long in the land. Peter Bowdoin, the father of JOHN BOWDOIN, rendered important services in the Burgesses from 1727 to 1732 and again from 1734 to 1740. The son, an outstanding member of the Virginia "Trade," ran up his political colors in 1766, when as a justice of the peace he joined his colleagues on the county bench in declaring the Stamp Act unconstitutional. Then in 1773 he was himself elected to the Burgesses, thereafter constantly to be returned. A man such as his constituents in the southern county of the exposed Eastern Shore could trust, he was present when after dissolution of the House in 1774, former members gathered in the Raleigh Tavern and proposed the meeting of an intercolonial congress. In August of that year he attended the first Virginia Convention and on 17 Dec. 1774 was elected chairman of the Northampton County committee. Elected to the second convention, he was unable to attend. His having recently lost a ship to His Majesty's service (25 May 1775, Norfolk Borough Town Meeting) probably placed him in a mood to attend the third convention, to which he was elected, in order to pronounce certain views; but a family "Indisposition" prevented his going to Richmond. Perhaps the "Indisposition" was his own, for in Oct. 1775 "a severe and painful illness" would snuff out the life of this genial, obliging, hospitable, prematurely gray patriot while he was yet in his early 40s (J. W. Allen, "The Bowdoin Family," *Va. Mag. of Hist. and Biog.*, XXXVIII [Apr. 1930], 191–94; W. Meade, *Old Churches, Ministers and Families of Va.*, I, 259–60 n.; *Rev. Va.*, I, 20–21, 98, 221, 235, II, 202, 303, 337; *JHB, 1773–1776*, pp. 4, 68, 164; *Va. Gazette* [Rind], 26 Nov. 1772; ibid. [Pinkney], 19, 26 Oct. 1775; Northampton Co. Will Book no. 19, microfilm in Va. State Library, pp. 244–48, no. 25, pp. 455–61).

13. Thomas Booth was from Gloucester County.

14. Corbin's "Copy" of the "opinion of the Gent. officers" is enclosed in Lord Dunmore's letter of 24 Sept. 1775 to Lord Dartmouth (P.R.O., C.O. 5/1353, fol. 293). That copy reproduced the language of Gilmer's transcript but is prefaced by the ominous observation that the officers were "Struck with Suspicions of the most dreadful Nature" compelling them to demand "a true and accurate Account" of His Majesty's revenues on hand. The officers had not yet received Peyton Randolph's letter of the previous day, and before doing so they would continue their self-assigned missions (28 July 1775, Third Va. Convention, Randolph to Officers; 1 Aug., same, Proceedings of Officers).

15. Reporting this "extraordinary" incident, Corbin informed the governor that he had no qualms in making the present statement, "as in truth" he had in possession no money "to remit on Account of Quitrents" (P.R.O., C.O. 5/1353, fols. 291–92). "The Independent Companys," stated James Parker, "are riding over all the Country to Seize what money is in the public offices," and he heard that they had gotten "what money Lewis Burwell," naval officer of the Upper James, had on hand (Parker to Charles Steuart, 4 Aug. 1775, Steuart Papers, National Library of Scotland).

16. RICHARD CORBIN, Esquire, a member of "his Majesty's Council of State for this Colony" since 1750 and receiver general since 1754, was carrying on a distinguished tradition of public service begun by his immigrant ancestor, Henry Corbin, who had been a burgess from 1658 to 1660 and was of the Council from 1663 until his death in 1676. Henry's descendants prospered, married well, and propagated prolifically, so when Richard Corbin married Elizabeth, daughter of the late councilor John Tayloe, he was already handsomely connected and in a position to pluck those public fruits to which gentlemen of eminent station were entitled. He represented Middlesex County in the Burgesses in 1749, thereafter removing to King and Queen County and establishing his seat at Laneville. Although a friend of George Washington and most of the outstanding patriots, he despised their cause. Back in the 1760s he had heaped scorn on those who protested passage of the Stamp Act, and now he took pains to inform His Excellency of his continuing fidelity: "my duty and Loyalty to the King, my Zeal for the Welfare of my Country, and my earnest endeavours in Support of its true Interest will remain unalterable." His perseverence did not go unnoticed, and there would be a day when His Majesty would tell Corbin's son Francis that his father was "the best subject I ever had in America." Now 67 years old, Richard Corbin did not exude that arrogance with which John Randolph could infuriate. Cast in a gentler mold, he continued to hold the respect even of those to whom his politics were anathema ([William G. Stanard], "The Corbin Family," *Va. Mag. of Hist. and Biog.*, XXIX [July 1921], 374, [Oct. 1921], 522–26, XXX [Jan. 1922], 80–85; *Exec. Journs. Coun. Col. Va.*, V, 316; *Col. Va. Reg.*, pp. 23, 74, 76, 125; Anderson, "Virginia Councillors and the American Revolution," *Va. Mag. of Hist. and Biog.*, LXXXII [Jan. 1974], 61, 69; P.R.O., C.O. 5/1353, fols. 291–92).

Sunday, 30 July 1775

Third Virginia Convention

John Bowdoin to The Honble Peyton Randolph Esqr President of the Convention now Sitting at Richmond per Express

Sir/   Northampton July 30. 1775
    Inclosed I send you a Petition [1] from our Committee to the Convention as we but yesterday heard that the Convention had come to a Resolution to stop the Exportation of Grain & Provisions after the 5th of next month, praying that the Exports for Indian Corn may be kept open, or permitted till 10. Septem[ber.] [2] should the Convention make no alteration in their first Resolution, many Traders & Planters will be greatly Injured here. I fully intended to have been at the Convention but the Indisposition of my family prevented which was the case with Mr ⟨John⟩ Burton our other Delegate
    I am with the Greatest Respect Sir yr mo Obt. Servt.
                                                          JOHN BOWDOIN

> Recipient's copy, autograph letter, signed, in papers of third Virginia Convention (Archives Division, Virginia State Library)

    1. For the "Petition" to which this is the covering letter, see 29 July 1775, Third Va. Convention, Northampton Co. Committee.
    2. The word here runs off the edge of the document and may originally have been abbreviated.

Monday, 31 July 1775

Third Virginia Convention

Proceedings of Eleventh Day of Session [1]

    The Order of the Day for the Convention to resolve itself into a Committee to take into Consideration the State of the Colony being read,

Resolved, that this Convention will Tomorrow resolve itself into the said Committee.[2]

adjourned till Tomorrow 9. oClock.

> Convention MS journal in hand of John Tazewell
> (Archives Division, Virginia State Library) [3]

Augusta County West: Journal of Captain James Wood

31st July we Arrived at the Shawanese Towns where I spoke to Kishanosity or the Hardman⟨.⟩ [4] desired him to call the Cheifs of the different Towns together as soon as Possible that I had something to say to them from the Great Council of Virginia⟨.⟩ [5] the Hardman [6] then informed me that Chenusaw [7] had returned home the night before and that he had brought the most alarming Accounts from Virginia (viz') that the People of Virginia were all determined upon War with the Indians except the Governor who was for peace but was obliged to fly on board of a ship to save his own life⟨;⟩ that the hostages found they were to be made Slaves of and sent to some other Country⟨;⟩ that the White People were all preparing for War and that they shewed him many Indian scalps among which Cuttemwha knew his Brothers⟨;⟩ that the Hostages determined if Possible to make their Escape and Accordingly sett off in the Night all of them together⟨;⟩ that the next day he being behind the other two at some distance was seized by three Men⟨;⟩ that he heard them determine to kill him on which one of them proceeded to Load his Gun while the other two held him by the Arms⟨;⟩ that before the Man loaded the Gun he found Means to disengage himself and made his Escape leaving his Gun and every thing also⟨;⟩ that he soon after heard Several Guns and was possitive that Cuttemwha and Neawau were both killed as he had been Sixty days travelling and had heard nothing of them⟨.⟩ I told Kishanosity that most of what Chenusaw had informed him was false and that I would be glad he would send for him which he did⟨.⟩ as soon as he came I explained the whole Matter to him and a Number of the other Indians and Informed them that Cuttemwha and Neawau were both well and on the Road and that they were bringing his Cloaths and every thing which he had left behind him and that it was very unlucky for him he did not turn back as the others had done to have got a horse and Saddle to ride home as they had

> Thwaites and Kellogg, *Revolution on the Upper Ohio, 1775–1777*, pp. 57–58

As Related to Augusta County West Committee

He arrived at the Shawanese towns on the 31st. He desired the Headman [8] to call the Headmen of the different towns together as soon as possible, that he had something to say to them from the Headmen of Virginia. The Head-men then informed him that Chenusaw, or the Judge, had returned home the night before; that he brought alarming accounts from Virginia, that all the people, except the Governor, were determined on war with the Indians, that the Governor was for peace, but was obliged to fly on board a ship; that the hostages found that they were to be made slaves and sent to some other colonys; that the white people were all preparing for war, and that they shewed him many Indian scalps, amongst which the Wolf [9] knew his broth-ers; upon which they determined, if possible, to make their escape, and ac-cordingly set off all together in the night; that the next day, he, being behind the others at some distance, was seized by three men; that he heard them say they would kill him, and one of them began to load his gun; while the other two before the gun was loaded, held him by the arm, he found means to disengage himself and make his escape, leaving his gun and every thing else behind him; soon after, he heard several guns go off, and was sure that Cuttenwa and Newa were killed, as he had been sixty days travelling, and had heard nothing of them.

Capt. Wood told the Headman that most of what Chenusaw, or the Judge, told him was false; and that he would be glad if he would send for him, which he did. As soon as he came Capt. Wood explained the whole matter to him and many more Indians, and informed them Cuttenwa and Newa were both well, and on the road; and that they were bringing his clothes, and what other things he left behind him; and that it was very unlucky for him he did not turn back, as the others did, and have a horse and a saddle to ride home as the others had.

> *Dunlap's Pennsylvania Packet, or, the General Ad-vertiser* (Philadelphia), 11 September 1775

Norfolk Borough Committee to Peyton Randolph

Sir,   Norfolk July 31. 1775.[10]

By order of the Committee for this Borough, I am directed to inform the Covention of the arrival of troops this day in this harbor in the sloop lately belonging to Mr. Bowdoin.[11] They are said to be from St. Augustine, and are about sixty in number,[12] under the command of one Captain and two Lieu-tenants: the Ensign, it is said, is coming by land. From good authority we learn, that another vessel with more troops may be hourly expected. At present we are under no apprehensions from them, but we find exceeding bad effects have arisen among the blacks from the neighborhood of the men of war, which we have great reason to believe will be very much encreased by the arrival of these troops.[13] The Committee think it their duty to give the Honorable the Convention the earliest information of this occurrence, that such measures may be taken as shall be judged most expedient.

I have the honor to be, sir, by order of the Committee [14]
   Your most obedt Servt.
Hon. Mr. Randolph.   WILLIAM DAVIES secy.

> Recipient's copy, autograph letter, signed (Miscel-
> laneous Manuscripts, Library of Congress)

Sussex County Committee

Exoneration of Suspects

At a meeting of the committee for Sussex *county, held at the courthouse, on*
   Monday *the* 31st *of* July, 1775.[15]
A CHARGE being laid against a certain WILLIAM NELSON, merchant, of Prince
George, that he had purchased wheat for the use of our enemies at Boston,[16]
and having voluntarily appeared before this committee, declared, that he had
instructions from a correspondent in England to purchase certain commodities, the produce of this country, to be shipped to the port of London; and
having read part of a letter relative thereto, the committee are of opinion, that
mr. Nelson is altogether clear of the said charge.

   Mess. ⟨Glaister⟩ HUNNICUTT and ⟨Peter⟩ WILLIAMS having been suspected
of aiding and assisting mr. Nelson in the said purchase, have also cleared themselves of such suspicion, to the satisfaction of the committee.

   A charge being laid also against RICHARD BLOW, of Sussex, merchant, that
he had purchased, or been employed to purchase, for or on account of mr.
JOHN HAY, merchant, of Surry, a quantity of provisions for the use of our
enemies at Boston, the said Blow, being examined, has also fully cleared himself of the said accusation, to the satisfaction of the committee.

                                        Michael Blow, chairman.
                           (a copy)
                              John Massenburg, clerk.

> *Virginia Gazette* (Purdie), 11 August 1775

1. The membership on this day could not have exceeded 104 in number, or 103 if
George Stubblefield was awaiting Peyton Randolph's letter of 28 July 1775 in Williamsburg.

2. The "Order of the Day," voted on 27 July 1775, was that the "Letter from the
Deputies appointed to represent this Colony in General Congress together with the
papers inclosed therein" and the "Letter from Oconestoto," together with "the other
Papers relative to Indian Affairs," be taken under consideration. On 29 July consideration was voted to be deferred until "Monday next."

The abbreviation of this day's session may be ascribed to the time desired and
needed for committee labor. The work of 3 committees at this time called for special
diligence: the committee for defense and protection, appointed on 19 July, with
Richard Bland chairman; the committee of elections, appointed on 25 July, with
Archibald Cary chairman; and the committee on war claims, also appointed on 25 July,

with Isaac Zane, Jr., chairman. On the 4 committees now sitting (including the 1 appointed on 18 July, with Robert Carter Nicholas chairman, to investigate the Fincastle Co. committee–William Preston controversy), there was a total of 46 memberships filled by 33 individuals, or fewer than a 3d of the delegates.

Hence to such fainéants as Robert Wormeley Carter, who had not and would not be appointed to anything, learning what was being done was a matter of buttonholing those who were doing. And there was the concomitant problem of keeping himself entertained. It is difficult to envision "Wild Bob" not finding outlets, when the convention should not be in session, for indulgence in his unconventional propensities; but confined as he was to existence in or near the small town of Richmond and restrained by prohibitions of the Continental Association, he was already restless and sighed, "God knows when we shall rise" (R. W. Carter to Landon Carter, 29 July 1775, Sabine Hall Papers, Dept. of MSS, Univ. of Va. Library).

3. Tazewell wrote "No. 10 & 11" edgewise at the bottom of the 4th of 4 pages (the 3d of which is blank) on which he entered the journal for this day below that for the preceding day.

4. Following their departure from the "Wyandots Town" on 29 July, Capt. James Wood and Simon Girty "travelled very fast and Constant," their "Course South East," for the most part "thro' extensive Plains and Meadows." On the 30th they arose "before sun rise" and rode southward along the banks of the Scioto River until at noon they reached the town of Pluggy, a Mohawk leader of a mixed and undisciplined band. But Pluggy being "from home" and his followers "drunk and very troublesome," Wood left a string of wampum and a "Speech" for Pluggy, purchased some dried meat, and set off with Girty for the "big Salt Licks." They arrived at that destination at dark and took "Lodging" with "an old Squaw in a Cabbin." On the present day they departed at 7:00 A.M. and rode "very Constant" for 8½ hours (Thwaites and Kellogg, *Rev. on the Upper Ohio*, pp. 56–57).

The 2 travelers were now in one of the several Shawnee villages located in the Scioto River Valley between the present-day towns of Circleville and Chillocothe, Ohio. If, as the identity of their host seems to make probable, they were in the town visited in Jan. 1773 by Rev. David Jones, they found it small and pleasant. "The buildings here are logs," the missionary had noted in his journal, "their number about twelve." And it was "a peaceable town," unlike those adjacent, which were full of "robbers and villains," the "chief men" of which were the greatest "scoundrels guilty of theft and robbery without any apology or redress" (ibid., p. 57 n. 87; D. Jones, *Journal of Two Visits Made to Some Indian Nations*, pp. 52–54).

5. The "Great Council of Virginia" was the Council and House of Burgesses.

6. Although a Shawnee "king," Kishanosity, or THE HARDMAN, was distinguished neither in appearance nor life-style. But the Rev. Mr. Jones found him to possess "some degree of hospitality," and when the monarch served him a breakfast of "fat buffalo, beaver tails, and chocolate," all in a solemn manner whilst acknowledging "the goodness of God," the 39-year-old divine concluded that he was also "a man of good sense" (D. Jones, *Journal of Two Visits Made to Some Indian Nations*, pp. v, 52–54).

7. For Chenusaw, or The Judge, see 18 July 1775, n. 11.

8. Either the unidentified copyist or someone at John Dunlap's printing office mistakenly designated The Hardman as "the Headman."

9. "The Wolf" was Cutemwha's English name.

10. The captain of the war sloop *Otter*, Lord Dunmore's floating palace at Gosport, entered notice of the troops herein mentioned in his log on 31 July 1775 (P.R.O., Adm. 51/663, unpaged).

11. John Bowdoin's merchant "sloop" was the *Betsy,* seized by Lt. Henry Colins of the *Magdalen* late in May 1775 (25 May 1775, Norfolk Borough Town Meeting; Clark, *Naval Docs. of the Am. Rev.,* I, 1025).

12. The troops, a light-infantry contingent from the 14th Regiment of Foot, were estimated by the governor to be "about Seventy in number including Officers" (Clark, *Naval Docs. of the Am. Rev.,* I, 1025; P.R.O., C.O. 5/1353, fol. 232).

13. The "elopement of their negroes" had caused white owners in Norfolk to become "much disturbed." Notwithstanding assurances given by the officers commanding His Majesty's warcraft in the harbor "that not the least encouragement" would be extended to runaway slaves, many bondsmen had "made application for service on board." They were turned away. A committee of the gratified members of the borough Common Hall waited on Captains John Macartney and Matthew Squire "with the thanks of the Corporation for their conduct" (*Va. Gazette, or the Norfolk Intelligencer,* 2 Aug. 1775).

14. The meeting may have run late into the night before the committee completed its business. In reporting the information contained in the present letter, the *Va. Gazette, or the Norfolk Intelligencer* of 2 Aug. 1775 added that "early yesterday morning" the committee "dispatched an express to the Honorable the Convention of the colony." The letter would be laid before the convention on 3 Aug. 1775 (Procs., 3d para.). His Excellency was delighted with the alarm occasioned by the arrival of the royal troops and gloatingly hyperbolized to Whitehall that it was "the cause of many expresses from here to the Convention" (P.R.O., C.O. 5/1353, fol. 232).

15. This is the 1st record found of a meeting of the committee of Sussex County since that of 8 May 1775, and it is the last record for that committee within the present volume.

16. That is, Nelson was charged with contravening a resolution of the Continental Congress passed on 2 June, printed in Purdie's *Va. Gazette* of 16 June 1775, and officially noticed by the House of Burgesses 3 days later (11 July, Third Va. Convention, In Congress and n. 12). Consideration of the resolution by the convention was a part of the present "Order of the Day," for which see n. 2 above.

Tuesday, 1 August 1775

Third Virginia Convention

Proceedings of Twelfth Day of Session [1]

A Petition and Remonstrance from the Merchants of the Borough of Norfolk, and also Instructions from the Committee of the said Borough to their Delegates in Convention setting forth the great Hardships & Inconveniences to which they should be reduced, by this Convention for stopping the Exportation of Grain and Provisions after the fifth Day of this Month and praying that the same may be repealed, was presented to the Convention & read.

Ordered, that the said Petition and Remonstrance together with the said Instructions do lie on the Table.[2]

The Convention then according to the order of the Day, resolved itself into a Committee to take into Consideration the State of the Colony, and after sometime spent therein Mr President ⟨Peyton Randolph⟩ resumed the Chair & Mr. ⟨Richard⟩ Bland reported that the Committee had had the State of the Colony under their Consideration, but not having Time to go through the same, had directed him to move for Leave to sit again.[3]

Resolved, that this Convention will on Thursday next, resolve itself into a Committee to take into their further Consideration the State of the Colony.

Adjourned til Thursday 9. oClock.

> Convention MS journal in hand of John Tazewell
> (Archives Division, Virginia State Library) [4]

Matthew Tilghman to the Honorable Convention of Virginia

Gentlemen,   Annapolis 1st August 1775.

The Resolution of your Convention, That no Flour, Wheat, or other Grain, or Provisions of any kind, should be exported from your Colony to any part of the World after the fifth Day of August, came to Hand by your Express Yesterday Afternoon.[5] The Delegates from this province have communicated to this Convention, That the Utility and propriety of stopping Exports had been fully considered by the Congress, and that they had not thought proper to stop the Exports before the 10th day of September. We have received Information that the Congress intended to adjourn the Beginning of this Week, so that this Subject cannot again be brought before them.[6] This Convention on mature Consideration do not see that the Advantages to the common Cause by an immediate Stoppage of the Export of provisions could equal the Inconveniences and Distresses of Individuals which would certainly be occasioned thereby, nor that any Distress could be brought on the common Enemy by our coming into your Resolution without the Accession of the Colonies of Pennsylvania and New-York, which cannot be brought about sooner than the 10th of September as the Convention of New-York will probably rise about the same Time as the Congress, and the Assembly of Pennsylvania hath already adjourned.[7] For these Reasons, we have unanimously resolved not to prohibit Exports before that Day.

We are with great Respect your mo. obdt Servts.

Signed by order of the Convention,[8]   MAT. TILGHMAN
                                                             President of the Convention

> Recipients' copy, MS letter in hand of Gabriel Du
> Vall, with Tilghman's autograph signature (Etting
> Collection, Historical Society of Pennsylvania)

John Connolly to George Rootes Esqr: at Richmond

[Dear Sir: Winchester August 1st. 1775.

I yesterday ar]rived [9] here from the warm springs, to which place [I intentionally] conducted three Indians sent with m[e, to] give them an opportunity of seeing as many Gentlemen of Virginia, as that place, & this Season generally bring together.[10] I have finished a treaty with the Shawanese, which I have also brought with me, & I flatter myself it will prove satisfactory to the Gentlemen of the Convention, at Richmond, as it has been particularly so, to the Inhabitants in our Country.[11] You must well know Sir, from a finale retrospect upon the necessary business in which I have been for some considerable time past engaged, that I must have been exposed to considerable expense, & that the mere subsistence of a Militia Officer in my Rank, could not be sufficient to have indemnified me. add to this consideration the trouble I have experienced from the Government of Pennsylvania,[12] & the necessity I was under of conducting the military affairs of this Government, during our late troubles, throughout the great extent of that remote part of Augusta; a due attention to which important business, caused me entirely to relinquish every other pursuit, & devote myself solely to the publick Service. I should have even blushed to mention any of [the]se Circumstances, did not I fin[d that the malice of my] Ene[mie]s pushes them on to every vile s[tep to prejudice my] character, & depreciate the value of my [publick services.]

Pecuniary acknowledgment alone [would be very unsatisfactory] to my Mind, did it not also bespe[ak the care of the] Government which I have faithfully served, & must therefore silence effectually, the slanderous tongues of the ungenerous.[13]

It has been diligently propagated thro' this Country that I, as a ministerial Tool, would be extremely sollicitous to forward their designs; & should be ready to support every measure which Lord Dunmore might recommend to me. I have only to assure you that such insinuations are malicious, & far foreign to truth; & that no person would sooner shun an Act, which must draw down upon Him, the censure of His Countrymen than myself: & altho gratitude, & honor call upon me to testify upon all occasions, the good offices which I experienced from His Excellency Lord Dunmore; yet you may be satisfied, that such impression should operate no farther upon me, than it ought to do; & that I justly distinguish between a ministerial officer, & a Friend, a Gentleman in a private character.

I have some business with, & a letter to the Honorable Peyton Randolph,[14] as well as a desire to see Jno Randolph Esqr. & some other my Acquaintances at Williamsburgh, & must confess that I should also if agreeable, desire to see the Governor & I did not care under whatever restrictions was it judged necessary.[15]

I am &c Sir your most obedt Srvt

JNO CONNOLLY

Autograph letter, signed, in loose papers of third Virginia Convention (Archives Divisions, Virginia State Library)

Augusta County West: Journal of Captain James Wood

1st August Kishanosity sent me word he had sent for the Cheifs of the other Towns and that they would meet me in the Council house to Morrow

Morning⟨.⟩ Employed ourselves the remaining part of the day in enquiries of the Squaws concerning the Speeches and belts sent to the Shawanese by the French at Fort D'Troit who all gave the same Accounts we had before heard with this addition⟨,⟩ that the Picts and Tawixtawees had Accepted the Belts but that the Shawanese had dug a hole in the Ground and buried them never to rise again [16]

> Thwaites and Kellogg, *Revolution on the Upper Ohio, 1775–1777*, p. 58

As Related to Augusta County West Committee

That on the first of August he enquired of sundry squaws concerning the speeches and belts sent to the Shawanese by the French at Detroit. They all gave the same accounts he had received before, with this addition, that the Picts and Tightwees had accepted the belts, but that the Shawanese had dug a hole in the ground, and buried them never to rise again.

> *Dunlap's Pennsylvania Packet, or, the General Advertiser* (Philadelphia), 11 September 1775

Proceedings of Officers of Gentlemen Volunteers of Independent Companies in Williamsburg

At a Meeting of the officers of the Volunteer Companies now in Wmsbgh Present Charles Scott, James Innes George Gilmer Frank Eppes Samuel Harwood Oliver Towles Richd. Kidder Mead⟨e⟩ Everard Mead⟨e⟩, Edwd. Walker, Wm. Finnie, Joseph Jones, Edmund Ruffin John Nicholas & Humphrey Harwood, gent'n.[17]

Resolved that Mr Robert Prentis do immediately appear before the Gent of this meeting & make known his reasons for alledging by letter [18] to the Honble. Rd. Corbin that he was by the sd. officers informed they were instructed by the Convention to stop the public money in his hands as clerk to the Receiver General and ordered that Everard Mead do wait on Mr Prentis with a Copy of the order.[19]

A Resolve of the Convention made the 28th last month having this day come to the hands of the Gentn. of this meeting declaring that they cannot approve of the proceedings mentioned in this letter to the sd Convention [20] it is therefore unanimously resolved that the several sums of money & Bills of Exchange Received by Capt. Geo⟨rge⟩. Stubblefield of the Honble Lewis Burwell, Esqr, be restored to him immediately & ordered that Richd. Kid. Mead Thos. Ruffin & Ed. Ruffin Gent do wait on the Treasurers Clerk & receive from him the money & bills lodged in his hands by order of a former meeting [21] & that the sd. Meade proceed from thence to the house of the sd.

Burwell & after delivering to him the said money & bills to obtain his receipt for the same⟨.⟩ it is also resolved that, Mr Robert Prentis affidavit be delivered up & he discharged from the Obligation⟨,⟩ therefore that the said Mead wait on him for that purpose.

> Document MS transcript in hand of George Gilmer, in autograph diary and Revolutionary memoranda of Dr. George Gilmer (Virginia Historical Society)

Officers to President and Gentlemen of Convention

The repeated alarms we daily receive induces us to beg you would lay down some certain line for our conduct, lest in our excessive Zeal we should precipitate our Countrymen into unnecessary Calamities.

The Governors Cutter has carried off a number of Slaves belonging to private Gentlemen⟨.⟩ we think it high ⟨time⟩ to establish the doctrine of repraisal & to take immediate possession (if possible of his person) at all events of his property.[22]

It is certain that one Phillips commands an Ignorant disorderly mob who are in direct opposition to our plan.[23] It is our desire to crush these matters in embryo & take every advantage a kind providence may make us masters of.

We beg liberty to acknowledge to you the execution of those matters before related to you, tho ever so proper ought first to have received your sanction⟨.⟩ we stand reproved for our precipitate conduct, & ready to execute any matters under your authority that you shall please to direct at the expense of life & fortune.[24]

The bearer Capt Js. Innes in whom we place the most implicit confidence will explain much fuller than we can by letter, & we therefore request you would for your fuller information call upon him.[25]

With the most profound respect we Subscribe ourselves

> your Soldiers & Servts.

> Letter MS transcript in hand of George Gilmer, ibid.

1. The membership present this day would not have exceeded 104 if George Stubblefield had returned from Williamsburg. That he is not listed among the "officers of the Volunteer Companies" meeting this day in the capital (6th item below) suggests that he may have left for Richmond. That the officers sent another of their number to explain their actions to the convention after their convocation would seem to indicate that Stubblefield did not go back to the convention with the latest "information."

2. For the "Petition and Remonstrance," see 28 July 1775, Third Va. Convention, Merchants and Traders of Norfolk Borough and Portsmouth Town; for the "Instructions," same, Norfolk Borough Committee.

3. The "Order of the Day," voted on 27 July 1775, was that "the Letter from the

Deputies appointed to represent this Colony in General Congress together with the papers inclosed therein" and the "Letter from Oconestoto," along "with the other Papers relative to Indian Affairs," be taken under consideration. On 31 July consideration was voted to be deferred until "Tomorrow."

4. Edgewise on the top of the 4th of 4 pages (the 3d of which is blank) Tazewell wrote "No. 12."

5. For the "Resolution of your Convention," see 24 July 1775, Third Va. Convention, Proceedings, 3d resolution. Peyton Randolph's letter of transmittal is under the date heading of 27 July 1775, Third Va. Convention, 2d entry.

6. It was on this same day, 1 Aug. 1775, that the second Continental Congress "Adjourned to Tuesday, the 5 of Septr next" (*JCC*, II, 239).

7. Contrary to expectations in Maryland, the "Convention," or first Provincial Congress, of New York would not adjourn until 4 Nov. 1775 (Becker, *Hist. of Pol. Parties in the Prov. of N.Y.*, p. 227). In Pennsylvania constitutional evolution was taking a different course. There the "Assembly," while maintaining nominal relations with Gov. John Penn, had created its own executive agency in a Committee of Safety empowered to prepare vigorously for war. On 30 June 1775 the Assembly had "adjourned to *Monday*, the 18th of *September* next, at Four o'Clock, P.M." (Gertrude MacKinney and Charles F. Hoban, eds., *Pennsylvania Archives*, 8th ser. [8 vols., Philadelphia, 1931–35], VIII, 7249).

8. Tilghman's letter would be laid before the Virginia Convention on 8 Aug. 1775 as the initial business of the day.

9. Bracketed words, syllables, and letters are those borrowed from the printed copy edited by William G. Stanard and printed in the *Va. Mag. of Hist. and Biog.*, IV (July 1906), 78–79, when the letter was in a much better state of preservation. In addition to wears and tears along the edges and folds of the original, a portion measuring approximately 2½″ × 3″ is missing from the upper left of the manuscript, a result of which is that there is a loss of an even greater amount of writing on the verso.

10. The "warm springs" in question were the Berkeley Warm Springs in present-day Morgan County, W.Va. For the "three Indians" who accompanied Connolly, see 10 July 1775, Third Va. Convention, Augusta Co. West, and n. 1; 18 July, same, and n. 14.

11. Connolly's letter is to be understood only when accepted for what it was, a tissue of lies. At the distance of 2 centuries his recourse to trickery may be forgiven when it is recalled that even in a more enlightened age, all continues to be considered fair also in war. The writer's statement that he had "finished" a treaty with the Shawnee was an attempt to increase his credit with the delegates in Richmond and so to procure for himself a shield against incarceration or worse by distrustful patriots while he made a break to reach Lord Dunmore. At the same time, whether he knew it or not, the major's protestations of wounded innocence were abetted by James Wood's letter of 9 July asserting that he had conducted negotiations with the Six Nations and the Delawares "in the Most Open and Candid Manner," and by John Campbell's of 3 days later to the same effect (9 July 1775, Third Va. Convention, Augusta Co. West, Wood to Randolph; 12 July, same, Campbell to Harvie and Rootes).

In his "Narrative," written 7 or 8 years after the events delineated, Connolly stated that at about this time there arrived in Winchester a letter to him from Peyton Randolph enclosing the "entire approbation" of the convention for his services. No such documents have been found. This fact does not of itself disprove Connolly's allegation. But what alone is demonstrable is that whereas there is in the convention journal no resolution extolling the major's accomplishments, no directive for the president to address him, and no authorization to hire a courier to go to Winchester, there is an expression of approbation for developments at Fort Pitt and a commendation bestowed on "the Committee of the County of Augusta" as a whole (John Connolly, "Narrative," *Pa. Mag. of Hist. and Biog.*, XII [1888], 322; 25 July 1775, Third Va. Convention, Procs. and nn. 6, 8).

12. For this "trouble," see 22 June 1775, n. 2; 26 June, n. 4.

13. For some "reports" that had "been propagated" to the "Prejudice of the Principal Inhabitants" and to "Major Connolly in Particular," see 12 July 1775, Third Va. Convention, Campbell to Harvie and Rootes and n. 5 above. According to Connolly, the "suspicious valetudinarians of the warm spring" and "the clerk" of the committee of West Augusta, James Berwick, had alerted the Frederick County committee at Winchester to the traveler's "dangerous and Tory principles." But while being interrogated by that committee, the examinee was apparently vindicated by the arrival of the "express" from Richmond bearing the aforementioned letter and enclosures from Peyton Randolph (Connolly, "Narrative," pp. 321–23).

14. The "business" was unintended and the "letter" probably nonexistent.

15. There can be but little doubt that George Rootes received the present letter and made its contents known to his convention colleagues. Edgewise on the address cover there is written in an unknown hand: "a well regulated & appointed army of Sixty men to be reinforced by forty more." This clause comports with the floor resolution contained in the 2d paragraph of the proceedings of 7 Aug. 1775 directing John Neville "to march with his Company of one hundred Men and take possession of Fort Pitt."

Connolly himself later asserted that the letter was penned as a ruse to aid his journeying unmolested to Dunmore's headquarters. The assertion is supported by his actions. He proceeded not to Richmond but to the lower Tidewater. Stopping at Fredericksburg to dine with Hugh Mercer, he sat in uneasy silence while "inflammatory and unconstitutional toasts and sentiments were drank" by his host and other guests. The silence kindled such suspicions that a spy was sent after the major "under the appearance of an accidental traveller on the road to Richmond." But Connolly gave him the slip and hurrying through Williamsburg at night, went on to Yorktown in a blinding rain. Thereafter he hastened down the peninsula, crossed the James River, and at Gosport found haven with the governor (Connolly, "Narrative," pp. 323–24).

16. Captain Wood had heard the "same Accounts" several times before, most recently from the "King and Cheifs of the Delawares" on 23 July 1775. He would duly record the meeting of "to Morrow."

17. Officers not heretofore identified by home county are Everard Meade of Amelia, and Edward Walker, Joseph Jones, Edmund Ruffin, and John Nicholas, all of Dinwiddie.

18. Not found.

19. If the officers desired to set the record straight—that is, to impress on Prentis that their actions had been taken anterior to receipt of any warrant by the convention—that was one matter. Lacking their "Instructions" to whoever delivered the document, it is impossible to declare whether Prentis deliberately overstated the case to Corbin or was justifiably confused. His affidavit of 26 July 1775 (Third Va. Convention, 2d entry) asserting that he would "pay away" no sum of money "but to such purposes as shall be directed by the convention" does nothing to clarify but does hint at possible misconstruction. Yet to summon him to appear "before the Gent" of

the independent company was another matter. The young officers at Williamsburg were arrogating to themselves all of the powers of a committee of correspondence. Thereby they were underscoring the validity of a traditional article of faith of their British heritage—that unless completely subordinated to the civil power, the military would end by subverting the rights and liberties of the people. The penultimate paragraph of the officers' letter next following reveals that subversion was not their intent. But absence of intent did not invalidate the article.

20. For the "Resolve of the Convention made the 28th last month," see the Proceedings of that date.

21. The "former meeting" at which the decision was reached to deputize Robert Carter Nicholas's "Clerk" to hold the confiscated funds, though at the time without the "Treasurers" knowledge, was held on 26 July 1775 or shortly thereafter.

22. For the concern of white masters of the borough of Norfolk over the behavior of bonded blacks living in "the neighbourhood of the men of war," see 31 July 1775, Third Va. Convention, Norfolk Borough Committee to Randolph, and n. 13.

23. Josiah Phillips was a "laborer" formerly of Lynnhaven Parish, Princess Anne County. Sporadically over the next 2 years he would compensate for a previously humdrum existence by leading a band of loyalist murderers and plunderers on forays throughout the southeastern corner of Virginia. He would be honored by being the only principal designated in an act of attainder passed by a General Assembly of the commonwealth and, although not as a result of that act, would condignly terminate his career on the gallows (William P. Trent, "The Case of Josiah Phillips," *American Historical Review*, I [Apr. 1896], 444–54; *Va. Gazette* [Purdie], 11 Aug. 1775).

24. The "matters before related" to the convention are contained in the officers' letter of 26 July 1775.

25. Capt. James Innes would deliver the present letter to the convention on 3 Aug. 1775 (Procs., and n. 4).

Wednesday, 2 August 1775

Third Virginia Convention

Augusta County West: Journal of Captain James Wood

2d August [1] at 10 o'Clock a runner came and Informed me the Cheifs were Assembled in the Council House ready to receive me upon which I went and was received in the most freindly manner when I delivered the following speech to Kishanosity [2] in the Presence of the Shade and Snake the Milkman Shawanese Ben and many other Cheifs and Warriors *Brothers the Shawanese* your Elder Brothers of Virginia in their great Council have appointed me with five others [3] to meet all the Cheifs of the different Nations of Indians on the Ohio and Lakes in forty one days from this time at Fort Pitt in Order to Brighten the Chain of Freindship [4] between them and the People of Virginia and have ordered me to come to this Place to assure you that their Hearts are good towards you and that they will be glad to meet the Cheifs of

your Nation fully to Confirm the Peace agreed upon last fall between Lord
Dunmore and the Shawanese⟨,⟩ and Expect you will be fully prepared to
Comply with your part of the Conditions at that time⟨.⟩ [5] I am very Glad to
see your Brother Chenusaw is returned safe⟨.⟩ he left us without any reason
that we know of but Imagine it must be Owing to some Mistake or other⟨.⟩
as soon as we found he was gone we sent many People on Horseback with
written papers directing all our people to treat him kindly so that he might
return to you in Safety⟨.⟩ your Brothers Cuttemwha and Neawau are well⟨.⟩
they are now on the way and you may depend will be safely brought to the
Treaty⟨.⟩ [6] Cuttemwha desired me to tell you to be Strong and to come at the
time I appoint and to bring some of your wise Women along with you [7] *A
String of White Wampum* [8]

after delivering the Speech I called for Chenusaw but was Informed he
was ashamed to Appear⟨.⟩ I then at their Desire Explained the nature of the
dispute with Lord Dunmore and Convinced them that Chenusaw had not
told them the truth and also Explained to them the dispute with Great Britain
in the same Manner which I had before done to the Wyandots and other
Nations of Indians⟨.⟩ [9] the Hardman then made the following Answer to my
Speech⟨:⟩

Brother the Big knife I am very thankful as well as all my freinds here
present for your good speech delivered to us at our Council fire⟨.⟩ It gives us
great Pleasure to think that our Brothers the big knife have not forgot us and
that we shall have an Opportunity of talking to them in Freindship at the time
you now Mention⟨.⟩ we are much Oblidged to our Brothers of Virginia for
their Care in directing all their People to let our Brother Chenusaw come to
us without receiveing any hurt⟨.⟩ his coming away in the Manner he did proceeded from Mistake in not Understanding your Language⟨.⟩ we are fully
Satisfied with what you have told us and hope you'll not think hard of us for
his bad behaviour⟨.⟩ after which Kishanosity and other Cheifs enquired after
News whether a great Many of our Young Men were not going to Boston to
War against the English Red Coats and if we had not several Engagements
with them⟨;⟩ to which I answered that but few Men were to go from Virginia
as there were a great Sufficiency of Men in New England to Manage all the
Regular Troops in America or which they were Able to send and as for the
Engagements there had been several in all of which we had beatten them with
great loss on their side and very small on Ours⟨,⟩ but that we were in daily
Expectation of all differences being setled between the two Countries to the
Satisfaction of both. [10] The Shade then Informed me that he had Just returned
from the Miami River⟨;⟩ that he met Catfish and a Number of other Delawares on the Ohio with many things which they had Robbed the Inhabitants
of on the Great Kanhawa⟨;⟩ that he gave me this Information least his Brothers
the Big knife should blame the Shawanese for it⟨.⟩ Kishanosity then Complained of the Encroachments of the Virginians⟨;⟩ he said they were now
settling in Great Numbers in the Midst of their Hunting Grounds on the
Kentucke River and that many of our people Crossed the Ohio killed and
drove off their Game⟨.⟩ he then Asked my Advice whether they should go

and talk to the People on Kentucke about it⟨;⟩ to which I replied that I thought it would be very Improper least some of our bad people might do them an Injury⟨,⟩ but advised them to let the Matter alone till the Treaty when I made no doubt but we should be able to make them sensible that we had already purchased the Lands on Kentucke River from the Six Nations at the Treaty of Fort Stanwix⟨;⟩ [11] and as to our Hunters Crossing the River and Killing the Game we should do every thing in our power to prevent it in future⟨.⟩ he then desired me to beg their brothers the big knife not to listen to any bad stories which they might hear as he had great reason to Beleive that David Duncan [12] would make many false reports that he had been talking a Great deal to the foolish Women and paid no regard to what the Men said to him⟨.⟩ I then told him that I had been Informed that the Commanding Officer at Fort De Troit and Monseiur Baubee ⟨Duperon Baby⟩ had sent a Belt and String of Black Wampum to their Nation with a Speech that the people of Virginia intended to drive them off and to take their Lands⟨,⟩ recommending them and the other Nations to Join together in Order to Oppose them and at the same time advised them not to Listen to any thing which might be said to them by the Virginians⟨,⟩ that they were a people not to be depended upon – all of which the Shawanese Acknowledged⟨.⟩ [13] they said that whatever they had heard or received from them they had Dug a hole in the Ground and Buried them never to rise again⟨.⟩ [14] I was then Informed by a Mohicon Indian [15] who spoke good English that he had Just Returned from Kacayuga where he saw a Greater Number of Indians than he had ever seen before and that we might Expect Warmer Work this fall than had ever happened before⟨.⟩ [16] I was likewise Informed by James Bavard a Trader in the Shawenese Towns that the Indians were Constantly Counseling and that the Women all seemed very uneasy in Expectation that there would be War⟨.⟩ I then set off from the Shawanese Towns

Thwaites and Kellogg, *Revolution on the Upper Ohio, 1775–1777*, pp. 58–63

As Related to Augusta County West Committee

The 2d of August he delivered a speech to the Shawanese, the same in substance to what he had delivered to other nations. He explained the nature of the dispute with Lord Dunmore, and convinced them that Chenusaw had not told the truth, and likewise explained to them the nature of the dispute with Great Britain. The Headman [17] returned them the following answer,

"Brother, the Big Knife,

"I am very thankful, as well as all my friends, who are now present, for your good speech this day delivered to us at our council fire. It gives us great pleasure to think that our brothers, the Big Knife, have not forgot us; and that we will have an opportunity of talking to them in friendship at the time you mention. We are much obliged to our brothers, the Big Knife, for their care in directing all their people to let our brother Chenusaw come to us. His coming away in the manner he did, proceeded from a mistake. We are fully satisfied with what you have told us, and hope you will not think hard of us for his bad behaviour." [18]

Dunlap's Pennsylvania Packet, or, the General Advertiser (Philadelphia), 11 September 1775

1. Wood's journal continues from the previous day, 1 Aug. 1775.

2. Or The Hardman.

3. The "great Council" was the governor's Council and the House of Burgesses. For the 5 other appointees, see 9 July 1775, n. on provenance, 1st para.

4. See 19 May 1775, n. 5.

5. For "the Peace agreed upon last fall between Lord Dunmore and the Shawanese," see ibid. and n. 3.

6. For the 3 hostages and the escape of Chenusaw, or The Judge, see 18 July 1775, Third Va. Convention, Augusta Co. West, and n. 11; 31 July, same.

7. That squaws often knew what occurred in council is evident from Wood's having received on 1 Aug. information verified this day by the Shawnee chiefs. Indian tribes with sociopolitical organizations similar to that of the Iroquois often gave women prominent roles in intratribal discussions. This was true of the Shawnee. In 1706 Thomas Chalkley, a Quaker missionary, found that "some of the most Esteemed of their Women do sometimes speak in their Councils." On his inquiring why, the Friend was told that *some Women were wiser than some Men.*" This was primitive philosophy, of course, but even in the male-dominated world of white Virginia a logician in 1775 would have found the proposition easier to slither around than to argue down (Hodge, *Handbook of Am. Indians*, pt. 2, 971; [Thomas Chalkley], *A Journal, or, Historical Account of the Life, Travels and Christian Experiences, of That Antient, Faithful Servant of Jesus Christ, Thomas Chalkley* . . . [Philadelphia, 1749; 2d ed., London, 1751], p. 50).

8. See 20 May 1775, n. 7.

9. Speeches "in the same Manner" were those delivered to the Delaware chief White Eyes and to the Wyandots on 10 and 27 July 1775 respectively.

10. For the "few Men" of Virginia, some from Wood's home county, Frederick, who by this date had reached Boston, see 11 July 1775, n. 16; see also 28 July, Third Va. Convention, Augusta Co. West, and n. 19. If Wood had truthfully anticipated an Anglo-American settlement of "all differences," he would have been writing off half the purpose of his mission; but here was the diplomatist in a play for further time.

11. For the purchase at Fort Stanwix of "the Lands of Kentucke," see 28 July 1775, n. 18.

12. For David Duncan, see 1 July 1775, n. 5.

13. Wood upon his arrival at Fort Pitt on 9 July was first "Informed" of the Shawnee's having been put in contact with the agents of the Detroit commandant. On 23 July 1775 the captain was given a "Belt and String" that the Delawares had received from those agents.

14. Wood here repeats a phrase with which he had concluded his interrogation of "sundry squaws" on the day immediately preceding.

15. The Mahican (Mohegan) Indians had jointly occupied the Hudson River Valley with their kinsmen the Mohawks before breaking up into several bands, one

of which around the 1730s filtered into the Wyoming Valley in Pennsylvania, thence into Ohio, and there were absorbed into the Delaware tribes (Hodge, *Handbook of Am. Indians,* pt. 1, 786).

16. "Kacauga" was probably the Indian village of Caughnawaga on the St. Lawrence River opposite Montreal. Near there on or shortly after 17 July 1775, Col. Guy Johnson, northern Indian agent, recuperated from his recent flight, had assembled "the Northern Confederacy to the amount of 1700 & upwards" and procured their promise "to assist his Majesty's Troops in their operations" (O'Callaghan, *N.Y. Col. Docs.,* VIII, 636).

17. The Hardman.

18. Here ends the information given by Captain Wood to the committee of the District of West Augusta. The narrative was probably put down on paper by James Berwick, committee clerk. Then on 24 Aug. 1775 congressional Indian commissioner James Wilson forwarded the "information" to Benjamin Franklin in Philadelphia, probably at whose urging the document was published (Wilson to John Montgomery, 24 Aug. 1775, Ferdinand Julius Dreer Autograph Collection, Hist. Soc. of Pa.). The public image of Virginia (its governor withdrawn) working to safeguard the lives of frontiersmen could be made to stand in brave contrast to that of Pennsylvania (its governor present) bent on jeopardizing lives by haggling over a patch of earth. But if so, did the committee miss a point? The natural line of communication from Fort Pitt was eastward to Philadelphia, not tortuously southeast to Williamsburg, where, if it was sent, the narrative was printed in none of the 3 gazettes.

The next printed entry from Wood's journal is under the date heading of 11 Aug. 1775, when he returned to Fort Pitt (Third Va. Convention, Augusta Co. West).

Thursday, 3 August 1775

Third Virginia Convention

Proceedings of Thirteenth Day of Session [1]

A Letter from the Committee of the County of Northampton complaining of the great Hardships and Inconveniences to which the Inhabitants of their County would be particularly exposed by the Resolution entered into by this Convention for stopping the Exportation of Grain and Provisions after the fifth Day of this Month and praying that they might have Liberty to export their Grain till the tenth of September agreable to the Resolutions of the Continental Congress, was presented to the Convention and read.[2]

Ordered, that the said Petition do lie on the Table.

A Letter from the Committee of the Borough of Norfolk informing the Convention of the Arrival of Troops from St. Augustine, about sixty in Number, under the Command of one Captain and two Lieutenants; that they had learned from good Authority another Vessel with more Forces might be hourly expected: that at present they were under no Apprehensions from the Troops but found exceeding bad Effects among the Slaves from the Neighbourhood of the Men of War, which they had great Reason to believe would be very much increased by the Arrival of these Troops.[3]

Also, a Letter from the Officers of the Voluntier Companies in Williamsburg, requesting that some certain Line for their Conduct might be laid down, lest in their Zeal to serve their Country, they might precipitate their Countrymen into unnecessary Calamities—informing the Convention, that the Governor's Cutter had carried off a Number of Slaves belonging to private Gentlemen, & that they thought it high Time to establish the Doctrine of Reprisal—that one ⟨Josiah⟩ Phillips commanded an ignorant disorderly Mob, in direct Opposition to the Measures of this Country and they wished to crush such Attempts in Embryo and to take every Advantage a kind Providence might make them Masters of—acknowledging the Execution of the Measures they had formerly laid before the Convention, though ever so proper, ought first to have received the Sanction of this Convention—that they stood reproved for their too precipitate Conduct on that Occasion, and held themselves in Readiness to execute any Instructions the Convention should be pleased to give at the Expence of Life & fortune[—That they placed implicit Confidence in Capt. James Innes, the bearer of their Letter, and wished refered to him for a fuller Explanation of Matters—],[4] were laid before the Convention and read.

Resolved, that the said Letters be referred to the Committee appointed to take into Consideration the State of the Colony.

The Convention then, according to the Order of the Day,[5] resolved itself into the said Committee[—examined[6] Capt. Innes relative to the Contents of the Letters

Resoln. for raising one thousand Men agreed to.[7]

Wm Woodford Esq; appointed first in Command of the said Men, and &c.[8]

Com. to be appd. to draw up proper Articles of War.][9] and after sometime spent therein Mr. President ⟨Peyton Randolph⟩ resumed the Chair and Mr. ⟨Richard⟩ Bland reported the Committee had according to Order had under their Consideration the State of the Colony but not having time to go through the same had directed him to move for Leave to sit again.

Resolved, that this Convention will tomorrow resolve itself into a Committee to take into their further Consideration the State of the Colony.[10]

Adjourned till Tomorrow 9. oClock.

Convention MS journal in hand of John Tazewell
(Archives Division, Virginia State Library)[11]

1. George Mason being ill this day (Rutland, *Papers of Mason*, I, 246), and George Stubblefield presumably returned from Williamsburg, the number of members attending could not have exceeded 103.

2. For the "Letter from the Committee of the County of Northampton" and the covering letter under which it was forwarded by John Bowdoin to Peyton Randolph, see 29 July 1775, Third Va. Convention, 2d entry; 30 July, same. This was the 3d protest received respecting George Mason's nonexportation resolution adopted 24 July 1775. The others, from merchants and traders of Norfolk and Portsmouth, and from the committee of Norfolk Borough, had been laid before the convention on 1 Aug. 1775.

3. For the "Letter" from the "Committee of the Borough of Norfolk," see 31 July 1775, Committee to Randolph.

4. The bracketed portion of this paragraph is taken from Tazewell's 1st attempt to compose the manuscript journal for the day. He began carefully but was soon writing in a hastier hand, as though resolved to set down the transactions in a proper sequence, and then to delete some that would have made the record more accurate, complete, and informative. One may suppose that in the present instance Tazewell perhaps conceived an admission that members of the convention had been dependent on a volunteer captain for "A fuller Explanation of Matters" might lessen the dignity of the august assemblage in the public eye, or that a record of a volunteer captain's appearing before the bar of the convention would too greatly enhance the dignity of the independent companies.

5. For the standing "Order of the Day," voted on 27 July and taken up on 1 Aug. 1775, with leave to sit again "on Thursday next," see 1 Aug. 1775, Procs. and n. 3. Tazewell's minutes have value in specifying what parts of the broad "Order" were under immediate discussion.

6. This bracketed section is drawn from Tazewell's minutes for the day. It is preceded by the entry "Letters from the Voluntiers in Wms.burg & the Committee of Norfolk laid before the Convention & referred to Com: on State of the Colony" and is itself the last entry.

7. In contradistinction to those of the Continental Line, the "one thousand Men" were meant to be regulars of a standing Virginia line. Since any number decided upon by the convention would affect the pertinent ordinance, this "Resoln" was in effect an instruction to the committee for defense and protection initially appointed on 19 July 1775 (Procs., 4th para. and n. 6). But though the number here set forth was close to the 1,020 ultimately to be agreed upon (*Statutes at Large*, IX, 9), the resolution appears to have been tentative—which may have been the cause of Tazewell's not entering it in the official journal. Not only on 29 July had Robert Wormeley Carter understood that "3000 men are to be embodied," but again on 5 Aug. he was "imagining" in a letter to his father that "3000 Regulars will be raised." This number was verified on the last-indicated date by George Mason, a member of the committee, who informed a correspondent that "3,000 Men are voted as a Body of standing Troops" (R. W. Carter to Landon Carter, 29 July, 5 Aug. 1775, Sabine Hall Papers, MSS Dept., Univ. of Va. Library; Rutland, *Papers of Mason*, I, 245).

William Wirt stated that after Patrick Henry on 23 Mar. 1775 had successfully moved that "this Colony be immediately put into a posture of Defence," Robert Carter Nicholas moved to "raise ten thousand regulars for the war." The treasurer's motive was said to have been to give Henry's resolution "its greatest effect." John Taylor of Caroline, a spectator at the second convention, declared that Nicholas wished 20,000 regulars. Wirt's authority was the recollection of Thomas Marshall, as in turn cited by his son John Marshall. Taylor's recollection was his own, 43 years after the alleged event. It is possible that Nicholas did so move in an attempt to render Henry's motion reductio (or amplificatio?) ad absurdum, but there is nothing in the extant contemporary records to suggest it. The present editors are much of the opinion that both Marshall and Taylor recalled a development of the third convention and ascribed it to the second. As a conservative realist who moved with the times, Nicholas was much more likely by Aug. 1775 to propose that since war seemed inevitable (as had not been apparent to him in March), the colony make a greater effort than now was being proposed to prepare for the struggle. "Our Friend the Treasurer," George Mason wrote to General Washington on 14 Oct. 1775, "was the warmest Man in the Convention for imediatly raising a standing Army of not less than 4000 men, upon constant Pay" (*Rev. Va.*, II, 366–67, 368–70 nn. 8, 9; Wirt, *Sketches of the Life and Character of Patrick Henry* [Philadelphia, 1817], pp. 124–25 n. 2, [9th ed.], p. 143; David John Mays, *Edmund Pendleton, 1721–1803: A Biography* [2 vols., Cambridge, Mass., 1952], II, 353–54 n. 18; Rutland, *Papers of Mason*, I, 256).

8. Evidence is substantial that this and other resolutions were introduced, probably by Nicholas, vice-chairman of the committee for defense and protection, and were either withdrawn or defeated. There is in the convention loose papers the greater portion of a document in an unidentified hand:

"Resolved, that it is the Opinion of this Committee, that five hundred effective men, part of the Regulars of the Colony, be raised and sent for the defence and protection of the towns of Norfolk and Portsmouth and the neighbourhood thereof.

"Resolved, that it is the Opinion of this Committee, that William Woodford Esqr: be appointed Colonel and Commander in chief of the forces so to be raised.

"Resolved, that it is the Opinion of this Committee, that Charles Scott Esqr: be appointed Lieutenant Colonel.

"Resolved, that it is the Opinion of this Committee, that George Matthews ⟨Mathews⟩ Esqr: be appointed Major.

"Resolved, that it is the opinion of this Committee that 500 effective men be immediately raised for the defence and protection of the City of Williamsburg and the lower parts of the Country.

"Resolved, that it is the Opinion of this Committee, that Thomas Nelson⟨, Jr.⟩ Esqr: be appointed Colonel and Commander in chief of the said Forces."

No provision was made for a lieutenant colonel, the document continuing, "Resolved, that it is the Opinion of this Committee, that Thomas Fleming Esqr. be appointed Major.

"Resolved, that it is the Opinion of this Committee, that the forces so to be raised be in the pay of this Colony, and that they be under such Regulations and Restrictions as shall be established by the convention, for the Government of the provincial army."

A floor resolution then being offered, Tazewell continued on the verso of the same sheet of paper: "Resolved, that it is the Opinion of this Committee, that all publick Arms and Accountrements lately taken from the City of Williamsburg be immediately delivered to Thomas Nelson⟨, Jr.⟩ Esq: Colonel & Commander in chief of the Forces to be raised for the Defence of the City of Williamsburg & lower parts of the Country." This last resolution clearly referred to the arms removed from the powder house by sundry citizens without authorization (pp. 15–16 above).

There was "Some talk," Robert Wormeley Carter reported on 29 July, of electing a "General to our Regulars," though "some are for their being governed by the oldest Colonel." And in another paragraph he added that "the Contest" seemed to "lye" between Thomas Nelson, Jr., and Patrick Henry (R. W. Carter to Landon Carter, 29 July 1775, Sabine Hall Papers, MSS Dept., Univ. of Va. Library). "Mr. Henry," stated his grandson, had made "it understood that he desired a military command" (William Wirt Henry, *Patrick Henry: Life, Correspondence and Speeches* [3 vols.,

Philadelphia, 1891], I, 312). The younger Henry specified no time at which his grand-father made his desire known, but in view of Carter's comment, that desire must already have been communicated to the orator's supporters in Richmond.

In this light, it is possible to interpret the document in any one of 3 ways. First, that it was pro-Henry, forced to the floor by his adherents on the committee and designed, by boxing in Nelson to the command of 500 troops in or near Williamsburg, to re-move him from "the Contest" for supreme command. Second, that it was anti-Henry, forced to the floor by his opponents on the committee and designed by its very transparency to be defeated, so reassuring those opponents that they also had com-manding strength on the floor. Or third, that it was no more than it appeared to be—an effort to get the convention moving, for what, after all, had nearly 2 weeks of sessions produced? Whatever the truth, perhaps Robert Wormeley Carter struck the proper chord when in his letter of the 5th he complained to his father, "We are of as many different opinions as we are Men."

9. Although it seems clear that agreement was reached that a special committee should be appointed to deal with "proper Articles of War," members of the committee for defense and protection evidently understood the resolution to be an instruction to themselves. This understanding would lead to what on 8 Aug. 1775 appears to be a false move (Procs. and n. 6).

10. The convention on the morrow would spend most of the session in committee "on the State of the Colony" in consideration of the petition mentioned in n. 2 above.

11. Edgewise at the bottom of the 4th of 4 pages Tazewell wrote "No. 13."

Friday, 4 August 1775

Third Virginia Convention

Proceedings of Fourteenth Day of Session [1]

Ordered that the Petition & Remonstrance from the Borough of Norfolk, the Instruction from the Committee of the said Borough and the Petition from the Committee of the County of Northampton be referred to the Com-mittee appointed to take into Consideration the State of the Colony.[2]

The Convention then according to the Order of the Day[3] resolved itself into a Committee on the State of the Colony and after sometime spent therein Mr. President ⟨Peyton Randolph⟩ resumed the Chair and Mr. ⟨Richard⟩ Bland reported that the Committee[4] had, according to Order had under Con-sideration the State of the Colony & had come to several Resolutions thereon which he read in his Place and afterwards delivered in at the Clerk's Table where the same were again twice read & agreed to as follows.

Resolved, that the Instructions from the Committee of the Borough of Norfolk and the Petition from the Committee of Northampton are decent & respectful & that they merit due Consideration.

Resolved that the Petition & remonstrance of the Merchants and traders of the Borough of Norfolk is indecent highly reflecting on the honor of the General Convention and directly tending to destroy that necessary Confidence reposed by the good People of this Colony in their Representatives, regularly deputed to guard & preserve their just Rights & Privileges.[5]

Resolved, that the former Resolution of the Convention for restraining the Exportation of Provisions was not adopted with great Haste as unjustly insinuated in the said Petition and Remonstrance, but that it was done in the Maturest Deliberation—a Member of the Convention having given previous Notice, that at a future Day, he intended to move for such a Resolution the Substance of which was fairly and candidly laid open for the Consideration of the Different Members and the Motion not made til several Days after such Notice.[6] Resolved, that the Merchants and traders of the Borough of Norfolk, being as properly and fully represented in the Convention as other Parts of this Colony, it is unreasonable in them to expect especially at this alarming Crisis, that any important Business in which not only this Country, but the whole Continent is essentially and deeply interested, should be suspended till their particular Opinions can be asked on the Subject.

Resolved, that, altho' it is with Concern this Convention at any time adopts Resolutions by which Individuals may be materially affected, yet it becomes their Duty as good Citizens to acquiesce in such Measures as are calculated for the general Publick Weal.

Resolved, that the Resolution complained of was adopted on the fullest Conviction of its Utility founded on certain facts some of which the Continental Congress in all probability could not be well acquainted with, and that the Convention considered it as their indispensable Duty to pursue such Measures as are necessary for their own Security but that of the whole Continent.

Resolved, as the Opinion of this Committee that the primary and true design of the Resolution of the Continental Congress in allowing a free Export till the tenth of September next could only be intended to respect the Crops of the last Year, That the Members of this Convention as well for themselves as most of their Constituents offered the greatest Sacrifice to the publick Good in adopting the Resolution complained of as many of them have large Crops of Wheat now on hand equally liable to perish with such grain as may be in the hands of the Petitioners and Remonstrants. willing however so far as is consistent with the Interest of the Country to remove every colourable Complaint, this Committee doth resolve that any of the Inhabitants of this Colony who may have purchased and have now on hand any Quantities of Indian Corn of the last Crop for the Exportation of which they had actually provided or chartered Vessels previous to the former Resolution of this Convention upon their making these facts appear by proper Proofs, that they be allowed to export the same at any Time between this Day and the tenth of September next provided they give a proper and satisfactory Assurance to the Committee of each County, from whence such Commodity is to be exported, that they will not directly or indirectly suffer the same to be carried to either of the Northern Colonies.[7]

Resolved, that the Committee of each County in this Colony except the

Counties of Accomack & Northampton do immediately appoint, one Captain one Lieutenant and Ensign within their County and that the Officers proceed immediately to enlist a Company of fifty Regulars in each County to be marched as soon as enlisted to such place of Rendezvous as shall be hereafter appointed by this Convention.[8]

Resolved, that five hundred effective Men part of the Regulars to be raised for the Defence of this Colony be sent for the protection of the Towns of Norfolk & Portsmouth & the Neighbourhood thereof.[9]

Other Resolutions to lie on Table.

[Officers to be chosen to Morrow.] [10]

Adjourned till Tomorrow 9. oClock.

> Convention MS journal in hand of John Tazewell
> (Archives Division, Virginia State Library) [11]

1. George Mason being ill and absent on this day, the number of members present could not have exceeded 103 (Rutland, *Papers of Mason*, I, 246).

2. For the "Petition & Remonstrance from the Borough of Norfolk," the "Instruction from the Committee of the said Borough," and the "Petition from the Committee of the County of Northampton," see respectively 28 July 1775, Merchants and Traders to Delegates and Borough Committee to Newton, Holt, and Hutchings; 29 July, Committee to Randolph. The petition and remonstrance and the instruction had been laid before the convention as the 1st transaction of 1 Aug., the Northampton petition as the 1st transaction of 3 Aug.

3. The "Order of the Day," that the convention resolve itself into a committee on "the State of the Colony," had been the last transaction of 3 Aug. 1775.

4. At this point in the manuscript journal Tazewell began writing rapidly. The result was that the equivalent of 3 full pages have little in common with those on which he exercised calligraphy.

5. Obviously the majority of convention members were stung by the "remonstrance" of the "Merchants and traders" of Norfolk—why those of Portsmouth escaped censure must remain a minor mystery. To inform a representative body that its actions are calculated "to destroy all confidence" in itself, that it is violating "public faith and order," and has built on "deceitful expectations" is not to reach the high-water mark of tact. It is probable that the total of 3 seats assigned at this time to Norfolk Borough and County were in fair proportion to the 128 seats to which the freeholders of the entire colony were entitled to elect delegates (Sutherland, *Pop. Dist. in Col. America*, pp. xii, 198, 206). If, moreover, it is assumed that on 24 July 1775, the day on which George Mason's resolution was adopted, Thomas Newton, Jr., James Holt, and Joseph Hutchings were present, while no more than 100 others could have been, it can even be argued that borough and county were overrepresented.

The fact remains, however, that Mason's resolution was adopted by a body dominated by planters, and even though some of them were also "in trade," it must have been primarily as planters that they voted. The posture of Congress, the sacredness of contracts, the possible nonconcurrence of other colonies with the resolution, and the improbability of procuring concurrence within the time allotted—all of these considerations, however ably or poorly debated, had been swept under the carpet. This was Mason in all his resoluteness, but in thought it was not Mason at his best. Nor was it a convention at its best.

6. See 19 July 1775, Third Va. Convention, Procs., n. 1.

7. It seems reasonable that the convention members did understand something of "the primary and true design," at least as interpreted by Richard Bland, who had attended and perhaps patricipated in the debates of the first Continental Congress. Nevertheless, the convention was yielding ground, and more than by any other factor it may have been impelled to do so by the incisions inflicted by the "Petition & Remonstrance" of the merchants and traders.

By "either of the Northern Colonies" was apparently meant Massachusetts Bay and, sweepingly, eastern Canada ("Quebec, Nova Scotia the island of St. Johns, Newfoundland"), set off limits by resolutions of the Continental Congress (11 July 1775, Third Va. Convention, In Congress and nn. 8, 11).

8. This was a floor resolution, a copy of which in Tazewell's neat clerical hand is in the convention loose papers. The exception of the "Counties of Accomack & Northampton" was evidently made on the ground that 50 "Regulars" raised in each could not "be marched" anywhere except on the Eastern Shore. The effect of the resolution was to close off an area of concern properly that of the committee for defense and protection initially appointed on 19 July 1775 (Procs., 4th para.). The anomalous nature of the resolution would lead to its recission on 12 Aug. 1775 (Procs. and n. 14).

9. This too was a floor resolution, in which the "Neighbourhood" was meant to include the capital, for in his minutes for this day Tazewell wrote, "Also, as to forces for Norfolk & Wms.burg." On 12 Aug. 1775 the resolution would automatically expire with the rescission of the one immediately preceding.

10. The bracketed phrase is taken from Tazewell's minutes for this day. It follows the entry "Other Resolutions to lie on the Table" and is itself the final entry. That an "Order" for choosing "Officers" was voted is confirmed by the fact that 3 regimental commanders would be elected "to Morrow," 5 Aug. 1775.

11. Edgewise on the bottom of the 4th of 4 pages Tazewell wrote "No. 13." then marked over the last digit heavily with a "4" and followed the whole with a bold check mark.

Saturday, 5 August 1775

Third Virginia Convention

Proceedings of Fifteenth Day of Session [1]

On a Motion made,

Resolved, that any Person who shall hereafter accept any Office of Profit or pecuniary Appointment under the Crown shall be disqualified from sitting in this Convention, the General Congress, Council of Safety [2] or County Committee.

Resolved, that no person who shall accept of a Commission as an Officer

to command any of the regular Forces now to be raised or which may hereafter be raised, for the Defence of this Colony be capable of sitting or voting
as a Member of the Convention, General Congress or Committee of Safety
during his Continuance in the said Office.

Ordered, that it be an Instruction to the Committee appointed to prepare
and bring in an Ordinance for regulating the Election of Delegates & Committees, that they receive a Clause or Clauses pursuant to the foregoing Resolutions.[3]

On a Motion made,

Ordered that there by a Call of the Convention on Wednesday next.[4]

On a Motion made,

Resolved, that this Convention will immediately proceed by Ballot to the
Appointment of Officers to command the regular Forces to be raised for the
Defence and protection of this Colony.[5]

Ordered, that the Members of this Convention do immediately prepare
Tickets to be put into the Ballot Box with the Name of the Person to com-
mand the first Regiment which being accordingly done, Mr. Rob⟨er⟩t. Carter
Nicholas, Mr. Charles Carter of Lancaster, Mr. ⟨Robert⟩ Lawson and Mr.
⟨Bartholomew⟩ Dandridge were appointed a Committee to examine the Ballot
Box, and report to the Convention upon whom the Majority falls.

The Committee then withdrew and after sometime reported that they had
according to Order examined the Ballot Box, and that the Numbers appeared
as follows.

for Hugh Mercer Esq:	41.
Patrick Henry Esq.	40.
Thomas Nelson⟨, Jr.⟩ Esq.	8.
William Woodford Esq.	1.[6]

The Question being then put whether the said Hugh Mercer or Patrick
Henry upon whom the greatest Numbers fell on the Ballot should be ap-
pointed to command the said Regiment, the Majority appeared in favour of
Patrick Henry Esq.

Resolved, therefore that the said Patrick Henry be appointed Colonel of
the said first Regiment.[7]

The Convention then proceeded in the same Manner to the Appointment
of a Colonel to command the second Regiment, and it appearing from the
Report of the Committee appointed, to examine the Ballot Box, that there
was a Majority of the Convention in Favour of Thomas Nelson⟨, Jr.⟩ Esq.
Resolved that the said Thomas Nelson be appointed Colonel to the said
second Regiment.

The Convention then proceeded in the same Manner to the appointment of
a Colonel to command the third Regiment and it appearing from the Report
of the Committee appointed to examine the Ballot Box, that the Numbers
stood as follows

for William Woodford Esq	44.
William Christian Esq	36.
Hugh Mercer Esq.	8.[8]

The Question was then put whether the said William Woodford or Wm Christian on whom the greatest Numbers fell on the Ballot should be appointed to command the said Regiment, the Majority appeared in favour of William Woodford Esq.

Resolved, therefore, that the said William Woodford be appointed Colonel of the said third Regiment.

Resolved, that the further Appointment of Officers be postponed till Wednesday next.[9]

A Letter & Deposition on the subject of Indian Affairs were laid before the Convention and read.

Ordered, that the said Letter & Deposition do lie on the Table for the perusal of the Members.[10]

Ordered, that Leave be given to bring in an Ordinance for paying the Delegates of this and two former Conventions, the same Wages as are allowed the Burgesses of this Colony and that Mr Henry Lee do prepare and bring in the same.[11]

Resolved, that this Convention doth applaud the Zeal of the Gentlemen Officers and Voluntiers in the City of Williamsburg and do recommend that they keep themselves on the defensive, exerting their utmost Endeavours & Vigilance to discover and defeat any hostile Attempts of the Enemies of this Country.[12]

Adjourned till Monday next 9. oClock.

> Convention MS journal in hand of John Tazewell
> (Archives Division, Virginia State Library)[13]

1. With George Mason returned to the convention this day, the number of delegates in attendance may have been 104, but a pseudonymous "Cato," who himself seems to have been a delegate, later stated that William Woodford was absent (Rutland, *Papers of Mason*, I, 246; "Cato" in *Va. Gazette* [Dixon and Hunter], 30 Mar. 1776). By the time the ballot was cast for "the Name of the Person to command the first Regiment," the number was 91, President Randolph presumably not voting.

2. Heretofore unmentioned in the journal, the "Council of Safety" leaps from the page, to be followed by a 2d start when in the paragraph following the proposed executive arm becomes the "Committee." That such an arm was in contemplation Mason had informed a friend on 24 July 1775 (Rutland, *Papers of Mason*, I, 241); for it was clear that during adjournment of the convention the armed forces the colony might raise must be held in strict subordination to an agency of the civil authority. By the present date the committee for defense and protection probably had provided for that subordination in the proposed ordinance being drafted. But no ad hoc committee had as yet been appointed to consider the creation of a committee of safety per se, let alone to deliberate on the extents and limitations of its powers. "We are," lamented Mason on this very day, "getting into great Confusion here" (ibid., I, 245).

3. With the possibility that Patrick Henry might be elected commander in chief of the colony's "Regulars," the above resolutions could be interpreted as a victory of conservatives determined that he should be permitted no opportunity to combine the power of a roused rabble with that of a disciplined soldiery. Undoubtedly individual delegates had Henry much in mind. But undoubtedly also there were broader bases in

the thought of the majority. In the debates attending adoption of the resolutions the classicists probably drew on antiquity for examples of the danger of combining powers. In Greece they could point to men who had left council or assembly to direct a phalanx, and in Rome to others who had quit the senate to command legions, and all to return to their civil roles once the battle was done. Yet the end of the glory that had been Greece was tyranny, and the grandeur that had been Rome, debasement. And closer to home in time and space was the example provided by the 3 generals who had joined Thomas Gage at Boston: Sir William Howe, Henry Clinton, and "Gentleman Johnny" Burgoyne. Each was a member of Parliament. Yet the end of the splendor that had been the empire was corruption.

Philip Mazzei later related an account of his having dined with "about thirty persons" in Williamsburg. Present was Robert Carter Nicholas, who said, "Mr. Mazzei, what I am afraid of is that we may lose the Constitution."

"Mr. Treasurer," Mazzei replied, "had I such a Constitution, I would think myself in consumption."

There was general laughter, and Richard Bland evidenced the "greatest satisfaction" with Mazzei's rejoinder. What the Italian meant was that encouraged by English writers, the colonists had for generations been assuring each other that adhered to and its provisions observed, the British constitution was the most nearly perfect ever devised by man, a masterpiece of checks and balances, a model of the division of powers. But in reality that constitution was replete with "defects" (Mazzei, *Memoirs*, trans. Marraro, pp. 204, 204–5).

By adoption of the above resolutions, then, the convention was attempting to correct in part the defects of the royal constitution as evolved in Virginia, by establishing a real system of checks and balances and a genuine division of powers. And Henry's most ardent supporters must have joined in voting adoption.

4. By a "Call of the Convention" was meant a roll call to determine who was present or absent. To be recorded absent in Purdie's printed journal would be a source of embarrassment. Since according to the concurrence of 17 July 1775, the convention was following in its "Proceedings, the same Rules and Orders as are established in the house of Burgesses of this Colony," an absent delegate could be tracked down by a "messenger" and readmitted "on paying fine"—or he could be expelled for delinquency, a source of even greater embarrassment. Because it is manifest that the overwhelming majority of delegates were present on this day, it is somewhat puzzling as to why the "Order" should have been adopted. It may have been erected as a block against threats to withdraw—no block could be set up against grumbling. But adoption was at best psychological, for on 9, 11, 12, 19, 21, 22, 23, and 24 Aug. 1775 the order will be found revived or postponed, and on 10, 14, 15, 16, 17, 18, 25, and 26 Aug. as a standing order, ignored.

5. If the anti-Henryites, granting such to have been their motive, conceived that their maneuvers of Thursday past (3 Aug. 1775, Procs. and n. 8), coupled with the first 2 resolutions adopted on this day, disclosed domination of the floor, now was the time to move. At worst they could congratulate themselves on having safeguarded their sylvan commonwealth against the peril of the rise of a man on horseback, be the rider Henry or another.

6. Since 29 July, when Robert Wormeley Carter had foreseen the probability of a Henry-Nelson contest for supreme command of the regulars, the anti-Henryites had substantially regrouped around Mercer. Although the message did not get entirely through or was not sufficiently diffused, Nelson (possibly because of bouts with recurring asthma) let it be known that he did not wish ranking command and on 17 Aug.

1775 would be recorded in the journal as declining command even of the 2d Regiment (Procs. and n. 8). He meanwhile nodded toward Mercer and "acknowledged" the latter's abilities. And in a buzz of politicking, Woodford made the rounds declaring that he would gladly serve under Mercer, "as he knew him to be a fine officer."

On the floor objections were raised to Henry's having command on the grounds that "his studies had been directed to civil and not to military pursuits," that he knew nothing of the "art" of war, and that he was "very unfit" to lead troops against crack British regulars. To these objections a delegate replied that since "Mr. Henry had solicited the appointment," he surely knew what he was doing, and that was good enough for *him*.

Mercer in turn was attacked for being a native Scotsman. In his defense it was observed that the subject had arrived in America in his "early years," that he thereafter had never left these shores, that he had "uniformly distinguished himself as a warm and firm friend to the rights" of the colonies, and that he "possessed great military as well as literary abilities" ("Cato" in *Va. Gazette* [Dixon and Hunter], 30 Mar. 1776).

7. Assuming that the same number of votes was cast on the 2d ballot as on the 1st, Henry picked up 6 of the total of 9 that had gone to Nelson and Woodford. Although command of the 1st Regiment (which as yet had no existence) made Henry ranking commander, he would not specifically be denominated commander in chief until adoption by the convention on 26 Aug. 1775 of the "Form" of his commission.

8. The total of votes being 2 fewer than that cast on the 1st ballot of which there is a recorded count, 1 deletion may be accounted for by the abstention of Christian, who according to the standing rules of the House of Burgesses (adopted by the convention on 17 July 1775), was ineligible to vote on a "Question, in the Event of which he" was "immediately interested" (*JHB, 1766–1769*, p. 324). It is also possible that John Syme of Hanover County abstained, owing to the nicety of his circumstance, for he was Colonel-elect Henry's half brother, and Henry was Christian's brother-in-law (*Rev. Va.*, II, 224 n. 4, 257 n. 4).

9. Other important business arising, the resolution would on "Wednesday next," 9 Aug. 1775, and thereafter successively on 10, 11, 12, 14, and 16 Aug. be postponed or ignored, finally to be taken up on 17 Aug.

10. For the "Deposition" (the "Letter" has not been found), see 20 July 1775, Third Va. Convention, Augusta Co. West, 2d entry.

11. Although in their 3d instruction of 4 Mar. 1775 the freeholders of Hanover County had requested Patrick Henry and John Syme to use their "influence" to procure reimbursement for the delegates attending the second and future Virginia conventions, there is no record that such a proposition reached the floor (*Rev. Va.*, II, 312). With delegates now having been in or near Richmond for 20 days at their own expense, monetary compensation would have a special appeal. On 7 Aug., Lee would be discharged from his duty, with the transfer of the subject of wages to the committee of elections appointed on 25 July 1775, Archibald Cary, chairman. But this should have caused no surprise, for on this same day confirming George Mason's lament at "Confusion," Robert Wormeley Carter was complaining, "We are undoing one day, what we did the day before" (R. W. Carter to Landon Carter, 5 Aug. 1775, Sabine Hall Papers, MSS Dept., Univ. of Va. Library).

12. The applause for "Zeal" was in response to the letter of the officers dated 1 Aug. 1775 begging for "some certain line" by which to establish their "conduct" (Third Va. Convention, Officers to President and Gentlemen), and laid before the convention on 3 Aug. 1775 (Procs., 4th para.). But the key phrase was "that they keep themselves on the defensive," with the implication that dutiful accountings by the king's servants of money rightfully his not be regarded as "hostile Attempts"

against his subject's liberties. Transcripts of orders and papers maintained by Lt. George Gilmer in his autograph diary and Revolutionary memoranda (Va. Hist. Soc.) disclose that by the time the officers received Peyton Randolph's letter of 28 July 1775 (Third Va. Convention, Randolph to Officers), the volunteers had commandeered "Twelve hundred dollars, weighing one thousand and thirty-nine ounces, four penny weights of silver" from Jacquelin Ambler, collector of the port at Yorktown, and almost £900 from Lewis Burwell, naval officer for the District of the Upper James River. In addition, affidavits had been gathered from Alexander Purdie and John Dixon that £300 14s. were at the Williamsburg post office, and from several other officials that they held smaller amounts. And apparently his word had been procured from the deputy naval officer for the District of the Rappahannock River that nearly £900 would not be disbursed without authorization of the convention.

The resolution presupposes another letter from Randolph to the officers, but none has been found. Unfortunately, his sword unblooded and he bored beyond measure, Lieutenant Gilmer appears to have withdrawn to the quietude of his Albemarle hills, a potential Lion-Heart lost to battle forever; and so he was not present to transcribe anything that Randolph might have written. Yet with the volunteers this was not the end. On 11 Aug. 1775 the delegates would learn that confused by the convention's own confusion, the independents had once again struck a misdirected blow (Procs., 3d para.).

13. Edgewise on the bottom of the 4th of 4 pages John Ruffin wrote "No. 15."

Monday, 7 August 1775

Third Virginia Convention

Proceedings of Sixteenth Day of Session [1]

RESOLVED that this Convention will proceed on Friday next to the appointment of Deputies to represent this Colony in General Congress and that such appointment be made by ballot.[2]

RESOLVED that John Nevill⟨e⟩ be directed to march with his Company of one hundred Men and take possession of Fort Pitt and that the said Company be in the pay of this Colony from the time of their marching.[3]

ORDERED that Edward Sniggars ⟨Snickers⟩ be employed to furnish Provisions for the Forces under John Nevill directed to march to and take possession of Fort Pit.

RESOLVED that it be an Instruction to the Committee ordered to prepare an Ordinance for regulating the Elections of Delegates and Committees in the several Counties and Corporations in this Colony to receive a clause or clauses for settling the allowances to Delegates in future and for their attendance at former Conventions.[4]

ORDERED that the Committee appointed to prepare an Ordinance for paying the Delegates for their attendance at this and two former Conventions be discharged from preparing such Ordinance.[5]

RESOLVED that the Convention will on Thursday next resolve itself into a Committee to take under their consideration the state of the colony.[6]

Adjourned til Tomorrow 9 OClock.

> Convention MS journal, in hand of John Ruffin
> (Archives Division, Virginia State Library)[7]

1. The number of delegates in attendance this day could not have exceeded 104 but according to the total of votes cast for regimental commanders on Saturday, 5 Aug. 1775, was probably around a dozen fewer; and Tazewell apparently was absent, for the journal for the day is in the hand of John Ruffin, a delegate for Dinwiddie County.

2. This order would be honored in the keeping, for which see 11 Aug. 1775, Procs.

3. The resolution, a copy of which in the convention loose papers is probably in the hand of George Rootes, was in favorable response to the letter of 12 July 1775 from John Campbell to John Harvie and Rootes (Third Va. Convention). Although too ill the previous March to represent the inhabitants of western Augusta County in the second Virginia Convention (16 May 1775, Augusta Co. West, 1st entry and n. 8), Capt. John Neville had recovered his health and would occupy Fort Pitt on 11 Sept. 1775 (W. H. Smith, *St. Clair Papers*, I, 361 and n. 2).

4. This was the committee on elections, appointed on 25 July 1775, Archibald Cary chairman. A copy of the resolution in the convention loose papers is in the hand of John Ruffin, the acting clerk this day.

5. The "Committee" now discharged was Henry Lee, appointed on 5 Aug. 1775 (Procs. and n. 11).

6. On "Thursday next," 10 Aug. 1775, the convention would duly so resolve itself (Procs. 3d para.).

7. On the top of the 4th of 4 pages (the 3d of which is blank) John Ruffin wrote "No. 16."

Tuesday, 8 August 1775

Third Virginia Convention

Proceedings of Seventeenth Day of Session[1]

A Letter from the honorable Matthew Tilghman Esq; President of the Convention of the Province of Maryland, in Answer to a Letter from the President of this Convention inclosing the Resolution entered into the ⟨twenty-⟩ fourth of July[2] last to prevent the Exportation of Flour, Wheat or other

Grain or Provisions of any kind from this Colony to any Part of the World from & after the fifth day of this month, was laid before the Convention and read, and it appearing that the Convention of Maryland will not come into a similar Resolution & that the good Purpose intended by the said Resolution cannot be effected without a general Agreement of the Neighbouring Provinces,[3]

Resolved therefore, that the abovementioned Resolution of this Convention for the Non Exportation of Flour, Wheat or other Grain & Provisions be repealed and rescinded.[4]

Mr. Rob⟨er⟩t. Carter Nicholas from the persons appointed to prepare and bring in an Ordinance for raising and embodying a sufficient force for the Defence and Protection of this Colony presented to the Convention according to Order the said Ordinance, which was read the first time and ordered to be read a second time.[5]

[Mr. Treasr. repd. Articles of War—agreed to be read second time.]

The Ordinance for raising and embodying a sufficient Force for the Defence and Protection of this Colony was read a second Time and ordered to be committed.

[Articles of War to be comm. to Comm. of whole Tomorrow.] [6]

Resolved that this Convention will Tomorrow resolve itself into a Committee on the said Ordinance.[7] Adjd. till Tomorrow 9. oClock.

> Convention MS journal in hand of John Tazewell
> (Archives Division, Virginia State Library) [8]

Norfolk Borough Committee

An Officious Pointing Out

Norfolk borough, Committee Chamber, August 8, 1775

WHEREAS it appears from undoubted testimony, that a certain JOHN SCHAW of this borough, did in the presence of Lord Dunmore, officiously point out to the soldiery at Gosport, one Alexander Main, fifer to one of the volunteer companies of this place, as a person who ought to be apprehended for his impudence (as the said SCHAW expressed himself) in wearing a hunting shirt[9] in their presence; in consequence of which the unhappy man was apprehended, and is now by his Lordship's order, confined on board the Otter sloop of war.—We therefore, think it our duty to declare, that the said SCHAW has herein shewn himself a busy tool, and an enemy to American liberty, and as such we advise every friend to his country to have no farther dealing or connection with him.[10]

> Published by order,
> William Davies, Secretary.

In Committee, August 8, 1775

RESOLVED, that it be strongly recommended to the inhabitants of this borough, to furnish themselves with a hunting shirt and cockade, and the provincial uniform complete, with arms, ammunition and all the necessary accoutrements for war, as recommended by the Convention.[11]

Extract from the minutes,

William Davies, Secretary.

Virginia Gazette, or the Norfolk Intelligencer, 9 August 1775

1. The delegates in attendance this day could not have exceeded 104 in number but probably were about a dozen fewer; and John Tazewell apparently was absent, for the minutes for the day are in the hand of John Ruffin, a delegate for Dinwiddie County.

2. For the "Resolution entered into" on 24 July 1775, see the proceedings of that day. Tazewell's 20-day error is repeated by Purdie in the printed journal, p. 22.

3. For the "Letter from the President of this Convention," see 27 July 1775, Randolph to Delegates of Md.; for the "Letter from the honorable Matthew Tilghman Esq;" see 1 Aug. 1775, Third Va. Convention, 2d entry.

4. Tilghman's "Letter" was an exploding grenade. In effect the Maryland speaker reiterated the arguments coming out of Norfolk, Portsmouth, and Northampton County; he rendered nugatory the time and labor spent on the justificatory and backtracking resolutions adopted by the Virginia Convention on 4 Aug.; and he contributed nothing toward ending the "Confusion" originating in and emanating from that convention (28 July 1775, Third Va. Convention, Norfolk Borough Committee to Newton, Holt, and Hutchings and Merchants and Traders of Norfolk and Portsmouth to Delegates; 29 July, same, Northampton Co. Committee to Randolph; 4 Aug., same, Procs.; 11 Aug., same, Procs., 3d para.). But George Mason, who might have been expected to be most disappointed by the contents of Tilghman's letter, stated matter-of-factly: "The Maryland Convention not concurring in the Resolve for imediatly stoping the Export of Provision⟨s⟩, it became necessary to rescind ours; that our ports, as well ⟨as⟩ theirs, might be kept open til the 10th of Sept." (Rutland, *Papers of Mason,* I, 251). Authenticated as by "John Ruffin for John Tazewell," the resolution of recission would appear successively in each Williamsburg *Va. Gazette* (Pinkney), 10 Aug. 1775, (Purdie), 11 Aug. 1775, and (Dixon and Hunter), 12 Aug. 1775—too late to prevent "the Officers of the Voluntier Companies in Williamsburg" from delivering another unnecessary coup (11 Aug. 1775, Third Va. Convention, 3d para.).

5. Nicholas was vice-chairman of the committee for defense and protection appointed on 19 July 1775. Richard Bland was chairman (Procs., 4th para.). If Nicholas himself read the proposed ordinance (as was occasionally done by a burgess "in his place"), he may have done so because of the chairman's poor eyesight; but it is more likely that John Ruffin read the document the "second Time."

6. The bracketed phrases anent the "Articles of War" are drawn from Ruffin's minutes. In composing the manuscript journal for this day, John Tazewell may well have been startled to see those phrases. Drawing on memory and glancing back at his

own minutes for 3 Aug., he could have reassured himself that agreement had been reached only that a committee was "to be" appointed to "draw up proper Articles of War" (Procs. and n. 9). But that was hardly authorization for the committee for defense and protection to undertake the task. Or if it was, the matter of articles is not mentioned here or again in the official journal until the appointment of an ad hoc committee on 21 Aug. 1775 (Procs., 1st para.).

The present editors believe the self-assigned role of the committee of defense and protection to have been an error. On the assumption that it was, Peyton Randolph, following conversation with Tazewell and others, may have delivered an unrecorded ruling from the chair. Or the president may have reached a private agreement with Nicholas to drop the subject without further ado. Coupled with the meanderings of the proceedings, these possibilities raise a question: Was the convention still in confusion partly because Randolph had never had real control of it? In only 8 days hence, 16 Aug. 1775, the members would express their "Concern" by unanimously requesting him to retire from the "Fatigues" of presiding. No contemporary mentions his ineptness in guiding the convention—members would have been very hesitant to criticize the "Father of His Country"—but it is possible that he was already suffering from minute cerebral hemorrhages, or "little strokes," that were building to what on his death in Philadelphia on 22 Oct. 1775 Richard Henry Lee would describe as "dead palsey" (James Curtis Ballagh, ed., *The Letters of Richard Henry Lee* [2 vols., New York, 1911–14], I, 153).

7. Consideration of the "Ordinance" that was properly the business of the committee of defense and protection would be the 1st transaction "Tomorrow," 9 Aug. 1775.

8. Tazewell wrote an economical "17" edgewise on the top of the 4th of 4 pages (the 3d of which is blank).

9. "The hunting shirt" was a "kind of loose frock, reaching half way down the thighs, with large sleeves, open before, and so wide as to lap over a foot or more when belted" (Joseph Doddridge, *Notes on the Settlement and Indian Wars of the Western Parts of Virginia and Pennsylvania, from 1763 to 1783, Inclusive . . .* , ed. Alfred Williams [Albany, 1876], p. 140).

10. John Schaw was probably "in the presence of Lord Dunmore" on 1 Aug. 1775, when at Gosport His Excellency "reviewed his 60 body-guardmen, lately arrived from St. Augustine" (*Va. Gazette* [Purdie], 4 Aug. 1775, postscript). For the "body-guardmen," see 31 July 1775, Norfolk Borough Committee to Randolph and n. 12. On that day the governor appointed Schaw "Commissary" to supply the troops being assembled at the royal headquarters (P.R.O., A.O. 13/32, folder S). After "undergoing a strict examination by Lord Dunmore," Main would be released in the evening of 8 Aug. (*Va. Gazette, or the Norfolk Intelligencer*, 9 Aug. 1775). Schaw, on the other hand, will be found offering a "sincere repentance" for his officiousness under the date heading of 10 Aug. 1775, Norfolk Borough Committee.

11. On 25 Mar. 1775 the second Virginia Convention had "recommended" that in the volunteer infantry "every man be provided with a good Rifle if to be had, or otherwise with a Common Firelock, Bayonet and Cartouch Box; and also with a Tomahawk, one pound of Gunpowder, and four pounds of Ball at least fitted to the Bore of his Gun; that he be cloathed in a hunting Shirt by Way of Uniform" (*Rev. Va.*, II, 375).

Wednesday, 9 August 1775

Third Virginia Convention

Proceedings of Eighteenth Day of Session [1]

The Order of the Day for the Convention to resolve itself into a Committee on the Ordinance for raising a sufficient Force for the Defence and Protection of this Colony being read,[2] the Convention accordingly resolved itself into the said Committee and after sometime spent therein Mr. President ⟨Peyton Randolph⟩ resumed the Chair and Mr. ⟨Richard⟩ Bland reported that the Committee had according to Order had under their Consideration the Ordinance for raising & embodying a sufficient force for the Defence and Protection of this Colony [Amendments To be one thousand & 20 men only] [3] but not having Time to go through the same had directed him to move Leave to sit again.

Resolved, that this Convention will Tomorrow resolve itself into a Committee on the said Ordinance.[4]

The Orders of the Day for a Call of the Convention and for the Appointment of Officers being read, ordered that the same be put off till Tomorrow.[5]

[*Patrick Henry, Edmund Pendleton, Benjamin Harrison*, and *Thomas Jefferson*, Esquires, appeared in Convention, and took their seats; and the gentlemen appointed to represent their counties, during their necessary absence, retired.] [6]

[Mr. Pendleton, Mr. Jefferson, & Mr. Harrison added to the Committee of Ways & Means.] [7]

Ordered, that Mr. Pendleton, Mr. Harrison, Mr. Henry and Mr. Jefferson be added to the Committee appointed to take into Consideration the Governor's Proclamation relative to granting Lands in this Colony.[8]

adjourned till tomorrow 9 oClock

> Convention MS journal in hand of John Tazewell
> (Archives Division, Virginia State Library) [9]

Charles Duncan of Prince George County to President and Members of Convention [10]

To The Honourable The President & the other Members of the Convention The Memorial of Charles Duncan of the Town of Blandford in the County of Prince George

Humbly Sheweth,

That your Memorialist, who had long carried on business as a Merchant in this Colony, has for some Years had a Store in the County of Brunswick on Account of himself & divers others his Partners which has for some time past been under the care and management of one Thomas Crawford, who has always been in the esteem, and good opinion of his Customers and acquaintances, and has, ever since the present unhappy dispute with Great Britain began, endeavoured to conduct himself in such manner, as to avoid all cause of offence towards any of the inhabitants of the Colony, & has also endeavoured as far as in him lay, to conform to the regulations, laid down, and recommended, by the Honorable General Congress and Convention of this Colony by acceeding to the General Association, and by a chearful Submission, and conformity to the Terms thereof.[11]

Under these circumstances, your Memorialist, as well as his Partners, Factors, and Servants hoped they shou'd have been permitted to transact their business, and conduct their own affairs in Quiet and Security, without being called upon, or compelled, by any Set of Men, under an assumed authority, either to enlist as Soldiers, or take part in any Military regulation, other than they are bound to adopt, either by the Laws of the Colony, or the recommendation of the Convention.[12]

But such is the unhappy Situation, as well of your Memorialist, as his Partner & Servants in the County of Brunswick, that they have been called upon by the Gentleman who commands the Volunteer Company in the Said County, to enlist as Soldiers therein, under pain of incurring the Displeasure of the Said Company, and of being treated as Enemies to the Country, and exposed to all the Violence, that may happen from the mistaken Zeal of Men heated by Passion, & prejudice, and who treat with disregard the peaceable remonstrances of your Memorialist With no other alternative left than either to desert the property, and Interest which they have in the Said County, or remain therein to protect their property, at the hazard of all that is dear and Valuable to Freemen, & good Citizens.[13]

Your Memorialist, presumes, humbly, to hope that this Convention will take this matter into Consideration, and So provide for the Safety and protection of his Factors and assistants aforementioned, and others under like circumstances, as to them in their wisdom Shall Seem meet.

And your Memorialist as in Duty bound will every pray &c.

CHARLES DUNCAN [14]

> Autograph document, signed, in loose papers of third Virginia Convention (Archives Division, Virginia State Library)

Norfolk County Committee

Summons for Mr. Andrew Sprowle

Norfolk County, in Committee Augt the 9th 1775.
Ordered that the Messenger Summons Mr Andrew Sprowle to appear on
Wednesday the 16th. Inst. to give his Reasons, why he suffers the Store
House to be Occupy'd by the Soldiery as Barracks.[15]

Extract from the Minutes
Edward Archer Secretary

Document MS transcript in unidentified hand (John
Norton & Sons Papers, Colonial Williamsburg Foundation, Research Archives)

1. The delegates in attendance this day could not have exceeded 104 in number
but were probably a dozen or so fewer.

2. The "Order of the Day" was the final transaction of 8 Aug. 1775.

3. The bracketed "Amendments" are drawn from Tazewell's minutes for this day.
The effect of reducing the establishment of military "Regulars" from the originally
proposed 3,000 to 1,020 rank and file was to eliminate the equivalent of the 3d Regiment and other units and so to leave William Woodford, elected on 5 Aug. 1775 to
command the 3d Regiment, without prospective employment. Still irritated by Patrick
Henry's election to ranking command, "Some" of his foes thought "to bring on that
matter again," but Robert Wormeley Carter correctly predicted that a motion to reconsider would "be to no purpose" (R. W. Carter to Landon Carter, 10 Aug. 1775,
Sabine Hall Papers, MSS Dept., Univ. of Va. Library).

4. Implementation of the resolution would be the 1st order of business "Tomorrow,"
10 Aug. 1775.

5. The "Orders of the Day" had both been voted on 5 Aug. 1775.

6. The bracketed paragraph is taken from Purdie's printed journal, p. 23. In the
manuscript journal Tazewell did not record the appearance of the 4 deputies returning
from Congress until the next day; yet in the bracketed phrase next following he accounted for 3, and in the final paragraph, for 4 of the deputies; and Randolph was not
accustomed to appoint committeemen in absentia.

7. The bracketed phrase is drawn from Tazewell's minutes for this day. By "the
Committee of Ways & Means" he meant the committee for defense and protection,
instructed on 21 July 1775 to "provide the ways & Means" of supporting the armed
forces to be raised (Procs. and n. 7). The committee now totaled 34 members, with
11 a quorum.

8. Appointment of these 4 additional delegates brought to 13 the total membership
of the committee on western lands first appointed as the last business of the day on
18 July 1775, Robert Carter Nicholas chairman, to investigate the controversy between
the Fincastle County committee and William Preston. On 19 July 1775, again as the
last business of the day, there was referred to the committee the governor's proclamation that was the intermediate cause of the controversy. Each of the present appointees

had been a member of the committee appointed on 27 Mar. 1775, the final day of session of the second Virginia Convention, to "enquire whether his majesty may of right advance the terms of granting lands in this colony, and make report thereof to the next General assembly or Convention" (*Rev. Va.*, II, 383).

9. Edgewise on the top of the 4th of 4 pages (the 3d of which is blank) John Ruffin wrote for Tazewell "No. 18."

10. This undated document is here arbitrarily placed. It will be found laid before the convention on the following day, 10 Aug. 1775.

11. The "General," or Continental, "Association," adopted by the first Continental Congress on 20 Oct. 1774, was "entirely & cordially" approved by the second Virginia Convention on 22 Mar. 1775 (*Rev. Va.*, II, 361).

12. For the "recommendation" of the second Virginia Convention respecting the revival of the militia as independent companies of volunteers, see 1 May 1775, n. 4.

13. The records for Brunswick County in 1775 do not identify the nominal county lieutenant, who may have commanded "the Volunteer Company," but John Jones was later, if not already, county lieutenant and was possibly the "Gentleman" in question.

14. CHARLES DUNCAN, living at this time in Blandford but also occasionally identified as being of Chesterfield County, was a prosperous merchant with other lands and interests in Brunswick, Dinwiddie, and Prince George counties. On 22 June 1770 he had joined fellow merchants and members of the House of Burgesses at the Raleigh Tavern, where arms were raised 17 times in the drinking of toasts, and pens put to work in subscribing to a nonimportation association in protest against the duty on tea. The evolution of his thought since that time appears in no available documents, but it is evident that he conceived his business to be business, not war. Of uncertain age, but apparently thought still vigorous enough to bear a firelock, he was wed to Jennie Gilliam Duncan (*JHB, 1773–1776*, p. 235; *Rev. Va.*, I, 79–82; *Va. Gazette* [Purdie and Dixon], 15 Oct. 1772).

15. The "Store House" was one of Sprowle's warehouses at Gosport, the "Soldiery" a part of Lord Dunmore's command, as the addressee would state in his reply of 12 Aug. 1775 to the Norfolk County Committee.

Thursday, 10 August 1775

Third Virginia Convention

Proceedings of Nineteenth Day of Session [1]

The Convention according to the Order of the Day resolved itself into a Committee on the Ordinance for raising and embodying a sufficient Force for the Defence and Protection of this Colony and after sometime spent therein Mr. President ⟨Peyton Randolph⟩ resumed the Chair and Mr. ⟨Richard⟩ Bland reported that the Committee had according to Order had under their Consideration the State of the Colony but not having time to go through the same had directed him to move for Leave to sit again.[2]

Resolved, that this Convention will tomorrow resolve itself into the said Committee.[3]

The Order of the Day for the Convention to resolve itself into a Committee on the State of the Colony being read, the Convention accordingly resolved itself into the said Committee and after sometime spent therein Mr. President resumed the Chair and Mr. Bland reported that the Committee had according to Order had under their Consideration the State of the Colony but not having time to go through the same had directed him to move for Leave to sit again.

Resolved, that this Convention will tomorrow resolve itself into a Committee to take into their further Consideration the State of the Colony.[4]

A Memorial of Charles Duncan of the Town of Blandford merchant was presented to the Convention & read, setting forth that he had for some Years past had a Store in the County of Brunswick on Account of himself and others his partners, which had for sometime past been under the Care and Management of Thomas Crawford, who had always been in the Esteem of his Customers & Acquaintences, and has ever since the unhappy Dispute with Great Britain endeavoured to conduct himself in such a Manner as to avoid giving Cause of Offence to any of the Inhabitants of this Colony, & has also endeavoured, as far as in him lay, to conform to the Regulations of the General Congress & Convention of this Colony—that under these Circumstances he hoped he should have been allowed to transact Business & conduct his own Affairs in quiet & Security without being called upon or compelled to enlist as Soldiers or take part in any Military Regulations other than such as were prescribed by the laws of the Colony or the Recommendation of the Convention: but that such was the unhappy Situation of himself his partners & servants in the County of Brunswick that they have been called upon by the Gentleman who commands the Voluntier Company in the said County to enlist as Soldiers therein under pain of incurring the Displeasure of the said Company and of being treated as Enemies to the Country, with no other Alternative left them than either to desert the property & Interest which they have in the said County, or remain therein to protect the same at the Hazard of all that is dear & valuable to Freemen & good Citizens & praying that this Convention would take the same into Consideration & do therein as should appear just and reasonable.[5]

Ordered, that the President be desired to write to the commanding officer of the said Company requiring them to desist from a further prosecution of the Measures mentioned in the said Memorial.[6]

On a Motion made,

Resolved, that the Powder purchased by Patrick Henry Esq: for the Use of this Colony be immediately sent for and applied by the Deputies appointed to represent this Colony in General Congress, in such Manner as they shall judge most for the Interest of this Colony.[7]

Mr. Henry Pendleton a Member for the County of Culpeper appeared in Convention & took his Seat.[8]

Lewis Burwell Esq. a Member for the County of Gloster ⟨Gloucester⟩ appeared in Convention & took his seat.

The Order of the Day for the Convention to proceed to the appointment of Officers to command the regular Forces to be raised for the Defence of the Colony being read,

Resolved, that this Convention will tomorrow proceed to the said Appointment.[9]

[Adjourned till to-morrow, 9 o'clock.] [10]

> Convention MS journal in hand of John Tazewell (Archives Division, Virginia State Library) [11]

John Goodrich, Jr., to Matthew Phripp [12]

Sir

I wass Informed this Morning that the Goviner has got 13 Fieldpeacis fited up & on board of his Ship & that he Intends to Wmsburg with them⟨.⟩ I think it Highly Nessesary that the Volinteers at that place Should Informed of it as they may be in Readyness to Receive his Lordship [13]

I am Sir yours &c

Portsmouth Thursday forenoon   JOHN GOODRICH JUNR: [14]

> Recipient's copy, autograph letter, signed, in loose papers of third Virginia Convention (Archives Division, Virginia State Library)

Norfolk Borough Committee

Sincere Repentance and Determined Resolution of John Schaw

To the Public.

WHEREAS it has been proved to the Committee for Norfolk borough, that I did in the presence of Lord Dunmore and in open disrespect to the good people of this country, point out to the soldiery at Gosport, a certain Alexander Main, fifer to one of the volunteer companies of this borough, as a person who ought to be apprehended for his impudence, as I very imprudently expressed myself, for appearing in our presence habited in a hunting shirt, by which means the unhappy man was taken into custody and confined for some time; I do therefore most humbly ask pardon for my indiscretion, and do solemnly declare my sincere repentance, and determined resolution, in all points hereafter to conduct myself as a zealous advocate for the rights and liberties of America.[15]

Norfolk, August 10, 1775   John Schaw.[16]

Virginia Gazette, or the Norfolk Intelligencer, 16 August 1775

1. With the appearance of Henry Pendleton and Lewis Burwell, the number of delegates attending this day could have risen to 106 but was probably a dozen or so fewer. The number could have been determined by recourse to the standing order of the previous day that there be a "Call of the Convention" (Procs. and n. 5), but the existence of the order was either overlooked or ignored.

2. Tazewell's botching of the opening paragraph is initially repeated by Purdie in the printed journal, p. 24, but under "Errata," p. 59, the printer amends "*state of the colony*" to read "*said ordinance.*"

3. On a crowded agenda, the order to resolve "into the said Committee" would on "tomorrow," 11 Aug. 1775, be "postponed" (Procs. and n. 16).

4. Not since Friday, 4 Aug., had the convention sat as a "Committee on the State of the Colony," then to adopt a series of resolutions set off by petitions received in opposition to the passage of George Mason's nonexportation resolutions (Procs. and nn. 2–7). The nature of the "Consideration" of the committee during the present and subsequent days is not to be found until the session of 16 Aug. 1775, with the passage of resolutions respecting the creation of the Committee of Safety (Procs. and nn. 4–7).

5. For the "Memorial of Charles Duncan," which Tazewell probably had in hand when he composed the above paragraph, see 9 Aug. 1775, Third Va. Convention, 2d entry.

6. No copy of the president's letter has been found. The treatment of neutrals—one of which Charles Duncan pretty obviously was—posed a problem of some delicacy. What to do with an enemy civilian's property, and in extreme cases with his life, might more easily be ascertained. But concepts of the nation in arms and of total war were of the future, and in 1775 simple justice dictated that an individual, one perhaps even opposed to the patriotic cause but willing to obey the mandates of those in power, able to play a useful role in society, and pledged to abstain from giving aid or comfort to the enemy, be as well protected in his rights and liberties as the most ardent patriot.

And once again, an example of what might be expected from a soldiery not "melted down" by known rules and regulations in complete subordination to civil authority had been demonstrated.

The immediate response to Duncan's petition established a serviceable precedent when, on 25 Aug. 1775, there would be laid before the convention a petition by "sundry merchants, and others, natives of *Great Britain,* and resident in this colony" (pp. 490–92 below).

7. The floor resolution in the convention loose papers was written by Tazewell in a hand more careful than that in which he completed the journal for the day. Robert Wormeley Carter in reporting the appearance of the Hanover County delegate in the convention on the previous day stated: "Henry informed us he had purchased a ton wt. of Gunpowder which is now at Baltimore, with the money he got from old Corbin, and today his transaction relative to that affair is to be considered by the Convention. I imagine it will occasion great altercation and perhaps some battles; as

some are too warm. I wish it had never been thought of again, but it seems Braxton insisted when he carried him the money, that the Convention should determine it" (R. W. Carter to Landon Carter, Sabine Hall Papers, MSS Dept., Univ. of Va. Library).

How much "altercation" or how many "battles" occurred on the floor Tazewell could be trusted not to record. Yet throwing the disposition of the gunpowder into the hands of deputies still to be elected to the Continental Congress was rather a curious dodge for a colony desperate for munitions. This was especially so since the previous deputation to Congress had thrown Henry's note of exchange back into the hands of "the Colony Assembly or convention" (4 May 1775, Hanover Co. Committee and n. 2).

Still outstanding was the question of what to do with the money in excess of that judged the proper equivalent for the gunpowder which the governor had spirited away, but Carter Braxton "by motion prevented the discussion of the question relative to Corbin" (R. W. Carter to Landon Carter, 10 Aug. 1775, Sabine Hall Papers, MSS Dept., Univ. of Va. Library). The question would not be resolved until 25 Aug. 1775 (p. 488 below).

8. Following this entry, Tazewell wrote his erroneous sentence first placing 4 of the deputies returned from Congress in the convention as of the present day (9 Aug. 1775, Procs. and n. 6). What is most probable is that the clerk penned the official proceedings for both 9 and 10 Aug. 1775 (and perhaps for another day or days as well) in a single night and in this instance drew from a loose paper out of proper position. If so, it was also probably he who pointed out the error to Purdie, who does not repeat it.

9. By "Officers" were meant those in grade of lieutenant colonel and major. On "tomorrow," 11 Aug. 1775, the order would be "postponed" (Procs. and n. 16).

10. Tazewell did not record the fact of adjournment. The bracketed phrase is borrowed from Purdie's printed journal, p. 25.

11. Edgewise at the bottom of the 4th of 4 pages John Ruffin wrote for Tazewell "No. 19."

12. Although the letter is dated only "Thursday forenoon," it is assuredly this particular Thursday. The information contained herein would be reported in Williamsburg on Saturday, 12 Aug. 1775 (*Va. Gazette* [Dixon and Hunter], 12 Aug. 1775; ibid. [Purdie], 11 Aug. 1775, postscript, delayed one day in publication).

13. This letter on this same day would be forwarded by the recipient and Joseph Hutchings of Norfolk to the chairman of the Elizabeth City County-Hampton Town committee, William Roscow Wilson Curle. The action of the latter upon receiving Goodrich's letter will be found under the date heading of 11 Aug. 1775, Third Va. Convention, 3d entry.

14. JOHN GOODRICH, JR., was probably the eldest of his namesake father's 5 sons. Although not yet a practiced merchant, the son had a sharp eye and would act for the family during the ensuing winter when his father should fall into such disfavor with the patriots as to be clapped into jail. The present letter makes it obvious that the younger Goodrich did not suspect that he too might espy profit in attaching his interests to those of the "Goviner." At this time, John, Jr., was probably 26 or 27 years of age (Sabine, *Biog. Sketches of Loyalists*, I, 481; Fairfax Harrison, "The Goodriches of Isle of Wight County, Virginia," *Tyler's Qtly. Hist. and Geneal. Mag.*, II [Oct. 1920], 130).

15. For the condemnation of John Schaw as "a busy tool, and an enemy to American liberty," see 8 Aug. 1775, Norfolk Borough Committee. Unhappily for the principal, he fell victim to unfortunate timing. Thus although this "sincere repentance" was

this day acknowledged to the borough committee, the source through which that sincerity was to be evinced to the public would not be in print for another 6 days. For this reason, he was yet to experience a frightening misadventure, for which see 11 Aug. 1775, Norfolk Borough Committee, 1st entry.

16. JOHN SCHAW, a Scot merchant of Norfolk, was frequently to be found in the Virginia colonial gazettes advertising his other employment, that of collector of debts owed defunct enterprises. When the firm of Andrew Sprowle and Robert Crooks was dissolved upon the death of the 2d-named partner, Schaw collected its outstanding credits. He was now doing the same for William Duncan and Company, late owners of the Norfolk newspaper, following dissolution of that partnership after censure of the junior, John Brown, by the Norfolk County committee for violations of the Continental Association (*Va. Gazette* [Purdie and Dixon], 31 Oct. 1771; *Va. Gazette, or the Norfolk Intelligencer*, 28 June 1775; *Rev. Va.*, II, 307–8; Clarence S. Brigham, *History and Bibliography of American Newspapers, 1690–1820* [2 vols., Worcester, Mass., 1947], II, 1129).

Friday, 11 August 1775

Third Virginia Convention

Proceedings of Twentieth Day of Session[1]

Ordered, that Mr. Thomas Walker and Mr. John Walker have Leave to be absent from the Service of this Convention for the Remainder of the Session.[2]

[Mr. *Richard Henry Lee* appeared in Convention, and took his seat as a member for the county of *Westmoreland.*][3]

A Letter from the Officers of the Voluntier Companies in Williamsburg was presented to the Convention & read, setting forth that they had seized a Vessel outward bound laden with Bread and Flour, that the Captain informed them the Convention had come to a Resolution posteriour to that by which the Exportation of Grain & Provisions was stopped after the fifth Instant, and had allowed a free Export till the Time limited by the General Congress, that under these Circumstances, they applied themselves to the Convention for Information and requested certain Directions by which they might regulate their Conduct on similar Occasions.[4]

Resolved, that the President ⟨Peyton Randolph⟩ be desired to write to the Officers of the said Voluntier Companies informing them, that the Convention is well pleased with the Zeal they have shown on this Occasion, to carry into Execution their Resolutions—that it is true, as the Captain had informed them, that the Convention had rescinded their former Resolution, in consequence of a Letter from Maryland, by which they were informed that Province could not come into a similar one.[5]

On a Motion made,

Ordered, that the Commissioners appointed by the House of Burgesses to examine State and Settle the Accounts of the Militia lately drawn out into actual Service, do also state and report the Cases of such wounded Soldiers & poor Widows & Orphans as may have suffered by the late Expedition agst. the Indians.[6]

The Convention being about to proceed to the Choice of Deputies to represent this Colony in General Congress, Edmund Pendleton Esq. expressed his most grateful Acknowledgments for the honour done him in two former Appointments to that important Trust, but on Account of the declining State of his health,[7] entreated to be excused from the present Nomination; which Excuse being accepted,

Resolved, unanimously, that the Thanks of this Convention are justly due, to George Washington Patrick Henry & Edmund Pendleton Esquires three of the worthy Deputies who represented this Colony in the late Continental Congress, for their faithful Discharge of that important Trust; and this Body are only induced to dispense with their future Services of the like Nature, by the Appointment of the two former to other Offices in the publick Service incompatible with their Attendance in this, and the infirm state of Health of the latter.

Mr. President acccordingly delivered the Thanks of the Convention to Mr. Henry & Mr. Pendleton in their Places who expressed the great pleasure they received from this distinguished Testimony of their Country's Approbation of their Services.

Resolved, that the President be desired to transmit the Thanks of this Convention by Letter to his Excellency General Washington.[8]

The Convention then proceeded, according to the order of the Day, to the Appointment of Deputies to represent this Colony in general Congress for one Year,[9] and the Members having prepared Tickets with the Names of the Deputies to be appointed & put the same into the Ballot Box, Mr. Robert Carter Nicholas, Mr. ⟨Archibald⟩ Cary, Mr. Pendleton, & Mr. ⟨Richard⟩ Adams were appointed to examine the Ballot Box and report upon whom the Majority fell, who retired and after sometime returned into Convention & reported that they had according to Order examined the Ballot Box & that the Numbers appeared to be as follow

for Peyton Randolph Esq.	89.
Richd. Henry Lee Esq.	88.
Thomas Jefferson Esq:	85.
Benjamin Harrison Esq.	83.
Thomas Nelson⟨, Jr.⟩ Esq.	66.[10]
Richd. Bland Esq.	61.
George Wythe Esq.	58.[11]
[Carter Braxton	24
Geo. Washington	22
Geo. Mason	19

Jos: Jones	6
Jno. Banister	4
Edmd. Pendleton	3
Thos. ⟨Ludwell⟩ Lee	3
Fras. L⟨ightfoot⟩. Lee	3
Jas. Mercer	2
Wm. Cabell⟨, Jr.⟩	2.
Dudley Digges	1.
Paul Carrington	1
Robt. Lawson	1] [12]

Resolved, that the said Peyton Randolph, Richard Henry Lee, Thomas Jefferson, Benjamin Harrison, Thomas Nelson, Richard Bland & George Wythe Esquires be appointed Deputies to represent this Colony in General Congress for one Year, and that they have Power to meet & to adjourn to such time & to such Place or places as may be thought most proper.[13]

Resolved, that the said Deputies or any four of them be a sufficient Number to represent this Colony.[14]

Ordered, that Mr. George Mason & Mr. ⟨John⟩ Harvie be added to the Committee appointed to inquire into the Petitions of W⟨illia⟩m. Preston Gent: & the Committee of the County of Fincastle.[15]

The Orders of the Day for the Convention to proceed to the Appointment of Officers to command the regular forces to be raised for the Defence and Protection of this Colony,—for the Convention to resolve itself into a Committee on the State of the Colony, & for a Call of the Convention, being read,

Resolved, that the Call of the Convention be postponed till Tomorrow & that the Convention will then proceed to the Appointment of the said Officers, & resolve itself into a Committee on the State of the Colony.[16]

The Convention, according to the Order of the Day[17] resolved itself into a Committee on the Ordinance for raising a sufficient force for the Defence & Protection of this Colony, and after sometime spent therein Mr. President resumed the chair & Mr. Bland reported that the Committee according to Order had under their Consideration the Ordinance for raising a sufficient force for the Defence and Protection of this Colony, but not having time to go through the same had directed him to move for Leave to sit again.

Resolved, that this Convention will tomorrow resolve itself into the said Committee to take into their further Consideration the Ordinance for raising & Embodying a sufficient force for the Defence & Protection of this Colony.[18]

Adjourned till tomorrow 9. oClock.

Convention MS journal in hand of John Tazewell
(Archives Division, Virginia State Library)[19]

Augusta County West: Journal of Captain James Wood

11th August Arrived Fort Pitt about 3 oClock in the afternoon[20] where I found several Senecas who had Just come from a Treaty which had been held at Niagara by Guy Johnston⟨.⟩ I Interrogated them but found that they had got their Lesson not to make any Discovery's⟨.⟩ they said that the Indian Agent told them to lie still and not to Concern with the Dispute between the People of Great Britian and America [21]

Thwaites and Kellogg, *Revolution on the Upper Ohio, 1775–1777*, p. 65

William Roscow Wilson Curle to the Chairman of the
Committee at Williamsburg [22]

Sir,   Hampton Augt. 11th 1775
    The inclosed Letr.[23] I received this Morning from Colo. ⟨John⟩ Hutchings and Capt. ⟨Matthew⟩ Phripp of Norfolk with a Request to forward it to the Volunteers at Williamsburg. Those Gentn. inform me that seven Officers arrived the night before the last in Hambletons ⟨John Hamilton's⟩ Brig from Boston but as far as they cou'd learn no men were expected to follow them.[24]
    I am &c. &c.

W. R. W. Curle [25]

Autograph letter, signed, in loose papers of third Virginia Convention (Archives Division, Virginia State Library)

Norfolk Borough Committee

Retirement of the Little General

On Friday evening last, a number of people assembled and took into possession, Mr. John Schaw merchant of this place, being highly incensed against him, for advising the soldiery at Gosport in the presence of ————,[26] to apprehend the Fifer of one of the volunteer companies of this borough, only for appearing before them with a hunting shirt on, as it was proved and published by the Committee. The populace were parading him into town to the tune of Yankee Doodle, as played by the Fifer he had caused to be apprehended, when the Little General, (a name Schaw is commonly known by) choosing to retire from his honorable post, effected his escape into the house of one of the Aldermen. Great persuasions were used with the people to disperse, but to no purpose; till at length three gentlemen offered themselves as securities, that they would see the General (who had been all this while endeavoring to get up a chimney) should be forthcoming and delivered into the hands of the Committee at eight o'clock next day.[27]

Virginia Gazette, or the Norfolk Intelligencer, 16 August 1775 [28]

1. With the granting of "leave to be absent" to Dr. Thomas Walker and his son, coupled with the appearance "in Convention" of Richard Henry Lee, the delegates in attendance this day could have numbered 105; but the ballot cast for deputies to the Continental Congress strongly suggests that the number was nearer to 90, for Peyton Randolph, who received the highest number of votes, 89, probably did not vote for himself.

2. The Walkers were on their way to Fort Pitt via Berkeley Warm Springs, in the latter community to meet George Croghan, whom they had supplied with money in a private deal to purchase several million acres of land from the Shawnee. It is possible that Patrick Henry was also involved and that this was one of the "deep Schemes" that Robert Wormeley Carter mysteriously reported as being more easily smelled than fingered. But to the Walkers self-interest was not a thing confined to itself when the commonweal was likewise served. Both men had been appointed agents of the House of Burgesses to treat with the northwestern Indians, and in continuation of the work undertaken by John Connolly, would be at Fort Pitt on 10 Sept. 1775. Even before that date "A correspondent" would unwittingly "inform" John Pinkney of a tactic of this double-ended service, and Pinkney as unwittingly instruct his readers in a paragraph in which pronouns evolved into ghostly antecedents: "doctor Walker and his son, of Albemarle, lately went out upon an expedition, in company with a few Indians, in order to shew them the strength and activity of the volunteers in one of the back counties. They expressed great astonishment at the sight, and gave the gentlemen who conducted them sufficient tokens to believe that they would never take up the hatchet against us" (Abernethy, *Western Lands and the Am. Rev.*, pp. 120–21; R. W. Carter to Landon Carter, 10 Aug. 1775, Sabine Hall Papers, MSS Dept., Univ. of Va. Library; 9 July 1775, Third Va. Convention, Augusta Co. West, n. on provenance; Thwaites and Kellogg, *Rev. on the Upper Ohio*, pp. 27, 28; *Va. Gazette* [Pinkney], 14 Sept. 1775).

3. The bracketed sentence is taken from Purdie's printed journal, p. 25. Tazewell neither wrote the sentence in the manuscript journal nor jotted down an abbreviation of it in his minutes for this day. He may have supplied Purdie with the entry from a loose paper now long lost or destroyed. On his return from Congress, Lee did not proceed directly to "Richmond Town" but first "seized the opportunity of visiting" his "family" (Ballagh, *Letters of R. H. Lee*, I, 147).

It was perhaps at or about the time that he took his seat in the convention that Lee delivered what Governor Dunmore from a firsthand account described as "a very long and artful Speech" informing the delegates that if the petition that Congress had addressed to the king on 8 July 1775 (for which see 11 July 1775, Third Va. Convention and n. 1)—"in as humiliating terms as could come from free Men"—was not favorably received, Congress was disposed to act "by the Middle of January" 1776 "to open the Ports of the whole Continent to all Foreign Nations" in direct defiance of the navigation and the trade acts (P.R.O., C.O. 5/1353, fols. 310, 312).

Despite an assertion to the contrary that Dunmore would make in a report to London, Lee did not then or subsequently present to the convention a copy of a plan of colonial union that Benjamin Franklin had laid before Congress on 21 July—the same day on which that body had discussed throwing open the ports. Only a few months returned from London, Franklin did "not hesitate" to support the "boldest Measures" proposed in Congress but thought even them "too irresolute, and backward." He anticipated that "if the ministry continued pertinacious," colonial opposition would have to remain united for some years, and toward the end of erecting a firmer structure he offered a grandly revised text of his 1754 Albany Plan of Union, that the deputies might "have something more perfect prepared by the time it should become necessary." This proposed charter would have bestowed on Congress sovereign powers until king and Parliament should have repealed all obnoxious legislation or, on "Failure thereof," in perpetuity (ibid., fol. 310; Carl Van Doren, *Benjamin Franklin* [New York, 1937], pp. 534–35; Butterfield et al., eds., *The Adams Papers*, ser. II, *Adams Family Correspondence* [Cambridge, Mass., 1963–], I, 253; Boyd, *Papers of Jefferson*, X, 372–73; *JCC*, II, 195–99).

Shocked at the implications in this scheme, the "timid members" (the words are Jefferson's) prevailed in their insistence that neither should the plan be debated nor should even allusion to its existence be entered in the journal. Less daunted, the delegates for North and South Carolina sent information about the possible opening of the ports, along with copies of Franklin's plan, to the conventions of their respective colonies. The convention, or provincial congress, of North Carolina had copies of the plan made and circulated among its members (a result being that Dunmore procured possession of the text), and the 2 unapproved measures came to be regarded as a single package by those knowing little of their history (Boyd, *Papers of Jefferson*, X, 372; Burnett, *Cont. Cong.*, p. 91; P.R.O., C.O. 5/1353, fols. 316–18).

Even after Lee's "Speech" very little was known about the suggested confederation charter in Richmond. The "knowing ones in Convention" did discuss it "out of doors" but kept it a "secret" fairly well guarded from the other delegates. Lee and the other deputies returned from Congress may have been dissuaded from giving the plan wider circulation for the very reason that Dunmore would ascribe to the rumored rejection of that plan: "that the minds of the Delegates were not Sufficiently prepared" for "a total Subversion of the Constitution" (P.R.O., C.O. 3/1353, fols. 310, 312). But this statement represented an amount of backtracking by a governor who for months had insisted that the rebel leaders were moving steadily toward their true objective, independence, for examples of which insistence see *Rev. Va.*, II, 252–53; p. 12 above.

4. No copy of the "Letter" has been found. For the repeal of the nonexportation resolution and the cause for the officers' application for accurate information and "certain Directions," see 8 Aug. 1775, Third Va. Convention, Procs. and n. 4.

5. With Lt. George Gilmer retired to Albemarle County, there was none among the officers in Williamsburg to transcribe the letter that "the President" undoubtedly wrote.

6. As its final transaction on 24 June 1775, the House of Burgesses resolved that Archibald Cary, William Cabell, Jr., William Fleming, John Winn, and John Nicholas, with 3 a quorum, be commissioners for Fincastle, Botetourt, Culpeper, Pittsylvania, Halifax, and Bedford counties, and for "that part of the County of *Augusta*, which lies of the Eastward of the *Allegany* Mountains"; that Richard Lee, Francis Peyton, Josias Clapham, Henry Lee, and Thomas Blackburn, with 3 a quorum, be commissioners "for the other Counties," for the District of West Augusta, and for volunteers from Maryland and Pennsylvania, "to examine, state, and settle the Accounts of the pay of the Militia" that had participated in Dunmore's War, and of the accounts of "all Provisions, Arms, Ammunition, and other necessaries, furnished the said Militia" (*JHB, 1773–1776*, p. 283).

Thereafter Purdie's newspaper was filled with frequently amended schedules announcing when and where the separate groups would "attend" for the discharge of their functions, until the schedules were suspended "on account of our necessary attendance at the Convention." Finally the 1st group fixed times and places as of 11 Sept. 1775 at Staunton, 22 Sept. in Botetourt County, 4 Oct. in Fincastle County, and 16 Oct. in Bedford County; and the 2d group fixed 11 Sept. at Fort Pitt, 2 Oct. at

Romney, and 10 Oct. at Winchester (*Va. Gazette* [Purdie] 30 June, 21 July, 28 July, 18 Aug. 1775).

7. How far declined? On 17 Aug., having by then served on 2 temporary committees, still serving at that time on 3 special committees, and being yet to perform yeoman work in the convention, Pendleton would not reject election to the chairmanship of the colonial Committee of Safety. He would, nonetheless, comment on 1 Sept. 1775 that he was "unwell" (Mays, *Letters of Pendleton*, I, 118). It is not unlikely that he was experiencing a recurrent fever, for this was the "sickly season" in Virginia, and even in more northerly Pennsylvania, from which he had just returned.

8. The beauty of the 4 paragraphs of which the present paragraph is the last is that Tazewell had only to copy them from a loose paper entirely in Pendleton's hand. It is true that Pendleton may have transcribed the paragraphs from the manuscript journal, but then it is unanswerable as to why he amended words and a phrase to reproduce what was already written, or why he should have given the transcript to the clerk. It is most probable that desiring the record not be bungled, Pendleton first wrote the script, then played his role and handed the script to Tazewell.

The "Thanks of this Convention" would be transmitted to General Washington by Mr. President in a letter dated 6 Sept. 1775, a date beyond the compass of the present volume.

9. This "order" had been voted as the 1st transaction of 7 Aug. 1775.

10. On 5 Aug. the convention had resolved that no officer commanding "any of the regular Forces" of the colony should be eligible to serve in Congress and on the same day elected Thomas Nelson, Jr., commander of the 2d Regiment. The answer to the question that arises is that Nelson probably had already let it be known that he would not accept a regimental command, a declination that would be entered in the journal on 17 Aug. 1775.

11. The sudden appearance in the journal of the name of GEORGE WYTHE, who was not even a convention delegate, needed explanation to few who were present. Of an ancestry on both sides moderately distinguished, he had begun his education at his mother's knee and studied briefly at the College of William and Mary before setting up in the practice of law at 20 years of age, gradually to build a reputation so refulgent that many considered his the finest legal mind the colony had ever produced. For a few months in 1754, when Peyton Randolph was in England, Wythe had been acting attorney general, being then only 28. And although it would be years before he would become the nation's 1st professor of law, he had already begun to train students, among whom were a number whose names would be household words in the future nation and the commonwealth. Wythe had sat in the Burgesses for Williamsburg (1754–55), for the College (1758–61), and for his native Elizabeth City County (1761–68). In 1768 he was mayor of Williamsburg, and from 1769 to 1775 clerk of the House of Burgesses, thereafter perhaps to serve as clerk of the first Virginia Convention. Opposed to the precipitateness with which Patrick Henry seemed bent on bringing the differences with Great Britain to a crisis, Wythe yet was scarcely a "conservative" and might more readily be labeled a "measured-pace radical" who held that Parliament had no legitimate authority over the colony whatsoever. Men knew, of course, that he had appeared in the streets of Williamsburg attired in a hunting shirt and shouldering a musket to protect the community from Lord Dunmore after His Excellency had made off with the powder from the magazine. Now in his 50th year, Wythe was of medium height and weight, had a large head, a huge, domelike forehead, more of a long, curved nose than seemed really necessary, and he wore his hair long around the sides and back. Somewhat skeptical, he was always a faithful vestryman. No Benjamin

Harrison, he was a vegetarian. As a grammarian, he began only paragraphs with a capital letter and wrote the 1st-person singular pronoun as a modest *i*. He had married twice, to Anne Lewis in 1747 (she died soon thereafter) and to Elizabeth Taliaferro (whose surname, as all Virginians know, is pronounced Tol'-i-ver) in 1755, but no children survived. Bishop Meade's grandfather would remember Wythe as the only honest lawyer he ever met. Thomas Jefferson would declare that "he might truly be called the Cato of his country, without the avarice of the Roman; for a more disinterested person never lived." Wythe's reputation would follow him to Philadelphia, where meeting him, John Adams would note that Virginians held him to be a jurist "of the first Eminence" (Lyon G. Tyler, "George Wythe," in *Great American Lawyers*, ed. William Draper Lewis [8 vols., Philadelphia, 1907–9], I, 51–90; William Edwin Hemphill, "George Wythe, The Colonial Briton" [Ph.D. diss., Univ. of Va., 1937]; [John Sanderson and Robert Waln], eds., *Biography of the Signers to the Declaration of Independence* [2d ed., 5 vols., Philadelphia, 1828], IV, 171–88; *Wm. and Mary Qtly.*, 1st ser., II [July 1893], 69, X [Oct. 1903], 124–25; *Va. Mag. of Hist. and Biog.*, IV [Oct. 1896], 199, XX [Apr. 1912], 204; *Va. Hist. Register*, V (1852), 162–67; Butterfield, *Adams Papers*, 1st ser., II, 172).

12. The bracketed "Numbers" are taken from Tazewell's full list of the ballot, which he neatly inscribed on a loose paper. Votes cast for Washington and Pendleton may be considered as complimentary. Those cast for George Mason were that and a bit more.

"I was personally applied to," Mason wrote, "by more than two thirds of the Members, insisting upon my serving at the Congress." He assured them that he "cou'd not possibly attend": His health was precarious; a widower of 2 years, he was now both "Father and Mother" to 9 children, some of whom were still very young; and, as he probably did not add, public life irritated more than it inspired him. But notwithstanding this stance, there were 19 delegates "who wou'd take no Excuse" (Rutland, *Papers of Mason*, I, 250; Hill, *George Mason*, pp. 34–35).

13. In the resolution of 7 Aug. to proceed this day "to the appointment of Deputies" to Congress, nothing was said about the size of the delegation. Apparently it was understood that the number would continue at 7. This, then, was the total of candidates for which each member of the convention was entitled to vote. If we accept the supposition that Peyton Randolph did not vote for himself, the number of delegates present and voting was 90. There was a grand total of 601 votes cast, so signifying that in one combination or another the "Tickets" lacked 20 names that could have been written in.

According to the procedure apparently adopted by the first convention and seemingly followed by the second, deputies were elected only when their names appeared on two-thirds of the ballots. On this day that fraction would have been 60. Thus was Wythe 2 votes short of election. It is possible that the old rule was modified without record by the third convention. It is more probable, however, that Robert Carter Nicholas announced the totals for the 7 candidates standing highest, noted that there was a spread of 34 votes between those cast for "George Wythe Esq." and the candidate in 8th place, and successfully moved that Wythe be elected without resort to a 2d ballot. The motion would have had appeal to men by this date stapled to Richmond or its neighborhood for 26 days.

14. This was a floor resolution. A variant and awkwardly phrased version of the resolution in Tazewell's hand is in the convention loose papers.

15. The appointment of Mason and Harvie, accompanied by the departure of Dr.

Walker, raised to 13 the number of members on the committee first appointed on 18 July 1775, with Robert Carter Nicholas the chairman.

16. The order "to proceed to the Appointment of Officers" had been standing since 5 Aug. (Procs. and n. 9); that for the "Committee on the State of the Colony" only since the previous day, 10 Aug. (Procs. and n. 4); and that for "a Call of the Convention" also since 5 Aug. 1775 (Procs. and n. 4).

17. This "Order of the Day" resulted from the 1st proceeding of the previous day, 10 Aug. 1775.

18. The committee will be found sitting again "tomorrow," 12 Aug. 1775.

19. Edgewise at the bottom of the 4th of 4 pages near where John Ruffin wrote "Fryday. No. 20." Tazewell inscribed "No. 20."

20. Captain Wood and Simon Girty had left the Shawnee towns on 2 Aug. 1775 (Third Va. Convention, Augusta Co. West and n. 18). Sometimes through driving rain, and for 2 days subsisting only on "Blackberry's," they pushed determinedly on, to pause on the 6th and attend a trilingual church service at one of the Indian missions. The night of the 10th they spent at John Gibson's trading post at Logstown and on the next day "sett off after Breakfast" (Thwaites and Kellogg, *Rev. on the Upper Ohio*, pp. 63–65).

21. For "discovery" the 20th-century English-speaking American substitutes "disclosure." The evidence is that silence was the only "Lesson" successfully taught by Col. Guy Johnson, royal northern Indian agent. Meeting several tribes in southeastern Ontario early in June—that is, before the council at Caughnawaga (for which see 2 Aug. 1775, Third Va. Convention, Augusta Co. West and n. 16)—he futilely attempted to win them to the royal cause. His failure he attributed to "their minds, having been corrupted by New England Emissaries and most of them discouraged by the backwardness of the Canadians" in rallying to the Crown (William L. Stone, *Life of Joseph Brant* . . . [2 vols., Albany, 1865], I, 83–88; O'Callaghan, *N.Y. Col. Docs.*, VIII, 636).

Captain Wood will be found reporting to the president of the convention under the date heading of 18 Aug. 1775, Augusta Co. West.

22. The "Chairman of the Committee of Williamsburg" was Peyton Randolph, the vice-chairman Robert Carter Nicholas. Since both men were in Richmond, the letter was received and forwarded to the convention by a 3-member subcommittee (12 Aug. 1775, Third Va. Convention, 3d entry). Curle sent the letter by mail; the postmark "Hampton / Aug: 11" is on the cover.

23. The "Letr." was that of John Goodrich, Jr., to Matthew Phripp, for which see 10 Aug. 1775, Third Va. Convention, 2d entry.

24. Hamilton's brig was the *John*, in which Capt. Hugh Kennedy had intended to sail for Antigua late in June. Seized by the governor, the vessel sailed instead to Boston and had now returned with a letter for Lord Dunmore from Vice Adm. Samuel Graves, and with 2 captains, a lieutenant, 3 ensigns, and a surgeon for the royal 14th Regiment of Foot (Clark, *Naval Docs. of the Am. Rev.*, I, 823, n. 1, 998; *Va. Gazette, or the Norfolk Intelligencer*, 21 June, 5 July 1775; *Va. Gazette* [Purdie], 11 Aug. 1775, postscript). In his Norfolk newspaper of 16 Aug. 1775 John Hunter Holt noted that some of the officers "expressed great surprise" that Gosport was not swarming with armed loyalists, for the officers "had been made to expect that government, as it is called, could raise troops here at will."

John Hamilton of Nansemond County, part owner of the brig, was a merchant whose business extended widely through Virginia and North Carolina. He may by now have returned from the latter colony, to which he had recently eloped with the wife of a neighbor and creditor (P.R.O., A.O. 13/95, Pt. I, folder H II, fols. 71–311; petition of Christopher Godwin, 1 Nov. 1779, Va. Legislative Petitions, Nansemond Co., Archives Division, Va. State Library). Not for this foible but on another charge he would a week from today present himself to the county committee (18 Aug. 1775, Nansemond Co. Committee).

25. WILLIAM ROSCOW WILSON CURLE, lawyer, was one of the younger sons of the happy union of Wilson and Priscilla Meade Curle. A native of Hampton, where his family had already dwelled for a century, he was equally at home in Norfolk and would represent the borough in the convention of May 1776. In 1766 he had served as clerk for the Norfolk Sons of Liberty. His domestic happiness blighted but shortly before by the death of his wife, Euphan Wallace Curle, he on 22 Nov. 1774 accepted election as chairman of the Elizabeth City County–Hampton Town joint committee, perhaps to lose himself further in work. He was now taking only cash in payment for his legal services, but despite the total or partial closing of many courts, he would within the year add a carriage to his properties. He was by this date probably entering the 5th decade of his years. His personal copy of Purdie's printed journal of the third convention, bearing his unmistakable, bold signature, is in the Archives Division of the Virginia State Library and is the one to which the present editors refer when need arises (*Wm. and Mary Qtly.*, 1st ser., IX [Oct. 1900], 125–26 n. 12; *Col. Va. Reg.*, p. 209; *Va. Gazette* [Purdie and Dixon], 30 Dec. 1773; *Va. Mag. of Hist. and Biog.*, XXVI [Apr. 1918], 154; W. Meade, *Old Churches, Ministers and Families of Va.*, I, 292; *Rev. Va.*, I, 45, 47, II, 173–74, 247 n. 4).

26. That is, L——d D——e, a name too despicable to print.

27. For the condemnation of Schaw by the borough committee and his as yet unpublished "repentance," see 8, 10 Aug. 1775, Norfolk Borough Committee. "The General" could have sought out the chimney of any one of 8 aldermen, but if he had the time to be selective, his natural refuge would have been the "Elegant" house of William Aitchison, business partner of the loyalist James Parker and friend of L——d D——e. Although Aitchison within 10 days would join his aldermanic colleagues in protesting against threats made by Capt. John Macartney (21 Aug. 1775, Norfolk Borough), his heart was with the "Interest of Great Britain" (P.R.O., A.O. 13/27, folder A II). Writing 7 weeks later, the governor was to charge that the crowd had seized Schaw in "the middle of the Town," then "beat and bruised" him in "a most Cruel manner," and tore "all his Cloathes" from his back, with intent "to have tarred and feathered him" (P.R.O., C.O. 5/1353, fol. 306).

As promised by his "securities," Schaw would be "forthcoming and delivered" on the "next day" (12 Aug. 1775, Norfolk Borough Committee).

28. The present item consists of the greater part of the 1st paragraph of a 3-paragraph notice.

Saturday, 12 August 1775

Third Virginia Convention

Proceedings of Twenty-first Day of Session [1]

[A Letter from Richd. Bland Esq: was laid before ⟨the⟩ [2] Convention & read.—to proceed to elect another on Tuesday next.] [3]

Richard Bland Esq. [one of the Deputies appointed to represent this Colony in General Congress] [4] returned the Convention his most grateful Acknowledgments for the great honour they had pleased a third Time to confer [5] on him by appointing him one of the Deputies to represent this Colony in General Congress & said this fresh Instance of their Approbation was sufficient for an old man, almost deprived of Sight, whose greatest Ambition had been to receive the Plaudit of his Country whenever he should retire from the public State of Life. [6]

That the honorable Testimony he lately received of this Approbation joined with his present Appointment should ever animate him, as far as he was able, to support the glorious Cause in which America was now engaged; but that his advanced Age rendered him incapable of taking an active part in those weighty & important Concerns which must necessarily be agitated in the great Council of the united Colonies, and therefore begging Leave to decline the honor they had been pleased to confer on him, & desiring that some person more fit & able, might supply his Place.

Resolved, that this Convention will on Tuesday next, proceed to the Appointment of a Deputy to represent this Colony in the Room of the said Richard Bland Esq. [7]

[Ordinance for Election of Delegates &c. read the first time & to be read a second Time . . .] [8]

The Committee appointed, presented to the Convention according to order, an Ordinance for regulating the Election of Delegates & ascertaining their allowances; and also for regulating the Election of Committee men in the several Counties & Corporations within this Colony & for other Purposes therein mentioned. and the same was read the first Time & ordered to be read a second Time. [9]

[Thanks returned to Richd. Bland Esq: by the President ⟨Peyton Randolph⟩.]

Resolved, unanimously, that the Thanks of this Convention are justly due to the said Richard Bland esq: one of the worthy Deputies who represented this Colony in the late Continental Congress, for his faithful discharge of that important Trust, and this Body are only induced to dispense with his future Services of the like Nature, on Acct. of his Advanced Age.

The president accordingly delivered the Thanks of the Convention to the said Richard Bland Esq. in his place, who expressed the great pleasure he received from this distinguished Testimony of his Country's Approbation of his Services.[10]

[A Letter from Voluntiers in Wmsburg recommending Farquharson was read.]

A Letter from the Officers of the voluntier Companies in Williamsburg was presented to the Convention and read, setting forth that the Bearer Mr. John Farquharson had supplied the Troops under their Command with all kinds of Vegetables & they had conceived an exceeding good Opinion of him & hoped he would meet with the favour & Approbation of the Convention.

Ordered that the said Letter do lie on the Table.[11]

[. . . and was read a second time and committed.

Committed to the whole on Monday next.]

An Ordinance for regulating the Election of Delegates and ascertaining their Allowances; & also for regulating the Election of Committee men in the several Counties & Corporations within this Colony & for other purposes therein mentioned, was read a second Time and Ordered to be Committed.

Resolved, that this Convention will on Monday next resolve itself into a Committee on the said Ordinance.[12]

[The Accts. of Arms &c. refd. to Mr. Bland, Mr. Lee, Mr. Henry & Mr. Pendleton & Mr. Cary.]

The Members from the County of Frederick informed the Convention that some Gentlemen in their County had purchased a Number of Rifles & a Quantity of Gun Powder at a low rate, which they were willing & proposed to deliver up for the Use of the public, at the same Price at which those Articles had been purchased by them.

Ordered, that Mr. ⟨Richard⟩ Bland, Mr. ⟨Edmund⟩ Pendleton, Mr. ⟨Patrick⟩ Henry, Mr. ⟨Archibald⟩ Cary & Mr. Richd. H⟨enry⟩ Lee be a Committee to examine & State the said Proposition & report the same together with their Opinion thereupon to the Convention.[13]

[Archibald Cary Esq. informed the Convention that Officers had been appointed by the Committee of Chesterfield County agreable to the Resolution of this Convention, & that they had in Obedience thereto inlisted the Number of Men directed by the said Resolution, who were now ready and desiring the Direction of the Convention in what was to be done with them.

Resolved, that the Officers and Men so appointed & enlisted & all others who may have been appointed & enlisted agreable to the foregoing Resolution, be in the pay of this Colony from the Time of their appointment & Enlistment, to this Day, and that they and

Resolved, that where][14]

[Officers of Chesterfield to discharge their Men & to be paid by the publick, & the same as to other volunters.

former Resolutions to be rescinded for raising Men.]

Resolved, that the Resolution of this Convention directing the Committees of the several Counties to appoint Officers & to have fifty Men immediately enlisted in each County be rescinded, and that where any Officers have been appointed and men inlisted, in pursuance of the said Resolution, they be immediately disbanded.

Resolved, that the Officers so appointed & Men so enlisted be in the Pay of this Colony from the time of their appointment & Enlistment to the time of their being discharged.

[Accts. to be brought in to the Committee appointed to settle other Accts. Mr. Adams, Mr. Randolph, Mr. Carrington, Mr. Mayo & Mr. Pendleton.]

Ordered, that Mr. ⟨Richard⟩ Adams, Mr. ⟨Richard⟩ Randolph, Mr. ⟨Paul⟩ Carrington, Mr. ⟨Henry⟩ Pendleton & Mr. ⟨John⟩ Mayo be a Committee to examine state & report the Claims of such Officers & Men who shall apply to them for that Purpose, and that the Committee appointed by the house of Burgesses to examine state & settle the Claims of the Militia lately drawn out into actual Service, do also examine state & settle the Claims of such Officers & Men as may have been appointed & established in the foregoing Resolution in the Counties of Frederick & Augusta.[15]

[Ordinance for pay of Militia read 1st Time & ordered to be read a second Time.]

The Committee appointed presented according to Order An Ordinance for appointing Commissioners, to settle the Accounts of the Militia lately drawn out into actual Service & for making Provision to pay the same, which was read the first time & ordered to be read a second Time.[16]

[Went into Committee on State of Colony but not having time to go through the same to sit again—on Monday.] [17]

The Convention according to the Order of the Day resolved itself into a Committee on the Ordinance for raising & embodying a sufficient force for the Defence & protection of this Colony, & Mr. Robert Carter Nicholas reported that the Committee had according to order had under their Consideration the said Ordinance but not having time to go through the same had directed him to move for Leave to sit again.[18]

Resolved, that this Convention will on Monday next resolve itself into the said Committee.[19]

[Order for Call put off till Tuesday] [20]

[Other Orders put off] [21]

[Leave to bring in Ordce
    Henry, Mr. Treasurer, Mr. Cary] [22]

Ordered that leave be given, to bring in An Ordinance to encourage the making Saltpetre, Gun Powder & Lead the refining of Sulphur & providing Arms for the use of this Colony, & that M⟨ess⟩rs. Richd. Henry Lee, Mr. ⟨Patrick⟩ Henry, Mr. Robert Carter Nicholas, Mr. ⟨Archibald⟩ Cary, Mr. ⟨Charles⟩ Lynch, & Mr. ⟨Edmund⟩ Pendleton do prepare & bring in the same.[23]

adjrd. till Monday 9. oClock.[24]

Convention MS journal in hand of John Tazewell
(Archives Division, Virginia State Library) [25]

Richard Bland to The honble. the President & Gentlemen of the Convention [26]

Gentlemen

Permit me to return you my most grateful Acknowledgment for the high Honour you have a third time conferred upon me by appointing me one of the Delegates to represent this Colony in the general Congress of the Confederated Colonies of North America.

This fresh Instance of your Approbation of my public Conduct, is sufficient for an Old Man, almost deprived of Sight, whose greatest Ambition has ever been to receive the Plaudit of his Country whenever he shall retire from the public Stage of Life.

The honourable Testimony I lately received of their Approbation joined with my present appointment must animate me as far as I am able to support the glorious Cause in which our Country is engaged: but my advanced Age renders me incapable of taking so active a Part in those weighty and important Concerns which must necessarily be Aggitated in the great Council of the united Colonies. I must therefore beg leave to decline the Honour you have been pleased to confer on me, and hope you will make choice of some Person more fit & able to supply my Place. I am Gentlemen with great Respect & Esteem

August 12th   Your most obliged & very humble Servant
   1775

                                                  RICHARD BLAND

> Recipients' copy, autograph letter, signed (Etting Collection, Historical Society of Pennsylvania)

Williamsburg Committee to President of the Convention

Sir,

The committee of Williamsburg thought it proper to send the inclosed letters, which came to their hands this morning, by express, to you, to be laid before the convention. We are, Sir, Your humble servants [27]

Williamsburg   JAMES HUBARD
12th Aug.   G: WYTHE
   1775   J DIXON

> Recipient's copy, MS letter in hand of George Wythe, with autograph signatures (Simon Gratz Autograph Collection, Historical Society of Pennsylvania)

Norfolk Borough

Captain John Macartney, Commander of His Majesty's Ship *Mercury*,
to Paul Loyall, Mayor of the Borough of Norfolk

I AM just now informed by his Excellency Lord Dunmore, that Mr. Andrew
Sprowle has received a summons to attend a committee in Norfolk, on Thursday next.[28] The accusations alledged against him are of a most extraordinary
nature. In the summons he is charged with having harboured his Majesty's
troops in stores at Gosport. I am not surprised that a summons grounded
upon such accusations should be alarming to Mr. Sprowle; particularly after
the cruel and oppressive treatment Mr. ⟨John⟩ Schaw lately received from a
mob in Norfolk.[29] As I do most earnestly wish, and shall upon all occasions
endeavor to promote the public peace of this province, I think it necessary
to explain to you, as chief magistrate of the town of Norfolk, the conduct
I mean to pursue, in hope of preserving that peace and obedience to the laws,
so ardently to be wished by all loyal subjects and good citizens. I am sent
hither to be a guardian of a British colony; to protect his Majesty's Governor,
and all the loyal subjects in the province of Virginia. This is my duty, and
should wish it to be known that my duty and inclination go hand in hand.
The same principles, which have innured me not to harbour the slaves of any
individual in this province, will operate with me to protect the property of all
loyal subjects.[30] As I have before observed, that I shall endeavor to promote
the public peace of this province, it is hardly necessary to mention that I
shall not remain an idle spectator, should any violence be offered to the persons or property of any of his Majesty's subjects. I have reason to apprehend
that many gentlemen in this province, from their connections with government, or their readiness to supply his Majesty's ships or servants with provisions, stores, &c. are held up as objects inimical to the liberties of America,
and unjustly censured for their loyal conduct. Men under these circumstances
are more particularly entitled to my protection. I have not the least doubt,
from your desire and readiness upon a former occasion to preserve harmony
in the town of Norfolk,[31] but you will heartily concur with me in my endeavors to suppress all party jealousies and animosities, so highly injurious to
the welfare of a country. More effectually to play my part, I shall the first
opportunity, place his Majesty's ship under my command abreast of the
town; and I must assure you that notwithstanding I shall feel the utmost pain
and reluctance, in being compelled to use violent measures to preserve the
persons and property of his Majesty's faithful subjects, yet I most assuredly
shall, if it becomes necessary, use the utmost coercive measures in my power,

to suppress all unlawful combinations and persecutions within the province of Virginia.[32]

I am, Sir, Your most obedient humble servant,

John Macartney.[33]

Virginia Gazette, or the Norfolk Intelligencer,
30 August 1775

Norfolk Borough Committee

An Humble Concession and a Satisfaction

The Committee met and the gentlemen, who had become surities for his appearance, produced him accordingly; when the Committee, interposing with the people, prevailed on them to disperse, after having an humble concession of Mr. ⟨John⟩ Schaw read to them, in which he promised to conduct himself hereafter as a friend to the country.[34] He has since thought proper to fix his place of residence at Gosport.

After the dismission of Mr. Schaw, some young gentlemen who had been concerned in apprehending him, waited upon one ⟨John⟩ Carmount in this town, who had expressed himself very freely to their prejudice on that occasion, and demanded satisfaction of him for the insult he had offered them, which he consented to give, and the expressions being proved to have been made, he, with bended knee, asked their pardon and was peaceably discharged.[35]

Virginia Gazette, or the Norfolk Intelligencer,
16 August 1775 [36]

Norfolk County Committee

Andrew Sprowle to Gentlemen of the County Committee Residing in the Borough of Norfolk [37]

Gentlemen

From your Secretary Mr ⟨Edward⟩ Archer I had of the 9th. Inst. a Citation to appear before you at Norfolk the 16th. to answer how I came to admitt Troops to be landed and take possession of one of my Stores.[38]

The whole Inhabitants at Norfolk on the Monday saw the Vessell proceed up the southern Branch off Gosport,[39] on the tuesday, all unknown to me or asked of as the Sloop was Crowded his Lordship sent some of the Soldiers into the different Ships and ordered thirteen of them into the Store house,

Sailmakers being mending Sails in that Store and doors open I went & found them in possession.

Now Gentlemen under these circumstances what was I to do, suppose yourselves in my situation what would ye have done under the Guns of two Men of War and Sixty Soldiers. suppose they had landed at Northfolk or Portsmouth would it not have caused much confusion if resisted; moderation appears to me most adviseable; the Gentlemen of the Navy and Army insists on it that I shall not appear before you without their escorting me & protecting me from the mob—from their behaviour to Jno. Schaw as they say it would appear the Committee has no government of the Mob.[40] Now I would by no means admit of any person or persons Escorting me least disturbances should arise. Therefore to prevent trouble & to have matters settled with moderation I beg leave to recommend to any the Gentlemen of the Committee to repair on board the Commodore when convenient or come over to my house in day light. I will wait on them pawn my life that no harm shall come to them & there will answer all reasonable questions asked of me. Self preservation is the first law of Nature I am old and an older American than any of ye to be used as Schaw was at my time of day was what no man durst in my younger days. I signed the Congress & promoted every person to do so in my power and complied with Colonel Arch⟨ibal⟩d Carys order last Assembly in answering the queries put to many of us and am as much attached to the American cause as any one (but more moderate than many.) I was appointed a Committee man my age & not wholly recovered of a severe fever prevented me from acting.[41] as I know most the Gentlemen of the Committee & suppose they may & believing them all reasonable Gentlemen hope my answers will be to them satisfactory.

I am with esteem Gent. Your most humbe Sert.

N.B. the Soldiers that were ashore are now on board of his Lordships Ship—which way am I to prevent them from landing again.[42]

> Letter MS transcript in unidentified hand (Tucker-Coleman Papers, Earl Gregg Swem Library, College of William and Mary in Virginia)

1. The number of delegates in attendance this day could not have exceeded 105 but was probably considerably fewer. On 15 Aug. a total of only 75 votes would be cast for a successor to Richard Bland as a deputy to Congress.

Tazewell's minutes for this day are hereafter separately bracketed as he successively wrote them and are followed by the full paragraphs as penned in the manuscript journal. There are variations in the order of proceedings in the 2 documents, but the minutes, which were written as transactions occurred, are far more trustworthy guides to facts of sequence.

2. The definite article is torn from near the right margin of the minutes.

3. For Bland's "Letter," see the next following item.

4. Tazewell deleted the descriptive clause here bracketed by lining it through with ink, probably because in rereading, he found the clause superfluous.

5. Tazewell wrote the verbal as "conferred," an error that Purdie silently corrects in the printed journal, p. 28.

6. The "old man" was 65.

7. Why Bland had not like Pendleton discouraged his reelection to Congress before the balloting began, only he knew. He may have been absent at the time of the balloting and attended later in the session of 11 Aug., when as chairman of the committee for defense and protection, he led discussions on the floor. Or he may have arrived at the decision to resign only after some hours of nocturnal soul-searching. One thing alone is certain: a stickler for accuracy and not unmindful of praise, Bland was set on seeing his resignation properly made a matter of record and his services duly acknowledged.

In the manuscript journal Tazewell made the resolution of thanks to Bland, and the president's delivery of that thanks, immediately follow the act of resignation. This would give to the public the impression of regret, gratitude, and encomium forthwith felt and expressed, but the minutes show that while the resolution was being prepared, the convention went on to other business.

8. The ellipsis deletes the phrase "& was read a second time & committed. Committed to the whole on Monday next." The nature of the writing indicates that Tazewell added the phrases later, with some squeezing in of the 1st phrase. In this single instance it appears that the journal gives a more accurate picture of the order of business than do the minutes, and that the 2d reading of the ordinance actually took place after receipt of the "Letter from the Officers of the voluntier Companies in Williamsburg."

9. The proposed ordinance was probably presented by Archibald Cary, chairman of the committee of elections appointed on 25 July 1775 (Procs., and n. 11).

10. There is no evidence to indicate who prepared and moved the resolution of "Thanks," but the action would most graciously have been that of Bland's colleague of many years' standing Robert Carter Nicholas.

11. In the manuscript journal presentation of the "Letter" follows introduction of the ordinance proposed by the committee of elections. Did the order to "lie"—and no further action on the letter would be taken—betray an amount of boredom or irritation by the influx of announcements and requests and the recommendation coming out of Waller's Grove?

12. From the manuscript minutes and journal it may be inferred that the bill was "Committed"—or more accurately, recommitted—, but then so many were the moot points in the document that it was voted they best be debated by the entire convention. Debate would not be resumed, however, until Tuesday, 15 Aug. 1775, as the final transaction of the day.

13. The "Number of Rifles & a Quantity of Gun Powder" were probably obtained by Andrew Cox, who was employed as agent for the Frederick County committee and sent to Lancaster, Pa., for the purpose (10 July 1775, Frederick Co. Committee and n. 14). If Tazewell's minutes were correct, Richard Henry Lee was appointed vice-chairman of the committee, not the last-ranking member. Fortunately, this probable slip was to cause no further confusion in a convention that needed no more, for if the committee ever formed an "Opinion" on the "said Proposition," none would be reported.

14. What was Colonel Cary saying? He was saying that his constituents in Chesterfield County had taken seriously the convention resolution of 4 Aug. 1775 that the county committees appoint officers who would "proceed immediately to enlist a Company of fifty Regulars in each County to be marched as soon as enlisted to such a place of Rendezvous as shall be hereafter appointed by this Convention" (Procs. and n. 8).

Well, yes, but on 9 Aug. the convention had reduced the regular establishment to 2 regiments (Procs. and n. 3). So if you excepted the 100 men sent to Fort Pitt (7 Aug. 1775 and n. 3), thereby exempting the District of West Augusta from further obligation, that left you 61 counties, the quotas for which (allowing for differences in sizes of population) would approximate 17 men each. Furthermore, the commander in chief had not been commissioned, his subordinate field officers had not been elected, there were no articles of war by which the troops could be governed, there was no committee of safety to ascertain that the troops were governed according to articles, and there was no ordinance by the reading of which such a committee could learn the limits of its own powers.

The portion of the manuscript journal here bracketed breaks off as though someone interrupted Cary. But it was Tazewell interrupting his own writing. With large, left-swinging loops of ink, he deleted this portion. To let it reach public print would have been unforgivable.

15. The key to distinguishing is in the term "other Accts." written in the minutes. This committee is not, in short, to be confused with that on war claims constituted on 25 July, when Isaac Zane, Jr., was alone appointed (Procs. and n. 10), to be joined 4 days later by 3 colleagues (29 July 1775, Procs. and n. 6). For the "Committee appointed by the House of Burgesses" to investigate the "Claims" of veterans of Dunmore's War and their dependents, see 11 Aug. 1775, Procs. and n. 6. The committee now appointed would report to the convention on 25 Aug. (Procs. and n. 15).

16. In the printed journal, p. 30, Purdie begins the paragraph, "Mr. *Zane*, from the persons appointed, presented. . . ." Mr. Zane was presenting for the committee of which he was chairman, as mentioned in the note immediately preceding.

In the convention loose papers is the 5-page draft of the proposed ordinance, docketed "Sat. Aug. 12. 1775 read first time" by Tazewell. This draft in general followed the provisions of the bill passed by the General Assembly in June past that was rejected by the governor because it would have imposed a duty on imported slaves and contained no suspending clause pending royal approval (pp. 21–23 above; *JHB, 1773–1776*, p. 278). Prefaced by a summary of the inability of the Assembly and the governor to concur on a bill to provide for claims, the present document designated the same commissioners and deputed them to undertake the same tasks as the House of Burgesses had appointed and specified during its final day of session on 24 June 1775 (ibid., pp. 282–83; *Statutes at Large*, VIII, 63–64).

This much of the Zane draft occupied 2 pages and 4 lines of closely written script. The remaining pages provided for the emission of a quantity of "treasury bills" wherewith to pay veterans or their dependents; because of the "low State of the Treasury," the imposition of "duties or taxes" on 4-wheeled carriages, on certain legal processes, and on land; and the levying of a modest poll tax on tithables.

In the 1st portion of the bill Tazewell filled in blanks according to the directions of the whole house. The document (though unnoted in the journal or minutes) was recommitted, for the draft that was to be submitted by the committee on 24 Aug. 1775 would be better organized and more coherent.

17. Here the minutes bear no relation to the paragraph in the journal immediately following. The convention had last sat as a "Committee on the State of the Colony" on 10 Aug. 1775 and at that time had debated the establishing of the Committee of Safety (Procs. and n. 4).

18. The "Order of the Day" for the convention to resume consideration of the ordinance introduced by the committee for defense and protection had been standing since 10 Aug. 1775 (Procs. and n. 3).

19. Deliberation on the ordinance would be duly continued as the 3d transaction of "Monday next," 14 Aug. 1775.

20. The order for a "Call" of the roll of the delegates, standing since 5 Aug. (Procs. and n. 4), would on "Tuesday," 15 Aug. 1775, be overlooked or ignored.

21. On a separate page and in the clear, clerical hand that was his best, Tazewell wrote: "The Orders of the Day for a Call of the Convention & for the Appointment of Officers to command the regular Forces to be raised for the Defence of this Colony being read,

"Resolved, that this Convention will on Monday next proceed to the Appointment of the said Officers, & that the order for the Call of the Convention be put off till Tuesday next."

This, with variations in harmony with his editorial style, is the form in which Purdie prints the concluding proceedings of the day, p. 31. The order "for the Appointment of Officers" had been standing since 5 Aug. (Procs. and n. 9) and on "Monday next," 14 Aug. 1775, would again be "postponed." The writing on the separate page may have been specially for Purdie, for in reviewing the journal, Tazewell (or Purdie) must have observed that not even the fact of adjournment was recorded.

The entire manuscript journal for this day is written in the hurried hand to which Tazewell occasionally resorted during the course of the third convention (for a comment on which see 4 Aug. 1775, Procs., n. 4). Or was it the hand of a man who was periodically ill? There is no evidence that Tazewell was under undue pressure because of his duties (any problems affecting his private life are unknown), but illness may have caused his absence on 4 Aug., when John Ruffin inscribed the journal, and on 8 Aug., when Ruffin produced the minutes. There were reasons enough for the confusion in which to this point the convention had proceeded. But if that body was under the guidance of a president uncertain of what he was doing and whose chief aide was unsure of what had been done, confusion was bearing a compound interest.

22. Here words and proper names are missing owing to a jagged tear in the manuscript minutes.

23. Whether anyone remembered the resolutions of 29 July 1775 respecting "Trash" and "Transfer Tobacco" (Procs. and nn. 3, 4), they were not referred to the committee now appointed but were left separately standing.

24. This phrase, which does not appear in the journal for the day, is taken from the separate page mentioned in note 21 above.

25. Edgewise at the top of the 6th of 6 pages John Ruffin wrote for Tazewell "Saturday No. 21."

26. This letter was presented to the convention as the 1st transaction of the present day. Although the text of the letter is in Colonel Bland's hand, the address is in Tazewell's careful script.

27. The documents enclosed in this letter were the letter of John Goodrich, Jr., to Matthew Phripp (10 Aug. 1775, Third Va. Convention, 2d entry), and William Roscow Wilson Curle's covering letter forwarding the 1st letter from Hampton to Williamsburg (11 Aug. 1775, same and nn. 24–27). An intermediate item, from Joseph Hutchings and Matthew Phripp to Curle of 10 Aug. is not among the convention papers and was probably not sent to Richmond. The present document and its enclosures would be presented to the convention on 14 Aug. 1775 (Procs., and n. 4).

The signatories, James Hubard, George Wythe, and Mayor John Dixon, were all appointed members of the Williamsburg committee on the day of its formation, 23 Dec. 1774 (*Rev. Va.*, II, 208).

28. For the "summons," see 9 Aug. 1775, Norfolk Co. Committee. Macartney or Dunmore was mistaken as to the day, which was "Wednesday the 16th Inst."

29. For the "cruel and oppressive treatment" meted out to the chimney-climbing Mr. Schaw, see 11 Aug. 1775, Norfolk Borough Committee.

30. For an application of the "principles" guiding Macartney in respect to slaves, see 31 July 1775, Third Va. Convention, Norfolk Borough Committee to Randolph and n. 1.

31. The "former occasion" may have been that in which the mayor and members of the Common Hall commended the captain for his conduct (ibid.).

32. For Loyall's reply, see 13 Aug. 1775.

33. In Virginia waters only a month, Capt. JOHN MACARTNEY, commander of H.M.S. *Mercury* (20 guns and a complement of 130), was not on the most amicable footing with the governor he had been sent "to protect" (p. 225 above). Described by Adm. Samuel Graves as "an experienced Officer, extremely diligent and punctual," the captain, who was now about 40 years of age, was building upon a career promisingly begun and enhanced by heroic service at Quebec in the cruel winter of 1759–60. But despite Lord Dunmore's admonishments, he insisted on fraternizing with rebels— why, the chap had even broken bread with Thomas Nelson, Sr.! Who argued loudest and longest is unrecorded (although His Lordship was not renowned for his reticence), but Purdie near the end of July had heard enough that he could report the 2 men "on very indifferent terms" and "lately" engaged in "some smart altercation." Indeed, branding him "utterly unfit," Dunmore had already demanded Macartney's recall. This demand Admiral Graves received with "Astonishment." He nevertheless, with "all possible dispatch," sent a sloop to Virginia and requested the governor's specific charges and "further Proofs" for Macartney's court-martial. But before the end of August unexpectedly confronted by "Proofs" of the captain's firmness in dealing with rebels, His Excellency would be astonished in turn and attempt to weasel his way out of the events he had set in train. Too late. Macartney would insist that he go to England to defend his reputation. "I think his heart is good," Graves was to inform the Admiralty, but "unfortunately" the officer was "bred a rigid dissenter" and was "too much of an orator" for his own good or that of the naval service. This judgment would have little influence on a bungling Admiralty seeking a scapegoat for the unsatisfactory progress of the Royal Navy in American waters, and in the end it was to be Graves who would be recalled and Macartney promoted (p. 225 above; Clark, *Naval Docs. of the Am. Rev.*, I, 47, 904, 998, 1083–85, II, 54, 55, 372, III, 454, 469, 541; Francis Parkman, *Montcalm and Wolfe* [2 vols., Boston, 1884], II, 343–44; *Va. Gazette* [Purdie], 28 July 1775; G[eorge] R. Barnes and J[ohn] H. Owens, eds., *The Private Papers of John, Earl of Sandwich* [4 vols., London, 1932–38], I, 80–81).

34. For the events leading to the meeting of the committee at 8:00 A.M. on this day and the necessity for 3 "gentlemen" to act as "surities" for the appearance of John Schaw, see 11 Aug. 1775, Norfolk Borough Committee. The "humble concession" read to "the people" was that which would appear in John Hunter Holt's local newspaper on 16 Aug. 1775 (10 Aug. 1775, Norfolk Borough Committee).

35. In Mayor Loyall's letter of 14 Aug. 1775 to Captain Macartney (Norfolk Borough), "some young gentlemen" will evolve into "a number of thoughtless youth."

36. The present item consists of part of the 1st paragraph and all of the 2d paragraph of a 3-paragraph notice.

37. This item is arbitrarily dated. The reference in the 3d paragraph to the "behaviour to Jno. Schaw" demonstrates that the letter could scarcely have been written before this date.

38. For the "Citation" of the date indicated, see Norfolk Co. Committee. The "Stores" were at Gosport, near Portsmouth.

39. That is, the "Southern Branch" of the Elizabeth River. The "Monday" was

probably 31 July 1775, the day when the troops of the royal 14th Regiment arrived in the river. The next day, "on the tuesday," His Lordship reviewed the additions to his command on shore (31 July 1775, Third Va. Convention, Norfolk Borough Committee to Randolph; 8 Aug. 1775, Norfolk Borough Committee and n. 10).

40. On 15 Aug. 1775 Captain Macartney was to state that his health permitting, he would personally accompany Sprowle "to the Committee" (Norfolk Borough).

41. The "Congress" that Sprowle "signed" and "promoted" was the Continental Association of 20 Oct. 1774 (*Rev. Va.*, II, 104–5, 108). "Colonel Archd Carys order last Assembly" was a summons dated 12 June 1775 that Sprowle not only "complied with" but endorsed, requesting the merchants then in Williamsburg to appear before a committee of the House of Burgesses in order to answer questions respecting the "commotions" that followed the governor's removal of the gunpowder from the capital Magazine (for which incident see pp. 4–11 above. A copy of the summons is in P.R.O., C.O. 5/1353, fols. 100–102, the results of the investigation in *JHB, 1773–1776*, pp. 231–37). No record of Sprowle's having been elected "a Committee man" under the Continental Association has been found. But his word on this subject may be accepted. He would hardly have risked fraying with a provable falsehood the tightrope on which he was now teetering.

42. Owner of "a very valuable property in Lands, Buildings, Wharfs, several vessels with much Merchandize and Effects, together with many valuable Negro Slaves, Stocks of Cattle, and all kinds of Utensils and Implements of Trade and Husbandry" altogether worth perhaps £20,000 sterling, ANDREW SPROWLE was one of the most outstanding merchants in the colony. Forty-eight of this Scotsman's 65 years had been lived in Virginia—and 36 of them as chairman of the colonial Merchants Association. As "Chairman of the Trade," he had signed the nonimportation association of 22 June 1770, and if not an ardent patriot, was yet not a convinced loyalist. His real concern was commerce and trade, not politics—if only someone with a magic wand would wave troubles away. But wands waved over mundane affairs are seldom magical, and when the businessman eschews politics, he historically has learned that those who do not eschew oft end by controlling business, even to the point of garroting it. No doubt the imminent implementation of the provisions of the Continental Association worked with a degree of subtlety on Sprowle's mind to move him to a certain sympathy with the governor. The Scotsman's ambivalence would leave behind him a bag of evidences so mixed that his real views remain clouded. His family would ultimately appeal for relief both in Great Britain and Virginia, avowing in one his loyalty, in the other his patriotism. Yet all is not commerce, trade, and politics. Late though was the "time of day" to which his life had run, he would take and cleave to a new wife in the winter coming (P.R.O., A.O. 12/54, fols. 142–66; Boyd, *Papers of Jefferson*, VIII, 243–44 n., 329–30; Isaac Samuel Harrell, *Loyalism in Virginia; Chapters in the Economic History of the Revolution* [Durham, N.C., 1926], pp. 44–45, 97–98 and n. 93).

As treacherous as was the act of balancing himself, Sprowle was not quite achieving the poise he wished. The implication contained in the printed proceedings of the Accomack County Committee of 27 June 1775 that he had perhaps given James Arbuckle's navigation chart of the Eastern Shore to Lord Dunmore, joined to the fact that he had now shown the summons of the Norfolk County Committee to His Excellency, was not likely to impress men with the belief that it was the governor who was seeking Sprowle's favor.

Sunday, 13 August 1775

Norfolk Borough

Mayor Paul Loyall to Captain John Macartney

Sr,

I just now received yours of yesterday's date, by Mr. ⟨Samuel⟩ Swan⟨n⟩. The summons you mention, I believe did not go from a committee of this borough. I will make the necessary enquiry, and will answer your letter tomorrow; [1] in the interim, I am,

Sir, your most obedient servant

Paul Loyall.[2]

Virginia Gazette, or the Norfolk Intelligencer,
30 August 1775

1. For the "summons" mentioned, see 9 Aug. 1775, Norfolk Co. Committee; for "yours of yesterday's date," 12 Aug., Norfolk Borough; for Loyall's answer "tomorrow," 14 Aug., same.

2. Capable, industrious, trustworthy, and prosperous PAUL LOYALL, previously mayor of Norfolk in 1763 and 1772, was now serving his 3d term. He was a leading merchant of the community, a vestryman of Elizabeth River Parish, a captain of militia, and a member of the board of overseers for the Cape Henry lighthouse. Of a Norfolk family distinguished before and after his time, he had long devoted himself to public service beginning at about the time that he and his partner, Peter Proby, had lost a sloop to the French in 1760. For uninterrupted years an alderman (when not mayor), in 1766 he signed the resolutions of the borough and county Sons of Liberty vowing resistance to enforcement of the Stamp Act. In the next year, when one of His Majesty's naval press-gangs appeared suddenly in the streets, the 6-foot Loyall, roused by the cries of the night watch, finished pulling on his breeches just as he dashed out of the door, shoes unbuckled. Leading a horde of townsfolk, he descended pell-mell upon the astonished impressers. With inebriate misdirection, the captain of the gang lunged at him with his sword and shouted to his men to fire. But in the melee fire at whom? Mayor George Abyvon arrived with a posse and restored order; the gang captain and a sailor escaped in a boat; impressed tars were released; some of the gang were let go; the more obnoxious were clapped into gaol. When in 1774 passions again flared, Loyall at once was chosen to serve on the Norfolk-Portsmouth joint Committee of Correspondence. And needing able, steady leadership in troublesome times, the borough Common Hall on 24 June 1775 again installed him as mayor. At this time Loyall was certainly well into his 5th decade (Edward W. Jones, ed., *The Lower Norfolk County Virginia Antiquary* [5 vols., Baltimore, 1895–1906], I, 21–30, 59, 108, 165; *Statutes at Large*, VIII, 539; Charles McIntosh, "The Proby Family of England

and of Hampton and Norfolk, Virginia," *Va. Mag. of Hist. and Biog.*, XXII [July 1914], 325, XV [Oct. 1907], 155–56 n. 7; *Va. Gazette* [Purdie and Dixon], 1 Oct. 1767; *Rev. Va.*, I, 47, II, 89, 95, 111, 134, 159–60; MS Minutes of the Common Council of the Borough of Norfolk, 1736–89, microfilm in Va. State Library, fol. 70).

Monday, 14 August 1775

Third Virginia Convention

Proceedings of Twenty-second Day of Session [1]

[Resolution about Saltpetre &c. refd. to same Committee.] [2]

A Resolution of the General Congress recommending the Making of Saltpetre and several Methods which had been practised with Success, was laid before the Convention & ordered to be referred to the Committee appointed to bring in An Ordinance to encourage the Making Saltpetre, Gunpowder & the refining Sulphur & providing Arms for the Use of the Colony.[3]

[Letter from Wms.burg read & to lie on Table.]

The Convention being informed that Lord Dunmore was meditating an hostile March with an armed Force to attack the City of Williamsburg.[4]

[Convention went into a Committee on Ordinance for raising Men. – to sit again tomorrow.]

The Convention then according to the Order of the Day resolved itself into a Committee on the Ordinance for raising and embodying a sufficient Force for the Defence and Protection of this Colony, and after sometime spent therein Mr. President ⟨Peyton Randolph⟩ resumed the Chair and Mr. Robert Carter Nicholas reported that the Committee had according to Order had under their Consideration the Ordinance for raising and embodying a Sufficient force for the defence & protection of this Colony, and had made a further progress therein, but not having time to go through the same, had directed him to move for leave to sit again.

Resolved that this Convention will to Morrow resolve itself into the said Committee.[5]

[Resoln. respecting Wms.burg &c. agreed to.]

Resolved, that the Committee for the said City and the Committees of York and James City be desired to pay particular Attention to the Subject and if Lord Dunmore or any other Person shall land or attempt to Land any armed Troops in their Neighbourhood, that they immediately request the Assistance of the Voluntier Companies now in the City to repel such Troops by Force, and if need be, to call in the Assistance of other Voluntier Companies or Militia for effecting that purpose.[6]

[Order to go into Com. on Election Ordinance put off.] [7]

[Mr. Nelson to have leave of Absence.]

Ordered that Mr. ⟨Thomas⟩ Nelson⟨, Jr.⟩ have leave to be absent from the Service of this Convention for the remainder of the Session.[8]

[Order for Appointment of Officers put off til Wednesday.] [9]

[Order on State of Colony put off til Tomorrow.]

The Orders of the Day for the Convention to resolve it self into a Committee on the State of the Colony and on the Ordinance for the Election of Delegates and ascertaining their allowances and also for regulating the Election of Committee men in the Several Counties and Corporations within this Colony and for the purposes therein mentioned, being read, Resolved that this Convention will to Morrow resolve itself into the said Committee.[10]

[Mr. R: H. Lee added to Com: abt. Lands.]

Ordered that Mr. Rich⟨ar⟩d. Henry Lee be added to the Committee appointed to enquire into the Petition of William Preston Gent, and the Petition from the Committee of the County of Fincastle.[11]

Adjourned till to Morrow 9 OClock

> Convention MS journal in hand of John Tazewell
> (Archives Division, Virginia State Library) [12]

Virginia Baptist Association to Honourable Peyton Randolph and Gentlemen in Convention

To the Honourable PEYTON RANDOLPH ESQ. and the several deligated Gentlemen, convened at Richmond, to concert Measures conducive to the Good and Well-being of this Colony and Dominion.

The humble Address of the Virginia Baptists, now Associated in Cumberland, by Deligates from their several Churches.

Gentlemen of the Convention,

While you are (pursuant to the important Trust reposed in you) acting as the Guardians of the Rights of your Constituents, and pointing out to them the Road to Freedom, it must needs afford you an exalted Satisfaction, to find your Determinations not only applauded, but chearfully complied with, by a brave and spirited People. We, however distinguished from the Body of our Countrymen, by Appellatives and Sentiments of a religious Nature, do, nevertheless look upon ourselves as Members of the Same Common-Wealth, and therefore with respect to Matters of a civil Nature, embarked in the same common Cause.[13]

Alarmed at the shocking Oppression, which in a British Cloud hangs over the American Continent, We as a Society and part of the distressed State, have in our Association considered what part might be most prudent for the Baptists to act in the present unhappy Contest. After we had determined "that in some Cases it was lawful to go to War—and also for us to make a Military Resistance against Great-Britain, in regard to their unjust Invasion, and tyrannical Oppression of, and repeated Hostilities against America," Our People were all left to act at Discretion with respect to inlisiting, without falling under the Censure of our Community—And as some have inlisted, and many more likely so to do, who will have earnest Desires for their Ministers to preach to them during the Campaign, We therefore deligate and appoint our well-beloved Brethren in the Ministry, Elijah Craig, Lewis Craig, Jeremiah Walker and John Williams, to present this Address and to petition you that they may have free Liberty to preach to the Troops at convenient Times without Molestation or abuse; And as we are conscious of their strong Attachment to American Liberty, as well as their soundness in the Principles of the Christian Religion, and great usefulness in the Work of the Ministry, We are willing they may come under your Examination, in any Matters you may think requisite. We conclude with our earnest Prayers to Almighty God, for his Divine Blessing on all your patriotic and laudable Resolves, for the good of Mankind and American Freedom, and for the Success of our Armies in Defence of our Lives, Liberties and Properties.[14] Amen.

Sign'd by order, and ⎫   SAML HARRIS [15] Moderator
in behalf of the Association ⎬   JOHN WALLER Clk
the 14th: August 1775.— ⎭

> MS document in hand of John Waller, with autograph signatures, in loose papers of third Virginia Convention (Archives Division, Virginia State Library)

Norfolk Borough

Mayor Paul Loyall to Captain John Macartney

To John Macartney, Esq; Commander of His Majesty's ship, MERCURY.
   Sir,   Norfolk, August 14, 1775.
SINCE writing you yesterday,[16] I find upon enquiry, that the summons referred to in your letter, was sent from a number of Gentlemen who are freeholders, and compose the Committee of the county of Norfolk, and are therefore entirely without the jurisdiction of the magistrates of this corporation. I can only promise, that as the place of meeting for the purpose of considering Mr. ⟨Andrew⟩ Sprowle's conduct, is said to be within the limits of this borough, I will take proper care, that he shall not be molested or injured in his person by any riot or mob, if he shall think fit to attend to the Committee.[17] With respect to the treatment that Mr. ⟨John⟩ Schaw received, I was a stranger to it, till the disturbance was over; but can assure you that as soon as he put himself under the protection of a magistrate, he was secured from danger.[18] The conduct, which you are pleased to explain to me, as chief magistrate of this borough, as your intention to pursue in preserving peace and obedience to the laws, in the station assigned you by his Majesty, must be

commended by every good man; by that care in your department, particularly in discouraging the elopment of slaves, which of late it is notorious has frequently happened, from the countenance shewn them by some enemies to this colony as well as to the British constitution, much mischief and confusion may be prevented.[19] Your suggestion that gentlemen are in danger by supplying his Majesty's ships, &c. in this colony with provisions, I cannot account for. I am very sure the contractors for the Navy in this town are under no such apprehension of danger, as they have been assured to the contrary in the most explicit manner. I hope suspicions of this nature prejudicial to the loyalty of a number of inhabitants, who are as much attached to the just prerogative of their Sovereign, as any subjects in the empire, may not be hastily taken up and adopted without full and satisfactory proof. I am obliged by your favorable opinion of my readiness to concur in the suppression of all animosities: It has hitherto been, and I trust ever will be, the tenor of my conduct. I have always found the authority of the magistracy sufficiently complete for the maintenance of government and good order; and while I thank you for your chearful offers of assistance for that laudable purpose, yet I presume your intention is only to act within the line of your department. I confess I feel myself somewhat astonished at the last paragraph of your letter, which seems to me to imply a threatening, that would eventually prove destructive to the persons and properties of his Majesty's subjects. A personal insult offered to an individual, by the ill guided zeal of a number of thoughtless youth, can never justify a hint of this nature. At any rate it is to be presumed, that gentlemen in military departments, will not intermeddle in that capacity, unless particularly required by the civil authority; as I am determined, whenever I find any unlawful combinations or persecutions to prevail within the sphere of my jurisdiction, to take every legal method to suppress them. I have nothing further to add, but the strongest assurances of the earnest desire of the inhabitants of this borough, to live in the most perfect harmony with the gentlemen of the Navy, and hope that no little incident may interrupt it.[20]

I am, Sir, Your most obedient humble servant.

Paul Loyall.

Virginia Gazette, or the Norfolk Intelligencer,
30 August 1775

1. The number of delegates in attendance this day could not have exceeded 105 but was probably considerably fewer. On 15 Aug. 1775 a total of only 75 votes would be cast for a successor to Richard Bland as a deputy to Congress.

Tazewell's manuscript minutes for the day are hereafter separately bracketed as he successively wrote them, and insofar as possible each entry is followed by the pertinent paragraph penned in the journal. As with the proceedings of 12 Aug. 1775, there are variations in the order of transactions in the 2 documents, but the minutes, which were written at the time the transactions occurred, are far more trustworthy guides to facts of sequence.

2. In the manuscript journal, and in Purdie's printed journal, p. 31, this 1st transaction is made to appear the 2d.

3. For the "Resolution of the General Congress," see 28 July 1775, Continental Congress. The "Committee appointed" was that of 6 members, Richard Henry Lee chairman, named in the final transaction of the day on 12 Aug. 1775.

4. In the manuscript journal, and in Purdie's printed journal, p. 31, this 2d transaction is made to appear the 1st. Tazewell ended the prefatory dependent clause with a period, Purdie correctly with a comma. In both journals the resultant directive is made to follow immediately. For the "Letter from Wms.burg," see 12 Aug. 1775, Third Va. Convention, 3d entry and n. 27. The statement "that Lord Dunmore was meditating an hostile March" was derived from the enclosure in the letter from the capital (for which see 10 Aug. 1775, Third Va. Convention, 2d entry), in which it had been reported that His Lordship had "13 Fieldpeacis" mounted on a warship and "that he Intends to Wmsburg with them."

5. The committee for defense and protection had been initially appointed on 19 July, with Richard Bland as chairman (Procs. and n. 6). The vote on the "Order of the Day" was one of the last transactions of the session of Saturday, 12 Aug. (Procs. and nn. 18–19). On "to Morrow," 15 Aug. 1775, the present resolution would be overlooked or ignored, except by Purdie in the printed journal, p. 32.

6. As Tazewell's minutes disclose, the convention took up the "Letter from Wms.burg" only after having deliberated on the bill for defense and protection. A copy of the floor resolution in the convention loose papers is in Tazewell's hand. By whom the resolution was introduced is not clear, but it logically would have been by Robert Carter Nicholas, vice-chairman of the Williamsburg committee (2 May 1775, Va. Committee and n. 3). It is perhaps worth noting that the convention chose not to communicate with officers commanding independent companies but with the committees of the counties most likely to be affected by an armed threat by "Lord Dunmore or any other Person."

7. This "Order" must stand isolated, because Tazewell in the manuscript, and Purdie in the printed journal, p. 32, incorporated it as part of a later paragraph.

8. It is possible that after 22 days of session, Nelson, whose near-claustrophobia induced asthmatic attacks, had suffered about all of the convention that he could. Elected on 5 Aug. colonel of the nonexistent 2d Regiment (Procs.) and on 11 Aug. a deputy to Congress (Procs. and n. 10), he now had a choice of field or forum. On 17 Aug. 1775 he would select the latter by rejecting the former (Procs. and n. 8).

9. The "Order" for the election of the subordinate field-grade officers had been standing since 5 Aug. 1775 (Procs. and n. 9) and had most recently been fixed for action on the present day by the session of Saturday, 12 Aug. (Procs. and n. 21).

10. The last time the convention can be shown to have sat as a "Committee on the State of the Colony" was 10 Aug., when it deliberated on the establishment of the Committee of Safety (Procs. and n. 4). The "Order" can, however, be demonstrated to have been standing since the following day, 11 Aug. (Procs. and n. 16). The bill of elections had been introduced, twice read, and debated on 12 Aug., with the order to resume consideration standing since that day (Procs. and nn. 8–9, 12). The convention would next sit as a Committee on the State of the Colony on 16 Aug. 1775 (Procs. and nn. 4–5) and on the same day would order "postponed" further consideration of the ordinance to govern elections (Procs. and n. 11).

11. With the appointment of Lee to the committee established as the last transaction of 18 July 1775, with Robert Carter Nicholas as chairman, the number of members thereon was again raised to 14 (11 Aug. 1775, Procs. and n. 15).

12. Tazewell wrote "No. 22" edgewise at the top of the 4th of 4 pages.

13. As "some ease to scrupulous consciences in the exercise of religion" might be "an effectual means" of uniting English Protestant subjects "in interest and affection," Parliament in 1689 passed the Toleration Act. Thereby official persecution of dissenting Protestants ceased, and such nonconformists were permitted to practice their persuasions unhindered, provided they took oaths of loyalty to the Crown and, if required by local magistrates, posted bonds ("An Act for Exempting Their Majesties' Protestant Subjects Dissenting from the Church of England from the Penalties of Certain Laws," 1 William and Mary, *cap.* 18 [A.D. 1689], in Browning, *English Historical Documents,* gen. ed. Douglas, VIII, 400–403). But an act of an English Parliament did not produce instant (or even delayed) toleration in Virginia. Indeed, in consonance with political tenets noted elsewhere in these volumes, there were men who challenged the constitutionality of the act as applied to the colony.

Since about 1770 a group in the colony known as Separatist Baptists had become the objects of concerted harassment by more orthodox practitioners of Christianity. Distinct from, though by 1775 doctrinally rejoined with, the less boisterous Regular Baptists of the northern and western parts, the separatists derived their spiritual inspiration mainly from North Carolina. It was the practice of most of the preachers of this sect to refuse to take the oaths or to post the bonds. Their defiance of the law, together with the deplorable "enthusiasm," noisy exhortations, uproarious conversions, and almost uniformly ungenteel deportment, purchased them much trouble. Quite "poor, very plain in their dress, unrefined in their manners, and awkward in their address," they spent almost as much time in jail as they did in meetinghouses, particularly when they disturbed the repose of such law-enforcing stalwarts as Archibald Cary. Hounded from their pulpits by showers of sticks and stones, and lashed and incarcerated by indignant devotees of the Prince of Peace, they yet found overseas tyranny less endurable than that at home (Robert Baylor Semple, *A History of the Rise Progress of the Baptists in Virginia* [Richmond, 1810], G[eorge] W. Beale, continuator [rev. ed., Richmond, 1894], pp. 15–88; Reuben Edward Alley, *A History of the Baptists in Virginia* [Richmond, n.d. (1974)], pp. 31–89).

14. The "humble Address" would be presented to the convention as the 1st transaction of the day on 16 Aug. 1775.

15. For years SAMUEL HARRIS lived in "easy circumstances" and was one of the most respected citizens of that portion of Halifax County from which Pittsylvania County was formed in 1766. He held numbers of local offices and served as a church warden. But in 1758 he announced his conversion to the Baptist denomination, the next year set about preaching, and in 1769 was ordained. During the French and Indian War he kept 2 wagons constantly on the road between his home and Petersburg that his neighbors might not lack salt or other necessities. Notwithstanding this evidence of orderliness, he let his personal affairs fall into disarray and concentrated his great capacity for organization on the work to which his life was dedicated. A "large new dwelling house" that he had built he turned into a place of worship and remained in his old, smaller home. Or more accurately, he returned there when not crisscrossing the lower and central Piedmont on missions. If as "a doctrinal preacher" he displayed talents "rather below mediocrity," as an emotional evangelist he could reduce a congregation to hysteria. Braving hurlings of wood, stone, and rubbish, and shedding contumely as a drake would rain, he sermonized and prayed, sometimes at nearly every house he passed and to which he could gain admittance, and he even unnerved solitary travelers on dusty or muddy roads with dire warnings of the wrath to come. His appearance at an association of Baptist ministers was equivalent to his being chosen

moderator. At this time Harris was 51 (Semple and Beale, *Hist. of the Rise and Progress of the Baptists in Va.*, pp. 17–28, 65, 73, 74, 81–82; James B. Taylor, *Lives of Virginia Baptist Ministers* [Richmond, 1837], pp. 28–37; William B. Sprague, *Annals of the American Pulpit* . . . [9 vols., New York, 1866–69], VI, 79–82).

16. For Mayor Loyall's letter of "yesterday," see 13 Aug. 1775.

17. For the "summons" see 9 Aug. 1775, Norfolk Co. Committee, and for Sprowle's response, 12 Aug. 1775, same.

18. For the "treatment that Mr. Schaw received," see 11 Aug. 1775, Norfolk Borough Committee.

19. For Captain Macartney's "intention," see 12 Aug. 1775, Norfolk Borough.

20. For Macartney's reply, see 15 Aug. 1775, Norfolk Borough. If noticing, the captain would fail to comment on the mayor's well-put distinction between being set upon by a mob of emotional youths and a mob of reflecting gentry.

Tuesday, 15 August 1775

Third Virginia Convention

Proceedings of Twenty-third Day of Session [1]

On a Motion made. RESOLVED. that Robert Carter Nicholas Esq. be directed to pay the Officers & Soldiers of the two rifle companies sent from the Counties of Frederick & Berkeley to serve in the Continental Army such sums of Money out of the public Treasury as will make their pay equal to the pay of the Officers of the like rank and soldiers who were on the late Indian Expedition Commanded by Lord Dunmore including the pay Allowed by the Continental Congress.[2]

The Committee to whom the petitions of the Committee and Surveyor of the County of Fincastle and a Proclamation of Lord Dunmore dated the 8th. of May 1775 were refered REPORTED that they had had the same under their consideration and had come to the following resolution RESOLVED that untill the Committee appointed by the Convention in March last to inquire whether the King may of right advance the terms of Granting Lands in this Colony shall have made their report the recommendation then made that all persons should forbear to purchase or accept grants of Lands under the late instructions from the Governor be observed and that in the mean time all surveyors be and they are hereby directed to make no surveys under the said instructions nor pay any regard to the said Proclamation—and delivered the same in at the Clerk's Table where the same was again twice read & unanimously agreed to [3]

The Convention then according to the order of the Day proceeded to the appointment of a deputy to represent this Colony in General Congress in the

room of Richard Bland who hath resigned[4] and the Members having prepared tickets with the name of the deputy to be appointed, and put them into
the Ballot Box Mr. Robert C. Nicholas, Mr. ⟨Edmund⟩ Pendleton, Mr.
⟨Patrick⟩ Henry, Mr. George Mason & Mr. ⟨Archibald⟩ Cary were appointed
a Committee, to examine the Ballot box and report on whom the Majority
fell, who retired and after some time reported that the Numbers stood as
follows.

for Francis Lightfoot Lee Esqr.	37
Carter Braxton	36
[John Banister, Esq.	1
George Mason, Esq.	1][5]

and the question then being put whether the said Francis L. Lee or Carter
Braxton who appeared to have the greatest numbers on the Ballot should be
appointed a deputy to represent this Colony in General Congress, the majority appeared in favor of Francis L. Lee Esquire.

Resolved therefore that the said Francis L: Lee be appointed a deputy to
represent this Colony in General Congress.

The order of the day for the Convention to resolve itself into a Committee
on the Ordinance for regulating the Elections of Delegates and ascertaining
their[6] allowances and also for regulating the Elections of Committee men in
the several Counties & Corporations in this Colony and for other purposes
therein mentioned being read[7] the Convention resolved itself into[8] the said
Committee and after some time spent therein Mr. President ⟨Peyton Ran-
dolph⟩ resumed the Chair and Mr. Robert Carter Nicholas reported that the
Committee had according to order had under their consideration the said
ordinance and had made Considerable progress therein but not having time
to go through the same had directed him to move for leave to sit again.[9]

Resolved that this Convention will to Morrow resolve itself into the said
Committees.[10]

Adjourned till to Morrow 9 o Clock.

> Convention MS journal in hand of John Ruffin
> (Archives Division, Virginia State Library)[11]

Norfolk Borough

Captain John Macartney to Mayor Paul Loyall

His Majesty's ship Mercury, at Norfolk August 15, 1775.
Sir,
I was favored with your letter of yesterday's date,[12] and it gives me real
satisfaction to find, that the inhabitants of Norfolk are so earnestly desirous

of living in harmony with his Majesty's servants. You are pleased to assure me that no violence or insult shall be offered to the person of Mr. ⟨Andrew⟩ Sprowle, and upon the faith of your letter I have requested of him to attend the Committee tomorrow.[13] For some days past I have been much indisposed, but if I find myself well enough tomorrow, I mean to accompany Mr. Sprowle to the Committee, and will call upon you about 11 o'clock tomorrow morning. I must beg that you will go along with us. You, I am sure, will agree with me that the summons sent Mr. Sprowle (a copy of which I have enclosed you) must be truly alarming to all good citizens. When any set of gentlemen assume to themselves the power of arraigning an individual for furnishing barracks for his Majesty's troops, and pretend to censure a conduct, which I must think highly laudable, it gives me but too much reason to apprehend, that the authority of the civil magistracy is not competent for the support of government and good order.[14]

I am, Sir, Your most obedient humble servant:

John Macartney.

Virginia Gazette, or the Norfolk Intelligencer,
30 August 1775

1. With the granting to Thomas Nelson, Jr., of "leave to be absent" (14 Aug. 1775, Procs. and n. 8), the number of delegates in attendance this day could not have exceeded 103. But the total of votes later cast this same day for a deputy to Congress would be 75, so that if President Randolph withheld a casting vote, the number was probably 76.

2. For the rifle companies dispatched to Boston by the committees of Frederick and Berkeley counties in response to a resolution of Congress, see 11 July 1775, Third Va. Convention, In Congress and n. 16. The present "Motion" was a floor resolution, the manuscript original of which in an unidentified hand is in the convention loose papers. The pay scale for militia participants in Dunmore's War had been fixed in a bill passed by the General Assembly in June 1775 but not assented to by Lord Dunmore (p. 23 above; 12 Aug. 1775, Procs. and n. 16). Whether when introduced by the committee on war claims on 12 Aug. or subsequently written into the bill by the convention, the ordinance as passed would incorporate the identical pay scale (*Statutes at Large,* IX, 61, 62–63).

What was meant by the phrase "including the pay allowed by the Continental Congress" was that the Continental pay scale was lower than that to be fixed in the ordinance in question; hence the colonial treasurer was to make up the difference and remit it to the commanders of the rifle companies that the pay of officers and men be raised "to the Virginia Standard" (Ballagh, *Letters of R. H. Lee,* I, 150–51). Expressed in terms of Spanish milled dollars, the Continental pay scale ranged from $6⅔ per month for a private to $20 a month for a captain. Converted to the same terms, that for veterans of Dunmore's War would range from $6⅞ for a private to $25²¹⁄₃₃ for a captain. Yet lacking a knowledge of the facts behind the paragraph, a careful reader of the Purdie printed journal, p. 32, must be forgiven if he glances back in an attempt to determine what he has overlooked or forgotten, for there is no previous allusion to a transaction to which the resolution can be pegged.

3. "The Committee to whom the petitions" and "a Proclamation" were "referred"

had been initially appointed on 18 July 1775, with Robert Carter Nicholas designated chairman (Procs. and nn. 3–6). Dunmore's proclamation is under the date heading indicated, Royal Chief Magistracy. The "Committee appointed by the Convention in March last" was established on the final day of session, the 27th, and consisted of Patrick Henry, Richard Bland, Thomas Jefferson, Robert Carter Nicholas, and Edmund Pendleton (*Rev. Va.*, II, 383–84).

Thomas Lewis had been quietly circulating among the "Leading members" of the convention on William Preston's behalf and on 19 Aug. 1775 would write to the surveyor that "no blame was laid or attempted to be Charged to you." The members of the committee "of march last," he would continue, had individually been much engaged and were unable at present to deliver a report "for want of Some Original papers & Charters." He might hope that they would be able to "attend to this matter Soon." But, he would sigh, "as to what passes here it is difficult to Say with Certainty⟨.⟩ not an Ordinance is yet Compleated. a variety of opinions retards this Bussiness" (Draper MSS, 4QQ29, State Hist. Soc. of Wis.).

Before long it would be clear that there was no need for the committee "of march last" to report, for to whom western lands belonged would be merged with the larger question of to whom the 13 colonies belonged.

4. The "order" to elect a deputy on the present date had been standing since Bland's resignation on 12 Aug. 1775, for which see Procs. and nn. 3–7. On 13 or 14 Aug. "a strong Party" led by Patrick Henry, Thomas Jefferson, and Paul Carrington brought pressure to bear on George Mason to reconsider his refusal to serve in Congress, "laying it down as a Rule" that he could not decline "if ordered" by his "Country." Mason stood fast, but "just before the Ballot" he was "publickly called upon in Convention, & obliged to make a public Excuse" and to give his "Reasons for refusal." More "distress'd than ever" he had been before, he undoubtedly retraced the ground previously covered in private (11 Aug. 1775, Procs., n. 12). He glanced at the chair. Tears were running "down the President's cheeks." Mason accepted the sight as a lachrymal acknowledgment of abilities lost to the colony, and perhaps also of the pathos with which he spoke. He may have been correct. Or he may have been witness to a symptom of emotional instability.

"I took Occasion," said Mason, "at the same time, to recommend Colo. Francis Lee; who was accordingly chosen in the room of Colo. Bland" (Rutland, *Papers of Mason*, I, 250); but the ballot that follows will be found to involve a contest that could have been closer only by the shift of a single vote.

5. The bracketed portion of the report is taken from the Purdie printed journal, p. 33. The votes cast for Banister and Mason appear neither in manuscript journal nor minutes. Evidently Robert Carter Nicholas handed Tazewell (who in turn supplied Purdie with) the full tally on a loose paper that is no longer extant.

6. John Ruffin wrote "there," an error Purdie silently corrects in the printed journal, p. 34.

7. The "order of the day" had been adopted on the previous day of session, 14 Aug. 1775 (Procs. and n. 10).

8. Ruffin wrote "in," an error that Purdie silently corrects in the printed journal, p. 34.

9. On the next day of session, 16 Aug. 1775, the sitting would be "postponed" (Procs. and n. 11).

10. In the printed journal, p. 34, Purdie amends the short paragraph with its meaningless phrase "the said Committees" to read: "The orders of the day, for the Convention to resolve itself into a committee on the state of the colony, and on the

ordinance for raising and embodying a sufficient force for the defence and protection of this colony, being read,

"*Resolved,* That this Convention will to-morrow resolve itself into a committee on the said ordinance, and on the state of the colony."

The order to sit as a Committee on the State of the Colony had been standing since 12 Aug. (Procs. and n. 17), most recently to be postponed on 14 Aug. (Procs. and n. 10). Debate on the ordinance proposed by the committee for defense and protection had been a transaction of 14 Aug. 1775 (Procs. and n. 5).

Probably because he had no earlier portions of the manuscript journal at hand, Ruffin employed the phrase "the said Committees" to cover as best he could Tazewell's final minute for this day—"other Orders put off." It may have been that Purdie made his amendment after having reread earlier portions of the original manuscript journal or of a manuscript copy of the journal given him by Tazewell. If so, he overlooked or ignored the "order for the Call of the Convention" specified on 12 Aug. 1775 to be implemented this very day (Procs. and n. 21).

11. Tazewell wrote "No. 23" edgewise at the top of the 4th of 4 pages.

12. Q.v. under Norfolk Borough.

13. For the summons by the "Committee" and Sprowle's expression of hesitation to abide by the terms laid down, see respectively 9 and 12 Aug. 1775, Norfolk Co. Committee.

14. For the proceedings of the committee "tomorrow," see 16 Aug. 1775, Norfolk Co. Committee. Captain Macartney's correspondence with Mayor Loyall on this subject might have ended here and never have become public knowledge, but the mayor had other plans and submitted the letters to the Common Hall on 21 Aug. 1775 (Norfolk Borough).

Wednesday, 16 August 1775

Third Virginia Convention

Proceedings of Twenty-fourth Day of Session [1]

An Address from the Baptists in this Colony was presented to the Convention & read setting forth that however distinguished from the Body of their Countrymen by Appellatives and Sentiments of a religious Nature, they nevertheless consider themselves as Members of the same Community in respect to Matters of a civil Nature, and embarked in the same common Cause—that alarmed by the Oppression which hangs over America, they had considered what part it would be most prudent to take in the unhappy Contest, and had determined that in some Cases it was Lawful to go to War, and that it was Lawful for them to make a military Resistance against Great Britain, in her unjust Invasion, tyrannical Oppression & repeated Hostilities—that their Sect were left at Discretion to enlist without incurring the Censure of their religious Community and under these Circumstances many of them had enlisted as Soldiers and many more were ready to do so, who had an earnest Desire their Ministers should preach to them during the Campaign, that they had therefore appointed four of their Brethren to make Application to this Convention for the Liberty to preach to the Troops at convenient Times without Molestation or Abuse & praying the same may be granted them.[2]

Resolved that it be an Instruction to the Commanding Officers of the Regiments or Troops to be raised to permit dissenting Clergymen to celebrate divine Worship and to preach to the Soldiers or exhort from Time to Time as the various operations of the Military Service may admit for the Ease of such scrupulous Consciences, as may not chuse to attend divine Worship as celebrated by the Chaplain.[3]

The Convention then according to the Order of the Day went into a Committee on the State of the Colony [4] and after sometime spent therein Mr. President ⟨Peyton Randolph⟩ resumed the Chair and Mr. Robert Carter Nicholas reported that the Committee had according to Order had under their Consideration the State of the Colony and had come to several Resolutions thereupon which he read in his Place, and then delivered in at the Clerk's Table where the same were again twice read and agreed to as follows

Resolved, that for the more effectual carrying into Execution the several Rules and Regulations established by this Convention for the Protection and Defence of this Colony a Committee of Safety be appointed to consist of eleven Members to be chosen by Ballot by the Members of this Convention, who are to continue until the next sitting of the Convention or for one Year in Case the Convention should not meet within that time.[5]

Resolved, that no Member of the Committee of Safety shall hold any Military Office whatsoever after the End of this Session of the Convention.[6]

Ordered, Mr. Robert Carter Nicholas, Mr. ⟨Patrick⟩ Henry, Mr. Richard Henry Lee, Mr. ⟨Joseph⟩ Jones & Mr. ⟨Thomas⟩ Jefferson be a Committee to prepare & bring in an Ordinance pursuant to the said Resolution.[7]

Ordered, that Leave be given to bring in an Ordinance for establishing a General Test in this Colony and that Mr. ⟨Josiah⟩ Parker & Mr. Geo⟨rge⟩. Mason do prepare & bring in the same.[8]

A Letter from the Committee on the Western Waters of Augusta inclosing several papers on the subject of Indian Affairs was laid before the Convention and ordered to lie on the Table.[9]

Ordered, that Mr. Jefferson have Leave of Absence from the Service of this Convention for the Remainder of the Session.[10]

The Orders of the Day for the Convention to resolve itself into a Committee on the Ordinance for regulating the Election of Delegates and ascertaining their Allowances; and also for regulating the Election of Committee men in the several Counties & Corporations within this Colony and for other purposes therein mentioned—for the Convention to proceed to the Appointment of Officers to command the regular Forces to be raised for the Defence of this Colony—and for the Convention to resolve itself into a Committee on the Ordinance for raising and embodying a sufficient force for the Defence & protection of this Colony, being read,

Resolved, that the same be postponed till Tomorrow.[11]

It being observed with much Concern that the President was indisposed, and that the Time of his Departure for the General Continental Congress was nearly approaching, it was unanimously recommended to him to retire for the present from the Fatigues of the Business of this Convention, in which he was pleased though with Reluctance to acquiesce.

It was then unanimously resolved that the Thanks of this Convention be presented to his honor the President for his unremitted Attention to the important Interests of this Country & his unwearied Application to, and able faithful & impartial Discharge of the Duties of his Office, assuring him that he hath the warmest Wishes of this Convention for a speedy Return of his Health & an uninterrupted Enjoyment of every Felicity.[12]

adjourned till Tomorrow 9. oClock.

> Convention MS journal in hand of John Tazewell
> (Archives Division, Virginia State Library) [13]

Norfolk County Committee

Remissness and Most Unfriendly Disposition

NORFOLK COUNTY, Committee Chamber, Aug. 16.
PRESENT,
Col John Willoughby⟨, Sr.,⟩ Chairman, and 21 Mem⟨bers⟩.

MR. ANDREW SPROWLE agreeable to summons waited upon the Committee,[14] and being examined relative to soldiers occupying his warehouse as barracks, declared, that no application had been made to him by Lord Dunmore, or any other person for the use of the said house, previous to the soldiers taking possession of it. That as soon as he found they were there, he expostulated with Lord Dunmore, and told him such a proceeding was highly disagreeable to him, that it would give great offence to the community in general, and insisted upon his removing them immediately; that Lord Dunmore paid no attention to his repeated solicitations, but still continued to keep forcible possession, for the space of ten or twelve days, until the ship which he had pressed, and was then fitting up, should be made ready for their reception.[15]

RESOLVED, that Mr. ANDREW SPROWLE has been REMISS in not giving this Committee the earliest information that his private property had been seized upon, soldiers quartered in his house, contrary to his inclination and solicitations.[16]

RESOLVED, that it be recommended to the inhabitants of this county that they have no connections or dealings with LORD DUNMORE or CAPT. SQIRES ⟨Matthew Squire⟩, and the other officers of the Otter sloop of war; as they have evinced on many occasions, the most unfriendly disposition to the liberties of this continent, in promoting a disaffection among the slaves, and concealing some of them for a considerable time on board their vessels.[17]

ORDERED, that the stated meetings of this Committee be the first Thursday in every month, (if fair) if not the first day afterwards.[18]

Alexander Skinner, Sec'ry.

Virginia Gazette, or the Norfolk Intelligencer,
23 August 1775

1. The number of delegates in attendance this day could not have exceeded 103, but if the vote on 17 Aug. 1775 for the members of the Committee of Safety be indicative, the number was probably in the mid- or high seventies.

2. For the "Address from the Baptists in this Colony" and the 4 "Brethren" designated to present the address, see 14 Aug. 1775, 2d entry.

3. The original manuscript resolution in the convention loose papers is in the hand of Patrick Henry. Whether he introduced the resolution immediately after the conclusion of the reading of the address is indeterminable, for in his minutes for this day Tazewell made no entry respecting the subject. The resolution evidently was left to stand by itself and was not regarded as an instruction to the committee for defense and protection; nor would the committee to be appointed as the 1st transaction of the day on 21 Aug. 1775 for the purpose of drafting articles of war touch on the purpose of the resolution other than to penalize officers and men who should "behave indecently and irreverently in any place of divine worship" (*Statutes at Large*, IX, 36).

4. The convention's resolving itself into a "Committee on the State of the Colony" was in compliance with "the Order of the Day" of 10 Aug. (Procs. and n. 4) and thereafter twice postponed (11 Aug., same and n. 16, 14 Aug. 1775, same and n. 10).

5. The deficiency of the journal from the reading public's viewpoint is that although the delegates must have known reasonably well what "Rules and Regulations" they would probably pass "for the Protection and Defence of this Colony," not a single ordinance had yet been enacted, and to elect a committee of safety before authorizing, empowering, and limiting it, was to put the cart before the horse.

6. Whereas a resolution of 5 Aug. 1775 had prohibited any officer commanding "regular Forces" from election to the Committee of Safety (Procs. and n. 3), the present resolution extended that prohibition even to militia officers. In this wise, none of the plural executive exercising control over the commander in chief would, by serving in the field, become his subordinante; nor would a temporary subordinate be able to promote the interests of a particular command by resuming his seat on the committee. Either the present resolution was considered an instruction by the committee of elections, appointed on 25 July 1775, with Archibald Cary as chairman (Procs. and n. 11), or it was later incorporated by the convention as a whole in the final paragraph of the ordinance regulating elections (*Statutes at Large*, IX, 53).

But to every appearance there was more to the matter than is evident from reading the journal. On a page now in the convention loose papers, Tazewell wrote the words of the floor resolution. For the number of members on the committee he first wrote "sixteen," then deleted the word with a line of ink and above it wrote "eleven."

Writing on, he later deleted by ink crosshatchings a much interlineated 2d resolution: "Resolved, That no Member of the Committee of Safety, shall, after the End of the present Session of this Convention, continue a Member of this Convention, or hold any Military Office whatsoever in this Colony, and that one member be chosen out of each District"—the districts being 16 military entities yet to be formed from conjoined counties or from counties conjoined with Williamsburg and Norfolk (*Statutes at Large*, IX, 16). If offered, this resolution must have been withdrawn or defeated, in part because it was unnecessarily repetitious in its military restrictions, in greater part because the vote to limit membership on the Committee of Safety to 11 rendered membership by districts impossible.

On the verso of the page, however, Tazewell at some unknown date wrote more intriguingly and in his best crabbed hand: "After the disolution of the present Convention, Bribery was tendered to a Person in this Country—If it wou'd make them after ⟨alter⟩ their votes he wou'd be for the Motion." One may imagine that the "Person" selected as being the best positioned to disperse vote-altering douceurs was Tazewell himself, and that he rejected the tender. But beyond this point further speculation becomes so tenuous as to command its own rejection. What alone is evident—if the clerk was correct—is that at least 1 delegate among a probable 70-odd was not the reincarnation of Aristides.

7. A bill for establishing a committee of safety would be introduced under curious circumstances on 19 Aug. 1775 (Procs. 3d para.).

8. George Mason would introduce a "General Test," or oath of allegiance to the revolutionary government, on 19 Aug. 1775 (Procs. and n. 6).

9. "Letter" not found; it is possible that among the "several papers" was a copy of Virginia and Pennsylvania Delegates in Congress to Inhabitants on West Side of Laurel Hill, 25 July 1775, 4th entry.

10. Thomas Jefferson desired "Leave" that he might enjoy some repose at Monticello and there attend to personal business before returning to Congress, which on 1 Aug. had adjourned until 5 Sept. 1775. Before leaving, he handed Carter Braxton an order for £13 for the purchase of a treasured violin from Atty. Gen. John Randolph, who was engaged in selling such personalty as he could spare preparatory to sailing for "home" (*JCC*, II, 239; Malone, *Jefferson and His Time*, I, 159, 209–10). The convention journal for Thursday, the 17th, will show that the Albemarle delegate remained in Richmond one more day (Procs., 5th para., and n. 6).

11. The order to consider further the bill of elections was contained in the final transaction of 15 Aug. (Procs.); the order "to proceed to the Appointment of Officers" of subordinate field-grade rank, standing since 5 Aug. (Procs. and n. 9), had on 14 Aug. been postponed until the present day (Procs. and n. 9); the order to resume consideration on the bill for defense and protection had been standing since 14 Aug. (Procs. and n. 5) and on 15 Aug. was postponed until the present day (Procs. and n. 10). Once again the order for a "Call" of the members, standing since 5 Aug. 1775 (Procs. and n. 4), was overlooked or ignored.

12. A trial copy of the resolution in Tazewell's hand is in the convention loose papers. The copy reads: "The Convention observing that the President is indisposed, requested him, to retire from the Business for the remainder of the Session, and unanimously resolved that, the Thanks of the Convention are justly due for his faithful able & impartial discharge of the Import[ant] Office he had so worthily filled."

On the verso of his minutes for this day Tazewell wrote: "A member of the Convention moved that the president might be excused from the Service of the Convention for the remainder of this Session, he being indisposed."

It is doubtful that the resolution was introduced without Randolph's foreknowledge. If he did not himself mention his indisposition to others and suggest that the convention might be better served by his withdrawal, it then may be supposed that such old friends and political allies as Robert Carter Nicholas, Richard Bland, Edmund Pendleton, and Benjamin Harrison constituted themselves an informal committee to wait, and gently urge, on him that he seek to recoup his strength before returning to Philadelphia.

However the transaction was brought about, the end to which it was directed was to seem achieved when on 25 Aug. 1775 Purdie announced in his *Va. Gazette* that "his Honour" had reached his home in Williamsburg on the 19th, was since then "greatly recovered," and intended "setting out next sunday morning," the 27th, "for Philadelphia."

13. Tazewell wrote "No. 24" edgewise at the top of the 4th of 4 pages.

14. For the summons, see 9 Aug. 1775, Norfolk Co. Committee. Sprowle had begged to be excused from attending the committee from fear of "the Mob" (12 Aug., same), but a correspondence between Mayor Paul Loyall and Capt. John Macartney (14, 15 Aug., Norfolk Borough) emboldened him to present himself. Almost assuredly Sprowle was accompanied by the mayor. It is less certain that he was also accompanied by the hitherto "much indisposed" captain. If he was, the picture of a committee of determined patriots in confrontation with an equally determined British sea dog is framed only by the limits of individual imagination. But assuming Macartney's presence, it was most likely that when so much of his mission as seeing Sprowle safely to the "Committee Chamber" had been accomplished, he was left to cool his heels, which is not necessarily the same as cooling one's temper, in a waiting room.

15. The "ship" that Lord Dunmore "had pressed" into royal service on 16 July 1775 was the *William*, a large merchantman from Jamaica, upon which by last report His Excellency had mounted "13 field-pieces" (*Va. Gazette, or the Norfolk Intelligencer*, 19 July 1775; *Va. Gazette* [Purdie], 11 Aug. 1775, postscript).

16. Having learned, or thinking himself to have learned, a new trick or two in the art of tightrope-walking, Sprowle next would write an unlocated informative "Letter" that on 21 Aug. 1775 will be found drawing the "warmest" but private "acknowledgments" of the Norfolk County committee.

17. "Last week," it was reported—in stark contrast to previous notices (31 July 1775, Third Va. Convention, Norfolk Borough Committee to Randolph, and n. 13)— "several slaves, the property of gentlemen in this town and neighbourhood, were discharged from on board the Otter, where it is now shamefully notorious, many of them for weeks past have been concealed, and their owners in some instances illtreated for making application for them" (*Va. Gazette, or the Norfolk Intelligencer*, 16 Aug. 1775).

18. The "first Thursday" of September in 1775 was the 7th, a date not encompassed within the present volume, beyond which no record of the scheduled meeting of the Norfolk County committee on that date has been found.

Thursday, 17 August 1775

Third Virginia Convention

Proceedings of Twenty-fifth Day of Session [1]

[Robt. C. Nicholas Esq. unanimously chosen president during the Absence of the late President.]

The Delegates being assembled,[2] Edmund Pendleton Esq. a Member for the County of Caroline reminded them, that the honorable Peyton Randolph Esq. having in Consequence of what was yesterday recommended to him by the Convention[, retired,] it became necessary that they should proceed to the Choice of another president to act in that office during the Indisposition or Absence of Mr. Randolph; and he recommended Robert Carter Nicholas Esq: as a Gentleman in every Respect qualified to fill that important office. Mr. Nicholas was then by general Consent called to the Chair,

[Mr. No returned thanks]

and after being seated he arose & returned thanks to the Convention for the honour they had been pleased to confer on him. Professions of unworthiness he said he considered as more trite than sincere & therefore should decline every thing of that Sort; but candour obliged him to acknowledge he felt the great Diffidence, in succeeding to an Office lately filled by a worthy gentleman of confessed Abilities so much to his own honor & so greatly to the Advantage of this Convention.

The President then reminded the Convention how much a due observance of Order and Decorum redounded to the honor & Dignity of every Society & hoped a Continuance of the same Attention to those Objects, which he had been hitherto happy to observe; that on his part he should conduct himself with the utmost Impartiality.

[Balloted for Committee of Safety.] [3]

[Leave to Mr. Thornton.]

Ordered that Mr. ⟨Peter Presley⟩ Thornton . . .[4] have leave of Absence from the Service of this Convention for the Remainder of the Session.

[Com: Mr. R. Lee, Mr. Henry, Mr. Harrison, Mr. Jefferson. Eleven first to be chosen.]

The Convention then proceeded by Ballot to the Appointment of the Committee of Safety and the Members having prepared Tickets with the Names of eleven Persons to be of the said Committee & put the same into the Ballot Box Mr. Richard Henry Lee, Mr. ⟨Patrick⟩ Henry, Mr. ⟨Benjamin⟩ Harrison and Mr. ⟨Thomas⟩ Jefferson were appointed a Committee to examine the Ballott Box and report on whom the Majority fell who retired [5]

[Edmund Pendleton, &c.]

and after some time [6] returned into Convention and reported that the Numbers stood as follow.

for Edmund Pendleton Esq:	77
George Mason Esq	72.
the honble. John Page Esq	70
Richard Bland Esq	66
Thomas Ludwell Lee Esq	63
Paul Carrington Esq	54
Dudley Digges Esq	42.
William Cabell⟨, Jr.⟩ Esq	39
Carter Braxton Esq	38.
James Mercer Esq	38.

John Tabb Esq	36
[B⟨artholomew⟩. Dandridge	35
G⟨eorge⟩. Rootes	29
A⟨rchibald⟩. Cary	26
Jos⟨eph⟩: Jones	26
J⟨ohn⟩. Banister	23
Charles Carter ⟨of⟩ L⟨ancaster⟩	23
J⟨ame⟩s. Holt	17
J⟨ohn⟩ Harvie	15
⟨William⟩ Fitzhugh	8
Robert Carter Nicholas	8
Ga⟨brie⟩l: Jones	6
J⟨ohn⟩. Tazewell	5
John Blair	4
N⟨icholas⟩. Lewis	4
John Nicholas	4
B⟨enjamin⟩. Martin	3
Theo⟨dorick⟩: Bland⟨, Sr.⟩	2
Joseph Hutchings	2
H⟨enry⟩. Lee	2
And⟨rew⟩: Lewis	2
Fielding Lewis	2
James Madison junr	2
Ja⟨me⟩s. Madison⟨, Sr.⟩	2
Thomp: ⟨Thomson⟩ Mason	2
M⟨ann⟩. Page Junr.	2
R⟨ichard⟩. Randolph	2
The revd Mr. ⟨Charles Mynn⟩ Thruston . .	2
T⟨homas⟩. Whiting	2
J⟨ohn⟩. ⟨Augustine⟩ Washington	2
Theod⟨orick⟩. Bland junior	1
J⟨ohn⟩. Bowyer	1
John Lewis ⟨of⟩ Spotsyl⟨vani⟩a	1
T⟨homas⟩. Lewis	1
Dav⟨i⟩d Mason	1
John Page Junr.	1
P⟨eyton⟩. Randolph	1
T⟨homas⟩. M⟨ann⟩. Randolph	1
Thomas Walker	1
I⟨saac⟩. Zane⟨, Jr.⟩	1][7]

Resolved therefore that the said Edmund Pendleton, George Mason, John Page, Richard Bland, Thomas Ludwell Lee, Paul Carrington, Dudley Digges, William Cabell, Carter Braxton, James Mercer & John Tabb Esqs. be appointed Members of the said Committee of Safety.

[Wm. Woodford Esq. in the Room of Thos. Nelson Esq.]

Resolved that William Woodford Esq. be appointed Colonel to the second

Regiment of regular Forces to be raised for the Defence & protection of this Colony[, in the room of *Thomas Nelson*, Esq. who hath declined the said appointment].[8]

[Balloted for Lieutenant Colonel of first Regiment
Mr. Mason, Mr. T. Lee, Mr. Banister, Mr. Holt.]

The Convention according to the Order of the Day proceeded by ballot to the Appointment of a Lieutenant Colonel to the first Regiment and the Members of the Convention having prepared Tickets with the Name of the person to be appointed & put the same into the Ballot Box Mr. George Mason, Mr. Thomas Ludwell Lee, Mr. ⟨John⟩ Banister and Mr. ⟨James⟩ Holt were appointed a Committee to examine the Ballot Box and report on whom the Majority falls

[Mr. Christian appd. 1st. Lieutenant Colo. of majority]
it appearing from their Report that there was a Majority of the whole Convention in favor of William Christian Esq.

Resolved, therefore that the said William Christian be appointed Lieutenant Colonel to the said First Regiment.[9]

[Mr. Scott – 2d. Lt. Col. a Majority of whole.]

The Convention proceeded in the same Manner to the Appointment of a Lieutenant Colonel to the second Regiment and it appearing from the Report of the Committee that there was a Majority of the whole Convention in favor of Charles Scott Esq.

Resolved, therefore, that the said Charles Scott Esq. be appointed Lieutenant Colonel to the second Regiment.

[Mr. Jones, Mr. R. Lee, Mr. Dandridge, Mr. Lawson] [10]

The Convention proceeded in the same Manner to the Appointment of a Major to the first Regiment and it appearing from the Report of the Committee appointed to examine the Ballot Box that the Numbers stood as follow

Francis Eppes Esq. 39
Alexander Spotswood Esq. . . . . 20.
George Matthews ⟨Mathews⟩ Esq. 12
Alexander McClanahan ⟨McClenachan⟩ Esq. . . 9

The Question was then put whether the said Francis Eppes or the said Alexander Spotswood on whom the greatest Numbers fell on the Ballot should be appointed Major to the first Regiment

[Mr. Eppes Major to first Regiment.]
the Majority appeared in favour of Francis Eppes Esq.

Resolved, therefore that the said Francis Eppes be appointed Major to the said first Regiment.

The Convention then proceeded in the same Manner to the Appointment of a Major to the second Regiment and it appearing from the Report of the Committee appointed to examine the Ballot Box, that the Numbers stood as follows

for Alexander Spotswood Esq. . . . . . . 31.
Geo. Matthews Esq. . . . . 15.
Alexander McClanahan Esq. 13

    William Grayson Esq. 12
    [Tho⟨ma⟩s Elliott 8
    James Hendrick . . . . 3] [11]

The Question was then put whether the said Alexander Spotswood or the said George Matthews on whom the greatest Numbers fell on the Ballot should be appointed Major to the second Regiment⟨;⟩
[Mr. Spotswood–Majr. to 2d. Regiment.]
the Majority appeared in favour of Alexander Spotswood Esq. Resolved, therefore that the said Alexander Spotswood Esq. be appointed Major to the said second Regiment.

The Convention proceeded in the same Manner to the Appointment of an Adjutant General to the first & second Regiment aforementioned And it appearing from the Report of the Committee appointed to examine the Ballot Box that there was a Majority of the whole Convention in favour of Thomas Bullitt Esq.

Resolved therefore that the said Thomas Bullitt be appointed Adjutant General to the two Regiments aforesaid.

[John Harvie to have Leave of Absence.]
Ordered that . . . Mr. Harvie have leave of Absence from the Service of this Convention for the Remainder of the Session.[12]

[Orders of Day put]
The Orders of the Day for the Convention to resolve itself into a Committee on the Ordinance for regulating the Election of Delegates & ascertaining their Allowances; and also for regulating the Election of Committee men in the several Counties & Corporations within this Colony & for other purposes therein mentioned–& for the Convention to resolve itself into a Committee on the Ordinance for raising and embodying a sufficient force for the Defence & protection of this Colony being read

Resolved, that the same be postponed till Tomorrow.[13]
    Adjourned till Tomorrow 9. oClock.

                        Convention MS journal in hand of John Tazewell
                        (Archives Division, Virginia State Library) [14]

Augusta County West: Journal of Captain James Wood

the Committee recommended that I would send off an Express to the Convention at Richmond who were still sitting . . .[15]

                        Thwaites and Kellogg, *Revolution on the Upper Ohio, 1775–1777*, p. 66

1. With the withdrawal of Peyton Randolph from the presidency (16 Aug. 1775, Procs. and n. 12), the number of delegates present this day could not have exceeded 102. Although Thomas Jefferson had been "granted Leave of Absence" on 16 Aug.

(Procs. and n. 10), he will be found active in this day's session. But according to the highest vote recorded this same day—that for "a Major to the second Regiment"—the number at no time exceeded 82, or with the president holding a casting vote, 83.

Tazewell's manuscript minutes for the day are hereafter separately bracketed as he successively wrote them, and insofar as is possible each entry is followed by the pertinent paragraph or part thereof as penned in the journal. As with the proceedings of 14 Aug. 1775, there are variations in the order of business, but the minutes, which were written at the time transactions were effected, are far more trustworthy guides to facts of sequence—and in one instance to the appointment of a committee unnoticed in the journal.

2. The majority of them tutored in the procedures of the House of Burgesses, the delegates did not now fall into confusion owing to the absence of a presiding officer. Tazewell brought the chamber to order by ringing a bell—use of a gavel was foreign to the House—silently pointed a finger at Edmund Pendleton, who had arisen, and himself "then sat down" (*JHB, 1773–1776*, p. 73). The bracketed verbal and punctuation in this paragraph are taken from Purdie's printed journal, p. 36.

3. More apparently, it was successfully moved that balloting for the Committee of Safety take place, but before a committee could be appointed to count the votes, Peter Presley Thornton procured recognition on a point of privilege and requested "leave of Absence."

4. The ellipsis deletes the name of John Harvie, who although his name is coupled to that of Thornton in the manuscript journal and in Purdie's printed journal, p. 37, did not request leave until near the end of the day's session.

5. The meaning of "Eleven first to be chosen" as confirmed by the results that follow was that the men procuring the top 11 places, whether by or without a majority of votes cast, would be elected.

6. Tazewell failed to write "time," an oversight silently corrected by Purdie in the printed journal, p. 37. Ordinarily Tazewell joined adjective and noun as a single word, "sometime."

7. The portion of the ballot within regular brackets is drawn from a convention loose paper in the hand of Thomas Jefferson. The contents are here further idealized by the alphabetization of surnames according to descent in the number of votes individually received. In preparing the list, Jefferson wrote the names as they were announced by those reading the "Tickets." Hence, assuming 11 names to have been inscribed by the individual elector, the 1st ticket contained 1 vote each for "John Page, R. C. Nicholas, R. Bland, E. Pendleton, A. Cary, D. Digges, C. Carter L, T. L. Lee, Jos: Jones, John Nicholas, John Blair." The totals must then have been tallied on another page or pages, next to be entered on Jefferson's complete list; but in all probability thereafter there was made from the rather disorganized list a perfected report, now missing, for presentation to the convention.

The ballot discloses the majority judgment as to the relative worth and potential of those who, not having been elected to Congress or designated for "regular" military command, would guide the colony into and through at least a part of a civil war. Within this limitation, the capable Edmund Pendleton was now to be the 1st citizen of Virginia. But since the 1st citizen had declined reelection to Congress because of ill health (11 Aug. 1775, Procs. and n. 7), it is a valid question as to why he did not also reject election to the committee. The answer may be that indisposed though he was, he conceived acceptance to be a duty, that as chairman of the supreme executive authority and a practiced politician, he would be enabled to keep an eye on Patrick Henry, who, though well, was commander in chief and an unpracticed soldier.

The 2d citizen, on the other hand, was distraught. Having in private protests and an embarrassing public pronouncement fended off election to Congress (11 Aug. 1775, Procs. and n. 12; 15 Aug. 1775, same and n. 4), he now found that "in Spite of every thing" that he "cou'd do to the Contrary," he was seated on the committee. This assignment he found even "more inconvenient & disagreeable" than service in Philadelphia. "I endeavour'd to excuse myself," he wrote to a kinsman, "& beg'd the Convention wou'd permit me to resign; but was answer'd by an universal NO" (Rutland, *Papers of Mason*, I, 250).

The election of 3d place of "the honble. John Page Esq," youthful former member of the governor's Council, was proof that knowledge of his patriotism was not confined to a fuming Lord Dunmore and a select few. Page's placement at this time did not represent genuine political power, but because he symbolized the highest magisterial connection with the ancien régime, acquisition of his services could not but have a striking influence on the public mind.

Other positionings on Jefferson's list do not signify the absence or loss of political power by those in whose hands power had lain. Robert Carter Nicholas, for example, would have been honored by more than 8 votes had not other considerations been compelling. Charged by law with custody of the colonial treasury and by ordinances soon to be enacted with issuing paper money and paying members of Congress, convention delegates, and army officers and enlisted men, Nicholas had his hands full. He undoubtedly, and others almost certainly, would shy away from placing the administrator of the treasury on the board which was to direct his actions; the memory of the fiscal chaos wrought by the late speaker-treasurer John Robinson was too fresh. For similar reasons, Nicholas had never drawn much support in elections for deputies to the Continental Congress—less than a handful for that of the first (*Rev. Va.*, I, 228), and none for either of the 2 elections for the second (ibid., II, 366; 11 Aug. 1775, Third Va. Convention, Procs.). For if Mr. Treasurer's presence was needed in Virginia, he could not be in Pennsylvania.

And certainly the 1 vote on the present ballot cast for Peyton Randolph did not indicate a sudden vanishing of esteem. He received the only vote cast for any of the deputies to Congress. The case was, rather, since Mr. Speaker was best qualified to represent the colony in Pennsylvania, he could not be in Virginia.

Yet the composition of the committee elected may have caused some furrowing of brows. Among the 1st half-dozen members Pendleton was ill; Mason was ill almost chronically; Bland was by his own profession "an old man, almost deprived of Sight"; Lee had little taste for public life; and Carrington was lost in melancholy.

Too, committee membership was heavily weighted in favor of the Tidewater and the Piedmont; and James Mercer, who alone represented the West (and that the northern part only), was living in Spotsylvania County. This did not mean that there was an indifference to the concerns of the West—there is too much evidence within the present volume to indicate otherwise. It did mean that the extremely slow means of travel and communication at the time practically barred western membership on a plural executive body the separate parts of which could not be disjoined by great distances and which in an emergency must needs be reunited as quickly as possible. If, further, a westerner were to live in the East, not only would he suffer social sacrifices beyond those demanded of his colleagues but he could subsist only at the plantation seat or the town house of another, his dependency relieved alone by an allowance the source of which foreseeably would be suspect. Back in July, while admitting he had "no certain intelligence from the Convention at Richmond," John Hunter Holt had added that "it is said all the plate is to be called in and coined" (*Va. Gazette, or the Norfolk Intelligencer*, 26 July 1775). It might have been better had the rumor been fact. But by now the members of the convention understood that all Virginia money would be paper. Until recognizability of the issue should be established, the paper would infrequently be accepted; and after establishment it probably would be accepted only at a substantial discount.

It now remained for the Committee of Safety to learn definitely what were to be its functions and powers.

8. The bracketed clause is taken from the Purdie printed journal, p. 38. Nelson's declination presumes a letter that has not been found. The effect of the resultant resolution was to reinstate Woodford, who though elected colonel of the 3d Regiment on 5 Aug. (Procs. and n. 8), lost title to his command when the regular forces were reduced to 2 regiments on 9 Aug. 1775 (Procs. and n. 3).

9. Christian, wrote Thomas Lewis, was a man "of whose military powers much have been Said here" (Draper MSS, 4QQ29, State Hist. Soc. of Wis.). Seemingly Lewis did not know how neat was the family arrangement made by this election, but Christian was Colonel Henry's brother-in-law (*Rev. Va.*, II, 257 n. 4).

10. In neither manuscript nor Purdie printed journal is notice taken that Joseph Jones, Richard Lee, Bartholomew Dandridge, and Robert Lawson were appointed a committee to count ballots for the election of the majors of the 2 regiments of regulars.

11. The bracketed additional names are taken from a convention loose paper in Tazewell's hand.

12. The entry in the journal accompanying n. 4 above is here repeated by the present editors. The ellipsis deletes the name of Peter Presley Thornton, who had already been granted leave of absence.

13. The order to resume consideration on the bill of elections and on the bill for defense and protection was carried over from the previous day (Procs. and n. 11). Again overlooked or ignored was the order for a "Call" of the membership, standing since 5 Aug. 1775 (Procs. and n. 4). But at last the convention was moving.

14. Edgewise at the top of the 6th of 6 pages Tazewell wrote "No. 25."

15. Captain Wood had left Fort Pitt on 12 Aug. for Winchester, where he "Arrived in five days." Although his negotiations had been conducted in the District of West Augusta, the recommending "Committee" was that of Frederick County. The captain completed the sentence by writing, "which I did the next Morning with the following Letter Directed to the Honble Peyton Randolph Esquire" (Thwaites and Kellogg, *Rev. on the Upper Ohio*, pp. 65–66). For the "Letter," see 18 Aug. 1775, Third Va. Convention, 2d entry.

Friday, 18 August 1775

Third Virginia Convention

Proceedings of Twenty-sixth Day of Session [1]

The Convention according to the Order of the Day resolved itself into a Committee on the Ordinance for raising and embodying a sufficient Force for the Defence & protection of this Colony and after sometime spent therein

Mr. President ⟨Robert Carter Nicholas⟩ resumed the Chair and Mr. ⟨Benjamin⟩ Harrison reported that the Committee had according to Order had under their Consideration the said Ordinance for raising and embodying a sufficient Force for the Defence & protection of this Colony and had gone through the same & made several Amendments thereto which he read in his Place and delivered in at the Clerk's Table.

Ordered that the Consideration of the said Amendments be postponed til Tomorrow.[2]

The Order of the Day for the Convention to resolve itself into a Committee on the Ordinance for the Election of Delegates and ascertaining their Allowances; and also for regulating the Election of Committee men in the several Counties and Corporations within this Colony and for other Purposes therein mentioned being read

Resolved, that this Convention will Tomorrow resolve itself into a Committee on the said Ordinance.[3]

Adjourned till Tomorrow 9. oClock.[4]

> Convention MS journal in hand of John Tazewell
> (Archives Division, Virginia State Library)[5]

Captain James Wood to the Honble Peyton Randolph [6]

Sir—I am just now returned from my Expedition to the Indian Towns and have Inclosed you Extracts from my Journal which Contains every Material Occurance that happened Dureing my tour through the Nations of Shawanese Delawares Senicas and Wiandots⟨,⟩ the Cheifs of which have Engaged to Attend the Treaty at Fort Pitt the 10th of the next Month⟨.⟩[7] from every discovery I was able to make the Indians are forming a General Confederacy against the Colony having been led to beleive that we are a people Quite different and distinct from the other Colonies⟨.⟩[8] I Intend myself the Honor of Waiting on the Convention if they should not rise before the 25th in Order to give them every Information in my power⟨.⟩[9] I wou'd beg leave to make an Observation that there is no Garrison at Fort Pitt⟨,⟩ that the Inhabitants in the Neighbourhood of it are in the most defenceless situation⟨,⟩ and that there will be in my Opinion at least five hundred Indians at the Treaty⟨.⟩[10] I have the Honor to be &c

> Thwaites and Kellogg, *Revolution on the Upper Ohio, 1775–1777*, pp. 66–67

Nansemond County Committee

Exoneration of Merchant Shippers

At a committee held for Nansemond county, August 18, 1775, it being reported that Mess'rs ⟨Samuel⟩ Donaldson and ⟨John⟩ Hamilton, merchants in the town of Suffolk, had intentionally shipped a considerable quantity of provisions to Boston, in the brigantine John, Hugh Kennedy master, contrary to a resolution of the Committee of New-York, made April 27, 1775, and acceded to by the several provinces,[11]

The aforesaid gentlemen appeared, and several depositions and protests being read, fully convinced this Committee that the said Donaldson and Hamilton intended the voyage of the said brig for Antigua, and that it was by the express direction of the Governor and captain of the man of war, (who had information of her loading three weeks before she sailed) that the said brig was taken and carried to Boston.[12]

The aforesaid gentlemen being charged with shipping some hemp and butter the 17th of April last to Henry Lloyd a gentleman in Boston, Resolved, that the said Gentlemen in so doing have not violated the association, the said articles being shipped prior to any resolution to the contrary.[13]

By order of the committee   John Gregorie,[14] clerk.

Virginia Gazette, or the Norfolk Intelligencer,
23 August 1775

1. With the departure on "Leave" of Thomas Jefferson (16 Aug. 1775, Procs. and n. 10), Peter Presley Thornton, and John Harvie (17 Aug. 1775, Procs. and nn. 4, 12), the number of delegates in attendance this day could not have exceeded 99. The leave-taking of Robert Wormeley Carter is more problematical. Writing on "the last Piece of Paper" to which he could lay hand, he had expressed the belief as of 10 Aug. that the convention would adjourn on the 19th and made a qualified promise to be at Sabine Hall on Landon Carter's 65th birthday, 18 Aug. This letter the colonel docketed: "My Son August 10, 1775 He offers to be here by the 18 let the Convention rise or not." But the son's qualification was that the convention should "compleat the business now before us," and by 17 Aug. it was palpable that there still remained much to be "compleated" (Sabine Hall Papers, MSS Dept., Univ. of Va. Library; J. P. Greene, *Diary of Colonel Landon Carter,* I, 3).

There is within the remaining 7 days of session only one more ballot by which probable attendance can be reasonably well judged. "Cato" was later to assert that on 26 Aug., the date of final session, there were only "fifty-five members present" (*Va. Gazette* [Dixon and Hunter], 30 Mar. 1776), a statement largely substantiated by the vote on the place for holding the next convention (p. 500 below). On this basis and the assumption that there were on the present day 99 members in attendance (although because of illness and other considerations the number was probably less by a score), one may establish a "Cato formula" and from the 99 decrease the number by 5½ for each of the succeding 9 days of session. It is not a completely satisfactory formula, because (even to sidestep a theological awkwardness by counting fractions), its accuracy can in no way be demonstrated. Yet it is conceivably within striking distance of the truth, for the reason that although the delegates knew that eventually they would be paid for their attendance in paper notes, many by this date were surely out of funds and in debt to colleagues or others who had command of money or credit. Hence, it is not improbable that with or without the formality of asking "Leave," as many as 5 or 6 a day buckled their saddle bags and silently stole away.

2. "Consideration of the said Amendments" would be the 1st order of business "Tomorrow," 19 Aug. 1775.

3. The "Order of the Day" to sit as a committee on the bill of elections, introduced

on 12 Aug., had been standing since that day of session (Procs. and n. 9). Routinely bypassed was any reference to the order to "Call" the roll of members, standing since 5 Aug. 1775 (Procs. and n. 4).

4. Lacking knowledge as to the amount of time consumed in debating the bill for defense and protection, it is impossible to say whether the brevity of the journal for this day indicates a short session. What is certain is that as much time as possible was needed to forward the work of the committees, unless business was to be protracted beyond the ends of delegates' means of sustaining themselves in Richmond. Still to be heard from was the committee of munitions, appointed on 12 Aug. (Procs. and n. 23), and the committee for establishing the Committee of Safety, as well as the committee for establishing an oath of allegiance, both appointed on 16 Aug. (Procs. and nn. 7, 8).

Beyond these considerations lay others. Despite the seemingly false move by the committee for defense and protection on 8 Aug. (Procs. and n. 6), articles of war were needed. The forms of officers's commissions were still to be determined. And the establishment of wages for the deputies to Congress was a matter remaining yet untouched. A committee for officer's commissions would be appointed on 21 Aug. and introduce a bill 5 days later (pp. 471, 498–99 below), but a committee for articles of war, appointed on 21 Aug., would bring a bill to the floor on the same day; and a committee appointed on 25 Aug. to propose wages for deputies to Congress would also introduce a bill on that day (pp. 471, 487, 489 below). Such smooth follow-through hints strongly at activities not reaching the journal and suggests that President Nicholas, perhaps in consultations with the systematic and legislature-wise Edmund Pendleton, was moving steadily toward the day of adjournment by behind-scenes, informal "appointments" of committees, with the understanding that at the propitious moment the appointments would be made formal.

5. Tazewell wrote "No. 26" edgewise at the top of the 2d of 2 pages.

6. Captain Wood wrote his letter at Winchester. He could not have known that at the end of the session of 16 Aug. his addressee had retired from the presidency of the convention. The letter would be delivered to Robert Carter Nicholas and laid before the convention as the 1st order of business on 22 Aug. 1775.

7. The "Extracts," at least as selected by the present editors, are those to be found in this volume intermittently between 9 July and 17 Aug. 1775.

8. From a reading of Wood's own journal, it is evident that this sentence is too sweeping and overly alarmist. Reporting the arrival of "An Express from Capt. Wood, which arrived in Richmond a few days ago," Dixon and Hunter in their *Va. Gazette* of 26 Aug. 1775 more accurately stated: "the Mingo, Wyandot, and Shawanese tribes of Indians appear to be friendly, and have promised to attend the treaty at Pittsburg, the 10th of next month," but "many of the more western and south western tribes seem determined to take up the hatchet against us."

9. The convention was to "rise" on 26 Aug. If Wood appeared in Richmond on the 25th, it was to find the delegates engrossed in terminal business. Once he understood the shape of things effected, his most logical course would have been that evening to find the ears of Edmund Pendleton and other members of the Committee of Safety. Otherwise, he may have met with members of the committee for defense and protection, of which Richard Bland had been appointed chairman on 19 July (Procs. and n. 6), for it was to that committee that Indian affairs had been referred (21 July 1775, Procs. and n. 4, 27 July 1775, same and n. 3). By the date of Wood's possible arrival, the work of that committee had been completed, but by saving grace, of the 11 elected to the Committee of Safety 8 had also served on the committee for defense and protection.

10. The convention had already provided for the garrisoning of Fort Pitt (7 Aug.

1775, Procs. and n. 3). The captain's "Opinion" that there would be "at least five hundred Indians at the Treaty" was in the same pattern as had been his caution to Peyton Randolph on 9 July 1775 that peace on the Northwest frontier could not be purchased cheaply (Augusta Co. West, n. 5).

11. On 5 May the Committee of One Hundred in New York City had approved a nonexportation resolution adopted by the Maryland Convention on 1 May (for which see 17 May 1775, Cumberland Co. Committee and n. 2). The New Yorkers then addressed "*to the other colonies*" a circular letter that was printed in the *Va. Gazette* (Dixon and Hunter) of 27 May 1775.

12. The *John* had recently returned from Boston to Virginia with dispatches and with officers to augment Lord Dunmore's "army" (11 Aug. 1775, Williamsburg).

13. More pertinent than the Continental Association was the resolution of Congress of "Friday June 2. 1775" prohibiting the shipment of "provisions or necessaries" of any kind that might fall to "the use of the British Army or Navy in the colony of Massachusetts bay" (11 July 1775, Third Va. Convention, In Congress and n. 12), but the date of the resolution was itself exculpatory of anything wrought on "the 17th of April last."

14. Gregory.

Saturday, 19 August 1775

Third Virginia Convention

Proceedings of Twenty-seventh Day of Session [1]

The Amendments to the Ordinance for raising and embodying a sufficient force for the Defence & protection of this Colony yesterday reported by the Committee appointed were twice read, and on the Question severally put thereon, agreed to by the Convention.

Ordered that the said Ordinance with the Amendments be fairly transcribed & read a third Time.[2]

Mr ⟨Patrick Henry⟩[3] from the persons appointed presented to the Convention according to Order, An Ordinance for appointing a Committee of Safety for the more effectually carrying into Execution the several Rules and Regulations established by this Convention for the protection of this Colony, and the same was read the first Time and ordered to be read a second Time.

Mr. ⟨Archibald⟩ Cary from the persons appointed presented to the Convention according to Order An Ordinance to encourage the Making Saltpetre Gun Powder Lead the refining Sulphur & providing Arms for the Use of this Colony, and the same was read the first Time and Ordered to be read a second Time.[4]

An Ordinance for appointing a Committee of Safety for the more effectual carrying into execution the several Rules & Regulations established by this Convention for the protection of this Colony was read a second Time and Ordered to be committed.

Resolved that this Convention will on Monday next resolve itself into a Committee on the said Ordinance.[5]

Mr. ⟨George⟩ Mason, from the persons appointed presented to the Convention according to Order an Ordinance for establishing a general Test which was read the first time and ordered to be read a second time.[6]

[read a second Time & to be committed to the whole on Monday next.] [7]

An Ordinance for establishing a general Test was read a second Time and ordered to be committed.

Resolved, that this Convention will on Monday next resolve itself into a Committee on the said Ordinance.

[A Call of the Convention on Monday next. to proceed to Severity.] [8]

Ordered that there be a Call of the Convention on Monday next.

[Mr. Gray to have leave of Absence] [9]

Ordered that Mr. ⟨Edwin⟩ Gray & Mr. ⟨Nicholas⟩ Faulcon have leave of Absence from the Service of this Convention for the Remainder of the Session.

The Order of the Day for the Convention to resolve itself into a Committee on the Ordinance for the Election of Delegates and ascertaining their Allowances & also for regulating the Election of Committee men in the several Counties & Corporations within this Colony & for other purposes therein Mentioned, being read,

Resolved that this Convention will on Monday next resolve itself into the said Committee.[10]

adjd. till Monday 9. oClock.

Convention MS journal in hand of John Tazewell
(Archives Division, Virginia State Library) [11]

1. The number of delegates in attendance this day could not have exceeded 99. According to the "Cato formula," the number would not have exceeded 94 (18 Aug. 1775, n. 1, 2d para.). But the tone of "A Call of the Convention on Monday next" (n. 8 below) implies that the number must have been considerably smaller. For one proveable example, Jonathan Clark this day quit the convention without any indication of his having been authorized to do so (Autograph Diary of Jonathan Clark, Filson Club Docs., I, unpaged).

2. An order for consideration of the "Amendments" on this day was a transaction of "yesterday," 18 Aug. 1775 (Procs. and n. 2). There is no bill for defense and protection among the manuscripts of this convention.

3. Henry's name is here substituted for Tazewell's erroneous "Mr. Cary," repeated in the Purdie printed journal, p. 40. Not having been one of "those persons appointed" on 16 Aug. 1775 (Procs. and n. 7) to prepare a bill for establishing the Committee of Safety, Archibald Cary could not have introduced the proposed legislation. Of those who had been appointed to the 5-member committee, the chairman, Robert Carter Nicholas, was now presiding over the convention, and the last-named, Thomas Jeffer-

son, was on leave of absence. If Henry, vice-chairman of the committee, did not introduce the bill, then Richard Henry Lee or Joseph Jones did. Tazewell's pertinent minute for this day offers no cue: "Ordinance for appointing Com: of Safety read first time & to be read a second Time."

4. Tazewell began this paragraph with "The Com," deleted the definite article and the abbreviation with a line of ink, and restarted the sentence, "Mr. Pendleton." He then canceled the title and the surname and above them wrote "Mr. Cary." Cary was 4th-named, Edmund Pendleton 6th-named of the 6-member committee of munitions appointed as the last transaction of 12 Aug. 1775. Tazewell's pertinent and slightly mutilated minute for this day reads only, "Ordinance for making Saltepetre [&c.?] read 1st. time & to be read a second Time."

5. On "Monday next," 21 Aug. 1775, the convention would postpone consideration of "the said Ordinance" until Tuesday, 22 Aug. (Procs. and n. 9).

6. The "persons appointed" on 16 Aug. 1775 to prepare "a general Test," or oath of allegiance to the nascent Revolutionary government, were Josiah Parker and George Mason (Procs. and n. 8). It was Mason who took the lead in drafting the proposed ordinance. On 22 Aug. he would write that in drawing it up, he "endeavoured to make it such as no good Man would object to" and found "the Merchants here declared themselves well pleased with it." No draft of this document is known to be extant. A subsequent draft of 4 pages (the internal contents alone of which establish it as of a later date), which was prepared by a committee created in the fourth (or 2d session of the third) convention on 14 Dec. 1775, is extant. That draft's being dated, probably years later by an unknown archivist, "AUG. 19, 1775" has caused it to be confused with Mason's work.

Even as Mason was pleasing the "Merchants here," he had in hand a "very sensible petition" from merchants elsewhere. The latter were "Natives of great Britain" who prayed that the convention prescribe "some certain Line of Conduct" for them and recommend to the people at large that they not be treated as enemies (Rutland, *Papers of Mason*, I, 246–49, 251). The libertarian Mason wished no oppression of men willing to pledge obedience to patriot authority but unwilling to confront their kin on the field of battle. Yet could lenity be reconciled with imposition of the "Test"? Apparently not, and something had to give way. In the end it would be the test. For the petition, see 25 Aug. 1775, Procs. and n. 16. The next mention of the test will be on 21 Aug., when as part of the final transaction of the day, the order to debate provisions of the bill will be "put off till Tomorrow."

7. To this point Tazewell's manuscript journal and minutes are in accord, but whereas the journal has the 1st reading of the Parker-Mason test followed by the granting of leave to Edwin Gray and Nicholas Faulcon, the minutes, which were jotted down at the time business was transacted, disclose that the 2d reading immediately followed the 1st.

8. The journal places the granting of leave to Gray and Faulcon before the order for a "Call of the Convention." The minutes disclose that the order to call preceded the granting of leave. Such a call, standing since 5 Aug. 1775 (Procs. and n. 4), had been repeatedly overlooked or ignored. The "Severity" mentioned in the minutes and carefully omitted in the journal (hence kept from the knowledge of the reading public) indicates an alarming decrease in attendance.

9. As in the cases of Peter Presley Thornton and John Harvie (17 Aug. 1775, Procs. and nn. 4, 12), Gray and Faulcon almost certainly requested and were granted leave at different times, the latter probably toward the end of the day's session; but beyond this point the rest of the minutes have been torn away and are missing. In the

manuscript journal after Gray's name Tazewell inserted a caret and above it wrote "& Mr. Faulcon," in consequence of which the names are thus coupled in Purdie's printed journal, p. 41.

10. "The Order of the Day" was carried over from the previous day of session, 18 Aug. 1775 (Procs. and n. 3).

11. Edgewise on the 3d page of 4 pages (the 4th of which is blank) Tazewell wrote "No. 27."

Sunday, 20 August 1775

Third Virginia Convention

Freeholders and Inhabitants of Chesterfield County to President and Gentlemen of Convention

To The Honourable The President and Gentlemen of the Convention of the
    Colony of Virga.
    The Petition of the Freeholders and Inhabitants of the County of Chester-
    field
Humbly Sheweth. That agreable to The Eleventh Resolution of The Continental Congress, The Delegates Of this County Proceeded to the Election of a Committee for said County, In a Short time after being Resolved on by The Honourable Congress, with a Design to bring the people into the Measures off Associating. As well as doing the Other Business to them Recommended, for which reasons, but Very Few had it in Their Power to Vote in the choice of the committee, at that time not well Understanding what they Ware to do, or the Intent of Associating, and Then not being Associates, by which Means Some Persons Was by Then Few, Voted in, that we by no Means can think Propper, we now conceiving that the Committees are to Do business of much Greater Importance, then we Could possible then conceive.[1] We humbly Pray that it may be Dissolved before they proceed to further business and Another Elected To Execute and do all things that you in Your wisdom Shall think proper, that we may have no Divisions amongst us, but all unite and be as one man in this Critical Time in the great & Common Cause, and we as in duty Bound Shall Ever Pray &c.[2]

August 20. 1775

EDWD. MOSELEY [3]	JESSE TRAYLER	WILLIAM THWEATT −50
JORDAN ANDERSON	JOHN ELLIS	JOHN HILL
WM. FLOURNOY JR.	NATHAN SIMS	GEORGE ROBERTSON
MATHEW TURPIN	BARKLEY ELAM	JEFFERY ROBERTSON
WILLIAM RUX	JOEL FOLKES	HENNERY TURPIN

HENRY BRANCH
RICHD. WILKINSON
LEONARD CHEATHAM
JAS. ELAM
CREED HASKINS −10
WILLIAM ROBERTSON
WM. RUDD
HEZEKIAH TURPIN
HALY TALBOTT
GEORGE CLEBORN
ALEXANDER MOSELEY
ALEXANDER BASS
THOS. BASS
THOS BASS JUNR
WILLIAM HILL   20
FRANCIS PATNAM
OBEDIAH CHEATHAM
JAS WHITE

WILLIAM RUCKS
HENRY COX   30
SAML. CHEATHAM
HENRY BURTON
JOHN GARRETT
JAS. GATES SENR.
RICHD. REARBUCK
ELAM HARMER JUN.
JAMES RUCKS
GEORGE RAIBOURN
JNO. CALDWELL
JAMES SIMS   −40
FRANCIS LOCKETT
THOMAS BOWLES
COLLINS GOODING
JEREM. NUNNELY
JOHN STRINGER
MORCAS GELLINGTON
EDWD ANDERSON
BENJ. BAYLEY
THOS RUDD JUNIOR

JOHN BAKER
THOS. CHEATHAM
JOHN ROBERTSON
JOSEPH ROPER
JOHN WOLDRIDGE
EDWD. BRANCH   −60
THOMAS RUDD SENR
HENRY BASS
ARTHUR MOODY
JONAS CLEBORNE
ARCHIBALD MCROBERT
JOSIAH TATUM
DAVID NUNNELLEE
MORGAN LESTER
JAMES BALL
HENRY WINFREY
  SNR.   −70
EDWARD OSBORNE SEN
VALENTINE WINFREY

MS document in unidentified hand, with autograph signatures, in loose papers of third Virginia Convention (Archives Division, Virginia State Library)

1. At Chesterfield Court House on 25 Nov. 1774, "Proper Notice having been given requesting the Freeholders of the County to meet here on this Day, in Order to choose a Committee for the said County, a great Number assembled, and made choice" of a 19-member committee, some of whom were not themselves present (*Rev. Va.*, II, 176). For the "Eleventh Resolution of The Continental Congress," in compliance with the recommendation of which the "choice" was made, see 8 Apr. 1775, n. 5.

Evidently word that in erecting a de facto government, the convention was bent on greatly enhancing the powers of the local committees was getting around. But the statement of the petitioners that their conception of the "Importance" of the committee had undergone change, might be construed as a confession that they had not heretofore taken their responsibilities seriously. "The Delegates of this County" who "Proceeded" to effectuate the recommendation of Congress by rallying the arguably "Very Few" who read broadsides, or attended church services, and knew the time of day were Archibald Cary and Benjamin Watkins.

2. "The Petition" would be laid before the convention as the 1st business of the day on 23 Aug. 1775.

3. The autograph signatures are printed in the 3 columns in which they were inscribed. Every 10th signature is numbered in the original document.

Monday, 21 August 1775

Third Virginia Convention

Proceedings of Twenty-eighth Day of Session [1]

[Ordered that Leave be given to bring in an Ordinance for the better Government of the Force to be raised & employed in the Service of the Colony & Dominion of Virginia & that Mr. ⟨Edmund⟩ Pendleton & Mr. ⟨Archibald⟩ Cary do prepare & bring in the same.] [2]

An ordinance for raising & embodying a sufficient Force for the Defence & protection of this Colony having been fairly transcribed and read the third Time & the blanks therein filled up

Resolved, that the Ordinance do pass.[3]

[Mr. ⟨Edmund⟩ Pendleton from the persons appointed presented to the Convention according to Order an Ordinance for the better Government of the Forces to be raised & emploied in the Service of the Colony and Dominion of Virginia, and the said Ordinance was read the first time and ordered to be read a second Time.] [4]

Ordered, that Mr. ⟨John⟩ Banister, Mr. ⟨Robert⟩ Lawson, Mr. ⟨Benjamin⟩ Watkins and Mr. ⟨James⟩ Holt be appointed a Committee to draw up & report the Forms of proper Commissions to be granted to the Officers of The regular Forces, Minute Men & Militia of this Colony.[5]

An Ordinance for the better Government of the Forces to be raised and employed in the Service of the Colony & Dominion of Virginia, was read a second Time and ordered to be fairly transcribed & read a third Time.[6]

Ordered, that Mr. ⟨Isaac⟩ Zane⟨, Jr.⟩ have Leave to be absent from the Service of this Convention for the Remainder of the Session.

An Ordinance for the Better Government of the Forces to be raised & employed in the Service of the Colony & Dominion of Virginia having been fairly transcribed was read a third Time & the blanks therein filled up.

Resolved, that the said Ordinance do pass.[7]

Ordered, that the Clerk do immediately send the said Ordinance to Mr. John Pinkney, and the Ordinance for raising & embodying a sufficient Force for the Defence & protection of this Colony to Mr. Alexander Purdie, requesting them to print 500 Copies thereof with all possible Expedition.[8]

The Orders of the Day for the Convention to resolve itself into a Committee on the Ordinance for appointing a Committee of Safety for the more effectual carrying into Execution the several Rules & regulations established by this Convention for the protection of this Colony, – To encourage the making Saltpetre, Gun Powder, Lead, the refining Sulphur & providing Arms for the Use of this Colony—for establishing a general Test—for the Election of Delegates & ascertaining their Allowances, and also for regulating the Election of Committee men, in the several Counties & Corporations within this Colony & for other purposes therein mentioned,— & for a Call of the Convention being read,

Ordered, that the same be put off till Tomorrow.[9]

Adjourned till Tomorrow 9. oClock.

> Convention MS journal in hand of John Tazewell (Archives Division, Virginia State Library)[10]

Essex County Committee

Several Times in Liquor

At a committee for the county of Essex, *at* John Whitlock's, *in* Tappahannock, *on* monday *the* 21st of August, 1775.

GEORGE STEWART having been accused with saying, at different times and places, that he had bread and flour on board his vessel designed for the man of war,[11] and that *Peyton Randolph*, and *Thomas Nelson*, jun. esquires, would supply the man of war now, for that a peace was made; and that a young man, whom he saw in a hunting-shirt, had better go home, for that the *English* would be an overmatch for the *Americans*, or words to that effect: And the said *George Stewart* having appeared, and the witnesses against him having been examined, who proved the charge, he endeavoured to excuse himself, by saying he was in liquor at the several times of the afore-mentioned conversations; and the matter aforesaid having been considered by the committee, they are of opinion that the cargo of the schooner *Enterprise*, of which the said *George Stewart* is master, consisting of 26 barrels of bread, be landed and stored with mr. *James Lang*, at the expense of the owners, under the direction of *John Upshaw*, chairman, and any three of the committee, until the owners of the said bread shall satisfy the chairman, or any three of the committee, that it is not intended for any purpose injurious to the cause of *American liberty*.[12]

Ordered, that the above be published in the *Virginia* gazette.

Jack Power, clerk.

> *Virginia Gazette* (Purdie), 15 September 1775, supplement

Norfolk Borough

Proceedings of Common Hall respecting Conduct
of Captain John Macartney

Norfolk Borough—
At a Common Hall summoned and held the 21st day of August—
                              Present
Paul Loyall esquir Mayor
George Abyvon   Lewis Hansford
Archibald Campbell   Cornelius Calvert   } Gent: Aldermen
Charles Thomas   William Aitchison

The following letters were laid before the Hall by the Mayor viz: (Reference to the letters).[13] The Hall took the same into their serious Consideration, and being greatly surprized at the Contents, it was thereupon RESOLVED, that the Letters from Captain McCartney to the Worshipful the Mayor were evidently intended to alarm and intimidate the Inhabitants of this Borough, were disrespectful to the chief Majistrate of this Corporation, are an Officious intermedling in the Government of the Town, an[d] Contains an implied threatening which the Hall conceive to be unjustifiable, premature and Indecent. Unjustifiable inasmuch as no Reason can be deduced from fact, nor any Authority derived from Law, to empower Capt. McCartney unsolicited by the Majistracy, to interfere in matters within their Jurisdiction alone, and much less to hold up to them the Idea of Violence & compulsion in a transaction so entirely without the line of his Department; Premature as his Conduct in this Instance, originates from ill grounded suppositions and mistaken Apprehensions, and without any Sanction from facts to support them;—Indecent, because it implicitly charges the Majistracy with a willful remissness in the exercise of the powers legally Vested in them, because the menace is as perticularly pointed against them, as if they were the Abbettors of Riot and persecution: because it operates towards the destruction of the persons and properties of a Number of his Majisties Subjects, chiefly on Account of some accidental insults Alledged to have been offered by a few incautious Youth to an Individual;—because so little regard is shewn to the understandings and feelings of the people, as at the same moment, in which this haughty declaration, so big with ruin, is denounced, it is pretended that the execution of it, is to preserve the persons and properties of his Majistys subjects, as if the utter distruction of their Lives and estates could ever be deemed a preservation of their persons and properties. RESOLVED that the Military power agreeable to the British Constitution, is and Ought to be under the control of the civil: and notwithstanding the Utterly defenceless state of the Town, the Body Corporate of this Borough, will never Tamely submit to the invasion of their privilidges by the dangerous and untimely interposition of Military Force.

RESOLVED that this Corporation will continue steadfastly to adhere to those substantial principles of Good Government, which ought ever to Actuate the Minds of all his Majistys faithful Subjects: and they Embrace this Opportunity to make this public and Solemn Declaration, That notwithstanding their exposed and defenceless Situation which cannot be remedied, unbiassed by fear, Unappalled by the threats of unlawfull power, they will never desert the righteous cause of their Cuntry, plunged as it is, into dreadful and unexpected Calamities.

ORDERED That a Copy of the Above Resolution be by the Mayor Transmitted to John McCartney esquire: Commander of his Majisties Ship the Mercury.[14]

> MS Minutes of the Common Council of the Borough of Norfolk, 1736–89, in hand of John Boush, town clerk (original in office of city clerk, Norfolk, Va.; mcirofilm in Virginia State Library), fols. 71–72

Norfolk County Committee

Alexander Skinner to Andrew Sprowle [15]

Sir

I have laid your Letter before the Chairman,[16] and as many of the Committee as could be conveniently got together. They highly approve of your Behaviour to the Officers and think you entitled to their warmest Acknowledgments for the Early information you have given them.

The Committee in Course will meet in a few days & such steps will then be taken as shall be judg'd most prudent for your Redress. In the Mean time they see the fatal Necessity of Your Submitting to this Arbitrary & Unprecedented Act of Tyranny. A Cruel situation indeed when every petty Officer in His Majesty's service assumes the Authority of an absolute Monarch, and the private property of a peacable Citizen is seized upon as Lawful prey: But they trusts that Almighty providence will not permit those *Lawless Harpies* to continue long in their pride & insolence.

Your polite Letter shou'd have had an Answer before this, had I not been out of Town 'till Yesterday. I am Sir

Your Respectful Hble Servt.   A Skinner Secy

Norfolk Augt. 21st. 1775
To Mr. Andrew Sprowle Merchant at Gosport
Copy of Committee of Norfolk—Letter of Thanks to Mr. Sprowle

> MS transcript in unidentified hand (Tucker-Coleman Papers, Earl Gregg Swem Library, College of William and Mary in Virginia)

1. With the granting of leaves of absence to Edwin Gray and Nicholas Faulcon (19 Aug. 1775, Proceedings and nn. 8, 9), the number of delegates in attendance this day could not have exceeded 97. According to the "Cato formula," the number would not have exceeded 83 (18 Aug. 1775, n. 1, 2d para.). Whatever the actual number, the order for "a Call of the Convention," with severe penalties to be visited on delinquents, evidently brought results; at least there was produced on the chair and the house an equanimity that permitted the order for a call to be overlooked or ignored.

2. Tazewell's minutes for this day are missing, so that the actual order in which business was transacted can never be known. The bracketed 1st paragraph, originally penned in the manuscript journal, he deleted with a single large crosshatch. In the Purdie journal, pp. 41–42, the paragraph reads as follows: "THE articles for the better government of the forces to be raised and employed in the service of the colony and dominion of Virginia, which had passed through the several stages as part of the ordinance for raising and embodying a sufficient force for the defence and protection of this colony, were separated therefrom, read a third time, and passed, under the title of *An ordinance for the better government of the forces to be raised and employed in the service of the colony and dominion of Virginia*." As set against the manuscript journal for this day, the paragraph is manifestly untrue.

Other elements respecting this matter are more debatable. Tazewell on 3 Aug. entered in his minutes the note that the convention, sitting as a Committee on the State of the Colony, reached agreement that it would be necessary that a committee be appointed "to draw up proper Articles of War" (Procs. and n. 9), but he made no such entry in the journal, and nowhere did he indicate that the topic was assigned.

The committee for defense and protection did, however, apparently construe the agreement as an instruction to itself, and on 8 Aug.—according to John Ruffin's minutes—Robert Carter Nicholas introduced a bill. Debate must have been rather thorough, and first having been ordered read a 2d time, the proposed ordinance was then committed to the Committee of the Whole "Tomorrow" (Procs. and n. 6). These facts Tazewell also excluded from the journal, very possibly for the reason that there was no authorization for the proceedings. And thereafter mention of the articles is to be found neither in journal nor minutes until the session of the present day.

Notwithstanding that activation and discipline of troops are closely related, they are separate functions. Activation without discipline produces a mob. Discipline without activation produces paper. But paper had already been produced, and from the full proceedings of the present day, it is apparent that Pendleton and Cary drew on a document which, though no longer extant, they may already have caused to be engrossed—the ordinance is a long one, in Hening covering 13½ pages (*Statutes at Large*, IX, 35–48). What alone can be demonstrated is that Pendleton could have had nothing to do with the introduction of the bill on 8 Aug., because he did not attend the convention until the day following (9 Aug. 1775, Procs. and n. 6).

What seems most likely is that President Nicholas, Pendleton, and Cary on or soon after 18 Aug. (Procs. and n. 4) reached a private understanding that the 2d- and 3d-named should proceed to complete a bill on the articles, and on the present day Nicholas formalized their appointment. This is admittedly editorial opinion only, a case not proven. But if, as Tazewell caused Purdie to print the record, the measures of activation and discipline were separated, it becomes inexplicable as to why one part of a bill that had "been fairly transcribed and read the third Time" was forthwith enacted while a 2d part that had passed through the same "several stages" was reintroduced and treated as a new bill entirely. The complete reversal in handling the 2 parts would have been equally justifiable, or equally unnecessary. If separated from an original bill, all

that would have been involved for a part having passed 3 readings would be the providing of an appropriate title. But no known rule of the House of Burgesses, under
which the convention was conducting business, permitted reading of a new bill by title
only—it was the whole bill or nothing—and it is as a new bill, not a separate portion of
another bill, that the one on articles of war was to go through the requisite "several
stages."

3. No manuscript of the bill for defense and protection is known to be extant. The
ordinance is printed in *Statutes at Large*, IX, 9–35.

4. With a single large crosshatch, Tazewell also deleted this bracketed paragraph. Its
inclusion in the printed journal would have warred with the doctored 1st paragraph.

5. The committee on military officers' commissions would introduce a bill on the
last day of session, 26 Aug. 1775 (Procs. and n. 4).

6. Tazewell failed to delete this paragraph as he had the 1st and 4th above but took
care that it not find its way into the Purdie printed journal. The only manuscript in the
Va. State Library relating to this measure contains a brief proposed article. In an unidentified hand, the document reads: "74th. The foregoing Rules & Regulations shall
be read by each recruiting Officer to every Person offering to inlist himself either as a
Soldier or minute man before his Enlistment under the Penalty of   Pounds to be
paid by such Officer for every Neglect; & shall be publickly read at the Head of each
Regiment under the Penalty of   Pounds to be paid by such Colo. for every
Neglect."

This "74th." appears to have been the original draft of what became the final of 73
articles adopted. Article 73 reads: "The foregoing rules and regulation shall be publickly
read at the head of each regiment, once in three months, by order of the colonel or
commander in chief of such regiment, under penalty of fifty pounds, to be paid by
such colonel or commander for every neglect" (*Statutes at Large*, IX, 48).

7. Aside from the fact that the committee for defense and protection had already
drafted a bill for articles of war (8 Aug. 1775, Procs. and n. 6), quick reintroduction
was made possible by the adoption of articles, or "Rules and Regulations," by Congress
on 30 June 1775 (*JCC*, II, 111–22). There is no evidence that a copy of those articles
was transmitted to the convention, but they were available as printed in 2 separate sec-
tions by Dixon and Hunter in their *Va. Gazette* of 22 and 29 July 1775 respectively.
Article after article of the Virginia code was verbatim copy of the Continental. The
codes, George Mason would inform the commander in chief on 14 Oct. 1775, were
"principally" the same, except that in the one of the colony "a Court Martial upon Life
& Death is more cautiously constituted, & brought nearer to the Principles of the common Law" (Rutland, *Papers of Mason*, I, 256).

Mason's reference was to Article XXXIII. After repeating the Continental article, that
of Virginia continued: "Provided, that when any person is to be tried for his life,
under any of the foregoing or subsequent articles, the commanding-officer shall appoint
twenty four members, at least, to be of the court-martial, two of which shall be field-
officers, and ten shall be captains, out of which the offender may choose fifteen, one of
whom shall be a field-officer, and five of them captains, and sentences of death shall not
be pronounced unless twelve of the court-martial concur in such sentence" (*JCC*, II,
117; *Statutes at Large*, IX, 41–42).

8. Although copies of an undated Purdie printing of all of the ordinances of the third
convention are to be found in several repositories, none of the "500 Copies" of the
separate ordinance struck off by him and Pinkney appears to have survived.

9. The order to resume deliberation of the bill for establishing the Committee of
Safety was carried over from the previous day of session, 19 Aug. (Procs. and n. 5); the

bill of munitions, introduced on 19 Aug., had on that day been "Ordered to be read a second time" (same and n. 4); the 3d reading of the "general Test," also introduced on 19 Aug., had been ordered for the present day (same and n. 6); consideration of the bill of elections, last debated on 15 Aug. (Procs. and n. 9), had since that date been constantly postponed; and the "Call of the Convention," revived on 19 Aug. (Procs. and n. 8) had as of the moment seemingly accomplished its design by increasing attendance of those able to attend.

10. Tazewell wrote "No. 28" edgewise on the 4th of 4 pages (the 3d of which is blank).

11. The man-of-war most likely referred to was the *Mercury*, Capt. John Macartney, in ill odor with the mayor of Norfolk and this same day to be rebuked by the Common Hall of that municipality.

12. The action of the Essex County committee was taken in compliance with the recommendation of 17 May by Congress, as strongly endorsed on 19 June by the House of Burgesses (11 July 1775, Third Va. Convention, In Congress and n. 8).

13. The "letters" are those of 12, 13, 14, 15 Aug. 1775 (Norfolk Borough).

14. John Hunter Holt would correct the clerk's misspellings and reparagraph the document for publication in the *Va. Gazette, or the Norfolk Intelligencer*, of 30 Aug. 1775. The exchange of letters thus far had been confidential and would remain so with the mayor's transmitting the present document (26 Aug. 1775, Norfolk Borough); but within 2 more days it would be public knowledge that Macartney had written an "insolent letter" and received a "suitable reply" (*Va. Gazette, or the Norfolk Intelligencer*, 23 Aug. 1775).

15. Lacking Sprowle's "Letter" of undesignated date, Skinner's reply is a mysterious exception to the other documents treating of the case of the Gosport merchant (9, 12, 16 Aug. 1775, Norfolk Co. Committee; 12, 13, 14, 15 Aug. 1775, Norfolk Borough). A number of theories may be posited to explain the reply, but the only one that can be made to stand is the simplest; namely, that in an attempt to keep his balance, Sprowle at some time on or after 16 Aug. imparted "Early information" of a 2d "Arbitrary & Unprecedented Act of Tyranny" by Lord Dunmore or his "*Lawless Harpies.*" This information, Skinner's delay in responding considered, would have been hard on the heels of the 1st seizure of the merchant's "private property." The weakness in this theory is that there is no record of a 2d seizure. That fact does not, however, disprove the possibility. And possession of the present paper would provide Sprowle with the means of fending off an upsetting visit by bumptious patriots.

16. The "Chairman" was John Willoughby, Sr. (16 Aug. 1775, Norfolk Co. Committee).

Tuesday, 22 August 1775

Third Virginia Convention

Proceedings of Twenty-ninth Day of Session[1]

A Letter from James Wood Esq. on the Subject of Indian Affairs was laid before the Convention, read and ordered to lie on the Table.[2]

Whereas the Quiet of this Colony will greatly depend upon the County-Courts attending particularly to the Suppression of all Irregularities in their respective Counties, and whereas the Courts held at Pittsburg are by Writs of Adjournment, which renders it impossible to hold Courts for Suppression of Irregularities or Trial of Criminals at Staunton in East Augusta when the Adjournment is to Pittsburg and so vice versa,

Resolved, that the Courts at Staunton and Pittsburg do proceed in all Matters relating to keeping the peace and good Behaviour and in all criminal Matters as if they were distinct Counties.[3]

A Resolution of the Continental Congress was laid before the Convention in the words following, to wit, Whereas the Government of Great Britain hath prohibited the Exportation of Arms and Ammunition to any of the Plantations and endeavoured to prevent other Nations from supplying us,

Resolved, that for the better furnishing these Colonies with the necessary Means of defending their Right[s], every Vessel importing GunPowder, Saltpetre, Sulphur, provided they bring with it four times as much Saltpet[re] brass field Pieces or good muskets fitted with Bayonets within nine Months from the Date of this Resolution shall be permitted to load and export provisions to the Value of such Powder and Stores aforesaid, the Nonexportation Agreement notwithstanding and it is recommended to the Committees of the several provinces to inspect the Military Stores so imported and to estimate a generous Price for the same according to their goodness & permit the importer of such Military Stores aforesaid to export the Value thereof and no more in Provisions of any kind.

Ordered, that a Copy of the said Resolution be sent to the Committees of the several Counties & Corporations for their Government on this Subject; and that they be desired to take Care that no Copy of the said Order be printed or published.[4]

Ordered, that Mr. Richard Lee, Mr. ⟨Francis⟩ Peyton, Mr. ⟨Josias⟩ Clapham, Mr. Henry Lee, & Mr. ⟨Thomas⟩ Blackburn have Leave to be absent from the Service of this Convention they being necessarily called away to settle the Accounts of the Militia lately drawn out into actual Service.[5]

Ordered, that the Committee appointed to examine state, and settle the Accounts of the Militia lately drawn out into actual Service, do make a special Report of the Expence of building & repairing Forts, which is not to be paid without the further Order of the Convention or Assembly, & that the said Committee do also make a strict Inquiry for all the publick Muskets & Bayonets lately used in the Expedition against the Indians & cause the same to be sent to the Commander in chief of the Forces to ⟨be⟩[6] raised for the Defence & protection of this Colony.

The Convention resolved itself into a Committee on the Ordinance for appointing a Committee of Safety for the more effectual carrying into Execution the several Rules & Regulations established by this Convention for the Protection of this Colony and after sometime spent therein Mr. President ⟨Robert Carter Nicholas⟩ resumed the Chair & Mr. ⟨Benjamin⟩ Harrison reported that the Committee had according to Order had the said Ordinance under their Consideration & had gone through the same & made several Amendments thereto, which he read in his Place and afterwards delivered in at the Clerk's Table where the same were again twice read, and on the Question severally put thereon agreed to by the Convention.

Ordered, that the said Ordinance together with the several Amendments be fairly transcribed & read a third Time.[7]

The Convention then resolved itself into a Committee on the Ordinance for the Election of Delegates & ascertaining their Allowances, and also for regulating the Election of Committee Men in the several Counties and Corporations within this Colony & for other Purposes therein mentioned and after sometime spent therein Mr. President resumed the Chair & Mr. Harrison reported that the Committee had according to Order, had under their Consideration the said Ordinance & had made a considerable Progress therein, but not having time to go through the same had directed him to move for Leave to sit again.

Resolved, that this Convention will tomorrow resolve itself into a Committee on the said Ordinance.[8]

The Orders of the Day for the Convention to resolve into a Committee on the Ordinances for establishing a General Test—To encourage the making Saltpetre Gun powder Lead the refining Sulphur & providing Arms for the Use of this Colony—And the order of the Day for a Call of the Convention being read,

Ordered that the same be put off till Tomorrow.[9]

Adjourned till Tomorrow 9. oClock.

> Convention MS journal in hand of John Tazewell
> (Archives Division, Virginia State Library)[10]

Surry County Committee

Ostracism of Robert Kennan

Surry, *August* 22, 1775.

At a committee held at Surry court-house this day, a complaint being lodged by Henry Cook and Joseph Warren, against Robert Kennon ⟨Kennan⟩, at Cabin Point, factor for ⟨William⟩ Cunningham and company, for violating the ninth article of the continental association by selling salt at an advanced price,[11] the said Kennon being called on by this committee, and appearing; confessed he had acceded to the association, and that he had sold salt, within these twelve months last past, for 2s. and 2 s. 6 d. per bushel, and is now selling off the same cargo at 3 s.

Resolved therefore, that it is the opinion of this committee, that the said Kennon has violated the association and ought to be held up to public censure and it is recommended to the good people of this county, and others, to break off all intercourse and connection with the said Kennon.

Ordered that the clerk of this committee do transmit the above proceedings to the different printers in Williamsburg and beg they will publish the same in their papers.[12]

James Kee, c. c.

Virginia Gazette (Pinkney), 24 August 1775

1. With the granting of leave of absence to Isaac Zane, Jr., on the immediately preceding day of session, 21 Aug., the number of delegates in attendance this day could not have exceeded 95. According to the "Cato formula," the number would not have exceeded 77 (18 Aug. 1775, n. 1, 2d para.); but whatever the actual number, the "order of the Day for a Call of the Convention" being "put off" as the last transaction of the present day's session would indicate the presence of a comfortable quorum.

2. For the "Letter from James Wood Esq.," see 18 Aug. 1775, Third Va. Convention, 2d entry.

3. The District of West Augusta needed no more justices of the peace than the 42 to whom Lord Dunmore had issued commissions on 6 Dec. 1774—the court for the eastern district of Augusta County routinely operated with as few as 4 in attendance at any one time. What was needed was another clerk, for John Madison alone was authorized to inscribe and maintain the official records both at Staunton and Fort Pitt. As the court "adjourned" from place to place at intervals of from 4 to 10 weeks, he became a frequent traveler through the mountains. The present resolution would scarcely help him. What ultimately would were to be receipts of commissions for a "Deputy Clerk" in each district—one for Richard Madison in the east on 19 Mar., and for John Madison, Jr., in the west on 20 Aug. 1776 (*Rev. Va.*, II, 316 n. 2; Augusta Co. Order Book no. 16, 1774–79, microfilm in Va. State Library, p. 99; Loveless, *Recs. of the Dist. of W. Augusta*, p. 565).

Just how the separate Augusta courts—or the courts of any other constituency—were to proceed in the "Trial of Criminals" facing capital charges would be interesting to learn. In instances involving slaves and free blacks the county courts were competent tribunals, but all trials for life and death of whites could be adjudicated only by the General Court, which consisted of a flown chief magistrate and a dispersed Council; and it was not proposed that this power be transferred to the Committee of Safety or any other body of men (*Statutes at Large*, III, 292, 293, VI, 106–7).

4. For the "Resolution of the Continental Congress," see 15 July 1775. The mode of transmission to the convention is unknown. While committing variations, Tazewell evidently worked from a copy of the resolution, now in the convention loose papers, in the hand of Richard Henry Lee. If Lee was the agent of transmittal, the question arises as to why he had so long delayed introducing the resolution. But evidence indicates that his document was at best unofficial, because at the bottom of the page he wrote, "Pay of Men 6 dols. & 2 thirds pr. Month, Men to find Arms & Cloaths"—a reference to the pay of Continental privates as established by Congress on 14 June (p. 285 above) and laid before the convention in the 1st transaction of 24 July 1775.

As to how a "Copy" of the resolution was to be made and "sent to the Committees of the several Counties & Corporations" there is no word. Tazewell's minute for this transaction is unhelpful: "Resolutions about Powder &c. agreed to." If it was decided that he, perhaps aided by John Ruffin and William Dandridge, Jr., should transcribe copies, each scribe would have work enough. A quicker and more effective method would have been to swear the highly trustworthy Alexander Purdie or John Pinkney to secrecy and have him print a sufficiency of copies, but no committee copy, whether in handscript or print, has been found.

For an obvious reason, no reference to the secret resolution appears in the Purdie printed journal. There, p. 43, the resolution on the jurisdictional division of Augusta County is followed immediately by the order granting leave of absence to the commissioners for war claims.

5. For the election by the House of Burgesses of the 5 men to serve as commissioners for war claims, see p. 24 above; 11 Aug. 1775, Procs. and n. 6.

6. Although Tazewell did not complete the verb, Purdie does so in the printed journal, p. 43.

7. The committee for establishing a Committee of Safety had been initially appointed, with Robert Carter Nicholas as chairman and Patrick Henry as vice chairman, on 16 Aug. 1775 (Procs. and nn. 5–7). It was probably Henry who introduced a bill on 19 Aug. 1775 (Procs. and n. 3). On the present day Nicholas was presiding over the convention, and the deliberations were conducted by Benjamin Harrison, because in keeping with the order of the immediately preceding day of session, 21 Aug. 1775, the convention was sitting as a Committee of the Whole (Procs. and n. 9).

The draft copy of the bill introduced on the 19th is not extant. There are, however, the texts of 5 amendments in the convention loose papers. Four are in unidentified hands. Each amendment was adopted. Two in the same hand are written on a single page. The 1st of these provided for the calling of emergency meetings of the Committee of Safety "if Exigencies should occur" between regularly scheduled meetings (*Statutes at Large,* IX, 49–50). The 2d empowered the committee "in case of any extraordinary Exigency" to "call in any assistance that may be necessary & can be procured from either of the neighbouring Colonies & if required by such Colonies as may be exposed to danger shall likewise have power to send them any assistance from this Country that can be conveniently spared" (ibid., IX, 51, 2d para.).

Tazewell, probably jotting down an amendment offered orally from the floor, wrote: "Line 30, after the word *that* insert any person who shall hereafter accept of any Office of profit, or pecuniary Appointment under the Crown shall be disqualified from sitting or voting in the Committee of Safety and" at the bottom of the same page. These words were incorporated in the final paragraph of the ordinance (ibid., IX, 53). The amendment was in harmony with and reiteration of the floor resolution adopted as the 1st transaction of the day on 5 Aug. 1775.

Writing on a 2d piece of paper, a delegate successfully moved giving the Committee of Safety authority to elect and commission officers of minutemen and militia when a district committee ("composed of deputies from different counties") should, with the vote of the chairman included, be "equally divided," and in such district elections giving chairmen regular as against casting votes (ibid., IX, 52, 4th para.).

On a 3d piece of paper a delegate scrawled a 5th amendment. Following the words "And that the said committee of safety shall continue in office, and exercise the powers hereby given them," he successfully moved that there be added the clause "until the next sitting of the Convention, or for one year in case the Convention should not meet within that time" (ibid., IX, 53). As the case was to be, the fourth Virginia Convention (or, more exactly, the 2d session of the third) would proceed to a new "appointment of the Committee of Safety" on 16 Dec. 1775, or short by just 1 day of 4 calendar months after the 1st election (*The Proceedings of the Convention of Delegates, Held at the Town of Richmond, in the Colony of Virginia, on Friday the 1st of December, 1775, and Afterwards, by Adjournment, in the City of Williams-burg* [Williamsburg: Alexander Purdie, n.d. (1776)], p. 21).

8. The bill of elections, drafted by a committee appointed on 25 July, with Archibald Cary as chairman (Procs. and n. 11), had been introduced on 12 Aug. (Procs. and nn. 8, 12), and taken up again on 15 Aug. 1775 (Procs. and nn. 6–9), but further deliberation thereon was successively postponed until the current day of session.

9. The bill "for establishing a General Test," introduced on 19 Aug. (Procs. and n. 6) had been ordered read a 3d time on 21 Aug., when the reading was "postponed" (Procs. and n. 9). Consideration of the bill of munitions, also introduced on 19 Aug. (same and n. 4) had twice been deferred. The order "for a Call of the Convention" standing since 5 Aug. and revived on 19 Aug. 1775 (same and n. 8) was by this late date becoming Damocles' sword suspended by a hawser.

10. Edgewise at the top of the 4th of 4 pages Tazewell wrote "No. 29."

11. For the "ninth article of the continental association," see 8 Apr. 1775, Norfolk Borough Committee, 2d paragraph.

12. This notice appeared also in the *Va. Gazette* (Purdie) of 25 Aug. 1775 and ibid. (Dixon and Hunter) of 26 Aug. 1775.

Wednesday, 23 August 1775

Third Virginia Convention

Proceedings of Thirtieth Day of Session [1]

A PETITION from the freeholders and inhabitants of the county of *Chesterfield* was presented to the Convention, and read; setting forth, that, agreeable to the eleventh resolution of the Continental Congress, a committee had been chosen in their county, very shortly after the said resolution had been entered into; that not many of the freeholders attended the said election, as few persons had then associated, by which means some persons were chosen of the said committee whom they could by no means think proper; and as the committee is now to transact matters of greater importance than was conceived at the time of their election, they prayed that the said committee might be dissolved, and a new one chosen.

Ordered, that the said petition do lie on the table.[2]

The Convention then, according to the order of the day, resolved itself into a committee on the ordinance for regulating the election of delegates and ascertaining their allowances, and also for regulating the election of committee-men in the several counties and corporations within this colony, and for other purposes therein mentioned; and after some time spent therein, mr. President ⟨Robert Carter Nicholas⟩ resumed the chair, and mr. ⟨Benjamin⟩ *Harrison* reported, that the committee had, according to order, had under their consideration the said ordinance, and had made a considerable progress therein, but not having time to go through the same, had directed him to move for leave to sit again.

Resolved, that this Convention will to-morrow resolve itself into a committee on the said ordinance.[3]

The orders of the day, for the Convention to resolve itself into a committee on the ordinances For establishing a general Test,—To encourage the making saltpetre, gunpowder, lead, the refining sulphur, and providing arms for the use of this colony,—and the order of the day for a call of the Convention, being read.

Ordered, that the same be put off till to-morrow.[4]

Adjourned till to-morrow, 9 o'clock.

> *The Proceedings of the Convention of Delegates For the Counties and Corporations In the Colony of Virginia, Held at Richmond Town, in the County of Henrico, On Monday the 17th of July, 1775* (Williamsburg: Alexander Purdie, n.d. [1775]), pp. 44–46

Norfolk Borough Committee

Censure of Walter Chambre Published to the World

NORFOLK BOROUGH, in COMMITTEE, August 23, 1775.

Present, Mr. Deputy Chairman[5] and 19 Members

RESOLVED, that WALTER CHAMBRE of Whitehaven, is an enemy to American Liberty, and is guilty of an attempt to break the association by shipping goods for this place in direct opposition to the non-importation agreement.[6]

ORDERED that this censure be published to the world, that all persons may withhold any further commercial connexion with the said CHAMBRE.

By order of the Committee,
William Davies, secretary.

> *Virginia Gazette, or the Norfolk Intelligencer*, 30 August 1775

1. With the granting of leaves of absence on the immediately preceding day, 22 Aug. 1775, to Richard Lee, Francis Peyton, Josiah Clapham, Henry Lee, and Thomas Blackburn (Procs. and n. 6), the number of delegates present this day could not have exceeded 90. According to the "Cato formula," the number would not have exceeded 72 (18 Aug. 1775, n. 1, 2d para.). Whatever the actual number, "the order of the day for a call of the Convention" would as the final transaction of the day be "put off."

2. For the "PETITION," see 20 Aug. 1775. Tazewell's précis of the petition improves the original. There was no reason to act on the document, for debate on the bill of

elections introduced on 12 Aug. 1775 (Procs. and nn. 8, 12), was to be the next business of this day, and part of the bill, providing for uniform, annual elections of county committees, was designed to obviate just such objections as the petitioners had raised. Interestingly enough, the 2 "Delegates Of this County"—Archibald Cary and Benjamin Watkins—who stood accused of conducting an election by means not "Propper," were chairman and member respectively of the reforming committee of elections.

3. The "Convention" or its clerk would "to-morrow" overlook or ignore the order to resume debate on the "said ordinance," but on 25 Aug. 1775 the bill would again be taken up and on that day passed (Procs. and n. 11).

4. The bill "For establishing a general Test," introduced on 19 Aug. (Procs. and n. 6), had been ordered read a 3d time on 21 Aug., when the reading was "postponed" (Procs. and n. 8). Consideration of the bill of munitions, also introduced on 19 Aug. (Procs. and n. 4), had thrice been deferred. The order "for a Call of the Convention," standing since 5 Aug. (Procs. and n. 4), and revived on 19 Aug. 1775 (Procs. and n. 8), remained in suspension.

5. "Mr. Deputy Chairman" was probably Dr. James Taylor (6 June 1775, n. 10).

6. For the attempt of Walter Chambre of Whitehaven, Cumberland County, England, surreptitiously to ship goods to his Virginia partners, Jonathan Eilbeck, David Ross, and Company, in violation of the 10th article of the Continental Association, see 3, 4, 6 June 1775, Norfolk Borough Committee and 6 June, James City Co. Committee; for the probable suspicion of "Sly-Boots, junior," that Eilbeck was the home-based villain in the case, see 15 June 1775, Norfolk Borough Committee.

As required by the borough committee, the good ship *Molly* had now returned to Norfolk with customhouse dispatches to prove that the prohibited goods had been re-landed in England. She had, however, made the round trip in the astonishingly short space of 11 weeks and 3 days. Although some of the committee smelled a rat, they were convinced that there was none when the crew produced a July issue of the *Cumberland Pacquet* (W. Hutchinson, *Hist. of Cumberland*, II, 85). But from the present resolution and order of the committee, it is evident that the *Molly* returned with more in her hold than a newspaper. Already on 21 July 1775 the committee had threatened publication "to the world for such misconduct."

Thursday, 24 August 1775

Third Virginia Convention

Proceedings of Thirty-first Day of Session [1]

THE Convention, according to the order of the day, resolved itself into a committee on the ordinance for appointing commissioners to settle the accounts of the militia lately drawn into actual service, and for making provisions for the same; and after some time spent therein, mr. President ⟨Robert

Carter Nicholas⟩ resumed the chair, and mr. ⟨Benjamin⟩ *Harrison* reported, that the committee had, according to order, had under their consideration the said ordinance, and had gone through the same, and made several amendments thereto, which he read in his place, and afterwards delivered in at the clerk's table, where the same were again twice read, and on the questions severally put thereon, agreed to by the Convention.

Ordered, that the said ordinance, together with the several amendments, be fairly transcribed, and read a third time.[2]

An ordinance, appointing a Committee of Safety, for the more effectual carrying into execution the several rules and regulations established by this Convention for the protection of this colony, having been fairly transcribed, was read the third time, and the blanks therein filled up.

Resolved, that the said ordinance do pass.[3]

The orders of the day, for the Convention to resolve itself into a committee on the ordinances To encourage the making saltpetre, gunpowder, lead, the refining sulphur, and providing arms for the use of this colony,—For establishing a general test,—and the order of the day for a call of the Convention, being read,

Ordered, that the same be put off till to-morrow.[4]

Adjourned till to-morrow, 9 o'clock.

Proceedings of the Convention (Purdie), p. 46

Isle of Wight County

A Suit of Tar and Feathers and a Shower of Eggs

We hear from Isle of Wight that a certain Anthony Warwick, being lately summoned to appear before the committee of Nansemond county, on a suspicion of having violated the association, in a letter addressed to that committee, declared he would not appear without a promise of protection from the people of Isle of Wight county, and in the said letter abused them in the most scurrilous manner; some worthy gentlemen of Nansemond immediately gave information thereof to the injured people. Upon which a number of respectable inhabitants of Isle of Wight assembled, and seized the said Anthony Warwick (he being in the neighbourhood) and conveyed him to Smithfield, where they detained him some time, in order that a committee might determine in what manner he ought to be dealt with; but a sufficient number of members not attending, and the said Warwick not giving any satisfactory reason for his illiberal abuse, the populace very deliberately led him to the stocks, and having prepared him for the purpose, gave him a fashionable suit of *tar and feathers*, being the most proper badge of distinction for men of his complexion. They then mounted him on a horse, and drove him out of town, through a shower of eggs, the smell of which, our correspondent informs us, seemed to have a material effect upon the delicate constitution of this *motleyed* gentleman. At parting, the gentlemen gave Mr. Warwick a friendly piece of advice, which it is hoped he will observe, if only for the sake of his own interest.[5]

Virginia Gazette (Pinkney), 24 August 1775

1. The number of delegates present this day could not have exceeded 90. According to the "Cato formula," the number would not have exceeded 66 (18 Aug. 1775, n. 1, 2d para.); but whatever the actual number, there was a quorum, the convention was moving expeditiously toward adjournment, and once again the order "for a call of the Convention" would as the final transaction of the day be "put off."

2. The "said ordinance" was that introduced on 12 Aug. by Isaac Zane, Jr. (Procs. and n. 16), granted leave of absence on 21 Aug. 1775. By the present date more than providing for the veterans and bereaved dependents of Dunmore's War had found its way into the bill. There was also incorporated "provision for the pay and subsistence" of the 2 regiments of regulars and the units of minutemen, "as well as the residue of the militia" that might "be drawn into actual service." That provision necessitated increasing the tax levies. But whereas "the remote payment of the said taxes" was "unavoidably suspended, to suit the distressed circumstances of the inhabitants of this colony," the treasurer was directed to issue additional "notes" in anticipation of future collections (*Statutes at Large*, IX, 64, 67–68).

It was proposed that suspension be for 3 years. George Mason successfully argued that the time be reduced to 1 year. But glancing at like emissions rolling or soon to roll from the presses of other colonies, he was uneasy, for he feared that the flood of paper money might "have fatal" inflationary "Effects" (Rutland, *Papers of Mason*, I, 256).

Under an amended and expanded title, the "said ordinance" would be enacted on the next day of session, 25 Aug. 1775, p. 489 below.

3. The bill for establishing a Committee of Safety had been introduced, probably by Patrick Henry, on 19 Aug., that day twice read (Procs. and nn. 3, 5), taken up again on 22 Aug., amended and ordered, "with the several Amendments," to be "fairly transcribed & read a third Time" (Procs. and n. 7). At last the plural executive elected on 17 Aug. 1775 (Procs. and n. 7) knew the boundaries of its powers, which George Mason had correctly predicted would be "very extensive" (Rutland, *Papers of Mason*, I, 251).

4. The bill of munitions had been introduced on 19 Aug. (Procs. and n. 4), with further consideration thereof postponed (Procs. of 21 Aug. 1775 and n. 9, 22 Aug. and n. 9, 23 Aug and n. 3); consideration of the Parker-Mason bill for "establishing a general test," also introduced on 19 Aug. and twice read, was postponed at the same times as the bill of munitions; the order for a "call of the Convention," first directed on 5 Aug. (Procs. and n. 4) and revived on 19 Aug. (Procs. and n. 8), continued an increasingly innocuous threat.

5. The summons may have been in connection with the "certain" Warwick's recent shipment in a merchantman of "upwards of Six hundred barrels of Pork" to Boston for use by General Gage's troops (P.R.O., A.O. 12/32, folder W I). The "said letter" has not been found, but the action it induced bespeaks the imprudence in its contents. This was not the 1st time that the merchant's fidelity to the common cause had fallen under suspicion (*Rev. Va.*, II, 172–73). Although the information would not be widely

disseminated in Virginia for another month, on 5 Aug. the committee of Northampton County, N.C., had examined Warwick and impounded selections of his papers. The cause was his having spirited into the more southern colony from Virginia a quantity of gunpowder in a "clandestine manner." Thus he had, the committee ruled, "violated" the Continental Association, "shewed himself in the highest degree an enemy to the rights and liberties of America," and rendered himself an object fit "to be held in the utmost detestation by all lovers of American freedom" (*Va. Gazette* [Dixon and Hunter], 23 Sept. 1775).

Unnerved, Warwick withdrew to Norfolk and published his intention "to leave the Colony soon, for a few months" (*Va. Gazette, or the Norfolk Intelligencer,* 25 July 1775). But the temptation of making another fast shilling apparently lured him into the "neighborhood" of Isle of Wight County, where he fell into the hands of "respectable inhabitants." According to Pinkney, it was the "populace" of Smithfield who wrought violence on the merchant's person. According to Warwick, the Isle of Wight gentry were themselves a "rabble," who from the point of his seizure dragged him by "the hair of the head" for part of the 10 miles to the whipping post in Smithfield. But however these events may have been, and however "friendly" was the "advice" of his patriotic tormentors, by their own confession they paid little heed to the olfaction or comfort of the beast on which he departed the town.

Within 2 weeks of his discommodity Warwick would undertake to dispose of "about twelve hundred pounds sterling of dry goods," but alack, the impossibility of retaining the services of an agent willing to handle his business affairs was to delay his departure until Apr. 1776, when he would sail for Great Britain with an empty purse (*Va. Gazette, or the Norfolk Intelligencer,* 6 Sept. 1775; P.R.O., A.O. 13/32, folder W I).

Friday, 25 August 1775

Third Virginia Convention

Proceedings of Thirty-second Day of Session [1]

[Leave to bring an Ordinance to provide for paying the Exps. of Delegates to general Congress, & Mr. Pendleton to prepare & bring in the same.] *Ordered,* THAT leave be given to bring in an ordinance to provide for paying the expenses of the delegates from this colony to the General Congress, and that mr. ⟨Edmund⟩ *Pendleton* and mr. ⟨James⟩ *Mercer* do prepare and bring in the same.[2]

[Resolution to compel Returns of Executions] [3]

[Resolution for erecting a Magazine, agreed to.]

Resolved, that it be an instruction to the Committee of Safety that they forthwith cause to be erected a magazine, at some fit and convenient place, for the reception of arms and ammunition; and that they appoint a guard, to be drawn out of the minute-men or militia, for the safe keeping and preservation of the same, from time to time, as the exigence of affairs may require.[4]

[Resolution respg. Soldiers &c. agd. to.]

Resolved, that no person whatsoever shall sell to any non-commissioned officer or soldier in the regular service any kind of spirituous liquors within a mile of the head-quarters, under penalty of subjecting himself to every regulation prescribed for suttlers.[5]

[Resolution respecting Tithables &c. agd. to.]

Resolved, that it be recommended to the committees of the several counties and corporations to appoint proper persons of their body, within such districts as to them shall seem convenient, to take a list of the number of persons therein of all ages and sexes, distinguishing whether they be male or female, white or black, and of the males whether they be above or under sixteen years of age; from which lists the committee shall cause a general county or corporation list to be made and returned to the President of the Convention, without delay, who is desired, from them, to cause a general colony list to be formed, and certify the same to the Continental Congress.[6]

[Resolution about Powder agreed to as amended.]

It appearing to the Convention, by receipt of *Patrick Henry*, esq: and other testimony, that it was referred to them, at this meeting, to determine how much of the three hundred and thirty pounds which had been received of the receiver-general ⟨Richard Corbin⟩, on the 4th of *May* last, to compensate for the powder taken out of the magazine by the governour's orders, should be restored to the said receiver-general,

Resolved, as the opinion of this Convention, that sufficient proof being had of there being only fifteen half-barrels of powder so taken by lord *Dunmore*'s order, that no more money should be retained than one hundred and twelve pounds ten shillings, which we judge fully adequate to the payment of the said powder, and that the residue of the said three hundred and thirty pounds ought to be returned to the said receiver-general, and it is hereby directed to be paid to him by the treasurer of this colony ⟨Robert Carter Nicholas⟩.[7]

[Resolution of Thanks to the Voluntiers agd. to, Nem: con.]

Resolved unanimously, that the thanks of this Convention are justly due to the several volunteer companies in this colony for their zeal and attachment to the cause of *American* liberty, manifested by their attention to the resolutions of the last Convention in arming and disciplining themselves, and the readiness they have shewn, upon all occasions, to defend their country against the dangers with which it was threatened, and that they be desired to exert themselves in promoting enlistments into the regular and minute services adopted by this Convention; and it is recommended to the several district committees to pay proper attention to the merit of the said voluntiers, in their choice of officers.[8]

[Resoln. to pay Com: of Safety agd. to.]

Resolved, that the treasurer ⟨Robert Carter Nicholas⟩ do, from time to time, advance to the members of the Committee of Safety fifteen shillings per day, to defray their reasonable expenses during their attendance on duty.[9]

[Ordce. for pay of Delegates read 1st. time & to be read a second time]

Mr. ⟨Edmund⟩ *Pendleton*, from the persons appointed to prepare and bring in an ordinance to provide for paying the expenses of the delegates from this colony to the General Congress, presented to the Convention, according to order, the said ordinance; which was read the first time, and ordered to be read a second time.[10]

[Election Ordce. read & passed.]

An ordinance, for regulating the election of delegates and ascertaining their allowances, and also for regulating the election of committee-men in the several counties and corporations within this colony, and for other purposes therein mentioned, having been fairly transcribed, was read a third time.

Resolved, that the said ordinance do pass.[11]

[Ordinance for pay of Delegates read a second Time, & to be transcribed & read 3d. time.]

An ordinance, to provide for paying the expenses of the delegates from this colony to the General Congress, was read a second time, ordered to be fairly transcribed, and read a third time.[12]

[Ordinance appointing Commissioners read a third Time passed & Title amended.]

An ordinance, for appointing commissioners to settle the accounts of the militia lately drawn out into actual service, and for making provision to pay the same, having been fairly transcribed, was read a third time.

Resolved, that the said ordinance do pass.

Ordered, that the title of the said ordinance be *An ordinance for appointing commissioners to settle the accounts of the militia lately drawn out into actual service, and for making provision to pay the same, as well as the expense of raising and providing for the forces and minute-men directed to be embodied for the defence of this colony.*[13]

[Ordinance for pay of Delegates read a third Time blanks filled up & passed]

An ordinance, to provide for paying the expenses of the delegates from this colony to the General Congress, having been fairly transcribed, was read a third time, and the blanks therein filled up.

Resolved, that the said ordinance do pass.[14]

[Report of Com. for Chesterfield & Officers & Men to be paid as Regular forces.]

Mr. ⟨Richard⟩ *Adams*, from the committee appointed to examine, state, and report the claims of such officers and men as had been appointed and enlisted pursuant to a former resolution, reported, that they had examined the claims of the officers and soldiers in the county of *Chesterfield*, and that it appeared to them that the said officers were chosen by the committee of the said county, and directed to raise the men, in consequence of which they were accordingly enlisted, and entitled to pay as follows:

To *John Markham*, captain, four days, at 6 *s.*	£ 1	4	0
To *William Black*, lieutenant, four days, at 4 *s.*	0 16	0
To *George Hancock*, ensign, four days, at 3 *s.*	0 12	0
To *Thomas Bevington*, and *Meriwether Fowler*, serjeants, four days each, at 2 *s.*	0 16	0
To thirty three privates, four days each, at 1*s.* 4 *d.*	8 16	0
To five privates, three days each, at 1 *s.* 4 *d.*	1 0	0

£ 13   4   0 [15]

[Order on Test put off till 1st. day of next Convention]
The order of the day, for the Convention to resolve itself into a committee on the ordinance for establishing a general test, being read,
Ordered, that the same be put off till the first day of the next Convention.[16]
[Resoln. respecting Fines agd. to]
Resolved, that it be recommended to the committees of the several counties and corporations in this colony to call all collectors and receivers of fines heretofore imposed by any court-martial, and all other persons who have any money in their hands arising from such fines, to an immediate account for the same, and, after paying any arrears which may be due for arms or trophies formerly purchased, apply any such money for providing arms and ammunition for the use of their respective counties and corporations, in such manner as they shall think best.[17]
[Resolution to pay Chesterfield Officers & Men agreable to report.]
Resolved, that the treasurer ⟨Robert Carter Nicholas⟩ do pay the said 13 *l.* 4 *s.* agreeable to the foregoing report.[18]
[Resolution about Return of Exns. agreed to.]
Whereas, by a resolution of the Convention held in the month of *March* last, the several courts in this colony were directed to proceed to give judgments against sheriffs and other collectors for money or tobacco received by them, and it is represented to this Convention, that several sheriffs, in order to evade paying the money received on executions levied by them, refuse to return such executions,
Resolved therefore, that it be recommended to the several courts of justice in this colony to put in execution the laws now in force to compel the sheriffs to return executions, and to call all publick creditors to account.[19]
[A Petition of the Natives of Great Britain presented to the Convention & read & Resolutions agreed to Nem: Con.]
A petition of sundry merchants, and others, natives of *Great Britain*, and resident in this colony, was presented to the Convention, and read; setting forth, that being chiefly agents, factors, and persons who, from their youth, have been bred up to and employed in commerce, they have at no time interfered with the civil institutions of the country, but have always acted in conformity to the laws, under which they have enjoyed the best security for their persons and property; that with this experience of the protection derived from salutary laws, as well as from the happy intercourse they have

enjoyed with the inhabitants, many of them had formed connexions of the most endearing nature, and had invested considerable portions of their property in real estates, with a view of continuing their residence among a people with whom they had hitherto lived in much harmony; that their fears were much awakened from the ill-grounded prejudices which they are informed actuate the minds of some of the people of this colony against them, as a body who are not natives of the land, a circumstance which being accidental, cannot be imputed to them as a fault, and therefore hoping to stand in the same light with other subjects who conform to the laws; that they are very sensible the unhappy differences subsisting between the parent state and her colonies have given rise to distinctions to their prejudice amongst the natives of the country, and excited jealousies of them which otherwise had never existed; that, discriminated from the rest of society, and placed in a suspicious point of view, they presume to lay before this Convention the hardships of their situation, and, in the sincerity of their hearts, declare, that they hold the people of this colony in the highest estimation as friends and fellow-subjects; and that, in war or peace, they will cheerfully contribute, with them, to the exigencies of their common state; that in all internal commotions, or insurrections, they pledge their faith, at the risk of their lives and fortunes, jointly with their fellow-subjects of this colony, to defend the country; and that, in case of an attack from the troops of *Great Britain*, they will not aid in any manner, or communicate intelligence to them or otherwise; that they beg leave to assure this Convention they wish not an exemption from the hardships and burthens to which the people of this country are exposed, from the civil contest subsisting with the parent state, but are willing, and ready, to participate in all instances, except taking up arms against the people among whom they were born, and with whom, perhaps, they are connected by the nearest ties of consanguinity; that they entreat the impartial and favourable attention of the Convention to this circumstance, and beg that a line of conduct might be marked out, by which, in this dangerous crisis, they may move as useful members of the community, without being held to the necessity of shedding the blood of their countrymen, an act at which nature recoils, and which every feeling of humanity forbids; that, allowed this, they repeat their readiness to stand up, with the foremost, in defence of the country against internal insurrections, and in its support, by the most liberal and cheerful contributions; and that the supreme director of the universe might inspire this Convention with wisdom to put a period to this unnatural contest, and restore this once happy land to peace, safety, and union with its parent state, was their most ardent wish.

Resolved unanimously, that the said petition is reasonable; and it is recommended to the committees of the several counties and corporations, and others the good people of this colony, to treat all such natives of *Great Britain* resident here, as do not show themselves enemies to the common cause of *America*, with lenity and friendship; to protect all persons whatsoever in the just enjoyment of their civil rights and liberty, to discountenance all national reflections, to preserve, to the utmost of their power, internal peace and good order; and to promote union, harmony, and mutual good-will, among all ranks of people.

Resolved also, that the said petition, together with this resolve, be forthwith published in the *Virginia* gazettes.[20]

[Went into Com: on Ordce. for making Saltpetre &c – Mr. Harrison in the Chair to sit again]

The Convention then, according to the order of the day, resolved itself into a committee on the ordinance to encourage the making saltpetre, gunpowder, lead, the refining sulphur, and providing arms for the use of this colony; and after some time spent therein, mr. President ⟨Robert Carter Nicholas⟩ resumed the chair, and mr. ⟨Benjamin⟩ *Harrison* reported, that the committee had, according to order, had under their consideration the said ordinance, but not having time to go through the same, had directed him to move for leave to sit again.

Resolved, that this Convention will to-morrow resolve itself into a committee on the said ordinance.[21]

[Remember the list of Names tomorrow.

Adjourned til Tom Adjourned.][22]
Adjourned till to-morrow, 9 o'clock.

> Convention MS minutes in hand of John Tazewell (Archives Division, Virginia State Library); *Proceedings of the Convention* (Purdie), pp. 46–52

1. The number of delegates present this day could not have exceeded 90. It was probably far less. According to the "Cato formula," the number would not have exceeded 61 (18 Aug. 1775, n. 1, 2d para.); but there was a quorum, and at the end of the day's session filled with accomplishments, the order to "Call" the roll would be overlooked or blandly ignored.

Tazewell's manuscript journal for the proceedings of this day is not extant, but his minutes are, and they show considerable variation in the order of the proceedings as noted at the time of occurrence and as set forth in the Purdie printed journal, pp. 46–52. The minutes are hereafter separately bracketed as Tazewell sequentially penned them, and each entry is as far as possible followed by the pertinent printed paragraph.

2. The bill for paying the expenses of the Virginia delegates to Congress will be found introduced, thrice read, and enacted on this same day (p. 489 above).

3. Unnoted in the Purdie printed journal, where the appointment of the foregoing committee is immediately followed by the resolution respecting the sale of "spirituous liquors" to Virginia army regulars, pp. 46–47 (for which see p. 488 above), the present resolution – to compel delinquent sheriffs to pay into the treasury "money received on executions" – was at this time introduced from the floor; but the resolution was not to be adopted until later in the day (p. 490 above).

4. The resolution "for erecting a Magazine," minuted by Tazewell as being the 3d transaction of the day, is shown in the Purdie printed journal as being the 17th, adopted only toward the end of the day's session, p. 52. The original manuscript copy of the resolution in the convention loose papers is in the autograph of Patrick Henry. If at first sight the resolution seems a surrender of authority by Henry, as being

amendatory of the resolution adopted on 22 Aug. 1775 that "all the public Muskets & Bayonets lately used in the Expedition against the Indians" be "sent to the Commander in chief," it may be recalled that in his prospective role, the supreme field commander as yet had no troops.

5. Whereas Tazewell's minutes disclose that the introduction and adoption of the "Resolution respg. Soldiers &c." was the 4th transaction of the day, the Purdie printed journal presents it as the 2d, immediately following the appointment of the committee to prepare a bill for paying the expenses of the Virginia delegates to Congress, pp. 46–47. This resolution, the manuscript original of which is in the convention loose papers, is also in Henry's autograph.

An awkward 1st draft of the resolution Henry canceled with ink crosshatches, probably because on rereading it, he realized that it would be a guardhouse lawyer's delight. As rephrased and adopted, the resolution placed a civilian selling liquor under specified conditions in the status of a sutler—that is, of a nonmilitary supplies merchant attached to troops. Under Article XXXII of the ordinance "for the better government" of the armed land forces, or the articles of war, introduced and passed on 21 Aug. 1775 (Procs. and nn. 2, 4, 7), a sutler was "subject to the articles, rules, and regulations of the provincial army" as though sworn to the colors (albeit there were yet no colors) and hence amenable even to the death sentence imposed by a general court-martial (*Statutes at Large*, IX, 41).

6. Tazewell's minutes show the resolution "respecting Tithables &c." to have been the 5th transaction of the day. In the Purdie printed journal it is the 18th, or last, p. 52. The manuscript original of this floor resolution in the convention loose papers is in the highly legible autograph of Edmund Pendleton. His resolution was in response to the professed expectation that "at the next Congress," to reconvene in Philadelphia on "the 5 of Septr," the "delegates from the respective colonies" would "come provided with an exact account of the number of people of all ages and sexes, including slaves." Until Congress should have such censuses, that body would continue unable to ascertain "the importance of each Colony" and Virginia have only a single vote. Well acquainted with the subject, Pendleton had been a signatory to the letter suggesting that "The Convention will provide for this" (*JCC*, II, 239; *Rev. Va.*, II, 108; 11 July 1775, Va. Delegates to Randolph).

7. Tazewell minuted passage of the amended "Resolution about Powder" as the 6th transaction of the day. In the Purdie printed journal it is the 3d, p. 47. Not surprisingly, the original manuscript copy of the resolution in the convention loose papers is in the autograph of Carter Braxton, Receiver General Corbin's son-in-law.

The amendments were 2. In the prepositional clause in the preamble respecting the quantum of money yielded by his father-in-law, Corbin originally wrote, "of the Three hundred & thirty Pounds which had been taken." To every appearance, before offering the resolution he deleted "taken" and replaced it with "forced." That alteration must have brought a quick and stormy reaction from the Henryites. The portion of the verb was changed back to "taken." But even in that form it was too strong for Henry and his followers, and it is found deleted in turn and replaced in Tazewell's hand by "received."

To the prepositional phrase "of powder so taken by Lord Dunmores order" Braxton added "& the Property of that after the most diligent Enquirys remaining uncertain" in the paragraph containing the resolution proper. Those words must have raised a storm even among the anti-Henryites and are deleted by a heavy line of ink, probably from Tazewell's quill. For the background of the affair of the gunpowder, see pp. 4–11, above. Having dropped the disposition of the powder purchased by Henry into the collective laps of the Virginia delegation to Congress (10 Aug. 1775, Procs. and n. 7), by adoption of the present resolution the convention sought to guard its reputation for probity; it would take from the king nothing that was rightfully his.

8. Tazewell minuted the "Resolution of Thanks" to the volunteer companies as the 7th transaction of the day. In the Purdie printed journal it is the 4th, p. 47. For passage of the ordinance "promoting enlistments into the regular and minute services," see 21 Aug. 1775, Procs. and nn. 2, 3. The "several district committees" were the 16 into which the ordinance for defense and protection divided the colony for purposes of recruitment and appointment of field- and company-grade officers (*Statutes at Large*, IX, 16).

9. Tazewell minuted the "Resn. to pay Com: of Safety" as the 8th transaction of the day. In the Purdie printed journal it is the 5th, p. 47. The "shillings" would be paid in paper "treasury notes" (17 Aug. 1775, n. 7, final para.).

10. Tazewell minuted introduction and 1st reading of the bill "for pay of Delegates" as the 9th transaction of the day. In the Purdie printed journal it is the 6th, pp. 47–48. In the 1st transaction, Pendleton and James Mercer had been appointed to draft such a bill (above and n. 2). The proposed "Ordce." is brief and could have been prepared without a prior understanding; but it was carefully drawn. By its provisions, delegates were to be paid 45 shillings for every day's attendance in Congress, and 1 shilling, "besides all ferriages," for each mile of round-trip travel. "And for the greater convenience of the said delegates," the treasurer was authorized to advance to each before his departure a "sum of money not exceeding two hundred pounds," any surplus beyond his "allowance" to be refunded by the delegate upon his return (*Statutes at Large*, IX, 73–74). If the allowances seem generous, the "pounds" and "shillings" were, again, to paid in Virginia treasury notes, to which in far-off Philadelphia would be attributed what value?

The 2d reading of the Pendleton-Mercer bill would be the 11th transaction of the day.

11. Tazewell minuted the enactment of the "Election Ordce." as the 10th transaction of the day. In the Purdie printed journal it is the 7th, p. 48. The amendments made to the bill before it was "fairly transcribed" can be discerned from the changes made by Tazewell and John Ruffin either in committee or as a result of the debates in the Committee of the Whole on 15, 22, and 23 Aug. 1775. The draft bill in the convention papers is in the hand of Ruffin and is docketed by Tazewell, "sat. Aug. 12. 1775 read 1st Time read 2d Time & committed to Com: of whole." This manuscript is not divided into numbered articles as is the completed version in *Statutes at Large*, IX, 51–60.

The nature of the amendments, which were numerous, gives in general the impression that the 6-man committee of elections, appointed on 25 July 1775 (Procs. and n. 11), was so rural-oriented that it overlooked the municipalities. At the same time the resolution of 22 Aug. 1775 authorizing the eastern and western portions of Augusta County to proceed "as if they were distinct Counties" (Procs. and n. 3) necessitated revisions by the Committee of the Whole that could not have been foreseen by the special committee.

One alteration was the restoration to Jamestown "City" of its right to representation in future conventions. Then in the original bill, only sheriffs were deputed to hold elections for convention delegates. But there being no sheriffs in towns traditionally entitled to elect a burgess, it was necessary to find substitute authorities, and therein sheriffs were replaced by the "Mayor of the City of Wmsburg & Borough of Norfolk" (*Statutes at Large*, IX, 54, Arts. II, III). Moreover, the date for holding elections in

Jamestown and the College of William and Mary was overlooked and subsequently penned in (ibid., IX, 55, Art. IV).

The provision of Article II reading, "and the landholders of the district of West Augusta shall be considered as a distinct county, and have the liberty of sending two delegates to represent them in general convention, as aforesaid," was obviously moved from the floor and was cryptically noted by Tazewell on the manuscript bill by the entry "& the Landholders &c." The portion of Article X reading "and the landholders in the district of West Augusta, hereafter described" is also an addition. And the entire text of Article XII describing the suffrage provisions to apply to West Augusta County, where land titles were chaotic, was voted for inclusion where in the manuscript Tazewell inserted only "and whereas &c." (ibid., IX, 54, 58–59). Who successfully moved these amendments safeguarding the rights of the West Augustans is unknown, but George Rootes is the candidate most eligible for the honor.

12. Tazewell minuted the 2d reading of the "Ordinance for pay of Delegates" as the 11th transaction of the day. In the Purdie printed journal it is the 8th, p. 48. Enactment of the "fairly transcribed" bill will in the minutes be the 13th transaction.

13. Tazewell minuted passage of "An ordinance, for appointing commissioners" as the 12th transaction of the day. In the Purdie printed journal it is the 9th, p. 48. This ordinance, introduced on 12 Aug. 1775 and recommitted (Procs. and n. 16), was returned to the floor and debated in Committee of the Whole and therein amended on 24 Aug. 1775 (Procs. and n. 2). What engrossed the time of the committee on that day was the substituted revenue section. The manuscript text of the revision in the convention papers is penned in an unidentified, miniscule autograph on the rectos and versos of 2 sheets of paper and half the recto of a 3d. In this draft Tazewell filled in the sums of the "treasury notes" voted emitted, as well as the names of the designated signers of the notes and of the "overseers of the press." Several lines, probably at the behest of the Whole, he deleted as being superfluous.

Three amendments written by Edmund Pendleton were incorporated. On the bottom recto of the 3d sheet of the revised draft he penned the text of the provision for burning treasury notes received in payment of taxes (*Statutes at Large*, IX, 70, 3d para.). This concise provision replaced the florid version of the original draft, which had been omitted altogether from the revision. On a separate, small piece of paper, Pendleton submitted what became the final paragraph of the ordinance, granting the Committee of Safety authority to appoint another to act in the "room" of Robert Carter Nicholas "in case of the death" of the treasurer, or his "inability" to act (ibid., IX, 71). The careful lawyer from Caroline County also wrote on another piece of paper the passage that reads, "Provided always & be it further Ordained that nothing herein contained shall be construed so as to alter any Contract heretofore made between Landlords & their tenants, whereby the Payment of taxes shall have been stipulated to be made by either of them" (ibid., IX, 65, 3d para.).

On the piece of paper containing the last-mentioned contribution by Pendleton there are 2 additional amendments, both in a single unidentified hand. That these were written with different quills suggests that the amendments may have been penned at different times and in collaboration attending the final marking up of the bill. The 1st of these amendments specified that "the Landholders in the County of Fincastle & the district of West Augusta whose Rights of Voting at Elections of Delegates & Committeemen are Stated & allowed by an Ordinance of this Convention, shall give in a List of their said Lands, and the Land tax aforesd, shall be collected & paid for the same notwithstanding no Patents may have been obtained for such lands" (ibid., IX, 66, 2d para.). Although the convention had on 15 Aug. 1775 left the matter of western lands rather in the air (Procs. and n. 3), and although frontiersmen have seldom been far-famed for their dedication to paying taxes, this phase of the ordinance was to them gain, for it presumed their claims to have a degree of legitimacy.

The 2d amendment required "every Sherif or Collector of the duties or taxes" to pay revenues to the "Treasurer aforesd. on or before the twentieth day of November in every year" after deducting a "Salary of five per Centum" (*Statutes at Large*, IX, 66, 2d para.)—a stipulation qualified, however, by the fact that the actual payment of taxes had been suspended for a year (24 Aug. 1775, Procs. and n. 2).

In the convention papers there is likewise another amendment in Tazewell's hand. The amendment designated 5 "Commissioners" to "examine state and settle an Account of the pay and provisions of the volunteer Companies who have been lately called into actual Service for the Defence of the Lower parts of the Country," according to the pay scale elsewhere enacted for the "regular Forces" of the colony. Near the middle of the amendment there is inserted an asterisk, which is matched at the bottom of the page by a 2d, following which in an unidentified hand is written, "excepting that Charles Scott commander in Chief of the sd. Voluntiers at Wms.burg, shall be allowed 12/6 per day from the time he was chosen to that Command" (*Statutes at Large*, IX, 71, 1st para.).

14. Tazewell minuted passage of the "Ordinance for pay of Delegates" as the 13th transaction of the day. In Purdie's printed journal it is the 10th, p. 48. The "blanks" were probably the sums of money mentioned in n. 10 above.

15. Tazewell minuted presentation of the "Report of Com. for Chesterfield," appointed on 12 Aug. 1775 (Procs. and n. 15), as the 14th transaction of the day. He then deleted the entry with swinging loops of ink, with the result that Purdie, undoubtedly drawing from the missing manuscript journal, consolidates the report and its subsequent adoption as a single 13th transaction, p. 49.

16. Tazewell minuted the postponement of further consideration of the Parker-Mason "Test," introduced on 19 Aug. 1775 (Procs. and n. 6), as the 15th transaction of the day. In the Purdie printed journal it is the 11th, p. 48. On this same day Mason was in the 20th transaction to present the "Petition of Natives of Great Britain," and the incompatibility of enforcing some provisions of the proposed oath of allegiance while acceding to the "reasonable" request of the petitioners was clear. By private conversations or by open motion from the floor, he may have suggested or moved that deliberation on the test by "put off." The subject of allegiance would not be taken up on the "first day of the next Convention"; but on 14 Dec. 1775, James Mercer and Richard Adams would be appointed a new committee "to bring in an ordinance for establishing a general test" (*Proceedings of the Convention of . . . the 1st of December 1775*, p. 18).

17. Tazewell minuted adoption of the "Resoln. respecting Fines" as the 16th transaction of the day. In the Purdie printed journal it is the 12th, pp. 48–49. Fines "heretofore imposed by any court-martial" would be both those levied before the breakdown of the royal militia system and after the "recommended" establishment of the independent companies under the "Militia Law passed in the Year 1738" (*Rev. Va.*, II, 374). The present resolution was an instruction specifically to the "several" local committees, not to the committee of munitions appointed on 12 Aug. 1775 (Procs. and n. 23), on the proposed ordinance of which debate would be resumed in the final transaction of the day.

18. Tazewell minuted adoption of the "Resolution to pay Chesterfield Officers & Men" as the 17th transaction of the day. In the Purdie printed journal presentation of

"the foregoing report" and adoption of the resolution are consolidated as the 13th, p. 49.

19. Tazewell minuted adoption of the "Resolution about Return of Exns." as the 18th transaction of the day. In the Purdie printed journal it is the 14th, p. 49. By "a resolution of the Convention" on the 25th "of *March* last," it had been recommended "to the several Courts of Justice" not "to give Judgments but in the Case of Sherif[f]s or other Collectors for money or Tobacco received by them" (*Rev. Va.*, II, 373). The "laws now in force" were "An Act to Amend an Act for Raising a Public Levy, and for Other Purposes Therein Mentioned" (A.D. 1765) and "An Act to Amend an Act, Intituled An Act Declaring the Law concerning Executions, and for Relief of Insolvent Debtors" (A.D. 1769) (*Statutes at Large*, VIII, 178–82, 326–32). The resolution points up the peculiarity of the situation. Presumably all Virginia legislation to which His Majesty had graciously assented and which did not expire because of specified dates of termination would continue effective until the present or another Majesty-defying convention should repeal, amend, or supersede it.

20. Tazewell minuted presentation of the petition and the adoption of the resultant resolutions as the 19th transaction of the day. In the Purdie printed journal it is the 15th, pp. 49–51. The "said petition, together with this resolve," was printed in Pinkney's *Va. Gazette* of 31 Aug. 1775, in Purdie's of 1 Sept., and in Dixon and Hunter's of 2 Sept.

21. Tazewell minuted discussion of the proposed "Ordce. for making Saltpetre &c" as the 20th transaction of the day. In the Purdie printed journal it is the 16th, p. 51. The bill of munitions, introduced on 19 Aug. 1775 (Procs. and n. 4), had until the present occasion not again been brought to the floor. It would be enacted on the morrow, the final day of session (Procs. and n. 25).

22. Although Tazewell's minutes end at this point with a mystery and a spasm, in the Purdie printed journal the 18th and final transaction is the resolution respecting the preparation of a census, p. 52. In the minutes it was the 5th (above and n. 6). Tazewell's note to "Remember the list of Names tomorrow" was a memorandum for his own use. What recollection he intended to jog is not solved by anything that was to occur "tomorrow," unless it be the listing of the 9 men appointed officers of the convention (pp. 499–500 below) or, for Purdie's use, the names of the delegates who had attended the convention at any time.

Saturday, 26 August 1775

Third Virginia Convention

Proceedings of Thirty-third and Final Day of Session [1]

[Ballotted for the Place of Meeting and Mr. Carrington, Mr. Braxton, Mr. Stubblefield, & Mr. Cary . . .] [2]

THE Convention proceeded, by ballot, to appoint a place for the meeting of the next Convention; and the members having prepared tickets with the name of the place to be appointed for the purpose aforesaid, and put the same into the ballott box, mr. ⟨Paul⟩ *Carrington*, mr. ⟨Carter⟩ *Braxton*, mr. ⟨George⟩ *Stubblefield*, and mr. ⟨Archibald⟩ *Cary*, were appointed a committee to examine the ballott box, and to report on which place the majority falls, who retired . . .

[Draughts of Commissions reported & agreed to.]

Mr. ⟨John⟩ *Banister*, from the persons appointed to draw up and report the forms of proper commissions to be granted to the officers of the regular forces, minute-men, and militia of this colony, reported the following forms of the said commissions, which were read, and on the questions severally put thereon, agreed to by the Convention.[3]

Form of a commission for the COLONEL *of the first regiment, and commander in chief of the* REGULAR FORCES.[4]

The Committee of Safety for the colony of VIRGINIA to PATRICK HENRY, esq; WHEREAS *by a resolution of the delegates of this colony, in Convention assembled, it was determined that you the said* PATRICK HENRY, *esq; should be colonel of the first regiment of regulars, and commander in chief of all the forces to be raised for the protection and defence of this colony, and, by an ordinance of the said Convention, it is provided, that the Committee of Safety should issue all military commissions: Now, in pursuance of the said power to us granted, and in conformity to the appointment of the Convention, we the said Committee of Safety do constitute and commission you the said* PATRICK HENRY, *esq; colonel of the first regiment of regulars, and commander in chief of all such other forces as may, by order of the Convention, or Committee of Safety, be directed to act in conjunction with them; and with the said forces, or any of them, you are hereby empowered to resist and repel all hostile invasions, and quell and suppress any insurrections which may be made or attempted against the peace and safety of this his majesty's colony and dominion. And we do require you to exert your utmost efforts for the promotion of discipline and order among the officers and soldiers under your command, agreeable to such ordinances, rules, and articles, which are now, or hereafter may be, instituted for the government and regulation of the army; and that you pay due obedience to all orders and instructions which from time to time you may receive from the Convention or Committee of Safety; to hold, exercise, and enjoy, the said office of colonel and commander in chief of the forces, and to perform and execute the power and authority aforesaid, and all other things which are truly and of right incidental to your said office, during the pleasure of the Convention, and no longer. And we do hereby require and command all officers and soldiers, and every person whatsoever, in any way concerned, to be obedient and assisting to you in all things touching the due execution of this commission, according to the purport or intent thereof.*

Given under our hands, at   , this
   day of   , anno dom. 177

COMMISSION TO A COLONEL of the MINUTE-MEN.

The COMMITTEE *of* SAFETY *of the colony of* VIRGINIA *to* esquire.
WHEREAS *it is provided, by an ordinance of the Convention, that a battalion of minute-men should be enlisted, trained, and disciplined, in each of the districts therein-mentioned, and by the same authority it is ordained that all commissions for officers to command the said minute-men should issue from the Committee of Safety: Now, in pursuance of the said power and authority to us given, we do by these presents constitute and commission you the said colonel of the battalion of minute-men in the district of . You are therefore to act as colonel, by duly exercising the officers and soldiers under your command, taking care that they be provided with arms and ammunition, agreeable to the ordinances of the Convention; and you are to pay a ready obedience to all orders and instructions which from time to time you may receive from the Convention, Committee of Safety, or any of your superiour officers, agreeable to the rules and articles ordained by the Convention. And we do require all officers and soldiers under your command to be obedient, and to aid you in the execution of this commission, according to the intent and purport thereof.*

*Given under our hands, at , this
day of , anno dom.* 177

COMMISSION TO A COUNTY-LIEUTENANT.

The Committee *of Safety for the colony of* VIRGINIA *to*
BY *virtue of the power and authority invested in us by the delegates and representatives of the several counties and corporations within this colony, in General Convention assembled, we, reposing especial trust and confidence in your patriotism, fidelity, courage, and good conduct, do by these presents constitute and appoint you to be county-lieutenant of the militia of the county of ; and you are therefore carefully and diligently to discharge the trust reposed in you, by disciplining all officers and soldiers under your command; and we do hereby require them to obey you as their county-lieutenant. And you are to observe and follow all such orders and directions as you shall from time to time receive from the Convention, the Committee of Safety for the time being, or any superiour officer, according to the rules and regulations established by the Convention.*

*Given under our hands, at , this
day of , anno dom.* 177

[Voted to the revd. Mr. Selden . . £ 40.
     To J. Tazewell . . . . . . 150.
     To Mr. Dandridge . . . . 25.
     To Mr. Claiborne . . . . . 50.
     To the several Doorkeepers
     including the Sexton . . . . 20 each.]

Resolved, that the several sums following be paid to the several officers of this Convention, for their services during the present session.

To the rev. *Miles Selden*, chaplain to the Convention, £. 40 0 0
To mr. *John Tazewell*, clerk of the Convention,   150 0 0
To mr. *William Dandridge*, junior.   25 0 0
To mr. *Thomas Claiborne*, messenger to the Convention,   50 0 0
    To *Robert Hyland, John Creagh, William Drinkard, William Hix* ⟨Hicks⟩,
and *Richard Williams*, door-keepers to the Convention, 20 *l*. each.⁵
    [reported Richmond 25. Wms.burg 22. Fred. 8.
    Meeting to be at Richmond.]
and after some time returned into Convention, and reported, that the numbers
on the ballot appeared as follows:
    For the town of *Richmond*,   − 25
    For the city of *Williamsburg*,   − 22
    For the town of *Fredericksburg*,   − 8
    And the question being then put, whether the town of *Richmond*, or the
city of *Williamsburg*, should be the place for holding the next Convention, a
majority appeared in favour of the town of *Richmond*.
    Resolved therefore, that the next meeting of this Convention be at the said
town of *Richmond*.⁶
    [Declaration setting forth Reasons &c passed Nem⟨. con.⟩] ⁷
A DECLARATION *of the* DELEGATES *deputed by the several counties and corporations in the colony and dominion of Virginia to represent them in General Convention, setting forth the cause of their meeting, and the necessity of
immediately putting the country into a posture of defence, for the better protection of their lives, liberties, and properties.*⁸
THE advantages resulting from the wisest institutions, and the price of all
sublunary enjoyments, are best to be estimated from their loss or diminution.
By this accurate scale, we are taught to weigh the many blessings derived to
this once happy country from our excellent constitution. So long as this was
maintained on its original principles, and remained inviolate, all was well with
us; every thing flowed in a proper, peaceful channel; all were quiet, and at
ease. But, how great the change! how dreadful the reverse!
    The times were, and these not very distant, when the representatives of
the people, with much pleasure, met their governours in General Assembly. In
these assemblies the greatest harmony prevailed, till a fatal change of ministerial systems took place. A causeless, hasty dissolution, drove the representative body to the unhappy dilemma of either sacrificing the most essential
interests of their constituents, or of meeting in General Convention, to assert
and preserve them. The unlucky incidents here alluded to are of publick
notoriety, and need not a particular enumeration.⁹
    Repeated prorogations of our Assembly, when the country was in the
greatest distress, rendered a Convention, in the month of March last, absolutely necessary. The delegates of the people then met in full Convention,
the most numerous Assembly that had ever been known in this colony,¹⁰
taking a view of our unhappy situation; considering the country exposed to
the most eminent dangers, as well from invasions as insurrections; knowing
its then defenceless state, and seeing no prospect that opportunity would be

given them in General Assembly to provide and guard against such extensive evils, judged it their indispensable duty to put the country into a posture of defence. They recommended a due attention to the militia law; but considering this inadequate to the purpose, they farther advised the raising one or more volunteer companies in each county. In all their transactions, however, a proper regard and respect was paid to government.[11]

In a short time afterwards, a most extraordinary manoeuvre was exerted by the governour to render this country still more defenceless, by removing our small stock of gunpowder from the public magazine, and stripping of their locks a great number of the publick arms.[12] It is very remarkable, that this was done at a time when he acknowledged to have received information that an insurrection was apprehended in a neighbouring county. This, together with his lordship's threats of emancipating our slaves, and reducing to ashes the principal city in this colony, added to the many alarming accounts received from the northern colonies, could not but excite jealousies, and awaken the fears, of the people.[13]

The country, by these means, being thrown into a ferment, and there being little ground of hope that the Assembly would be called, it was thought advisable that a General Convention should be speedily held, to take under their consideration the state of the colony. The governour, however, on receipt of despatches from England, was pleased to issue his proclamation for convening the General Assembly. The design of calling a Convention was then laid aside, in hopes that matters might, in another place, be settled and adjusted in the usual mode. The proceedings of the House of Burgesses, the governour's conduct towards them, his withdrawal from the seat of his government, and taking up his residence on board one of his majesty's ships of war, the many obstructions given by his lordship to the business of the Assembly, and his determined resolution to render abortive those very measures he had recommended, are faithfully and impartially submitted to the publick, in a pamphlet published by order of the House of Burgesses.[14]

The two other branches of our legislature, his majesty's Council and the Burgesses, finding that his lordship had resisted their joint and most earnest entreaties, and that he was resolved not to return to the duties of his station, adjourned themselves to the month of October next.[15]

The governour still continuing on board the man of war, if his former conduct, his repeated and horrible threats, his at least connivance at the detention of some of our slaves on board the same ship, and a too well-grounded report of his having solicited troops to be sent amongst us, some of which are now arrived, could have left no doubt of his hostile intentions towards this country, the hurrying his most amiable lady and his children across the Atlantick, under a frivolous and groundless pretence of their being in danger amongst a people by whom they were universally esteemed and respected, holds out to us an irrefragable proof of his fixed determination to do this unhappy country every injury in his power.[16]

Under these embarrassments, seeing an unusual resort of ships of war and other armed vessels in our harbours, knowing the threats of one of their commanders, in short, when exposed to such accumulate dangers, what could be expected of this country? [17] That we should sit supinely down, and suffer the views and machinations of an arbitrary and relentless ministry to be carried into execution, without opposition or controul? The justice to this community, every motive to publick virtue, conspire in forbidding it. We therefore, deputed for this important purpose, have met in General Convention, and taken into our most serious consideration the state of the colony. Since our assembling, we have received authentick intelligence of the remorseless fury with which general ⟨Thomas⟩ Gage and his coadjutors are endeavouring to spread fire, famine, and the most horrid desolation, throughout a sister colony; of their insidious and cruel attempts to stir up the barbarous savages against the inhabitants on the frontiers of the different colonies.[18] We have seen a declaration of the Continental Congress, which proves the necessity of an immediate preparation for our security, by putting the whole country into a full state of defence, both against invasions and insurrections.[19] In the present untoward and distressful situation of our affairs, and the better to preserve the peace and good order of the community, we are farther driven to the very disagreeable necessity of supplying the present want of government, by appointing proper guardians of the rights and liberties of our country. But, lest our views and designs should be misrepresented or misunderstood, we again, and for all, publickly and solemnly declare, before God and the world, that we do bear faith and true allegiance to his majesty George the third, our only lawful and rightful king; that we will, so long as it may be in our power, defend him and his government, as founded on the laws and well known principles of the constitution; that we will, to the utmost of our power, preserve peace and good order throughout the country, and endeavour, by every honourable means, to promote a restoration of that friendship and amity which so long and happily subsisted between our fellow-subjects in Great Britain and the inhabitants of America; that as, on the one hand, we are determined to defend our lives and properties, and maintain our just rights and privileges, at every, even the extremest hazard, so, on the other, it is our fixed and unalterable resolution to disband such forces as may be raised in this colony whenever our dangers are removed, and America is restored to that former state of tranquility and happiness, the interruption of which is so much deplored by us and every friend to either country.

It remains a bounden duty on us to commit our cause to the justice of that supreme being who ruleth and ordereth all human events with unerring wisdom, most humbly beseeching him to take this colony, and the whole continent, under his fatherly and divine protection, and that he will be graciously pleased to soften the hearts of those who meditate evil against our land, and inspire them with the purest sentiments of justice, moderation, and brotherly affection.

[Went into Com: on Ordce. for Saltpetre]

The Convention, according to the order of the day, resolved itself into a committee on the ordinance to encourage the making saltpetre, gunpowder, lead, the refining sulphur, and providing arms for the use of this colony; and after some time spent therein mr. President ⟨Robert Carter Nicholas⟩ resumed the chair, and mr. ⟨Benjamin⟩ *Harrison* reported, that the committee had, according to order, had under their consideration the said ordinance, and had gone through the same, and made several amendments thereto, which he read in his place, and afterwards delivered in at the clerk's table, where the same were again twice read, and on the question severally put thereon, agreed to by the Convention.

Ordered, that the said ordinance, together with the several amendments, be fairly transcribed, and read a third time.[20]

[Publick Printer to send 22 Copies of the Ordinances of this Convent. to Coms. &c.]

Ordered, that the publick printer do send twenty two copies of the ordinances of this Convention to the committees of the several counties and corporations within this colony.[21]

[Resoln. abt. Gun Powder agreed to.]

Resolved, that it be recommended to the committees of the several counties and corporations, where it is not already done, to complete the collection of the money by them judged requisite for the purchase of gunpowder, lead, flints, and cartridge paper, according to the resolution in *March* last, in order to place the whole colony on an equal footing in that particular, and return a state of such collection to the next Convention.[22]

[Resoln. abt. Slitting Mills agreed to.]

Resolved, that in case the *British* ministry shall attempt to enforce the act of parliament for preventing the erecting of plating and slitting mills in *America*, this Convention will recompense to the proprietors of the two first of such mills as shall be finished and set to work in this colony all losses they may respectively sustain in consequence of such endeavours of administration.[23]

[Resolution respecting Otway Byrd agd to]

It appearing to the Convention, that ⟨Francis⟩ *Otway Byrd*, esq; had, on account of his attachment to *American* liberty, resigned his provision and prospects in the *British* navy, and may be destitute of employment,

Resolved, that the said *Otway Byrd*, esq; be strongly recommended to his excellency general ⟨George⟩ *Washington*, and the Conventions of our sister colonies to the eastward, for promotion in the army in that neighbourhood; and that until such promotion shall take place, or it be otherwise ordered by this Convention, that he be allowed ten shillings per day to support him as a cadet in the continental army, to commence the day he joins the said army, and that he be also allowed the sum of 50 *l.* to be paid immediately.

The foregoing declaration was presented to the Convention, maturely considered, and unanimously agreed to.[24]

[Salt petre Ordce. agreed to & Title amended]

An ordinance, to encourage the making saltpetre, gunpowder, lead, the refining sulphur, and providing arms for the use of this colony, having been

fairly transcribed, was read a third time, and the blanks therein filled up.
  Resolved, that the said ordinance do pass.
  Ordered, that the title of the said ordinance be *An ordinance for providing arms and ammunition for the use of this colony.*[25]
  [Adjourned till 1st. Monday in next Month] [26]

Ro. C. Nicholas, president *pro tempore.*
(A copy)
John Tazewell, clerk of the Convention.
Finis.

Convention MS minutes in hand of John Tazewell
(Archives Division, Virginia State Library); *Proceedings of the Convention* (Purdie), pp. 52–59

Virginia Committee of Safety

The First Meeting and Summons for the Second

At a meeting of the Committee *of* Safety, *in the town of Richmond, the 26th of August,* 1775: [27]
Ordered, that the chairmen of the several committees in this colony do deliver the public arms, to be by them collected, pursuant to an order of convention, to the captains who shall be appointed to command the companies of regular troops to be raised from their respective districts, taking their receipts for the same; and that the said captains take proper measures for *their* safe conveyance to the place of general rendezvous.[28]
  And it is farther ordered, that the said chairmen do respectively correspond with the president of this committee, informing him of their progress in the minute service, and when they shall have compleated each the number of regulars required from their respective districts.[29]

John Pendleton, junior, clerk.[30]

The Committee of Safety, at a meeting appointed at Hanover town [31] on the 18th of next month, intend to proceed to the choice of all officers within their appointment, particularly a commissary of provisions, or contractors for each of the regiments to be raised pursuant to an ordinance of convention, previous to which all persons inclined to contract, or to be appointed commissary, are desired to send their proposals, in writing, to Edmund Pendleton, esquire, president of the committee, enclosed and sealed. At the same time, the committee will be ready to deliver the commissions, and administer the oaths to the field officers of the regulars, chosen by the convention; and all captains, and subalterns, who may be chosen by the district committees, are also to attend, to receive warrants for the money necessary in recruiting, and their instructions.[32]

By order of the committee,

John Pendleton, junior, clerk.

Virginia Gazette (Purdie), 31 August 1775

Norfolk Borough

Mayor Paul Loyall to Captain John Macartney

Sir,   Norfolk, August 26, 1775.

WHEN I had the pleasure of seeing you last,[33] you mentioned having some letters that I had passed between you and me published, which I gave you to understand might be done, since which, as those letters concerned the public, I have thought proper to lay them before the Common Hall of this borough. The Hall have made some resolves on them, a copy of which I am directed to inclose you. My reason for not publishing the letters in this week's paper is, that as they are of a threatening nature, they might perhaps give the people of this colony great uneasiness; to prevent which, I think there cannot be too much precaution used, as I am willing to believe your intentions are only to act within your own sphere, and not to intermeddle with the internal policy of this corporation. If you still think proper to have the letters published, and will inclose them to me, I shall take particular care to have them put into the next Gazette.[34] My family joins me in best compliments, hoping you have recovered your health.

I am, Sir, your most obedient, humble Servant,

Paul Loyall.

Virginia Gazette, or the Norfolk Intelligencer, 30 August 1775

1. The number of delegates present this day could not have exceeded 90. But "Cato" was flatly to state that it was 55 (18 Aug. 1775, Proceedings and n. 1, 2d para.). This is a total precisely in accord with the vote cast as the 4th transaction of the day for the meeting place of the next session of the convention. Presuming, however, that President Nicholas withheld a casting vote, the actual number would have been 56.

Tazewell's manuscript journal for the proceedings of this day is not extant, but his minutes are, and they show considerable variation in the order of the proceedings as noted at the time of occurrence from those as set forth in the Purdie printed journal, pp. 52–59. The minutes are hereafter separately bracketed as Tazewell sequentially penned them, and each entry is as far as possible followed by the pertinent printed paragraph.

2. The ellipsis deletes the vote totals reported as the 4th transaction of the day but

which Tazewell brought up and entered in space left in the minutes at the end of the 1st transaction.

3. Banister was chairman of the committee appointed in the 4th transaction on 21 Aug. "to draw up & report the Forms of proper Commissions" (Procs. and n. 5).

4. This *"Form of a commission"* constitutes the 1st specific recognition of Colonel Henry as *"commander in chief."*

5. Tazewell minuted the vote to pay the officers of the convention as the 3d transaction of the day. In the Purdie journal, p. 56, it is the 8th.

6. Despite the danger that might be involved, a number of delegates undoubtedly sighed for the more commodious accommodations of Williamsburg. Whereas the second convention had resolved that "thanks" were "justly due to the town of Richmond, and the neighbourhood, for their polite reception and entertainment of the delegates" (*Rev. Va.*, II, 385), the third convention neglected to adopt a like resolution. A desire to be off after 41 days encompassing 33 days of session, of which the final one was long, probably caused the oversight.

7. The minutes are here torn at the right margin.

8. Tazewell minuted the reading and adoption of the "Declaration" as the 5th transaction of the day. In the Purdie printed journal, pp. 56–59, it is the 10th and last—for an obvious reason: the convention is made to adjourn only after justifying "the cause" for its convening and by issuing a ringing denunciation of the British ministry and its chief agent in Virginia.

Neither minutes nor journal during the days of session contains the slightest hint that a committee was appointed to prepare such a declaration, nor has anyone been found to claim or attribute authorship. It seems highly unlikely, however, that the convention would have proceeded without intending to issue a statement of this nature, or that the document was offered as a floor resolution. Whoever did the reading on the floor, the most probable author of the declaration, if single author there was, must be Richard Bland, who on 19 July had attempted to preface the resolution "that a sufficient armed Force be immediately raised" with a justificatory paragraph assailing His Lordship (Procs. and n. 4). For the task of composing the present justification Bland was well rehearsed. It had been he, for example, who was chairman of the "Committee of the whole House" of Burgesses that on 24 June bitterly censured the governor's conduct in a declaration of which the present one is in part a rehash (*JHB, 1773–1776*, pp. 281–83; pp. 22–23 above). It is well to observe, on the other hand, that the final paragraph of the present declaration bespeaks the touch of the deeply religious Robert Carter Nicholas.

9. The "dissolution," unarguably "hasty," but not entirely "causeless," occurred on 26 May 1774. It was followed on 31 May by the summons for the first Virginia Convention, which sat in Williamsburg from the 1st to the 6th, both dates inclusive, of the succeeding August (*Rev. Va.*, I, 94, 100, 223–39).

10. This was the second Virginia Convention, which met in Richmond, 20–27 Mar. 1775, and at one time or another during 7 days of session was attended by 120 delegates.

11. Although true, the statement disregards (and that naturally enough) the tempest of opposition roused in the second convention by Patrick Henry's motion that Virginia be placed in "a posture of Defence" (ibid., II, 366, 368–69 n. 8).

12. As early as 14 or 15 Apr. 1775 word has been passed by the keeper of the Magazine in Williamsburg that Dunmore intended to remove the firing mechanisms of the shoulder arms in that depot. Later the keeper informed the committee of inspection from the House of Burgesses that when he remarked to the governor that

a number of "Muskets were without Locks," His Excellency "rebuked him for taking notice of that Circumstance" (Burk, *Hist. of Va.*, 409 n.; *JHB, 1773–1776*, p. 223).

13. For His Lordship's "threats" and "alarming accounts" from the northern colonies, see pp. 6, 68, 69 n. 6, 72–73, 93–94 above. The gazettes of the time are replete with the reports of British troop movements and target areas.

14. Although no such authorization is recorded in the journal of the House of Burgesses, Purdie during the 1st week that the convention was in session published, "as directed by the House," a pamphlet purporting to contain "the most material transactions" of that body. The purpose was to expose to the "publick" the "many obstructions" that Dunmore had thrown in the way of the attempted enactments of fruitful legislation. The pamphlet, which consisted of 48 folio pages, sold for 2 s. 6 d. (*Va. Gazette* [Purdie], 21 July 1775). A copy is in the Va. State Library.

15. Here it is difficult to square statement with fact insofar as fact can be determined. In neither journal of the Burgesses nor of the Council is there any evidence but that the House adjourned itself and thereby caused the Council to adjourn perforce.

16. For the governor's "at least connivance at the detention" of slaves aboard the *Otter*, see 1 Aug. 1775, Third Va. Convention, Officers to President and Gentlemen and n. 22; 16 Aug., Norfolk Co. Committee and n. 17; for the "too well-grounded report of his having solicited troops," 31 July 1775, Third Va. Convention, 4th entry and nn. 11, 12; 3 Aug., same, 3d para.; for his "hurrying his most amiable lady and his children across the Atlantick," p. 223 above.

17. The "commander" was undoubtedly Capt. George Montagu, who had threatened to fire on Yorktown, for the threat by Capt. John Macartney to pay Norfolk a like disfavor was as yet privy only to a few (pp. 10, 431–32, 439, 442–43, 447–48, 473–74 above).

18. For "authentick intelligence of the remorseless fury" with which General Gage and assisting spirits were spreading "desolation" in Massachusetts, see pp. 283–84 above; for their "insidious and cruel attempts to stir up the barbarous savages," 20 July 1775, Third Va. Convention, 1st and 2d entries; 28 July, same, Augusta Co. West and n. 20; 2 Aug., same and n. 16; 11 Aug., same and n. 21.

19. For the "declaration" of Congress, adopted on 26 May and "seen" by the convention on 24 July 1775, see pp. 283–84, 338 above.

20. Tazewell minuted the business of the "Com: on Ordce. for Saltpetre" as the 6th transaction of the day. In the Purdie printed journal, p. 55, it is the 3d. This bill, for the manufacture and procurement of munitions, was the work of a committee appointed on 12 Aug. with Richard Henry Lee as chairman. On 19 Aug., Archibald Cary, 4th-named of the committee, introduced the proposed bill, further consideration of which was successively put off until 25 Aug., when renewed deliberation was ordered for the present day (pp. 429, 466, 492 above). Passage of the bill would be the 11th transaction of the day. No manuscript version of the ordinance having been found, the nature of "the several amendments" is indeterminable.

21. Tazewell minuted adoption of the order to the "Publick Printer," Alexander Purdie, as the 7th transaction of the day. In the Purdie printed journal, p. 55, it is the 4th.

22. Tazewell minuted the adoption of the resolution "abt. Gun Powder" as the 8th transaction of the day. In the Purdie printed journal, p. 55, it is the 5th. This was a floor resolution, the manuscript original of which, in the convention loose papers, is in the hand of Edmund Pendleton. The basic "Resolution of the Convention in March" had been adopted on the 25th (*Rev. Va.*, II, 375). Pendelton probably pointed out to

his colleagues that although the ordinance of munitions provided for future manufacturers and procurement of munitions, there was no standing mode by which "the
next Convention" could properly judge what by the time of its meeting should have
been accomplished by the various committees, or where might lie the greatest need.

23. Tazewell minuted adoption of the resolution "abt. Slitting Mills" as the 9th
transaction of the day. In the Purdie printed journal, p. 55, it is the 6th. This was a
floor resolution, the manuscript original of which, in the convention loose papers, is
also in the hand of Edmund Pendleton. The "act of parliament" alluded to was 23
George II, *cap*. 29 (A.D. 1750) (15 May 1775, Third Va. Convention, Brutus . . .
and n. 3).

24. Tazewell minuted adoption of the resolution "respecting Otway Byrd" as the
10th transaction of the day. In the Purdie printed journal, p. 56, it is the 9th. The
original manuscript of this floor resolution, by whom introduced is unknown, is in
Tazewell's hand. The son of compulsively gambling, estate-dissipating, suicide-destined
Colonel William Byrd III, a member of the governor's Council, Francis Otway Byrd
was now 3 months into his 20th year and only 1 year out of the College of William
and Mary. His father was vacillating between loyalism and patriotism but was steady
in his agitation at the threatened hostilities between colonies and mother country. In
July 1774 the colonel had provided in his will that "if my son Otway should quit the
Navy before the death of my dearest wife," the youngster should not share in the
cash devised to be distributed among many siblings. Otway was to serve in the Continental Army for 3 years and soon would begin to acquire such knowledge of soldier-
ing as might be learned by an aide-de-camp to the eccentric Maj. Gen. Charles Lee
(*Va. Mag. of Hist. and Biog.*, IX [July 1901], 81, 86–87; Francis R. Heitman, *Historical Register of Officers of the Continental Army during the War of the Revolution* [rev. ed., Washington, D.C., 1914], p. 138).

25. Tazewell minuted passage of the "Salt petre Ordce.," with amended "Title,"
as the 11th and final transaction of the day. In the Purdie printed journal, pp. 55–56,
it is the 7th. The ordinance is printed in *Statutes at Large*, IX, 71–73.

26. Tazewell minuted the fact of adjournment. In the Purdie printed journal, p.
56, the fact is omitted and the appended signatures of Nicholas and Tazewell made
to appear authentications and endorsement of the "DECLARATION *of the* DELEGATES,"
pp. 500–502 above. The adjournment until the 1st Monday—that is, the 4th day—of
Sept. 1775 was a device whereby the adjournment not being sine die, the convention
remained technically in session. In actuality, not until after having been summoned
by Robert Carter Nicholas, would the members reassemble, again in Richmond, on
Friday, 1 Dec. 1775 (*Va. Gazette* [Pinkney], 16 Nov. 1775; *Proceedings of the Convention of . . . the 1st of December 1775*, p. 1).

Although, wrote George Mason to General Washington, the early sessions had
been "so ill conducted" that he "was sometimes near fainting in the House," as time
passed, "several wholsome Regulations were made;" and with order restored, the
master of Gunston Hall would apparently have been willing to risk his health further
(he was ill even as he wrote), for "if the Convention had continued to sit a few Days
longer," he believed that "the public Safety wou'd have been as well provided for as
our present Circumstances permit" (Rutland, *Papers of Mason*, I, 255).

It now remained, assuming Mason to have been correct, to determine what that had
been left undone would prove necessary to be done. It also remained, for Mason as
well as his colleagues, to determine how effective those measures that had been taken
would prove in answering the challenges of the time.

27. Since the final day of session of the convention began at 9:00 A.M. and was a

lengthy one, it is almost certain that the 1st meeting of the Committee of Safety was not held until late in the afternoon, or perhaps even that night.

28. To what "order of the convention" the committee was referring is unknown. By combining various paragraphs of "An Ordinance for Raising and Embodying a Sufficient Force, for the Defence and Protection of This Colony," enacted on 21 Aug., with one in "the Ordinance Appointing a Committee of Safety," enacted on 24 Aug., such an "order" could be constructed. It was the 1st-named ordinance that provided for the appointment of captains of "companies of regular troops" raised in the 16 military districts into which the colony was divided and authorized members deputized by the committees in "each district" to designate "one certain place of rendezvous within their district" for the formation of the separate companies into battalions. The 13th paragraph of the 2d ordinance empowered the Committee of Safety to distribute "all arms purchased at the publick expense" (*Statutes at Large*, IX, 10, 10–11, 16, 17, 53).

29. Let alone by its general authority, the Committee of Safety could fall back on paragraph 7 of the ordinance by which it had been established. That paragraph (although relating to the procurement of intelligence) read in part that the committee should "keep up a correspondence with the committees of the several counties and corporations." Provisions by which "progress" in both "minute service" and that of "regulars" was expected to be made and reported were set forth in the ordinance for defense and protection (ibid., IX, 10–11, 12–13, 13–14, 16, 18, 19, 20–21, 51).

30. A nephew of President Edmund Pendleton, JOHN PENDLETON, JR., had been marking out a clerical path in Henrico County similar to that blazed by his distinguished uncle in Caroline County 30 years before. The younger man had worked for Thomas Adams in private employment, and at times for the county court. He had been succeeded in both positions by John Beckley, now also clerk of the Henrico County committee. Pendleton was in his mid-20s, and his being still celibate (if such was the case) would explain the apparent ease with which he was soon to remove self and luggage to Williamsburg, there to maintain the committee's records (Beckley to Adams, 26 Oct. 1775, Thomas Adams Papers, Va. Hist. Soc.; Hutchinson and Rachal, *Papers of Madison*, I, 190 n. 8; *Rev. Va.*, II, 171).

31. Hanover Town stood at the navigible headwaters of the Pamunkey River, some 4 or 5 miles north of Newcastle, and in better years had shipped as many as 1,600 hogsheads of tobacco to England. But with the gradual silting of the river, the community would lose its cause for being; its people would remove and its buildings finally fall into ruins, thereafter to vanish. Seventy years later the historian-lexicographer Henry Howe was to find that the previous existence of the town even then lay "within the memory of those living" (*Historical Collections of Virginia . . .* [Charlestown, S.C., 1845], p. 293).

32. A paragraph of the ordinance for defense and protection provided in part "That the committee of safety shall, and they are hereby required, to appoint some fit person, or persons, to provide arms and accountrements, clothes, waggons, tents, and bedding, upon the best and cheapest terms, and also to appoint one or more commissaries or contractors; who are hereby required to use all possible despatch in purchasing such provisions as shall be necessary for the army, and in laying of the same in such convenient place, or places, as may best suit their different stations and marches" (*Statutes at Large*, IX, 14–15).

The commissary was to be William Aylett, whose appointment, though 3 weeks in the future, was understood "from what dropt in Committee." The committee gave him "pretty General" instructions to obtain leggins, blankets, clothing, provisions, and "Salt, which the Committee wished to have engaged at all events" (Mays, *Letters and Papers of Pendleton*, I, 118). Already on 24 and 25 Aug., Aylett had purchased from Tate, Alexander & Company two "bales" of blankets "for the use of the Army." The bill was £29 15s. 16¾d., to be discounted 5 percent if paid before the end of October (Accompt of Colo Wm Aylett with Tate Alexander & Co., 29 Aug. 1775, Auditors MS Item 171, Archives Division, Va. State Library). Before the committee should meet at Hanover Town, Aylett would also from 4 other firms have purchased buttons, thread, silk, duffle, "Felt Hatts," "Knives & forks," and other supplies "for the use of the Army," at an additional cost of £345 3s. 9d. (Accounts of William Aylett with John Holloway, 29 Aug. 1775, Meades & Driver, 11 Sept. 1775, Sparling, Lawrence & Co., and Willis Cowper, undated, ibid.). Although Aylett was acting on his own account, it was with Pendleton's knowledge and approval, and both men were confident the committee would ratify the purchases (Mays, *Letters and Papers of Pendleton*, I, 118).

33. The mayor may last "have had the pleasure of seeing" the captain on 16 Aug., when the latter possibly accompanied him and Andrew Sprowle to the meeting of the Norfolk County committee (n. 14).

34. For the "letters," see 12, 13, 14, 15 Aug. 1775, Norfolk Borough; for the "resolve," 21 Aug. 1775, same. On 28 Aug. 1775 Captain Macartney would reply to Mayor Loyall thanking him for this "polite favour, which inclosed some strictures by the corporation of Norfolk." "I must beg you will be pleased," the captain would continue, "to publish the letters which passed between us in the Virginia News Papers, that a candid public may judge of the motives which actuate my conduct." He would affirm that he had no wish to "draw on a political discussion" or "to ascertain in particular cases the limits of the civil or military jurisdictions." He was, rather, desirous that His Majesty's "subjects should know I ardently wished the peace of this province" (*Va. Gazette, or the Norfolk Intelligencer*, 30 Aug. 1775).

The publication of this correspondence was to reveal Macartney in a light heretofore concealed from Lord Dunmore and to throw the latter into confusion (pp. 225, 437 n. 33 above). Upon receipt of Adm. Samuel Graves's request that he draw up charges and specifications for the captain's court-martial, His Excellency on 12 Sept. 1775 would respond in a letter the very model if inditements could be made to babble. The governor "really did not mean or wish that Captain Macartney should be brought to a Court Martial." His Lordship acknowledged that on "reexamining the first part" of his accusatory letter, "such an inference might be drawn." But he was "really sorry for the disagreeable Consequences." Macartney was in fact "a most diligent, punctual good Officer." He was simply "unequal" to dealing with the Virginia rebel leaders, "a very Artful, Subtle set of people." Yes, that was it: the captain's deficiencies consisted only of "a want of knowledge of Mankind." And it was certainly to be hoped that so fine a sailor would be reinstated not only to command of his ship but to the admiral's "good Opinion" (Clark, *Naval Docs. of the Am. Rev.*, II, 84–85).

Unaware of misunderstandings existing within the royal services, and with a different object in view, a Middlesex correspondent by the date of Lord Dunmore's reply would already have written a Scottish addressee: "We are in arms, exercising and training old and young to the use of the gun. No person goes abroad without his sword, or gun, or pistols. The sound of war echoes from north to south. Every plain is full of armed men, who all wear a hunting shirt, on the left breast of which are sewed in very legible letters, '*Liberty or Death*'" (Force, *Am. Archives*, 4th ser., III, col. 621).

Index

Index

Note: Boldface type below indicates pages on which persons are identified. Such pages for those identified in Volumes I and II follow their names immediately in parentheses.

Index